"The only new thing in the world
is the history you don't know."
— HARRY S. TRUMAN —

———————————————

"In Jefferson's famous line,
'When in the course of human events…'
the operative word is 'human.'"
— DAVID McCULLOUGH —

Previous works by Talmage Boston

Raising the Bar:
The Crucial Role of the Lawyer in Society

Baseball and the Baby Boomer:
A History, Commentary, and Memoir

1939: Baseball's Tipping Point

CROSS-EXAMINING
HISTORY

**A LAWYER GETS ANSWERS FROM
THE EXPERTS ABOUT OUR PRESIDENTS**

★ ★ ★ ★ ★ ★ ★

TALMAGE BOSTON

FOREWORD BY KEN BURNS

bright sky press

HOUSTON, TEXAS

bright sky press
HOUSTON, TEXAS

**2365 Rice Blvd., Suite 202
Houston, Texas 77005**

10   9   8   7   6   5   4   3   2

Library of Congress Cataloging-in-Publication Data on file with publisher.

ISBN 978-1-942945-20-8

Editorial Direction: Lucy Herring Chambers
Managing Editor: Lauren Adams Gow
Designer: Marla Y. Garcia

Printed in Canada through Friesens

To my parents,
Paul and Mary Jean Boston,
who inspired me
to begin loving presidential history
at the age of seven

Table of Contents

Foreword

KEN BURNS

Working on historical documentaries over the last thirty-five years, I've been interviewed thousands of times. Some of my questioners have had little knowledge about the subjects we've covered, but they have known enough to throw me softballs. Others have had a preconceived idea about the niche in history we've portrayed in a particular film and wanted to argue to show me how smart they were. Very few interviewers have removed their egos from our conversation and still challenged me to go deeper with my subject. Talmage Boston is among the few who do exactly that.

Two of my great loves in American history—Abraham Lincoln and the game of baseball—are what first brought Talmage and me together in 2009. We met at the Dallas Center for the Performing Arts shortly before my presentation there to promote PBS's first showing of *The National Parks: America's Best Idea*. Talmage said he was thinking about writing a book about similarities between Jackie Robinson and Abraham Lincoln and asked me to weigh in. When we finished our conversation, Talmage gave me copies of the two baseball history books he'd written. A few weeks later, when I returned to Dallas, he warmed me up in the Texas Rangers batting cage before it was time for me to throw out the first pitch at that night's ballgame (a strike!). Then we watched the game together, and I told him about my next film for PBS, *The Tenth Inning*, a four-hour sequel to my earlier eighteen-hour documentary, *Baseball*.

A few months after that game, Talmage made arrangements for me to talk about *The Tenth Inning* (shortly before it was shown on PBS) in front of a large crowd at an event sponsored by the Southern Methodist University Athletic Forum lecture series. That was the first time I was interviewed onstage by Talmage. Aware of how much he knew about baseball from our prior conversations and from reading his books, I expected him to hurl hard verbal baseballs over the plate—and no softballs. He didn't disappoint me, and every fan of our National Pastime knows that a veteran batter can hit a high-speed baseball much farther than a slow-pitch softball. "Haven't an increasing number of Latin American ballplayers gotten the opportunity to use their skills in Major League Baseball over the last three decades largely because of pure economics?" "If we wanted to carve a Mount Rushmore of the four most important people in the cultural development of MLB, would the faces on the cliff be Ruth, Robinson, Clemente, and Ichiro?" "What took baseball so long to realize which information is important in evaluating a player's offensive value?" These were fair questions, but not softballs. Knowing that Talmage was a commercial trial lawyer for over thirty years before he began conducting onstage interviews helped me understand where he got the capability to craft good, deep, tight questions.

After that program, Talmage and I continued to stay in touch. Shortly after *The Tenth Inning* aired on PBS, as we took steps toward the formation of The Better Angels Society, the non-profit that raises money to help provide funding for our films, I was pleased when he agreed to serve on our board of directors.

Our next onstage interview happened when I was on the promotional tour for our three-part film *Prohibition* in 2011. Again, Talmage put together a huge crowd in Dallas at a program co-sponsored by the Dallas Bar Association and the World Affairs Council of Dallas/Fort Worth, and again he came at me with some high, hard questions. "People's hypocrisy makes for good drama. What caused so many people to vote one way and drink another before and during Prohibition?" "How important to the US economy was the liquor business in 1919?" "How could 2/3 of Congress and 3/4 of the states not recognize in advance that upon Prohibition's going into effect, the liquor business would immediately be taken over by criminals?"

My most recent onstage interview with Talmage was in October 2014 when we discussed my series *The Roosevelts: An Intimate History* a month after it was shown on PBS. I'm pleased that the complete edited transcript of our conversation that night (again in front of an overflowing ballroom at an event sponsored by the Dallas Bar Foundation) appears in this book. You can see in these pages how much fun we had going deep into Theodore, Eleanor, and Franklin.

Having gotten to know Talmage over the last six years, having watched YouTube videos of some of his other interviews, and having read several of the transcripts in *Cross-Examining History*, I believe this book provides an important new angle on history. Getting some of our country's top historians and public figures into an onstage interview format in basically three years was obviously no small task in itself, but then coming up with the penetrating questions asked of them during the interviews turns this book from good to great. Talmage's editing the transcripts of those interviews into text that flows smoothly makes the book an easy page-turner.

Here's hoping you'll enjoy reading Talmage's book as much as I have. Those of us in the business of promoting the stories of America's rich history are well served by the information conveyed in *Cross-Examining History*.

KEN BURNS
Walpole, New Hampshire

Introduction

TALMAGE BOSTON

Enhancement: the process of taking something good and making it better. Think food. Icing on the cake. Butter on the bread. Whipped cream on the milkshake. Add one complementary ingredient and thereby ratchet up the taste.

Now, think presidential history. Start with something very good: the written work of a master historian or presidential insider. Add the complementary ingredient of interviewing him, using probing questions to encourage the author to go beyond his book and add new angles of insight to expand his message.

Sounds like an idea with possibility, but who should ask the questions? Perhaps someone who has spent his career digging below the surface with penetrating inquiries—someone like Perry Mason—with an instinct for the jugular?

Sadly, Perry Mason was not available for this project when it began in 2013. Someone else was needed to step up to provide the interviewing-expertise ingredient necessary to enhance public appreciation of history beyond our best presidential biographies. I volunteered.

As a commercial litigator for almost forty years, my goal in every case I've handled has been to seek the truth, then use it as a sword to achieve resolution. The quest to find out "what really happened" requires asking the right questions and getting responsive answers, most importantly in the cross-examination stage when a witness' credibility is ultimately revealed.

A presidential biography reflects the author's direct examination of his protagonist. Regardless of how thorough the research and how clearly stated the author's conclusions, even the best works of history inevitably raise questions that require answers before a subject's assessment can be completed. Hence the need for the professional cross-examiner to button up the loose ends and take the presidential historian to places he didn't go when he pursued the direct examination of his particular commander-in-chief.

What kicked off this effort?

In May 2010, Michael Lewis came through Dallas at the end of his national tour for *The Big Short: Inside the Doomsday Machine* (W.W. Norton & Company, 2010). In that book, Mr. Lewis profiled some of the intriguing winners and losers in the 2008 subprime meltdown. Because I had played a role in having the World Affairs Council of Dallas/Fort Worth land him for the event, and because Mr. Lewis preferred the interview format for his presentation, the Council's CEO Jim Falk asked me to be the interviewer in front of a sold-out ballroom at the Fairmont Hotel. When the program ended, Michael Lewis said to me, "Talmage, nobody on this tour pushed me harder than you did about Goldman Sachs' conduct." Seventeen days later, the SEC sued Goldman for the alleged fraud in its subprime transactions. Affirmation is good for the soul.

A year later, Pulitzer Prize winner David McCullough passed through town on his tour for *The Greater Journey: Americans in Paris* (Simon & Schuster 2011). He and I had only shaken hands before the program, meaning he knew nothing about me when our onstage conversation began. For my third question, I asked him to compare what he had done in writing *Journey* with what Samuel F.B. Morse had done in selecting the figures for his painting "Gallery of the Louvre" (a subject profiled in his book). At first, the question seemed to stun him, because after hearing it, he pivoted his head away for a pregnant pause. Then he turned back around, looked me in the eye, and asked, "What do you do for a living, Talmage? You've asked me something about my book I've never thought about before." That moment went past affirmation. It was a time of pure ecstasy.

In February 2013, I did a program in Dallas with another Pulitzer Prize winner, Jon Meacham, about his then best-selling biography *Thomas Jefferson: The Art of Power* (Simon & Schuster 2012). At mid-interview, I asked the following question: "If the Jefferson Memorial had never been built, and a Congressman submitted a bill today that called for funding the construction of a Jefferson Memorial in Washington, DC with federal tax dollars, given what we now know about Thomas Jefferson and his slaves, would that bill pass?" Jon paused, smiled, answered "No," and then explained why. After the program, he told me it was the best question he had been asked on his national tour. With feedback like that coming from Jon Meacham, on top of my experiences with Michael Lewis and David McCullough, I began wondering exactly where public interrogations might lead me. One thing was clear: I needed to start recording and transcribing the interviews to preserve what appeared to be increasingly important conversations.

The tipping point in understanding where the interviews might take me came in May 2013 when the opportunity arose to interview Henry Kissinger in front of a thousand people at Dallas' Hilton Anatole ballroom. As a newly-minted public interviewer, the prospect of examining a person of Dr. Kissinger's stature before a huge highbrow crowd was like climbing Mount Everest. The preparation consumed six months of my free time; the edited transcript of that conversation can be found in this book; and the reader can judge the final product. After the program, former US Senator Kay Bailey Hutchinson and Kissinger biographer Jeremi Suri (both in the audience that day) sent me congratulatory notes saying I had gotten Henry Kissinger to say things they had never heard him say before. Dr. Kissinger was also complimentary to the extent we exchanged correspondence and he later hosted my wife and me for coffee at his office in Manhattan.

Those circumstances started the ball moving down *Cross-Examining History*'s playing field, sparking the thirty-one play drive toward the goal line that comprises this book. One thing I knew before the ball snapped on the first play: America has an abundance of high-powered historians and presidential insiders whose insightful words have the power to open up new levels of understanding about our past. What I learned from watching prominent authors interviewed by Brian Lamb and Charlie Rose on television over the years was that not only do they write elegantly about our history, but they also talk about it with serious storytelling firepower.

My process for the interviews contained in these pages was the following:

- Line up the program with the expert at a time and place where a crowd would be present;
- Read the prospective interviewee's work thoroughly—underlining and making margin notes regarding any information that *might* frame a potential onstage question;
- Prepare a detailed summary of my notes;
- Draft and edit interview questions until they were ready for prime time;
- Conduct and record the interview in front of the crowd without letting my guest know the questions in advance, since spontaneity brings a higher energy level to the conversation, thereby enhancing the audience's experience;
- Have the interview tape transcribed;
- Edit the transcript to remove "uhs" and "you knows," eliminate false-starts/stops/start-overs, break up run-on sentences, divide long answers into paragraphs, and clarify and sharpen the text (consistent with what was said at the program) to ensure the final version reads as smoothly as possible;
- Transmit my final edited version to the interviewee with the instruction, "Make any changes that you believe will make this the best final product of our conversation. All your tweaks will be accepted, because I want everything that appears in this book to be wholly pleasing to you"; and, finally,
- Accept the interviewee's changes, and then forward the final product to my publisher for copyediting.

Those interviewed for this book fall into two categories: esteemed biographers of our most significant American presidents, as well as some public figures who have been presidential insiders. For those who may wonder why a few notable presidential historians were not interviewed for this book, rest assured they were contacted, but for different reasons were not able to participate. Similarly, for those wondering why certain presidential insiders were interviewed while others were not, recognize that in every presidential administration many people qualify as insiders. My simple selection process was that I interviewed those insiders who became accessible to me.

By my assessment, America has had twenty historically significant presidents—Washington, J. Adams, Jefferson, Madison, Jackson, Lincoln, Grant, T. Roosevelt, Wilson, Coolidge, Hoover, F.D. Roosevelt, Truman, Eisenhower, Kennedy, Johnson, Nixon, Reagan, Bush 41, and Clinton. For those wondering about the basis for some of these twenty being deemed "significant," the interview transcripts about them in the book will explain why they were chosen. A case can certainly be made to include a few others into the "significant" class, but this book is plenty thick as it is. I chose not to interview any biographers of Presidents Bush 43 or Obama because I believe more time must pass before a capable historian can put their performances into context.

My presidential-biographer interviewees include Pulitzer Prize winners and finalists, Emmy Award winners, *New York Times* best-selling and "Notable Book" authors, scholars of the highest order, and a few newcomers well on their way to gaining national recognition. They are all respected by the serious history-reading crowd and, in their unique ways, have transformed our major presidents into flesh-and-blood fascinating people. Those interviewed who are designated as "presidential insiders" have served in the Cabinet, as White House chief of staff, as White House counsel, as national security advisor, and experienced life as a president's daughter. They are all great storytellers and big picture historical thinkers.

As with my previous three books, each chapter in *Cross-Examining History* stands on its own. The reader can select reading about those presidents who interest him (and ignore those who don't), without fear of losing continuity.

Because all the interviews in this book were performed in front of a live audience, each lasted forty-five to ninety minutes, depending on the event. During the allotted time, my job as interviewer was to gently ramp up the conversation's energy and engage the crowd with meaty content in hopes that those in the room would hang on the conversation's every word. It's my hope that some of the excitement experienced during these interviews rises up out of these pages.

Given the realities of limited time onstage, my goal for each program was to cover in some depth as many subjects as time allowed. This sometimes caused choppiness between an answer and the next question (a problem I've attempted to address by headers interspersed throughout each chapter); but as the clock ticked toward "Time's up!"—when given the choice between smooth Q&A transition and maximum topic coverage—I always opted for covering more ground.

At the end of *Cross-Examining History*'s sustained drive, the goal line has two components: to answer many questions in history lovers' minds about what it was that made our major presidents tick and what influenced the trajectory of their lives; and to provide fresh insights on America's past to help us better understand the present and have a more informed expectation about our future. These are ambitious goals for someone with my limited credentials as a presidential historian, but when taking on the challenge of filling in for Perry Mason on this unique three-year "greater journey" (to borrow two words from David McCullough), why not shoot for the moon?

At age twenty-three, during his first campaign for political office, Abraham Lincoln expressed his "peculiar ambition": to become recognized by the end of his life as "being truly esteemed of my fellow men, by rendering myself worthy of their esteem." In keeping with young Abraham's earnest statement of purpose, my peculiar ambition for this book is for it to be deemed truly worthy of the reader's esteem because it offers enhancement to our understanding of American presidential history.

TALMAGE BOSTON
Dallas, Texas

CROSS-EXAMINING HISTORY

HISTORY
A LAWYER GETS ANSWERS FROM THE EXPERTS ABOUT OUR PRESIDENTS

I.

Founding Fathers

GEORGE WASHINGTON

JOHN ADAMS

THOMAS JEFFERSON

JAMES MADISON

THE FOUNDERS' BATTLE WITH FREEDOM OF SPEECH

Husband and wife historians **DAVID** and **JEANNE HEIDLER** have focused their eleven books on America's history from the founders' era through the Civil War. Jeanne retired as a long-time professor of history at the Air Force Academy in December 2015. I interviewed them in front of an audience of Academy history students on Friday, October 2, 2015, in Colorado Springs about their newest book *Washington's Circle: The Creation of a President* (Random House 2015), which received a very favorable review on April 2, 2015 in the *Wall Street Journal*.

"The idea that George Washington would be the first president was central to creating a system different from the British because first of all, he could not establish a dynasty since he had no children of his own. Secondly, he had demonstrated at the end of the Revolution a remarkable capacity to walk away from power, give up the army, resign his commission, and go home, with very little ceremony and no reluctance whatsoever." **– DAVID HEIDLER**

CHAPTER 1

DAVID AND JEANNE HEIDLER
ON
George Washington

WASHINGTON AND HIS AMBITION

BOSTON Early in the book, you mention George Washington's having had extreme ambition for most of his life, though he had satisfied it in his own mind before he became president.

Is that to say that his only real ambition in life was tied to his military career?

JEANNE In winning the American Revolution he had fulfilled his ambition of being admired by his peers, which meant a great deal to him since he did not come from the wealthiest of Virginians. With his military success, he felt he had reached the pinnacle.

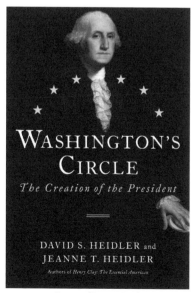

Courtesy of Penguin Random House LLC

DAVID I agree with that. Washington's ambitions receded as he grew older, as happens with many of us. When he was a young man, he was intent upon achieving a measure of celebrity, fame, and glory, especially in his military career, which began in the 1750s. When that came to an end, he devoted himself to the maintenance of Mount Vernon and attempted to build it up as a prosperous plantation and prove himself a good husband and adoptive father to his wife's children. When he was called back into public service in the political arena, he wanted to do his duty but was reluctant to make the sacrifice associated with leaving home.

BOSTON As I heard you both answer that question, I was reminded of Abraham Lincoln's famous statement when he was in his mid-twenties that his sole ambition in life was to be esteemed by his fellow man; and it sounds like that was George Washington's sole ambition as well.

JEANNE I think that's exactly it.

DAVID Isn't that true of all of us? We all seek the approval and admiration of those we admire, and Washington was no different. He wanted to be a good neighbor and a good citizen. Before the American Revolution, he had actually aspired to be a good subject of the king, until that became an impossibility.

WASHINGTON AS THE NATION'S "CONSCIENCE-IN-CHIEF"

BOSTON You mention in your book that the founders had a collective central virtue, which is what caused the American experiment in government to succeed—that virtue being "the celestial spark of conscience."

Did George Washington stand out among his peers as the leading conscience of his era and the nation's conscience-in-chief?

JEANNE I think that's how he saw himself as president—that it was his duty to not only do what was best for the country, but what was best for the country under the Constitution. He was scrupulous about adhering to the Constitution, which was why he sometimes saw himself as being not up to the job because he was not an attorney, like so many of the other founders. He felt that his judgment about the directives under the Constitution didn't have the honed legal knowledge that some of the other founders had, and that's why he depended on his advisors so much—because he saw them as having superior legal knowledge.

BOSTON Was there anything in particular in Washington's upbringing or background that caused him to have such a powerful conscience that he set the standard for his era?

DAVID Since his father died when he was young, because he was the eldest son in the family, he had to assume a level of responsibility that required a mature level of self-control and discipline at an early age.

Washington was not unique in losing his father at a very young age; this happened to a lot of our founders and to many people of that generation, when life expectancy was not very long. The males of Washington's family were remarkably short-lived, and he believed his time was limited.

Another factor that enhanced his conscience came when he undertook a penmanship exercise during his adolescence, and used as his basis for good handwriting a Jesuitical book devoted to the rules of civil behavior that had become popular in England in the middle of the eighteenth century. As Washington copied these rules of civil behavior, it became more than a penmanship exercise—it became a character definition exercise. Based on his subsequent behavior, Washington adopted almost all these rules to the letter in his daily conduct, including the point that a gentleman should speak slowly and deliberately.

Fully embracing these rules for civil behavior enhanced his desire to preserve at all costs the celestial spark of conscience in his own breath. It made him a man for whom private rectitude was as important as public posture.

BOSTON Throughout your book you reference his faith and that he often invoked God as a guide into his life. Were the Bible and his faith as important to his conscience as the rules of civil behavior he learned in the penmanship exercise?

JEANNE Definitely. His faith guided much of his action as president, and, before that, as commander of the Continental Army. It influenced not only his actions but also his attitude about what he had to do. He had a very private faith and showed no outward emotional signs of having it, although he attended church services regularly and devoted part of his mornings to reading devotionals.

WASHINGTON'S UNIQUE STATURE AMONG HIS CONTEMPORARIES

BOSTON As we try to visualize George Washington today and perceive exactly what it was that made him stand out among his peers, a relevant fact to me was that while he presided over the Constitutional Convention, he said very little on the record while the meetings were in session.

Since he barely spoke at the Convention, how did he keep the train on the tracks and bring it to its destination in producing a final, workable Constitution amidst all the major-league egos?

DAVID Washington's principal contribution to the Constitutional Convention was attending it. Making him the presiding officer was almost a foregone conclusion. After Benjamin Franklin, he was the most universally admired man in America, and the most admired American in the world in some respects.

Washington's presence at the convention was a major boost for the stature of the gathering, as was his support for the finished product—which was indispensable to its being ratified by the states. He rarely spoke during the sessions in Philadelphia because he didn't like public speaking. On the three occasions he did speak, the group listened to him intently. He spoke about mainly procedural matters, but his saying anything was very important. It reminded everyone of the gravity of the situation, especially of the need to maintain secrecy, and the necessity of creating something tangible that could put the new country on the right track. If they didn't achieve their goal at the convention, the future would likely be chaotic.

BOSTON While the convention was going on, they met during the days, but then they'd adjourn and go their separate ways, with many of them having dinner together or engaging in some type of off-the-record discussion of what had been said and where things appeared to be going.

What role did Washington play when the Convention was not actually in session, to motivate the attendees to stay on task?

JEANNE Although his diary is not very informative about what was said during his time in Philadelphia, it's clear Washington went out many nights during the convention, or else received visitors at the home of Robert Morris, where he stayed. He was careful about what was said during his conversations with the other delegates, so there could be no hint of anyone's disclosing what was going on in their sessions. It seems clear, however, in spite of Washington's instruction for the convention delegates to maintain confidentiality, that during the social events, they talked about what had happened during the day, and Washington likely participated in these discussions but only with the other delegates.

BOSTON Continuing on in search of identifying the certain something Washington had that no other Founder had, part of that something was his capacity to command universal respect regardless of where he was or whom he was with.

Give your best description of what it was that caused this unanimous reaction from all those in his presence who responded with one unified voice of admiration.

DAVID Washington was a physically imposing figure—a big man for his time—in fact, he would have been a big man in any time, but especially in his time. He towered over everyone.

He was put together in ways that were arresting. He did not have a classic physique. He was rather narrow-shouldered and pear-shaped in his body, but had a good face, with penetrating pale blue eyes, and a broad-bridged nose that gave him a lion-like look.

He was an impassive person in terms of his expression, but he listened intently to what people said. Washington could be quite retiring in his demeanor, which encouraged people to open up to him. At the same time, he always had an air about him of remote aloofness that discouraged familiarity, especially the kind that breeds contempt.

So Washington melded a physical presence, a striking countenance, and a personal demeanor that was unique, and almost everyone who came into his circle realized it. They picked up on the levels of familiarity he allowed and the level of formality he required—even among his closest associates.

Washington's appearance was unusual enough to have the portrait artist Gilbert Stuart regard him as an oddity. His hands were too large, his hips too wide, his chest too narrow or too shallow; yet Stuart regarded him as a magnificent person. When Stuart's wife first saw Washington enter his studio for a sitting, she said he was the most magnificent person she'd ever seen in her life. That kind of uniqueness in terms of physical presence and demeanor made

a great deal of difference in Washington as a leader, such that he was able to exert a magnetic and charismatic spell over people without effort.

WASHINGTON AND HIS FRIENDSHIPS

BOSTON Given the fact that he maintained his distance from others in his capacity as a leader, do you think he had any close friends?

JEANNE He definitely had close friends, though it wasn't the kind of friendship we see in the twenty-first century. He wasn't one to open up and unburden his soul to someone, except perhaps Martha; and I say "perhaps" because we don't know anything about their private conversations.

Gouverneur Morris was an extremely close friend and someone who could be very frank with Washington, and didn't stand on ceremony. Eliza Powel, the Philadelphia social maven, spent a great deal of time with both Martha and George Washington, and they seemed to have had a very open friendship. Before the Constitutional Convention, he was very close to George Mason, one of his closest neighbors in Virginia. They later came to a parting of the ways caused by their political differences over the Constitution—and it's not entirely clear exactly why that happened—but they certainly conferred quite a bit about farm matters and neighborhood issues prior to their falling out. George Clinton, the governor of New York, was also a good friend. At the beginning of Washington's presidency, James Madison would have certainly been considered a close friend. So yes, he had close friends.

BOSTON Do you think Washington ever became a close friend of Alexander Hamilton?

JEANNE He saw himself as a friend of Alexander Hamilton, and relied on him quite a bit, even after Hamilton left the government. They corresponded primarily on official matters, but he trusted Hamilton, which is certainly a sign of friendship.

DIFFERENCES BETWEEN THE NEW GOVERNMENT AND THE BRITISH SYSTEM

BOSTON Your book points out that a central concern of the founders in setting up the new government under the Constitution was a fear of having it emulate the British government because they had been our enemy and we'd just gained our independence from them in the Revolutionary War.

We didn't want our president to be like a king, we didn't want our Senate to be like the House of Lords, and we didn't want Congress to be like Parliament. In fact, though, the founders ended up creating something very similar to the British system; it was different enough to feel like something new and uniquely American.

In creating the government, what were the red lines the founders believed they could not cross or else they would have been guilty of creating a system that was too British?

DAVID One of the things that was paramount in the revolutionary experience and then carried over into post-revolutionary America was the role that virtue played in guiding our every move—whether it was in securing victory during the Revolutionary War or playing a central role in creating our new government. The original government following the Revolution had operated under the Articles of Confederation and in many respects it demonstrated all the fears and anxieties that had fueled the Revolution. The main fear was of a centralized authority, whether in a legislature like Parliament or an executive like a king. That was one of the problems the Constitutional Convention had to overcome—the hurdle of making sure that the parliament-type legislative body they created in the formation of Congress would not be viewed as

something remote, distant, and meddlesome like Parliament was perceived at the time, and that the executive would not be so powerful as to be likened to a king.

The idea that George Washington would be the first president was central to creating a system different from the British because, first of all, he could not establish a dynasty since he had no children of his own. Secondly, he had demonstrated at the end of the Revolution a remarkable capacity to walk away from power, give up the army, resign his commission, and go home, with very little ceremony and no reluctance whatsoever.

Relying on virtue to serve as the source of direction would provide an interesting test for the new government in that one of the things that had been so disturbing about the British system was its tendency to fall into political cronyism, wherein people gravitated into groups, factions, and actual parties for the purpose of advancing their self-interests ahead of the national interest. This would, in fact, carry over into the new federal government because factions were turning into parties during the 1790s; though everyone insisted that they were not "political parties" because of the taint associated with parties in the British system.

The main thing the founders attempted to create in their government was a body that would be both workable yet constrained; an executive who would be powerful yet not overbearing; and a Congress that would not exhibit the factional self-interest which had so badly marred parliamentary practices during the eighteenth century and had been instrumental in causing the American Revolution.

WASHINGTON AND HAMILTON

BOSTON Getting back to Hamilton, your book suggests that wherever he went, Alexander Hamilton was usually the smartest guy in the room, and his biggest flaw was that he knew he was the smartest guy in the room.

Did George Washington have a problem getting past Hamilton's arrogance or his capacity to make enemies?

JEANNE I don't think so. Washington had had experience with Alexander Hamilton during the Revolution. As soon as Hamilton reached adulthood, and perhaps even before, he had an arrogance borne of insecurity, given his background—the poverty he grew up in and the fact he was illegitimate. Washington knew Hamilton's story and understood how insecurity had necessarily come his way and influenced his personality. He probably saw a little bit of himself as a young man whenever he encountered Hamilton. So in a fatherly way, he was able to get past Hamilton's extreme ego.

As far as Hamilton's capacity to make enemies, Washington probably was unaware of what Hamilton did that contributed to the number of enemies he made or why so many people disliked him.

BOSTON One of the things Hamilton did that served to make an enemy was to pass along confidential information to the British envoy George Beckwith, obviously to the detriment of then Secretary of State Thomas Jefferson; and that was done without Washington's knowledge, as you just mentioned.

Can you hazard a guess on what Washington would have done had he known of Hamilton's communications with Beckwith?

DAVID Washington knew Hamilton and Beckwith were talking. He thought their conversations had value in providing information about what the British government was thinking. Beckwith was not really an official envoy so much as a visitor with ties to the Canadian government of the British Empire. By virtue of that, he had ties back to the British Cabinet in Whitehall. Where the conversations became irregular was when Hamilton divulged information about what was being deliberated inside

our government. His conversations with Beckwith were improperly candid, so much so that he often gave away points of leverage that Jefferson would have otherwise found useful in negotiating with the British.

Some of the most virulent Hamilton haters, who not surprisingly were supporters of Thomas Jefferson, have gone so far as to suggest that Hamilton provided confidential information to Beckwith in a nefarious, almost traitorous way, in hopes of pushing the United States into the arms of an alliance with the British, especially in the Anglo-French War. No credible evidence supports that claim.

Hamilton was not interested in selling out America to the British. He would not have done it for all the money in the world or all the fame it would have brought him. He was not a traitor; rather, he was a commercially-minded hard realist, who knew that Britain was our biggest trading partner and that our government was so insolvent and our economy so moribund that America could not function without some level of relationship with the most powerful trading entity in the world at that time—Great Britain.

Hamilton was not selling out America; he was selling America, and trying to make the British interested in doing business with us. That was the motivation which drove Hamilton in almost every conversation he had with Beckwith. Any suggestion that Britain was somehow alienated toward us and therefore might decide to shut off the valves of trade or at least constrict American trade on the high seas horrified him; because, if that occurred, it would knock the foundation out from his domestic financial plans.

BOSTON Are you suggesting that when Hamilton divulged confidential information, which thereby prejudiced Jefferson's negotiating powers, he was somehow not aware that he was divulging confidential information?

DAVID He knew exactly what he was doing, and sometimes he was called out on it, which caused him to fashion elaborate, complex lies that made no sense and were contradictory. Washington possessed a scintilla of knowledge about the information being passed from Hamilton to Beckwith, and it was basically acceptable to him for them to be talking. Washington even instructed Hamilton to inquire of certain things with Beckwith, but he did not know the level of information Hamilton was divulging.

Although Hamilton communicated confidential information to Beckwith, he was not giving away state secrets. He talked to Beckwith about there being differences of opinion in Washington's Cabinet, which suggested ways the British could influence American policy. His primary sin was to downplay Jefferson's influence, suggesting that Washington was not altogether in concert with Jefferson's attitudes about foreign policy. By doing that, Hamilton created an unfortunate situation that most of us would have a problem with, in terms of inhibiting our leading foreign policy officer (the secretary of state) from being able to move things forward with Britain in a positive way.

WASHINGTON'S ADMINISTRATIVE PRACTICES

BOSTON Regarding the historic rivalry between Hamilton and Jefferson—probably the biggest power struggle in American history, which led to the formation of political parties: did Washington's administrative methods play a role in causing that power struggle to arise and grow?

JEANNE They did to a degree. Early in the presidency, Washington held very few meetings with his entire Cabinet. He tended to confer with each man separately about all manner of things. Going back to his experience during the Revolution, he liked to get as many opinions as possible, and he preferred getting them in writing rather

than hashing things out in person—either individually or as a group.

As a result of Washington's preferred style of administration, Hamilton and Jefferson during the early years of Washington's presidency likely knew very little of what the other was advising the president to do. We'll never know, but perhaps if they had discussed things together, they might have found a way to reach consensus on issues. Since Cabinet officers mainly conferred separately with Washington, achieving consensus became impossible.

BOSTON Jefferson liked to avoid confrontation and conflict. That being the case, in the few early Cabinet meetings where both Hamilton and Jefferson were physically present in the same room, I'm guessing that there wasn't much arguing because of Jefferson's being gun-shy about discord—such that all discord between the two men arose from the separate communications they had with Washington. Is that what you're saying?

JEANNE Yes. The discord arose in large part because, early on, they did not know what the other was telling Washington to do because the president tended to take advice from a number of people and then form his own decision. It is true that Jefferson normally did not like personal confrontation, but once they started having more frequent Cabinet meetings—particularly over the French crisis—he wasn't shy during those meetings about expressing his opinion. There were some very tense meetings when he disagreed with not only Hamilton but also with the other Cabinet members, and on those occasions he expressed his opinion openly.

WASHINGTON'S PROCESS FOR MAKING DECISIONS

BOSTON Your book explains that Washington's method of operation in leading the country as president was to recognize that he was smart—but not necessarily the smartest guy in the room—and also recognizing he had two totally brilliant people operating in his Cabinet with often differing opinions in Jefferson and Hamilton.

Did you determine any process that Washington used in attempting to synthesize two equally persuasive, competing ideas coming from Jefferson and Hamilton?

DAVID Let me explain how these two officials gradually realized where each other stood on certain issues. When Washington sought their written opinions, he asked about issues that crossed Cabinet turf lines. If the president wanted input on the subject of establishing the National Bank, he asked for opinions from everyone—not just from his secretary of the treasury, Hamilton. If he sought advice about our position on the Anglo-French War, which broke out late in his first term, Washington asked for opinions from everybody—not just from his secretary of state, Thomas Jefferson.

This approach of gathering different opinions in hopes of using them to come up with the best final decision soon produced the unfortunate result of making people quite conscious of their respective areas of responsibility being invaded by others, which understandably caused Cabinet members to get very prickly about people meddling in their business.

Whenever Washington would get opinions on what to do on a foreign policy issue and the opinions would come in with opposing advice, especially when they were in direct opposition to each other, the president would copy the conflicting opinions in his own hand and would then send Jefferson's opinion to Hamilton and ask him to respond. Hamilton would prepare a voluminous rebuttal producing some of the finest state papers in American history in terms of constitutional interpretation and the powers of the central government. Through that process, Hamilton was certainly aware that he was responding to Thomas Jefferson's ideas.

When Washington made decisions in favor of Hamilton's position, Jefferson would know his opinion had been rejected. This process suggests that Washington was synthesizing conflicting positions, but in fact, he did not have the luxury of synthesizing opinions. He had to make a decision, and he made them based on what he found to be the most compelling argument presented in the most persuasive way, and that often turned out to be Hamilton's opinion.

Washington tended to agree with Hamilton more with regard to the national imperatives rather than the local ones. This grew out of their experience in the Revolution. Thomas Jefferson and Alexander Hamilton disagreed on the proper role of the federal government and of the state governments no matter what, but what's often overlooked is that Thomas Jefferson and George Washington also disagreed on this subject, regardless of Alexander Hamilton's influence—because Washington had a national vision, and it became increasingly at odds with the local or decentralized vision central to Thomas Jefferson's philosophy of government.

WASHINGTON, THE BROKEN ECONOMY, AND HAMILTON'S SOLUTION

BOSTON One of the national imperatives in front of Washington during his presidency was what to do about the country's financial condition. When Washington became president, the country was essentially broke and then Hamilton came along with his vision for economic recovery, which Washington soon embraced and put into practice.

Is there any evidence Washington had any ideas of his own, independent of Hamilton, regarding what should be done to get the US out of its economic problems?

JEANNE Not really. Washington came to the presidency with a visceral fear of debt, and he certainly knew of the country's insolvency. Throughout his adult life, he was an extremely frugal person with his own finances, and that influenced his opinion toward what Hamilton proposed.

Washington did not have any concrete ideas of his own about what should be done to rescue the economy. Until Hamilton came up with his plan, no one believed it was possible to pay off the national and state debts very quickly because there simply was no money available to do so. Hamilton miraculously arrived at a plan that would manage the debt in a way that the country would no longer be in any danger of bankruptcy, so Washington had no problem embracing Hamilton's plan.

DAVID Thomas Jefferson and James Madison were both on board with Hamilton's plan because everyone knew we were in a great deal of financial trouble. Debt for a government is baneful. It was a Jeffersonian idea that debt was enslavement because it puts the debtor at risk to the beck and call of his creditor. This was one of Jefferson's greatest fears throughout his time in France—that someone hostile to the United States would buy American debt from the French, who had been the principal financiers of the American Revolution. If that happened, whoever bought the debt would be in a position to exercise a greater leverage over American policy than was wise or prudent.

Hamilton came up with a plan that was sensible, and Jefferson understood all of it. His claiming ignorance about the plan was disingenuous. In fact, Hamilton used some of Jefferson's writings in formulating his plan. Everyone realized that our economic situation was a crisis, and being able to get out of it made Hamilton the most important person in the federal government.

BOSTON Given Hamilton's brilliant vision for successfully dealing with the severe economic problem the country was in, did the members of Congress, the Cabinet, and everybody else who ended up accepting Hamilton's plan actually understand it?

JEANNE A lot of people were confused by it and didn't understand the nuances of what he was proposing. His Report on Public Credit was an extremely detailed document, and undoubtedly many who read it didn't understand every part of it.

DAVID It's doubtful they felt it necessary to fully understand it. They trusted Hamilton and his plan and knew he had consulted with Congress about it and had simply persuaded Congressmen that the plan was feasible and likely to succeed.

The main problem opponents had with the plan was not with how paying off the debt would be funded—everyone understood this perfectly—but why it would be prudent for the federal government to assume the states' debts. The assumption of the states' debts led to the first serious internal opposition to a government initiative and became the most serious bone of contention until the National Bank issue arose, which was also tied to the funding and assumption plans.

Many believed that the assumption of state debt was unfair and overreaching. Some thought it wouldn't clear debt off the books. His opponents also believed Hamilton's plan was a way for the federal government to ultimately subsume the states, and move them closer to the role of being mere administrative entities instead of sovereign participants in the American experiment.

BOSTON When challenged by the breadth of his economic plan as to whether or not it was constitutional, Hamilton relied on the "necessary and proper" clause in the Constitution, and used his interpretation of that clause to expand the role of the federal government.

Is there any indication that George Washington fully embraced Hamilton's broad interpretation of the "necessary and proper" clause, which was obviously a huge factor in growing the federal government during his presidency?

JEANNE It's not really known. The constitutional issue did not come up in connection with the funding and assumption plan, and it became a far more important component of the arguments used against the Bank of the United States. I don't think Washington viewed the "necessary and proper" clause as being necessarily broad. He thought that if an advocate could demonstrate that the Bank was both necessary and proper, then Washington would deem the Bank to be constitutional. When it came to putting his argument in writing, Hamilton was very persuasive with Washington; and after much soul-searching, the president determined that Hamilton had satisfied both requirements.

BOSTON Is the consensus of historians today, as best you can tell, that Hamilton did the right thing by causing a major shift toward the executive branch in running the economy, given how quickly the state of the economy can change and how slow and contentious Congress typically is in responding to a crisis?

DAVID We need to sharpen the definition of what we're talking about. I think Hamilton would have been horrified to have anyone suggest he was "running the economy," because Hamilton did not endorse the mercantile notion of central control. He believed in a free-market economy. What he was trying to do was establish an environment where the economy could prosper and thrive. Hamilton's notions of governmental regulation of the economy would be regarded as highly laissez-faire today given the way the Federal Reserve now works.

What Hamilton did want was to have the Bank of the United States establish a way for national commerce to work in a facilitative fashion. Stable credit, a sound currency, an operating medium for economic transactions in both goods and services and in banking, all had to be in place for this to happen.

It's interesting to note that the French government and nation were in much better economic circumstances than Britain in 1789, except that there was no Bank of France. The difference between the two economies was that France had no way to make use of their economic advantage because they had nothing similar to the Bank of England. That's why Hamilton wanted a bank here like the Bank of England that could execute central economic planning sensibly. He thought his innovation of the Bank was particularly good because it would not need much government control over it like the Federal Reserve has. That's why he wanted the Bank incorporated as a private operation, though that turned out to be a principal constitutional objection to it—that the government had no right to incorporate private organizations.

Hamilton saw his plan as a way for the economy to operate through the Bank instead of through the government. With that perspective, he revealed a much more conservative view of economic fiscal activity than we see now in the way the government operates. It's important to recognize that the people who objected to Hamilton's bank plan did not see it as economically unsound; rather, they saw it as politically perilous because the federal government's involvement in any aspect of economic matters was seen as the camel's nose entering the proverbial tent. Once that happens, reversing its direction becomes difficult, as indeed it would be, but it was not Hamilton's original intent to make the federal government the arbiter of the national economy.

BOSTON I accept that and appreciate the clarification, but the way I read your book was that, in the very beginning, as the first presidential administration and its Cabinet was being set up, and with a new Congress operating, it was something less than clear as to who would take responsibility for coming up with the most important approaches to dealing with national economic problems. Because Hamilton happened to be Secretary of the Treasury and not a member of the Congress, and because he was such a visionary and came up with such a creative and successful plan that most people ultimately supported, he thereby seeded into the executive branch what Madison and others thought should have stayed within the jurisdiction of the legislative branch. If I misread that in your book, please correct me.

DAVID No, you're right to this extent, Talmage. The necessity of somebody in charge of the public till is a governmental principle that is sound and universally accepted. Hamilton's original charge within the definition of the scope of his office as created by Congress was that the Secretary of the Treasury was the only Cabinet position within the executive branch, which should have a direct relationship with Congress. That being the case, it created an erosion of the separation of powers, though it had to work that way because it was absolutely necessary for Congress (especially the lower house) to be in charge of the purse.

Giving Congress that ultimate power was by design and in accordance with the voice of the people because it was the people's money that was to be managed and preserved. As a result, Hamilton's and Treasury's relationship with Congress was much more intimate than that of any other officer of the federal government—even George Washington. That's why, when we talk about a part of the executive branch running the economy, it's an overstatement.

The first thing Congress did when Hamilton took his post at Treasury was to tell him, "We want a plan from you as soon as you can get one ready for us. Send it to us and we'll address it promptly." With that directive, it was clear who was in charge—and, thus, Congress was in charge of Hamilton. They told him to come up with a plan, they would review it, and then they would vote on it.

The locus of power concept in the executive branch was something that everyone was very mindful of. It was also something Hamilton had to be careful about because he wanted to avoid the appearance that he was running things, or was gathering power unto himself with a patronage network of lighthouse keepers and customs collectors. If perceptions like that arose, it would have definitely created political problems, though philosophically, everyone was on the same page regarding the necessity of having someone (the secretary of the treasury) administer the economy under Congressional supervision.

BOSTON We've talked at length about Hamilton's plan and the fact that it was not met with universal approval when he proposed it, although because of his successful persuasive powers, he succeeded in getting it approved.

Did his main adversaries, Jefferson and Madison, have a plan of their own that they tried to present to Congress as an alternative to Hamilton's plan?

JEANNE No, they did not. As David mentioned before, Jefferson had expressed some of the same ideas as Hamilton, and was very much aware of the need to manage the debt, and gradually retire it, so Jefferson and Madison were both in complete agreement with Hamilton on that point.

There was no argument about the desired "end"—it was just the "means" issue; and as David mentioned, the idea that the federal government should assume the states' debts was something Madison especially disagreed with. When the most serious debates over the issue of the states' debt assumption took place, Jefferson was just getting started as secretary of state, so he didn't participate. It wasn't until the Bank issue that Jefferson jumped into the fray and began opposing Hamilton's financial policies.

WASHINGTON AND MADISON

BOSTON Let's talk some more about Madison. He was devoid of charisma, physically unimposing, and yet was brilliant, driven, tactful, and usually got his way. In particular, he served as an important guide to Washington in suggesting ways the federal government should function in terms of how the gap should be bridged between the executive and the legislative branches.

Just as I asked a few minutes ago about how much Washington understood Hamilton's economic plan, I have basically the same question regarding how much Washington understood Madison's vision for how the government should work as between the executive and legislative branches.

Was it mainly Madison's idea that Washington embraced, such that Washington really didn't have a plan of his own but relied entirely on what Madison propounded?

DAVID Yes, that's how it was and there was a reason it worked out that way. Madison was arguably the most learned of the Constitution's framers with regard to the functions and structures of government. His reading on the subject was omnivorous, and

he brought that indispensable knowledge to the convention in Philadelphia. Once the federal government became a functioning enterprise, he became indispensable to George Washington in establishing protocols, precedents, and processes that would make it work better. Jefferson, Hamilton, Madison, and Washington knew better than anyone else that however the new government began working in its early days would essentially be written in stone as the way government would work going forward. If it started out operating incorrectly, then it would be like a machine assembled in a haphazard and unworkable fashion, which would be destined to fail.

Madison's vision for the federal government recognized the necessity of harmony between and among the workings of the judicial, legislative, and executive branches, such that together they could achieve a cohesive and coherent operation that would move things forward. For progress to happen without the government breaking down was the challenge Madison accepted and it made him the main advisor to George Washington, meaning he had more importance than anyone else on how the federal government should be run.

WASHINGTON AND SLAVERY

BOSTON I'm switching gears now in talking about George Washington and some of the other founders on a subject that comes up often in 2015. That is, I'd like to explore the fact that the founders who came from Virginia (Washington, Jefferson, and Madison being those who became president) all owned slaves on their respective plantations throughout their adult lives.

Given the nature of large scale farming, and the shortage of agricultural workers in the market place trying to sell their skills for a wage, how could an eighteenth century Southern plantation owner have managed a productive, successful farm without slaves?

JEANNE He probably could not have done it without slaves because of what you mentioned—the labor shortage. There was so much land available on the frontier that it was difficult to persuade free people to work for someone else when they could fairly easily acquire land of their own. People didn't want to farm for others.

Slavery in Virginia and then in other Southern colonies evolved gradually. If you go back to the seventeenth century, most large land-owners used indentured servants—people who had been sent over from foreign countries either voluntarily or involuntarily to the colonies—and that was the preferred source of agricultural laborers until it became increasingly too much of a financial strain on the landowners who used them. The strain came because of a condition in the indentured servitude contract which provided that at the end of the indenture, the landowner was required to provide his servant with clothes, tools, and land; and to do that, he had to carve out a piece of his own land and give it to his servant. That was a main reason why slavery became increasingly attractive over the indentured servant approach although slavery had also been around since the seventeenth century.

The increasing use of slave labor in the eighteenth century gradually evolved into the agricultural plantation system in the South, as opposed to its getting integrated into the system quickly as had already occurred in Latin America. This was the state of affairs that Washington, Jefferson, Madison, and other Southerners inherited. Slavery in America certainly troubled all of them to some degree—some more than others—but if they were going to maintain their large land holdings, it really was the only way to do so profitably. Sometimes they couldn't do it profitably, but they kept going anyway.

DAVID It's important to remember that there was a political component to this as well. Slavery put Washington into a fix, in both a moral and material sense. Morally,

he found slavery to be repugnant for all the obvious reasons, and materially he found it troublesome because it was bankrupting him.

Tobacco was the principal crop throughout Virginia for most of Washington's adult life. Cotton did not become the staple until after the early 1790s. Tobacco farming was incredibly labor intensive in every aspect of its production—from planting to cultivating to harvesting to processing. As a result, slavery fastened upon the upper South where tobacco was the principal money crop. Washington started moving away from growing tobacco almost immediately after he returned from the French and Indian War, and began turning his farm at Mount Vernon to grain production, which did not require as many slaves. By virtue of their natural reproduction, his slave population burgeoned as Washington's need for them decreased, and that caused an economic nightmare for him.

The compelling moral and economic factors when considered in a vacuum made emancipation sensible, but they were complicated by the political aspect of slavery. Washington knew emancipation was a charged issue in the South where slavery was intimately involved in people's livelihoods as well as social control measures. If he had decided to emancipate his slaves, it would very likely have diminished his standing with a significant part of the country, and that might cause the entire federal experiment to fail. He actually said as much in letters to foreign correspondents in which he spoke more candidly than he did with domestic correspondents. The fact that Washington was constrained by his position as an American icon meant he could only act in ways that were sometimes antithetical to his basic core beliefs.

BOSTON To summarize what you just said, David, had Washington emancipated his slaves, it would have been for him a serious social and political problem as well as a serious economic problem in that he simply would not have been able to operate Mount

Vernon at the level he had without having slaves there to do the work.

JEANNE He could have emancipated the slaves at Mount Vernon who belonged personally to him, and probably not suffered any economic problems. Approximately half of the slaves on Mount Vernon, however, were what were called "dower slaves" whom Martha had brought into the marriage. After she inherited them from her first husband, they were there for Martha's use during her lifetime; but then after her death, they were to go to her husband's estate. George Washington had no control over the dower slaves and neither did Martha because she had no legal right to free them.

DAVID Unless the estate of her late husband was reimbursed.

JEANNE Yes—if they had the money to reimburse the estate, they could have freed them, but George and Martha never had that kind of money. So it was a financial impossibility for the Washingtons to free the dower slaves who made up the substantial majority of the slaves who worked for them. It was not possible—legally or financially— for Washington to free his slaves because of the cost.

BOSTON You have just explained why Washington, Jefferson, and Madison kept their slaves, and how it made good sense to keep them for economic and political reasons.

Did anybody in the South during the founders' era overlook those two grounds and emancipate their slaves as a matter of moral purpose?

JEANNE There were a handful of people in the South who freed their slaves, but none of them were prominent Founding Fathers. The records are clear that they did it because they found such a conflict between the ideals of the Revolution while human beings were still being held as property. In

most cases, freeing one's slaves was not financially possible. Also, the state legislatures in the South increasingly made it more difficult for people to free slaves by passing laws that required freed slaves to leave the state. They didn't want freed African-Americans living in the midst of the slave population—thinking that might inspire the slaves to do what it took to gain their freedom. So it became very difficult legally for slaves to be freed. Plus it would have put an extreme burden on the freed slaves if they had to leave their friends and families behind and move to another state after gaining their freedom. For all these reasons, not many Southerners emancipated their slaves during the founders' era.

DAVID There was another problem with emancipation, and that was to recognize the reality that people in slavery, once freed, were not always prepared for the rigors imposed by liberty. George Wythe, for instance, freed his slaves with the stroke of a pen, but since he was not a planter, his household staff simply became his servant employees after he freed them, and he paid them a wage. John Randolph of Roanoke freed his slaves. It ruined him economically, but he freed them, and it ruined his plantation. It was a shuttered and dilapidated ruin by the time he died, but he did it and left in his will a provision to educate them with what money he had left, to make sure they were given educations—just like George Washington did in his will.

The slaves would need to be prepared for freedom by having trades and a level of education that would allow them to succeed in free societies as independent beings, rather than merely ciphers thrown out of slavery into another condition, often just as bad. These were thorny problems. Slavery was a blight on our country. Everyone knew it. It was not until later that some Southerners began to talk of slavery as having a positive side, and they said it as a defensive mechanism to respond to the growing abolitionist movement. At the beginning, everyone knew and agreed, as Daniel Webster would later say in the 1850s, "Slavery was awful." It was merely a question of how they would deal with it, and what they would do in light of the economic and political realities that it entailed.

WASHINGTON AND JOHN ADAMS

BOSTON Let's now talk about a founder who we have not yet mentioned. In the early part of your book, you're very critical of John Adams.

What were Adams' biggest flaws and how did he become such a revered Founding Father?

JEANNE I feel somewhat bad that it came across that we were extremely critical of him because I have great admiration for John Adams. Part of his problem was his being similar to Alexander Hamilton in that he was extremely bright, extremely well read, and he knew it. However, his mind was not as disciplined and he did not approach things looking for practical solutions like Hamilton did. As a result, Adams often came across as being pompous, arrogant, and undisciplined, because when he started expounding on something (as he often did in the Senate), while it might start out sounding quite brilliant, he tended to ramble and dominate any conversation or debate. It was very difficult for him to persuade others because of those personality traits.

BOSTON I'm looking at page 23 of your book, and you say there, "Even men who did not like Washington, admired him. But Adams often irritated people without any offsetting advantages. He could be petty in his jealousies and say acid things about people that he later had cause to regret." You also mention Adams having made a comment about Washington to the effect that "he never would have commanded the army or become president if he had not married a rich widow." Those were the words that leaped off the page at me that I regarded as not particularly positive comments about John Adams.

DAVID John Adams had the failing of many who never feel appreciated by their peers. That often happens to great people and they react differently to it. John Adams acted very predictably. He found the underestimation of his worth as a statesman, scholar, and politician to be most irksome, and he reacted badly to it. He would say things about people behind their backs that were petty and revealed a jealousy that was unbecoming.

There is no doubt though that he was a patriot. His behavior in the Senate was sketchy but, on the whole, effective in terms of supporting the administration—something Washington definitely appreciated. These traits I've mentioned do not diminish the fact that Adams was a great man, though we can't diminish that he had his flaws.

BOSTON As Washington began his second term, he started bringing Adams into his decision-making circle, which had not been the case during his first term.

What caused Adams' status to be upgraded in Washington's mind?

JEANNE A couple of circumstances caused it. First, Washington's second term was dominated by foreign affairs. There was a crisis in our country's having to deal simultaneously with both France and Great Britain because of the war between them, and Adams probably had the most experience in foreign affairs of anyone in the country. He had been a diplomat in France during the Revolution and in England during the Articles of Confederation period, so he knew how both of those countries worked, and that was something Washington definitely needed. He could rely with more confidence on someone with experience.

Another reason Adams became more involved during Washington's second term was because the team of advisors from his first term began resigning from their

Cabinet positions—starting with Jefferson, then Hamilton, and then Knox—and Washington increasingly found himself surrounded with Cabinet members and advisors who he didn't know very well and sometimes didn't really like. As his presidency continued, it became increasingly difficult for him to persuade people to make the sacrifice of accepting top positions in the government because it was truly a financial sacrifice. After all these departures, although Washington was never personally close to Adams, at least he knew him better and had been around him longer, so he began to feel more comfortable confiding in Adams as opposed to the newcomers in his administration.

WASHINGTON'S IMPOSSIBLE DREAM OF UNIFICATION

BOSTON Let's now talk about the increasing disharmony that occurred during Washington's presidency as two competing factions became more aggressive toward one another—Hamilton's Federalists and Jefferson's Republicans. Recognizing that Washington, above all, wanted to avoid factions and have the government's efforts be unified, did he finally recognize that consistent political harmony was just impossible?

You mentioned at the beginning of this interview about how throughout Washington's administration it was acknowledged that the British system had its disruptive factions, and, therefore, no one wanted to have divisive factions. Despite knowing all about British politics, did Washington finally recognize that political discord was just a fact of life because of the nature of mankind—that there will always be people who simply cannot agree and therefore cannot become unified?

DAVID Yes, he began to realize that consistent harmony and unity was simply not going to happen. It was Washington's belief that factions were bad and those who opposed him were indeed part of factions, while he never wanted to be part of a faction. It's unfortunately the way things work out in partisan contexts. It's always the "other guy" who's being the difficult, stubborn, and inflexible one. The government in George Washington's time was based on the concept of deference. He had embraced it during the colonial period when he was a member of the Virginia House of Burgesses. Deference is the notion that people should elect their representatives and then leave them alone to do their jobs. Officials should be elected on the basis of their character and reputations, and once they're in office, they should exercise their judgment accordingly. If an elected representative displeases the people, then they can remove him from office in the next election.

Washington did not believe it was productive or respectful for the people to object to an official's performance by responding in a voluble way either through public demonstrations or private correspondence. Under the deference theory, the role of the people was to express their pleasure or displeasure at the ballot box and not in public meetings—and certainly not in street protests or large petitions. So Washington found these public expressions of dissatisfaction with his administration increasingly distasteful as they became more vehement and impassioned.

The controversies of his second term that gave rise to people's expressing their disturbed feelings were associated with their perception that the federal government had become too pompous and formal, thereby making it resemble too much the governments of Europe. They also believed federal laws and policies had become too meddlesome, especially in western Pennsylvania where the whiskey excise was being collected; and also in foreign policy, where they felt their interests were being severely eroded by agreements such as Jay's Treaty, and in the inability of the federal government to secure navigation rights on the Mississippi River from Spain.

These disagreements led to the creation of private groups called "democratic societies" that gathered together to form organized coherent ways to protest government policy. Especially when the Whiskey Rebellion broke out, Washington found these "democratic societies" troubling, and ultimately concluded that they were not simply a means of protesting government policies but were actually subversive organizations designed to challenge the government in seditious ways.

Photo credit: Tom Darnell

David and Jeanne Heidler

WASHINGTON AND THE USE OF EXECUTIVE PRIVILEGE

BOSTON In talking about Jay's Treaty and the public's response to it, one of the historic accomplishments of Washington's presidency was his making the decision to invoke executive privilege in refusing to turn over to the House of Representatives the documents they had requested about the negotiation of Jay's Treaty.

When he invoked executive privilege, was there precedent for it?

DAVID Yes, there were precedents that had descended from the British common law system based on a concept called the "confidential deliberative process," which were based on the idea that executive departments in any organization (including government) have the right to conduct their business with some level of confidentiality. It allowed people in charge of making decisions to receive candid advice without there

being political, social, or any other kind of considerations that might impinge on their advice and make it less reliable. The notion of confidentiality during an executive's or a legislative body's deliberative process is embedded in any kind of government or organizational structure, and it frequently collides with the concept of transparency.

Washington invoked executive privilege based on something of a technicality, and he did it in a way that was fairly clever and, as it turned out, effective. Here's what happened as Congress considered Jay's Treaty. The House of Representatives had the responsibility to vote on whether to provide the necessary funding for the treaty. In the context of that, they wanted to know all about what had led to the treaty's being negotiated and signed. Because almost everyone in Congress found the treaty objectionable, the House sought an excessive amount of information from President Washington in hopes they could use it to support their desired goal of not providing the funding for the treaty.

Washington quite sensibly declined their request, saying, "No, I will not give you this correspondence because you have no constitutionally prescribed right or function in the treaty making process." Ratification of a treaty has always been purely a Senatorial prerogative. Since the Senate hadn't asked for the information from Washington—and they wouldn't have asked for it because of the political complexion of the Senate—he was able to stand on constitutional grounds in invoking executive privilege and refusing to deliver the documents. The use of executive privilege had been used in certain parliamentary circumstances in the British government long before Washington, so it came out of the English common law.

IMPACT OF WASHINGTON'S FAREWELL ADDRESS

BOSTON The end of Washington's presidency concluded with his farewell address, which you say, "Was a political document for the present but a guiding doctrine for the future."

What impact did George Washington's farewell address actually have on guiding America's future?

JEANNE First of all, regarding future foreign affairs policy, he spoke of the need to avoid permanent alliances in the world. The French treaty we had made during the Revolution had increased our involvement in the European crisis. For the most part, his desire to avoid lasting alliances has been something that's guided many presidents over the years. Most alliances typically have an end date, but that was not the case with the French treaty.

Politically, when he criticized parties and factions in his farewell address, it was really a statement about the undesirability of partisan politics. To this day, partisan politics are viewed in a derogatory way, and he set the tone for the future by addressing that in his farewell address.

WASHINGTON AND THE ALIEN AND SEDITION ACTS

BOSTON When Washington departed the presidency, he was succeeded by John Adams who seemed just fine with Congress' passage of the Alien and Sedition Acts in 1798. George Washington, the most revered person in America at the time, refused to condemn those Acts even though they obviously violated the Constitution's guarantees of freedom of speech and freedom of the press.

Was Washington's refusal to condemn the Acts because he had simply grown tired of being part of any political controversy upon leaving the presidency, or did he actually think the Alien and Sedition Acts were good pieces of legislation?

DAVID The latter. Washington didn't recommend the Acts completely, but he certainly did not condemn them and, therefore, he tacitly endorsed them. He did it because he had been criticized too many times by disgraceful attacks from newspaper editors who had bent the truth and misrepresented

his character, and thereby created a false impression of him. The attacks were a personal affront to him and Washington, like most human beings, took them personally and certainly wanted to advocate any effort to suppress them in the future. Since he was no longer president, he had no actual power to do anything about them, but was willing to applaud someone else trying to do something about the situation.

Absolute freedom of the press is imperative for a healthy republic and it's unfortunately one of those rights that tends to get modified depending on the victim. Even the most principled of the founders would stray from the path of fully supporting freedom of the press when they were targeted in an especially vicious campaign of character assassination by a member of the press. Jefferson was probably the most staid and staunch defender of absolute freedom of the press, and he suffered lies and mischaracterizations, and was willing to put up with it to a certain extent, though he did not necessarily think the press should have an untrammeled and open ability to lie. If anything, he thought maybe state governments could issue appropriate restrictions on the press. This approach played into his core belief that the government closest to those being governed is best; and, thus, the decisions about these types of issues should not be made by a central authority.

WASHINGTON'S PERSONALITY CHANGE IN HIS FINAL YEARS

BOSTON My last question has to do with Washington's final years in retirement after he left the presidency; went back to Mount Vernon; and, as I read your book, finally loosened up for the first time in his life, and started shaking hands with strangers, telling jokes, and laughing heartily.

Is it your perception that his whole personality changed during his final years?

JEANNE Apparently it did. People who had known him during the presidency and then saw him after he went back to Mount Vernon said that he was not as deliberate in his speech. Until then, during both his military and political careers, he had always been quite slow in his speech, measuring every word before it came out due partly to the gravity of his responsibilities, but also because he just felt more comfortable expressing himself in that manner. Henrietta Liston, the wife of the British minister to the United States, is probably the person who is most often quoted on this.

In retirement, Washington could finally relax. He had done his duty during the American Revolution and yet people believed he still was required to serve his country some more in the new nation and its government that he had helped create. After serving two terms as president, there was really nothing else they could ask of him. For some reason, he still said "yes" to serving when President Adams asked him to command the American army during the French crisis, but for the most part, he now felt that he could go through each day in a more relaxed frame of mind.

I won't say he could "be himself" by being more relaxed, because he was being himself when he was the more formal George Washington; that was also a facet of his personality. He maintained two very different personas—the serious Washington in the midst of fulfilling duties to the American people, and the man at Mount Vernon who relaxed around the people he loved and cared for.

BOSTON David, how do you believe George Washington communicated his words while he was still in a position of power during his presidency—and even before, during his military career when he had all the responsibility leading the troops—as opposed to how you envision he spoke after all those responsibilities had been lifted?

DAVID Here again Washington invoked those rules for civil behavior coming into play that he had learned early on as he improved his penmanship, believing that a civil person should choose his words carefully because words can hurt, persuade, injure, and inspire. Washington's very deliberative way of speaking that he used until his retirement years was exasperating to those people with more nimble and agile minds. They thought intellectual fluency should normally reflect a person's mental agility.

This wasn't the case with Washington. He was perfectly acute in terms of his mental agility, but he was extremely careful in the way he spoke. In Cabinet meetings for example, when he was called upon to address some issue, he would halt whenever he spoke, such that there would be in his statements implied ellipses, so he would say, "I…am of the opinion…that this…particular…circumstance…requires…a level of…consideration that…would…result…in a more…felicitous…result." That kind of speech in a setting where there's an agenda for things that need to be addressed exasperated people. Jefferson found himself wanting to pull the words out of Washington's mouth.

His extremely deliberate pace of speaking dropped away during his retirement years when he spoke off the cuff and made jokes, witticisms, and quips. He made observations with his words strung together in facile fashion for extended periods. So there was a major change in how he spoke that amazed people who had seen him in both situations. As he flowered in personal conversations late in life, he became a fascinating conversationalist and it was a delightful change, and it reflected the fact that his final years were a happier and more carefree time for him.

BOSTON I cannot thank both of you enough for your time, your insight, your wisdom, your capacity to articulate, your knowledge in such a thoughtful manner, so this concludes the interview.

DAVID McCULLOUGH is regarded as one of America's leading historians. His books are not only major best-sellers, they also receive critical acclaim as evidenced by the many awards he's won including the Presidential Medal of Freedom. On November 19, 2015, I interviewed David in front of a sold-out ballroom at the annual fundraising dinner for the Dallas Bar Foundation. In forty-five minutes, we covered his two Pulitzer Prize-winning biographies, *John Adams* (Simon & Schuster 2001) and *Truman* (Simon & Schuster 1992). This chapter is devoted to the John Adams portion of the interview and a later chapter is devoted to the Truman discussion—and I've included David's comparison of Adams and Truman in both interview transcripts. He told me that our onstage conversation was the first time he had ever made a public presentation talking about both of his Pulitzer-winning presidential biographies.

"An aspect of Adams' life that I wanted to accentuate was his all-important role on the floor of the Continental Congress where he battled for the passing of the Declaration of Independence as did no one else. Jefferson hardly had a word to say on the scene. John Adams, a successful courtroom lawyer by trade, was brilliant and tough on his feet and would not give up until he had persuaded Congress that we must have the Declaration." **– DAVID McCULLOUGH**

CHAPTER 2

DAVID McCULLOUGH

ON

John Adams

BOSTON David McCullough is regarded by most as America's leading historian. What a special occasion it is for us to welcome him. He's won many awards, including the Presidential Medal of Freedom, though I suspect that the two awards he treasures the most are the Pulitzer Prizes he won for his biographies of John Adams and Harry Truman. His thoughts on those two historic presidents will be the subject of our interview tonight. Please welcome David McCullough.

THE COMPELLING LIFE STORY OF JOHN ADAMS

BOSTON David, before your John Adams biography came out in 2001, Adams' place among the Founding Fathers was underappreciated. Ben Franklin, George

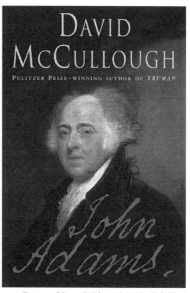

Courtesy of Simon & Schuster, Inc., New York, 2001

Washington, and Thomas Jefferson had all gotten plenty of historical recognition through the years, but not John Adams.

Then your book came out, became a best-seller, and was made into an HBO Emmy Award-winning miniseries, and that's caused us to put John Adams on the same high pedestal with our other leading founders.

Of John Adams' many contributions to America during his era, which ones do you think your book revived that people for the most part had either overlooked or forgotten?

McCULLOUGH I started out to write a dual biography of both Adams and Jefferson, who were about as different as any two men could be and came from two very different worlds. Yet they became fast friends, then rivals and almost enemies, and then, in their final years, restored their friendship. And they would wind up dying on the same day—the Fourth of July—which is one of those examples of how history can be far stranger than fiction. If you were a novelist and said, "I'm going to have them die on the same day and it will be the Fourth of July," no editor would accept that. And rightly so.

At the start, I didn't know much about Adams, though I knew quite a bit about Jefferson, or at least thought I did. As soon as I started reading Adams' letters and diaries and began to appreciate all that he'd done, I realized he was going to be my man.

I've been very motivated in my work to give credit where credit is long overdue. With both Adams and Harry Truman, this was a powerful, compelling motivation. Both of them served in the presidency between taller, more glamorous presidents, iconic Americans—Washington and Jefferson on either side of Adams; Franklin Roosevelt and Eisenhower on either side of Truman. To a large extent, both Adams and Truman had been ignored by history far too long.

The life of John Adams is a great story, and he told us nearly everything about himself in his letters and diaries, where Jefferson by contrast told us almost nothing about himself. He destroyed the letters he wrote to his wife and those she wrote to him; and, as a consequence, there is much of personal importance about Jefferson we simply don't know.

Something that sets John Adams apart from others of the Founding Fathers that wasn't widely known before my book came out was his being the only one of them who never owned a slave—as a matter of principal. His wife Abigail was even more adamant on the subject.

Another aspect of his life that I wanted to accentuate was his all-important role on the floor of the Continental Congress where he battled for the passing of the Declaration of Independence as did no one else. Jefferson hardly had a word to say on the scene. Adams, a successful courtroom lawyer by trade, was brilliant and tough on his feet and would not give up until he had persuaded Congress that we must have the Declaration.

John Adams was a man of absolute integrity, who spoke his mind. At times, he could be truthful to the point of being less than diplomatic, even rude.

He came from origins as modest and simple as Abraham Lincoln. He grew up on a hard rock farm in Quincy, Massachusetts. The only book in his house, as far as we know, was the Bible. His mother was almost certainly illiterate. He got a scholarship to go to Harvard at a time when it was far from the grand university of today, but a small college with few students. It was there he discovered books; and thereafter, as he said, he "read forever." I don't think there's ever been a better-read president in our history than John Adams, except possibly for his son, John Quincy. Abigail, too, was a marvel in this respect.

THE IMPORTANCE OF ABIGAIL ADAMS

BOSTON Which brings me to my next question: Your book may have done more to enhance Abigail Adams' place in history than it did for her husband. I loved the way you kept describing her as John Adams' "ballast."

What were the most important ways Abigail provided her "Dear Friend"/ husband stability and strength during his decades of public service?

McCULLOUGH Keep in mind that when people went off to Philadelphia to serve in the Continental Congress during the eighteenth century, they were largely out of touch with their family until they returned home. They couldn't pick up the phone and say, "How's everything going?" or send e-mails. In their time, one communicated only by letters carried on horseback, and it could take two weeks for them to reach their destination.

When Abigail ran the house for months on end while John was away, she had to make all the decisions for their household and family, and she never complained about it. She understood perfectly the importance of what John was doing and wanted to support him in every way she could. Later, after he sailed to Europe to serve as an American envoy, she stayed home to run everything.

ADAMS AS THE AUTHOR OF MASSACHUSETTS' CONSTITUTION

McCULLOUGH One of the most important of all John Adams' achievements was the writing of the Constitution of the Commonwealth of Massachusetts, which predated our US Constitution by nine years. Its content is very like that of our national Constitution, providing the same three-part structure of government—a legislative branch with a house of representatives and senate; an executive to lead the government in the form of a governor; and, finally, a supreme court.

But, the Adams constitution for Massachusetts also contained a clause that I want to read aloud, but before I do, please remember that at the time this was written,

there were no public schools to speak of and education had not yet been established as a fundamental necessity of our American system. With profound wisdom, Jefferson once said, "Any nation that expects to be ignorant and free, expects what never was and never could be." Adams did something about making sure that his state's government accepted its responsibility to provide children with a quality education.

Here's an excerpt from what Adams wrote in the Massachusetts Constitution:

"Wisdom and knowledge, as well as virtue, are fundamentally the right of the people, being necessary for the preservation of rights and liberties; and as these depend on starting opportunities and advantages of education in various parts of the country and among the different orders of the people, it shall be the duty of the legislators and magistrates of all periods of this Commonwealth to cherish the interests of literature and the sciences and all seminaries of them."

There are two operative words in there: the "duty" of the government to "cherish the interests of literature and the sciences and all seminaries of them—especially the university at Cambridge [Harvard], public schools, and grammar schools in the towns, to encourage private societies and public institutions rewards and immunities for the promotion of agriculture."

And listen to this line—he's really describing what a great university is about today: "...for the promotion of agriculture, arts, sciences, commerce, trades, manufacturers, and the natural history of the country"—and (and this is my favorite part)—"to countenance and inculcate the principles of humanity and general benevolence, public and private charity, industry and frugality, honesty and punctuality in their dealings, sincerity, good humor," (There shall be good humor!) "and all social affections, and generous sentiments, among the people."

ADAMS' CENTRAL ROLE IN THE DECLARATION OF INDEPENDENCE

McCULLOUGH I would like to mention one more thing before moving on. The painting that's been seen by more people than any other is that of the signing of the Declaration of Independence. It is by John Trumbull and hangs in the Capitol rotunda in Washington, where it's seen year in, year out by millions of visitors.

The painting is almost entirely inaccurate. First of all, there never was one gathering when all members of the Continental Congress signed the Declaration on the same day in the same room. Instead, they signed it when they came into town. The doors in the painting are in the wrong place, and the chairs are the wrong kind. The emblem of military symbols that decorates the rear wall never existed.

What is accurate, however, and what is so important and symbolically powerful are the men's faces. Every one is accurate. Trumbull painted preliminary studies of something like thirty-six of the signers from life.

To determine the exact center of a painting, you draw a diagonal line from the top left corner down to the bottom right, then another diagonal line from the bottom left up to the top right. Where the two

lines cross is the exact center. In Trumbull's painting, the lines cross on John Adams' chest. And there's a reason for that. He was the most important man at the Continental Congress, because he was the fellow who fought for it on the floor with the most persuasive force and as nobody else could have.

As it was, on the fourth day of July, 1776, there was no signing by anyone. The day the Declaration of Independence was signed by the most members of Congress was July second, and John Adams wrote about this, too, in a memorable letter to Abigail. Please keep in mind that nobody else who was there, nobody writing for the press at the time said anything with such foresight as Adams did:

> "The second day of July, 1776, will be the most memorable epoch in the history of America. I am apt to believe that it will be celebrated by succeeding generations as the great anniversary festival. It ought to be commemorated as the day of deliverance by solemn acts of devotion to God Almighty. It ought to be solemnized with pomp and parade, with shows, games, sports, guns, bells, bonfires, and illuminations from one end of this continent to the other from this time forward forever more." Bravo!

BOSTON Strike up the Star Spangled Banner!

McCULLOUGH Adams was not just predicting that this would become our national day of celebration every year. He was saying it would happen from one end of the continent to the other. Think about that! America then hardly even reached to the Allegheny Mountains. But he could see what was coming—he really could!

Sadly, despite all he did to get our country off the ground, John Adams has never been appropriately honored. There are no monuments or tributes to him in our nation's capital. We have statues of all kinds of people in Washington, but none of Adams, nothing to remind us of all he did.

Well, we know who he was. And if we know our history, we know how indispensable he was.

THE SIGNIFICANCE OF ADAMS' LEGAL SKILLS

BOSTON David, you've got four hundred lawyers in this ballroom tonight and, of course, one of the reasons John Adams did such a great job in writing the Constitution of Massachusetts was because of his being a great and noble lawyer. In fact, he was the Atticus Finch of his era in the way he stepped up to represent unpopular clients—in Adams' case, by representing the British soldiers who had fired the shots at the Boston Massacre—except unlike Atticus Finch, John Adams won his jury trial.

How did John Adams' being a top-notch lawyer impact his contribution as a Founding Father?

McCULLOUGH Most importantly, he had the capacity to get up on his feet and make his case with power. It should be remembered that when he defended the British soldiers involved in the Boston Massacre, he thought taking on that representation would be the end of any ambitions he had for a public career. But he felt that if we really believed in the principal of "innocent until proven guilty," then somebody had to represent those soldiers, and if nobody else would, he would. Friends warned him not to do it. "I've got to," he said, and then he prevailed and got the soldiers off.

I am hugely grateful to Tom Hanks, Paul Giamatti, Laura Linney, and the others involved in making the magnificent film for HBO based on my Adams biography; and the scene at the start of the series, where Adams defends the British soldiers, is a powerful testimony to his courage and effectiveness.

ADAMS AND JEFFERSON

BOSTON One of Adams' chief virtues was his capacity to develop and maintain friendships. In particular, for most of his life, he worked very hard to maintain a friendship with Thomas Jefferson, which (as you mentioned earlier) was challenging not only because of their political differences, but also because of Jefferson's "want of sincerity."

How hard was it for John Adams to refuse to let the Jefferson friendship slip away, and to take the initiative to rekindle it, and to forgive him despite Jefferson's betrayal of him during Adams' presidency?

McCULLOUGH It was hard. Abigail didn't want him to do it. She had no use for Jefferson from then on, and she was feisty. Adams was a true Christian. He believed in forgiveness, and, too, he was lonely. He missed his old comrades from the founding days. His outreach to Jefferson worked. Correspondence resumed. They got back to talking about much they both cared about—things like books written in Latin and Greek. Imagine two retired presidents of the United States discussing the proper pronunciation of certain Greek words. That was a different crowd back then! We never can underestimate the importance of their lives in history. How lucky we are to have had leaders of such stature during the eight and a half years of the Revolution— the longest war in our history except for Vietnam. A great many thought we had no chance to defeat the British, but we had leaders who refused to give up.

One of the most powerful scenes of all was when Adams went to meet George III after the war ended. Here were two men of the same age, and in many ways not dissimilar, greeting each other and starting the relationship between the two countries anew again.

I think the reconciliation had much to do with the English language. One of the things we can gain from studying the founders is an appreciation for their use of the English language and its importance to them not only professionally, but as a means of expressing their innermost feelings. Even Washington, who had comparatively little education, was very good at expressing himself. It's important not only that we read what the founders wrote, but read what they read.

I was reading a letter from John Adams to Abigail in which he said, "We cannot ensure success [in this struggle], but we can deserve it." I thought, "Imagine someone in a leadership role having that kind of attitude." What a great man!

Then, shortly after, I was reading a letter Washington wrote and there was the same line! I thought, "Wait a minute!" I picked up my trusty *Bartlett's Familiar Quotations,* and started through the eighteenth century, and there it was! It's a line from Joseph Addison's play *Cato,* the most popular play of the time. Washington, who adored the theater, probably saw *Cato* four or five times.

In eighteenth-century correspondence, no one used quotation marks, so it's almost impossible to know when they were quoting someone else. When Nathan Hale was about to be hanged as a spy by the British, he famously said, "I only regret that I have but one life to give for my country." It turns out that, too, was a line from *Cato*! Of course, the soldiers who were about to hang Hale also knew the line. I like to think Hale delivered it this way: "I only regret that I have but one life to give for my country"—not your country, you bastards!

COMPARISON OF JOHN ADAMS AND HARRY TRUMAN

BOSTON David, here's my transition question between our two subjects in tonight's interview. When John Adams was elected president, a Baltimore newspaper gave this description of him: "a tough, hardy, laborious little horse that works very hard and lives upon very little and is very useful to his master at small expense."

When I read that description of him in your biography John Adams, I thought to myself, "Couldn't those same words be used to describe Harry Truman?"

Photo credit: William B. McCullough

David McCullough

McCULLOUGH Absolutely. The two men had many similarities. Both grew up on farms, and lacked money or advantage. Neither was handsome or particularly charming in terms of first impressions, although that could change once people got to know them. Both enjoyed a good drink. Both liked to tell stories. Both were tough physically. Both did what they thought was right when they had major responsibility.

As president, both had to make unpopular decisions—and they made them. During his presidency, Adams kept us out of a war with France, which at the time would have been catastrophic. Most of the politicians, including Adams' fellow Federalists, were ready to go to war with France. But Adams knew better.

Like Adams, Truman was a great reader. Truman, as few could have imagined, read Latin for pleasure, and we're talking about a man who never went to college! One of the things to remember is that high school education at the time of Truman's adolescence was in many ways comparable to a college education of today. I've seen the history test Truman passed in his senior year in high school. I doubt many history majors in our colleges and universities today could pass that test. I'm not sure I could. Truman had an excellent history teacher in high school,

Miss Margaret Phelps, and he loved history all his life.

His knowledge went beyond history. During his presidency, Truman would go to the national symphony, not for a photo opportunity, but because he wanted to hear what was on the program that night. If it were one of his favorite composers like Mozart, he would take the score with him.

Harry Truman was no simple Missouri-nobody who had failed as a haberdasher. He was in many ways a born leader. Look at what he did in World War I and you see exactly what kind of leader he was, even as a young man.

At the heart of the story of these two remarkable men are character and courage. Not just physical courage, but the courage of their convictions. And Truman knew who he was. "I tried never to forget who I was, where I came from, and where I would go back to," he said.

One of my favorite Truman stories took place in the Oval Office when he was about to appoint General George Marshall secretary of state. One of his political advisors cautioned him, saying, "Mr. President, you might want to think twice about making that appointment." Truman asked why. "Because," said the advisor, "if you appoint General Marshall Secretary of State, in two or three months people will start saying he'd make a better president than you are."

"He would make a better president," Truman answered, "but I'm the president, and I need the best people possible around me."

Consider what he accomplished in his presidency. Imagine desegregating the armed services with one sweep of his pen. He just used his right as commander-in-chief and signed the military desegregation into law.

The Marshall Plan, one of our greatest steps ever as a nation, came to fruition during Truman's time in office. His accomplishments just go on and on. This supposed nobody became one of our best presidents ever.

It's important to keep in mind about Truman that he'd been through a great

many setbacks in his life. He had learned how to handle failure, as Adams had. If you want to judge someone on how they're going to act in the office of the presidency, take a look at how many times they experienced failure, because every president is eventually going to have failures of some sort to contend with. How does he handle it? Does he get feisty, angry, touchy? Does he start blaming others? Or does he get back up on your feet and keep going? Does he learn from mistakes and failures? Does he let those around him see that he has the courage of his convictions?

I would like to tell one more story because I think it's important. After he was appointed as secretary of state, General Marshall held a press conference. A reporter asked him if he thought he had received a good education at the Virginia Military Institute where he went to college. "No," Marshall answered. The reporter followed up, "Why not, sir?" "Because they didn't teach us history," Marshall said.

Truman once said, "The only new thing in the world is the history you don't know." Truman's passion for history was essential to his life in general and his presidency in particular.

It is not coincidental, in my view, that some of the most effective presidential leaders we've had were those who had a major interest in history. A number of them actually wrote history themselves—Woodrow Wilson and Theodore Roosevelt, for example. It is a sad statistic that today 82% of American universities and colleges no longer require any history in order to graduate. What a mistake that is! We have to know who we are, and how we got to be where we are, and how very much we owe to those who preceded us and provided us with so many blessings and opportunities that we ought not ever take for granted.

PETER S. ONUF is the Thomas Jefferson Memorial Foundation professor emeritus at the University of Virginia. He has written five books and many articles on the life of Thomas Jefferson. On October 7, 2015, I interviewed Peter in front of a group of students, faculty, and staff at Franklin Pierce University in Rindge, New Hampshire, about his book *The Mind of Thomas Jefferson* (University of Virginia Press 2007).

"I used to describe myself as a Jefferson therapist. We all need to work through the stuff that's repellent about his legacy and face it. It can't be ignored, but there is a way out. It's not enough to say, 'Oh, we're all human; we're all original sinners,' as my New England ancestors would say. Yes, we have human bodies and are all flawed and make mistakes. For Jefferson, however, we have to say more than that because he had a uniquely important vision." **– PETER S. ONUF**

CHAPTER 3

PETER ONUF
ON
Thomas Jefferson

JEFFERSON'S LEGACY IN THE TWENTY-FIRST CENTURY

BOSTON   Peter, these days, whenever anyone sings Thomas Jefferson's praises as "America's inventor" or "the great apostle of democracy and national self-determination," the common reaction is, "Yes, but ..., what was going on with the slaves at Monticello?" It's an issue that's recently caused members of the Democratic Party in Iowa to change the name of their annual Jefferson-Jackson Day dinners because "they want to align with the values of the modern day Democratic Party—inclusiveness, diversity, and quality," and they don't want their party in the twenty-first century to have any association at all with the name "Thomas Jefferson."

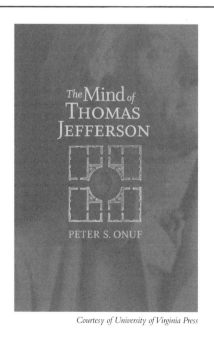

The Mind *of* THOMAS JEFFERSON

PETER S. ONUF

Courtesy of University of Virginia Press

How does the current national obsession over Thomas Jefferson's private life impact his public service legacy?

ONUF The issue of Jefferson's status as a slave-holder has been absolutely central ever since the American Civil Rights movement began. The great Julian Bond was a colleague of mine at UVa, and an African-American leader of the Civil Rights movement. In 1993, we had a celebration of the 250th anniversary of Jefferson's birth. On that occasion, Julian said, "The words of the Declaration of Independence are America's Holy Scripture. They define our experiment in republican government."

My distinguished predecessor as the Thomas Jefferson professor of history at the University of Virginia, Merrill Peterson, said similar things. In fact, Merrill really didn't want to know about Jefferson's personal life—didn't want to go there. He only wanted to take Jefferson for what he did—for his contribution to America.

For me, it's more what Thomas Jefferson said than what he did, because he provided the words that have defined who we are as a people.

BOSTON In April 1962, President John F. Kennedy had a big dinner at the White House. Those in attendance were winners of the Nobel Prize in different fields. In a crowded ballroom, in front of the Nobel Prize winners, President Kennedy said, "I think this is the most extraordinary collection of talent, of human knowledge, that has ever been gathered together at the White House, with the possible exception of when Thomas Jefferson dined alone." The universal response to JFK's statement was that he had said something wonderful on that occasion about Thomas Jefferson as a full-blown American hero—one of our leading Founding Fathers; the author of the Declaration of Independence; our third president; the man who acquired the Louisiana Purchase; the guy who's honored by one of the three presidential monuments

in Washington, DC; and the founder of the University of Virginia.

That's where things stood in America in 1962 regarding our assessment of Jefferson, but now we find ourselves in 2015. Can you imagine any United States president in the twenty-first century in a public forum offering the kind of praise for Jefferson that President Kennedy did, now that he's so tarnished by reason of the DNA information about his relationship with his slave Sally Hemings with whom it appears he fathered several children, and the fact that he owned so many hundreds of slaves over the course of his life at Monticello?

ONUF Let's invoke another great president, Abraham Lincoln. It's important to know that, like Lincoln, Thomas Jefferson's reputation has gone up and down throughout history. In fact, it's a wonderful way to study American history—by recognizing and understanding the changing reputations of our leaders over time. Merrill Peterson, who I just mentioned, wrote a classic book, *The Jefferson Image in the American Mind*.

BOSTON That book came out in 1960. Presumably, it's the book Kennedy had just read when he made his statement to the Nobel Prize winners two years later.

ONUF Jefferson was definitely on the upswing in 1962, but there was at least some awareness of there being a darker Jefferson at that time, and, of course, the Civil Rights movement was going on then. The conflict over Jefferson's doing what he did with his slaves revolves in many ways around the position of the South in American history and recognizing that Thomas Jefferson was a Southerner.

How does the South figure into our great nation's history? Before the Civil War, Jefferson's stock was falling rapidly, not only in the North with all the anti-slavery people who knew he had been a slave-holder; but also in the South where Jefferson was viewed unfavorably because he was associated with having declared that "all men are created equal"—a statement he could never unsay, and that Southerners could never agree with. Southerners insisted that all men were *not* created equal.

For over two hundred years, Jefferson has been for us the carrier of natural-rights thinking, which we'd like to believe is a given in America—because we believe in natural rights. We have a very robust sense of what's owed to all of us as a universal principle, and we call that "natural rights." It's right there in the Declaration of Independence.

Jeremy Bentham was a British utilitarian philosopher in Great Britain in the nineteenth century who famously said, "Natural rights is nonsense upon stilts." What rights? People like John C. Calhoun said there was no such thing as natural rights.

To talk about natural rights is to talk about nothing. All rights must be viewed as being specific. For them to have any meaning, they must be enforced. Lincoln said, "All hail Jefferson!", although he knew Jefferson had declared that "all men are created equal" in the context of the argument many patriots were making before the Revolution seeking lower taxes. By framing the issue in terms of natural rights, Jefferson gave us the most important sentence in history about who we are, or at least who we should be as a people.

The Stamp Act and the Sugar Act threatened to deprive colonists of their hard-earned property. So those laws caused a tax revolt, which led to the American Revolution. As for me, I'm glad Jefferson articulated our key principles that we can still rally around, glad we had the Revolution, and glad that Lincoln recognized the most important part of Jefferson's legacy.

Lincoln said that if Jefferson hadn't given us his rhetorical magic, and thereby given us a greater cause, then all that we've been through as a country—all the carnage—would have been pointless. Of course, Lincoln presided over the greatest carnage in American history, and though it

was tragic, there was something redemptive about it. I think the revival of Jefferson has carried through over time, and that he will be reconsidered favorably at some point by the Democratic Party.

BOSTON I hope you're right.

You say in the book, consistent with what you just said, that Jefferson's legacy is so complex because he forces us to think about our past, our present, and our future, and therefore serves the American people like no other founder.

Is that to say that all the controversy that continues to emanate from his life keeps the buzz going, and the ideas flowing, and motivates every generation to keep coming at him with new angles in hopes of explaining what often appears to be unexplainable?

ONUF I think that's exactly right. We shouldn't want to get rid of him just because there are some unattractive things about him we don't like. Jefferson left such a powerful legacy, not just because of the things he said and did that we can feel good about, but also because of some of the things he said and did that we need to feel bad about.

BOSTON We have a tendency to put our Founding Fathers on a pedestal. In many ways, they deserve to be there; but they *were* human beings, and thus flawed. Therefore, when we put them under the microscope, particularly after more than two hundred years of study, their flaws become more pronounced and publicized, and that causes them to be distorted from the men who they actually were. A big part of your analysis and perspective is in pursuit of the goal of putting these people in their time and in their circumstances, because that's really the only way to understand them.

ONUF I used to describe myself as a Jefferson therapist. We all need to work through the stuff that's repellent about his legacy and face it. It can't be ignored, but there is a way out. It's not enough to say, "Oh, we're all human; we're all original sinners," as my New England ancestors would say.

Yes, we have human bodies and are all flawed and make mistakes. For Jefferson, however, we have to say more than that because he had a uniquely important vision. What we're talking about is a conversation between the past and the present. Jefferson imagined progress—that over time, society would improve. It's a concept that may be hard for today's young people to grasp, because they now wonder whether the world will become a better place in the future, or whether they can expect progress, or whether they're going to make as much money as their parents did, or whether they will have a grand and glorious future. In fact, today's young people should worry about the future. It's problematic.

Jefferson believed in the future. He always believed that the American people would achieve great things. Implicit in believing in the future is a critique of the present. Think of Jefferson's present. He knew his fellow American patriots were not a chosen race or a superior people. They were people who drank ten times more alcohol per capita than Americans do now. They also smelled really bad. Those facts about the people who lived in Jefferson's era may sound like a silly thing to say, but when we sanctify and idolize the founders, we neglect their bodily existence. Of course, in Jefferson's time, slavery was legal in every American state, and we realize *now* that it was a horrible, nationwide condition.

So it's not as if Jefferson is either uniquely good or uniquely evil, and I don't want to say he was just a man of his time. He knew the injustices of his own time, with slavery being the primary injustice. No one fought in the American Revolution in order to make the world perfect for future generations. It was fought in hopes that our people would continue to do good work and make things improve over time.

BOSTON Along those lines, Peter, of putting Jefferson into his place as a unique visionary who could verbalize the hopes for Americans that we still aspire to in 2015, in your introduction to *The Mind of Thomas Jefferson*, you raise questions that contrast Jefferson's hopes for what America would ultimately become in the world—the chosen people, and the proxies and exemplars for the human race—and you distinguish his hopes about what we would become from how we really are in the twenty-first century.

What's the most significant way Americans today fail to live up to the high aspirations Jefferson had for us?

ONUF What we are confused about with Jefferson today is that we think his whole purpose in life was to pass on a bundle of rights to each one of us, which will enable us all to be secure and prosperous. We think we're the fulfillment of his vision because we possess those bundle of rights, and we're a little complacent about it.

His greatest legacy though is to make us think in two ways: first, that those in each generation should come onto the stage at the same time with an expectation of doing their best to make society work better. Jefferson was fine with saying to each succeeding generation, "It's now your turn. You are a solidarity. You're connected to each other. Your relationships with each other are meaningful. You constitute the living nation, and you will determine the nation's future destiny." So the first part of Jefferson's legacy is his notion that with each generation, there should be progress.

The second part is his getting the country to think collectively. This one is hard to understand, because we're so obsessed with individual rights. We've taken the notion of rights and made it into a license for us to be self-sovereign. If that's how someone thinks, then his emphasis is *not* going to be on the rest of the world. Jefferson gave us a patriotic commitment to the idea of people joining together to make a nation that, through their collective efforts, will get better in the future. That notion of working together in a collective enterprise is something that too many people miss because they focus too much on his being a total libertarian, interested only in his own world where he maintained his own plantation domain, and a man who was not thinking beyond himself.

When we only think of Jefferson as a slave-holder, we thereby think of him as somebody so wedded to injustice that he must have been a selfish son of a bitch—and that was not Jefferson! He was always thinking beyond himself. He was thinking of a larger coming together of the American people.

This idea that "all men are created equal" is an idea that still resonates with us today. What's so important about that as far as Jefferson is concerned? It defines him as being a moral philosopher. In that capacity—and this is a paradox—his idea was that each person should be so secure in his rights that he will want to come together and cooperate with others fearlessly, because he should have no fear that connecting with others will compromise his rights. To feel secure in one's rights is a threshold for becoming collaborative. This idea of Jefferson's really evokes a classical notion of human flourishing—of being better than one is now—because realizing one's human potential is greater when it is an integrated part of a larger, more capable whole.

That's what Jefferson was talking about. He didn't think having his own plantation and his own wonderful life at Monticello was sufficient. The ultimate fact for people in any generation to realize is that we will all die. Most of Jefferson's children died before he did, as did his wife. He knew that his and everyone else's time on earth was evanescent. Despite that, he saw his own work and the work of others as being part of a collective body of work that was not only to be accomplished during his lifetime, but also as part of a body of work that would continue into posterity.

BOSTON Part of the legacy you've just described is exemplified by the fact that, as Jefferson aged and faced his own mortality, a big part of what he focused on at the end of his life was establishing the University of Virginia, which would serve to empower many future generations. He did this not only by creating it, but also by mentoring the young students who attended the university, knowing that they were going to be the next generation of leaders.

When you talked about his future aspirations for the American "collective enterprise," sitting here in 2015, with the United States as polarized today as it's been in many years, our people clearly are not now acting as a collective enterprise; rather, we're acting as a dysfunctional gridlocked enterprise.

Is that your answer to my last question regarding what we're doing now that would be most disappointing to Jefferson's aspirations for what he hoped we would do?

ONUF Let me answer that indirectly by emphasizing how tenuous and experimental the United States was at its very beginning. If Jefferson had analyzed his past hopes for us compared to our current state of affairs, he would be most upset about the fact that too many people in our nation take our liberties and security for granted. It's hard not to. This is where we've been born, and almost since birth we've had these expectations of having peace in our society.

We revere the Founding Fathers because we think they were powerful people who made a world. They didn't know they were making a world, because at the time, our new nation was only a third-rate power; and I'm using "power" as a euphemism. It took a while before the United States could effectively operate as a power even regionally, and in the early years, it could have easily fallen apart.

When I talk about Jefferson, and what his priorities and goals were, the key word is "union," and it's another dimension of this "collective enterprise" idea. The word "union" has meant nothing to us in recent years except to describe what laborers form when they want to organize themselves against management. Union was the sacred word for Jefferson, because it was what the American experiment hinged on. If the states came together, then clearly they would have to overcome incredible differences. There's a world of difference between the people of South Carolina and the flinty people of New Hampshire. They're not from the same planet. They're different and don't have much to do with each other until national political issues come into play and then they *have* to deal with each other.

People who came over to America from Great Britain during Jefferson's era were actually much more closely connected to the British people than they were to the other Americans who had come from other parts of Europe. What was an American before Jefferson's era? There was no such thing as "an American" until the movement that led to independence began, when for the first time people living in the thirteen colonies began to call themselves "Americans" and thought beyond their respective states toward a larger union that had the potential to be an empire that would progress into the future and expand across the continent.

JEFFERSON IN HIS OWN TIME AND PLACE

BOSTON Let's get back to what you said a few minutes ago about the fact that, in 2015, many are attempting to draw conclusions about Thomas Jefferson, and yet they don't do the heavy-lifting associated with trying to evaluate him in his time, his circumstances, and his part of the country. You say in the Introduction that your purpose in writing the book, per its title, was to focus on "the mind of Thomas Jefferson," and make him more vital today by restoring him more completely to his own time and place.

What was your process for getting into the mindset, lifestyle, and circumstances of Jefferson's life—a man born in 1743, who died in 1826?

ONUF The best approach to understanding today how Jefferson operated in his era is an oblique one. If you go straight at the guy, you'll end up getting lost. You can easily read through more than forty volumes of his letters and never grasp the man and his accomplishments.

For me, the process began by asking questions. My first question of Jefferson had nothing to do with slavery. I came on to that later. My early work was about federalism, which was a fundamental problem for Jefferson. He had backed the idea of there being a union; and, that being the case, why was he so concerned about states having rights? How can individual states form a more perfect union if we focus mainly on the rights each state should have?

The answer I gave to this seeming paradox for students of federalism is connected to my own personal life story. My brother Nick is a distinguished political scientist—a scholar in the fields of international law and international relations. He and I have written a couple of books together. He got me thinking about state systems—not just the states in the United States, but in Europe as well. He got me to think about the United States as part of the world and also as it existed *not* in our magical fictional idea of the United States as a young, strapping, adolescent nation inevitably about to become a world power. Histories of nations historically have been written in order to justify and glamorize its people's pedigree. For the United States in the Jeffersonian era, it was all invented in order to make us feel good about our history and give us a national myth.

I thought my job was to begin undoing this myth and then recover and invigorate the authentic Jefferson whose mind can still speak to us. To do that requires us to put ourselves into his world—and it was a dangerous world. He didn't know what he was doing half the time, but he had great ideas. He believed free trade would bring peace and prosperity to the whole world. He had a vision not only of the union of the United States surviving, but also that our American union would serve as an exemplar for a European union of civilized republics, which would in turn inspire republics across the world. That was his vision for a republican millennium that would come to pass in time.

It was a wonderful vision, but it was presented in the context that the world was a dangerous place; and it became more dangerous after Americans achieved their independence, and the French Revolution began. When that happened, it felt like the world was falling apart.

JEFFERSON'S GENIUS

BOSTON Let's go deeper on that. Here we are in 2015. Our country has been around a long time. Whenever we decide to do something now on any political issue, it can usually be supported by a precedent. Following precedent helps make the decision made seem logical. We have all this history we can use to guide us as we face complex decisions. In Jefferson's era, though, they were really starting from scratch and reading about the history of countries in other parts of the world, and trying to discern other countries' best practices, and which of them could be applied to our new "collective enterprise," the United States.

In the context of all that, you point out: "Jefferson's Declaration of Independence was supposed to constitute a more perfect world order with colony states, a transcendent and inclusive national identity for the American people, and a legitimate recognizable government to represent union and nation states, and also people in the larger world." This was the idea of an American in the 1770s.

Where in the world did Jefferson get those ideas that would cause him to use those words and make them sensible to Americans in his era, when there really wasn't any precedent for what he was envisioning?

ONUF Here's my answer. If Jefferson had not been born in Virginia, which had once

been part of the British Empire, he would have been absolutely clueless. His vision for what he wrote about in the 1770s didn't come from having read John Locke, though he loved John Locke. It didn't come from steeping himself in the classics of political philosophy going back for ages.

To me, when I try to assess Jefferson's journey through life, the key point is that he began life as a provincial British subject on the far side of nowhere. America was nothing—a savage land—a land that, from the British perspective, was a place where people went to make a killing and sometimes did some killing. They came to America to strip resources from the land with enslaved people in tow to help them make a buck. This was a nasty place. To the British, the standard stereotype of those living in our thirteen colonies before the American Revolution was that all the people here were degenerate slaveholders who were impregnating their slaves. They had only contempt and disgust for the American people.

Yet Americans had a totally reversed perspective toward the British. Most Americans were proud to be from Britain and able to act as "agents" of the British Empire—a key term I like to use. Americans had created enormous wealth for Britain. Slavery and Indian removal were crucial to the process of continental colonization that created great wealth. Because of the wealth they were providing to the British, Americans began talking about how they deserved more favorable recognition and a bigger piece of the pie. "Equality" becomes a key word for Americans of that era. They started using it in the abstract and now it means everything to us. For British Americans, "equality" meant equal recognition with the British people at home. In other words, Jefferson's vision for America started from that all-inclusive imperial perspective, and Virginia would become great as part of an expanding empire that would include other new states or provinces.

BOSTON I understand what you've said, but here's my concern. The statement I read a few minutes ago was written by Jefferson in the era of the Declaration of Independence of 1776, which preceded the Revolutionary War. The Declaration was issued then in the context that, on the one hand, Jefferson liked the British a lot and thought there were many good things in their system. On the other hand, he didn't like the way they had been treating us. This ultimately led to our having a revolution against them. When the war ended with victory, and it came time to create a constitution, Americans wanted to be vigilant about not creating a system that would be essentially a mirror image of the British, who they despised and had just been at war with. Yes, on the one hand, they were respectful of what the British had done in setting up their government, but on the other hand, they were their bitter enemies.

ONUF Talmage, you put your finger on it. This is exactly what I'm talking about. Jefferson began life as an anglophile, and later he became an anglophobe. If we go back to our basic readings of Sigmund Freud, we know love and hate are very close. Our love and hate for Thomas Jefferson are not all that different. We're obsessed with him.

BOSTON It makes sense for you to bring Sigmund Freud into this conversation because the title of your book is *The Mind of Thomas Jefferson*. We can all rattle off the achievements of his life, and that's why so many people hate history, because fact rattling is so fundamentally boring. What you're trying to do, Peter, two-hundred-plus years after the fact, is get inside Jefferson's head and try to determine what made this guy tick. What was the source that put those important words into his mouth?

ONUF The words came to him because our Constitution is not that different from the English unwritten constitution—with a bicameral legislature and an executive who's not a king but nonetheless has prerogative powers like a king. George Washington became our first president and operated somewhat like a king and was the commander-in-chief. We now know that some Americans people feared that he would grab power, though they recognized him as the "father" of his country. Fortunately, for him and for us, he didn't have children; so he was not going to establish a king-like monarchical dynasty, and, therefore, he became highly regarded when he resigned from office.

JEFFERSON AND HIS SLAVERY COLONIZATION IDEA

BOSTON I want to go a little deeper on this issue of Jefferson and slavery. We know that even though Jefferson did nothing in furtherance of emancipation, he most definitely wrote about its undesirability and said that when the proper time came for emancipation, we should go about it by transporting the freed slaves away from the US to a foreign country, a notion that Lincoln later played with as he tried to identify his next step, post-emancipation. Lincoln ultimately realized that expatriation and/or colonization—i.e., deporting the freed slaves to a foreign country—was not practicable; because there were so many of them, and it would be too expensive to compensate the people who had owned the slaves prior to emancipation.

Long before Lincoln considered the issue, Jefferson came up with a way to deal with emancipation's logistics, and his approach was to deport all the freed slave children to a foreign land on the premise that eventually all the freed slave parents staying in America would die. When I read that, I wondered, "Here was Jefferson, a totally brilliant guy, and he was proposing to disconnect tens of thousands, maybe hundreds of thousands, of young children from their parents?" Does his plan of expatriating the slave children make Thomas Jefferson one of the most amazingly callous people in American history?"

ONUF Well, he's way up there on that issue, and you're right to raise the question.

BOSTON I raise it because I read your book.

ONUF It's a fair question, and a big issue. I'll invoke my brother again since we're getting a little personal on this. When I started thinking about international relations, it made me wonder what kind of nation we are. What kind of navel-gazing is characteristic of American studies? I wanted to get into it a little more, and it produced a big insight—maybe the most important insight I've ever had.

I'm proud of it, so let me explain it. It's the idea that the African people enslaved in America were a captive nation. If you think of nations at war, think of what was going on with slavery as an institutionalized cold war. The outcome of what Jefferson proposed (separating slave children from their parents and expatriating them) is horrific. You're right to be horrified by it, but Jefferson's idea started with this premise: there was one people, the master class, the white people of Virginia, who had enslaved and done radical injustice to another people—the black people. This conflict between the whites and blacks was a state of war, even though war technically occurs when two nations are actually fighting and have no prospect for peace. Slave-holders throughout history have known that a slave insurrection was always a possibility, since slaves always posed a threat of rising up.

Here is the liberal dimension to what Jefferson was saying: We've got two nations at war. The white nation believed America was *its* land, because it was they who owned it. Whites had once obtained a grant from the king, and it had become theirs because they improved the land—as John Locke said people should. The slaves were like foreign people with whom white people were at war and against whom they were committing radical injustices—because they thought blacks did not belong here.

If the slaves could have ownership of property in any country in the world, it would not be the United States. The white nation believed that the slave nation simply was not capable of having love of country—and, thus, couldn't be patriots and couldn't be true Americans.

We know what Jefferson wrote in the first draft of the Declaration of Independence, which was excised by his Congressional editors, where he blamed George III, the British Crown, for the existence of American slavery—an idea that was way over the top. There was some plausibility to his argument; because if it hadn't been for the British extending credit, the American slave-owners could never have bought slaves in the first place, and the thirteen colonies wouldn't have become a slave empire.

So, yes, the king had some responsibility for slavery in America. The horrible injustice, however, was committed against the black people when they were removed from their homes in Africa, and then transported to America, and then the white people acquired the slaves once they got here. These feelings of conflict between the whites and the blacks became exacerbated when Lord Dunmore, the British governor of Virginia, issued his proclamation of 1775 which invited slaves to escape from their owners, and cross over to British lines to fight and attempt to kill their masters. The idea of that happening was just horrible from the white planters' perspective.

So Jefferson's solution to this looming strife between the white nation and the black slave-nation was that the two nations needed to come apart. To Jefferson, the *humane* thing to do—and I emphasize this—was to declare the slaves be to free and independent people *once they were expatriated*. The black nation would then become an independent nation, post-emancipation, and they would find a place outside the thirteen colonies where they could put the freed slaves.

That's a liberal vision, Talmage. It's repugnant to us now because it's precisely opposite to our understanding of our forefathers coming together to form a new nation.

HOW JEFFERSON WOULD VIEW THE AMERICAN JOURNEY OF AFRICAN-AMERICANS

BOSTON Along those lines, and as part of his thoughts about the need for the expatriation of the slave children, Jefferson predicted a "genocidal blood-bath" if emancipation occurred without expatriation. In other words, if we emancipated everybody but then left all the freed slaves here in America, then there would be a genocidal blood-bath. Now we know that full emancipation, in fact, occurred with the passage of the Thirteenth Amendment in early 1865 before Lincoln was killed, and we also know of the treachery that's been inflicted on black Americans since 1865.

If Thomas Jefferson was to be reincarnated in 2015 and he learned of what's been happening to African-Americans in our country over the last 150 years, knowing his mind as you do, would his response be, "I told you so," or would his response be something else?

ONUF No, I think Jefferson would acknowledge that he was wrong about there being a genocidal blood-bath if the freed slaves stayed in America following their emancipation.

BOSTON We didn't actually have a genocidal blood-bath, but we have had a lot of bad stuff happen to black people—lynchings, etc.

ONUF It's all been one way—all white on black historically. Emancipation for African-Americans never gave them a chance to retaliate. This is one of the main impacts of Christianity in the slave South—the idea and power of forgiveness. It's something Jefferson couldn't have begun to imagine, given his perspective that the white nation and the slave nation were essentially engaged in a type of war, and, therefore, were mortal enemies. The forgiveness that took place after the slaves were emancipated would have been deeply surprising to him.

He would be surprised because, first of all, all feeling of union among the states had fallen apart during the Civil War; and that fact alone would have triggered the end of everything as far as Jefferson was concerned. Second, he would be surprised about the impossibility of implementing his plan of deportation; although during his lifetime, he must have begun to sense it wasn't going to work.

The best way to assess the future of slavery during Jefferson's life is to look at what happened to the price of slaves. If the price of slaves had gone down, it would have meant that people were turning away from the institution. To the contrary though, the price of slaves increased to an all-time high right before the Civil War. Slaves had become more and more valuable ever since the 1820s at the beginning of the great cotton boom. Jefferson surely knew this.

So would evidence-based history show Jefferson that he was wrong about what would happen after emancipation if the freed slaves stayed in the country? I'd like to think so. Even though he saw the nation as white and embraced the idea that white people should always be on top everywhere, I don't see him as an Anglo-Saxon racist. What he really believed was that George III was to blame for putting us in a state of war with the enslaved people.

The most important aspect for Jefferson in his plan for emancipation and expatriation was to create the conditions in which Africans, in the abstract, could return to either Africa or someplace else and become a free, independent, self-governing people. He believed that once peoples became equal across the world, they would all come together, and in time, the enmity between black and white people would dissolve.

JEFFERSON'S PHILOSOPHY OF GRADUALISM ON THE SLAVERY ISSUE

BOSTON All right. So he *was* a deep thinker—thinking about the need for expatriation as a means of furthering peaceful relations between the races, after drawing far-fetched conclusions about why slavery started in America. We all recognize that he wrote and spoke a lot about the evils of slavery, but he never *did* anything about it. During his lifetime, he never emancipated his own slaves or proposed any legislation in any way aimed at freeing the slaves.

So recognizing all these facts, surely he recognized that every journey starts with a single step. Did Jefferson see no wisdom in the concepts of leading by example or that progress usually takes place only incrementally?

ONUF Talmage, you're my kind of guy. You're an incrementalist. You say, "Let's get it started." So let me reconstruct Jefferson's logic about why he never got started doing anything about slavery. Recognizing that the mother principle of republicanism is that majority rules, Jefferson always advocated the need for people to see the world as he saw it. Through his plan of emancipation and expatriation, he could look ahead and see a better future for everybody—white and black people. He saw what slavery was doing to us, and what was wrong with it. In particular, he said what was mainly wrong with slavery was that young white people were growing up on their parents' plantations and learning from their parents the habits of despotism. We know Jefferson always placed a huge emphasis on education and how people can't be free if they're not enlightened and vigilant. He saw parents who owned slaves as turning out the lights on a huge part of their children's moral education by showing them how to rule over their slaves.

BOSTON What kind of parent was Thomas Jefferson? Wasn't he, as a slave-owner, guilty of training his own children to be despots over the family's slaves?

ONUF This is getting good. Remember his perspective that we've got to believe in both enlightenment and progress. In colonial days, people owned slaves and regarded them as property that came with the plantation—as if they were something like horses and cattle. The American Revolution taught us something we needed to know—that African-American slaves were human beings who could and would ultimately strike out for their rights. The first right is self-preservation. They were never going to be satisfied to live as slaves; and we realize now that, during Jefferson's life, the lid started coming off, and the situation was getting ready to explode.

Jefferson wanted all slave-holders to realize that they were doing great harm to their children by creating a legacy where it was perfectly fine to count as part of a family's estate the value of its slaves because, after all, they were property. You could sell them. Jefferson wanted people to recognize how short-sighted that type of thinking was because, in the long term, the republic simply would not survive if we didn't do something to eradicate this shameful legacy being passed down through generations.

Now your question recognizes that Jefferson didn't *do* anything about taking even a single step toward ending slavery; I maintain that what he *did do* was make a pitch to all enlightened people in hopes that they would soon constitute the majority in a land where the majority ruled. Jefferson essentially said to them, "You successfully fought a revolution for liberty; now follow through on it." That's why he said to Edward Coles in his 1814 letter, "It's up to your generation. My generation did the heavy lifting on independence. Now, it's up to your generation to do something about slavery."

JEFFERSON, SLAVERY, AND OPERATING A PLANTATION

BOSTON That position he advocated was nonetheless made in the context that, when he said it, he was still functioning in public life; and yet all he was doing about the evil of slavery was to talk about it.

Let me ask one more question on the slavery issue. My wife and I went to Monticello a month ago and saw his massive plantation. During Jefferson's life, managing a farm that size was necessarily a labor-intensive operation if the owner wanted his plantation to function productively. Given that there was no massive labor pool seeking employment on tobacco farms in those days, the only available workers were slaves.

So there was Jefferson trying to operate Monticello. It was a big place, and he wanted it to be a productive farm. He had to have manpower to do it, and there was no workforce in his part of the country knocking on his door trying to get hired. Even if laborers had been available, they would work only for someone who paid a daily wage. Put all those facts together and if Jefferson was going to make Monticello run productively, his only option was to use slaves like everybody else did.

In light of all that, were there any racially enlightened large-plantation-owner/farmers in the Southern United States in the last quarter of the eighteenth century or the first quarter of the nineteenth century, (i.e., during Jefferson's adult life), who were able to operate large farms without slave labor?

ONUF No there weren't. If someone decided to liberate his slaves, then they would leave the plantation, and the owner would also have to leave; and in some instances, that happened. Quaker slave-owners took the lead in doing that.

BOSTON So once a plantation-owner made the decision to free his slaves, then he necessarily would have to throw in the towel; since, without them, he couldn't have a productive farm?

ONUF That's what young James Madison thought when he was at the College of New Jersey (later named Princeton). Because of that aspect of plantation farming, Madison talked with his friends about the possibility of relocating permanently in the North after he finished college. William Short, a Jefferson protégé, ended up living in Philadelphia. Edward Coles, the man I just mentioned, was supposed to stay in Virginia and lead the fight for enlightening the public about what the institution of slavery was doing to America. He ultimately moved to Illinois, took his slaves with him, and gave them their freedom. It could be done, but Jefferson didn't do it on his own plantation, which, by the way, wasn't very productive.

BOSTON I realize Jefferson died insolvent, and most of his fellow plantation owners like Washington and Madison did the same, but surely they were at least trying for their farms to be productive.

ONUF There was a lot of wasted labor at Monticello. He had one period in the 1790s where he was determined to be an improved farmer, but he never had any real success.

BOSTON So he was a much better president, secretary of state, and Founding Father than he was a farmer.

ONUF And he spent a lot of money being an unsuccessful farmer. This is an unpleasant truth. In many ways, Monticello was a showplace home, but from an economic standpoint, it was built in a really inconvenient place (from a construction standpoint) on the top of a hill. We love it because it has a great view of the surrounding area, but just imagine the labor that went into leveling the land at the top where the home was built. How did he get water up there? There were all sorts of logistical problems, but building it as the showplace it was is another example of Jefferson the visionary in architectural terms.

When we call someone a "visionary," it's usually a compliment, because it connotes a person who can envision a better future. Visionaries, however, often overlook things. There's a lot a visionary doesn't see up close, because he's looking at things far off in the future.

Eventually, despite not having a productive farming plantation, Jefferson nevertheless owned a large population of slaves who had great value in the marketplace. It would be insulting and ridiculous to call him a slave-breeder, but what many Virginia and Maryland planters did was sell their slaves to plantation-owners who lived farther south. They would prepare slaves for the market and then take them to Richmond, which became a major center for sending slaves south in the slave trade. The domestic slave trade picked up in the last decade of Jefferson's life, and it became a big business. Virginians were selling slaves from that market up to the time of the Civil War.

BOSTON It sounds horrible, even though I know it happened.

ONUF People could make money with slaves in Virginia during the first half of the nineteenth century. You could also make money with slaves in industry—not just in agriculture. There were plenty of slaves who became productive laborers in ironworks. One of the unpleasant things to realize about slavery is that economically-speaking, it was *not* a dying system. Before the Civil War, slave prices were increasing. It was a robust and vital institution that supported the rest of the American economy. The richest county in America in 1860 was Adams County, Mississippi, and that was because of all the slaves being used where there was such a productive plantation area, because of its location in the fertile fields of the Delta.

BOSTON We've spent a lot of time on Jefferson's relationship with slavery, but we did it because it's the elephant in the room as far as his legacy is concerned; but now let's move on to some of the other aspects of his life.

JEFFERSON AND THE EXERCISE OF POWER AMIDST PARTISAN POLITICS

A few years ago, Jon Meacham wrote a biography of Thomas Jefferson, and its subtitle was *The Art of Power*. Meacham talked about how Jefferson exercised power in his political dealings by the way he went about manipulating relationships for his own end. In your book, Peter, you basically affirm that fact.

ONUF Jon Meacham saw that aspect of Jefferson's *modus operandi* as a good thing, and was not pejorative about that aspect of his personality.

BOSTON Correct. Anyway, in your book, you say, "The imperatives of partisan politics led Jefferson to secrecy and concealment, and, therefore, he would conscript others to do his pamphleteering and newspaper writing." He wouldn't come out publicly and make harsh statements regarding the political issues of the day. Instead, he would hire other people to write what he wanted to be said, so they would put their names into the marketplace expressing ideas that were actually Jefferson's.

Does that mean Jefferson believed that refusing to state his position in a transparent method on a controversial issue in order to avoid personal confrontation outweighed the benefits of expressing his authentic self in an honest manner?

ONUF Think of Jefferson as an anti-partisan in a partisan age. He was partisan in spite of himself. As a party leader in the 1790s when he was hiring people to write and put their name on editorials advocating the positions he favored, Jefferson did so because he wanted to stay above the fray. He was conflict-averse. It gets back to his aspirations for harmony and cooperation, like he said in his first inaugural address—"We are all Federalists. We are all Republicans." He wanted to wish-away party conflict.

He had a vision for how America could move toward a higher level of understanding. To do that would require us to overcome the vicious divisions that had characterized the American Revolution itself, which was a party conflict between Tories and patriots; the debate over the ratification of the Constitution was also a party conflict. He had hoped and expected that the first Washington administration would be a group of likeminded men working toward the common good.

BOSTON Of course, Washington thought that, too, but it didn't take long for that pipe dream to go away because of the fundamental differences in how the factions wanted the country to be run—with Hamilton and the Federalists on one side, and Jefferson, Madison, and the Republicans on the other side. They soon recognized that they were not going to be unified and would be in conflict.

To me though, it just seems devious to say, "Okay. We're in conflict. I don't like what you're saying because it's just flat wrong, but I'm not going to come right out and criticize you. I'm going to hire

Joe Blow to criticize you, so that when I see you in polite company, I'll keep a smile on my face and pretend like we're friends and everything between us is hunky-dory; when, in fact, behind the scenes, I'm doing everything I can to find a way to defeat your point of view." I have trouble recognizing that the way Jefferson acted using this mindset constituted "the art of power." I regard it as dishonest behavior.

ONUF As I suggested, we can reach higher levels of understanding. When the Republicans mobilized in the 1790s, it was because Jefferson and Madison were convinced that monarchists and aristocrats had taken control of the federal government. What Jefferson believed was that the high Federalists, who had dominated the second Washington administration and the Adams administration, were not good Americans; and it was only the Republicans who still stood up for the country's founding principles. That's why he talked about the need for a political revolution with the election in 1800 that he hoped would restore the spirit of 1776—thinking his desired revolution could come about only by his being elected to the presidency. That sounds awfully self-serving to say: "Once I'm president, everything will be great," but he really believed it.

He believed that the controversies between Federalists and Republicans had spilled over into America from the French Revolution. I emphasize again the importance to Jefferson of international relations. In the 1790s, one thing combatants had learned was that in America, they were part of a worldwide movement defined in terms of insurgent democrats all over the Western world. That had happened in France; and there had almost been a revolution in Britain—and the leaders of this great insurgency would be called "democrats."

What's a democrat? It's someone who believes "all men are created equal." In furtherance of turning that goal into reality, they would need to organize a political system based on the equality of all citizens, and that would require power sharing.

Those who supported hierarchy, monarchy, and aristocracy believed that all men were created *unequal*. They wanted to preserve the privileges of the rich and well-born or, even more insidiously, they wanted to destroy the republic and build a new aristocracy upon its ruins. This perception of there being these two disparate factions is one of Jefferson's most powerful legacies today in the realm of democratic thought.

We now have the moral equivalent of an aristocracy, because we have some families in America in 2015 with dynastic ambitions, and yet voters keep returning them to office. It provides a horrifying image of a republic degenerating into an aristocracy or a monarchy. The idea of this taking place in America was a nightmare to Jefferson. It's why he was so much less concerned about what to do with slaves (since he always saw himself as a benign and benevolent master)—than he was about the possibility that the gains achieved by the American Revolution would soon be lost because people like Alexander Hamilton had George Washington's ear. To Jefferson, if Hamilton succeeded in gaining control of the federal government, then everything would go downhill.

JEFFERSON AND HAMILTON

BOSTON I'm glad you brought Hamilton into our discussion because there was Jefferson, who didn't want to have direct conflict with any of his adversaries, except for the one clear conflict he had with Hamilton. Those two were simply oil and water, which made open conflict between them inevitable. As members of Washington's Cabinet, they were always at loggerheads over many key issues.

Did Jefferson, in his mind, essentially throw up his hands and surrender to the impossibility of harmonizing with Hamilton, much like he surrendered to the impossibility of taking any action to end slavery?

ONUF He had an answer to Hamilton. The title of our upcoming book, *Most Blessed of the Patriarchs* (co-authored with Annette Gordon-Reed, and to be released in April 2016), is taken from a letter Jefferson wrote to Hamilton's sister-in-law, Angelica Schuyler Church. In the letter, Jefferson talked about how he intended to go home after his tenure as secretary of state, and become a "blessed patriarch," supervising all the good folks at Monticello. He was going to look out for the welfare of the people who had looked out for him, and that would include his family and his slaves. He planned to retreat from political life.

His retreat, however, would be tactical and temporary, because he intended to return to public life; and when he did, he had definite objectives he planned to pursue. Even though he hated political parties, (and it's important that he hated parties), he was an absolutist. He loved his idea of the true nature of "the people," and it bothered him that they didn't have enough honest representatives in Congress who would stand up for the people's rights. He believed there were too many people who could be bought off by Hamilton with some crumbs from the Treasury Department's table. He wanted federal legislators who would not be corrupt, and would be independent vigilant defenders of the people's rights.

The Republican Party's partisan press printed editorials advocating all the things which Jefferson believed but wouldn't write himself. They led a vicious assault on the Washington and Adams administrations, accusing them of being monsters who wanted to destroy the republic and return the country to a monarchy. Jefferson believed that these partisan editorials would persuade the people and cause them to come back into having the same mindset that had powered our quest for independence and liberty. When it happened with his election in 1800, it was Jefferson's triumphant moment.

Photo credit: Kristin K. Onuf

Peter Onuf

JEFFERSON, THE SEDITION ACT, AND THE KENTUCKY RESOLUTION

BOSTON His triumphant moment was tied into the incredible, partisan discord between politicians and belligerent partisan newspapers, which had led Adams and the Federalists to pass the Alien and Sedition Acts in 1798, which provided that anyone criticizing the president was committing a crime for which he could be imprisoned; and, in fact, people were imprisoned under the Sedition Act.

ONUF But not if they criticized the vice president.

BOSTON That's right. There was only one non-Federalist in Adams' administration, and that was Vice President Thomas Jefferson. The Sedition Act made it a crime to criticize the president or anybody in his Cabinet, but it was legal to criticize the vice president because he was on the other team. So most people became angry over the Federalists' extinguishing the First Amendment's right to free speech and freedom of the press.

In response to the Sedition Act, in 1799, Jefferson authored a nullification resolution on behalf of the State of Kentucky which basically said that the people of Kentucky believe the Sedition Act to be unconstitutional; and, therefore, they had the right to void it—not avoid it, but void it, ignore it, pretend like it did not exist. Madison did the same thing in Virginia, although not with quite the edge to it, because he didn't use the word "nullification."

So there was Jefferson, advocating the position that a state had the right to ignore a federal law, in the context of his being the grand champion of building, strengthening, and preserving the union.

How could he believe a state had the right to nullify a federal law?

ONUF A state's having the right to nullify depended on what the federal government was all about. Once the anti-republican bad guys had taken control of the federal government, then there was no viable option to address the bad guys' wrongs except by the states. He did not see the states as being an end in themselves, because it was the ideal of the union that he cherished all his life, but since the states were his only remaining option as a means of acting upon the federal government's evil and unconstitutional Sedition Act, Jefferson decided he would make his pitch to void the Act acting under the authority of a state—in this case, the State of Kentucky.

I talk about the central importance to Jefferson of the idea of union and states' rights, just as I talked about love and hate being closely connected. Union and disunion are tightly wed to each other. At various moments, Jefferson looked over the precipice and saw the abyss. He believed the union might not survive. The Missouri Controversy (that led to the Missouri Compromise) is a wonderful example of this, when Jefferson heard "a fire bell in the night," because he believed that what was happening in the attempt to restrict the spread of slavery in Missouri might well become the death knell of the union. It was a nightmare for him.

Jefferson had a gift, for what we psychologists call "projection"—that is, believing that all evil impulses come from one's enemies—in this case, from those north of the Mason-Dixon line. He saw them as hypocrites because they pretended to have sympathy for enslaved people; but in fact, they aspired to enslave everybody by depriving Virginians (and those in the other slave states) of liberty by imposing *their* will on the whole country. Imagine this terrible idea of an engorged, bloated federal government in Washington—does this again sound familiar?—simposing law on the states.

Dissidents always rally at the lower level of people, like defending personal liberty laws in Wisconsin. The litmus test for the federal government was: are the people governing themselves through the agency of the federal constitution? If so, then they believed a legitimate national government was working.

Asking these sorts of questions was and is deeply corrosive and subversive. When you start to ask them—and thereby challenge the federal government as many people are doing today—you're on the slippery slope that leads to the abyss. I can't emphasize strongly enough how fragile the American experiment was during Jefferson's era. What Jefferson feared most was that his political enemies, with their misbegotten, hierarchical ideas, would extinguish all that had been gained by the American Revolution.

BOSTON I understand what you're saying. In 2015, we hear the term "start-up"—start-up companies, start-up enterprises, start-up all kinds of things. In the Jefferson era, we had a start-up country, with a start-up form of government. When something happened that shattered the promise of the ideas that got the ball rolling—things like freedom of speech and freedom of the press, as guaranteed by the First Amendment to the Bill of Rights—and the federal government started enacting laws that caused people to get

thrown in jail because they expressed their freedom of speech—then, in Jefferson's eyes, it would be just fine for this start-up country and its government to fail.

JEFFERSON AND THE LOUISIANA PURCHASE

BOSTON One final question: As president, one of the most important things Thomas Jefferson did was consummate the Louisiana Purchase. He did it without amending the Constitution, which violated his prior pronouncement that if the US was going to buy property from a foreign government, it required a constitutional amendment. So regardless of his past position on how the government was supposed to work, all of a sudden, now that he was president, he had the opportunity to acquire the Louisiana Purchase for an amazingly low price; and to wait on a constitutional amendment would might cause the deal to get away.

Having said all that, can we draw the conclusion that, in Jefferson's mind, there were times when the ends justified the means—thereby providing a precedent for future presidents like Lincoln? That is, was Jefferson the father of this idea of the law of necessity—of doing whatever it took when an extraordinary situation arose, regardless of its constitutionality?

ONUF You sound just like the second coming of Henry Adams. You must be a lawyer to make those kinds of criticisms, and I deeply respect that, Talmage. Now—doing my best to channel Jefferson—there is a higher law, and that's the law of nature and nations, and it was international law in the eighteenth century.

Recognize that the Louisiana Purchase would double the size of the US. The dilemma which Jefferson recognized was that with the Mississippi watershed flowing through New Orleans, it could potentially open a way for the French (or any great imperial power) to establish a beachhead at New Orleans, and then go from there to take the continent away from the Americans. What Jefferson celebrated as the great legacy of the American Revolution was that in our country, there would be land for the thousandth to the thousandth generation; but that would not happen if a foreign country took control of New Orleans, and then the Mississippi River, and then used those strategic locations to take over the rest of the country.

Business people think that their business will either expand or contract; and if it contracts, it will fail. The same thing applied to countries, at least in Jefferson's mind. He thought that if he didn't take Louisiana and New Orleans, then the French would soon move in and establish a French empire.

Napoleon clearly had a vision of a French empire in America. If that happened, then what would the French do with their empire? Jefferson feared that they would unleash Native Americans on the American frontier just like George III had done, and they would also foment a slave insurrection, since the first French Revolution had attempted to bring an end to slavery.

It was in the context of this scenario that Jefferson talked about the necessity to acquire Louisiana very quickly. He knew that if he didn't move quickly, the opportunity to make the deal could go away, and if it did, it would be dangerous to our union to have a foreign presence on our borders.

Jefferson was not stupid. He knew that we would have to have the right kind of power to meet the challenges the United States would face. The marvelous thing about Jefferson is that in his conception of an expanding union, he developed an approach to politics and state-making that brought new states in and connected them with the other states. This integration process for the new states didn't happen because we offered them a big powerful government in Washington, DC. It happened because representatives of the new states were brought into Congress, and public lands were distributed to them, and public spending was used to improve them, such

that all the tools of the federal government reversed the centrifugal tendencies that could easily have left western settlers disconnected from the union.

The possibility that adjacent territories would not readily join into the union as states was one of the greatest threats in American history. We think of frontier people as our heroes—that they were the great settler/conquerors of the continent—yet at the outset, the loyalties of these people toward the union were definitely up in the air. Jefferson had a vision of how they could be brought into our union by offering them the promise of equality. Every state in the union, old and new, would in some fundamental sense be equal—certainly equal in the Senate. That principle of state equality was vital to Jefferson's conception of how the union could grow and prosper.

America has always provided many ways up the ladder. That's the genius of American federalism. It has had its failures, but at its core, it always maintained a vision of an expanding union made up of equal and free states, with all Americans equal to one another. That's something we need to remember as we nitpick Jefferson on how he handled the Louisiana Purchase, and second-guess him on many of his policies.

BOSTON I'm not criticizing his decision to consummate the Louisiana Purchase, because obviously we've all enjoyed the benefits of that massive acquisition. If it had gotten away, it would have been a crime. I'm just asking you, as my Jefferson expert, the question regarding his thought process in going forward with the purchase without the support of a constitutional amendment, as he had stated previously was needed. It's a question that has been thrown around for years, and reasonable minds have differed about Jefferson's legal justification for bringing the Louisiana lands into our fold.

You've done a wonderful job of explaining the marvelous complexity of Thomas Jefferson, but now our time is up. Thanks so much, Peter.

DAVID O. STEWART had a distinguished career as a top-flight lawyer before deciding to become a top-flight historian and historical novelist. He came to Dallas on February 10, 2015, the first day of publication for his presidential biography, *Madison's Gift: Five Partnerships That Built America* (Simon & Schuster 2015) that later won the William H. Prescott Award for Excellence in Historical Writing. We had our interview at Arlington Hall in front of a crowd of clients and professionals of my law firm and Ernst & Young.

"Despite all the harsh attacks made on him during the War of 1812, Madison (unlike Adams and Jefferson) never retaliated against a newspaper or anybody else. When the war finally ended, and it ended reasonably successfully, the country proceeded to have an incredible rebirth. He's the only president I can think of who had a better second term than his first term." **– DAVID O. STEWART**

CHAPTER 4

DAVID O. STEWART
ON
James Madison

MADISON'S TRIUMPH OVER HIS LIMITATIONS

BOSTON David, let's begin with the personal side of James Madison. He was short—5'6". He was not handsome, had a soft voice, and was socially timid. If he walked into this room right now, no one would notice him. But for those in his day who made the effort to get to know him, they soon realized he was brilliant, hard-working, tenacious, and unflappable.

For the benefit of us social wallflowers, did you discern Madison's method of operation in connecting with high-horsepower people in a way that made them overlook his physical and social limitations in order to appreciate his subsurface virtues?

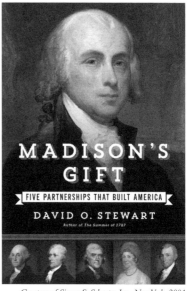

Courtesy of Simon & Schuster, Inc., New York, 2001

STEWART That is the core of what I tried to do with this book. He really was a fellow with a remarkable intellect. What he did principally to rise above his limitations was figure out, (and essentially say to himself), "Okay, I am short. I am skinny. I don't much like going to big events and have zero charisma when I get there. But I'm smart, I work harder than anybody else, I work effectively with other people, and I can get the job done." So he figured out ways to connect with people who could help him do great things. He executed on what we recognize as a modern self-assessment process that young professionals these days are trained to do, though I think it was a natural thing for Madison to do to make himself more effective. He figured out a way to be proactive about using his gift of connecting with people, which was a rare gift.

In history, we think of a great leader as sort of the man on horseback, and the guy who demands to be in charge. Madison didn't worry about being in charge. He worried about getting the job done. One of his longtime aides said, "What was wonderful about President Madison was he always worried about what was due from him to others." When was the last time we had a leader who worried about that instead of worrying about what was due *to him*? That's the prevailing model of leadership. Madison presents a different model and one worthy of study.

MADISON'S UNIQUE GIFT

BOSTON Regardless of his personal and social deficits, per your book's title, Madison made his place in history by using his "gift" for developing partner relationships with those—Washington, Hamilton, Jefferson, Monroe, and his wife, Dolley—who had the star power he lacked.

Has there been anyone operating in American politics in the last hundred years who had Madison's gift for filling his personality toolkit with the tools he lacked by cultivating a steady stream of complimentary partnership relationships, *or* was his gift a unique emotional-intelligence talent that disappeared when Madison died?

STEWART It was a unique gift. You can find people during the last century who were not embarrassed and not nervous about having really powerful people around them. Although Franklin Roosevelt was full of star power, he also was happy having stars around him. They didn't make him nervous, because he had so much confidence. You can see other characters with quieter personalities (Dwight Eisenhower, for example) who were able to enter leadership positions. Madison's particular talent for forming partnerships by working with so many different kinds of people as peers, and then causing those partnerships to put him in line for leadership positions, were what made him unique.

MADISON'S BEING UNDERAPPRECIATED

BOSTON When the United States won the Revolutionary War, it essentially became a start-up country, and start-ups often fail. Twice during Madison's political career, our American start-up was on the ropes. First, when the United States operated under the Articles of Confederation, a time when George Washington said the country was connected by "a rope of sand;" and second, during the War of 1812 when the country was almost taken back by the British. Both times, aided by his friends, Madison saved the start-up country and empowered it to survive, allowing him to emerge as the Father of the Constitution and later America's first successful wartime president.

Despite these extraordinary achievements, accomplished in large part by his unique gift for getting things done through partnerships, Madison's picture isn't on our money and contemporary historians don't rate him among our top ten presidents. Why is Madison so underappreciated?

STEWART Well, he was short. He was quiet. I always try to point out, however, that he had the hottest wife.

I think a good bit of his being under-appreciated came from that terrible day in August 1814, when the British troops burned the public buildings in Washington, DC—a day that badly tarnished Madison's historical legacy. There were lots of reasons Washington, DC burned in 1814. Mainly it was because of bad military planning on our part, but it's important to remember that, after it happened, we came back and ended the War of 1812 fairly successfully. That image of our burned capital is something that has stuck with Madison, along with his quietness. It's a shame, because when you go through the first thirty years of our history, up to the end of Madison's presidency, there's nobody there in the middle of everything and making a difference like Madison.

BOSTON How far do you have to expand Mount Rushmore before you get to Madison?

STEWART I'm still fighting with the Washington Nationals over the presidents' race that they run at every ballgame. I can't believe they put William Howard Taft in there before Madison, and I actually wrote them about that. We've had some wonderful presidents, but if you saw Ken Burns' documentary *The Roosevelts*, there was this great moment where David McCullough said, "You have to realize that our extraordinary presidents—well, they're extraordinary!" There aren't many of them. We have plenty of presidents who do their best, but because of the times or their own problems, they are not regarded as being extraordinary.

I think Madison as president turned out to be extraordinary, and here's why. Both John Adams and Thomas Jefferson threw newspaper editors in jail for writing nasty things about them. Lincoln had newspapers shut down if they became too critical of him during the Civil War. This stifling of freedom of speech and freedom of the press is something we cover up about our history. During the War of 1812, James Madison was vilified around the country, particularly in New England. He was called awful names, particularly after the burning of Washington's public buildings. A "coward" was just the beginning of what the critics called him. Despite all the harsh attacks made against him, he never retaliated against a newspaper or anybody else. When the war finally ended, and it ended reasonably successfully, the country proceeded to have an incredible rebirth. He's the only president I can think of who had a better second term than his first term. For those reasons, I would put him up there on Rushmore if it were my mountain.

MADISON AND SLAVERY

BOSTON Despite his being in the middle of the action when good things happened during our republic's early years, part of your book focuses on Madison's Achilles' heel—what he thought, said, and did about slavery throughout his lifetime. To use St. Paul's term, the slavery issue was "the thorn in his flesh," as it was with Jefferson.

What kept Madison from rising above the fray on slavery, particularly in the context that he was perhaps the first to see that the slavery issue had a good chance of dividing the country between North and South in the not too distant future?

STEWART Yes, he felt slavery personally. His family owned slaves—one hundred slaves worked at Montpelier. As a young man, he actually bought land in upstate New York and wrote about leaving Virginia so he would no longer live on the labor of slaves. He wanted to be free of slavery but he never succeeded.

Some of his inability to address slavery came about because he was the oldest son of a family who owned lots of property and many slaves. Part of the reason why he never took steps to free the family slaves was because it was really comfortable to run

Montpelier with all those slaves taking care of it. When Madison finally retired, he continued to struggle with the slavery issue but did nothing about it.

Madison felt he had attacked all the great issues facing the country—the need to demonstrate that a self-governing republic could be established that preserved the liberty of its citizens, the need to deal with the British and French threats at the beginning of the nineteenth century—all the great issues except one. Slavery was the one thing he never was able to figure out. He wrote memos to himself and letters to people about it. He was constantly trying to figure it out. He believed that for there to be government-sponsored emancipation, the government would have to buy slaves from the slave-owners. That would require plenty of money, which the country simply couldn't afford without selling off the public land out West. He didn't think freed slaves could live in America, because he believed racial prejudice was so terrible at that time that it would be necessary to move the slaves out of the country. Of course, that was ridiculous. We couldn't do that. There were two million slaves in America by the time he was in retirement, and that was way too many to think about deporting to another country. And most of them didn't want to go, anyway.

The issue of what should be done about slavery became the one issue where Madison's intellect was not equal to a problem he faced. He never confronted the fact that dealing with slavery was a problem of his human heart. Solving the economic and political challenges were not enough. He also had to overcome racial prejudice. He never figured out a way to deal with it.

MADISON AND HAMILTON

BOSTON Moving beyond his lack of success in addressing slavery, let's talk about all the success he had with the five partnerships you profile in the book. The first was with Alexander Hamilton, with

whom he partnered in calling together the Constitutional Convention, negotiating and drafting the Constitution, co-authoring *The Federalist Papers*, getting the Constitution ratified by the states, and then getting the nation's capital moved from Philadelphia to the site on the Potomac that became Washington, DC. Madison and Hamilton enhanced each other and accomplished more together than they ever could have separately.

As the years passed though, these two founders lost their chemistry, diverged, and clashed. What caused them to go from connect to disconnect?

STEWART It's a great story. They were always very different. Hamilton was this dynamic guy from the West Indies who came from nothing. He was an orphan at age thirteen and became a completely self-made man. Madison was quiet, a man who didn't have a home of his own until he was forty-three. He lived with his mom until he was seventy-eight. He was not one of the world's adventurers. Despite his differences from Hamilton, together they made tremendous things happen.

The real nub that led to their disconnect arose early in George Washington's administration, and it was a problem anybody working with Hamilton had to deal with. Madison was Washington's closest adviser for the first half-year of the new government, but then Hamilton arrived as secretary of the treasury and supplanted him. Madison had fundamental disagreements with Hamilton's financial policies, and that drove them apart. There are people who explain the separation between Hamilton and Madison in personal terms, that Jefferson came back from Paris and seduced Madison away from Washington and Hamilton used his overpowering intellect and wily charms—I think that's baloney.

Madison made up his own mind to split with Hamilton. and it was over basic questions of what the government should look like. The Constitution was originally adopted to give us a stronger, better federal government. In Hamilton's hands, it became much stronger than Madison ever expected. Hamilton and Madison had fights over the federal assumption of state debts from the Revolution, and over the centralized Bank of the United States. These were government control issues Madison had not actually foreseen when the Constitution was signed and ratified. Hamilton was this incredibly creative, vibrant guy who had Washington's backing, and with Washington's backing—as Madison well knew—you could make things happen in America.

We ended up with several financial panics in the early 1790s, thanks in substantial part to Hamilton's financial initiatives. Madison was a country guy who distrusted finance, who was alarmed by the panics, and just didn't buy what Hamilton was doing, so he opposed Hamilton's big government initiatives.

The fascinating thing is that even though Madison was a determined, consistent adversary of both Hamilton and Washington after the first few years of Washington's presidency, the disagreements never became personal. After five years of that adversary relationship, with Madison serving as the leader of the opposition in Congress, Washington needed a new ambassador to France. Hamilton suggested he appoint Madison. Washington sent out feelers to find out if Madison would take the job, but Madison refused because he didn't want to be part of that administration. That situation gives you a feel for how Madison could maintain personal relationships with other leaders even though he was completely opposed to them on their policies.

MADISON AND WASHINGTON

BOSTON The second partnership described in your book was the one Madison had with George Washington. Washington was nineteen years older—almost old enough to be Madison's father. What Washington had in stature with his command presence and leadership ability, Madison had in brains. They worked hand-in-hand at the Constitutional Convention; then shortly thereafter during Washington's pre-presidency they planned the new governmental enterprise; and then during the early years of Washington's administration, Madison served essentially as America's prime minister until the disconnect occurred over Hamilton's plan to expand the role of the federal government. While their partnership lasted, Washington plus Madison was a case of one plus one equaling at least three, and maybe ten.

Would it be fair to say that Madison owed more of his ultimate political success to Washington than to any of his other partners?

STEWART That's fair. Washington was the trump card of American politics when the country was being formed. He was unassailable. Some of you will get how this worked by an analogy: At my first law firm, there was a guy named Jack, the fellow who founded the firm, and then there were the rest of us. We used to say, "You and me, Jack. We can make this thing happen." With George, as long as you had him on your side, you could make things happen, and Madison understood that. He cultivated Washington, and in short order made himself indispensable to the country's indispensable man. That was incredibly smart on Madison's part. I'm sure it was very painful for Madison to separate himself from Washington over the financial policy issues I mentioned a minute ago because he knew Washington was the key to getting things done.

For his own ideological reasons, however, Madison didn't feel like he could maintain his political alliance with Washington, even though the partnership they had maintained for years was very important. Getting the Bill of Rights through Congress was something that in many ways was a solo act by Madison, but having Washington's support put him and the Bill of Rights over the goal line.

MADISON AND JEFFERSON

BOSTON The third partnership Madison had was with Thomas Jefferson. Jefferson was eight years older, so in some ways was an older-brother figure. He gained his fame earlier, writing the Declaration of Independence in 1776, and then preceding Madison as president. Together they formed the first political party in America, which is today's Democratic Party. On page 125 of your book, you have a great quote about them from John Quincy Adams: "The mutual influences of these two mighty minds upon each other is a phenomenon like the invisible and mysterious movements of the magnet in the physical world."

How did these two alpha males stay in sync for such a long period of time with very little traces of disharmony?

STEWART I may sound a little syrupy here—they just loved each other. They were both the eldest sons of great landowners and grew up thirty miles apart, so they came from and continued to live in the same world. They were interested in everything

and knew something about most things. They shared so much between themselves. Their friendship developed into a lifelong seminar—an exploration of learning and thinking between them.

Politically, they agreed on almost everything, though they had occasional differences. There were times when Jefferson, who was more of a visionary and a little less analytical, would get ahead of himself, and Madison would have to pull him back into reality. Because of that dynamic in their friendship, Jefferson developed a habit of sending his ideas to Madison first (before disbursing them for public consumption) to get Madison's reaction, because he trusted Madison's judgment to keep him out of trouble. They were great soulmates and it gave them amazing pleasure to be with each other.

MADISON AND MONROE

BOSTON The fourth partnership Madison had was with James Monroe. At times, they were rivals. They ran against each other for the US House in 1789, and then later competed against each other for their party's presidential nomination in 1808. Yet when the contested races were over, they reconciled. The greatest time for their partnership came during Madison's presidency when together they did what it took to get the country through the dark days of the War of 1812.

Explain how Madison's bonding with Monroe kept our star-spangled banner waving through the perilous fight, from the twilight's last gleaming through the dawn's early light.

STEWART It's not easy to follow the national anthem! Monroe, at heart, was a soldier—not an intellect. In doing my research for the book, it was shocking to find the number of people who wrote during Monroe's lifetime, (and I'm going to paraphrase), "This fellow Monroe is a little dumb." But he was a person of good heart, had shrewd political judgment, and was very charismatic. He and Madison were warm, personal friends; political allies; and they socialized as families; but Monroe didn't provide the sort of intellectual exchange Madison had with Jefferson.

When Madison became president, he wanted to go to war with Britain. It was not a reason why he got elected, but he believed America could not continue to endure the seizure of its ships and sailors by both Britain and France. The United States had to establish its own identity and credibility in the world. Despite that worthy goal, there were plenty of good reasons *not* to go to war with Britain, the most important being that the British were really powerful, and we weren't. Regardless of that reality, Madison was determined to go to war.

I know I keep coming back to this—but Madison was short, skinny, quiet, and nobody would think of him as a military leader. He was never in the military. To lead the country during a war, he needed what we might call today an image upgrade. In particular, he needed some steel in his administration. He and Monroe had been on the outs for four years because of their contested campaign in 1808 when Monroe ran against him for president. They finally made up, and Monroe came into the Cabinet as Madison's secretary of state, and for part of the war, he was both secretary of state and secretary of war, if you can imagine that.

Monroe became a critical player and was important for giving much needed strength to Madison's administration. For a president in time of war, it helps to have a strong friend around. So they became highly important to each other, and that connection lasted through their retirements, even though they were very different people.

BOSTON As you read David's book about the War of 1812, and you think of the lyrics to "The Star-Spangled Banner," our national anthem is the ultimate statement on the subject of how we barely survived that war. Knowing the dire straits our country was in when Francis Scott Key was inspired to write the lyrics makes the singing of that song before sports or civic events that much more important to me.

MADISON AND DOLLEY

BOSTON The fifth and final partnership, the one you've all been waiting for—the one involving the hot wife—was Madison's marriage to Dolley. From your book, it sounds like Dolley had more star power than all the rest of our First Ladies combined. She totally dominated the social scene in the nation's capital for sixteen years. Jefferson was a widower, so Dolley served as his First Lady and then stayed on in that role when her husband became president. She had a radiant personality, was a flashy dresser, was the vivacious life of the many parties she organized, was a patriot who famously saved Gilbert Stuart's portrait of George Washington when the British burned down the Executive Mansion, and was a devoted, politically savvy wife who truly elevated her husband.

Is there any woman in American history who had as much social fire-power as Dolley Madison?

STEWART It's good to get these questions on the first day of my book's release so I'll be ready for them after today! There has been nobody like Dolley Madison because, for heaven's sake, we're still eating her ice cream and cake! More seriously, we've had First Ladies who made a great impact, but not like Dolley did. Eleanor Roosevelt was a historic First Lady in many ways but she was certainly not a great social figure. Jacqueline Kennedy was not the sort of dazzler or dominant social character that Dolley was—although she could dazzle in a social setting, but in a quieter way. It's a measure of Madison that he wanted his wife to shine. He knew he wasn't going to shine in any social setting, so the fact that she was a couple of inches taller, a little bit broader, and would wear turbans with feathers and fruit...

BOSTON Yeah, you couldn't miss her in the room. She was the one with the turban and the feathers on top of her head.

STEWART Coming into a room like this, as Talmage said, you couldn't find Madison, but you couldn't miss Dolley. She was always lively. One of her nieces described her as "a foe to dullness," and it was a wonderful quality.

DAVID STEWART READS A FAVORITE PASSAGE FROM THE BOOK

BOSTON Before we open it up for questions from the audience, I think it's important for you to have an appreciation for David's gifts as a writer; particularly the rhythm of his language and how he puts so much information into so few words. So I've asked him to read just a very short passage from *Madison's Gift* to whet your appetite for what I think you'll find as a delicious read.

STEWART The setup for what I'm about to read is that on February 13, 1815—about two-hundred years ago exactly—a senator had heard a rumor that the US had entered into a peace treaty with Britain; and he went to see President Madison at the Octagon House, his temporary residence after the burning of the White House, to find out if it was true.

"He found the house dark, the president sitting solitary in his parlor . . . in perfect tranquility, not even a servant in waiting. The senator asked if the rumor was true; Madison bade him sit down. 'I will tell you all I know,' he said, then confirmed that he thought there was peace but he had no official confirmation. The senator recalled with some wonder what he called the president's self-command on the occasion, and his greatness of mind.

That war had truly been Mr. Madison's war, as his opponents called it. It was about principles, not gain. It was fought with a quiet tenacity, often ineptly, and with endless tolerance of those who opposed it. As a friend of Madison's wrote years later, the war had been conducted in perfect keeping with the character of the president, of whom it may be said that no one ever had to a greater extent firmness, mildness, and self-possession. And when peace came, Madison welcomed it in a darkened house, sitting alone with his thoughts."

BOSTON Let's give a hand for David Stewart. Do we have any questions from the audience??

DAVID STEWART'S CONNECTION TO MADISON

AUDIENCE MEMBER How long have you been interested in Madison? How did you become interested in him? And did you believe he was extraordinary before you wrote the book or did you decide he was extraordinary as you wrote it?

STEWART As Talmage mentioned, my first book was about the Constitutional Convention. You can't write about that without dealing with Madison, and I came away from that book with a kind of counterintuitive or counter-opinion. I didn't (and still don't) think of him as "the Father of the Constitution," and he actually objected to being called that. He said the Constitution was the product of many hands and many heads, and he was right.

I became more interested in him when I did a later book on Aaron Burr, and it was Burr who introduced Madison to Dolley. After surviving all the fallout that arose from his arguably treasonous misconduct, Burr was finally able to come back to the United States only because President Madison looked the other way.

I began noticing that Madison was always within the four corners of history's picture throughout his era. In fact, he was usually at the center of the picture, and I wanted to understand him better and learn how he became so prominent for so long with so many Founding Fathers also aspiring to be in the center of the picture. That's what led me to want to write this book.

I thought Madison was not getting his due and still has not. The more I examined him, the more I realized that it was his personal qualities that allowed him to make these contributions to the development of our government. We tend to think of him as this disembodied intellect—this great mind. He definitely had a great mind, and political philosophers love him and have analyzed him to death; but I don't think his great mind was the key to his greatness. Going beyond his mind to his unique personal qualities was what I wanted to capture.

MADISON'S HEALTH CHALLENGES

BOSTON One of our honored guests here is Alan Lowe, the head of the George W. Bush Presidential Library. Alan, where are you on Madison? Last year, you hosted Lynne Cheney, who had a *New York Times* best-selling biography of Madison in which, for whatever reason, she devoted very little attention to the slavery issue. Whereas, David, as you'll read, gives Madison's complicated relationship with the slavery issue his full attention.

ALAN LOWE Can't wait to read your book, David. One thing I've been thinking. Mrs. Cheney talked a great deal about Madison's health challenges. Do you talk about that in your book and how they affected his public service and private life?

STEWART You can't write about Madison and not talk about his health. He had two chronic conditions. One was an intestinal condition that you don't need to know more about. The other was a form of epilepsy, and people have tried to figure out what the heck it was. It caused him as a young man to go into a depression, because he thought he was not long for this world. He turned out to live to be eighty-five,

longer than all his peers. His health issues were always there and caused him to seem frail and timid to others. I feel like his health issues were something he was able to manage. He had lots of bad nights; but I don't think it ended up defining him, which I regard as a triumph of his will.

Photo credit: Patrice Gilbert

David O. Stewart

MADISON'S ROLE IN LOCATING THE CAPITAL TO WASHINGTON, DC

AUDIENCE MEMBER Joseph Ellis, in his book *Founding Brothers*, deals with the move of the capital from New York to Philadelphia to the Potomac. Can you give us your take on Madison's role in that?

STEWART Congress fought ten years over where to put the capital and it was very contentious. Madison and Washington wanted to get it on the Potomac. They were concerned that if it stayed up North, they would have a lot less influence over the government. The politics of the issue were intricate, but most people realized it should be in the center of the country, which at the time was really just the Atlantic seacoast.

The politicians ultimately arrived at this convoluted deal that had a bunch of winks and nods, and allowed for the assumption of states' debts by the federal government in return for putting the capital on the Potomac. It ultimately became a deal made by Madison and Hamilton, though it was Madison and Washington who wanted the capital near Virginia. So, once again, Madison's alignment with Washington was a key to achieving a successful result.

Madison was central to the deal. One of his great gifts as a legislator—and he was a talented legislator—was his ability to work the stall. If you have ever watched the process of legislation, stalling can sometimes be a very important tactic. It can help avoid a bill's getting pushed through at the wrong moment when the right people aren't in the room to vote no. To execute the stall, Madison would come up with some procedural motion, or some reason to send the bill back to the committee. For example, he stalled the issue of locating our nation's capital two or three times until he got an adjournment, a recess, or whatever it took to get the time necessary so he could reboot the politics. He was very definite about it, and it was a real talent of his.

MADISON'S VIEW OF HIS LEGACY

AUDIENCE MEMBER Thomas Jefferson put on his tombstone his assessment of the most important accomplishments of his lifetime. You said a minute ago that Madison didn't claim to be the "Father of the Constitution." What would Madison have put on his tombstone?

STEWART I think he would have taken great pride in his having played an important role in getting the Constitution written and ratified, though he wouldn't have claimed it for himself. He would have just said he was an important part of the process that led to the execution and adoption of the final document. He was proud of *The Federalist* essays. He was proud he had gotten the country through the War of 1812 at a time when he was flying solo. There was no

Jefferson or Washington around to help him then. He was *the* guy, he got us through it, and it wasn't pretty. I think those were his high points.

He was a genuinely self-effacing guy. It is a little frustrating (though it doesn't keep me awake at nights) that when you walk around Washington, DC, you see the Jefferson Memorial, the Washington Monument and the Lincoln Memorial, and I don't mean to denigrate them. We've now got an FDR Memorial. All we have named after Madison in DC is the Madison Building at the Library of Congress. That's all there is. It seems a little less than he's entitled to.

BOSTON But in your book, you say that there are more counties and cities across the country named after Madison than anyone else?

STEWART Yes, his contemporaries appreciated him.

MADISON AMIDST THE GENIUS OF THE FOUNDING FATHERS

AUDIENCE MEMBER During Madison's era, how did our country end up with such a great collection of minds at a time when America was largely a backwater country?

STEWART Other than to say it was a wonderful coincidence, I would say that it was also an amazing opportunity in human history. In the late eighteenth and early nineteenth centuries, our founders had the chance to build off of the English constitutional tradition. They got to write on a nearly blank slate at the moment of the Enlightenment when human rights were taking center stage. You have to give these guys credit for the fact that they recognized the opportunity. They had a chance nobody ever had before, and they were determined not to botch it. What came into the picture during Madison's lifetime was a combination of talent, opportunity, and recognition of opportunity, and those three things made it one of those wonderful moments in our history.

BOSTON In closing, we think about Doris Kearns Goodwin's being so shrewd in coming up with the "team of rivals" angle on Lincoln. Along those same innovative lines, David has come up with a new angle on Madison that connects certain dots never connected before regarding Madison's unique "gift" for building what proved to be historic partnerships. Let's give a final round of applause to our guest, David Stewart.

CHARLES SLACK is an emerging Harvard-educated historian whose newest book, *Liberty's First Crisis: Adams, Jefferson, and the Misfits Who Saved Free Speech* (Atlantic Monthly Press 2015), received the following endorsement from Pulitzer Prize-winner Jon Meacham: "Slack brings one of America's defining crises back to vivid life. This is a terrific piece of history." On October 6, 2015, I interviewed Charles on the subject of his new book at The King's College in New York City before a large audience of students, faculty, staff, and friends of the school.

"Americans don't recognize injustice immediately. Sometimes we've been agonizingly slow, but finally we wake up to doing what it takes to restore justice. It took a couple of years under the Sedition Act for people to fully realize how bothered they were about the specter of having Americans being thrown in jail just because they had used their First Amendment rights."

– CHARLES SLACK

CHAPTER 5

CHARLES SLACK
ON
The Founders' Battle with Freedom of Speech

WASHINGTON'S FAILURE TO ACHIEVE THE IMPOSSIBLE

BOSTON Charles, early in your book, you say that by 1798, in the second year of John Adams' presidency, the nation was in danger of total collapse.

What does that tell us about the effectiveness of Adams' predecessor, George Washington?

SLACK It was really a fall from Eden. The early founders led by Washington had a belief that seems naïve in retrospect—that our leaders of the federal government could somehow represent all Americans, and any disagreements would be fought out at the ballot box. They thought that, once elected, the winners would all be able to lead as a unified body.

"Powerful and engaging . . . Slack brings one of America's
defining crises back to vivid life. . . . This is a terrific piece of history."
—JON MEACHAM, Pulitzer Prize–winning author of *Thomas Jefferson*

Liberty's First Crisis

Adams, Jefferson,
and the Misfits Who Saved
FREE SPEECH
Charles Slack

The idea of there being political parties was deplorable. They were viewed as vehicles for serving factions and special interests, their playing a role in the government would clearly conflict with there being a unified government acting in support of the president.

From the moment George Washington took office, people began aligning themselves with factions and special interests. Over the course of Washington's presidency, the country awakened to the reality that we would not all get along, and having one unified body of people running the government wasn't going to be the norm.

The country then divided into two distinct and opposing parties: the Federalists and the Republicans. Because of this division, contrary to what the founders had expected, many feared that the country might fall apart at the seams at the end of Washington's presidency.

BOSTON So although Washington attempted to be the great political unifier in the midst of major discord in his Cabinet, Congress, and elsewhere, was he essentially a failure at achieving harmony among those serving in the federal government?

SLACK He was a failure to the extent we can now look at the initial model and recognize that it was doomed to fail from the start. It was a wonderful idea, and if anyone could have made it work, it was George Washington, given how beloved he was. The reality is that we had a country attempting to live under an idea of freedom that hadn't been tried before. It soon became clear that those in our government were going to be fractious, argumentative, and at each other's throats as a function of human nature. That's just the way it was then, and it's stayed that way ever sense.

THE AMERICAN DEMOCRATIC SYSTEM EVOLVES FROM THE BRITISH

BOSTON There were clearly many egos trying to call the shots in the new government during John Adams' presidency, at a time when the start-up country was in danger of collapse.

Was our only real hope for survival having strong centralized power in the federal government, regardless of how much it looked and felt like monarchial government system of the British, with whom we had just fought against in the American Revolution?

SLACK That's certainly the way people like Alexander Hamilton felt. Everybody knew the country was in danger of collapse, and there were two principal ways of looking at it. The first was to be pessimistic about the intelligence of average Americans and their ability to govern themselves—and Hamilton was the leader of that camp who really believed in that—and, therefore, we needed a muscular federal government and a strong centralized economy. On the other side, we had people like Jefferson who feared having a government that essentially was a replica of that of the British and would thereby raise the possibility of an incipient monarchy, causing these thinkers to believe decentralized power in the form of states' rights was the way to go.

We ultimately came around to how our government operates in the middle of those two extremes. Madison is my favorite founder because he was the one who could grasp both sides' position. He aligned with Hamilton in collaborating on *The Federalist Papers*, then gravitated in the other direction when the centralized government became too muscular for his taste, such that it alarmed him and caused him to move over to Jefferson's camp.

THE FALLOUT OVER PARTISAN POLITICS

BOSTON As each year passed in the United States during the 1790s, the individuals in the faction that ultimately became the Federalists mainly lived in the North and were increasingly aligned with the British, and those who ultimately became the Republicans mainly lived in the South and were more aligned with the French. This caused major "competing interests and divided loyalties" between the two groups, which to me seems not too different from the division in our country a half century later that led to the Civil War.

Given that division, is there any likelihood that the competing interests and divided loyalties between the pro-British Federalists and the pro-French Republicans at the end of the eighteenth century might have led to a civil war absent the Sedition Act?

SLACK Certainly, the Republicans (also called the Democratic Republicans, which is a great term in our own age) accused the Federalists and John Adams of trying to incite a civil war by attempting to stamp out their view by means of the Sedition Act. What was mainly happening was an awakening by both factions to the reality that Americans were going to disagree and, therefore, could we find a way to disagree peacefully without disrupting the work of those who had been elected to govern?

The Federalists tried to stamp out their opposition's voices through the Sedition Act, which made it illegal to criticize the government and thereby attempted to create a one-party system. Ultimately, everyone recognized that maintaining a "free" country while attempting to stop freedom of speech simply wasn't possible. We found out and ultimately accepted the fact that the way we would do our fighting amongst ourselves would not be by arms, but through newspapers and words. We managed to get by with the division for a while, and it was several decades later before we had a Civil War.

BOSTON You say that the Sedition Act was a "wartime measure without a war," but based on your last answer, is it your opinion that the Sedition Act did not serve as a leading factor toward preventing a civil war between the two factions?

SLACK Correct. I don't think the Sedition Act served to prevent a civil war. If anything, it forced us to the brink of war. The Sedition Act was passed in 1798 by the Federalists, and the idea was that those people who criticized the then leader of government, and made doing his job difficult, were thereby endangering the republic. So the Federalist leaders decided they had to stop all the disruptive criticism and accomplished this by passing a law that made it illegal for anyone to criticize the elected leaders. Any violators of the new law called the Sedition Act would face criminal penalties of two years in prison and a $2,000 fine.

The Act pushed us to the brink, because it forced us to reckon with a direct contradiction to the First Amendment—which contained arguably the most glorious words ever produced by a government. The ultimate issue became: would we govern in a way that permitted us to live up to those words? In essence, the Sedition Act invoked a bloodless civil war once people woke up to the specter of having their fellow citizens being thrown in jail for using their First Amendment rights. Everyone finally realized how wrong that was.

Over history, one of the great characteristics about Americans has always been that we don't recognize injustice immediately. Sometimes we've been agonizingly slow, but finally we wake up to doing what it takes to restore justice. It took a couple of years under the Sedition Act for people to fully realize how bothered they were about the specter of having Americans being thrown in jail just because they had used their First Amendment rights.

WHAT PROMPTED THE SEDITION ACT?

BOSTON You say that "President Adams had good reason for feeling besieged on all sides in a pincer between the hawkish Federalists who pressed for conflict with France and the staunch Republicans who loved France and hated England, such that Republican newspaper publishers were not just making Adams' life and job difficult, they were directly impeding his ability to govern the country at a precarious time."

Does that mean that circumstances existed which provided clear justification for President Adams and the Federalists to abandon the commitment to free speech that they had made in the decades before Adams became president?

SLACK I'm certain President Adams felt that his critics had become so aggressive that they were making governance virtually impossible, but one of the realities of living in a country where people often disagree on political issues is that when the president has an agenda that's being impeded, he clearly thinks that's bad; but his opponents believe that that's exactly what they are there for— to impede the president from pursuing policy that they view as harmful to the country.

ADAMS' ROLE IN THE PASSAGE OF THE SEDITION ACT

BOSTON The Sedition Bill was passed by Congress on July 14, 1798.

What role, if any, did President John Adams play in its passage, or was he merely a bystander?

SLACK Toward the end of his life, John Adams realized what a mistake the Sedition Act had been, and his biographers and his reputational caretakers over the years have attempted to distance him from the Sedition Act. They have described him as a very reluctant bystander who signed the Act into

law, but did not take an active role in getting it passed or in enforcing it. My research revealed that just about everybody prosecuted for violating the Act got prosecuted because he had criticized John Adams. From my perspective, the commander-in-chief is the top dog; and when people are being thrown in jail for criticizing you, even if you think of yourself as "a bystander" to those prosecutions and incarcerations, you are still culpable for letting it happen.

President Adams actually took an active role in a couple of the prosecutions, and refused to pardon a defenseless loner named David Brown in Massachusetts who sat in jail longer than anybody. Furthermore, Adams attempted to reward with high office a prosecutor who had gone after a guy named Luther Baldwin whose single act of "misconduct" was that he had made a street-corner joke about John Adams.

So, in my opinion, President Adams should not get off scot-free, as some people have attempted to do. I think he was a great man. Whenever you tell the story of the founding era, John Adams is one of our greatest heroes. In the case of the Sedition Act though, he was not a hero; and it was a tragedy, because he had been one of the most principled proponents of free speech as a younger man.

JEFFERSON AND MADISON'S RESPONSE TO THE SEDITION ACT

BOSTON Regarding Jefferson and Madison, in 1798 and 1799 they both protested the Sedition Act by writing the Kentucky and Virginia Nullification Resolutions— Jefferson did Kentucky; Madison did Virginia. The resolutions claimed that every state had the right to disregard the Sedition Act, a federal law, if it believed that the law violated its constitutional rights.

Do you think either Jefferson or Madison grasped the precedent they were setting by authoring these resolutions, which were later claimed to be manifestos for the right of any state to secede from the Union shortly before the Civil War?

SLACK I think Madison anticipated that danger more than Jefferson did. One of the interesting things about those resolutions is, at that time, the United States Supreme Court did not act in the role of having the power for judicial review. They didn't decide that until *Marbury v. Madison* a few years later. When you read about the Kentucky and Virginia Resolutions attempting to nullify the Sedition Act, you probably wonder, "Where was the Supreme Court? Why didn't they declare the law in those two states unconstitutional?" At that time, Supreme Court justices rode the circuit, and they were scattered all over the country. That was a main reason why the early presidents had trouble getting people to serve on the Supreme Court, because it was a great hardship to travel all over the country. Some of our Supreme Court justices actually presided over Sedition Act cases where the defendants were railroaded into a conviction under the statute. The Supreme Court justices at that time were all Federalists, so they were on board with enforcing the Act.

There really was no mechanism at that point to pursue getting a federal law declared unconstitutional, so Jefferson and Madison apparently felt that their only recourse was to write these resolutions and threaten secession. If you read the two resolutions side by side, Jefferson's is a lot darker. It's the one that says, "Hey, we don't have to hang around if we don't like what you're doing." Ultimately, that was the one cited as precedent for a state's having the power of nullification decades later in the time leading up to the Civil War.

Madison's Virginia resolution is softer. It opens by recognizing the essential nature of our federal government and the union as compared to what the Sedition Act was doing to the country. Madison essentially said that Virginia wanted this resolution in order to preserve the union. That's why he's my favorite of the founders; because he

recognized the beauty and necessity of the national government, but he also saw the dangers of there being a government that became so strong that it overreached.

BOSTON In typical Thomas Jefferson fashion, he did not publicly acknowledge that he had written the Kentucky Resolution until much later.

SLACK Right, and in fact, he knew that he might have been open to charges of violating the Sedition Act for having written it, so he did not put his name on the resolution. Madison ultimately outlived Jefferson by quite a few years, and in the years leading up to the Civil War, people began citing the Kentucky Resolution as proof of their position that "We can leave the Union if we don't like what's going on." Madison sharply criticized those who claimed such a precedent, and came to Jefferson's defense, saying: "That's not what Jefferson intended."

THE SEDITION ACT'S IMPACT ON THE 1800 ELECTION

BOSTON Did Thomas Jefferson and the Republicans beat Adams and the Federalists in the 1800 presidential election primarily because of the unpopularity of the Sedition Act?

SLACK Yes. That was the leading cause. The threat of war with France had been a powerful bolster for the Federalists as they sought to retain power. As long as we were under threat of war with them, and thought that they (a superpower) might invade us, and were clearly attacking our ships on the high seas, that was the main focus of what the Federalists addressed during Adams' four-year term; and it was the threat of war with the French that kept their popularity going. Then, Adams helped seal his fate by doing something good for the country (but bad for the Federalists) when he achieved a resolution with France, one of the greatest achievements of his presidency.

Once the direct threat of war with the French went away, people began waking up to the evils of the Sedition Act, and it became the real driver in the 1800 election. One of the lesser-mentioned parts of the First Amendment is our right to petition the government. This right became widely used to express the public's dissatisfaction with the Sedition Act during the last two years of Adams' presidency. Congress began getting flooded with thousands of petitions coming in from average citizens who were demanding repeal of the Act, and it became a major factor in the outcome of that election.

BOSTON The Sedition Act was rare, in that Congress enacted it with a provision that it would not be the law into perpetuity.

SLACK The Federalists were very crafty about this. The Act made it illegal to criticize anybody in the federal government except the vice president, because Jefferson was the vice president, they didn't like him, and he wasn't a Federalist, so it was permissible for him to be criticized. The other thing they did when they wrote the Sedition Act was to let it expire at the end of Adams' term. They wrote it that way to ensure that if they lost the 1800 election, when the Act expired, they would have some protection from prosecution if they criticized the victorious opposition.

JEFFERSON'S ROLE IN BRINGING AN END TO THE SEDITION ACT

BOSTON We've talked about this some, but let's get some clarity on exactly what Thomas Jefferson's role was in bringing about the end of the Sedition Act. We know he funded some people who wrote editorials criticizing Adams publicly and thereby exposed themselves to prosecution. We know he authored the Kentucky Resolution. We know he ran for president, won the 1800 election, and then made sure the Sedition Act was not renewed.

Is there anything else that Jefferson did that was prominent in bringing an end to the Act other than those things?

SLACK He was the figurehead of the emerging Republican Party. The Republicans were called several things: Democratic Republicans, Republicans, and Jeffersonian Democrats. Jefferson was the party's figurehead and leader.

The 1800 election between Adams and Jefferson was the first election in which the candidates were openly acknowledged as being backed by political parties. We look on that as a great occurrence, not just in US history but in world history, because it was the first time there were two parties going at it; and when the election ended, the losing party peacefully departed and the winning party came to power.

After Jefferson got elected president, he gave his inaugural address—one of the most beautiful addresses ever given by an American president—where he acknowledged that we were all going to have to find a way to get along. In it, he said, "We are all Republicans. We are all Federalists." What he meant by that wasn't, "Now it's time for all of us to get along." His real message was, "We're all *going* to disagree, but we're going to have to learn to live with it."

In fact, Jefferson even said in his first inaugural address, "If someone wants to advocate the dissolution and downfall of the United States, then let him have his say and let wiser heads prevail, and let's prove we're a strong enough country to hear, but then rebuff voices like that." Of course, I'm paraphrasing, but that was the essence of what he said.

Compare Jefferson's perspective to what Washington had said in his farewell address just four years before, which was a very pessimistic address talking about the baneful effects of party politics, and how if we didn't all learn to get along, then the country would to be doomed. Four years later, Jefferson acknowledged there was now a new reality of political discord, and we were going to have to learn to live with it.

BOSTON Just so everybody's clear, when we talk about Thomas Jefferson and the Republicans, we're talking about the party that evolved and ultimately became today's Democratic Party.

SLACK More or less. It was certainly not today's Republican party. I made it clear at the beginning of my book that when I use the word "Republicans," I was referring to a party that had no connection to today's Republican Party. One of the things I liked about exploring this era was that although there were certain qualities of each party that apply to today's parties, anyone would have a hard time aligning himself 100% with either of the two parties who sponsored the candidates in the election of 1800. The Federalists were the party of big government, which we normally today associate with the Democratic Party; but they were also the party of big business and anti-immigration, which we associate with today's Republican Party. The Republicans in 1800 were the party of open immigration (which we associate with today's Democrats) and small government (which we associate with today's Republicans). So, you can find enough in both parties to make it hard to align them with today's parties. My hope is that by looking at that, the reader won't automatically side with one side or the other, but will be able to see the danger to our liberty when one side gets in power and starts outlawing free speech.

THE SEDITION ACT'S IMPACT ON JOHN ADAMS' LEGACY

BOSTON Yesterday evening, we heard Evan Thomas talk about his new biography of Nixon, which means we spent some time talking about Watergate.

From a presidential history standpoint, is it accurate to say that the Sedition Act was to John Adams what Watergate was to Nixon—that is, by far the biggest scar on his presidency?

SLACK Absolutely. It contributed greatly to his being a one-term president, because the Federalists got thrown out of office in the next election and, in fact, never held another major office again. I suspect that in John Adams' heart of hearts, he considered what had occurred under the Sedition Act as the greatest error of his presidency.

BOSTON You have a great quote in the book: "The greatest national test of our first generation Americans was: Would they live up to and appreciate the words they wrote in the Bill of Rights?"

Did John Adams ever recognize that he failed that test?

SLACK The Federalists in general, and John Adams in particular, did not recognize that they failed that test. It's very easy to recognize that one's own First Amendment rights are in jeopardy when there's a law that says you can't say what you want. When an outside authority (like the British) are clamping down on what can be said, it's easy to say, "We want our freedom to say what we want." What we hadn't gone through before the Sedition Act was the reality that giving everyone First Amendment freedom of speech would also mean allowing opinions to be expressed in person or in the press that are believed to be dangerous to our nation's stability—not just wrong, not just obnoxious, but dangerous. We hadn't been through that test until John Adams' presidency, and, in some ways, it was Adams' bad luck to be our nation's chief executive at that time.

Plenty of people then and to this day advocate curbs on free speech with the idea that the guys who are making threatening comments are such lunatics that shutting them up will actually enhance freedom. That's a great mistake. Whichever side of the political spectrum one favors, the great danger for whoever is in power is not recognizing that by deciding to clamp down on antagonistic voices, that will actually cause the biggest danger to freedom. With respect to the Sedition Act, Adams believed what he did in terms of, "We'll just shut these guys up for now, but our freedom will continue on."

BOSTON Compare the conflict between the Republican newspapers, like the *Aurora,* and the Federalists newspapers, like *The Gazette,* in the late 1790s, to the level of today's antagonism between WSNBC and Fox News or between *The New York Times* and *The Wall Street Journal.* How does that level of media conflict and antagonism and political conflict during Adams' presidency compare with what we're seeing today?

SLACK Anyone who looks back fondly to an earlier age and believes that it was more civil then than our political arena today needs to start reading the things people said about one another in the newspapers in America's earlier history. One difference between now and the end of the eighteenth century is that what is happening today is clearly very rancorous, but it doesn't end in physical violence, like it did then. Benjamin Franklin Bache, the Philadelphia publisher of the vigorously anti-Federalist newspaper the *Aurora,* became engaged in several fist-fights over what he had put in his newspaper. Mobs would show up at his newspaper office where he and his family lived and throw bricks through their windows. In those days, anyone who published strong political opinions was risking his physical safety.

Beyond that, there are parallels between what happened then and what's happening now. Before the age of the Internet and cable television, there were fewer voices in the media and more gatekeepers. The big newspapers and television stations felt more of a responsibility to be objective than they do today. I started my career in the newspaper business at a time when there was typically only one newspaper in a city. At that time, regardless of what the editorial page said, all journalists felt a mandate to be objective. What's happened in the Internet and cable television age is that there are all these outlets and all these voices, all over the place.

In that respect, it's much more like 1798. The year 2015 is more like 1798 in terms of there being a multitude of media commentators, as compared to the way things were in 1950 or 1980. Today, things have gone back to being a free-for-all, like it was in John Adams' time.

THE INTENT OF THE FOUNDING FATHERS

BOSTON When we talk about the Bill of Rights and what it means, and what it was supposed to mean, we always get to the question of founders' intent. You say that, "In the end, the search for the founders' intent amounts to a sort of quest for the Holy Grail. The intents of the figures involved were so varied that parsing their pre-Constitutional writings and speeches for specific intentions behind this or that phrase in the Bill of Rights becomes a game of post-Colonial whack-a-mole." Can we say anything with confidence in its accuracy, about the founders' intent in creating the Bill of Rights, other than we know they agreed on the words?

SLACK What it came down to when the Constitution was written was that everybody wanted to live in freedom and enjoy freedom. So they wrote the Bill of Rights, which, in the case of free speech, seems to say unequivocally, "Congress will not mess with my life." They were afraid of having a government that would interfere with their lives. They wanted freedom from intrusion, so that's why to me the Bill of Rights is our most beautiful government document. How many times in history has a government put into words its desire to limit its own power? Every other government in history has set out to inform its citizens that they need to hand over their rights and then the government will take care of you, but our Bill of Rights set out to limit the government's capacity to do that.

There was no practical experience as of 1798 about what this level of freedom meant, so that's what I mean about the need to look through the practical experiences of 1798 or 2015 and then begin to think about how the founders envisioned this or that occurrence. I don't think they foresaw how strong published political criticism might impact our leaders' capacity to govern, because it hadn't been tried yet, though the one thing they all agreed on was the desire to live in freedom.

BOSTON These days, many people want to opine on the founders' intent. Having done all the research you've done and drawn your own conclusions, when somebody puffs up his chest and says, "Well, here's what Thomas Jefferson really intended…or George Washington or James Madison," what's your response?

SLACK It's too easy to find opposite examples of what the different founders intended. That's the problem with claiming that there was one intent only. We tend to get lulled into thinking that the founders were operating as a monolithic group carved in stone. In fact, they were fractious and often disagreed with one another.

During that era, many people didn't think we needed a Bill of Rights. That's what's fascinating. Alexander Hamilton felt very strongly we didn't need a Bill of Rights, and that it would actually be dangerous to have one, because any rights that weren't included in those Ten Amendments were susceptible to the claim that they weren't protected. Hamilton said that we've already got free speech, because Congress will only have powers that are outlined in the Constitution. Hamilton's thinking was that if it's not prohibited by the Constitution, then people have the freedom to do it. So Hamilton thought that to take the trouble of adding free speech as an amendment was superfluous; because there was nothing in the Constitution saying the government can't outlaw free speech, though that was something of a stretched argument. However, if we look at what

Photo credit: Denise Bosco

Charles Slack

Congress has done over the years, there are many issues not addressed in or prohibited by the Constitution that Congress has decided it has the power to address.

TALES OF MISFITS JAILED UNDER THE SEDITION ACT

BOSTON You just mentioned Hamilton. Obviously, he was one of the dominant public figures of Adams' presidency, and like so many politicians throughout history, Hamilton was brought down by his libido—carrying on an affair with Maria Reynolds for years that was ultimately revealed in the press by James Callender in 1797. If you haven't seen the Broadway musical *Hamilton*, they go into it in great detail. You suggest that Callender may have gotten his information about the Hamilton–Conway affair from Hamilton's arch-enemy, Thomas Jefferson. Is that true?

SLACK Well, it's true that he may have. We don't know for sure. Don't want to spread rumors, but there's a possibility. Jefferson was a great politician, though very wily.

BOSTON Behind the scenes.

SLACK Yes, he definitely acted behind the scenes when he was Washington's secretary of state. Jefferson bankrolled a journalist named Philip Freneau who published many critical editorials about Washington. When Washington got wind of what Jefferson was doing, the president asked him: "Do you have anything to do with Freneau's criticisms?" Jefferson replied, "Who me? What?" The same thing happened when Jefferson was Adams' vice president and gave $50 checks to James Callender to write political editorials that attacked Adams. He also financially supported Benjamin Franklin Bache and other opposition journalists who wrote horrible things about Adams, but Jefferson almost always managed to keep his hands clean.

Jefferson certainly supported Callender in writing his harsh editorials over the years; and he was certainly an enemy of Hamilton's, because he felt Hamilton was dangerous to the country. It would have been absolutely in Jefferson's method of operation to get Callender to tell the world about Hamilton's ill-fated affair with Maria Reynolds. Callender, by the way, is one of the most amazing characters of this time period.

BOSTON Isn't he the guy who ultimately revealed the story of Thomas Jefferson and Sally Hemings? Wasn't he essentially the *National Enquirer* of his day?

SLACK Yes. He hated Hamilton and revealed the Reynolds affair, and then ultimately became one of the guys who was charged with sedition. He was put on trial in Richmond, Virginia, and Jefferson helped arrange for his defense. Callender got convicted and spent time in jail. By the time he got out, Jefferson was president and Callender assumed he would be in line to receive a political appointment. In fact, he wanted to be the postmaster of Richmond.

Jefferson, however, being the great politician he was, recognized that although Callender had been very useful as an opposition journalist, he was an unhinged, unreliable alcoholic—so he was the last person Jefferson wanted in his administration. So Callender didn't get any appointment, though Jefferson did send him another check for $50.

Callender then became incensed and immediately started a Federalist newspaper, and he took off after Jefferson and was the one to reveal the Sally Hemings affair, which was denied for two centuries until the DNA test established the Jefferson-Hemings connection. The preponderance of opinion among historians now is that the affair did exist and the children she had were Thomas Jefferson's. It's a great story of how James Callender made news two hundred years after his death. I think he would have been happy about that.

BOSTON That's what you call being immortal. In another kind of amazing coincidence, as I read your book, the person who really made the connection between the arguments made in the Kentucky Resolution and how it could serve as a precedent for a state having the right to secede from the Union before the Civil War was a fellow named Thomas Cooper, who was one of the people convicted under the Sedition Act.

SLACK Yes, that was Thomas Cooper. One of the realities of these types of situations is how people convicted under the Sedition Act became victims and martyrs, so they were looked upon as being saintly. Then, as they moved on with their lives, they went back to being real people with flaws. Thomas Cooper was an Englishman who came over to the United States. He operated a newspaper, was charged with and convicted of sedition. He was brilliant and courageous in standing up for his rights of free speech; but after leaving jail, he moved to South Carolina, became enamored of life in the old South, became a slave owner, and did some very disappointing things. Of all the victims of the Sedition Act, his legacy is probably the most disappointing.

BOSTON The subtitle to Charles' book is: *Adams, Jefferson and the Misfits Who Saved Free Speech.* The audience is probably wondering, "Who are these misfits who saved free speech?" Besides James Callender and Thomas Cooper, one of the leading misfits was someone I had never heard of before reading Charles' book. I suspect none you has ever heard of him either—a guy named Matthew Lyon, who became a misfit hero. He was a loose-cannon immigrant who served in Congress as a Republican from Vermont in its earliest years and then was prosecuted and imprisoned for exercising his right to free speech. Upon being released from prison, he was the guy who cast the deciding vote to make Jefferson our third president.

Charles, had you ever heard of Matthew Lyon before you began researching your book?

SLACK I hadn't and I was delighted to learn of him, because he has an amazing story. When writing a book, an author tries to find great stories to tell in order to keep the narrative going. Matthew Lyon certainly kept it going. He came over to America at age fourteen as an indentured servant from Ireland. He was once traded from one owner to another for a pair of bulls. When he told that story later in life, he was actually quite proud of it. He went up to Vermont and fought with the Green Mountain Boys in the Revolutionary War. He then built a business empire and became a congressman. When he arrived in Philadelphia, he was the Federalists' worst nightmare—remember the Federalists were the party of anti-immigration. In 1798, they somehow felt that the country had already become too crowded. They were particularly afraid of Irish and German immigrants. Harrison Gray Otis, a congressman from Massachusetts, gave what's known as the "Wild Irish" speech, where he said, "We have nothing against honest industrious immigrants, but we can't have these hordes of wild Irishmen invading our shores and taking places in Congress."

It was amazing. If you substitute in a few words here and there, you've got 2015 and the same debate that's going on now about immigration.

Anyway, when Lyon got himself elected to Congress, the Federalists said, "Gosh, it's bad enough to have this guy in the country, but here he is essentially trying to be part of Congress." His greatest contribution to US history was that he couldn't keep his mouth shut. At one point, someone on the floor of Congress accused him of cowardice during the Revolutionary War and Lyon turned around and spat in the guy's face. Some members of Congress tried but failed to toss Lyon out; they lost by a couple of votes. So House member Roger Griswold then took matters into his own hands a couple of weeks later, walked into Congress carrying a big cane, and proceeded to beat Lyon over the head. Lyon then grabbed a pair of tongs from the fireplace, started beating Griswold with them, and they went at it for a while right there on the House floor.

Ultimately, Lyon became one of the Federalists' chief targets. When they couldn't vote him out of Congress, they figured they had to do something to get rid of him, so they passed the Sedition Act. When it came time for Lyon to hit the campaign trail seeking reelection, he said John Adams belonged in a madhouse and some other critical things. Immediately, he was arrested, put through a kangaroo-court trial in Rutland, Vermont, got convicted, and was sent to jail for four months. The Federalists expected him to be a wild lion in jail and hoped he would try to escape and prove himself unfit for office. Instead, he became a model prisoner. He said, "If they put a thread across my cell, I won't overstep it."

While in jail, he started a newspaper called *The Scourge of Aristocracy*, and it was run by his son. In it, he continued to write terrible things about President Adams and the Federalists, while being a model prisoner. In the end, the Sedition Act turned Matthew Lyon from being regarded as a scalawag and widely disliked political figure into a martyr and a saint.

He was re-elected to Congress while in his jail cell. When he stepped out of jail, he was worried he was going to be re-arrested for what he'd written in his newspaper, so he proceeded to invoke the Constitutional provision that said someone can't be thrown in jail on his way to conducting business in Congress. When he stepped out of jail, he announced, "I'm on my way to Washington," and got into a carriage festooned with two American flags. His supporters lined the streets all the way, and he traveled in the carriage down to Philadelphia to take his seat back in Congress.

SUBSEQUENT SEDITION ACTS

BOSTON You point out at the end of your book that although the Sedition Act ended in 1801, it has reared its ugly head a few times since then in the US in times of emergency—during the Civil War, World War I, World War II, and post-9/11.

In America, is it safe to say that freedom of speech will always come under fire and be restricted in times of national emergency?

SLACK Yes, that's always a danger. Inevitably, we can look back at those periods in history when we abridged freedoms because we had gotten so worried about something; and then inevitably, when the crisis passed, the infringement on free speech became a footnote or maybe a paragraph in American history.

What we must remember is the folly of the people who tried to get past the crisis of their era by abridging unalienable rights. When we look back at the Sedition Act, we don't remember Luther Baldwin and his drunken joke about John Adams' rear end; instead, we remember how the Sedition Act was passed to improperly silence him. When we look at World War II, we don't look at the danger of those Japanese-Americans who suffered internment because of their ancestry;

we look back on what a terrible thing the internment was. When we look back at the activities of the House Un-American Activities Committee, we think mainly about Joe McCarthy's going after people who had exercised their free speech rights.

Regardless of which side of the political fence we're on, we must endeavor to keep in mind that the greatest danger faced usually isn't the unhinged person we don't like and would like to silence; rather, the danger comes from ourselves when we go overboard and abridge freedoms we hold dear, as we attempt to solve a temporary problem.

CURRENT EFFORTS TO LIMIT FREE SPEECH

BOSTON Last question. You mention the threats to free speech that are now arising due to the efforts of the left-wing intellectual movement—you mention Jane Fonda, Gloria Steinem and Cass Sunstein, to name a few.

What's your prediction on whether that movement is going to gain traction?

SLACK I sure hope it doesn't. When you study different periods of history—like during the 1950s—it was those on the political right who were more inclined to intimidate free speech, so it's clearly not a partisan thing. At this moment in history, I find it troubling that the extreme left is seeking to restrict free speech. I don't call them "liberals" because I think of myself as a liberal in the sense I believe in there being maximum liberty for people. That's what our country is all about. When you have people trying to solve problems by limiting freedom, whether they're from the left or the right, I refuse to call those people "liberal."

There's some intellectual cachet these days on the left with the idea that we should limit free speech because allowing it is not as important as preventing people's right to engage in what's known as hate speech. For those of us standing up for protecting free speech, in that context it doesn't mean we agree with people who want to say racist or sexist things; but the danger a hate-speech law presents to our liberty is real. At every period in history, whoever has been in power has had to encounter people who were saying things they thought were hateful. Once we start outlawing it at every phase when strong conflicting positions are being expressed, we won't have much free speech left.

There's also a position put out there gaining credence on the left that free speech is only a part of a collective value; that free speech exists only to help us create a better government. It's sort of a nuanced point that really needs to be understood because it gets things backwards. The Bill of Rights exists to protect us from government overreach. When people say there's a more important collective right that exists to make government better, the problem becomes creating a basis toward censoring all speech that doesn't serve that collective purpose. I think there's a lot of that going on now; and the danger, of course, is that free speech then becomes not a right, but a privilege that's granted by whoever's in power and thinks that their speech is serving the greater good.

ADAMS' EVOLUTION ON FREEDOM OF SPEECH

BOSTON We have a few minutes for questions from the audience. Does anyone have a question?

AUDIENCE MEMBER As a lawyer, John Adams courageously represented the British soldiers who fired the shots at the Boston Massacre. So principles of justice and proper respect for law were near and dear to his heart. Was it solely his annoyance over these partisan publishers that motivated Adams to support the Sedition Act or was there something else that made him support it? I find it hard to reconcile how he stood up for justice earlier in his career, and then later allowed people convicted under the Sedition Act to languish in jail without pardoning them.

SLACK I agree with you 100%. John Adams had been arguably the most principled founder on the subject of free speech. He wrote an essay in his thirties where he actually invoked the term "sedition," and he sent it to printers and editors. In it, he said, "Don't let the controlling authorities tell you that what you write is sedition because the jaws of power will always try to clamp down on you." I emphasize that in the book as a fervent message to his future self.

So the question becomes: How did he then turn around and as president sign the Sedition Act into law? One factor in play was having the misfortune of being the second president. The Federalists thought that whatever they were doing was mild in light of the fact that through the long, grizzly train of human history, shutting up your opponents is what leaders always did when they were in power. Whenever somebody said something that criticized the current regime, the leaders historically started rounding up the usual suspects and doing what it took to take their discordant voices out of commission. The Federalists looked on the Sedition Act as mild. If you went back to the British governors in the colonies before the American Revolution, they had felt under siege, too. Adams really felt himself caught between the hardliner Federalists who really seem to want a war with France (who he was trying to hold off), and the Republicans who painted him as a monarchist and a warmonger who wanted war with France. He was finding being caught in that position very, very difficult.

We can't discount the role Abigail Adams played. She was brilliant and her husband's staunchest supporter. There's no question which side she came down on. She compared the journalists attacking her husband to vipers who needed their heads cut off. She essentially said, "Hey, in any other country in the world, these people would be rounded up and thrown in jail."

I've always said, "It's great to be an American," but lots of people say that, in any other country, they wouldn't put up with these partisan attacks. That's true, but John Adams had to wake up to how hard it was to maintain free speech when vipers were coming at him from two sides. He found himself at this crisis point in history and felt allowing the Sedition Act to be enforced was something he had to do in order to be able to function as president.

JEFFERSON'S MOTIVATION BEHIND THE KENTUCKY RESOLUTION

AUDIENCE MEMBER Regarding the Kentucky and Virginia Resolutions, was Jefferson's primary purpose for crafting the Kentucky Resolution to set up his platform for the coming presidential election?

SLACK That's a great question, and something I've never thought of before. That's a great insight—sounds like a good subject for a paper—though I don't want to give you an assignment if you haven't written it already.

I have no idea whether Jefferson had already decided formally in his mind to run for president in the next election (in 1800) at the time he wrote the Kentucky Resolution in 1798. But he was a great politician; I don't think he would ever have put something to paper of that magnitude if he weren't working out his own thoughts. Certainly, at that time, he wasn't trying to claim credit for the resolution, because he didn't claim credit for it until many years later, so the resolution wasn't put out there like a position paper for the public. But certainly I think he did write it as a means of working out his own ideas.

SLACK'S THOUGHTS ON MAINTAINING FREE SPEECH TODAY

AUDIENCE MEMBER In today's marketplace, we see reporters, CEOs, athletes, and actors lose their jobs and get ostracized for making comments that are perceived as offensive. Is there a way to fight this attack on free speech while pursuing successful careers in those fields where people are no longer allowed to speak their minds?

SLACK When it comes to free speech, the key thing is to maintain the lack of government involvement, and make sure the coercive power of government isn't used to shut somebody up. There was a case in Connecticut where there was a flea market, and someone was selling Nazi memorabilia in a stall. Somebody who was the grandson of someone who had been imprisoned in Germany during World War II walked by the vendor's stall, and he took offense to the sale of the merchandise.

Now we can certainly understand the man's anger, frustration, and sadness; and he clearly had recourse available to him. He could have protested on public property. He could have written a blog. He could have written a letter to the editor of a newspaper. Instead, he called the police and tried to invoke the coercive power of government to shut the flea market vendor people up. To me, that's what we have to preserve.

In terms of your question, I do think that it's particularly frustrating about what's now going on at certain college campuses where whenever a politically prominent person says something controversial, he either gets disinvited to speak at the college or else shouted down. These things are very troubling, but the key thing to focus on is the government's involvement in attempting to restrict free speech. There will always be fractious give-and-take, and opinions will rise and fall and go in and out of fashion, but we've got to maintain government neutrality.

FREE SPEECH ISSUES CONCERNING EDWARD SNOWDEN

AUDIENCE MEMBER Where does Edward Snowden fit on this spectrum? Is he a modern James Callender or is he something more problematic?

SLACK Probably the closest parallel to Snowden in 1798 was journalist Benjamin Franklin Bache who was the publisher of the *Aurora,* an anti-Federalist newspaper. Bache was Benjamin Franklin's grandson, and he actually got possession of government documents and published them. He was ultimately charged with sedition over publishing a letter from the French foreign minister to John Adams that Bache's subscribers in Philadelphia got to read before John Adams did. Publishing of leaked government documents was going on back in the eighteenth century.

Regarding Snowden, I don't know. I would like to see what he did played out in a court. The biggest gripe I have with Snowden is that if he was going to take the step of getting confidential documents and publishing them, then he should have to face the music in the United States and play out his decision in court. We can see what he did as courageous in one sense, but seeking refuge in foreign countries that have demonstratively fewer rights than we have certainly tarnished his image in my mind.

THOUGHTS ON PREVENTING LIMITATIONS ON FREE SPEECH

AUDIENCE MEMBER Politicians are notoriously sensitive to public opinion. I would assume there was some kind of public support for the Sedition Act when it became the law. What could have been done then and what can be done now to counter this culture where certain members of the public don't seem to put enough importance on the right to free speech?

SLACK There was a lot of support for the Sedition Act at the time. The Federalists used marvelous logic in getting the Act passed by claiming that they had been elected by the American people, and that whoever was then doing the criticizing of President Adams was thereby undermining the will of the American people who had voted Adams and the other Federalists into office. It was a great piece of logic: any criticism of any public figure's behavior was an indictment of the entire American system.

I don't know what lessons we can draw from how that argument was used. Politicians are always going to be sensitive to criticism. There was some guy out in Michigan who wanted to require journalists to be licensed because he didn't like what they were saying. I think politicians are always going to have thin skins, so as a people, we just need to constantly be on guard.

People don't think about their First Amendment rights every day. If they did, my book would be a huge best seller right now. There are books which I think are about subjects not as important as freedom of speech that become huge best sellers. I'm with you regarding your concern. We have to make sure we don't go too far in abridging our rights or in allowing these errors to be committed and then not getting them repealed. We must maintain the ability to recognize injustice, but sometimes it can be frustratingly slow.

BOSTON Okay. Our time is up. Thanks so much, Charles Slack!

SLACK Thank you. I want to say to those in the audience that it's a real honor to be here. Your college is a great institution. Thank you for listening and for your great questions. It's been a great day.

II.

Nineteenth Century, After the Founders

ANDREW JACKSON

ABRAHAM LINCOLN

ULYSSES S. GRANT

H.W. ("BILL") BRANDS is among America's most passionate and accomplished historians. He has twice been a finalist for the Pulitzer Prize and holds the Jack S. Blanton, Sr. Chair in History at the University of Texas at Austin. On October 15, 2015, I interviewed Bill in front of his large American History class at the University of Texas about his book *Andrew Jackson: His Life* (Doubleday 2005) in Austin, Texas.

photo credit: Terry Tottenham

"Andrew Jackson believed that the whole point to being president was to accomplish good things for the United States. His controlling principle was, 'What's good for the United States is what Andrew Jackson thinks is good for the United States.' Members of Congress could have their own opinions, members of the Supreme Court could have their own opinions, but Jackson said, 'The people of the United States elected me to be president of the United States and I'm going to do whatever I think is necessary to further the interests of the United States.'" **– BILL BRANDS**

CHAPTER 6

H.W. BRANDS
ON
Andrew Jackson

JACKSON FULFILS MADISON'S PROPHECY IN FEDERALIST PAPER NO. 10

BOSTON Let's begin, Bill, by talking about why Andrew Jackson is so important in American history. You note that in Federalist Paper No. 10 written in November 1787, James Madison said that, "extending the republic through a greater variety of parties and interests would make it stronger." While president a quarter of a century after writing Federalist No. 10, Madison had major dealings with Andrew Jackson during the War of 1812, and then later, Madison lived through most of Jackson's presidency.

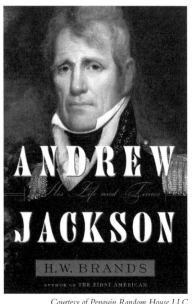

Courtesy of Penguin Random House LLC

Did Madison ever recognize the role that Andrew Jackson played in proving the accuracy of *Federalist Paper No. 10?*

BRANDS That's a very good question. I don't recall reading anything Madison wrote about Jackson as president, but one of the things Madison appreciated was Jackson's role in extending the boundaries of the United States.

Jackson was a key figure in America's expansion. Part of the expansion was essentially defensive expansion. Jackson was the hero of the Battle of New Orleans—the battle at the end of the War of 1812 in which American forces prevented the British from marching up the Mississippi River and accomplishing what their grand strategy of the West was intended to accomplish—to cut the American republic in two.

The United States had acquired Louisiana roughly ten years before and it was still tenuously held by the American grasp. The British believed the United States could be split in two, by using a strategy of having one of their armies march up the Mississippi River, getting past New Orleans, and then connecting with their army coming down from Canada. The idea was to hem in the United States.

The British looked upon the United States in the early nineteenth century like the United States looked at the Soviet Union during most of the twentieth century—as a troublesome expansionist power that embraced a rather disturbing ideology. Our ideology was committed to democracy, which was in conflict with many values the British government held.

The British wanted to contain the United States by blocking us to the West at the Mississippi River. In fact, "containment" was the name of the strategy the United States used during the Cold War against the Soviet Union. Jackson frustrated the British plan for achieving containment by defeating the British at New Orleans, thereby putting an end to their strategy that sought to divide the United States.

BOSTON With Jackson's extending the republic by preventing the British from setting up a barrier to the West, he strengthened the republic—and thereby did exactly what Madison had predicted in *Federalist No. 10.*

BRANDS Madison's *Federalist No. 10* flew in the face of the conventional wisdom of the time in that most people then believed republics needed to be small and the people living within them needed to know each other, in order for civic virtue to blossom. Madison turned this idea on its head by arguing the need for extending the republic if it was to fulfill its potential. Prior to *Federalist No. 10,* America was a diverse republic, and the issue was how could we make it more stable and permanent. Madison pointed out that strength would come from both the diversity of interests and the eventual extension of our geography.

Jackson lived to be the person who definitively proved that by extending our geography, it brought great strength. There were moments in Jackson's early career when growing America's lands was not a forgone conclusion. There was a concern in those days that by extending the boundaries of the republic west across the Appalachian Mountains, it would prove to be a recipe for dividing the republic. In those days, it was very difficult to get from the East Coast to the Mississippi Valley, and the geographic obstacles seemed to be pulling the country apart. Jackson was one who believed that the future of the West lay with its being part of the United States, and as the first Westerner elected president, he demonstrated that the West would have a sizable role to play in our country's future.

The Northwest Ordinance of 1785 allowed for the creation of new states on precisely equal footing to the original ones; and if not for that plan of equality among the states, Andrew Jackson would have never become president—because a Westerner would never have become president. In the Roman Empire, there were people from the provinces who ultimately became emperor. If America's leaders had not allowed for growth in our republic, we would not have achieved what the framers of the Constitution intended.

JACKSON AND SLAVERY

BOSTON Let's talk about Andrew Jackson and slavery. For most of his life, Andrew Jackson owned slaves, and at the time of his death, he was one of the largest slave owners in Tennessee. Late in his life, as the abolitionist movement gained traction, Jackson said he opposed abolition for several reasons. George Washington, Thomas Jefferson, and James Madison all owned slaves, and although they did nothing to bring slavery to an end, they at least wrestled emotionally, intellectually, and morally with the evils of slavery in America. Did Andrew Jackson ever acknowledge that slavery was evil?

BRANDS Jackson accepted slavery as part of the imperfect world he lived in. He believed it was incumbent on slave-holders to be as kind as possible to their slaves, but he opposed abolitionism. He was against the immediate emancipation of slaves because he believed it would be destabilizing to the slave states and disruptive to the union.

Jackson's one pole star in his political philosophy was that the union must hold together. It's really important for anyone who tries to understand Jackson and this early period in American history to remember that Jackson's generation did not take the permanent existence of the United States for granted. Because of what had happened throughout his life, Jackson believed life for Americans would always be a struggle and there existed forces outside the United States—starting with Britain and including Spain and potentially France—who wished the United States ill, and would do whatever they could to break up the United States.

Now we live in the early years of the twenty-first century. The United States has been the great power in world affairs for over a century, and it's very tempting for us to think that somehow there was an inevitability in our nation's becoming a world power. Jackson lived his entire life on the knife's edge of uncertainty as to whether the United States would survive at all. Anything that threatened the security of the United States—whether it was British designs on the American West, or attacks by the renegade Seminole Indians in Florida, or the residual power of the Spanish in Florida—any divisive, potentially threatening influence had to be dealt with and suppressed. Jackson believed anything that stirred up the slavery issue would likely break up the union and he was absolutely right about that. In fact, the pressure of the abolitionists was instrumental in causing the slavery issue to rise to the level where it broke up the union.

Jackson as president had to deal with the political instability that the slavery issue brought on and also had to deal with the questions of nullification and potential secession. All this made him believe that there was nothing preordained about the success of the American experiment in self-government, and that survival was something that had to be fought for almost every year. Slavery had the potential to disrupt the union, and Jackson didn't want to try to eliminate it because he knew that would cause disruption.

Jefferson is probably the best example of a slave-holder who wrestled intellectually and morally with the issue of slavery, but he was wealthy enough where he could afford to indulge in this kind of philosophizing. Jackson was orphaned as a young teenager, and had to fight for whatever he got. He allowed that another world in the future without slavery might be better than his current world, but the current world had given him all the problems he could handle.

JACKSON'S STATURE IN TODAY'S DEMOCRATIC PARTY

BOSTON What's your reaction to the Democratic Party's decision in Iowa and other states in 2015 to change the name of their annual Jefferson/Jackson Day fundraising dinner because they no longer want their party to recognize a connection with anyone who was a slave owner?

BRANDS If I was responsible for branding the Iowa Democratic Party as my primary job, I'd probably do what they did because Jackson is identified in the popular mind with favoring slavery and pursuing harsh policies toward the Indians.

As a historian though, I believe that to try to erase Jackson from our historical memory does disservice to us as a people—and as a republic. It's easy these days not to like Andrew Jackson because of the things that stick out in Jackson's history—his owning slaves and treatment of Indians—and they're things that are difficult for anybody in today's world to understand.

The fact of the matter is that Jackson was absolutely essential to the evolution of American history. Regarding his being a slave-holder, Jackson *had* to be a slave-holder to accomplish what he accomplished. He grew up professionally and politically in Tennessee, which was a slave state. To be successful in Tennessee in his era required men to be planters—and to succeed as a planter required owning slaves. Jackson never would have achieved national prominence had he not first been successful in Tennessee.

It's no coincidence that every Southern president before the Civil War—and there were plenty of them—was a slave-holder, because that was a measure of success in their part of the country during their eras. The whole Southern system was built on slavery.

Today, we can regret that slavery is part of America's past and say it was a bad thing for our country, but the fact of the matter is

that the people who have been successful in moving the United States forward throughout our history have been the people who stayed at best only a half step ahead of their time. In Jackson's case, he was ahead of his time on the subject of democracy.

The absolutely revolutionary idea of democracy sent chills through the spines of most of the Constitution's framers. Many of them didn't really believe in democracy. The idea that ordinary people should actually be able to exercise political power was the most bizarre thing most of them could imagine. They thought of democracy as the first step on the slippery path down to anarchy and chaos.

Then along came Jackson and his generation, who heeded and read the words of Thomas Jefferson and believed that "all men are created equal." In the West, people actually were more equal to each other than they were in the East. With Jackson as their leader, they began to demand more rights for themselves to exercise political power, and this was his great contribution to American history.

He is known as "the people's president"—the one who gave the presidency to the people. Jackson was the first president elected under a regime where the popular vote was recorded. Until Jackson's day, most electors were chosen not by ordinary voters, but by the legislatures of the various states, such that there was an indirect way of electing presidents.

Nowadays, as we're in the thick of the 2016 campaign for the presidency, every candidate has to knock himself or herself out to demonstrate the common touch showing his capacity to connect with ordinary voters. This all goes back to what started with Andrew Jackson.

The two main things we have to thank Jackson for are the emergence of democracy and holding the country together in moments of great trial. It's easy to forget that our democratic nation's survival didn't just happen. Jackson would have said it wasn't inevitable at all and it took great effort by people like him and other leaders of his generation to make it happen.

This happens again and again in history. We forget the great accomplishments of past generations because we accept what they did as the norm, and tend to think that there was an inevitability about what they accomplished and somehow think individual people weren't required to take the tough decisive actions they took. Instead, we focus on what in their particular day were the individuals' comparatively menial sins.

JACKSON AND AMERICAN INDIANS

BOSTON Given his history of defeating Indians and causing them to relocate throughout his military career, is it safe to say that during the first twenty-five years of the nineteenth century, as far as American Indians were concerned, Andrew Jackson was public enemy number one?

BRANDS Jackson was certainly perceived that way, but his view of the Indian situation was a widely shared view during his time, though most of the outrage gets directed at Jackson because he was president then. His view of how best to deal with the Indians was more complex than it's often presented. For example, he believed that Indians who lived east of the Mississippi River needed to relocate if they intended to live in tribal form under their tribal government. The Cherokees were the tribe at the heart of this controversy during the Jacksonian era. If the Cherokees had been willing to live simply as citizens of Georgia and make themselves subject to the laws of Georgia, then they could have stayed where they were; but they *didn't* want to live that way. They wanted to live under their own government, so Jackson said to them, "If you want to live under your own government, then you need to go somewhere beyond the bounds of state governments."

Jackson was a states' rights guy, though he was a different kind of states' rights guy than would be common in the 1850s. Jackson was a states' rights unionist which meant he thought most laws should be made at the states' level because states were better at determining what was best for their inhabitants, though he stopped short of saying that it would ever be permissible for any state to leave the union.

Jackson believed that Georgia, as a state, had the right to make laws for the people who lived in Georgia. The Cherokees didn't want to live under Georgia law; they wanted to live under their own law. He said to them, "If that's the case, you need to go west of the Mississippi River where you can live in territory outside the states." Under Jackson's plan, the territories set aside for the Indians would never have been made states.

There was also a bit of what might be called "tough love" involved because if Jackson was nothing else, he was a realist. He looked at the world as it was—not the world that someone might hope it might become. In speaking to the Indians of the Eastern United States in the late 1820s or early 1830s, he asked, "Where are the Indians of New England? They have vanished. Where are the Indians of the East Coast? Where are the Indians of New York? They have vanished."

Jackson believed white civilization was superior to the Indians' civilization, and his belief was shared by probably 99% of white Americans at the time. He believed that if the representatives of the Indian civilization tribes in Georgia insisted on standing their ground, then they would surely be destroyed—just like what had happened to the Indians in New England and New York. Jackson didn't say moving the Indians west of the Mississippi would be a good thing or a bad thing. He just thought it was the way the world worked in his day, and had been working for the previous two-hundred years, and would probably continue to work in the future.

He believed that for the good of the Cherokees, they needed to get out of the way of the expansionist white

juggernaut—because if they stayed in Georgia, they would be annihilated. This was a tough thing for the Cherokees to hear. It was harsh and probably in violation of some treaties, but the Cherokees should have acknowledged that Jackson was telling them the truth.

It was a very uncomfortable truth then and an uncomfortable truth for us today, but to sugarcoat the truth was impossible for Jackson. What he said to the Cherokees aligned with the policy toward the Indians of every president from George Washington to Ulysses Grant, though Jackson has become the poster boy for this harsh policy toward the Indians of making them relocate west of the Mississippi River, such that he is often blamed for the "Trail of Tears"—the forced migration of the Cherokees from Georgia to Oklahoma. In fact, Jackson had left office when the Trail of Tears took place.

BOSTON If Jackson had not had his great success over the Indians in furtherance of American expansionism, can you estimate how long Manifest Destiny would have been delayed?

BRANDS I don't think there was much that could have delayed Manifest Destiny. Again, this policy to get the Indians to move to the territories west of the Mississippi was not just Jackson's policy, it was the policy of virtually all white Americans. I'll cite an example of it from a subsequent president who tried much harder than Jackson to preserve the rights of the Indians—Ulysses Grant—who originated the policy where Indians would have reservations designed to become their permanent homes. The Sioux Indians had a reservation in the Black Hills of what is now South Dakota. Unfortunately for the Sioux, gold was discovered in the Black Hills and Grant did his best to keep prospectors and miners out of the area, and sent the army there to keep people from moving in on the Sioux. This outraged ordinary people who thought that the whole point of having American resources was so they could be exploited. Congress wouldn't give Grant the appropriations he requested to beef up the army and allow it to have the strength needed to prevent the invasion of the Sioux reservation at the Black Hills. This type of steamrolling over the Indians on their reservations happened again and again.

It also happened after the Cherokees and other tribes had been moved to Oklahoma on land which was supposed to be theirs forever, but then white settlers in the regions around it decided they liked the land in Oklahoma, and wanted to own it. So new laws were passed—not by President Jackson, but by Congress—which diminished and eventually dissolved the reservations and opened the territory to others.

One of the reasons many people are uncomfortable with Andrew Jackson today is because taking an honest look at him makes us uncomfortable about our history as a nation—and there are parts of our history that we ought to be uncomfortable about.

JACKSON AS A MILITARY LEADER

BOSTON Let's go deeper on the subject of Andrew Jackson as a military leader. During and after the War of 1812, as Andrew Jackson did his own thing in Florida and with the Indians, you say that President Madison recognized that Jackson "wasn't an ordinary general, had his own moral compass, and his popular prestige gave him the freedom to chart his own course." Therefore, President Madison basically let General Jackson do his own thing, and allowed him to operate as essentially a rogue military leader who answered to no one; and then James Monroe basically did the same thing when he became president.

With that as the predicate, please compare the president/military leader relationship between Madison/Monroe and Andrew Jackson, on the one hand, with President Truman and General MacArthur, on the other hand, which is the subject of the book you're now writing.

BRANDS As historical background, Andrew Jackson, essentially on his own, took a military force and marched into Florida at a time when it was still legally claimed by Spain. Jackson did this mainly because the Spanish were not governing Florida well, and had essentially lost control of it. Slaves would escape from plantations in Georgia, go into Florida, and then ally with Indian tribes there who would attack settlements in the American territory that abutted Florida. Jackson believed it was bad policy to let the Indians have their way where it adversely impacted America's people and property.

He also believed Spain was not a particular problem to the United States, but Spain's ally Britain was. Jackson had this longstanding, deep hostility toward Britain. Almost anything the British might be capable of doing in creating problems for the United States, he thought they would do. Jackson believed that as long as Florida was beyond the control of the United States, then there would be trouble because of the Indians and the escaped slaves, and these lawless circumstances invited the British to intervene and thereby meddle in American affairs.

Because of these concerns, Jackson determined—against international law and against the policy of his president—that Florida needed to become a part of America. He marched his troops in, battled the Spanish, and took control of Pensacola, a major city in that part of Florida. This intimidated the Spanish who, as a result of losing Pensacola, felt obliged to negotiate away Florida via treaty with the United States in 1819.

Presidents Madison and Monroe liked what Jackson allowed them to accomplish without their having to get their hands dirty. The president of the United States did not want to acknowledge that he was authorizing a military adventure against Spain in violation of America's treaty obligations, but both of them knew perfectly well that Jackson's tactics gave them, as presidents of the United States, leverage in negotiating with the Spanish. By 1819, when the treaty negotiations concluded, Spain realized there was no way it could hold on to Florida, so they might as well give it up.

BOSTON Let's compare Jackson's operating in free-wheeling style during the Madison and Monroe administrations with the way MacArthur operated during Truman's presidency.

BRANDS In 1950-1951, Douglas MacArthur was the American commanding general in the Korean War, and became quite frustrated by the restraints President Harry Truman placed on him in dealing with Chinese forces that entered the Korean War. General MacArthur complained bitterly that he was being required to fight a war with one hand tied behind his back. MacArthur then proceeded to make his complaints public against Harry Truman, his commander-in-chief, by writing a letter to a member of Congress, giving interviews to the press, and writing letters to people that got published. Ultimately, this caused Harry Truman to fire him.

In that case, Harry Truman fired MacArthur because he was challenging the authority of the president. That was true enough, but if MacArthur had been challenging the authority of the president in a direction that Truman actually wanted to go, then he almost certainly would have given MacArthur a longer leash. The difference between 1819 and 1951 is that Jackson in 1819 was accomplishing what the American presidents wanted to accomplish, but clearly didn't want to have to accept direct responsibility for. What Harry Truman held against Douglas MacArthur in 1951 was that his top general wanted to pursue a policy that Truman thought was very dangerous and might well lead to World War III.

JACKSON AS PRESIDENT

BOSTON As president, Jackson didn't always show a great deal of respect for the separation of powers, although in his early political career, he had served in the US House and in the US Senate. You say he wasn't cut out for legislative politics because he had only an executive temperament—meaning he could make decisions much easier than he could make compromises. With that executive bent in his approach to leadership, if Andrew Jackson was president in 2015, would he likely attempt to govern by issuing executive orders whenever Congress blocked his path like President Obama has been doing with increasing frequency during his administration?

BRANDS The answer is almost certainly yes. Andrew Jackson believed that the whole point to being president was to accomplish good things for the United States. His controlling principle was, "What's good for the United States is what Andrew Jackson thinks is good for the United States." Members of Congress could have their own opinions, members of the Supreme Court could have their own opinions, but Jackson

said, "The people of the United States elected *me* to be president of the United States and I'm going to do whatever I think is necessary to further the interests of the United States."

BOSTON Keeping with Jackson's disconnect with the Constitution's separation of powers, during his presidency, he refused to believe that United States Supreme Court decisions bound the president, such that when Chief Justice Marshall and the Court ruled in favor of the Cherokees in a case against the State of Georgia, Jackson disregarded the decision, moved the Indians west of the Mississippi, and said publicly, "John Marshall has made his decision; now let him enforce it." When that was happening, did John Quincy Adams, Henry Clay, or anyone else take any action in response to Jackson's refusal to abide by the Supreme Court's ruling?

BRANDS This is another case where it's very tempting to think about what we know to be the case today, and then look at what Jackson did during his time, and say, "this guy was out of control." In fact though, in Jackson's day, the idea of judicial supremacy—the notion that the Supreme Court had the final word in American politics—was novel and widely disputed. By and large, Daniel Webster and the other Congressional leaders didn't believe the Supreme Court had the power to bind them. They thought the Supreme Court had its name only because it was supreme among the courts. Thus, Jackson and Congress believed that a decision of the Supreme Court surely bound the lower courts, but Jackson certainly didn't believe the Court could bind the president of the United States. In a number of important cases, Jackson simply gave the back of his hand to the authority of the Supreme Court.

For example, when Andrew Jackson vetoed the bill to recharter the Bank of the United States, he claimed he did so because he thought the bank was unconstitutional. He asserted this position despite an earlier Supreme Court decision authored by Chief

Justice John Marshall that had explicitly held that the Bank of the United States *was* constitutional.

Citizens at the time threw up their hands and asked, "Who are you going to listen to?" Jackson's perspective was "That's why we have separation of powers. So that as chief executive, I can do what I think I need to do as chief executive."

In the case of Jackson's allegedly having said "Justice Marshall has delivered his opinion; now let him enforce it," in fact, there was nothing in the opinion that enjoined the president of the United States from doing anything in particular. The Supreme Court's ruling dealt with a dispute between the State of Georgia and the Cherokees, so Jackson didn't have to get involved in that case if he didn't want to.

There's a deeper lesson here. Jackson understood that if the Supreme Court's decision was carried out—that is, if the Cherokees were allowed to remain in Georgia—then he would have to raise an army to fight against the citizens of Georgia. At the time, he didn't have an army, so he would have had to go to Congress and seek appropriations to fund an army and there probably weren't more than a handful of votes in Congress who would support the US Army in a fight against the citizens of Georgia on behalf of the Cherokees.

BOSTON When he said what he said and did what he did about the Supreme Court's decision, did anybody in Congress challenge his position or were they all likeminded with him, and, thus, were just fine with the Supreme Court's ruling being ignored? In 2015, clearly everyone in Congress would be outraged if the president attempted to ignore a Supreme Court ruling.

BRANDS Yes, Congress was fine with Jackson's response to the Supreme Court's opinion in the Georgia case. Today, the idea that the Supreme Court has the last word on the constitutionality of issues that come to its attention is generally accepted

and recognized as a good thing because it means all disputes eventually get resolved. In the 1820s and 1830s though, the Supreme Court was still a work in progress.

There were people at the time who criticized Jackson for rejecting the court's authority, but they mainly raised their criticism because they disagreed with him on the outcome. There was almost nobody who agreed with Jackson on the merits of the case, but disagreed with his ignoring the Court's ruling. There simply weren't enough defenders of the Court's having ultimate authority to put together any kind of critical mass to challenge what Jackson did. When he spurned the Supreme Court, plenty of people said, "That's exactly what we expect our president to do."

JACKSON AND THE NULLIFICATION CRISIS

BOSTON The biggest crisis of Jackson's presidency came from his vice president, John Calhoun, who in protesting a tariff passed by Congress, claimed that the State of South Carolina had the power to nullify the tariff law, claiming that liberty trumped the union. In February 1833, in furtherance of its desire for nullification, South Carolina held a convention that threatened secession if Congress attempted to enforce the tariff against it.

President Jackson responded to South Carolina's threat to secede with overwhelming force and justified his aggressive conduct on the basis that secession would be treason and that his oath of office required him to take action. Soon thereafter, South Carolina rescinded the nullification ordinance after Congress made a slight modification to the tariff.

By doing what he did about South Carolina's attempted nullification and threatened secession, did Andrew Jackson set the precedent that Abraham Lincoln later followed in responding to secession with force as a constitutionally mandated duty for the president?

BRANDS Jackson certainly did set the model Abraham Lincoln followed. I'll elaborate a little bit on how Jackson handled this. There was a longstanding dispute over what could be done if Congress passed a law that a substantial number of people thought was either unconstitutional or simply violated their interests. This was still a time when people weren't sure what the relationship between the states and the federal government was.

The tariff had been passed in 1820, and it outraged many people in the South, especially in South Carolina which was then and later the hotbed for advancing the idea that the states had supreme authority over the federal government. If South Carolina didn't like this particular tariff law, they believed they had the power to nullify it, meaning they would block the enforcement of federal law within its boundaries. If they couldn't stop its enforcement, then South Carolina believed it had the right to secede from the Union.

Jackson had always been a states' rights guy, who therefore believed South Carolina probably made better laws for the people of South Carolina than the government in Washington could make for them; but Jackson would not for a moment tolerate the idea of nullification or, its logical conclusion, secession.

Remember that Jackson was the great military hero of his age. He was often described as the second George Washington—Washington had won independence on the field of battle for the United States during the Revolutionary War, while Jackson had ensured that the United States would continue to maintain independence during and after the War of 1812. So when Jackson got wind that there was secessionist sentiment rising in South Carolina, he told a South Carolina congressman (who visited the White House before heading home on the holiday break) that he should, "Tell my friends in South Carolina" (and Jackson had been borne either in South Carolina or North Carolina; it was a little unclear

exactly where and he would play it either way depending on how it served his purpose)—that if a single drop of blood is shed in opposition to the laws of the United States, then I will come to South Carolina myself, and will hang every traitor from the first tree I can find."

Now when Andrew Jackson—the hero of the Battle of New Orleans, the only president ever to have killed a man in cold blood in a dual, the person who had shot several of his own soldiers during the War of 1812 for desertion—when Jackson talked about hanging secessionists in South Carolina, the South Carolinians truly feared his wrath. At the same time, he instructed his secretary of war to start pulling together provisions for an army of two hundred thousand that he would soon march into South Carolina in order to crush any secession effort.

Now, the South Carolinians decided to back down, but as you mentioned, it wasn't all because of Jackson's threatened use of force. He also, behind the scenes, encouraged Congress to make a new compromise on the offending tariff, which met with the approval of the South Carolinians and was an important factor in their backing down on the threat to nullify or secede.

Jackson made it clear that people in states can talk all they want to about being upset with federal laws, but that doesn't give them the right to disregard them or secede from the Union. If they tried, attempted secession would bring on war.

One can wonder: What if Abraham Lincoln had threatened to pursue war against the Southern states that had seceded right after the election of 1860? A striking thing about Abraham Lincoln was that he didn't say what he was going to do about the Southern states after they seceded before his inauguration. Several people told him, "Mr. President-elect, you need to tell us what you're going to do about the states that have seceded." Lincoln responded, "I'm not president yet; I can't do anything."

One can also wonder: what if Andrew Jackson had been elected president in 1860 and then several states had started seceding? Jackson would *not* have kept silent and would have made it very clear that if you guys try to secede, it will mean war.

One of the reasons there was a Civil War was that many Southerners weren't at all sure the North would fight to preserve the union. Jackson made it very clear early on that he would fight; and because everyone knew his history of fighting, his threat to hang traitors and bring federal troops into South Carolina forced them to back down, though Jackson understood that the problem had not ended. In fact, he predicted that the secession problem would return, and the next time, he said it would be over the Negro question—by which he meant slavery—which is exactly what happened.

JACKSON AND HARDBALL POLITICS

BOSTON Recognizing the success he had in the nullification crises, as well as the success you mentioned earlier when the Bank of the US renewal came up and he succeeded with his veto in preventing the renewal of the US Bank, when it came to playing hardball politics during his presidency, did Andrew Jackson ever lose a major battle?

BRANDS He essentially lost the war aimed at having a sound economy in the case of the Bank of the United States, even though he won the battle by destroying the Bank. Jackson believed that the Bank of the United States, which was the forerunner of the modern Federal Reserve, was a bad idea because it gave too much power to the bankers, and took too much power away from ordinary people. Jackson distrusted bankers and especially distrusted Nicholas Biddle, who was the head of the Bank of the United States. Biddle tried to pull a fast one on Jackson by finding allies in Congress for an early renewal of the charter of the Bank of the United States. Henry Clay, who was behind this, wanted to run for president

Photo credit: Marsha Miller

H. W. Brands

in 1832 on the issue of the need to preserve the Bank of the United States.

When Nicholas Biddle and Henry Clay colluded to challenge the president's authority by getting Congress to override his veto after Congress had passed the bill to renew the Bank's charter, Jackson declared to his vice president, "The Bank is trying to kill me, Mr. Van Buren, but I will kill it." He then succeeded in killing the Bank by withdrawing federal deposits from it. The Bank's biggest customer by far at the time was the federal government. By pulling federal assets out of the Bank, Jackson doomed the Bank to collapse.

You might think this was a victory for democracy based on the idea that ordinary people should run the United States' monetary policy, but it turned into a disaster for the American economy because ordinary people are simply incapable of running our monetary policy. It's just too complicated. It's too tempting for people to say, "Let's increase the money supply and we'll all feel richer."

So this was a case where Jackson's vigorous embrace of democracy demonstrated the limitations of democracy. There are certain things democracy does not do very well and one of them is monetary policy. Jackson's victory over the Bank of the United States by causing it to collapse was certainly a victory for democracy, but it proved to be a disaster for the economy, which demonstrates that democracy isn't the answer to everything.

BOSTON But right or wrong, did he ever lose a major political fight? As I read your book, it seemed like all he had was one success after another. He would go to the mat, play hardball, and win.

BRANDS His biggest setback during his presidency—and I wouldn't call it a defeat exactly in part because Jackson never admitted defeat—had nothing to do with pursuing a major policy. It had to do with the personalities in his administration. His Secretary of War John Eaton, was married to Peggy, a beautiful woman of somewhat suspect background. Partly because she was beautiful and partly because of her background, the wives of the other Cabinet members decided to avoid having anything to do with Peggy Eaton. This caused a virtual paralysis of Jackson's administration because not only did the wives not get along with each other, but they also insisted that their husbands not go to state dinners and receptions and the like. Jackson found he couldn't even get a quorum present from his own Cabinet to attend any function.

Somebody truly enamored of playing hardball politics would have simply fired the whole bunch and brought other people into his Cabinet. Eventually, Jackson was forced to do this; but for quite a while, he insisted on taking the side of Peggy Eaton. He didn't have any particular good reason for thinking she was innocent of everything she was accused of, but Jackson had a memory of his mother who had died saving him from a prisoner of war camp, which caused him to be incapable of believing anything ill about almost any woman. He believed Peggy Eaton was being unfairly slandered by the other members of his administration.

What he should have done was recognize that there's a difference in the code of ethics between being a private individual and being president of the United States. As a private individual, he was not going to throw John Eaton and Peggy Eaton under the bus for something they hadn't done, so he insisted on keeping them as part of his official family as a matter of his personal code of ethics; but as president, he should have realized that regardless of the merits of Peggy Eaton's case, she was preventing him from getting anything done. He should have gone to John Eaton and said, "John, you've got to take one for the team here." He didn't do that though, and as a result, for about a year and a half, nothing good got accomplished in the administration.

It's probably good for the country that a whole lot less was happening in America during the 1820s and 1830s which demanded the attention of a president. One of the striking differences between then and now is that being president today is a 24/7/365 job. Being president in the 1820s and 1830s meant being on the job for a few months while Congress was around, and then being off for four or five months while it was in recess. For the most part, presidents did not lead full-time the way presidents are expected to today.

The other difference between then and now is that presidents today—every hour of every day—have to deal with foreign policy. Presidents in the 1820s and 1830s had almost nothing to do with foreign policy. I had to work hard to come up with one chapter in my book that provided coverage of President Jackson's decisions and activities in foreign policy—because the United States simply didn't have much foreign policy during his presidency.

JACKSON ON AMERICAN FOREIGN POLICY

BOSTON For my final question, Jackson wrote a letter to James Monroe in 1808 in which he explained favoring Monroe over

Madison for president that year because "in the event of war, the mind of a philosopher cannot dwell upon blood and carnage with any composure and is not well fitted for a stormy sea." Does that observation by Andrew Jackson explain why Barack Obama, who leads the country in the mode of being a philosopher, and has no personal or family history in military service, has been reluctant to pursue any significant military action throughout his presidency at a time when so many problems have arisen around the world?

BRANDS In my opinion, Obama's foreign policy has been exactly the right policy. I think the United States is better served today by restraint than by sending our troops into power vacuums.

What Jackson would have had to say about how to respond to power vacuums though is a different matter. Jackson was always a forward thinking guy and was also one who was careful of protecting what he saw as American interests. If he thought our interests were at risk, he would do whatever was necessary to protect them. If he thought American interests were not at stake, then he would leave those entirely alone.

BOSTON Thanks very much, Bill. We're out of time.

RONALD C. WHITE, JR., is the author of my favorite single volume cradle-to-grave biography of our sixteenth president, *A. Lincoln*, (Random House 2009), a *New York Times* bestseller that came out during the Lincoln bicentennial, and won the coveted Christopher Award which salutes books "that affirm the highest values of the human spirit." It was his third book devoted to Father Abraham. I interviewed Ron on a Sunday afternoon, April 12, 2015, at a large gathering of family and friends at Old Parkland in Dallas.

"Lincoln *started* the Civil War *only* to save the Union. His decision to free the slaves came about in the middle of this war. I would argue that the Emancipation Proclamation was not simply a military maneuver. It was also a moral maneuver. There could be no freedom unless freedom was given to all people." **– RONALD C. WHITE, JR.**

CHAPTER 7

RONALD C. WHITE, JR.

ON

Abraham Lincoln

LINCOLN'S RELATIONSHIP WITH HIS FATHER

BOSTON Ron, let's begin at the beginning with Lincoln's early years. One of the most fascinating things about that time was his very complicated relationship with his father. Tom Lincoln, like most of us, was a mixed bag of strengths and weaknesses. For his strengths, he didn't drink or smoke—which was unusual for a man in those days. He was a faithful husband, a regular churchgoer, a great storyteller, and he made a subsistence living as a farmer and a carpenter, though always managed to feed his family and keep a roof over their heads.

For his weaknesses, Tom was essentially illiterate; he groused at his son whenever Abe tried to read

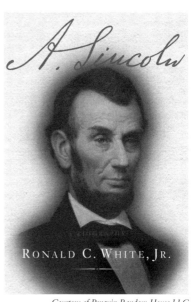

Courtesy of Penguin Random House LLC

because Tom wanted him working in the fields; and he farmed his son out to neighbors and kept every dollar earned from the boy's hard work—meaning Abe was essentially an indentured servant until the time he left home.

When Lincoln finally left the family at age twenty-one, he almost never came back; and had very little communication with his father. When Tom was dying, Abe refused to go see him; and when he finally died, Abe refused to go to the funeral.

With that predicate, throughout your book you point out that even at a young age, Lincoln knew his Bible well. The Fifth Commandment is "Honor your father and mother."

Why did Abe Lincoln choose not to honor his father?

WHITE I'm glad you asked that question because I sometimes find myself falling into the trap of simply being only superlative about Lincoln. Often towards the end of my remarks whenever I'm speaking somewhere, someone will ask, "Were there any dark sides to him?"

I'll start by saying I don't think Abraham Lincoln fully understood his father's background. When Tom was only six years old, his father (named Abraham) was killed by Indians in Kentucky. Because of the way land was divided in those days, Tom didn't get any land but his older brothers did. So Tom didn't have the benefit of having something passed onto him by his father, and Abe never fully appreciated what a difficult spot that put Tom in from an economic standpoint.

It is true that Tom aspired for Abe to become a farmer, since all prior generations in the Lincoln family had been farmers. Tom could not understand for a moment why his strapping young son growing up on the frontier wanted to read, think, and write instead of farm.

Theirs was a conflicted relationship and hard to understand. You said Abe "refused" to visit his dying father. Maybe that's the

right word, but when he heard that his aging father was ill, Abe wrote a letter to his stepbrother saying, "I don't think it would do any good right now if I were to return to see him. Our seeing each other again really wouldn't be helpful." His father recovered, and then when he died, Lincoln, by then a busy politician, did not go to the funeral.

This is one of those authentic gray areas where it's hard to fully understand what was going on. Just a quick contrast: those of us who are parents and grandparents know how the world has changed. Until the last twenty-five years or so, most Americans lived in what I call a "vertical world," such that when Ulysses S. Grant's father said, "I think you should go to West Point", his son said, "I don't want to go to West Point, but if that's what you think I should do, then I will." Now how many of your children would say that? That's the world in which Lincoln grew up—the father and mother were the authority figures and the children obeyed whether they like it or not.

What went on between Abraham Lincoln and his father was strange and has never been fully explained. Lincoln's own words don't help us understand this. The basis of their disconnect was ultimately that Tom never understood or appreciated his son; and never gave Abe the space to become the young man he wanted to be.

BOSTON From a young age we know that Abraham Lincoln was very ambitious. I've often wondered if his fractured relationship with his dad had something to do with that ambition. Tom, being a poor farmer, was never going to be in a position to advance his son's political career, legal career, or anything else, and maybe that's why Abe kept his father in the rearview mirror. Is that a possibility?

WHITE Maybe so. I think Lincoln's reading opened up a world his father never knew and could not imagine. That's the beauty of reading. It opens up a new world—be it novel or non-fiction. Lincoln saw that world out there which he could walk into, and wanted to walk into, and his father never could appreciate it though Abe's stepmother did. Shortly after his mother died of milk sickness when Lincoln was about nine years old, Tom went back to Kentucky and reacquainted himself with Sarah Bush, a young widow. Tom proposed to her on the spot, she accepted, they married, and then they went back and rejoined the family.

Sarah came into Abe's life and brought order, love, and affection and became a key person in his life because of the way she nurtured him. Sarah didn't understand the world that reading opened up, but she wanted to support her son. In many ways, she was the important parent during Abe's early years.

CONGRESSMAN LINCOLN'S ATTACK ON PRESIDENT POLK

BOSTON Switching now from his family to his early political career, more than a decade before he became president, Lincoln served one term in the US House of Congress from late 1847 through 1848. That term was dominated by one issue: his being an outspoken critic of President Polk's handling of the United States' engagement in the Mexican War.

When Lincoln ran for the US House of Congress in 1846, he had initially supported the United States pursuing the war with Mexico; but then his political hero, Henry Clay, came out and blasted the president on the basis that Polk claimed it was Mexico who had been the aggressor and started the war, while Henry Clay claimed the opposite—believing that the United States had started the war. Lincoln jumped on the Clay bandwagon. After serving in Congress less than a month, Abe tore into President Polk on the floor of the House with his famous "Spot Resolution" speech, which soon became an unpopular position in his Springfield district.

What was behind Lincoln's decision to attack President Polk for the way he started the Mexican War?

WHITE Let me begin with your opening lines. A few years ago, on behalf of the State Department, I gave a speech in Mexico on the subject of Abraham Lincoln. When I mentioned the Mexican War, the people in the audience looked confused for a minute, but then said to me, "Oh, you mean the *American* War." So in my Grant biography (that will be coming out next year), I'm calling it "the War with Mexico."

Lincoln was part of what was called a rotation system in his Congressional District. At the outset, there were three able young men who were Whigs and wanted to represent the Springfield district in Congress—all lawyers, all veterans of the Blackhawk War, and Abe drew straw number three, meaning he became the third person nominated in the congressional district of which Springfield was the heart. Each of the three men served one term.

When Lincoln began his term, he almost immediately was faced with a dilemma: How could he support American troops fighting in the Mexican War, but not support Polk's policy rationale in starting the war? That was the nub of Lincoln's complicated position. The war was already going on when Lincoln began his term, and there were great patriotic rallies going on all over the country in support of America's involvement in the war, so it took people by surprise when Lincoln challenged Polk about misrepresenting who started the war. He said to Polk, "You must remember that you sit in the seat where George Washington sat and you must answer honestly." Lincoln became convinced that the United States started the war and had drawn the Mexicans across the border.

Ulysses S. Grant called it "the most wicked war our nation has ever fought, where we dared to be the aggressor against a poor, impoverished country." Grant went on to say, "I should have had the courage not to fight that war. I didn't, but I'm going to tell you what I think of it now when I write my memoirs." So Lincoln stood up to Polk in December and January, and challenged the war.

After his term ended, when he went back home to Springfield, the people in his district said, "Thank you very much, Mr. Lincoln. You will never be elected again. We do not appreciate the position you have taken on the war." Then the next person in the rotation lost the Congressional seat, which made Lincoln's Whig electorate all the more angry. His unpopularity over his stance on the Mexican War was the reason Lincoln relegated himself into becoming a full-time lawyer from 1849 to 1854 with the expectation he would never run for political office again. Only the Kansas-Nebraska Act of 1854, which opened up the possibility that slavery might be expanding into American territories and new western states, brought Lincoln back into the political arena.

His single term in Congress became quite dramatic, and in that time, he was guided by his own internal moral compass. Whatever other people thought, Lincoln had to advocate his unpopular position because he thought it was the right thing to do.

PRESIDENT-ELECT LINCOLN'S BEING MUM ON SECESSION

BOSTON Moving on from his one term in Congress to being elected president twelve years later in November 1860, upon his getting elected, several Southern states seceded immediately. In that era, a president wasn't inaugurated until March of the following year. So there were four months between Lincoln's election and when he was actually sworn in. During those four months, as Southern states seceded, Lincoln essentially said and did nothing to address this situation, and he seemed focused entirely on selecting his Cabinet and preparing his First Inaugural Address, apparently believing that a stirring address to the country after he was sworn in might persuade the South to change its mind and rejoin the Union. Your book is critical of Lincoln's silence as the states seceded, saying it was one of the greatest errors of political judgment in his life.

Why do you think President-elect Lincoln chose to say nothing publicly between November 1860 and March 1861 about the national and constitutional crisis associated with the Southern states seceding from the Union?

WHITE This is what we call "The Long Secession Winter." In those days, presidential inaugurations took place in March, and it wasn't until the second term of Franklin D. Roosevelt when it was changed to January. During the four months after his election, Lincoln was essentially isolated in Springfield, removed from the tension building in the nation. Although people came to see him before he left for Washington, I don't think he fully grasped what was going on with the secession.

He also was very discouraged with President James Buchanan, who had handled this issue so poorly. Buchanan had asked Edward Stanton (who would soon become Lincoln's Secretary of War) to join his Cabinet and Stanton was kind of a mole for Lincoln inside Buchanan's Cabinet. Through Stanton, Lincoln knew what was happening during the four months preceding his inauguration, but didn't have the power to act until he was sworn in on March 4. We've seen this situation arise often with our modern president-elects. For Lincoln to say something about the Southern states seceding before he could do anything about it might have triggered something bad happening and gotten his presidency off on the wrong foot before it even began.

It became a frightening moment in early 1861 when Seward wrote Lincoln in Springfield and said, "You'd better come to Washington in February when we count the votes for the electoral college. I hear there's going to be a Confederate raid that day attempting to prevent your inauguration from happening. Give up this idea of taking a twelve-day train trip to get here." Lincoln replied, "No, I'm not giving up that idea. I trust that no one will be able to stop the

Electoral College. I will make my twelve-day train trip."

He was seen and heard by more people in those twelve days than any other person in history before that time. Although he didn't say much publicly in revealing his policies toward secession during the trip, in his own way he was rallying people throughout the Union for his important cause: to unify the country. During the trip, he gave more than a hundred short speeches and also met with mayors and governors. His strategy was to poll the country and its leaders during the trip. When he finally arrived in Washington, DC, the time came for him to deliver his inaugural address, and he could then speak with authority about his thoughts on the situation as president—not president-elect.

BOSTON His doing anything else would have been essentially premature?

WHITE Premature. Thank you. That's much better said.

LINCOLN'S DESIRE FOR THE CIVIL WAR TO BEGIN

BOSTON Regarding another area of controversy that arose in 1861, there are many people who believe it was Lincoln who started the Civil War and their position is based on how the Civil War began at Fort Sumter. During President Lincoln's second day in office, he learned that the federal government's Fort Sumter located in the Charleston Harbor (with South Carolina having been the first state to secede), was in serious need of provisions. After much deliberation with his Cabinet, Lincoln sent ships to Fort Sumter with the purpose of providing provisions and food. He expressly made it clear to the Southern leaders that the ships would carry no arms or ammunition, and would only carry food and supplies.

As the Union ships approached Charleston Harbor, Confederate General Beauregard demanded the surrender of Fort Sumter. When the fort's commander refused, Beauregard ordered his Confederate battery to fire. Two hours later, the federal soldiers inside Fort Sumter shot back. For you baseball fans, the first Union shot was fired by Abner Doubleday.

On page 408 of your book, you say Lincoln was pleased that his provisions strategy had worked because it caused the South to start shooting first. It kept him from violating what he had said in his First Inaugural Address to the seceding states: "Our federal government will not assail you. You can have no conflict without being yourselves the aggressors".

Is it accurate to say Lincoln actually wanted the Civil War to begin, but didn't want the Union to fire the first shot?

WHITE This is a tough area and it shows Lincoln's shrewdness. He came into office recognizing his own inexperience. In the first days after his inauguration, he not only assembled his Cabinet, he called in all the military officers who he respected, and listened to them. He finally asked for an informal straw vote in his Cabinet regarding how to handle the Fort Sumter problem. The vote was six to two *against* resupplying Fort Sumter.

How he responded to that vote says much about Lincoln's leadership. In a sense, the president said to his Cabinet in the early days of his administration, "Thank you very much. We *will* supply Fort Sumter." I think he *did* want the South to fire the first shot. He understood that war was inevitable. He was going to resupply that fort and if the Confederates fired the first shot, so be it. It would mean, "Now we're in the war and we'll come back." That's my judgment and it's certainly open to people disagreeing with it. I think it shows Lincoln's sagacity in understanding how best to handle the situation, after he had taken the time to educate himself before making his final decision.

BOSTON Does what happened at Fort Sumter tie into Lincoln's perspective on

Polk and the Mexican War? Since he was outraged that the United States had been the first to fire the shot against the Mexicans, he darn sure didn't want his Union army to fire the first shot against the Confederates. Is there a connection there?

WHITE That's a fascinating question. There's no evidence that there was a connection but maybe there was. This obviously could have been in Lincoln's mind as he came up with his Sumter strategy since the two situations were so similar.

BOSTON At the time of the battle at Fort Sumter, the states of Virginia, North Carolina, Tennessee, and Arkansas had not yet seceded. Was Lincoln's thinking that by having the South fire the first shot, it would increase the likelihood that those four states would not secede?

WHITE No, engaging in battle at Fort Sumter was a huge risk. Lincoln knew it would increase the likelihood that those four remaining states *would* secede. And they did.

BOSTON After the surrender of Fort Sumter, Lincoln immediately called for seventy-five thousand troops to enter the Union army. When that happened, those four states *did* secede in short order.

LINCOLN AND THE SUSPENSION OF HABEAS CORPUS

BOSTON We often hear that Lincoln, as commander-in-chief, violated the Constitution by reason of certain actions he took during the Civil War. This controversy arises at least in part, if not mainly, because although the Constitution designates the president as commander-in-chief, it's not specific about the job responsibilities of the commander-in-chief. In performing his duties, Lincoln acknowledged, "I concede that I may in an emergency do things on

military grounds which cannot be done constitutionally by Congress."

The first alleged constitutional violation (and the one we hear the most about) was Lincoln's suspending the writ of habeas corpus beginning in April 1861 and then later in the war. Yes, there was a constitutional provision, Article 1, Section 9, that said it was okay to suspend the writ of habeas corpus if necessary to defend against a rebellion, but that provision was in the section of the Constitution that pertains to Congress' powers, not the president's.

Did Lincoln violate the Constitution by suspending the writ of habeas corpus in 1861 without first gaining Congressional approval?

WHITE I've been asked that question hundreds of times. If I were addressing a group of lawyers, the lawyers would probably say, "Yes, he did." If I was addressing a group of historians, they might say, "No, he didn't."

We must remember that Lincoln was a very astute lawyer and almost a constitutional lawyer. He really valued, understood, and respected the Constitution. I think what is sometimes missed was his great appreciation for precedent. This came out in what we call his State of the Union address in December of 1862, just before he issued the Emancipation Proclamation, where he said, "The dogmas of the quiet past are inadequate for the stormy present." He didn't spell out what those dogmas were. He talked about the quiet past in the context that, "as our case is new, so we must think anew and act anew." He said at one point, "You mean I'm supposed to follow everything in the Constitution so that our Union can be destroyed? Or do I act in this particular situation in a way that I would not have acted in 1830, 1840, 1850, or 1860? I have to find out and act based on the historical forces at work."

After suspending the writ of habeas corpus, he came back to Congress and asked them to ratify what he had done, but he had most definitely engaged in a radical act of presidential leadership in going beyond the Constitution because he believed it was necessary due to the exigency of the situation he faced.

LINCOLN AND THE EMANCIPATION PROCLAMATION

BOSTON The second alleged constitutional violation involved his issuing the Emancipation Proclamation. At the time he signed it, the Constitution was clear that slavery would be permitted in places where it already existed (i.e. in the South and the border states). By issuing the Emancipation Proclamation, Lincoln knew he was violating that provision but believed it was permissible because he claimed emancipating the slaves was a matter of military necessity.

Do you have an opinion on whether Lincoln's issuing the Emancipation Proclamation violated the Constitution?

WHITE Let me answer that by putting it in a larger context. One of the great debates of the last few years was: Did Lincoln start the Civil War to save the Union or did he start it to save the Union *and* free the slaves? He *started* the Civil War *only* to save the Union. His decision to free the slaves came about in the middle of this war. I would argue that the Emancipation Proclamation was not simply a military maneuver. It was also a moral maneuver. There could be no freedom unless freedom was given to all people.

Yes, knowing exactly what the powers of the commander-in-chief were was very tricky because of the way it was described or basically *not* described in the Constitution. So he issued the Proclamation on the basis of freeing the slaves in the seceded states being a military necessity.

The whole point of the *Lincoln* movie was that Lincoln understood the need for the Thirteenth Amendment to get passed because the Emancipation Proclamation could be overturned by another president, another Congress, or the Supreme Court.

One of the most amazing things about how it all played out was that the man who tried so hard to upstage Lincoln during his presidency and was always against him, Salmon P. Chase, was who Lincoln chose to serve as Chief Justice of the Supreme Court when the position opened up in late 1864. Lincoln knew Chase was anti-slavery and would stand rock solid for the emancipation of the slaves, and that was much more important to Lincoln than the fact that Chase had backstabbed him throughout his presidency.

So, yes, the Emancipation Proclamation was a military maneuver, but I want to step back from saying, as has been said by some and by many African-Americans, that it was only a military maneuver. It was *more* than a military maneuver. It was a moral commitment that Lincoln believed the nation needed to make.

BOSTON It was a moral maneuver but he put in the language of "military necessity" so it would hopefully pass Constitutional muster.

WHITE Right. When he first issued it, he had no idea that black soldiers would fight on the front lines. There's a little provision in the Proclamation which allowed blacks to serve in the military, but Lincoln expected them to stay behind the battle lines, thereby allowing more white soldiers to fight in the front. Grant wrote Lincoln in August of 1864, "I want to tell you about the courage of these black soldiers." That caused Lincoln to change his mind. Grant and Stanton told him, "You've got to start arming these black soldiers. They will fight for the Union."

BOSTON Do you recognize the issuance of the Emancipation Proclamation on January 1, 1863, as *the* turning point in the war?

WHITE I recognize it as *a* turning point in the war. *A* turning point.

LINCOLN AND THE FREEDOMS OF SPEECH AND THE PRESS

BOSTON The third alleged constitutional violation was Lincoln's interfering with freedom of speech and freedom of the press. He had a harsh critic, Congressman Vallandigham from Ohio, who was very critical of everything Lincoln did as commander-in-chief. Lincoln got fed up with him, so he caused Vallandigham to be taken from Ohio and delivered over to the Confederacy in Tennessee as a way of shutting him up. So much for freedom of speech for Congressman Vallandigham! Also, during the war, there were certain newspapers who were critical of Lincoln's policies, and he was instrumental in getting those newspapers shut down.

What happened to the Bill of Rights' freedom of speech and freedom of the press?

WHITE This is part of that larger question again: "Does the exigency of a particular moment demand that we do something we would not normally do?" What was happening to the country during Lincoln's presidency was not "normal." Lincoln was willing to say, "I hear the criticism. I may be wrong, but I must do this to save the country."

President Lincoln believed that what was called "the Fire in the Northwest" (being the criticism of his policies by Congressman Vallandigham and his cohorts) was almost as damaging to the Union as what was happening below the Mason-Dixon line. So Lincoln arrested Vallandigham and took him to the Confederacy's border and turned him loose. When Vallandigham was dumped in their laps, the Confederate soldiers surely wondered, "Who is this guy?" Lincoln was willing to say, "I may be in error here, but I must do this as the leader of the country."

POLITICAL ADVANTAGES OF LINCOLN'S BEING A LAWYER

BOSTON In addition to his pushing the envelope of the Constitution to deal with the major crisis that arose throughout the war, in your book you repeatedly reference how the skill set Lincoln developed as a lawyer during his twenty-three year legal career in Springfield made him a better president. You talk about his being a man who could frame an argument with lawyerly reasoning, marshal his evidence, and rely on precedent after engaging in thorough research; a man who chose his words and deeds carefully in hopes of withstanding US Supreme Court scrutiny; a man who as a trial lawyer was a proactive peacemaker and knew how to mediate disputes, but also recognized that sometimes peaceful resolution is not possible, in which case the lawyer has to go to trial (i.e. go to war in order to achieve a final resolution); and a man whose eloquence flowed from his jury trial-honed capacity to tie together law and literature with eloquence.

Given the challenges he faced during his four-plus years as president, was Lincoln's being a consummate trial and appellate lawyer (which caused him to possess these skills I've just described) absolutely essential to his having the horsepower to perform his duties as commander-in-chief at a high level during the Civil War?

WHITE How many lawyers are here tonight? In 1988, a professor at what was then called Sangamon State University (now the University of Illinois at Springfield), got into his head that if Lincoln had practiced law all over the State of Illinois in the mid-nineteenth century, could it be that some of Lincoln's legal papers might still exist in the 102 county courthouses? So he got a group of masters program students and sent them out across the State of Illinois. They found thousands of Lincoln's legal documents, which had turned blue with age. In almost all of them, Lincoln's signatures were razor-bladed out. He was the first real celebrity in American history so his signatures had been cut out by people who wanted his autograph. Lincoln's handwriting was so distinct though, that you could tell these were his papers even after his signature had been removed. Because of that professor's work, we now have a huge corpus of what Lincoln did as a lawyer. I have to tell you though that in writing this biography, my editor came back to me again and again and said, "Ron, this isn't very sexy. All you're talking about is what a great lawyer he was."

BOSTON Saying good things about lawyers? He was right. That's not very sexy.

WHITE I think knowing about Lincoln the lawyer is critical to understanding why he was such a great president. In my biography, I mention how Lincoln taught himself to be a good war president by checking books out of the Library of Congress; but he also looked forward to being a peace president after the war ended. He wrote a wonderful piece called his "Lecture to Lawyers," which we don't believe he ever delivered as a speech but it's in his Lincoln papers. In it, he says at the end, "The lawyer has a grand opportunity to be a mediator of peace." And I think Lincoln was a great mediator. He would say to people, "You may think you're

going to win your case in front of the judge or jury, but you may end up losing because the folks in small town rural America aren't going to accept your position. And if you pursue your case through trial and lose, then you're going to damage your relationship with the people you have to live with."

I believe we have undervalued the importance of Lincoln's legal skills as being the key to being such a great president.

BOSTON Were his legal skills *essential* to his success as president?

WHITE Yes, they were essential.

LINCOLN'S MARRIAGE

BOSTON Now we're going to get to the sexy part. We're going to talk about Lincoln's relationship with his wife Mary—particularly during their years in the Executive Mansion (it wasn't called the White House until Theodore Roosevelt's presidency).

Like Abe's father Tom, Mary was truly a mixed bag of strengths and weaknesses. Her strengths: she was smart, well-educated, ambitious, passionate about politics, and she enjoyed socializing and entertaining. For her weaknesses: she had a hot temper; she over-spent recklessly on shopping sprees; she had a rocky relationship with many people who were key to Lincoln, including his Secretary of State William Seward, and she was very critical of Ulysses Grant; and finally, her having family members who fought and died for the Confederacy complicated things during the Civil War.

Recognizing all these conflicting strengths and weaknesses, was having to deal with Mary among Lincoln's toughest challenges during his presidency?

WHITE Who can get inside someone else's marriage? I think the *Lincoln* movie did a good job of depicting Mary, and she has been depicted across a wide spectrum of interpretations. There are Lincoln historians who despise her. There are others who defend her. I would be more sympathetic to Mary in this guise. She had quite a good education for a girl of her era, in that most girls growing up then, if they had any education at all, didn't go beyond the fourth grade. She went beyond that, and also studied and learned French. Her sisters all thought she was marrying beneath herself when she chose Abe. One of them visualized their relationship as Mary and Abraham sitting on the couch, and he's sitting there in rapt attention as she carries the conversation. She was a very able person. I think she saw his ability before he saw it himself, and she was his chief counsellor in Springfield.

When she got to Washington in 1861, she was at first badly treated by the high-ranking women there who erroneously thought she was a Western rube without any sophistication. Second issue for her in DC was that Lincoln chose Seward, Stanton, and other men who had been Lincoln's rivals for the presidency and Mary had a hard time warming up to her husband's rivals.

Finally, you saw this in the movie, that the death of Willie in February of 1862 absolutely crushed Mary. I don't think she ever recovered from it. Lincoln was also crushed by Willie's death, but he had to go forward because he was the president.

Another brief comment in her defense. In those years when Lincoln was a lawyer, he rode the Eighth Judicial Circuit in Illinois (an area the size of the State of Connecticut), and would be gone 180 or more days a year—meaning he left his wife to be essentially a single mother half of each year to preside over their active young sons. That wasn't being a very good husband on his part. When trains finally arrived as public transportation in Illinois, Abe began coming back to Springfield on the weekends during his months on the circuit. While he was home, whenever Mary got mad at him, and she did have quite a temper, he would simply say, "I think I need to go to my office," and he'd walk out the door.

Then, think at the end of his life—when she held her husband's hand as he was assassinated. Her first son had died at age three and a half, Willie died at eleven, Tad (who you saw in the movie) died at age seventeen. Only one of her four sons lived into adult life. This woman suffered a great deal of difficulty in her life.

BOSTON One thing we can say—she had an eye for talent. Because nobody else wanted to date or marry Abraham Lincoln, and she said early on, "I think this guy can be president one day."

WHITE Right. He was six feet four. People were much smaller in the nineteenth century than they are now. If he were with us tonight, and we compared his height differential to a man's normal height in 2015, he'd stand six feet nine and we would all take notice of him.

LINCOLN'S FAITH BEING OVERLOOKED BY HISTORIANS

BOSTON Moving past the dynamics of the Lincoln marriage, your book broke new ground when it came out during the Lincoln bicentennial year of 2009 as a *New York Times* critically acclaimed best seller because it fully detailed Lincoln's lifelong spiritual odyssey culminating with his attempt to divine God's will throughout the Civil War, as reflected most eloquently in his Second Inaugural Address, which you've called Lincoln's Sermon on the Mount. You're aware of dozens, maybe hundreds, of esteemed Lincoln biographies written by distinguished historians who have decided to pay almost no attention to the fact that Lincoln's faith grew so dramatically throughout his presidency.

What's your explanation for why so many high-powered scholars have ignored the reliable evidence identified in your book, and given short shrift and sometimes no shrift to the impact of Lincoln's faith on his presidency?

WHITE I think it's a shortcoming of the historians. I'm sad to say that I think they don't think his faith story is interesting. They're not interested in it themselves and they don't have the tools to tease out what I see as his very sophisticated theological language in the Second Inaugural.

Lincoln's faith journey compares favorably with Dwight Eisenhower's, who was raised in a Mennonite family in Kansas, and didn't get baptized until he was president of the United States. As president, he joined the Presbyterian church in Washington, DC, and became an active member. When he retired to Palm Desert, he became a very active member in the Presbyterian church there. You won't find much about that in any Eisenhower biography, but it's the truth and the facts about it are easy to find. I've spent time with David Eisenhower and he told me, "I'm so disappointed that my grandfather's faith from the time of his presidency until the day he died was not at all represented in any of these biographies."

Lincoln traveled a fascinating spiritual odyssey. He was born during the Second Great Awakening into a Baptist family—no disrespect to any Baptist here. Theirs was a very emotional faith. For whatever reason, Lincoln from an early age was always suspicious of emotion. He became a highly rational person in his youth and that's one reason he became a lawyer. When he went to church at ages nine, ten, and eleven, he listened to the pastor's emotional sermons, and then would go out and repeat the sermons word-for-word on a stump, mimicking the preacher until his father ripped him down from the stump, whipped his backside, and sent him home. Lincoln did what many of us have done or our children have done— that is, as a child, he pushed against not the Christian faith but against his parents' Christian faith, and became a deist or what he called a fatalist.

After he left his father and stepmother, he moved to New Salem. There, we have a number of accounts about his having written a paper criticizing the Bible and religion. One of his best friends ripped the paper out of his hands and tossed it in a fire since the friend knew of Abe's political ambition and how his distributing the views he had written on the paper—criticizing Christianity—would not have been a smart thing to do if he wanted to have any success as a politician in Illinois in the 1830s.

Then what happened to Lincoln happens to many of us. His second child died at age three and a half. Reeling from that tragedy, he reached out to find the Episcopal minister in town but he was out of town that day. So Lincoln connected with a young Presbyterian minister who had been in his Springfield pulpit less than twelve months. This man, Reverend James Smith, had written a marvelous eight hundred page book defending the authority and authenticity of the Bible. Lincoln got to know him well over the next few years and Robert Todd Lincoln said Smith's book was one of the few books on the bookshelf in their home.

So Lincoln started his spiritual journey before becoming president, and then it continued during the Civil War, and most definitely picked up its pace as he kept wrestling with the question, "Where is God in the midst of this horrible war?"

In his Second Inaugural Address, in 701 words, Lincoln mentioned God fourteen times, quoted the Bible four times, and invoked prayer three times. He did nothing more than what a shrewd politician did in those days. We know that all politicians, then and now, want to have some invocation of religion. We are a religious nation and that's an important thing for a politician to do. Lincoln quoted the Bible like one would quote Shakespeare.

Right after Lincoln's death, his young secretary, John Hay, was going through his boss' desk drawers, and he pulled out this little piece of lined paper with Lincoln's handwritten thoughts. I traveled to Brown

University to see it—John Hay was a graduate of Brown. The paper is untitled, undated, and was unsigned as were all of Lincoln's slips of paper. In this paper Hay found, Lincoln began: "The will of God prevails. In each contest, each side claims to be following the will of God. Both cannot be right. One must be wrong. It may be that in this war, God's purpose is something different from the purpose of either party, and yet he uses human instruments to make his purpose."

If you think about it for a moment, what was on that paper became a key part of his Second Inaugural Address. At the point in time when we think Lincoln wrote that paper, two and a half years before the address, he was writing a philosophical, theological reflection. Lincoln did this a lot. By the time he got to the Second Inaugural, he became very specific and more clear about his thoughts. At the end of that little "Meditation on the Divine Will," as John Hay called it, Lincoln said, "And the contest proceeds." You might want to say, "Hey, wait a second. You're the commander-in-chief. You're supposed to be ending this conflict." Lincoln the private person is asking himself, "Where is God in this conflict?"

So the Second Inaugural is a most profound theological statement. Where did Lincoln's thoughts come from? I argue in my book that the missing person in the Lincoln spiritual growth story was his minister in Washington, Phineas Dinsmore Gurley, a brilliant and persuasive pastor who had been number one in his class at Princeton Seminary. While president, Lincoln began to attend Gurley's church regularly. Gurley's sermons have been preserved for history and he also preached the sermon at Willie Lincoln's funeral. The connection between the two men was real and strong.

In the Second Inaugural, Lincoln was no longer a deist or a fatalist. He kept invoking Providence and the will of God. He acknowledged that the Almighty has his own purposes. Some of us may not think it was so surprising, but when you think of inaugural addresses, aren't they usually made

up of what a president believes is most important? In his Second Inaugural, Lincoln took his audience by surprise. I didn't call it his Sermon on the Mount; a newspaper reporter the next day after Lincoln delivered it called it his Sermon on the Mount. Another reporter said he had crossed the line between church and state. Another one said it sounded like an old sermon. Lincoln, knowing this strongly religious approach would be controversial, believed he was making a profound statement at a critical time in history.

In doing the research for my books, I was surprised to learn that before Lincoln's Second Inaugural, the Bible had been quoted only one time in the previous eighteen presidential inaugural addresses. I think this speech opened a window into Lincoln. We've opened all the other windows—politician, lawyer—but we haven't fully opened this spiritual window yet. I think it's quite amazing.

LINCOLN AND SPIELBERG'S FILM

BOSTON You've talked a few times already about the movie, *Lincoln*. In it, director Steven Spielberg and screenwriter Tony Kushner focused the script almost entirely on one month, January 1865, presumably believing that month was the Lincoln presidency's dramatic zenith.

If it had been your movie, and you wanted it set during the most dramatic month during Lincoln's presidency, what month would you pick?

WHITE January 1865 was pretty dramatic. What happened then was a story Spielberg and Kushner felt was not well understood and it involved the key figures surrounding Lincoln at the time.

You could argue that several months during Lincoln's presidency were as dramatic. One might be December 1862, the month before Lincoln issued the Emancipation Proclamation, when many people (including Mary) came to him and said, "You're not possibly going to offer this Proclamation. You *must* withdraw it. Do you understand what will happen if you do this? It will create total chaos." That would have been a very important month.

The darkest days of the war probably were in July 1863 after the battle at Gettysburg; and as important and often undervalued, the victory at Vicksburg. Those were important turning points in the war. So there were a number of critical dramatic months during his presidency.

PRESIDENT LINCOLN'S BATTLE WITH STRESS

BOSTON In recent years, there have been many after-the-fact psychological assessments of Lincoln's mental state throughout his life. Some have claimed he battled depression, though most seem comfortable using the word "melancholy" to describe his temperament.

If ever someone had a reason to be melancholy, it was Lincoln during his time as president. In those years, he had to preside over a war that cost over seven hundred thousand lives; had to grieve over the death of his eleven-year-old son, Willie; had to deal with Mary and her high-strung temperament and insane spending sprees; had to agonize over the many Union generals' incompetence and unwillingness to fight the enemy; and had to try to build consensus amidst the discord of his Cabinet, the Senate, and the leaders of the anti-war movement. During the years of his presidency, Lincoln was Job-like in not only holding himself together emotionally, but making consistently good decisions.

How do you explain Lincoln's superhuman capacity to handle stress?

WHITE We should start with the melancholy or the depression. I'm not a psychiatrist, but some psychiatrists have told me that people who suffer from depression (and, interestingly, women suffer depression

almost twice as much as men), do so in part because they are so sensitive to the feelings of others. They feel deeply the pain of other people and that is one way to understand the cause of Lincoln's depression—because he deeply felt the pain of those all around him, but it didn't overcome him. Even when they were both grieving over the death of Willie, he said to Mary, "I have to go on. I have to do this." Remember that great scene in the movie where she said, "Don't you care about the death of our son?" He replied, "Of course, I do!" This showed his internal moral strength.

I went to college long ago. While there, I read a book by David Riesman called *The Lonely Crowd*—a great sociological book. In it, Riesman argues that in the nineteenth century, people were inner-directed people. Starting after World War I, maybe in the 1930s or 1940s, we became other-directed people, focusing our attention on questions like "What will *she* think of me? What will *he* think of me?" With that other-directed focus, beginning in the mid-twentieth century, we stopped asking ourselves, "What do *I* think is right?" Politicians then began getting all their signals from other people, and started making decisions on the basis of what they believed other people thought.

Lincoln had this strong internal moral compass regarding what was right. He thought he had been elected to an office that wasn't about "me". He would say again and again to the crowds during that twelve-day train trip from Springfield to Washington, DC, before his inauguration, "I know you're not here to greet *me*. If Stephen Douglas had been elected, I'm sure you would have greeted him. You're only greeting me because I represent you in this nation."

What an amazing way to talk to people. He had this internal sense that he was on a mission, and had been called to do something that was larger than himself. I think that's what allowed him to navigate through all his stress and setbacks. I tried to put into my biography on what we call the "facing page" (the page that begins each chapter), successive photographs of Lincoln as he aged. You can see what happened to him over the four years he was president. He was barely fifty-six years old when he was assassinated, but by the end of his presidency, he looked so old and worn down by the office he had carried.

LINCOLN AND HIS HUMOR

BOSTON In finding ways to deal with stress, you often mention in your book about the importance of humor to Lincoln. In fact, he once said, "With the fearful strain that is upon me night and day, if I did not laugh, I should die."

How important was humor as a tool for Lincoln's maintaining his emotional equilibrium?

WHITE Humor was wonderful and probably essential to Lincoln. Remember in the movie how those people all wanted to hear Lincoln speak at a party, and Secretary of War Edwin Stanton said to him as the crowd gathered, "You're not going to tell us one of those stories again, are you?" When I saw the movie the third time I realized that when the results came in from a battle victory, Stanton was holding Lincoln's hand—that's how close they were to each other.

Stanton had once been a high-priced, powerful lawyer, and was lead counsel for one of the parties in the so-called "Reaper Case" in Illinois. There were two different men who had invented the reaper, and one of them hired Lincoln to do the due diligence on the case when they thought it would be tried in Chicago. Then the venue shifted to Cincinnati. Lincoln arrived for the trial there after doing months of preparing the case for trial. As lead counsel for Lincoln's client, when Stanton saw that Lincoln was going to be part of his co-counsel team, he said, "We don't want that baboon here at the table in front and we don't want him invited to the social event this evening." He treated Lincoln horribly. Yet when the opening came for the position of secretary of war in Lincoln's Cabinet, who did Lincoln hire? Edmund Stanton, who had treated him so abominably at the trial in Cincinnati, but who Lincoln believed had the skills and experience to handle that important Cabinet position better than anyone. What does that tell you about Lincoln's rising above the fray and abiding by his moral compass?

One of my favorite stories of Lincoln's humor took place when Lincoln was traveling with Seward on a buckboard after Lincoln and Seward had become great friends. It was very rocky and noisy on the wagon ride. Seward had a wonderful liquor cabinet—Lincoln didn't drink. Seward smoked twenty cigars a day—Lincoln didn't smoke. Seward had a vocabulary of profanity—Lincoln didn't swear. But they became great friends. So they were traveling together one day and suddenly the buckboard driver started swearing a blue streak. Lincoln tapped him on the shoulder and asked, "My good man, are you an Episcopalian?" The driver replied, "No. I'm a Methodist." Lincoln responded, "I thought you had to be an Episcopalian. You swear just like Mr. Seward."

Lincoln's humor was not joke-telling like we see these days on late night television, but was often geared to his particular cultural situation. It may not resonate today but it was geared to what was happening then. Humor was a wonderful release for him and he laughed most at himself, not other people. I'm troubled by much of today's humor because it's aimed at the expense of other people. Lincoln didn't do that with his humor—he laughed at himself.

LINCOLN'S PUBLIC RELATIONS EFFORTS

BOSTON There are two Lincoln biographies that came out in 2014 that attempted to focus on new angles. You actually delved into both angles in your book that came out in 2009. The first is Harold Holzer's *Lincoln and the Power of the Press*, subtitled *The War for Public Opinion*.

Did Lincoln have an overall public relations strategy behind the initiatives he pursued in his dealings with the nineteenth century media?

WHITE Lincoln was very astute at the power of the press, and Holzer's book is great. The largest immigrant community in Illinois was German. Lincoln wrote anonymously in their German newspaper because he knew it had such a great influence on the German population in his district. Since there were no press conferences at the time, Lincoln got press coverage by writing letters to newspaper editors. He frequently invited editors to talk with him. One of the most amazing things that happened regarding Lincoln's writing pieces for newspapers came right after Stonewall Jackson died. Lincoln wrote a letter to an editor praising Jackson as a Christian gentleman, and giving him the highest marks as a battlefield leader. He understood in ways that others didn't the power of the press and how to cultivate that power. It was a great political talent of his.

LINCOLN'S REVERENCE FOR THE DECLARATION OF INDEPENDENCE

BOSTON The second one is Richard Brookhiser's new book, *Founder's Son,* about Lincoln's philosophy toward the bellwether issue of slavery expansion being tied to the intention of our Founding Fathers when they signed off on the Declaration of Independence. You talk often in your book about how Lincoln repeatedly tied his speeches and his debate positions to the Declaration of Independence, particularly in his attacks on the Kansas-Nebraska Act. In fact, on his train ride from Springfield to DC before he became president, he stopped in Philadelphia at Independence Hall, and said, "I've never had a feeling politically that did not spring from the sentiments embodied in the Declaration of Independence."

photo credit: Cynthia Conger White

Ronald C. White, Jr.

Why was Lincoln more focused on the Declaration of Independence than the Constitution?

WHITE Lincoln believed that the Declaration of Independence was the true founding document. Its principles had been a radical departure from those of the mother country Great Britain. Lincoln's focus on the Declaration was no criticism of the Constitution, but came from his recognition that it was a different type of document and attempted to codify the laws and principles that we should have as a nation going forward.

Lincoln wanted to step behind the Constitution back to its original impetus. He said at one point that he was deeply troubled by the fact that the Declaration was gathering dust in people's minds during the early decades of the nineteenth century. He attempted to revive the Declaration of Independence by saying, "We've lost its reforming impetus and that's not simply an impetus that applied to 1776 or 1787, but an impetus that should *still* be reforming us today." Therefore, regardless of whether Thomas Jefferson thought so or not when he said, "All men are created equal," Lincoln believed the Declaration actually *meant* that all men are created equal.

For many different reasons, the Founding Fathers could not fully activate the equality promise contained in the Declaration of Independence into the Constitution. They knew that they needed to have thirteen colonies join together in this experiment in order to form a nation, and they became largely silent on the issue of slavery in the Constitution because if they had taken a strong stand against it in the document, several states would not have ratified it.

The Founding Fathers believed, as did Lincoln at first, that slavery would become extinct by its own momentum over time. Then along came the cotton gin and slaves became needed more than ever as the cotton industry surged. This caused the defense of slavery both politically and on religious grounds to take place and it became clear to all that slavery was not going to become extinct. That's why Lincoln argued, although with great fidelity to the founders, that "Regardless of the quiet past, it was inadequate for the stormy present. As our case is new, so we must think anew and act anew." That to me is the delicate balance. Lincoln was essentially saying, "Yes, all these wonderful propositions were laid down by our founders, but we now live in a different era and therefore we must look at our country differently." Lincoln was right at the crux of that difficult game-changing decision-making.

LINCOLN'S CONTINUING QUEST FOR HIGHER MORAL GROUND

BOSTON You will be relieved to know this is my last question. Lincoln has been revered since his death 150 years ago in large part because of his moral integrity and his capacity to express that integrity into words that have resonated for many generations of Americans. Your book talks about the process which he developed over the course of his life, beginning with reading "books laden with moral fruit" as a child, that he used to grow and refine his integrity toward the public good with no backsliding over the course of his life.

Describe Lincoln's process for finding higher and higher moral ground to stand on with each passing year of his life.

WHITE I have thought about writing a book called "Abraham Lincoln's Diary", even though Abraham Lincoln never wrote in a diary. Those who write biographies know that if you can find a diary or a set of letters, then you've got a new basis for providing insight into what the historic figure really thought. For example, Scott Berg found Charles Lindbergh's letters and his wife's letters and used them to create a book on Lindbergh with lots of new information.

In Lincoln's personal papers, which started being published in 1898 by his two secretaries Hay and Nicolay, they found curious papers they called "fragments." What was a "fragment?" Lincoln habitually took little slips of paper and wrote his ideas out on them. He stuck them in his top hat or put them in the back drawer of his desk. We have more than two hundred of these fragments and we're still recovering Lincoln's letters. You might have a Lincoln fragment in your attic and you wouldn't know what it was because Lincoln never signed his name to a fragment, he never titled them, and he never dated them. They are phenomenal because they show Lincoln carrying on intellectual conversations with himself.

Once there was a big rally in Albany, New York, made up of people in the Vallandigham camp who were critical of Lincoln. These people sent him a petition and Lincoln planned to use the press to answer it. So he sat down to write out his answer to the critics. There was a man in his office who saw Lincoln compose his response in short order, and he remarked, "This is amazing that you can prepare your answer so fast." Lincoln replied, "No. I've been thinking about this for the last two years, I couldn't sit down at the desk and write it up without preparation. Look at all the notes I compiled over time on this subject. That's the way I'm able to write this paper."

These days, I want to say to young people whenever I get a chance, that I'm worried about what's happening between them and this little cell phone device that is so addicting. It prevents us from taking time anymore to reflect and ruminate. I asked the young people at Poly High School in Pasadena, which is an elite school, "How long do you think it took Lincoln to write this meditation?" They answered, "Three minutes." I said, "How about two hours? Maybe three or four." He didn't come to these decisions that he wrote about just like that. He was carrying on an intellectual conversation with himself, just as Benjamin Franklin did, and that was the basis of his continual moral growth.

Many of his ideas that developed over time were on slavery. There's another fragment he wrote that said, "Stephen Douglas has risen to high eminence, and as for me, my life is nothing but a flat failure." Lincoln revealed his feelings in these fragments in a way he would never have revealed them in the printed word. They allow us to get a sense of the way he thought about all these prominent and deeply complex issues.

I hope diary keeping comes back into practice because that's a way a person can actually think aloud about his own moral sensibility. This is a key to understanding Lincoln's approach to getting answers to his questions that we've overlooked because Lincoln's fragments are here and there and spread around through all these years. If you put them all together, you really see Lincoln's intellectual, moral, and spiritual growth.

BOSTON Sorry, but we've run out of time. Thanks so much, Ron.

[NB: Because this was an oral interview, the reader needs to appreciate that when Ronald White attempted to remember Lincoln's exact words, although they are identified with quotation marks, they are not exact quotations.]

HAROLD HOLZER is one of America's leading authorities on the life and times of Abraham Lincoln. Because of his many books and articles written on our sixteenth president, he received the 2015 Gilder-Lehrman Lincoln Prize and serves as the chairman of the Lincoln Bicentennial Foundation. I interviewed Harold on October 5, 2015 at a presidential symposium hosted by The King's College in New York City about his recent book, *Lincoln and the Power of the Press: The War for Public Opinion* (Simon & Schuster 2014).

"As he put it in his Second Inaugural Address, when the war began, no one could have imagined the magnitude or the duration it would attain. He was deeply tortured about the war as it went on year after year, and famously turned more and more to Divine Providence to explain or rationalize the enormous sacrifices that were being made. He became so burdened and guilt-ridden by the fallout from the war that you can see it in his face in the photographic portraits—a man simply ravaged during his four years in office— going from a youthful looking fifty-two-year-old man to a prematurely old man who had somehow weathered the agonizing years of his presidency." **HAROLD HOLZER**

CHAPTER 8

HAROLD HOLZER

ON

Abraham Lincoln

COMPARING POLITICS
AND THE MEDIA'S INTERACTION:
THEN AND NOW

BOSTON Harold, in your introduction to this book, you say that, "In the age of Lincoln, the press and politics often functioned in tandem" and "newspapers became unreliable and stressed opinion over news, which kept the public in a perpetual state of arousal." To me, that sounds like media and politics in 2015.

What are the main differences between how the media and politics worked together in the mid-nineteenth century as compared to how the tandem work today?

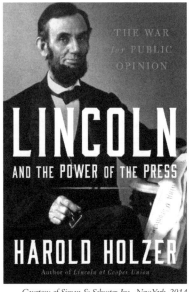

Courtesy of Simon & Schuster, Inc., New York, 2014

HOLZER Sure, there are similarities in the two eras, though I am going to attack the question from the other side. Let's say you are following a news story today on both Fox and MSNBC. You will obviously hear different and philosophically partisan views and interpretations of the same story. Certainly in interviews, you get that same sense, but "owned and operated" was a little bit different in Lincoln's era (and it actually started during Jackson's presidency) and became especially so when the slavery issue began roiling American politics into a fever that had been unimaginable previously.

In the mid-nineteenth century, unlike today, editors often ran for public office; office holders often founded newspapers, newspapers were part of the political parties' operations, and the Whig, Democratic, and Republican parties ran everything.

The reasons for the alliances between the press and political parties were not just philosophical; the alliances also involved remuneration. For example, if a Democratic newspaper worked closely with a Democratic candidate, the newspaper would print his flyers, brochures, pamphlets, speeches, and would cover his events in such a way that they were unrecognizable from the way the same events were covered in the Republican paper. Then if the Democratic candidate won, the Democratic newspaper would receive government printing contracts, and its editors might get appointed to political office—particularly to post office positions which were considered plumb assignments.

Legislators would buy newspapers, and then the newspaper would be designated as the official organ of the victorious candidate, meaning it would get the news from the candidate first and thus would be able to distribute news to its readers quicker than its competitors in the pre-telegraph days. That is how the press-politics interplay worked. Both the Democrats and the Republicans did it, and Honest Abe appointed many editors to public office, and he invested in newspapers, spent his time in newspaper offices, and helped to perpetuate this alliance.

HOW LINCOLN STAYED ABREAST OF PUBLIC SENTIMENT

BOSTON In the modern era, we criticize politicians who we call "flip-floppers" because they change their views in response to what the polls reveal about people's attitudes. Your book details that although Lincoln believed "public sentiment was everything," he would not change his opinions to align with public sentiment; rather, his goal was to mould public sentiment so it would embrace his positions.

That raises the question, what exactly did Lincoln do to stay abreast of public sentiment?

HOLZER Obviously, he functioned in an era long before there was polling, so gauging public sentiment was difficult. His first notion of how to do it was to evaluate the public sentiment of his own party. Wherever Lincoln traveled to practice law, political conventions and rallies were held repeatedly, and were always covered by the local newspapers. So Lincoln made it his business to visit the local newspaper editors wherever he had a lawsuit and ask them about the political campaigns and election returns in their areas. He'd commit their information to memory so he could follow the progress of Republican strength brewing in the central Illinois counties throughout the 1850s and up until his presidential election in 1860.

Lincoln measured public sentiment by what the newspaper editors told him about what they'd heard expressed at rallies, conferences, debates, speeches, and in their own private conversations. Remember that in the mid-nineteenth century, following politics and going to church were just about the only things people living in rural sections of the country did for "entertainment."

Lincoln was primarily concerned with where his party was going on the most vital issues of the 1850s, especially when the Democrats began suggesting that the Republicans favored full racial equality—an outlandish position for mainstream white Americans in 1858, the year of the Lincoln-Douglas debates.

HOW LINCOLN MOULDED PUBLIC SENTIMENT

BOSTON Through this ongoing process of gaining an understanding of the public sentiment, what was Lincoln's method for becoming a proactive factor in moulding the sentiment?

HOLZER The great politician is one who realizes that knowing public opinion is more important than enacting statutes—to paraphrase Lincoln himself. Lincoln had a unique way of leading on the political issues of his day. Certainly, one of the media he used to demonstrate his leadership was the newspaper. When he became president, there were many newspapers regarded as having been dedicated to supporting the new Republican administration. But when the time came for Lincoln to award the federal government's printing business to a single newspaper as a reward, surprisingly, Lincoln didn't give it to the leading Washington Republican paper; rather, he gave it to a very small newspaper that had been a brave abolitionist voice before the war and had been set upon by a mob in Washington, DC. Lincoln decided to help them out by giving them business in the form of government contracts for official documents that needed to be printed. This made a subtle but powerful statement about the incoming president's sentiments on black freedom.

Today, we'd call Lincoln's leadership style "leading from behind." It's been attributed to President Obama as his leadership style. It's when a person never seems to be leading, but is actually leading.

For example, Lincoln was extremely cautious about the greatest executive decision of his administration—the Emancipation Proclamation. He was being pushed to issue the Proclamation by the progressive voices within the Republican Party at the beginning of the war when blood was first shed, but he hesitated. He signed two congressional bills into law that authorized Union generals to confiscate the property of people who were in rebellion against federal authority, and the "property" permitted to be confiscated included human beings. These seizures of property had to be adjudicated in the federal courts, which were no longer operating in the states that had seceded from the Union. So the property confiscation bills were actually window dressing for what Lincoln really wanted to do—get out in front of the issue by issuing his own executive order to end slavery as the nation's commander-in-chief.

Let's look at the path he took to get to the day he issued the Proclamation on January 1, 1863. He wrote a famous letter to Horace Greeley, the editor of the *New York Tribune*, in 1862, and it's probably the most famous letter to the editor in American press history. Lincoln told Greeley that his paramount object in the Civil War was to save the Union. He said, "What I do about slavery, I do to save the Union. What I forbear, I forbear to save the Union. If I could save the Union by freeing all of the slaves, I would do it. If I could save the Union by freeing none of the slaves, I would do it. If I could save the Union by freeing some and leaving others alone, I would do that."

Those statements to Greeley were some of the most disingenuous declarations Lincoln ever made because at the time he wrote the letter, he had already written the preliminary Emancipation Proclamation, shared it with his Cabinet, and told them that he planned to issue it soon. His Cabinet cautioned him, though, that to announce it in the absence of a significant Union military victory would be premature. So he took his Cabinet's advice and waited for the right time to issue it. The Union won something of a victory at the Battle of Antietam in September 1862, and after a few days, the time was right to announce the Proclamation.

Before Antietam, and before he issued the Proclamation, Lincoln had invited a delegation of free African-Americans from Washington, DC to the White House. It was a classic good news/bad news story. The good news was that this was the first delegation of free people of color ever to visit the White House on official business to meet with a president. The bad news was that the president proceeded to launch into something of a diatribe against the visitors saying, "You are the cause of this war. If it wasn't for your presence among us, there would be no great war. It is better for us to be separated. We can never live on equal terms." Lincoln told the group he had a new plan for their future welfare that involved voluntary colonization in Central America and Santo Domingo, and asked them to give it serious consideration.

Why did he have this meeting with a few black people to discuss colonization three weeks before issuing the biggest freedom declaration in the history of the United States, with the possible exception of the Declaration of Independence? He did it because he was absolutely petrified that white public opinion would be strongly against the Proclamation, and he recognized that its issuance could help the Democrats triumph in the upcoming congressional elections, and might also cause his administration to sink in the public's eyes even before the congressional elections.

I've given you a very long answer, but his multi-layered approach to issuing the Emancipation Proclamation definitely could be classified as leading from behind. Lincoln had the Proclamation document in his desk drawer for several months. He was playing with and ultimately moulding public opinion, making sure that the people believed that he was only issuing it to save the union and not to promote the idea of an

integrated society. He still had this colonization scheme in the back of his mind, and by mentioning it to the black delegation, it showed that he was not intending to fully integrate society though he soon realized colonization was too impractical and would never work.

Unfortunately, there are historians who weigh the letter to Greeley against the Emancipation Proclamation and conclude that Lincoln was not a genuine liberator and had no commitment of his own to racial parity, and did everything for political reasons. Such a conclusion misses Lincoln's political artistry at doing what it took, by leading from behind, in order to accomplish his ultimate goal.

PRESS COVERAGE OF LINCOLN'S CRITICISM OF THE MEXICAN WAR

BOSTON I'd like to backtrack and ask you about a situation that occurred before his presidency, when Lincoln first attracted national media during his one term in Congress from 1847 to 1849 over his public criticism of President Polk's decision to pursue the Mexican War.

Was Lincoln's public stance on the Mexican War a clear instance of his desire to mould public sentiment and show the country that he was not a mere spineless politician who attached his political positions to the coattails of public sentiment?

HOLZER Almost every Whig in Congress opposed the Mexican War because they knew that winning the war would mean new territory being brought into the Union, which ultimately would become new states that would likely elect Democratic pro-slavery congressmen; and if that happened, Democrats would soon vastly outnumber Whigs in Congress. Lincoln emerged as one of the most eloquent opponents of the Mexican War though his speeches on the House floor sealed his doom as a member of Congress.

I need to gently change the record on one aspect of your question. Congressman Lincoln was dying to get national press coverage. He went to the newspaper offices in Washington seeking coverage of his anti-war speeches. He also made sure to see journalists when he spoke on his national political tours promoting the 1848 presidential candidacy of Zachary Taylor.

But from the record, it appears he received very little national coverage during his time in Congress, and had to work very hard just to get the Whig newspaper back in Springfield to cover what he was doing in Washington. He wrote angrily to his law partner William Herndon at one point and said, "You've sent me this batch of clippings, but I don't see any about myself. What's going on?" He functioned as his own press secretary and sent out mailings of his speeches in opposition to the Mexican War, but it didn't work to get him any more press coverage.

The one big piece of national coverage he received during his congressional career came when Horace Greeley of the *New York Tribune* served half a term as an unelected congressman from New York City—Greeley had stepped in to complete the term of someone who had been ousted from Congress. According to the laws of Congress at the time, congressmen who aspired to be reimbursed for their travel expenses in going from Washington back to their hometowns were required to travel on a direct route. In the summer of 1848, Lincoln sought and received reimbursement after he traveled the route from Washington to his home in Springfield, Illinois by going due north from DC and stopping in Baltimore to give some speeches, then going north again and stopping in Boston to give more speeches, then heading west and traveling to Niagara Falls because he'd never been there and wanted to see it, and then finally catching a boat on the Great Lakes and going to Chicago. Because of Lincoln's traveling such a circuitous route to get home, Greeley listed him among those who had abused the expense reimbursement system.

So that ill-fated, politically motivated trip produced his only national press coverage—and it was entirely negative.

THE MOTIVATION BEHIND LINCOLN'S RESPONSE TO THE KANSAS-NEBRASKA ACT

BOSTON Let's talk about Lincoln's political reawakening after the Kansas-Nebraska Act passed in 1854, a few years after he had left Washington after his one term in Congress. The Act was so alarming to Lincoln that it made him "thunderstruck," and it caused him to resume his political career. It upset him because it meant Congress had decided to nullify the Missouri Compromise and on a going forward basis, would permit the expansion of slavery in the West.

Harold, let's say you've got a hundred points to allocate regarding the true motivation behind Lincoln's becoming so active in response to the Kansas-Nebraska Act. How many of those points do you allocate to Lincoln's personal moral outrage over the prospect of slavery's expansion into the West and how many do you allocate to the Kansas-Nebraska Act's providing the absolute perfect opportunity for Lincoln to jump back into the national political fray to assert himself big-time on the evils of this controversial issue?

HOLZER I was worried that the second choice would be a little harder for me. I would allocate eighty-two points toward Lincoln's being totally dismayed about the Act's expanding the evils of slavery into the West. I take him at his word when he expressed his genuine moral outrage. He stepped up his passion in response to the slavery issue as he never had before; although he also stepped up his political ambition, but his doing that was a necessity if he wanted to be personally involved in attacking the Act.

There were several things about the Kansas-Nebraska Act that upset him. One was that Senator Douglas introduced the Kansas-Nebraska bill on the basis that it was democratic to ask settlers in new territories, on the verge of becoming states, to vote on whether to allow slavery in these new areas. Lincoln wondered why people would be asked to vote for the enslavement of a people who had no opportunity to decide their own fate. Holding elections on whether slavery should be permitted in new states was against all principles of free labor, and the right to rise, and equal opportunity that he believed in very deeply.

He was also concerned about the Act's proponents' claim that their position was aligned with notions of "popular sovereignty." The Republicans called Stephen Douglas' plan "squatter sovereignty" because they envisioned a voting class of pro-slavery people who would vote for slavery in Kansas, and then move to California or a different territory in the West and vote for slavery there, too. Voter registration was a very open thing in those days.

Lincoln also saw that the likely result of the Act would be the extension of Democratic control over all three branches of government in perpetuity, and perhaps could result in the annexation of Cuba and other distant territories to expand the grip of slavery even further. He thought the result was not only morally repugnant in terms of extending an evil, but also politically dangerous because it would create a super-majority for the Democrats.

Douglas and the Democrats believed that if Lincoln got his way and successfully drew a line in the sand prohibiting the extension of slavery, the result would be the election of Republicans in many western areas, which would eventually reduce their own power in Congress.

Never lose sight of how politics plays into social change. Why did the Southern states secede in 1860 in response to the election of a man who was pledged *not* to the idea of eliminating slavery, but only to the idea of stopping the *extension* of slavery? Because they could readily envision Republican senators and congressmen getting elected in the new free states entering the union from the West; eventually the Republicans could get to the point of having the two-thirds majority necessary to pass a constitutional amendment prohibiting slavery without resort to a civil war. That's what Stephen Douglas and the Act's proponents foresaw and feared.

So I give Lincoln credit for being inspired to respond actively in opposition to the Kansas-Nebraska Act mainly because of moral reasons, though he was certainly mindful of how the law could create the basis for the political landscape to change dramatically and quickly in favor of the Democrats.

LINCOLN'S REASON FOR INVESTING IN A GERMAN NEWSPAPER BEFORE THE WAR

BOSTON You mention in your book's introduction that as Lincoln started eyeing the presidency as time got nearer to 1860, he became part-owner of a German language newspaper in Illinois in 1859, which seemed to me to be a strange place for him to invest his money.

How much political mileage did he get out of being part-owner of a German language newspaper in Illinois?

HOLZER We'll never know for sure. Amazingly, not one copy of this German newspaper has ever been located! To my knowledge, Lincoln was the only politician of his century who would have been embarrassed about blending politics and journalism so openly. Others were very open about doing it. Lincoln did it in secret.

He entered into a contract which provided that the only reason he was investing in the enterprise was to retrieve the editor's printing press which had been seized by his creditors; and it took $500 to get it out of hock. His only requirement for the newspaper's content was that it endorse Republican platform principles through the 1860 election. He separated himself from the newspaper following the election and, upon becoming president, he appointed the editor, Theodore Canisius, as his consul to Vienna, a great political job with a salary of $2,000 a year. After his election, Lincoln also arranged for all unsold copies of the paper to be purchased by the Illinois State Legislature to provide the editor some pocket money to take to Europe. Lincoln had once attempted to take German lessons and apparently was such a cut-up in class that neither he nor any of the other students could learn any German, and so they got him out of the class.

Having said all that, let me explain the real reason why Lincoln invested in the German newspaper. Illinois was a genuine swing state in the 1856 and 1860 elections. If Lincoln wanted to get elected president, he had to gain support not just from native-born voters. German immigrants were pouring into the West in the late 1850s and there were very few requirements for citizenship or voting rights. At one point, Massachusetts had tried to impose a five-year residence requirement before an immigrant could qualify for voting rights, but that caused an outrage in the German population so it was repealed.

Since the Germans were in a position to swing the 1860 election in both Illinois and neighboring Indiana, Lincoln wanted a reliable voice in the German-speaking communities advocating not only Republican principles, but also that Abraham Lincoln was the best possible Republican candidate for president. Theodore Canisius, the German newspaper's editor, held a large rally in Springfield to support repeal of the Massachusetts law, and although Lincoln didn't attend it, he sent a note to Canisius that was later published in the local English-language newspaper.

In fact, Germans and Scandinavians voted overwhelmingly Republican, while Irish immigrants tended to vote overwhelmingly Democratic. I attribute the growth in the Republican Party's support in the Midwest to the German immigrants who came into Illinois and Indiana in the 1850s, and they became a big factor in Lincoln's winning the 1860 election. And they got their information from German-language papers like the one Abraham Lincoln purchased in 1859.

LINCOLN'S ARRANGING FOR HIS COOPER UNION SPEECH TO GO VIRAL

BOSTON In 2015, we talk about how quickly information can go viral. When Lincoln gave his Cooper Union speech in February 1860 in New York City, "the speech that made him president," the text of that speech soon went viral all over the country.

How much of that massive instant national circulation of his landmark speech can be attributed to Lincoln's media planning?

HOLZER A lot of it. First of all, it's never been fully explained how five daily morning newspapers obtained and had time to typeset and publish transcripts of the speech shortly after Lincoln finished delivering it, given the fact that the Cooper Union address was not recorded stenographically and was given from 8:30 to 10:30 p.m. The most likely answer is that Lincoln provided an advance copy of the speech to a newspaper pool operation before he actually delivered it. Then, to make sure the speech was perfectly reproduced, he took his original manuscript to the *New York Tribune*'s office after the event at Cooper Union ended and proofread it himself. Ultimately, the speech was reprinted in the five leading New York City papers, and also in Chicago, Washington, Detroit, and Boston, such that it was there for people all over the country to read immediately. Later, he also arranged for the publication and distribution of the speech as a pamphlet with footnotes added by two New York Republicans. But within a couple of days after he gave the speech at Cooper Union, the text of it could be found everywhere.

LINCOLN'S SILENCE ON SECESSION WHEN PRESIDENT-ELECT

BOSTON One of the mysteries of Lincoln's political career was his being silent in the press between his November 1860 election to the presidency and his March 1861 inauguration, during which time many Southern states seceded from the Union (and I know you've written a book about President-elect Lincoln).

What's your best explanation for Lincoln's going radio silent—at least to the press—during that critical time in our country's history when states were seceding from the Union?

HOLZER At that time, there was a strong tradition of candidates maintaining silence in campaigns and during the interregnum, which throughout the nineteenth century lasted four months, since presidents didn't get sworn in until early March. For President-elect Lincoln to speak publicly between his election and inauguration would have been deemed highly inappropriate.

The main reason for his silence, however, was not due to protocol, but because

Lincoln didn't want to be burdened with making the first public response to secession. He thought the response should be made by the president who was lawfully required to deal with it at the time the secessions occurred—James Buchanan.

Another reason he didn't want to address it before being sworn in was because he was being whipsawed between people who wanted conciliation and people who wanted confrontation. With that kind of political tension in the air, he didn't want to offer glimpses into his strategy until his inaugural address.

He believed over-optimistically that latent Union sentiment existed in many Southern states, and that South Carolina's December secession would not start a domino effect of states leaving the Union. Obviously, he was wrong about that.

So rather than publicly offering his thoughts between his election and inauguration on how the country should respond to secession, he wrote letters replying to those newspaper editors who had requested that he reassert that he did not plan to interfere with slavery in the states where it already existed. His response to the editors was always, "Those who have not believed what I've already said would never believe anything new. Those who've read it before and now ask me to re-explain it are doing injury to my manhood." It was a very Victorian response—"I've said what I've said, and you can trust what I've said." By doing what he did, he did not offend either faction within his own party.

LINCOLN'S COMMITMENT TO SEE THE WAR THROUGH

BOSTON Upon becoming president, Lincoln obviously believed he was required to uphold the Constitution—that's in the Presidential Oath—which he thought required him to dedicate the country toward bringing the seceded Southern states back into the Union. Ultimately, his commitment to fulfill that responsibility resulted in the death of over seven hundred thousand Americans.

Photo credit: Don Pollard

Harold Holzer

In the first few months of his presidency, is there any indication that Lincoln ever considered just letting the Southern states go their own way—particularly after the first battle of Bull Run, which made it clear that the war was going to be protracted and, therefore, costly in loss of lives?

HOLZER As he put it in his second inaugural address, when the war began, no one could have imagined the magnitude or the duration it would attain. He was deeply tortured about the war as it went on year after year, and famously turned more and more to Divine Providence to explain or rationalize the enormous sacrifices that were being made. He became so burdened and guilt-ridden by the fallout from the war that you can see it in his face in the photographic portraits—a man simply ravaged during his four years in office—going from a youthful looking fifty-two-year-old man to a prematurely old man who had somehow weathered the agonizing years of his presidency.

Having said that, he never for a minute thought he could responsibly allow the Southern states to leave the Union permanently, even though there were plenty of Republicans, especially anti-slavery Republicans, who thought secession was the answer to their dreams. They wanted the Southern slave states to go, thinking they would ultimately destroy themselves from within their horrific society that subjugated

a whole race of people and emphasized the white aristocracy at the expense of poorer whites.

But as Lincoln's contemporaries attested, the idea of the Union was almost sacred to him. The country had proven it could create itself and sustain a government for several decades, but it had not yet proven it could confront and successfully repel a challenge from within. Lincoln thought that the country's withstanding such a monumental challenge was crucial to its permanent survival, not only within this union of disparate states, but also within the idea of majority rule. So no, I don't think he ever questioned his own decision to attempt to preserve the entire Union—regardless of what it cost.

LINCOLN AND FREEDOMS OF SPEECH AND THE PRESS DURING THE WAR

BOSTON Before becoming president, Lincoln was a huge advocate of the Constitution, which included the Bill of Rights' freedom of the press and freedom of speech and how it was crucial to preserving democracy. Yet during the Civil War, he knew about the suppression of the press in different parts of the North. You say he remained "ambivalent" about what was being done to stifle or silence the voices of those who opposed his position, and seldom intervened to protect freedom of speech and the press.

In wartime, did Lincoln think that the rules change regarding freedom of speech and freedom of the press?

HOLZER Lincoln based his actions on the Constitution's words that in times of rebellion, it was permissible to suspend the right of *habeas corpus*, which he translated into meaning that arbitrary arrests ordered by the military or the president were permissible in cases of national emergency. A case of rebellion was clearly occurring throughout the country. Principally Democratic newspapers, which were much more inclined to be anti-war, appeared to some to cross the line from dissent to disloyalty to the government.

Lincoln may once have believed that any attempt to restrict what newspapers printed was censorship, but when the war came, he tolerated it, defended it, and once even ordered it personally. It was the military (not Lincoln) who censored the anti-war newspapers, destroyed the presses of some anti-war papers, and arrested those using their right of free speech to criticize Lincoln. The State Department also did it, and even courts did it.

The Daily News newspaper editorialized that the war Lincoln was waging was not a war for the country, but a war only for black people, and, therefore, people should not volunteer to serve in the Union army. After that editorial appeared, a grand jury indicted *The Daily News* editor. The government responded by ordering newspapers confiscated. Ultimately, *The Daily News* closed down, *The Brooklyn Eagle* was also briefly closed down, and other papers were closed down. Editors were transported to Washington to appear before military tribunals or congressional committees. Some were thrown into Fort Lafayette in Brooklyn, which was dubbed "The American Bastille."

Lincoln himself signed only one order that closed down two newspapers in New York City, when in 1864 they printed false presidential proclamation claiming that Lincoln was about to announce a draft call for four hundred thousand new troops. The story was totally fabricated, though Lincoln and Secretary of State Seward believed that the White House had been infiltrated by spies because Lincoln was actually working at the time on such a proclamation, though he was actually planning to draft five hundred thousand men.

It turned out that the article ran because of a hoax perpetrated by a former *New York Times* reporter who had become an associate editor at *The Brooklyn Eagle*. He had decided to create a false presidential proclamation about there being a huge upcoming draft because he believed that if such an announcement was made, the stock market would plummet. He and his friends then planned to buy plenty of stock after prices had fallen. Later, after the hoax was revealed, the market would quickly bounce back and he would make a killing by selling his cheaply-bought stocks at their actual market price. Lincoln was probably happy to sign the order having this conniving editor detained after he had engaged in such outrageous behavior.

Republican editors—like Horace Greeley and Henry Raymond of *The New York Times*—repeatedly editorialized that history would ultimately determine that Lincoln's administration arrested too *few* editors—not too *many*. There was certainly not much push-back from Republican editors at the time against the people in his administration and the military acting to restrain and/or censor the Democratic anti-war, anti-Lincoln newspapers.

One other thing about censorship. During my research on the book, I found more than two hundred cases where newspapers were shut down and editors arrested during the Civil War. To his credit though, Lincoln always re-opened the floodgates of press criticism at election time. So in 1864 here in New York, there was an editor who had been arrested and imprisoned. After his release, he mounted a vicious, racist attack on Lincoln in his newspaper. Lincoln almost lost New York state because of these hateful editorials—in fact, he did much worse in New York in '64 than he had done in '60—but he never again interfered with that editor or his newspaper. Lincoln never discouraged debate and criticism while political campaigns were going on because he regarded such wars of words as part of the democratic process.

LINCOLN AS THE MASTER LEAKER TO THE PRESS

BOSTON Regarding the Emancipation Proclamation, you mention in the book how Lincoln strategically leaked his future plans to issue it in order to prepare the public for his most important decision of the Civil War.

Was there any precedent for a president using a strategic leak like that?

HOLZER Never before on so big an issue was there a leak like that, though Andrew Jackson had leaked information to his favorite newspapers on issues of importance to him. Lincoln truly mastered the art of leaking. On subjects ranging from emancipation to the raising of African-American troops, he would leak information, and then take it back. For the Emancipation, he leaked much counterintelligence, particularly with his letter to Horace Greeley, which I mentioned previously, in which he said, "I really don't care about black people, I really only care about the Union." He also leaked stories about there being a "rumor that there was about to be a proclamation that would free Negroes." So he was putting out leaks on both ends. It was brilliant use of the media.

LINCOLN'S USE OF "PUBLIC LETTERS" TO GET GREAT PRESS COVERAGE

BOSTON For my final question, you say that by the end of the war, Lincoln had turned newspapers into his own personal sounding board and could address issues directly to the people through the press without the intervention of the big time editors like Horace Greeley.

What were the particulars in how Lincoln achieved this transformation in media coverage?

HOLZER He created a new phenomenon, which we call retrospectively "the public letter." Lincoln was a great orator and debater, but his voice was for the most part stilled not only during the 1860 presidential campaign, but also as president. Gettysburg was a huge anomaly because Lincoln thought that, for the most part, it was imprudent for a president to speak publicly except at

an inauguration. When he wrote the public letter to Greeley in which he said, "My paramount object is to save the Union," it was a reply to a vicious editorial in which Greeley had claimed that Lincoln's administration had been "strangely and disastrously remiss" by not recruiting African-Americans to fight for their own freedom.

Lincoln didn't want Greeley to have the satisfaction of running in his newspaper an important reply to his editorial from the president of the United States. So Lincoln released his letter to Greeley on a Friday to a newspaper in Washington, which published it on a Saturday—knowing that it would allow the Washington paper to print the scoop first. The next day, on Sunday, newspapers around the country published it. But Greeley didn't publish the *Tribune* on Sundays; he wouldn't be able to print until Monday, after everyone else in the country already knew about the reply. Lincoln orchestrated all of this on purpose.

After this played out so successfully for him, Lincoln realized he had a new avenue with which to communicate with the public. On future occasions, he went on to use the "public letter" format to advance, for example, his desire to arm African-Americans to serve as soldiers in the Union army. He was invited to give a speech in his hometown in the late spring of 1863. He wanted to do it, but he couldn't risk being away from Washington where the telegraph office and war rooms were. So he wrote what we now call "the Conkling letter" because it was read aloud at the rally by his friend, James Conkling. The letter was really an open letter to the country. In the Conkling letter, Lincoln said, "You say you will not fight to free Negroes, but some of them seem willing to fight for you."

Lincoln used the public letter format yet again with a reply to Erastus Corning, the Democratic political leader of Albany, as a means of speaking to the entire country on the subject of civil liberties. All these letters were published throughout the nation. Their success in being carried by newspapers made Lincoln realize that he didn't have to give speeches and he didn't have to write editorials to make his points to the public. He could stay in Washington and write letters and have other people read them aloud or have them published as open messages— and the approach provided for him the kind of positive coverage he had sought throughout his political career.

BOSTON Our time's up. Let's all say thank you very much to Harold Holzer.

JEAN EDWARD SMITH was a Pulitzer finalist for his biography *Grant*
(Simon & Schuster 2001), and has been called "America's greatest living biographer"
by George Will. This interview took place June 16, 2015 at the Alumni Center of
Georgetown College in Georgetown, Kentucky and was hosted for friends of the college
by my friend Dr. Todd Rasberry, the director of development there.

"After his death, Grant was trashed for almost four
generations largely by Southern historians because of his
stand on racial equality. The recent rebirth of appreciation for
Grant coincides with the fact that segregation is no longer
permissible in the United States." **– JEAN EDWARD SMITH**

CHAPTER 9

JEAN EDWARD SMITH
ON
Ulysses S. Grant

GRANT'S RISE IN STATURE AMONG HISTORIANS

BOSTON Dr. Smith, since your book came out on Grant in 2001, there's been a surge of interest in him by some of America's leading historians. Both Ronald Chernow and Ronald White are working on biographies of him that will be coming out next year, H. W. Brands' book on him in 2012 was a *New York Times* best-seller, and on your dust jacket James McPherson, the Pulitzer Prize-winning Civil War historian from Princeton, talks about the ongoing positive re-evaluation of Grant.

How do you explain Grant's rise in stature in recent years among the literati of American history?

Courtesy of Simon & Schuster, Inc., New York, 2001

SMITH Let me put that into context. When Grant left office, he was clearly the most popular president of his era and enjoyed great popularity for the remainder of his life. After leaving the presidency, he had a two-year tour of the world in which he was received by heads of state, and he actually negotiated peace between China and Japan during that world tour. When he died and was buried in New York, a million and a half people came to his funeral up Broadway to Riverside Drive to Riverside Park. So Grant was exceedingly popular during his lifetime and up until his death. And then his memoirs came out, which were equally popular.

Grant was then trashed for the next three generations, largely by Southern historians. This was a time of segregation in the United States, and he was trashed because of his stand on racial equality. So the recent rebirth of appreciation for Grant coincides with the fact that segregation is no longer permissible in the United States. With the end of segregation, and the advent of integration, it's probably inevitable that Grant's stature should be rehabilitated. I approached it from that standpoint and may have been the first to treat Grant in those respectful terms, but Grant was wrongly trashed for almost four generations because of his stand on racial equality.

GRANT AND HIS MEMOIRS

BOSTON You mentioned his memoirs. In your biography of Grant, you say it is the greatest military autobiography ever produced in the English language. Does this increasing respect for him in the last few years by our writers of history in the twenty-first century have anything to do with Grant's having been such a spectacular writer of history himself?

SMITH Sure, it's not unrelated. The fact is that Grant's memoirs are not only the best military memoirs ever written, but it's one of the best memoirs in the English language. Literary critics have always praised

Grant's memoirs. He wrote it just like he gave orders during the war—very crisp, very precise. And when reading them, there's no question about what Grant was thinking or what he was saying, just like when he was a commanding general.

BOSTON The publisher and presumed editor of Grant's memoirs was Mark Twain. Did Twain's involvement in Grant's book have anything to do with the prose being so elegant?

SMITH No, I think not. It has been suggested sometimes that part of it was written by Mark Twain and that is absolutely false. The book was written entirely by Grant. Twain was in the publishing business and this wasn't the only book he published. He made money and he lost money in the publishing business, though Grant's memoirs were the leading best-sellers in the United States up to that time. Grant died before the memoirs came out, but when the book got released, his wife received a check the next year of $200,000—that's $200,000 in the late 1880s! That was an awful lot of money.

BOSTON And that was a royalty check. Anybody who's ever written a book knows what a small percentage of the sales proceeds an author gets in royalties compared to what the book publisher gets. Mark Twain benefitted greatly financially by reason of Grant's memoirs.

GRANT'S IMPACT ON THE CIVIL WAR

BOSTON Let's move on to Grant's actual heroics during the Civil War, and recognizing that before he assumed command of the Union troops at mid-war, he had been preceded by Union generals who were flawed and passive in their approach to making war.

In your book you quote some Union soldiers who said that they believed that the delay in getting Grant into the army's top leadership position prolonged the war by an additional two years. Do you believe that?

SMITH That's an interesting question, but you have to realize where Grant was when the war began. He was working as a clerk in his father's leather goods store in Galena, Illinois. He had had a very difficult time during the nine years that preceded the war while he worked outside of the army. It would have been impossible for Grant to have been given a top military position at the beginning of the war given his lack of military stature as of April 1861. The war had to continue for a while with the grinding down on both sides that took place before it could be won, and Grant emerged through that process. It would have been premature for Grant to have been appointed to lead the army any sooner than when Lincoln appointed him.

BOSTON Yes, I understand that, but knowing Grant's offensive, aggressive approach to warfare, if that approach had been present in the mindset of the Union military leaders during the war's first two years, do you believe it's likely that the war would have been reduced in time by about two years?

SMITH On McClellan's first drive toward Richmond, if he had continued on as Grant did two years later, sure, the war would have ended sooner. But we're talking about Grant's mindset, and that can't be applied to McClellan's mindset.

BOSTON One of the great things about studying history is being aware of the "what ifs." Your book mentions how in May 1862, Union General Henry Halleck took control of the town of Corinth, Mississippi after it had been abandoned by the Confederates, and then began fortifying it. Halleck's inane defensive strategy so frustrated Grant that he was ready to quit the army then and there, and was making plans to do so. At the last minute, William Tecumseh Sherman realized what Grant was about to do and talked him

into staying in the army. As you say, that one conversation changed the course of the Civil War and Grant's life and thus it truly changed the course of American history.

Can you speculate on how the outcome of the Civil War might have changed had Sherman not had that conversation with Grant and the Union not had Grant as its leader for the balance of the war?

SMITH I think Grant is the only Union commander who recognized that the war would be won by grinding down the Confederate army. None of the other Union commanders recognized that. If Grant had not been there and done that, Lincoln probably would not have been re-elected in 1864, and we would be living in an entirely different world. Grant's determination to grind down the Confederate army was unique, was accepted by Lincoln, and it provided the path to victory.

BOSTON We've all heard the old story, "For want of a nail, the horseshoe was lost, for want of a horseshoe, the horse was lost, for want of a horse, the rider was lost, etc." Well, this was the reverse. Because of the conversation, Grant stayed in the army, and because he did, he ground down and ultimately defeated the Confederate army. So it's amazing how one little timely conversation can change the course of history like that one did.

SMITH I might add that soon after the Sherman-Grant conversation, Halleck was soon called back to Washington and Grant was placed in command in Mississippi.

GRANT AND HIS DETRACTORS

BOSTON Grant's detractors during the Civil War's final years called him a butcher because of the number of casualties sustained in his battles.

Is there any merit to that criticism?

SMITH Yes, there's some merit to it, but the key to Grant's strategy for winning the war was his recognition that the Union's troops he lost in battle could be replaced while the Confederate troops General Lee lost in battle could not be replaced. So in Grant's opinion, that kind of heavy casualty approach was clearly the best avenue toward achieving victory.

BOSTON His detractors also liked to slander him by claiming that he abused alcohol. We know from your book that during his life, Grant did get drunk from time to time, but did his drinking ever impact his performance during either the Civil War or his presidency?

SMITH Not during the war and not during his presidency. Grant had a problem with alcohol. He was a very small man, so he could not absorb more than one drink without becoming intoxicated. In 1852, when he was stationed at Fort Humboldt in California without his wife and family, he took to drinking and drank too much. Grant appeared drunk at pay call one day at Fort Humboldt and his commanding officer, Colonel Buchanan, gave him the option of either resigning from the army or facing a court martial, and Grant immediately resigned from the army. He then stopped drinking and went back to be with his wife and family in Illinois, and except for one occasion, he did not drink during the Civil War or during his presidency. Grant simply could not hold liquor, and he knew it.

Buchanan stayed in the army after Grant resigned, and later commanded a brigade of regulars during the Civil War. When Grant became general in chief, Buchanan was a brigadier general. Grant immediately promoted him to major general, continued to promote and encourage him throughout the war, and when the war ended, made Buchanan military governor of Louisiana. The point of this story is to say that Grant held no grudges. Buchanan had been the man who forced Grant out of the army and

into civilian life where he didn't do very well. Nevertheless, Grant recognized Buchanan's ability as a military leader and promoted him during and after the Civil War.

GRANT'S CIVILITY TOWARD THE ENEMY

BOSTON One of the many positive aspects of Grant's character during war time that you focus on throughout the book was his civility and compassion toward the Confederate military leaders and soldiers after he had defeated them in battle, as evidenced by the way he handled things after many of his victories, and most notably with Lee at Appomattox, which you regard as his greatest triumph.

From your perspective as a leading military historian, was Grant's attitude toward the enemy after conquest a rarity among military leaders?

SMITH It wasn't necessarily a rarity, but Grant certainly pursued it to the extreme. After taking the Confederate surrender at Fort Donelson, he allowed the officers who went into captivity to retain their side arms. After taking the Confederate surrender at Vicksburg, he allowed the Confederates to go home, and they weren't taken into captivity if they agreed not to take up arms again. Most importantly, at Appomattox, he effectively pardoned the Army of Northern Virginia for taking part in the rebellion. This was Grant's instinct. He did not take the war personally.

GRANT ON THE BATTLEFIELD

BOSTON Another positive aspect of Grant's character that you describe throughout your book was his serenity in times of chaos and his indomitable will that never flagged in the face of adversity. He repeatedly turned apparent defeat into victory at Belmont, Fort Donelson, Shiloh, and Chattanooga, and his fighting spirit and contagious optimism inspired his subordinates to rise to the challenge.

Do you regard him as being superhuman on the battlefield given his successful record achieved due to those aspects of his personality?

SMITH Let me draw a distinction regarding Grant's presence on the battlefield as compared to some of his contemporaries. Sheridan, as a battlefield commander, led his troops into battle. The poem "Sheridan's Ride" refers to what he did at the Battle of Winchester, where he rode out in front of his troops. Grant was not like that in battle. He gave very clear orders regarding what he expected his subordinates to do, and then he stayed aloof from the battle as it was taking place. He simply allowed it to continue and very forcefully intervened when necessary, but he was not a battlefield commander who operated from the front line.

BOSTON But let's talk about regardless of whether he was in the front of the troops or giving orders from behind, as chaos reigned at different times in different battles, he never lost his composure, and never thought he was going to lose.

In that respect, does he stand head and shoulders among his military leader peers?

SMITH There's no question about it. Grant understood what the operation was about and he simply continued to press the attack. After the first day at Shiloh is a good example of that. General Sherman came to see him in the evening prepared to ask Grant to withdraw across the Tennessee River. He saw Grant standing there in the rain contemplating, and Sherman recognized that Grant really did know what he was doing and so Sherman didn't mention or suggest withdrawing. Grant's comment to Sherman that night was, "Well, we'll lick them tomorrow."

Grant understood more than anyone else that the Confederacy could only lose so many people. So Grant's strategy during the war was to just keep pressing them. Grant did not attempt to capture cities and road

junctions, but instead kept his focus entirely on destroying the enemy army. Everything else took second place. "Lee's army will be your objective point," he told Meade. "Where Lee goes, there you will go also."

BOSTON You mention in your book a great description of Grant given by Abraham Lincoln during the war. He said, "Grant means business. He's the quietest little fellow you ever saw. But wherever he is, he makes things git. He makes things move."

Given that Grant was a quiet, almost sphinx-like person, was short in stature, always wore scruffy clothes because of his distaste for military uniforms, and the fact that he was not a good public speaker, how do you visualize exactly what he did to make his troops "git" and "move?"

SMITH What Grant did that prompted Lincoln's comment became apparent on the third day of the Battle of the Wilderness. After General Meade's Army of the Potomac crossed the Rapidan and moved south into Virginia, Lee and his Army of Northern Virginia hit the flank and the battle continued for three days. Lee had done that three times before in 1861, 1862, and

1863, and each time he did, the Union army always moved back. When it happened in 1864, rather than moving the army back toward the north, Grant told Meade, "Move south." Grant's orders to simply move south electrified the Army of the Potomac and they rejoiced. Grant was cheered massively because of that order. It was a decisive moment in history.

BOSTON So just by giving concise, direct orders with such a sincerity of purpose, it made his troops "git" and move?

SMITH That's exactly right. You see it at the Appomattox surrender ceremony as well, where Lee arrived in full dress uniform with his sword and so forth, while Grant came in from the field with muddy boots, wearing the uniform of a private with his stars on his shoulders. Grant's lack of pomp and circumstance simply endeared him to his troops.

GRANT AT APPOMATTOX

BOSTON Talking about the surrender at Appomattox, one of my favorite parts of your book was when they arrived there to discuss the terms of surrender, and Lee suggested that somebody needed to write out the terms of surrender. Grant instantly said, "I'll do it," went to a corner of the room, and with precision dictated his terms of surrender, which shows you what kind of a writer he was.

Talk about his spontaneous exhibition of coming up with the right words on that historic situation and his terms of surrender, and of being able to do what it took to come up with something Lee obviously could live with, and signed off on, which caused the war to end.

SMITH What Grant did at Appomattox, he did throughout the war. No commander under Grant ever doubted what his orders were. They were always very precise. The surrender document Grant wrote out on

the spur of the moment at Appomattox essentially pardoned the South. The Confederate soldiers who returned to their homes after the surrender and abided by the laws in force would not be disturbed by the authorities of the United States. Those words alone in Grant's terms of surrender kept Lee, Longstreet, and Johnston from being tried for treason later as President Johnson wanted to do. On his own authority, Grant simply issued a pardon at Appomattox to every Confederate soldier who had fought during the war. It was an amazing step in bringing the Union back together, which was what Grant intended.

BOSTON That's one of the interesting things about this time in history. Grant was a graduate of West Point and while there, he became close friends with many cadets who ended up becoming Confederate generals. In fact, Longstreet was the best man in Grant's wedding. At the Appomattox surrender meeting, when the armistice was signed, there was Longstreet along with two other Confederates in the room who had been ushers at Grant's wedding. So the people fighting, and trying to kill each other in the Civil War, had once been very close friends.

SMITH I might add to that the fact that Lee, on that morning before going to meet with Grant at Appomattox, talked to Longstreet and asked him what Grant was going to do. Longstreet told Lee, "Don't worry about it. He'll treat you decently and that will be it." It was Longstreet's discussion with Lee that gave Lee the confidence to go forward on to Appomattox that morning with the expectation that the terms of surrender would be fair.

BOSTON Getting back to Grant's humanity toward the enemy, by the time of the surrender, the Confederate troops in the Appomattox area had not had provisions and were actually very hungry. Tell our audience what Grant did in response to that situation.

SMITH He simply made the supplies that the Union had with them available to the Confederates. He fed Lee's army for the next several days.

GRANT'S PROBLEMS WITH CIVILIAN LIFE

BOSTON Looking at the entirety of Grant's amazing life in perspective, we know that as viewed by the likes of Abraham Lincoln, William Sherman, and even the Confederate General Longstreet, Grant was the greatest soldier of his time. Then as president, he had superior political skills. And as we discussed previously, he was a superb writer.

With all that emotional intelligence and intellectual horsepower, you note that "in civilian life he did nothing right." Why did Grant have such a hard time making a living in the private sector at the times in his life when he wasn't either fighting a war or being president?

SMITH Grant trusted people too much and that may have done him in. In the Grant and Ward Investment Company, which Grant took part in after he returned from his world tour following his presidency, Ward simply turned out to be a crook. Grant trusted him up until the very end when Ward's Ponzi scheme was exposed. I would put the fault on Grant's business failures simply on his trusting people too much.

BOSTON Regarding his personality deficit in trusting people too much, did that trait have something to do with his inability to control the corruption that occurred during his presidential administration?

SMITH Grant did take action on the corruption, but he had another problem, and it goes back to trust. He believed in his friends, and simply trusted people too much and some of the corruption that emerged in the Grant administration was attributable to the fact that some of the people were unethical and Grant simply let them get

away with it. The corruption never touched Grant himself because he was not involved in it, but his trust in his people caused him to not enforce discipline sufficiently either in his civilian business career or during his presidency.

GRANT'S DEALINGS WITH PRESIDENT ANDREW JOHNSON

BOSTON After Lincoln was assassinated in April of 1865, which was one month into his second term, Reconstruction began and it took place for the next four years under the incompetent and bigoted leadership of Andrew Johnson, Lincoln's successor as president, who was probably the worst president in American history. Grant was still the leader of the army when Johnson was commander-in-chief and, therefore, had to deal with President Johnson a great deal. As you point out, for the most part, Grant did not get too crosswise with the new president despite Johnson's many acts of stupidity and stubbornness that ultimately led to his being impeached.

Did Grant's knowing how to deal successfully with a difficult superior like Andrew Johnson arise, at least in part, from how he managed to stay calm and deal with the backbiting and slander he got from his nemesis superior Henry Halleck during the Civil War?

SMITH That's an interesting question. Grant and Halleck really did not like each other, but when Lincoln ordered Grant to Washington to become commanding general, thereby succeeding Halleck, Grant nonetheless recognized Halleck's ability and found a way to put it to use. Grant made Halleck his chief of staff, meaning Halleck had to deal with all the logistical and technical problems that needed to be addressed in the many Union regiments scattered throughout the country.

It's not generally recognized that when Grant became commanding general of the

Jean Edward Smith

United States army, he said, "Fine. I'm going to make my headquarters in the field." So, unlike his predecessors, Grant did not locate his headquarters over to the War Department in Washington, but had them in the field, and so he retained Halleck to run the details of handling the army from the War Department office, thereby allowing Grant to be free to operate in the field alongside General Meade. It's often overlooked that in that last Virginia campaign, Meade was in command of the Army of the Potomac as it marched south, while Grant, as commanding general of all armies, simply made his headquarters with Meade's army. In that position, Grant still remained in constant contact with General Sherman who was moving across Tennessee and Georgia at that time. It was totally unique for Grant, as general in chief, to have his headquarters in the field.

BOSTON My question was about comparing Halleck's difficult relationship with him (which I read as being entirely based on jealousy, in that Grant was so successful in the field and Halleck was not) and comparing that to his having to deal with another incredibly difficult and probably jealous superior in Andrew Johnson, and noting that in both situations Grant somehow

maintained his composure. I'm just wondering if his dealing with Halleck proved to be good preparation for his knowing how to deal with Johnson?

SMITH I think Grant handled each situation on his own through his own devices as a unique situation, and I'm not sure that what happened with Halleck was instructive on how to deal later with Johnson. At one point, Andrew Johnson relieved Stanton as secretary of war and appointed Grant in his place and Grant wouldn't have any part of it. Grant simply ignored Johnson's appointment and wouldn't obey it, and continued to serve as general in chief. Washington politics were simply different from army politics, and Grant was not going to get involved in the Washington politics in that situation.

GRANT AS PRESIDENT OF THE UNITED STATES

BOSTON When Grant was elected president after Andrew Johnson in November 1868, and inaugurated in March 1869, at the time he was the youngest president in American history—forty-six years old—and he served two full terms—eight years—making him the only president between Abraham Lincoln, our sixteenth, and Woodrow Wilson, our twenty-eighth president, to actually get elected for two consecutive elections.

In his first term, with his first string Cabinet, you summarize his many achievements: pursuing a sensible policy toward the American Indians aimed at assimilation, substantially lowering the national debt, preventing two leading entrepreneurs from cornering the gold market, keeping the US out of war with Spain over Cuba, restoring the US's relationship with Great Britain through the Treaty of Washington, and combatting the Ku Klux Klan terrorism in the South. Doesn't his first term alone qualify him as a top-ten president in the presidential rankings poll?

SMITH I don't disagree with you and I think you've ticked off his first term achievements very well.

Let me say a word about Grant's peace policy with the Indians. In the election of 1868, the frontier states were still under fire. Many people in those states had voted for Grant for president because they felt he would do to the Indians what he had done to the Confederate army. This proved to be a total misreading of Grant's attitude that was, in fact, pro-Indian. Grant's policy with the Indians during his presidency really made peace on the frontier, and allowed the Indians to move onto reservations much to the consternation of many white settlers who wanted the Indians destroyed, and over the objections of Sheridan and Sherman who also wanted them destroyed. Grant's policy was fully responsible for making peace on the frontier in the United States and ultimately bringing Native Americans into the US life.

BOSTON What was President Grant's relationship with the group known as the Radical Republicans in Congress during the war?

SMITH Frederick Douglas, the great black leader, once said that Grant was the last of the radicals. Grant was sympathetic to the radical viewpoint, and during his presidency, the American army stayed in the South throughout his terms, enforcing equality for African-Americans. Don't forget that one of the reasons the Democrats did not oppose the ultimate election of Hayes over Tilden in 1876, in spite of all the electoral college's difficulties, was because Hayes agreed to remove the American army from the South. Let me stress that point: this was the American army that was still in the South, and that was because Grant ordered them to stay there to protect black Americans. Throughout his presidency, Grant fought for black equality, and was determined to ensure it. As you mentioned earlier, he destroyed the Ku Klux Klan during his administration.

So, the answer to your question is that according to Frederick Douglas, Grant was the last of the radicals, and that's why he was trashed for the next three generations.

BOSTON During his second term, with his second string Cabinet in place, that was when the corruption took place in his administration. Despite the corruption, however, which obviously created a lot of controversy, Grant stood watch over the South essentially by himself, actively fought for black equality and for the re-integration of Southerners into the Union, refused to inflate our currency, and he prosecuted many tax evaders.

Was the corruption during his second term so extreme as to put a major stain on these otherwise terrific accomplishments?

SMITH No, it was not. There were minor incidents of corruption, and as I said in response to your first question, President Grant was trashed by Southern historians for three and a half generations beginning in the late 1870s, 1880s, and on because he was in favor of equality for African-Americans and against segregationists in the South. Thus, if you had asked historians for a ranking of presidents immediately after World War II, Grant would have ranked at the bottom along with maybe Warren G. Harding. It's only been recently that this has changed, and historians have come to respect Grant's concern for African-American equality and that's made a big difference.

GRANT AND THE PRESIDENTIAL POLLS

BOSTON President Obama is our forty-fourth president and in the most recent poll that I've seen, Grant is ranked at about twenty-third, so despite the three or four generations of Southern historians being so highly critical of Grant, there's been a lot of time (fifty-one years now—since the Civil Rights Act) for his ranking to go up.

Why is Grant still in the middle of the pack despite his many achievements during his presidency?

SMITH Significant movement in the polls doesn't take place over night, and let's face it, twenty-third is a lot better than being forty-third, so he's moved up half way. Your comment earlier is quite right that twenty years from now, he's liable to be listed in the top ten.

BOSTON Those are my questions. Thanks so much, Dr. Smith.

III.

Turn of the Century Until the New Deal

THE ROOSEVELTS

THEODORE ROOSEVELT

WOODROW WILSON

CALVIN COOLIDGE

HOOVER, COOLIDGE, & THE BIRTH OF
REPUBLICAN CONSERVATISM

KEN BURNS is the most successful history documentary filmmaker of all time. He's won many Emmy Awards, been nominated for Academy Awards, and taken history into more schools than all other historians combined. On October 20, 2014, a month after the first PBS showing of The Roosevelts: An Intimate History, I interviewed Ken in the Belo Mansion's Pavillion at the annual fundraising dinner of the Dallas Bar Foundation. That night was a magical time for all to hear first-hand Ken's profound thoughts about the Big Three: Theodore, Franklin, and Eleanor.

"Our kids don't have to work in mines seven days a week, fourteen hours a day. That's a Roosevelt thing. We have national parks. That's a Roosevelt thing. There are livable working hours and working standards. That's a Roosevelt thing. There's LaGuardia Airport and there are people in Chicago and people in the Tennessee Valley who turn on a light switch and they get power, as they do in the Southwest and the Northwest. That's a Roosevelt thing. If you've ever driven on the Skyline Drive or gone through the Lincoln Tunnel or over the Triborough Bridge, along with thousands of schools, thousands of bridges, hundreds of thousands of miles of roads that permit the commerce of this country to take place… those are all Roosevelt things. Hundreds of millions, if not more than a billion, trees planted…That's the Roosevelts." **– KEN BURNS**

CHAPTER 10

KEN BURNS

ON

The Roosevelts

THE ROOSEVELTS AND THEIR "EMOTIONAL ARCHEOLOGY"

BOSTON Ken, you've said that in the seven years you spent developing *The Roosevelts,* your objective was to pursue and present "emotional archeology," that is, reassembling in depth not only the outer lives of these three individuals, but their inner lives as well—"an intimate history."

Did Theodore, Franklin, and Eleanor take you deeper into emotional archeology than you've ever gone before in your prior films?

BURNS In a way, yes. Certainly, it's at the heart of all our films. The idea of emotional

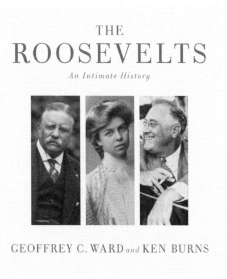

THE
ROOSEVELTS
An Intimate History

GEOFFREY C. WARD *and* KEN BURNS

Courtesy of Penguin Random House LLC

archeology is that we're not interested in trying to excavate the dry dates, facts, and events of the past, the sort of dry shards that makes history for most people like castor oil—something you know that's good for you but isn't good tasting—just another subject in the curriculum you didn't like—not the great pageant of everything—*everything* that's gone before this moment. And in some ways, our "subject" films like *The Civil War, Baseball,* and others have touched on that higher emotion.

We have to get our terminology straight though. Emotional archeology is not about sentimentality and nostalgia, which are the enemy of good anything. Too often as human beings we retreat to the rational world. To escape that baser sentimentality and nostalgia, we forget to evoke what our founders thought when they created our republic: that we would be able to have unleashed within the human spirit what we call "higher emotions." That's what I'm interested in, and all of us here are aspiring to these higher emotions—in the relationships we care about, the faith we have, the art we admire, and the music we love. All of us have to pursue these higher emotions with an improbable calculus that can transform the rational $1+1=2$ into $1+1=3$.

That's the emotional archeology I'm talking about and you can touch it time and time again, particularly in a major war where so many things are happening. With *The Roosevelts*, it was possible for us to go deeper into their emotional archeology because it's the first time we've ever done a biography over a major series. Normally our major series are on big subjects—*The Civil War, Baseball, Jazz, The West, The War, The National Parks.*

But here with *The Roosevelts*, we had three individuals who were related to one another, but strangely enough they had not been put together before in a major work. There had been a couple of books on the three of them, but nothing in the depth we wanted. I guess because Theodore was a Republican and Franklin was a Democrat,

some thought they should be separated, but that seemed arbitrary. They're very, very similar and there's no Franklin and no Eleanor without Theodore and his political underpinnings.

We thought it made sense to engage them not just on the more superficial idea of what they did, but asking questions about who they were, what kind of childhoods they had, what they were made of. That's "intimate history." It is not tabloid. It's "intimate" in the sense of not only what were their strengths, but also what were their weaknesses? How were they flawed? How did they overcome their flaws?

In fact, it becomes a hugely instructive kind of storytelling for us to dive deep into that. So in many ways, this was the most satisfying and the most deeply complex emotional archeology we've ever done.

THE NEED TO DETAIL HEROES' STRENGTHS AND FLAWS

BOSTON As you just mentioned, one thing that made *The Roosevelts* so compelling was how you explored Theodore, Franklin, and Eleanor by fully telling the story of their strengths *and* their flaws.

Now that millions have seen the film, and therefore know the extent of their flaws, will that impact the Roosevelts' legacy as American heroes?

BURNS No, I don't think so. I think it will actually strengthen them in a way—will impact their legacies in a positive way. I think too often we live in a media culture in which we're saturated with information with actually very little meaning or understanding. And because of the information avalanche, we rely on a kind of shorthand conventional wisdom to understand people and things. That causes us quite naturally to divide our world into red state or blue state, male or female, black or white, rich or poor, young or old, gay or straight, whatever it is—north, south, east, west—and we then make simple judgments. We find out again and again how fraudulent or inaccurate those judgments can be, how incomplete they are, and we yearn for something more substantial.

I remember very early on, when we were promoting the film, someone said that Franklin and Eleanor had a complicated marriage. I said "complicated marriage" is redundant. Somehow we've bought into our own Madison Avenue idea of ourselves or the presidency or greatness, and so we're stunned to realize that what we yearn for is the complexity we extend to the others who are close to us.

Our heroes are not perfect. In fact, the very definition of heroism that we've gotten from the Greeks is not perfection, but in fact a negotiation, sometimes a war between a person's very obvious strengths and his perhaps not so obvious but equal weaknesses. And it is that negotiation and that war going on inside us between our strengths and weaknesses that defines heroism.

Achilles had his heel and his hubris. All of a sudden, that opens up the flawed human condition, and we realize that we live in such a superficial media culture regarding our greatest leaders and heroes. It makes us lament, "Why if only we could have somebody like so and so!" Well, in fact, he's right in front of us. We just don't know how to look for him anymore because he makes one mistake and then we throw him out.

As I went through the process of trying to alert the country about the upcoming film, the great sorrow for me was my realization that today, none of the three Roosevelts would get out of the Iowa caucuses. That's a really sad commentary on us now, not on how America was during our earlier times.

BOSTON Theodore and Franklin Roosevelt both had a superhuman level of self-confidence, but also an inability to acknowledge anything in their lives that was personally unpleasant—from TR's first wife's death to FDR's social setbacks at Groton and Harvard, to TR's Brownsville incident during his presidency, to FDR's polio.

If TR and FDR were sitting here tonight at this table next to us and we asked them, "Theodore, Franklin, what were the biggest disappointments of your life?" or "What was your biggest weakness?" how would they answer those questions?

BURNS First of all, they wouldn't be sitting out there. They'd be sitting up here and asking you questions, and that's the only way they'd have it. You know, it's interesting that you phrase it that way, and you're absolutely right, Talmage. I think, though, that there's a very big difference among all three of them and Eleanor has to be in this picture.

For the sake of your question, as between Theodore and Franklin—Theodore was a depressive. We have to understand this. He had this wonderful phrase after his wife and mother died on the same day in the same house in Manhattan within hours of each other on February 14, 1884. He had dealt with the double tragedy by leaving New York behind—going out to the Dakotas—and said, "Black care can rarely sit behind a rider whose pace is fast enough," which is a nineteenth century way of saying, "You *can* outrun your demons." Theodore Roosevelt spent his entire life outrunning his demons. For example—the shame he felt at his father's having bought a substitute [for himself in the Union Army] in the Civil War. His mother, who was an unreconstructed southerner, insisted that her husband not go fight against her people, but that, instead, he should buy a substitute soldier for himself, as rich people could do at that time. Abraham Lincoln bought a substitute for his son because he was president of the United States.

So Theodore Roosevelt felt that his father, the man he admired most, wore a badge of dishonor because he didn't serve in the Civil War. Because of his feeling that way, he then spent his whole life adopting and living out a kind of belligerent posture, combined with this sense of, if you stop moving, if you aren't in perpetual motion,

then the demons *will* catch up with you. In fact, when he *wasn't* in perpetual motion, the demons *did* catch up with him. So throughout his life, his setbacks were largely unacknowledged.

In answer to your question though [about what was his greatest setback], he might say, "the loss of my wife and mother." He put an X over his calendar page on the day they both died, and said, "The light has gone out of my life." Maybe he'd admit that.

He also, in his belligerency, had strange behaviors. He was disappointed that he didn't have a disfiguring wound from the Spanish-American War on his day at San Juan Hill. He was proud of the fact (though the army was horrified by the fact) that his regiment had suffered the worst casualties—and a lot of it had to do with his recklessness that day. When that battle ended, he did something no one should ever do—those of you who have been in the military know this—he lobbied to get the Congressional Medal of Honor, which is just taboo.

Most important, and most tragically, he pushed all four of his sons not just into World War I, but into combat and danger, resulting in unspeakable tragedy, and it sat

on his shoulders the rest of his life. So in answering about his greatest disappointment, maybe he would say, "the loss of my wife", maybe it would be, "pushing Quentin, my youngest son, into fighting during World War I." There was a town in Pennsylvania named Bismarck that changed its name to Quentin when TR's son was killed in an air battle in the First World War in the nascent days of air combat.

Theodore was a very complicated figure and so very different in opacity than Franklin Roosevelt, who grew up absolutely without a shred of depression and self-doubt, and was over-confident, well-loved, but also troubled by the fact that because he was an only child, he interacted well socially when he was around adults, but not so well around people his own age. His classmates at Groton and Harvard found him sort of insufferable. He was, as Geoff Ward says in the film, a too-eager-to-please airedale that the adults adored and the kids just said "a-yee". In our research, we discovered at Groton a photograph that's never been published before that's so amazing. It's three boys from Groton, who are sharing some joke, and beside them is a column in front of a house, and separate and apart from the three boys is this morose-looking young Franklin Roosevelt, clearly excluded from their joke. He never mentioned how difficult Groton was socially to his parents. He was always cheerful to them, always had the mask in place for them. So in many ways, TR and Franklin share the same unwillingness to acknowledge disappointment, though they did it in really different ways.

Eleanor was more like Theodore. She came from the same branch of the family and was his favorite niece. TR's brother Elliott was Eleanor's father and was a hopeless alcoholic and a reprobate and mentally ill. She always worried about her tormented father and so she also was always in perpetual motion all of her life.

Franklin was her fifth cousin... That's really far away. I'm the fifth cousin, once removed, of Theodore Roosevelt. And I'm the sixth cousin of Franklin. So you can imagine how far distant they were in the family tree, even though they were all born in Manhattan; they all knew each other; and they had reunions, picnics, and holidays together. It's a really complicated dynamic, which we thought was a key to unlocking their leadership qualities as well as their later flaws.

THE ROOSEVELTS' ATTITUDE TOWARD THE CONSTITUTION, THE JUDICIARY, AND THE RULE OF LAW

BOSTON You've now got a ballroom full of lawyers here and we're talking about two men, Theodore and Franklin Roosevelt, who both at one time aspired to become lawyers.

BURNS Yes, and Franklin actually became one for a short period of time.

BOSTON Theodore abandoned the law while he was in law school and Franklin abandoned it after he practiced briefly in New York City because they both got bored with it. Both of them were outspoken critics of the Constitution's apparent inelasticity. As George Will said in the film clip we just saw, "They thought the Constitution was a nuisance."

BURNS That's George Will's opinion about them, yes.

BOSTON And they both disfavored the idea that the judiciary should be an equal partner in the Constitution's balance of power.

BURNS Wait. They felt the judiciary was behind the times. And it's so interesting that in the first episode of the film, Theodore decided to do what no gentleman of his social status would ever in his right mind think to do, which is enter the low business of politics—low because politics was perceived to be the business of only saloon keepers and ward heelers. Yet he was going to do it. His father had tried politics and lost an election through some boss' manipulation. Throwing his hat into the political ring sort of galvanized TR's actions and led him all the way to the presidency.

Theodore was always looking at the world in terms of things being either very right or very wrong. He felt the judiciary had not been quick enough to address these wrongs and these inequalities, particularly in the Gilded Age, when (like today) there was so much disparity in income. He thought the courts should be more active agents in trying to be, as he felt government should be, a countervailing force in people's lives, separating the people and their government from the monopolies and the trusts that owned the state senate, which truly owned the politicians.

In those days, there was no direct election of the senators, which meant the state legislatures were bought by the trusts— banking in New York, timber in Michigan, copper in Montana, railroads everywhere. The trusts in turn selected the senators, so the New York State senate was itself this incredibly corrupt institution. Theodore believed that the courts ought to play a role along with the executive branch of government in trying to sort of balance out the trusts' monopolistic control. It's so interesting that he was doing battle over this issue at the time and it's, of course, Franklin who's remembered for proposing what we now call the "court packing" incident.

BOSTON So, taking that to its conclusion, what's your perspective on this disconnect between Theodore and Franklin, on the one hand, and the legal profession and the rule of law on the other? You just said that it didn't move fast enough. Was there anything more than that?

BURNS No, I don't think so. In fact, their critics were always calling them, as George Will implies in his commentary (not just there in the film's introduction

but throughout the film), that they were treading very lightly on the Constitution. I think they had a fundamentally, philosophically different view of it, and Theodore and Franklin were alike in that they both felt the Constitution could and should be more muscular—as George Will said, they wanted it more "elastic" than it had heretofore been.

What they did was change the relationship between the citizen and the federal government in large ways, not by reinterpreting the Constitution, but by saying the government could take a more active role in people's lives, and that's what they succeeded in doing. Quite often, they were held in check by a judiciary who (in their eyes) was often not of the time and they rankled against it. The Roosevelts were hugely powerful people who were going to push at the borders of everything in order to achieve their goals.

ELEANOR'S UNRELENTING RESILIENCE

BOSTON One of the best parts of your film was how it deepened our appreciation for the indomitable Eleanor Roosevelt, who grew up with two toxic parents and was orphaned by the age of nine; then married FDR at age

twenty hoping to find a lifetime companion, but soon became overwhelmed by his mother's domination; then was betrayed by her husband in his affair with Lucy Mercer; and then had her husband struck down by polio. Yet she overcame all these setbacks and disappointments to become the greatest First Lady in American history.

What was the source of her amazing resilience?

BURNS She was a miracle of the human spirit. She should not have survived her childhood. It's really amazing. Her father was an alcoholic and mentally ill, though she idolized him. Her mother was a great beauty who was disappointed in Eleanor's not-very-good looks, though that picture we show in the film's introduction betrays that a little bit. Her own mother called her "Granny." But Eleanor learned very early on that she could be of use to other people; and if she was useful to other people, then she could be loved. It's in some ways almost pathetic, but that's what she did all her life— try to be useful to others.

What that did was translate from the intimate stage of her own upbringing, and then also translate from the more personal, relatively intimate stage of her family life, with all the dynamics and dramas that are probably not unfamiliar to people in this room. She had no role model for parents from her own mother and father, so she was actually a horrible mother. She had six children. Five survived infancy, and among those five, they had nineteen marriages. And her mother-in-law, who was herself a very *good* mother, as mother-in-laws are wont to do, stepped in and really took over Eleanor and Franklin's family. So you can understand that Eleanor, having survived her mother-in-law, Sara, made history. She comes down to us in conventional wisdom, that superficial view that I don't like too much, as the Dragon Lady.

Eleanor spent her life expanding the arena in which service to others took place. Early on, it was the *noblesse oblige* of the debutante class that caused them to go down to the Lower East Side, while keeping their white gloves on, and then scurry back up to Fifth Avenue as soon as their service to the poor was completed. Eleanor would take public transportation down there, and live their lives, and get involved with them. Later, as an Assistant Secretary of the Navy's wife, she was doing more within the circles of Washington. Then, in World War I, she was going to the depots, making sandwiches, going to the burn wards, and being with the shell-shocked soldiers, and really being stunned by it all. She said if you got up every day and did something you didn't want to do, then that was a good thing, and, therefore, she did it all her life.

I give her a pass on Prohibition. She had an alcoholic father and many alcoholic relatives who were a great physical threat to her. And her own younger brother for whom she felt responsible died in her arms of delirium tremens. You can say Eleanor's favoring Prohibition was a big mistake, but I think we can give her a pass on that because of all the trouble caused by the members of her family.

On absolutely everything else, she was right. She had what Stewart Udall said in our National Parks film about Teddy—that he had "distance in his eyes." I think all three Roosevelts had distance in their eyes. She, more than anyone else, understood the coming issues that are still on the forefront today, whether it's poverty or it's women or it's race or it's labor or it's children or it's health. All the things we continue to debate, she was on top of in the twenties, thirties, and forties—she did it all her life. I think that's what makes her so remarkable, that she accomplished what she did despite all the personal misfortune in her life that would have folded the tent of a lesser human being.

FEARLESSNESS IN THE ROOSEVELTS' DNA

BOSTON Another common trait in all three Roosevelts that your film developed was that they were each absolutely fearless—from Teddy's charging up San Juan Hill and busting trusts in his political career, to FDR's taking on the Great Depression and then Hitler and the Japanese after Pearl Harbor, to Eleanor's leading the fight to allow the Tuskegee Airmen to fly in World War II, and to release Japanese-Americans from internment on the West Coast during the war. Time and again, the three of them looked fear in the eye and never blinked.

Was such extraordinary courage in the Roosevelts' DNA or did it come from somewhere else?

BURNS It's a mystery. All history, certainly all biography, is about this failure to know where extraordinary intangibles come from, because as everyone in this room knows, the person closest to you has an aspect that is and will remain inscrutable. So how can we pretend to understand someone who lived a hundred years ago? If you look at the whole expanse of the Roosevelt family, I think you've got to say that many of them lived lives of idle luxury, dissipation, and alcoholism and, in that Oyster Bay branch, not infrequent madness and depression. That these three accomplished what they did is beyond remarkable.

Let me digress for one second. I've got four daughters. My second daughter, Lily, is in her late twenties. When she was little, she was petrified of the vacuum cleaner. She literally thought it was a monster. If we were going to vacuum the house, my wife and I would have to get her out of the house, get her asleep, over at friends, whatever. Then one day, when she was two years old, she walked into the room where this monster was roaring, and sat on it. From that day on, in our family, when we talk about confronting fear, we call it sitting on the vacuum cleaner.

Courage and fearlessness are all about facing the monster. What I think is so interesting about this human story is that these three people for three sets of entirely different, complicated reasons, became who they became, all with that hallmark of having been of privilege but dedicated to helping people less fortunate. There have been sociological studies that have ascribed lots of attributes of Democrats and attributes of Independents and Republicans; and one thing Americans share 100% is a sense of fairness—that things should be fair—that there should be a level playing field—and that we should have concern for those less fortunate. The Roosevelts put not just their money, where many of us do in politics, but their lives on the line for that principle. For all their deep flaws—and our film did not shirk from exposing them—they nonetheless were willing to do something that is admirable in that all three of them *did* change for the better the lives of ordinary Americans.

THE ROOSEVELTS' COMMITMENT TO ADDRESSING SOCIAL INEQUITIES

BOSTON To follow up on that answer, here they were, raised upper crust, wealthy, and yet when we look back on their presidencies and lives, they had this commitment to the lower class. There were many in their respective eras who called them "traitors to their class," because their social and political priorities did not align with the people who had been their neighbors and so forth; but instead they aligned with those less fortunate.

Where did their aspiration to challenge social inequalities come from?

BURNS I think it began with Theodore's father who was something new in the world. He was a philanthropist, well before the Carnegies, Rockefellers, and Fords in the nineteenth century. If you've ever been to the Metropolitan Museum or the Museum of Natural History in New York City, it was Theodore Roosevelt, Sr., who was responsible for those museums, with a lot of other men from this period who, as the good citizens of Dallas do (in this city unlike any other city in the United States), are so dedicated to the eleemosynary, the charitable organizations of the community. They did that. They helped provide for newsboys' homes and orphanages and did all these good deeds for the underprivileged, and they were committed to it.

In doing good things for the less fortunate, they ran up against the bosses all the time—both the political bosses and the people pulling strings behind the political bosses. So although they were "old wealth," they were not that wealthy. They had property, but they didn't have a lot of liquid cash the way the Vanderbilts, Carnegies, Fords, and Rockefellers did. So they developed a kind of social consciousness that said, "Our society ought to operate on a level playing field and the government is the only thing big enough to offer a countervailing force that helps level that playing field."

So now, and throughout our past, we debate, as we should, what the role of government should be and what a citizen should expect from the government. What goes along with that debate are questions about the nature of leadership and how is leadership formed, and what are the tensions between pragmatism and ideology that a leader might experience?

Our kids don't have to work in mines seven days a week, fourteen hours a day. That's a Roosevelt thing. We have national parks. That's a Roosevelt thing. There are livable working hours and working standards. That's a Roosevelt thing. There's LaGuardia Airport and there are people in Chicago and people in the Tennessee Valley who turn on a light switch and they get power, as they do in the Southwest and the Northwest. That's a Roosevelt thing. If you've ever driven on the Skyline Drive or gone through the Lincoln Tunnel or over the Triborough Bridge, along with thousands of schools, thousands of bridges, hundreds of thousands of miles of roads that permit the commerce of this country to take place…those are all Roosevelt things. Hundreds of millions, if not more than a billion, trees planted…That's the Roosevelts.

You've got to really balance sometimes the ideological impulse to sort of say, "I think I know who they are," and the fact that we all take for granted the world they ushered in. We take advantage of and of course, we are also heirs to its inevitable problems and that's what *The Roosevelts* series was trying to say. It is not a simple black and white choice.

THE ROOSEVELTS' PERSONALITIES AND GIFT FOR LEADERSHIP

BOSTON Maybe the two greatest strengths of all three Roosevelts that made them so successful and so fascinating was their force of personality and their gift for leadership.

Knowing what you know about their personalities and their leadership styles, which served them so well in their respective eras, and this is tying in to one of your prior answers, how do you think clones of Theodore, Franklin, and Eleanor would do if they entered the political fray in 2014? You said that you didn't think they could get out of the Iowa caucuses.

BURNS No, I don't. Okay. Let's start with Eleanor. She didn't have the telegenic looks that we require of female candidates today. Her own aunt, the wife of the president of the United States, Edith Carow Roosevelt, said that "her mouth and teeth have no future." This is coming from her own relative. There were thousands of Eleanor Roosevelt jokes from that period and almost all of them had to do with ugliness and unattractiveness. Just imagine how that would translate today to a media culture so unwilling to tolerate nuance.

Theodore Roosevelt wouldn't be able to get out of Iowa because he would have ten Howard Dean moments a day. "Bully! Dee-lighted!" He would be too, too, too hot for the cool medium of television. We expect a certain kind of behavior and he was just all over the place. Somebody called him "a steam locomotive in trousers."

He did have a magnificent presence. He always felt that you couldn't be judged a great president if you didn't have a crisis. As David McCullough says in the film, many people thought *he* was the crisis. And he did earn the undying enmity of those wealthy people who he was trying to sort of regulate or at least check.

The interesting thing (going back a little bit to that answer of the earlier question) is that this anti-wealth thing is not true. When he ran as the third party candidate for the Progressive Party, he said, "We are trying to enlist worker and wealthy alike." He really thought that in this republic, as it has always been when it's worked really well, in those little patches where it's really functioned like a well-oiled machine, there has always been during those rare times a kind of intense cooperation between the classes…and the disappearance of the distinctions of class, not because there weren't people who were rich and poor, but because there was more of a sense of participation. You can think of World War II as a classic example of that.

Those very people Franklin Roosevelt labeled as "malefactors of great wealth" during the Depression, the people whose unregulated speculation and greed had caused the collapse of the markets, and who he regulated and to whom he said, "I welcome their hatred"—he then turned around and, during the Second World War, went to them and said, "I'm going to make you really, really rich." And he did.

"You're going to make me fifty thousand planes this year." "Mr. President, we can't do that." And he said, "You're going to make me fifty thousand planes." You can look, and one of the great ironies in history was Eisenhower's warning about the military industrial complex in 1960. When he issued that warning, Ike was not talking about something that had just happened last Thursday. He was talking about something that started on September 2, 1945—the day after the Japanese surrendered. Because at that moment, more than 50% of the manufacturing in the world took place in the United States and Franklin Roosevelt was largely responsible for that by growing our military during World War II. Those businessmen, those corporations, did not want that production to end, and this is part of the irony of a complicated situation.

Franklin couldn't get out of Iowa today because he would be in a wheelchair, and CNN, Fox and MSNBC would compete to show the things that the media of that time, in restraint, did not show. What it took for him to stand up or sit down with sweat pouring off and his enduring a great deal of pain. Roosevelt knew that pity was political poison. He knew he could never advance if people pitied him, and pity would come from seeing that infirmity.

Photo credit: Cable Risou

Ken Burns

When we think of all of those reporters in his era who would not focus their stories or cameras on FDR's physical incapacity, we say, "Well, it was a simpler time." I don't think you can say the Depression and the Second World War were simpler times. It was actually probably more complex than right now. But they made a decision not to cover what polio did to FDR physically; although that didn't mean they didn't see it. Those audiences of 350 or 3,500 who watched Franklin give a speech and then watched the arduous nature of how he moved—and over seven years of research we were able to catch those few frames at the beginning or the end of that process, that had been edited out of the newsreels—to give a sense of how unbelievably infirm our president was. If a man in his condition were seen in the media today, we would decide on the basis of the nightly drumbeat of this information that this person couldn't possibly get us through a crisis. Yet Franklin Roosevelt got us through two of the greatest crises in American history since the Civil War: the Depression and World War II.

BOSTON Being in Texas, as you probably know, our Republican nominee for governor, Greg Abbott (who in November 2014, in fact, was elected Governor of Texas), became paralyzed when a tree fell on him thirty years ago. Yet he's in his wheelchair for every single commercial in this campaign. There's been almost an emphasis on his paralysis from the waist down. Certainly, he is beholden to FDR for awakening American consciousness to the fact that those with physical limitations still have all their horsepower and all kinds of things to bring to the table and that, to me, that's such a big part of FDR's legacy.

BURNS I think it's a huge part and I'm so glad you said that. The Americans with Disabilities Act would not have happened had we not had the memory of somebody who had been able to do what he did. Of the three Roosevelts, the one who would be the exception and able to compete in today's political arena would be Franklin—as much for the force of his personality, the outward cheeriness, the magnetism he had, in addition to what we see is the heroic extra effort all of those who have some sort of disability have to go through. They have to work that much harder just to get through the day. I'm glad you brought that up. I think that dynamic is changing in the United States.

BOSTON We have time for probably a question or two from the audience. We've got some serious Ken Burns fans out there. Yes, sir. Would you stand up, please?

ELEANOR'S SEXUAL ORIENTATION

AUDIENCE MEMBER Did you conclude that Eleanor Roosevelt was a lesbian?

BURNS I went into making *The Roosevelts* with the presumption or the understanding that she was a lesbian. Now, having thoroughly studied her life, I don't think there's any historical evidence to support that conclusion. We do know that she had very, very passionate—I don't mean sexual—very intimate, close relationships with a number of women, some of whom were committed to other women. But she also had an equal

number of relationships with men, like her bodyguard Earl Miller. We've got some footage of them playing Errol Flynn, or Douglas Fairbanks, and him kidnapping her as a pirate.

At one time, she was close to a man named Joseph Lash. She lived the last years of her life in a close friendship with David Gurewitsch, her doctor, who she told, "I love you more than I've loved anyone else." People always cite the letters and the intimacy of those letters. I could show you letters between Abraham Lincoln and Joshua Speed that had the same tenderness, "I wish to come back." They would sleep on the same pallet, the same bed, at rough frontier inns and when they were separated for some time, they would write each other long letters about "I can't wait until the nights we spend together", you know, things like that. And if you're going to make the judgment about Eleanor, then you have to go that far with Abraham Lincoln as well.

I feel in many ways that Eleanor was asexual. She had six children, as I said. Five survived. But I don't think that's how she was configured. A lot of the controversy about her sexual connotation arises from people reading into Eleanor what they want. Just as there's a presumption that Franklin Roosevelt's White House was this harem of secretaries and his distant cousin, Daisy Suckley, and the reappearance of Lucy Mercer Rutherfurd. He did have an affair with Lucy more than a decade before he became president. The presumption is that their affair was just sexual, but, in fact, they fell in love. The letters between them that Eleanor discovered I'm sure were burned in the fireplace on 86th and Fifth Street, so we don't have those letters.

Unlike Theodore and Eleanor, Franklin was someone who could not outrun his demons because of his physical infirmity. So he surrounded himself with people who were quite adoring and who he cared very deeply about. He had a secretary, Missy LeHand, who, having suffered a stroke, caused him to basically rewrite his will to give her half his estate. She predeceased him—you guys know that term—so it didn't obtain. But theirs was a relationship with great sensitivity and friendship. Later, Lucy Mercer Rutherfurd reemerged in his life during the final years of his presidency through meetings arranged by Franklin's daughter, Anna, who feared that her mother, who was always away from the White House with all of her causes, would find out about these meetings. Anna Roosevelt knew her father was alone much of the time, and was getting older and frailer. He'd asked Lucy to come back and visit him, which she did six times, the last time being when she was there with him when he died at Warm Springs, but there was nothing sexual about it during those six visits. Nor was there with Grace Tully, one of his secretaries, or Margaret LeHand, or his distant cousin Daisy Suckley. I think they were just among the women and larger company of men who spent their time adoring Franklin Roosevelt.

One other point I'd like to make, and it's related to what you're talking about regarding assumptions made about the Roosevelts: if you can remember the oldest portrait you've seen of Theodore Roosevelt, he looks like he's about eighty-five years old. I'm sixty. Theodore Roosevelt died at sixty. Think of the oldest image you have of Franklin Roosevelt. He looks like a cadaver—like he's ninety-five or one hundred. He was sixty-three when he died. Knowing this, you will have an idea of these lives—the kind of RPMs at which they lived their lives—the extent to which they burned themselves out. David McCullough once said of Theodore Roosevelt that he was "a high-intensity bulb that burned very brightly for a very short period of time."

Also remember that the three Roosevelts all did what they did in the service of their country, regardless of whether you agree or disagree with certain ideas or programs. They nonetheless were doing what few of us, except those who serve in the military, are doing. They put their lives literally on the line for this greatest of all countries, the United States of America.

BOSTON Let's have a great round of applause for Ken.

DOUGLAS BRINKLEY is a major American presidential historian, having written or collaborated on books about six presidents—many of which became *New York Times* bestsellers. He's also a professor of history at Rice University. His being an ardent conversationalist inspired him to write *The Wilderness Warrior: Theodore Roosevelt and the Crusade for America* (HarperCollins 2009). I interviewed Doug on the subject of Theodore Roosevelt in front of his history class at Rice University in Houston, Texas, on November 12, 2015.

"Theodore Roosevelt defined the American centrist. By not being part of either the right or left paradigms, and by not being about politics first and foremost, he was able to look at what made sense for the whole country to go forward. For anyone who considers himself an independent-minded voter, he is the number one president. For those who want a political leader who can deal with circumstances from a pragmatic perspective, and who's a visionary, and who aspires to do what's right without worrying about the political consequences, TR shines mightily." **–DOUGLAS BRINKLEY**

CHAPTER 11

DOUGLAS BRINKLEY

ON

Theodore Roosevelt

TR AS A SERIOUS NATURALIST BEGINNING IN CHILDHOOD

BOSTON Doug, let's start with Theodore Roosevelt's developmental years pre-college. To me, three things stand out that set the tone for the rest of his life. The first huge influencer from his childhood was his becoming a discerning naturalist before he was ten years old. I realize that his father was one of the founders of the American Museum of Natural History, but does that alone explain the extraordinary passion for nature that was in Roosevelt's DNA almost at birth?

BRINKLEY Theodore Roosevelt's love of nature, and ultimately conservation, was really part of the family ethos. As you mentioned, his father was the

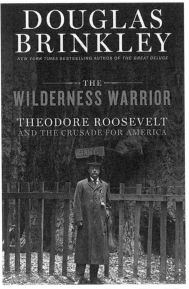

Courtesy of HarperCollins

co-founder of the American Museum of Natural History, which is one of our country's great places to go to study the natural world. But he also had his Uncle Robert Barnwell Roosevelt—considered the Audubon of the 1860s, 1870s, and beyond—as an influence. Uncle Rob wrote books about the game fish of Florida, the waterfowl in the Great Lakes, and especially Lake Superior. This was unusual in the 1870s, and we hadn't heard much about Uncle Robert until my book came out. He was an eccentric Dr. Doolittle-like character. He collected all sorts of animal species—monkeys, snakes, and the like. Young Theodore Roosevelt enjoyed and admired Uncle Rob because he'd walk into his house and there were critters everywhere. Young Theodore took to that a great deal.

What also attracted TR to nature was the enduring legacy power of John James Audubon. Knowing Audubon's work allowed him to identify the birds of North America. He'd prepare a checklist of all the birds in the New York City area and would check them off as he saw them. A few years later, he got a gun and started going into Central Park to shoot birds, and then would bring them back to his house and stuff them. He created his own in-house museum with these birds as the main attraction.

Add to all these reasons for embracing nature the fact that Theodore Roosevelt was born in 1858, on the eve of the Civil War. At that time, the big thing going on in our country beyond the Civil War was the exploration of the American West. During the Civil War, Abraham Lincoln connected the East to the West with the Transcontinental Railroad. Once that connection was made, it brought on the advent of new magazines filled with pulp western stories about the Wild West. Soon, boys' magazines had photographs of slick rock canyons in southern Utah or the blue Crater Lake up in Oregon or a volcano in Hawaii. Photography was starting to be used in magazines, so Theodore Roosevelt grew up reading these stories and seeing these photos showing a complete inventory of America's backyard in the West. To see all these wild and exciting places inspired him to want to go see them.

THE IMPACT OF TR'S SICKLY CHILDHOOD

BOSTON The second huge factor from childhood to consider was Roosevelt's being asthmatic and sickly most of his youth. That inspired him, at his father's behest, to start improving his body with vigorous exercise, pushing himself to the limit. What was it about his parents' upbringing or in his own wiring that made Theodore think, even as a boy, that whatever was worth doing was worth overdoing—in exercise and everything else?

BRINKLEY Asthma is very important in Theodore Roosevelt's life. He often had a hard time breathing and those days in New York City, before the regulation of factories, with the Industrial Revolution well underway, the air quality was terrible. He often had to search to find a place where he could breathe. He would take the train up to the Catskills in New York and then go up to the Adirondack Mountains. In the mountains, his lungs would open up in the fresh air. What he found was that nature could be a curative. This experience caused him later to focus his conservation efforts on pursuing clean air and water, because he knew how they impacted personal health.

The science on asthma is still sketchy even now, but in Roosevelt's day, they tried to figure out how to deal with it. I was stunned to learn that people thought kids should smoke cigarettes because they thought the tobacco would help asthma, when obviously it only irritated it. Some people still think asthma has a psychosomatic component to it, but we know from the polluted areas in the world that bad air makes people get horrible respiratory illnesses—and that's what happened to TR.

Another influence that caused Theodore Roosevelt to relentlessly build up his body when he was young came about one day when he was dressed up like a dandy and traveled to the Maine wilderness. At a train station, he encountered a bunch of boys who roughed him up, shoved him to the ground, and kicked him when he was up there on a holiday. It made Theodore Roosevelt so upset to be hazed that he talked to his father about it. His dad said, "Son, the only thing you can do is not be so sickly. We need to build your body up." So they put in a weight room at their home (unusual in those days), and Theodore Roosevelt began training there regularly by lifting weights.

By the time he went to Harvard, there are photos of him without a shirt on where he looked like a big-time wrestler. He had gotten so buff after being the sickly kid who used to get beat up. He realized that when he was in shape, it created confidence and made him feel better and made his mind sharper. So that hazing incident was a major factor in his becoming a huge promoter of physical activity, and allowed him to make the connection between vigorous exercise and having a good mind.

TR'S RESPONSE TO HIS FATHER'S AVOIDING MILITARY SERVICE DURING THE CIVIL WAR

BOSTON The final huge childhood influence was the major angst he suffered after learning that his father, who he idolized—Theodore Roosevelt, Sr.—had done what many rich people of his era did. He hired a substitute to fight for himself in the Civil War so that he wouldn't have to join the Union army, which his son believed to be an act of cowardice.

There was a perfectly logical and reasonable explanation for Theodore Sr.'s doing what he did. He was married to a Southern belle from Georgia, he had two brothers-in-law who were fighting for the Confederacy,

he had four young children under the age of five for whom he was responsible. So why did his father's decision not to join the Union Army drill down and stick in Theodore's craw?

BRINKLEY It's a very important point. Go back to the 1860s when Theodore Roosevelt was a young boy. Because his mother was from the South and loved Robert E. Lee and Jefferson Davis, and his father was from the North and felt the same toward Ulysses S. Grant and Lincoln, you can imagine what feuds would have taken place in their household if the father had gone off to fight for the Northern Army. Instead, the father decided to punt. He spent money to hire a surrogate to be his replacement so he didn't have to go to war.

Theodore felt that his father should have served in the military, because the entire Roosevelt family (not including his mother) believed so much in the Union cause, and they were all big Lincoln Republicans. He felt that his father, for all his piousness and greatness as a family figure, had let the country down by not putting his own life on the line to fight.

This situation came up over a century later when a lot of well-to-do people get deferments during the Vietnam War, and only inner city and working class people fought in the trenches of the war. Throughout history, people with wealth and means usually manage to stay out of harm's way.

That was not Theodore Roosevelt's way. He eventually redeemed his father's decision when he stepped up and volunteered to fight in the Spanish-American War. When it began, he immediately quit his job as Assistant Secretary of the Navy; traveled to San Antonio, Texas; recruited volunteers at the Menger Hotel (which still exists today in San Antonio); went to Tampa to train the Rough Riders; and then fought in Cuba. In combat, he served courageously leading the famous charge up San Juan (Kettle) Hill, for which he posthumously won the Congressional Medal of Honor. Roosevelt always said that his day in battle at San Juan Hill was the greatest day of his life, because it allowed him to redeem the sin of his father. He had the means, the money, and the prestige not to have served, but he never thought the country should send men into harm's way if all men weren't willing to go into battle themselves.

TR'S OBSESSION WITH "MANLINESS"

BOSTON A big part and a strange part of Theodore Roosevelt's mentality throughout his life was his obsession with being a "man's man." He often talked about desirable people and activities as being "manly"—his favorite adjective; while people or activities he deemed undesirable he labeled as "effeminate." Was this obsession typical of the men of his era or was it deemed excessive even then?

BRINKLEY Theodore Roosevelt always maintained the philosophy of the strenuous life. In a very male gender-driven culture at the time, men needed to be tough, loyal to their wives, have large families, and take full responsibility for raising their children. It was a manly-code, which is very antiquated today. Part of Roosevelt's manly-code, however, was not chauvinistic for this reason: His senior thesis at Harvard made the argument that women should not lose their names when they get married, an idea that still hasn't been fully resolved in the United States. He also favored giving women the right to vote long before they won it in 1920. So in some respects, he was ahead of this time, as far as women's rights are concerned, yet he maintained this "manly-code" which makes him a paradoxical figure to analyze.

There are a group of fine women scholars led by Patricia O'Toole and Kathleen Dalton who have argued that Theodore Roosevelt is actually a paradigm of a good male role model. This goes counter to what conclusions can be drawn from his extreme

macho-ism, but the fact is that if someone promotes women's rights to vote, and fidelity in marriage, and the husband's having the responsibility to share in raising children, those perspectives have caused some women scholars to say, "Look, for all his macho rhetoric about manly virtues, TR was not necessarily a bad role model."

His "manly code" came from an over-dramatic sense of men as gladiators and the need for men to engage in combat with each other, which was a kind of militaristic strain in him. He was overcompensating for something. It's hard to find the feminine side of Theodore Roosevelt. Often, when a man presents himself to society as being hyper-macho, there's something wrong there. Why is he having to prove his manliness all the time? Can't he just *be* a man? Why does he have to tell people that he is manly? So it was definitely an unusual and interesting part of his personality.

RESOLVING THE CONFLICT OF TR'S BEING A CONSERVATIONIST AND A HUNTER

BOSTON Like many great men in history, Roosevelt was paradoxical with his share of inconsistencies. A major one was his having, on the one hand, a passionate mission for conservation and preserving wilderness and wildlife, and always wanting to make sure there was no cruelty toward animals, while at the same time, relishing the killing of mass quantities of animals.

Explain that paradox.

BRINKLEY Nineteenth century America was still a very rural country, and guns were a big part of that culture. Hunting and fishing for food were the way many people survived. Market hunters, however, were slaughtering certain species into near extinction. Roosevelt went all the way to the Dakota territories looking to shoot a buffalo, and then hired the best game scouts, yet he couldn't find a buffalo there. Though there had once been about sixty million buffalo roaming the Dakota plains, all that remained by the time TR got there were 1,500 or so. Also, the passenger pigeon which John Adams wrote about, which used to darken the skies in Eastern America in huge flocks, had gone extinct toward the end of the nineteenth century. So species extinction became a serious problem in that era.

After Theodore spent a long week struggling to find a buffalo, he eventually found and then shot one, and proceeded to perform a Native American dance around the dead buffalo. After the dance, he cut the tongue out (a delicacy), and then the hunting party ate the hump considered to be the best meat on the buffalo. Finally, he chopped the head off the buffalo and sent it to a taxidermist in St. Paul, and it became a trophy on the wall of his home.

After he arrived back in New York after the buffalo hunt, he met George Bird Grinnell who was running *Forest and Field* magazine—a sportsman magazine. Together they created the Boone and Crockett Club, an organization for aristocratic hunters, which had as its aim the goal of bringing back the buffalo, elk, antelope, and deer to North America.

Doing his part to preserve the opportunity to hunt those animals in the future (after growing their numbers) was part of why TR wanted to start the club; but there was more to it than that. He also had started developing a post-Darwin view to the effect that all animal species were God's gifts to the planet, and to lose a species was like slashing all the paintings of Rembrandt or Goya, because each species in itself was not only to be treasured, but also was part of the natural order of things.

Because of this, he became biologically attracted to landscapes and species. In the late nineteenth century, many people went West looking for a new type of geography. They sought to tap the West for its minerals—gas, oil, zinc, asbestos, and copper. As a man of science and a Darwinian, Theodore Roosevelt was very interested in preparing

and getting published guidebooks of our native grasses, birdlife, and native species. That became his passion—to save North American wildlife.

RESOLVING THE CONFLICT OF TR'S BEING AN ARISTOCRAT AND A MAN OF THE PEOPLE

BOSTON Another paradox about Theodore Roosevelt was his having an aristocratic will *and* yet, at the same time, a Democratic desire to please. He was from a wealthy family who had gotten rich in the plate glass business and they were two generations into the wealth. He liked wearing tuxedos and going to fancy parties. Despite that, he became a huge trustbuster and, therefore, was attacking the business empires of many of the wealthy people in his part of the country with whom he went to high society social events.

Explain that inconsistency: his aristocratic upbringing, as opposed to his democratic philosophy toward American life.

BRINKLEY The inconsistency starts with the fact that Theodore Roosevelt was our only scientist president. He went to Harvard to major in wildlife biology, and took science classes there. While in college, he went to Maine and met a backwoods guy who looked like the Alaska bush people we now see on cable television. Theodore Roosevelt soon realized that this outdoorsman living on the land knew more about moose than the Harvard scholars in his classes who were studying them in the laboratory.

This lesson made him want to enlarge the field of wildlife biology. He wrote his first book on the summer birds of the Adirondacks; then he wrote a trilogy of books about the Dakotas and the mountain ranges in the West; and he also wrote two volumes about the War of 1812. He began to see himself as a writer about the outdoor life and US history, and it was by writing these books where he started making money on his own. He never had any interest in Wall Street, and actually turned against people who made their money there.

He became a believer that the real American heroes were not Wall Street financiers or the wealthy people, but were the explorers—people like Admiral Byrd who went to the Artic or people who traveled into the dense parts of South America or Africa, and then did mapping and discovered new species there. In recent generations, astronauts have had the same kind of mentality. Roosevelt felt that explorers like Lewis and Clark were the top of the human food chain—along with Daniel Boone and Davy Crockett.

Being an explorer (not a politician) was what made men great, in Roosevelt's eyes. Lincoln and George Washington were exceptions to that rule for TR, because they had started out as surveyors and rail-splitters. His pecking order was the great wilderness explorers at the top, followed by the farmers who produced agriculture crops from the land, and it went down from there.

In short, by the time he left Harvard, he had developed an anti-urban perspective on humanity and did not like or trust those who inhabited big cities. He felt their environment was unhealthy. He favored medium-sized cities with green belts and plenty of land outside the cities. Today, he would admire places like Boulder, Colorado or Ogden, Utah or Eugene, Oregon, which have a research university and an intellectual class, yet it's easy to get away from their downtown area and get out to the wilderness and be removed from urban life, which he thought was destroying the essential American character.

He was an original Boy Scout—not only in attitude but, in fact, he became a founder of the Boy Scouts of America. He thought every young man needed to know the name of every tree in his back yard, what kind of grasses were growing there, what each bird was, and how to read the weather. He thought having this type of knowledge gave a person the survivalist skills which were

essential to those who he identified as great Americans. Certainly, those skills are very useful for anyone who planned to become a soldier.

TR, RELIGION, AND NATURE

BOSTON You called your biography of Theodore Roosevelt *The Wilderness Warrior*, though you might have also called it "The Wilderness Theologian." In the book, you call him a "nature theologist" and say he absorbed "the gospel of the wilderness," and describe how Darwin's and Audubon's books essentially became his Bible substitutes. He saw Darwin as a Noah-like hero, more impactful to him than Jesus or anyone in the Bible. You believe that "Theodore Roosevelt watching a blue heron for an hour was worth more to him than saying one hundred Lord's Prayers."

Did he ever consider that everything in nature was created by a higher power; and, therefore, that a higher power might be a more worthy object of worship than earthly plants and animals?

BRINKLEY Charles Darwin was Theodore Roosevelt's ultimate hero—not just because Darwin wrote *On the Origin of Species*, but also because he was a world-class explorer, most famous for what he found at Galapagos Island. His being both a great explorer and an intellectual caused him to have uniquely elevated stature to TR.

Theodore Roosevelt believed that if you wanted to find God, He was there in a tree, in a species, in nature. Whenever he walked into a cathedral, he soon felt trapped—confined indoors—whereas when he walked outside and looked up at the stars, there he found his true God. His was a strand of transcendentalist philosophy, and it came from reading Thoreau, Emerson, and Whitman. Those American thinkers became his group of heroes because they were all saying that the natural world was God's great masterpiece. In fact, I write in the book about his sometimes holding Sunday church services in the outdoors.

After William McKinley was assassinated, and they rushed TR to Buffalo, when he got sworn in as president, he refused to put his hand on the Bible. It's a mystery why, though the official line was that nobody could find a Bible at the time, which seems impossible to believe. Religion mattered to him. But nature mattered more.

He wrote a letter once and said, "I am a foot soldier in the Darwin revolution." This did not mean he was an atheist. Far from it. He thought God created the Earth and that it was our job to protect it and be great stewards and custodians of it, though he perhaps didn't believe in the stories contained in the Bible, per se. He knew the Bible had great meaning to many people, and that religious services help build character and bring communities together, but he wasn't a hyper-believer or a "born again" type of evangelical figure. His evangelism was in the Whitman-Thoreau-Emerson perspective of "finding God in the outdoors."

TR'S OBSESSION WITH FORWARD MOMENTUM

BOSTON Given where religion and God were in his life, as I read your book, it seemed that he essentially saw himself as God. His favorite poem was entitled "Opportunity," and its punch line was "Master of human destinies am I." Another biographer of his, Edmund Morris, said he was "congenitally unable to question the rightness of his decisions." In other words, he basically saw himself as perfect—which sounds God-like.

Did he see himself as God-like and the "master of all human destinies"?

BRINKLEY Theodore Roosevelt lost his first wife, Alice, and his mother on the same day—Valentine's Day, 1884. Alice died of Bright's Disease while giving birth. That day, TR put a big X in his diary, and said, "The light has gone out of my life." Two deaths

of the two people he loved the most—and it happened on the same day. He had to do a dual burial for them, and that was a very gloomy day.

At that point, depression could have kicked in. Instead, he tried to run away from his grief, and immediately resumed the strenuous life, believing that it was up to every human being to write his own storybook and create his own chapters. He wanted his book to be honest, and he wanted it to show him as a person of integrity. Most important, he wanted to make himself the hero of his own storybook.

In addition to the impact of the dual death in his family, we need to remember that there were some addiction problems in the Roosevelt family. His brother had already become an alcoholic and ultimately committed suicide. These sad parts of his life caused TR to be a deeply unreflective person about himself. He was a doer—a person of action. Making a decision about his life involved simply moving forward. He was constantly using words like "onward" and "going forward." He never pulled back and did any "navel gazing" or contemplation.

This staying in a mode of moving forward can have positive effects for a leader—among other things, self-assuredness and self-confidence. In Theodore Roosevelt, those traits "runneth over." He believed he could do anything, and was afraid of nothing. A major factor in his fearlessness was that he wasn't afraid to die. If you're not afraid to die, then what's there to be afraid of?

I've never met anyone who, when they were young, was totally unafraid of dying, yet TR developed his mind with that perspective. Hunting taught him that when he shot an animal, it was gone. Like the poet Allen Ginsberg once said, TR believed that people and animals "were all hairy bags of water." He also believed that upon death, the soul left the body.

With this perspective, and having suffered through tragedies, he believed the world to be a brutal place, and it was up to each person to make his own way in it. Life was tough, and if someone was dealt a setback, or had an ailment, then he had to just pull himself together and go onwards—at all costs—and be vigilant in fighting against any weakness of mind and body. From that perspective, he authored his own storybook, became the hero of it, and felt fully satisfied with everything he had done in his life.

TR'S MANIC PERSONALITY

BOSTON Every great biography of Theodore Roosevelt, including yours, devotes many pages to his manic personality. At different parts of your book, you describe his passion for life as "double barreled," "double charged," that he was a "human blowtorch," that he lived by "throwing up skyrockets," that he was "radioactive," a "human tidal wave," and like a "boll weevil eating his way through a bale of cotton." These are the descriptions you use to describe his manic personality. As you point out though, sometimes manic depression can be brought on through excessive exuberance, and you assert that Theodore Roosevelt was the poster child for the exuberant manic depressive.

In his era, was there any medication to deal with this type of exuberant, over-the-top every-hour-of-every-day manic behavior that might have gotten him into a mode of having some sort of steady emotional equilibrium?

BRINKLEY Until writing *The Wilderness Warrior*, I didn't realize that exuberance can be a form of manic depression. It's a coping mechanism for depression. Whereas some people turn to drugs, and some to alcohol, people fight depression in different ways. There's one group who deals with it by going the exuberance route—that is, those people live every day for the moment, convince themselves that every situation is special, and refuse to explore pain.

Modern psychiatry suggests that people are supposed to work out their problems on the couch by talking to a therapist. The exuberant person deals with his pain and depression from the perspective that every day is wonderful. Theodore Roosevelt's favorite word throughout his life was "Bully!", which meant "Great!" If he walked into this lecture room today, he'd say, "What a bully day! The birds are singing outside! Do you feel the wind out there? Isn't it wonderful to be alive?"

Now when you're an historian, and see that characteristic in a person, the initial reaction is to think that was just TR spouting off some political blarney by telling people in the room how wonderful everything is and how optimistic he is; but Roosevelt did it everywhere he went, all day long, day after day. He never took a reprieve from that kind of attitude.

Exuberance sounds like a good condition for a person to have. It can make someone amazingly productive. TR wrote over thirty-five books and hundreds of thousands of letters and articles. He explored Africa, South America, and all over the American West. In his life, he achieved so much because he burned the torch at both ends. He was fueled by coffee—drank about a gallon every day. He had an amphetamine type of personality.

The ultimate result of living every day with that level of exuberance is a short life. It often causes a heart attack or a stroke. It ravages the body. In researching the book, I learned Roosevelt had a serious problem with insomnia. When it was midnight, and everybody else was sleeping, he would be reading a book until 4:00 in the morning. Because his brother had died from abusing opium and alcohol, TR didn't want to drug himself to sleep, so he ended up suffering long nights of insomnia. He would sometimes go days without sleep. Part of his love of the rugged outdoor life was because it exhausted his body. When he went on a twenty-five-mile hike, he could get tired enough to sleep, so he would totally exhaust himself physically just to get himself to sleep.

If someone today has this type of insomniac condition, we give him Ambien®, a sleeping drug, and it mellows a person out so he can rest, but Theodore Roosevelt was not wired that way. He did not want rest and relaxation. He wanted every day to be crowded with activity—getting the most out of life every minute because life was fleeting and it could end quickly.

The great Puritan theologian Jonathan Edwards once said, in paraphrase, "We're all standing on a platform, and any minute, the door might open and we might fall." Life is tenuous like that. A friend can get killed in an auto accident and "Boom!"—He's gone. Roosevelt was keenly aware that death can strike any of us at any minute, so for him the key to life was to treat every day like it was going to be one's last day. He rigged his mind that way and it made him accomplish so much and also be in a genuinely upbeat and happy mood all the time; but it also resulted in his having a short life. He died a burned out man at age sixty.

TR'S WALKING THE LINE BETWEEN GENIUS AND INSANITY

BOSTON The comedic pianist Oscar Levant once said, "There's a fine line between genius and insanity, and I have erased that line." Theodore Roosevelt was a bona fide high IQ genius and was also way beyond "over-the-top" in the way he conducted every aspect of himself. By that I mean over-the-top in the way he talked, the way he read, the way he wrote letters, the way he rode horses, the way he ate, the way he played tennis, the way he boxed, the way he gave speeches (constantly pounding his fist), the way he emasculated his critics, the way he bragged, the way he campaigned, the way he laughed, the way he played with his children. He did all those activities with his accelerator pushed hard to the floor.

Was there any identifiable line between genius and insanity in the way he conducted himself every day of his adult life?

BRINKLEY It's true about genius and insanity, and there's an element of insanity in most artists. They basically wake up every day to smash existing artistic paradigms and then create new art. I think Theodore Roosevelt was an American artist. His art was nation-building and nation-preserving. He believed that the United States was the greatest country God ever made and American exceptionalism was a fact of life.

His mind produced many novel ideas, and his spontaneity served to keep his opponents off guard. No one ever quite knew what TR would do and that gave him the power edge in many situations. He might point his finger into your face or he might pat you on the back. They used to say, "He wanted to be the groom at every wedding and the corpse at every funeral." He always had to have all the attention on himself and be the biggest star in every room he entered. In modern culture, we call this level of self-obsession narcissism.

Great things don't often get accomplished without having a genius around to provide the spark of big new ideas, and rarely are geniuses found in politics. Along with John Adams and Thomas Jefferson, Theodore Roosevelt was one of the three smartest presidents we've ever had. His brilliance didn't come from osmosis. Roosevelt learned how to speak foreign languages and was fluent in French and German. He read all the classics—read everything—read Latin.

Every available minute he spent building up his mind so he would know more than other people—and he knew that he was the smartest guy in the room. He became one of the great historians of his era, as well as a great politician; he was also one of the great explorers; and also one of the great ornithologists. Everything he took on, he became one of the best at it, and he was wired that way. I think he was more genius than insane, but by the time he left the White House, and started getting older, and his body started breaking down, then the insanity part of his personality started getting into this bloodstream more and more.

BOSTON The most obvious instance of his being taken over by insanity came a few years after he left the White House, when he ran for president on the Bull Moose ticket, and an assassin shot him in the chest right before he was supposed to give a campaign speech. Roosevelt insisted on giving the speech and proceeded to speak to the crowd for ninety minutes as blood poured through his shirt. That's what we're talking about regarding his insanity.

BRINKLEY That's a crucial moment. Put yourself in his place. If somebody comes up to you with a gun and shoots you, you would immediately go get medical help. Do you know any single human being who would not do that? TR took a bullet and was bleeding, and yet refused to let the assassin stop his speech. He held the shirt over his wound and kept speaking and said, "It'll take more than a bullet to kill a bull moose!"

What do you do with a person like that? To many, he became a folk hero. Anyone who can take a bullet and keep giving a speech is superhuman—and unusually wired. Finally, they rushed him to the hospital in Chicago where Jane Addams, founder of Hull House and of social work in modern America, and a socialist in her politics, came and sat by TR's bedside, and tried to help him recover. She was one of the strongest supporters of his Bull Moose Party campaign in 1912, which shows how far he had moved to the left of the political spectrum by that time.

TR'S MARRIAGE

BOSTON Let's talk a minute about his marriage. Senator Alan Simpson once said, "Show me a great man, and I'll show you a wife walking a few steps behind him who's rolling her eyes." Theodore Roosevelt's wife Edith appears to have been the only person who managed to tamp down her husband's exuberance. Using Alan Simpson's line, I'm guessing that her husband's antics caused Edith to roll her eyes a great deal.

Beyond that, what exactly did she do to tame the lion that no one else could tame?

BRINKLEY I'm not convinced he ever got tamed. She had the advantage of having a husband who firmly believed in the institution of marriage, which is always helpful when you're married; and he also strongly believed that the father had a big role to play in raising the children. His making that total commitment to their marriage and family made her rather happy, but then he would disappear for long periods of time. When he stepped down from the presidency in March of 1909, he declared "I'm going to Africa for a year." Well, he didn't take his wife on that trip. He just said, "Bye, Honey. See you in a year." That would be hard on any marriage, and he never checked to see what she thought about his prolonged departures. He continued to be irascible and irrepressible, so I don't think she ever truly calmed the beast.

TR'S STATURE AMONG HIS PRESIDENTIAL PEERS

BOSTON In this interview, we've obviously given plenty of attention to Roosevelt's emotional and psychological make-up. The reason for doing that is an attempt to grasp what made him tick because he's such a major figure in American history, regarded by our leading historians and scholars as a summa cum laude president. In every presidential ranking pole of the last sevnty-five years, he's always in the top five, and is well-deserving of his place on Mount Rushmore.

Doug, we may have had a couple of more successful presidents than Theodore Roosevelt, but have we ever had a more dominating president?

BRINKLEY Theodore Roosevelt created the modern presidency by using executive power in a new way that led America into the new century. He turned the office of president from being a lonely lighthouse into a citadel of direct action. When it comes to ranking the presidents, George Washington is in a league of his own for being the first, so he always gets ranked near the top, as does Lincoln for being the president who brought us through the crucible of the Civil War—so they are always ranked number one and two. Franklin Roosevelt usually gets ranked number three because he won four political elections and battled through the Great Depression and World War II. So those are the big three.

Theodore Roosevelt never makes the top three, but he's in the same league with Thomas Jefferson, and usually comes in at either number four or five. To be ranked that high while being president from 1901 to 1909 when America was not at war is simply amazing. With all his hawkishness and "manliness" and extreme strenuous life and big power bluster, he kept the United States at peace during his presidency and

actually won the Nobel Peace Prize for mediating an end to the war between Russia and Japan.

He defined the American centrist. By not being part of either the right or left paradigms, and by not being about politics first and foremost, he was able to look at what made sense for the whole country to go forward. For anyone who considers himself an independent-minded voter, he is the number one president. For those who want a political leader who can deal with circumstances from a pragmatic perspective, and who's a visionary, and who aspires to do what's right without worrying about the political consequences, TR shines mightily.

TR'S SUCCESSES AS PRESIDENT

BOSTON He famously made Pelican Island in Florida a federal bird reservation by saying "I declare it!" to be a federal bird reservation. Was there anything he declared as president that didn't come to pass?

BRINKLEY He tried in some ways to stamp out racial segregation as an opponent of Jim Crow laws in the South, and obviously didn't succeed in that. Most frustrating for him though was that by not staying on for an additional term, he never got into position to start putting his progressive agenda into effect. He believed in every child's getting a good public education. He believed science should be taught in all the schools. He believed that all children should be properly fed and never go hungry. He believed in universal healthcare. These progressive ideas began fermenting in his mind during his presidency from 1901 to 1909. When he ran for president in 1912, he thought he could take one step further and bring all of them to fruition, but of course, he didn't win that election—Woodrow Wilson won—and that was the beginning of the end of Theodore Roosevelt's life.

BOSTON How much of his success as president can be attributed to the fact that the press adored him?

BRINKLEY There was no president who got along with the press better than Theodore Roosevelt. That was partly because he was a writer. When TR was with fellow journalists and writers, he knew what they did and how they went about constructing sentences. He was a voracious reader. He read all the newspapers and magazines of his day, and had a photographic memory, such that whenever he'd see a reporter, TR would tell him what a great piece he had written. He'd then proceed to talk about specific points in the piece to prove he really had read it, which was very flattering to the writers to know that the president had actually read the editorial under their byline.

Another reason for TR's enjoying great relations with the press was because he was unafraid of any reporter because he never told a lie and strongly believed in whatever he said. He would hop on a train, greet a reporter, say, "Let's talk!", "Ask away!", and "What do you think?"; and then he'd answer every question. He would also call up members of the press and invite them to follow him on a trip or to an event.

He was also a great lover of political cartoons. Today, there are YouTube videos and different types of blogging on the Internet, but in the early twentieth century, the cartoon was king in the sense of providing satire. TR would invite leading political cartoonists like Clifford Berryman and Ding Darling to different events at the White House, and give them seats at state dinners, and treat them as if they were major American celebrities. Such generosity of spirit surely softened their attitudes toward him.

He also recognized that to move public policy, a book critical of an industry could be helpful. To go after the meat packing industry, he read and then promoted Upton Sinclair's *The Jungle*. He did the same with Ida Tarbell's book that detailed the problems of Standard Oil as a trust.

BOSTON With his extreme ferocity in all aspects of his life, how do you explain his great success in international diplomacy?

BRINKLEY It came about because he knew the world so well. He had a mind like a map. He knew every country and their leader. He spoke foreign languages. He believed America should have a global power presence, though he wasn't a knee jerk person about pursuing war. He wanted more world order and he accomplished that by negotiating formidably to end the war between Russia and Japan.

People recognized that TR was someone who was not only wildly popular in the United States, but also around the globe. In Europe, Theodore Roosevelt was honored like Benjamin Franklin had been in his era—a quirky, quintessential American figure. He had the bully pulpit of the American presidency, and with the full power of America behind him, he'd go to countries and say, "Let's talk. Let's solve this problem."

Douglas Brinkley

Part of his diplomatic perspective, however, was that if the international situation interfered with his objective for the United States, then he would throw the rulebooks out. He wanted the Panama Canal built so he supported the idea of creating the Republic of Panama, thereby stripping the land away from Colombia, and letting Panama declare itself as its own country. Then he supported the American take-over of a zone in the middle of Panama where the canal was ultimately located. In a modern day context, the United Nations would have frowned on this, but TR was willing to jeopardize international relations in order to advance America's interest.

"SPEAK SOFTLY AND CARRY A BIG STICK"

BOSTON Theodore Roosevelt's ultimate statement about successful diplomacy appears to be as true today as when he said it—the statement being: "Speak softly and carry a big stick." Obviously, one of the big criticisms of the Obama administration has been his refusal to carry and use a big stick, and instead, he prefers to watch from the sidelines while the world disintegrates. What is your thought as a historian, and bring it into today, whether big stick diplomacy is the most successful way to engage in international affairs?

BRINKLEY "Speak softly and carry a big stick" has become the slogan that supports America's decision to put a big part of our tax dollars into the military every year. Since World War II, we have kept a huge standing navy, army, air force—based on the belief that our military power will serve as a deterrent to countries' misbehaving, because it will make them fearful of us.

The problem President Obama had was when he drew a red line in Syria and then didn't enforce his statement after the red line was crossed. That was un-Theodore Roosevelt-like. If Theodore Roosevelt drew a red line and anyone crossed it, that was

it. There would be consequences. We were headed to war. He believed that if people around the world knew our position and knew of our military strength, then they wouldn't cross the red line because they knew the big stick would be coming after them. The slogan grew out of Theodore Roosevelt's obsession about the US Navy. Not only was he the Assistant Secretary of the Navy, but he also wrote the definitive history of *The Naval War of 1812,* and was a Naval historian, and believer in Alfred Thayer Mahan's principles of sea power.

BOSTON And in the days before airplanes and atomic bombs, the US Navy was America's big stick.

BRINKLEY It was our big stick and he was the one who built it. Nobody is more beloved in today's US Navy world than Theodore Roosevelt because he believed that for America to have the strongest military presence in the world, we had to have the world's strongest navy. He believed not only that naval power was the guiding power in global diplomacy, but also that it put the Americans on top of the Darwinian jungle.

Keep in mind, TR thought that there were always key species in the food chain. He was fascinated by grizzly bears out West and how they were the top of the food chain in the wilderness. He wanted the American military to be the grizzlies of the world—number one at all costs and recognized as such.

This nationalism of Theodore Roosevelt, combined with his belief in American exceptionalism, provided the side of him which conservatives admire, while his progressivism on social issues like universal healthcare makes him liked by the left. Somehow, he's revered by all Americans because of his different sides. He's not an easy person to pigeonhole because he favored both progressive and conservative traditions.

TR'S FINAL TEN YEARS IN DECLINE

BOSTON Doug, let's conclude our conversation by talking about the last ten years of Roosevelt's life—between the time he left the White House and the time he died. During that final decade, essentially nothing went right. He had political failures; he had one son killed and another badly injured in World War II, and another ended up committing suicide; the press turned on him; his body broke down; the books he wrote were panned; his friendships ended; he took an almost suicidal trip down the "River of Doubt" Amazon, and so you say he lived the last ten years in "a state of anti-climax" and suffered from "severe power deprivation."

What's the moral of his story about the relationship between having an incredible second act—his wildly successful presidency—and an incredibly unsuccessful post-presidency third act, when his train totally fell off the track?

BRINKLEY The train fell off the track because of sheer physical exhaustion from burning the candle at both ends. He wanted us to enter World War I long before most others did. In fact, when we had success and ultimate victory in the war after Woodrow Wilson belatedly entered it, TR felt redeemed. Yet, as you mentioned, he lost a son in the war which brought on massive grief. During his exploration of the Amazon, he picked up a malarial disease and told his whole group to leave him there to die—leaning up against a tree by the Amazon. They refused his request, and when he came home, he never again was truly healthy and never could get his energy level back up to what it had been.

The Bull Moose Party of 1912 looks better in history because even though TR lost that election, it proved to be the most successful third party effort in American history. Much of the Bull Moose Party's platform later became adopted by his cousin, Franklin Roosevelt. Young Bull Moosers

like Harold Ickes became FDR's Secretary of the Interior and Henry Stimson became his Secretary of War. These were people who had supported TR in 1912—and they later found a home in the New Deal of the 1930s and 1940s.

TR'S LEGACY

BOSTON I hope many of you in this class got to see Ken Burns' series on PBS last year, *The Roosevelts*. A big theme, developed throughout the series was the continuation of progressive policies, which were proposed by Theodore Roosevelt and were ultimately fulfilled by his cousin, Franklin Roosevelt.

For your epigraph, Doug, you quote Annie Dillard in her book *Holy the Firm*, where she said, "And learn power, however sweet they call you, learn power, the smash of the holy once more and signed by its name. Be victim to its abruptness and seizures, events intercalated swellings of heart. You'll climb trees, you won't be able to sleep or need to for the joy of it."

Doug, power does make people joyful, but what does it do to them in the end? Is that the story of Theodore Roosevelt?

BRINKLEY Regardless of what happened during his final decade, I think the story of Theodore Roosevelt is a triumphant one. Even though his was not a rags-to-riches story, it was a from-sickly-to-strength tale, and also a belief in the mind of America— the independent minded people, the rugged individual, the person who bucks the system, and is able to define his era by being brave and taking chances. Theodore Roosevelt did all that.

In addition, his triumph came because he was someone who believed in the power of education—that those who aspire to achieve have got to read, do homework, do math and fully understand situations.

He got honored. He was beloved. Every year, there's a bestselling book that comes out on Theodore Roosevelt. I once talked to President Obama's Secretary of the

Interior, Ken Salazar. He showed me a note he received from former Secretary of the Interior Stewart Udall. The note said, "Here's what you need to do to be a successful Secretary of the Interior. First and foremost: Whenever you go, always say Theodore Roosevelt's name as much as possible. It always pleases both the right and the left. If possible, throw a Theodore Roosevelt quote into every speech." Using Abraham Lincoln in a speech also always works as a way of pleasing people of both parties, but there are very few people today whose legacy and thoughts are truly universally admired.

Theodore Roosevelt, in the end, captured the imagination of the American people. That was what he always wanted to do—to be not only a great American president like Lincoln, but also to be a great explorer in the Lewis and Clark tradition—and he was able to accomplish both in his life.

BOSTON We're out of time. You've been a wonderful audience. Thanks so much, Doug.

SCOTT BERG is on the short list of America's leading biographers, and has a Pulitzer Prize to prove it. In 2013, he released the complete cradle-to-grave history of his lifelong hero, Woodrow Wilson. He came through Dallas October 4, 2013, on his national tour when *Wilson* (Putnam 2013) was a *New York Times* bestseller. My interview of Scott took place at the Rosewood Crescent Hotel ballroom at a luncheon sponsored by the World Affairs Council of Dallas/Fort Worth.

"The world in which we live today is almost entirely of Woodrow Wilson's making—whether it's our foreign policy, economic policy, or labor policy." – SCOTT BERG

CHAPTER 12

A. SCOTT BERG

ON

Woodrow Wilson

WHAT DREW BERG TO WOODROW WILSON

BOSTON Scott, your new biography *Wilson* shows the power of books. Forty-eight years ago, when you were fifteen years old, your mother gave you the best-selling book, *When the Cheering Stopped.* You've said in your new book's introduction that you devoured it, and fell in love with Woodrow Wilson. Now, almost a half century later, you've spent thirteen years in the preparation of your new book.

What is it about Woodrow Wilson that's driven your connection with him for almost a half century?

BERG When I was fifteen, after I read *When the Cheering Stopped,* I had on my bedroom wall

Courtesy of Penguin Random House LLC

four portraits—F. Scott Fitzgerald, Adlai Stevenson, Woodrow Wilson, and Don Quixote. I think you can see the thru-line. They were all quixotic figures, and tragic idealists. At fifteen, I was deeply into tragedy and idealism. Wilson just stuck with me and I've been reading about him ever since. I've read hundreds of books about him. In reading them, I kept thinking no book has fully captured the (i) personal side of this man and really developed his character that led to his presidency, and (ii) how his life affects the world we live in to this day.

BERG'S CONTEMPORIZING WILSON

BOSTON Wilson became our twenty-eighth president in 1913, and your book references many of his characteristics that match up with our president in 2013—a president elected on a meteoric rise primarily due to his gift for oratory; a president who sought to impose serious regulations on private enterprise and attempted to redistribute wealth; a polarizing president who's in gridlocked conflict with Congress, and has tried to turn Congress around by speaking to the public; and a president whose view of American foreign policy is idealistic, but he lacks the wherewithal to build consensus.

Is that part of the biographer's job—to contemporize your subjects by writing about historical figures from a different time in a way that connects them with today's historical figures?

BERG First, let me ask, do you think we have gridlock today? All right, wait till you read about how things were in 1913. Now that was gridlock!

My answer to your question is yes and no. I don't consciously think about contemporizing. However, I do think it's a nice layer to have within the book and it really did help me a great deal to have those similarities you just mentioned between President Obama and President Wilson. There are some very curious parallels between them.

What I try to do is not draw a big circle around things, but in writing about Wilson, I often used contemporary language so that the reader will get the reference.

It's a little like when I was writing my Lindbergh biography. Of course, the centerpiece of Lindbergh's life was the famous kidnapping of his child, which in his era was called "the crime of the century." As I was writing the Lindbergh book, the O.J. Simpson trial was going on at the same time, and everyone was calling that case "the trial of the century." So I wrote up the Lindbergh trial almost as though I were writing about the O.J. trial, talking about the mountain of evidence that was piling up against him and so forth—using the same lingo—just so people would realize, among other things, that things don't change much.

The parallels between contemporary society and Wilson's are so, so close. I think it makes a further point in the case of a president such as Wilson. One of the main themes of my book is that the world in which we live today is almost entirely of Woodrow Wilson's making, whether it's our foreign policy, economic policy, or labor policy. Just about everything going on today for good or for bad, love him or hate him, is largely of Woodrow Wilson's design.

WILSON'S DEEP FAITH AND CHRIST COMPLEX

BOSTON One of the aspects of your book that I liked best was the fact that you titled every chapter with one word that has a Biblical connection—Eden, Sinai, Advent, Reformation, Damascus. Then you started every chapter with a Scripture verse.

Did you Biblicize your book to drive home the point that Wilson, the son and grandson of a Presbyterian minister, was a "Christian soldier," who has been accused by the likes of Sigmund Freud and Clemenceau of having a Christ complex?

BERG Yes is the answer to that question. It occurred to me as I was researching the book, but I believe Wilson was the most deeply religious man we've ever had in the White House (although I don't know much about John Tyler, so I might be wrong in making this statement). He was deeply spiritual. As you said, he was the son and grandson of Presbyterian ministers; and if you shake the family trees of the Woodrows and the Wilsons, another twelve ministers would fall from the branches. So that was a big part of his life.

This was a man who got on his knees and prayed twice a day, a man who said grace before every meal, went to church every Sunday, read Scripture every night, and grew up really admiring his father. He went to church not just on Sundays but during the week when his father would practice his sermons. To be a little boy and sit in the churches, in Columbia, South Carolina, or Augusta, Georgia, (where his father preached and which are still standing), it's easy to recognize that Wilson grew up in a world of small cathedrals. As I walked into those churches for the first time, and actually sat in the pew that Woodrow Wilson sat in as a child, and imagined him looking up and hearing his father's booming voice (which was nothing less than the voice of God), and recognizing that Wilson did develop something of a Christ complex, using the biblical terms and Scriptures at the beginning of each chapter made sense.

I wanted to suggest to the reader not just his religiosity but through my research I knew certain passages of the Bible Wilson was reading at certain times in his life, and those began to inform me. Then I said to myself, "Gee, when he first came to Washington with very little experience in our federal government, he really had his baptism here." So "Baptism" became the title of the chapter there. Then at the end, when he fell into the public's disfavor, and then bounced back, I thought, "It's like getting resurrected," so "Resurrection" became the title of that final chapter. Suddenly, I thought, "I can do seventeen of these!" That's easy.

WILSON'S PERSONALITY DEFICITS

BOSTON Your epigraph is two stanzas from Wordsworth's poem, "Character of the Happy Warrior." It concisely states the theme for the 743 page book, yet some of Wilson's traits you develop in the book are quite unflattering: that he was a good hater, always looking for someone to hate; that he was a "genteel racist" who did virtually nothing to advance civil rights; that on at least three occasions he quickly and totally severed long-time friendships over disagreements; and that he was an enemy of compromise—"God save us from compromise."

How do Wilson's negative traits line up with "the Happy Warrior?"

BERG He was a complicated guy. Wilson would be the first to tell you that people are not consistent and he really didn't like labels, political or otherwise. Again, his religiosity kicks in here. I'm not going to say he felt that God spoke to him, but he definitely felt he was on a mission. He was so directed in whatever his mission was—over a lifetime or over a specific year—that if anybody or anything got in his way, he either just plowed right through them or passed them aside.

So in that regard, this man who really did believe "God is love," really did become a very good hater. If you crossed him (as his two or three of his closest friends in the world did), he would literally just draw the curtain down.

For years, his closest professional associate was a Texan, Colonel House. Wilson used to say, "Colonel House, he's my second personality, he's my other self." Then, Colonel House went with Wilson to Paris in connection with negotiating the Treaty at Versailles, which ended World War I. For that, Wilson went to Paris for six months. The president of the United States left the country for a half a year! These days, we get upset if a president even takes two days off in Martha's Vineyard. Here was Wilson drawing up the treaty to end World War I.

He came home for three weeks because Congress was closing down for the year and he had to be there for that. During that period, he left his man Colonel House in charge of things at Versailles.

When Wilson returned to France, he learned that Colonel House, (who before Wilson went to the US had been really in the shadows), suddenly liked the limelight. He was suddenly giving press conferences and being photographed. His son-in-law was there talking about how "Woodrow doesn't really do much, but my father-in-law is really doing everything." Wilson then learned House had actually been selling the country down the river a little, and going back on some of the things Wilson had already negotiated.

From that point on, they still had another couple of months to go where they were together at Versailles, but during that time, Wilson really began to lower the curtain on his friendship with House. By the time Wilson left Paris in June of 1919, all of Paris turned out to say goodbye to this great savior. And there was Colonel House with him on the platform. Wilson shook House's hand, said goodbye, never saw him again, and never spoke to him again. The man no

longer existed from Wilson's standpoint. It was as simple as that. And he did that with two or three other of his friends.

MOST IMPORTANT ASPECT OF WILSON'S PERSONALITY

BOSTON I am sure you were delighted to learn that Leonardo DiCaprio bought the film rights to your book, and plans to play Woodrow Wilson in the movie, hoping to duplicate the success of the movie *Lincoln*.

If Leonardo DiCaprio was sitting here in this ballroom, what would you tell him is the most important, or maybe the two most important characteristics in Wilson's personality that he needs to develop if he is going to play him straight, recognizing the complexity of his personality?

BERG The first thing I would say to Mr. DiCaprio is "Thank you!" That's mostly because for years a lot of people have come up to me and said, "Woodrow Wilson, he's so sexless!" Now I just say, "Leonardo DiCaprio."

Leonardo DiCaprio actually has the two most important qualities as an actor that Woodrow Wilson's character demands. First of all, he's got brains. He sells great intelligence. He can really do that. He's one of the few actors who can read complicated dialogue and make it sound as though he knows what he's saying.

The other thing is Leonardo DiCaprio sells great heart. He has a great inner core of romance to him. And most photographs of Wilson aside, that is actually who he was. He was a deeply romantic figure as evidenced by the thousands of passionate love letters he wrote to each of his two wives. He had two separate wives at the same time, I should add. What an interesting movie that would be! But his first wife did die in the White House and then he courted and married the second Mrs. Wilson. His letters to them are the most romantic love letters I've ever read—and I've read the Brownings', and the Adamses', and they're

Rebecca of Sunnybrook Farm next to Wilson's letters.

So I would say to Leonardo Dicaprio, "Don't be afraid to be as intelligent as you can." That was another characteristic of Wilson. He was the most educated president we ever had. He's our only PhD president. He never talked down to the American people. He never dumbed down his language. He never simplified his thoughts. That was one of his secrets to success because everybody felt uplifted by Woodrow Wilson. I would also say to Leonardo DiCaprio, "Don't downplay the heart. Don't downplay the romance." Wilson was a deeply emotional man.

WILSON'S MOST DRAMATIC TIME

BOSTON Now *Lincoln*, the film, dealt with only four months of Lincoln's life. If you were the director, and you decided the Wilson film should only be devoted to four months of his life, which four months would you pick?

BERG Well, I am a co-producer.

BOSTON Good!

BERG What we've been talking about and what I'm going to say is a tad premature because we're still in the process of selecting a screenwriter. We're talking to a number of people and we're waiting to hear their reactions to the overall material. If a writer came in and said, "I'd love to do this part or that part," we'd be happy to hear it and possibly do it.

My gut reaction is that the single most dramatic four to six months of his life would start with Wilson's going to Paris right after the war in December of 1918. That's the opening of my book actually. What I tried to establish especially for modern readers is that this was not just a great man making a trip abroad. At that moment, Wilson was the savior of the world. There

had never been such a march of triumph. There had never been such a greeting. There had never been so much adulation heaped on a single human being as what befell Woodrow Wilson when he landed in Paris. It was just extraordinary. Two million people turned out in the city with a population of only one million people. That was just for openers. And the reaction everywhere, in fact, was not surpassed until Charles Lindbergh flew the Atlantic.

I think that would be a splashy opening. From there, it would be good to see the negotiations that went on in Paris. Then came the real trauma, the real tragedy of Wilson's life—coming back to America with this treaty which he had been negotiating for six months. In it, was incorporated much of Wilson's Fourteen Points, the fourteenth of which was the most quixotic, a League of Nations. All of you know the president can draft and negotiate treaties, but he can't ratify them. Only the US Senate can do that, and Wilson came back to an increasingly hostile Republican Senate who was simply against anything Wilson brought back. If you can imagine a Republican Congress saying to a Democratic president, "We don't care what you've got, we're against it." And that's what Woodrow Wilson found.

Then he embarked on what I consider the most dramatic moment of his life—maybe it's one of the greatest dramas in American history—which was Woodrow Wilson's realizing that the Senate wasn't going to ratify the treaty, so he decided to take it to the people. Wilson went on a twenty-nine city tour around the country in very poor health, sometimes giving five speeches a day during a very hot summer, traveling in unairconditioned train cars that were more like ovens. He traveled around as his health declined with each day, with each speech. Then finally he collapsed, they rushed him home, and three days later he had a stroke, which they didn't tell the country about.

BOSTON I didn't realize until I read your book that there was no radio then; so

Wilson couldn't talk to the people unless he traveled around the country.

BERG That's true.

BOSTON And for these huge crowds, for the most part, there were no microphones.

BERG That's exactly right. I even make a statement in the book that if Wilson's cross-country tour had happened one or two years later, radio would have been hooked up over most of the country by then. Imagine what it would have been like if Woodrow Wilson could have just sat by the fireside and had a chat. But he couldn't. He had to go out there and not talk into a microphone, but talk to, in some cases, twenty thousand people who would show up to hear his speeches.

WILSON'S SURPRISING SUCCESS AS COMMANDER-IN-CHIEF

BOSTON Wilson's handling of the United States' intervention in World War I was masterful in that he entered the war only as a last resort after he exhausted all of his other options; he then got the country up to speed militarily in record time; he then pressed the Allied cause with full force; and he then obtained a quick German surrender once America intervened.

How did a historian and an academic like Woodrow Wilson figure out how to direct successful international war tactics as commander-in-chief with essentially no prior military background?

BERG Well, we've had dummies do that, too. I wouldn't hold his being smart against him. That said, Woodrow Wilson was a great historian. In fact, he was one of America's leading historians at that point. He was not only the only president who had a PhD, but the only real academician we've had that went on to the White House. He had written a biography of George Washington and

a five volume history of the United States. So he knew whereof he spoke, and he clearly had a lot of natural political instincts.

He was not a military historian per se, but he would say that he served as commander-in-chief using his morality more than anything else. He did consider himself a Christian soldier, and a lot of that really kicked in for him.

He made a couple of really wise decisions in leading this country into war. The first was his going to the military men, and telling them, "Fight the war." He hired General Pershing to run the war and he never second-guessed Pershing. Basically he said, "You know more about this than I do. Now do it! But be sure you win it," and Pershing did.

The second thing, (and this was a really smart Wilsonian idea), in sending our two million soldier army over there, he made it clear from the start that we were not an Allied country. We were sending what was called the American Expeditionary Force, and we were not sending these two million men over to replace all the empty uniforms of French and British soldiers who had been killed. We were going to fight alongside the French and the British, but separately. That was a smart thing to do because after four years of exhaustion on the parts of the European countries, along came these freshly trained, freshly uniformed eighteen-year-old American boys, and they proceeded to just mop up Europe.

WILSON'S DESIRE TO END ALL WARS

BOSTON When the war ended, we've talked about the six month negotiation in Paris. When it was over, Wilson received the Nobel Peace Prize in 1920 because his goal was that he wanted World War I to be "the war that ended all wars."

My question is, does that reflect Wilson's having glaring naivete about the nature of man to think that we're ever going to have a war that ends all future wars?

BERG When I was fifteen, I had four pictures on the wall. There are some people known as tragic idealists. I don't know. I hate to agree with what you just said.

BOSTON But you can.

BERG I can, but just on principle I don't want to. Naiveté? I'm not sure. I would call it more faith in mankind instead of naiveté. I think that's what Wilson felt. Wilson really felt his League of Nations wasn't a pipe dream, and that it was really practical. He drafted a really practical Constitution for this organization. He had a very clear understanding of how it could and should work. And he often said, "If we had had this League of Nations in place in the summer of 1914, when not even the leader of a country but a mere prince was assassinated, and all the countries of Europe had just come to a table and talked it through instead of sabre-rattling, we probably could have avoided World War I." That was his firm belief and nothing could shake that. He did believe in mankind at the end of the day, crazy though that might be.

EDITH WILSON AS AMERICA'S FIRST FEMALE PRESIDENT

BOSTON You go into detail that after he sustained the paralyzing stroke after the nationwide tour, there was a conspiracy of misinformation orchestrated by his wife Edith, his doctor Cory Grayson, and his secretary Joe Tumulty. We now face the prospect of Hillary Clinton seeking to be elected our first woman president in 2016.

During the last seventeen months of the Wilson presidency, is it safe to say Edith Wilson acted as our first woman president?

BERG Yes, I think it is safe to say that. It was Mrs. Wilson and a handful of doctors who basically conspired to keep the president's stroke from the world. I hasten to add a few things. Wilson did not lose his powers of speech or thought. He could still reason, but he was paralyzed completely on his left side. He developed (as we realize now), something that accompanies strokes very often, and that is great emotional swings—real major mood swings—and often they produce strange lapses in judgment.

During this period, the doctors came to Mrs. Wilson and said "Mrs. Wilson, your husband can endure no stress. Any stress could be fatal." And she replied, "That's what being president is—stress. That's all you do all day is deal with stress." One of the doctors then said, "I know you're very close," and they were. They were one of the closest presidential couples we've ever had. Even before the stroke occurred, Mrs. Wilson began accompanying the president when he visited Cabinet members. She was in on every memorandum. It was as though he innately had known of the need to train her. The doctors said, "You seem to know everything that's going on. Why not let everything come through you? And you decide what the president will even consider."

She would say she was only a steward, that she never made a decision her husband didn't make. That being said, for seventeen months, nobody saw the president of the United States unless they passed first through the second Mrs. Wilson. No document, nothing requiring a signature, no memorandum, no policy, no note went to the president of the United States without Mrs. Wilson first vetting it and then deciding if he should see it. And if he was going to see it, she would tell him what the arguments were, rather than suggesting what the answer should be.

One could say the wheels of the executive branch day-to-day were rolling because Mrs. Wilson was out there pushing them. So yes, she acted as president to a degree. It depends on what you define the president of the United States is, but she was definitely the person in charge of the White House for seventeen months. There's no question about that.

A. Scott Berg

CONDUCT OF WILSON'S DOCTOR AFTER THE STROKE

BOSTON With this national awareness that there was something keeping President Wilson out of the limelight, obviously one of the main sources of information about him to the Cabinet, the Congress, and the public, was his doctor, Dr. Grayson, who was in serious ethical limbo —because on the one hand, his patient and his patient's wife, didn't want the public to know what was going on. But on the other hand, the doctor was an American citizen.

Didn't he have a duty to the American public to provide them with an awareness of what condition the president was in? From your perspective, with these conflicting duties, if you were Dr. Grayson, which would be more important—the duty to the patient or the duty to the public?

BERG In Dr. Grayson's case, that was an easy choice. His duty was to his patient. We now have the Twenty-fifth Amendment to the Constitution which very specifically defines presidential disability. There's even a clause in the Amendment that says if a

certain number of Cabinet members decide that the president is incapacitated, he will be replaced by the vice president.

Now this raises a whole other question, which is why didn't they just call on the vice president? The problem here was the vice president, who in this case was a rather charming, lovable buffoon. I hope there are no relatives here of Thomas R. Marshall of Indiana, who became vice president of the United States and loved being vice president. In fact, and I never saw it, but I was told by somebody who knew him, that he had a business card that read, "Thomas R. Marshall, Vice President of the United States and Toastmaster." He loved nothing more than making toasts, and the rumor yet again is, and I got this from Teddy Roosevelt's daughter Alice Longworth (so, I know it's probably not true), but she claimed that in Washington, the word was that when they finally realized they had to at least break the news to the vice president, they said, "Vice President Marshall, the president has suffered a stroke," and Marshall immediately fainted. So this was not a man who really wanted to serve as president of the United States.

This raises to me, perhaps the most important unraised question in the book and in the life which is: "Who were Mrs. Wilson and a doctor to decide that?" Because who knows about Thomas R. Marshall? Everything they said about Marshall, they said about Harry Truman in 1945. Who is to say that Thomas R. Marshall couldn't suddenly become a Harry Truman once the light was on him? Who knows, and that's a decision Mrs. Wilson refused to consider.

WILSON'S LEGACY IN THE TWENTY-FIRST CENTURY

BOSTON You close your book with an absolutely dazzling paragraph to the effect that in 2013, you believe the shadow of Woodrow Wilson in Washington, DC is lengthening. How so?

BERG I do believe that. I wrote that paragraph a while ago. Now, as I read the newspaper every day, I underscore that Wilson's shadow is lengthening. Where to begin? Certainly our foreign policy to this day entirely goes back to one sentence in one speech Woodrow Wilson gave in April of 1917, when he called a joint session of Congress, and asked for a declaration of war against Germany. In the middle of that speech he said, (famously now), "The world must be made safe for democracy."

Now whether you like it or not, whether you agree with it or not, it is with us today, like when President Obama a few weeks ago was talking about Syria and raised the question, "Is America the policeman of the world?" On the other hand, can we sit and watch a dictator gas and kill a thousand of his people, children included? Can the United States look the other way? Is there not some moral component to foreign policy for this country?

Again, whatever your answer is, Wilson was the one who raised those questions. Therefore, every incursion we have had, whether it was Haiti and Mexico in Wilson's day, and later Haiti in Roosevelt's day, or whether it's Vietnam or Iraq or Afghanistan, all that goes directly back to April 1917 with Woodrow Wilson when he pledged the commitment for America to play a role in causing the world to be safe for democracy.

Our economic policy to this day is really built on the foundation of the Federal Reserve System which was something Woodrow Wilson presented in his first year in office. He said the Fed was essential to the American economy.

He also had a huge impact on labor law—the eight hour work day, and workman's compensation. He put the first Jew on the Supreme Court; which was really the first shattering of glass ceilings in this country. So I say now more than ever yes, the Wilson shadow is still lengthening.

BERG Thank you.

AMITY SHLAES is America's leading authority on Calvin Coolidge, and serves as the Chair of the Calvin Coolidge Presidential Foundation. For her historical writing, she has won the Hayek Prize and twice she's been a finalist for the Loeb Prize in commentary. On October 7, 2015, I interviewed Amity at The King's College in New York City where she serves as the school's Presidential Scholar. We discussed her 2013 *New York Times* bestseller, *Coolidge* (Harper 2013).

"He always underpromised and overdelivered, and that's a rare combination in a politician. Whenever Coolidge told people, 'I might do' something, he then proceeded to do one-and-a-half of whatever they'd requested. It took incredible personal discipline to accomplish that, but it was definitely his defining trait in the way he went about performing his political business." **– AMITY SHLAES**

CHAPTER 13

AMITY SHLAES

ON

Calvin Coolidge

COOLIDGE'S FAMILY HISTORY OF THRIFT

BOSTON Amity, the title of the introduction to your *New York Times* best-selling biography of Coolidge is "The Curse," and your opening sentence is "Debt takes its toll." Then you proceed to tell the story of Calvin Coolidge's great uncle who went to jail because he failed to pay a debt of $24.23 that he owed a neighbor.

Did his grandnephew Calvin know about this incident involving his great uncle, such that it became a factor that led him to become "thrifty to the point of harshness" and obsessed with reducing or eliminating debt throughout his life, particularly when he served as America's thirtieth president?

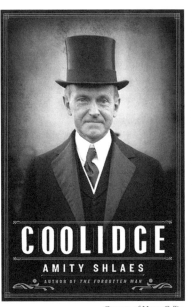

Courtesy of HarperCollins

SHLAES We don't know if Coolidge knew the details of what happened to his great uncle Oliver. But we do know Coolidge was raised in the shadow of debt. He did know there was a division in his family made up of the virtuous Coolidges and the less virtuous Coolidges. The less virtuous side of the family were the ones who weren't able to make it financially because they didn't save. Most were farmers, which meant they had to be thrifty and save to survive. Calvin had what we would in modern terms call a high level of consciousness about the need to save money and avoid debt.

Part of the family's history included this important story about Oliver Coolidge. Oliver went to prison over a small debt, when he was over sixty years old. He didn't die in prison, and when he got out, he went to the Midwest, where it was easier to make a living as a farmer. It's a great American story: pursue a new life at a late age in hopes of finding something better on the forgiving plains of the Midwest. John Deere, also of Vermont, did the same.

COOLIDGE'S PLACE IN HISTORY AS AN ECONOMIC HERO

BOSTON Along those lines, by focusing on Calvin Coolidge's success in elevating the economy by cutting taxes and at eliminating deficits during his presidency, you've basically done for Calvin Coolidge what David McCullough has done for John Adams and Harry Truman—that is, taken a president who was truly unappreciated from a historical standpoint and turned him into a hero. President Coolidge cut taxes and spending, the federal deficit narrowed, the economy grew, and the size of the federal government shrunk.

With all that success during his presidency, you describe Coolidge as an economic hero, a form of heroism that's subtle and hard to appreciate. Has America ever had a greater economic hero than Calvin Coolidge?

SHLAES Well, Coolidge was certainly one of the greatest heroes, and perhaps the greatest when it came to a challenge that seems impossible today: shrinking government. Before Coolidge, there had been great appreciation for Grover Cleveland's restraint and his willingness to pull back the forces of big government spending in Washington. Until Cleveland's presidency, excessive pork had been a common feature in federal spending. Cleveland got elected in part because he called for restraint in how federal tax dollars got spent, and he succeeded in reducing the amount of pork.

Besides Coolidge and Cleveland, other presidents regarded as economic heroes are Eisenhower, Reagan, and it might surprise you—John F. Kennedy. Today, we're satisfied with any amount of growth—even small growth—and we only use the word "recession" when there are two consecutive periods of the economy's shrinking with negative growth. Kennedy proclaimed that small growth was insufficient. Prior to his assassination, JFK planned to implement tax cuts. Lyndon Johnson succeeded in pushing through those cuts after Kennedy's death. This movement started by Kennedy became an act of heroism because the new rates caused the economy to grow faster after the cuts were made.

BOSTON From my perspective, regardless of the economic success of those other presidents, your book certainly persuaded me that during his presidency, Coolidge was our greatest economic hero. Do you put him at the top of the mountain or is he just part of the group at the top?

SHLAES For achieving economic success, Coolidge is at the top of *my* mountain. We Coolidge people have a running debate with the Reagan people about who's Number One. Shortly, I'll stand up for Coolidge and Steve Hayward, the Reagan stalwart, will stand up for Reagan, and we're going to debate the topic: "Reagan v. Coolidge" as our greatest economic hero in

Manchester, New Hampshire, on October 27. It will be covered by CSPAN.

"SILENT CAL" AS A GREAT PUBLIC SPEAKER

BOSTON In reading your book, some new information I learned was that although Coolidge was known as a man of few words (his nickname was "Silent Cal"), one of his most impressive political skills was as a fine debater and public speaker. Good public speakers usually like to hear themselves talk. What caused Coolidge to be so often silent despite having the verbal firepower to be persuasive when he needed to be?

SHLAES One reason was tradition. Coolidge came from a farming family, and it was said, "Farmers don't slop over." We all know families where the father rules at the dinner table and wants the sons to be very careful about the words that come out of their mouths. There's always some kind of penalty when the children express trivial thoughts. Calvin Coolidge grew up at a dinner table like that, with a stern father presiding. Farming also has a tradition of understatement. Farmers never show off what they have. They know ostentation is not wise. Another reason for Coolidge being quiet was temperament. This boy was shy.

Finally, Coolidge recognized the political value in not speaking too much. He said that when someone talks too much, that causes people to stick around him longer. For example, if you're sitting in a meeting, and another person keeps babbling while you stay silent, eventually the talker will wind down. Coolidge realized early in his political career that the longer people stayed in a meeting with him, the more inclined he was to say "yes," to their request. In private, he actually spoke a lot. We studied the off-the-record press conferences for the Coolidge book and he chatted away in them.

BOSTON So Calvin was talkative in some private circumstances, but just not in the public?

SHLAES Yes, and he also had the capacity to be a harsh critic. That in turn had the potential to get him into trouble. He knew that if he talked too much, he might also criticize another person attempting to show how clever he was. He knew that would not serve him well. He wrote in his autobiography that early on, he realized that there wasn't much utility in criticizing an opponent in a campaign debate. Instead Coolidge dedicated himself to spending his time at the podium arguing the merits of his case. To attack an opponent was to advertise that opponent. He didn't believe in doing what today's candidates do, trying to take down the other person.

COOLIDGE AND "THE RIVER OF LIFE"

BOSTON You reference throughout the book the metaphor, "the river of life," which Coolidge first learned from his favorite professor at Amherst, and how it became important to him as he went through life. It inspired him to make sure he got himself off the bank, (where he was probably most comfortable), and get out into the middle of the stream; and then later, when the time was right, the image motivated him to move forward into actually piloting his vessel. It's a wonderful image of life, but how much did it actually drive Coolidge toward being more active in life and ultimately move into leadership positions?

SHLAES At the beginning of college, students feel brave but also terrified. The Amherst professor who gave Coolidge and his fellow students the image of that ambivalence was Charles Edward Garman. Garman, by the way, was wildly popular among the student body because he used to criticize the university president. As today, kids thought there was nothing better than to watch adults go at each other, so Garman was regarded as the mutiny professor on the ship of the school.

Garman made Coolidge feel more comfortable about being in college because he let the students talk in his seminar, and he also introduced the metaphor about the river. The professor didn't say to his students, "You have to get in the river and be the fastest swimmer, win the race, or pilot the best boat right away." Garman essentially said, "Get in the river and just hang on to your raft; and the river will carry you forward, so long as you do hang on and don't run aground. Stay in and eventually you'll make progress and feel stronger and more confident, and finally you'll reach your destination and become a man of power." It was quite comforting for a young college student to hear that he didn't have to be a success in his first year. He just had to stay at Amherst and not lose his nerve; and by senior year, he'd be cruising. The same of course held true for the period after college.

COOLIDGE'S LIFETIME COMMITMENT TO PUBLIC SERVICE

BOSTON Coolidge became licensed to practice law in July 1897, and a little more than a year later, he began his political career, first winning a seat on the Northampton, Massachusetts (population twelve thousand) City Council. Thereafter, he was in politics nonstop. After serving on the city council, he became the mayor of Northampton, then a member of the Massachusetts House, then the Massachusetts State Senate, then Lieutenant Governor of Massachusetts, then Governor of Massachusetts, then Vice President of the United States, and finally President of the United States. Where did this more than thirty years of nonstop commitment to public service and politics (from 1898-1929) come from?

SHLAES The sense of service definitely came from his family. There were some very esteemed Coolidges in Boston. Some taught at Harvard, some were diplomats, and some were related to Thomas Jefferson. Then there was the part of the Coolidge family who lived out in the country, farming in Vermont. They became leaders in their community—squires, if not aristocrats. Coolidge's father served as a bailiff, a sheriff, a tax collector, a postmaster, and finally a state legislator who went up to Montpelier, the state capital. The president's grandfather also served in the state legislature. Another very distant relative, Carlos Coolidge, served as governor of Vermont. So every Coolidge took on the responsibility of public service.

Calvin Coolidge's public service stretched him financially. His letters home to his parents for many years into his political career read like this: "Dear Father, The weather is fine. Send $10. My wife needs a coat." "Dear Father, Rain is coming. Our son needs pants." I'm simplifying only a little. And this kept up into his thirties. He wasn't ashamed of asking his father for money because he thought of himself as being like a missionary or an ambassador, who were expected to impoverish themselves for the public good—and on behalf of all Coolidges.

It was accepted within the family that indeed it was necessary for one Coolidge to subsidize the other in this sacrificial line of work. Seeking additional funds seemed to him logical—not needy or greedy. His father apparently felt the same way because he never chastised Calvin for running short. We don't have his father's letters, but we have the son's letters, and in them, it's quite clear that the father really loved his son and wanted to help him any way he could.

When Coolidge became president and had a fine salary of $75,000 a year, he was getting ready to pay his father back. Unfortunately his father died while Coolidge was in the White House, and it added to Calvin's grief that he hadn't repaid the great debt, mainly emotional but perhaps also financial, before his father died.

BOSTON So basically public service, as far as the Vermont Coolidges were concerned, was in their DNA.

SHLAES Right.

BOSTON This thirty-plus years of non-stop public service obviously cut into the amount of time Calvin Coolidge practiced law, which meant his missionary service for the public good impacted his capacity to make the amount of money that a full-time lawyer made in those days—right?

SHLAES Yes, in your book, Talmage, *Raising the Bar*, you talked about the tradeoffs a lawyer has to make when he pursues a side career—whether he goes into government or maybe becomes a writer. You profile Louis Auchincloss, a New York lawyer, who was a good trust and estate lawyer, but who at night wrote novels and ultimately became a best-selling author. You also wrote about John Grisham, who found time to write his first two novels at night while he was still practicing law every day during business hours.

It's risky for a lawyer to devote several hours a day to an outside activity. Law partners often disapprove of a partner who practices law only part-time. Coolidge wanted to maintain a law office so he wouldn't be totally dependent on politics to make a living and support his family. But he needed a caretaker partner, and he found one in a Mr. Hemenway.

Another part of the tradeoff in having a split career as a lawyer and a public official was the possibility of there being conflicts of interest. For example, Coolidge was the attorney for a beer brewery. That obviously impacted his position on prohibition. He rated prohibition impractical.

Once Coolidge became governor, his activities for his law partnership as a practicing lawyer went dormant, though he threw business to his partner whenever he could.

COOLIDGE'S STUNNING WIFE

BOSTON Let's move on from Coolidge's finances and legal career, and now talk about his marriage. For such a quiet, physically unimpressive man, Coolidge succeeded in getting a stunning dynamo of a wife in Grace Anna Goodhue. What exactly did she see in him?

SHLAES Grace Anna Goodhue wins the prize as the most beautiful First Lady, if Calvin Coolidge wins for being the best economic president ever. This beauty was also energetic. Grace had gone to the University of Vermont and received professional training as an instructor for the deaf, which was pretty rare for someone born in 1879. She was an extrovert extraordinaire and could make anyone talk, not just as a matter of socializing, but because that was necessary in her line of work.

She saw in Calvin, who didn't speak much, a man of drive and ambition. Here was a young attorney who hadn't gone to law school because his family decided they couldn't afford it. In those days, an aspiring attorney could become a lawyer by clerking with an established firm—doing what they called "reading the law." Grace saw that Calvin had successfully negotiated this tough path and passed the bar in less time than it took everyone else.

They began life as a couple in Northampton, Massachusetts—which wasn't a sleepy college town, but was called a real "city"—meaning a town thought to have a bright future. Besides his legal practice, Calvin became involved in the trolley business there, trolleys would soon become the new mode of public transportation. He was already seen as a comer in politics, so she could see that although he was quiet, he appeared to be headed toward success.

COOLIDGE'S SUCCESS IN POLITICS

BOSTON Besides his capacity to speak and debate well in public, early on in his political career, Coolidge established himself as a politician who could work both sides of the aisle and find common ground.

What exactly did Calvin Coolidge do in working with his political colleagues interpersonally that allowed him to achieve the legislative and diplomatic success he had?

SHLAES Remember there were no cars when Coolidge started out in politics, and there were no microphones. To get around in an effort to get votes, a politician had to walk all over Hampshire County, or else ride around on horseback or in a cart. That walking got exhausting, particularly later when he started running for statewide office. When automobiles came along, they rescued politicians from the fatigue of campaigning, and made pursuing statewide office easier. Regardless of his mode of transportation in connecting with his constituency, Coolidge went to see every potential voter he could and visited every church. His question to them was always, "What do you need?" If he could fulfill their need within the law, he would do it. Calvin Coolidge was extremely diligent in representing the people of Hampshire County or the state of Massachusetts, and they appreciated him.

During that era, the beginning of the century through the teens, many in Massachusetts were worried about the change in the state's ethnicity. All of a sudden, there had come into the state a surge of Irish, German, and Italian immigrants. How would they fit in? Massachusetts was then a Republican state and the Republican Party was just as neurotic as it is now. The GOP leaders worried that the new arrivals would not vote for their candidates.

Coolidge became successful in attracting the ethnic vote because of how he reached out to a wide variety of people at their churches and attempted to meet their needs—even when they worshipped in different denominations than his. There's a dissertation about the Coolidge vote written by John Blair from the University of Chicago. Blair's research shows that Coolidge got the Irish vote and the German vote. In fact, Coolidge didn't join a church in his early years. I suspect one advantage of that was that he then could not offend anyone by his denomination. He also didn't put all his money in just one bank. Coolidge deposited in multiple institutions so he could attract all the bankers as his supporters.

I mentioned earlier that Coolidge had a brewery as one of his clients. He displayed quite an open attitude toward people and their use of alcohol. At the same time, he also did extraordinary amounts of legal work for social service organizations, like the Massachusetts versions of Hull House. These attempted to help immigrants learn the skills they'd need in the United States, such as reading, sewing, and cooking on an American stove. He didn't do the social work himself, but he did pro bono legal work for the nonprofits. It was another way to display both concern and optimism about immigration.

BOSTON One of the points you make that presumably tied into his being able to connect with all these ethnic groups was his being an eloquent listener. How did that play a role in his success at relationship building?

SHLAES Coolidge always underpromised and overdelivered, and that's a rare combination in a politician. Whenever Coolidge told people, "I might do" something, he then proceeded to do one and a half of whatever they'd requested. It took incredible personal discipline to accomplish that, but that was definitively his defining trait in the way he went about performing his political business.

COOLIDGE'S COMMITMENT TO PRINCIPLES

BOSTON We also know that a big part of Coolidge's success was his willingness to hold fast to his convictions, yet always doing so with a sense of calmness—whether breaking a labor strike or doing what it took to cut a government deficit.

Did his firm but calm personality come from channeling his father or from some other source?

SHLAES He got it mostly from his father, who was raised by a serious Baptist mother and ultimately became something of a father to his entire town. People liked John Coolidge's style of leadership. His father was like his grandfather, Calvin Galusha Coolidge, who was also a local political leader.

In addition to his family, Amherst College played a big part in forming Coolidge's deep commitment to principles. The college had originally been founded for the purpose of training poor young men to be ministers, and its motto was: "Let them illuminate the world." This statement of the school's purpose inspired its students to ultimately become beacons for illuminating the rest of the world, going forth as missionaries or ministers. At Amherst, there was truly a brotherhood devoted to embracing high principles and pursuing each day

with a strong work ethic. This stayed with Coolidge the rest of his life.

The toughest decision involving Coolidge's maintaining his commitment to his convictions came when he was the governor of Massachusetts, and the members of the Boston Police Department went on strike. That caused him to fire all the policemen. One of his Amherst classmates sent a letter to Coolidge saying how much he appreciated Coolidge's willingness to take such a risk. After all: the policemen he fired were voters, and their firing occurred very close to Election Day. Even though the policemen were kind people and hard-working public servants, Coolidge didn't think they had the right to go on strike—since the existing law prohibited the strike.

Coolidge wrote back to the Amherst classmate who had complimented his handling of the strike with a note saying, "I knew you would appreciate it." The brotherhood of Amherst sustained him at such moments.

BOSTON Coolidge's decision to hold fast to his commitment succeeded in breaking the Boston police strike, and that caused him to receive national recognition, and brought his name into Republican Party discussions about potential presidential candidates.

SHLAES Coolidge made a statement: "There is no right to strike against the public safety, by anybody, anywhere, any time." A local politician can turn into a possible national candidate when he upstages the president on a major issue. Coolidge broke the Boston police strike at a time when President Wilson was waffling over what to do with public sector unions and whether they had the right to strike. The background: Wilson came under fire when he asked big labor to help him get through World War I by not striking, basically telling them, "No strikes during the war. You can strike after it's over."

Samuel L. Gompers, head of the AFL at the time, acquiesced to President Wilson's request and it became their agreement. After the war ended, Gompers thought he had license to strike, and allowed police in Boston to affiliate. They went on strike, and Governor Coolidge proceeded to fire them. Wilson then followed Coolidge's lead and said, "Yes. There shall be no strikes by those in the public sector." So it became a situation where Governor Coolidge led the way in his jurisdiction on an important issue, and then the federal government followed suit.

In that situation, Coolidge resembled today's Governor of Wisconsin, Scott Walker. Think of what Walker did for Wisconsin by taking on the public employee unions. Successful governors take on major confrontations, and proceed to win them. By doing that, they earn national attention. This dynamic holds whether you agree with them or not.

COOLIDGE'S APPEAL TO "THE SILENT MAJORITY"

BOSTON Coolidge voters were said to be "the Silent Majority." Richard Nixon used that term with great success fifty years later. We know that Nixon was quiet in his private life, and inept at making small talk. Coolidge was also extremely quiet, at least publicly.

Does it take almost a silent personality to appeal to the Silent Majority?

SHLAES Not necessarily. Donald Trump appeals to the Silent Majority these days and he's pretty loud. I understand what you're saying, but what Coolidge did to attract the Silent Majority was to present himself to all voters as an outsider. That approach appealed to many people who also viewed themselves as outsiders—someone not in the club—and that's who makes up the Silent Majority. Nixon did the same thing. Basically, Coolidge was saying to voters, "I too am usually not in the mainstream. Still, I'm not sitting on the bank of the river either, I'm not." Many voters found that perspective very compelling because they felt they were drifting in the same way.

COOLIDGE'S CLASHES WITH LODGE AND HOOVER

BOSTON As vice president, Coolidge clashed with the most powerful Republican in Congress at the time, Henry Cabot Lodge, and as president, he semi-clashed with the fastest rising Republican star, Herbert Hoover, who was Harding's Secretary of Commerce. Hoover, of course, later followed Coolidge as president.

What caused Coolidge's two major personality clashes during his time in Washington, DC to be with the biggest leaders of his own party, as opposed to clashing with members of the Democratic Party?

SHLAES His battles were mainly with Republicans, which was understandable, because the party was not unified then— just as it's not unified now. The progressive movement began as a Republican movement, and made the party appear to be "the party of the future" and "where the action was." When Coolidge battled with Henry Cabot Lodge, it was over the Versailles Treaty ratification issue. Lodge was being very tough on Wilson, and Coolidge was more aligned with Wilson's effort to get the treaty approved. The two did not go head to head over the issue, but Coolidge resented the political capital Lodge spent.

There was personal context as well. Lodge, a Bostonian, thought Vermont too far west to be considered part of class New England. Thus, Lodge thought of Coolidge not as the former governor of Massachusetts but as some guy from Vermont and the Berkshires who he looked down upon. Lodge was an ass. Lodge even said, "I knew Coolidge only when it became necessary to know him."

Another dimension to the Lodge-Coolidge friction came from the fact that as vice president, Coolidge presided over the Senate, while Lodge served as the senate majority leader. Lodge suffered from a raging case of narcissism, and didn't like the fact that some other person from the Bay

State was in charge of the Senate, and not Lodge. After President Harding died, someone called Lodge to tell him the news, and his response was, "What? That means Calvin Coolidge is president." Paraphrase: "I can't believe it." So Coolidge's unpredicted outranking of Lodge also caused much of the friction between them.

In the case of Hoover, he and Coolidge clashed by reason of Hoover's being a businessman and progressive while Coolidge was a professional politician and free marketer. Hoover had been incredibly successful in business—the Warren Buffett of his day—a figure who everyone idolized. Hoover, as a progressive, featured a resemblance to Teddy Roosevelt.

Coolidge and Hoover also clashed by reason of their temperaments. Hoover was the kind of guy who would run up to the river and jump in as far from the bank as he could; whereas Coolidge entered into the river very gradually. The extreme boldness of Hoover caused Hoover to often overpromise, and anyone who did that drove Coolidge crazy.

BOSTON Was there a jealousy component to the friction between Coolidge and Hoover? After all, Hoover was very financially successful and also more extroverted, while Coolidge had no personal wealth and was much more withdrawn.

SHLAES Coolidge shocked the country at a press conference when he announced that he would not run for president in 1928. It was a difficult decision for him and perhaps he wanted the party to respond to the announcement by their attempting to get him to change his mind and run for reelection. Soon after the announcement, Hoover decided to run for president and started campaigning for votes that Coolidge would have otherwise claimed. Coolidge wanted the party to pick its next candidate, but he certainly didn't want him to be Herbert Hoover.

Coolidge was a little sanctimonious in the way he handled his decision not to run again, and the party didn't appreciate that. The withdrawal created a problem for the party. Coolidge was extremely popular at the time, so his dropping out of the race meant they were losing a good candidate. But the party also loved Hoover, so they turned around and got their bandwagon rolling for Hoover to lead the ticket.

Coolidge was disappointed when no one said, "Good job, President Coolidge! What an incredible saint you are for not running again." Once he took himself out of the race, it definitely hurt his pride that nobody paid much attention to him. Even saints don't enjoy being a lame duck.

BOSTON I had a different impression of that situation from reading your book, and maybe I misread it. When Coolidge announced: "I do not choose to run," he refused to give any explanation for his decision—which was strange. After making that announcement, I thought he received a groundswell of support, with the party essentially saying to him, "Come on, man. We need you to change your mind and run for reelection as our leader." I thought it was this reaction from the party that caused Coolidge to have to issue a second statement, to make his position about not running for reelection even clearer—essentially saying "I do not choose to run. Read my lips. I'm not going to run; and if you try to draft me at the convention, I'll refuse to accept the nomination."

The impression I got from reading your book was that the Republican Party's response to Coolidge's decision not to run in 1928 was more like, "What the heck's going on with you, President Coolidge? We love you. You've been successful. We need you to be our candidate in 1928." Coolidge responded to their request for him to reconsider by continuing to refuse providing an explanation for his decision.

So, as I read your book, the Republican Party most definitely attempted to persuade him to run again, but by issuing his second statement, Coolidge was trying to make it clear that he was not open to the possibility of being drafted as the party's candidate in the next election. In the first announcement, maybe he was essentially saying, "I'm not going to choose to run, but if you want to draft me, that might be okay;" but with the second announcement, he totally shut the door on the subject, saying, "No, I'm not even open to being drafted."

SHLAES At the time he made the first announcement, Coolidge may not have known what he wanted. One day, he decided, "I do not choose to run," which did leave open the draft possibility. Then, life happened. His wife was tired of Washington, tired of his being the president and her being the First Lady. She made a blanket which had in its design a marking for each month of his presidency, and she purposefully made sure that the blanket didn't have room for another four years' worth of months in the pattern.

Of course, Coolidge himself was tired. He had heart troubles. Regardless of what he told reporters, he was concerned that if he stayed on another four years, he wouldn't have the energy in a second full term to resist the expansion of government with the same fortitude he had demonstrated up till then. The presidency at that time was a totally exhausting, all-consuming job, and they didn't have angiograms then.

BOSTON And he was a ferocious cigar smoker.

SHLAES He was a ferocious smoker, he ate nothing but butter and pudding, and he knew something was wrong with his breathing system.

But to be clear: the main reason though for Coolidge's choosing not to run again for president in 1928 was that he agreed with Lord Acton, "Power corrupts. Absolute power corrupts absolutely." In my research for the book, I searched to see whether

Coolidge ever made a reference to Lord Acton, but didn't find it. He knew he shouldn't run again because he thought an additional term would corrupt him, as men in power so often are corrupted.

I don't think the party tried hard enough to get him to run again. They just took him at his word. He expected that he would get more praise instantly for not running, such as there had been for George Washington when he refused to run for an additional term, but the anticipated praise for Coolidge never came.

COOLIDGE'S ECONOMIC POLICIES

BOSTON The key to Coolidge's astounding budgeting success during his presidency was an idea from his partner on the budget, Andrew Mellon, his Secretary of the Treasury. Mellon had an idea he called "scientific taxation," which was much like "supply side economics," the policy later favored by President Reagan. On the subject of "supply side economics" or "scientific taxation," whichever label you want to call it, was the main difference between Reagan and Coolidge's performance in implementing the policy that Reagan essentially did nothing to stop the ballooning deficits, whereas Coolidge stayed focused on eliminating the deficit?

SHLAES Yes, that's the main difference. At some point during the Coolidge presidency, the White House received a gift of twin lion cubs from the mayor of Johannesburg, South Africa. Coolidge named the cubs, "Tax Reduction" and "Budget Bureau." Thus suggested that the two goals of cutting taxes and balancing the budget were "Even Steven" in his eyes.

That budget and tax story was why this book was very hard to write. Writing about a governor who breaks a labor strike is good copy and a fun story to tell. But chronicling a president getting a tax reduction law passed or a budget's being approved is

Photo credit: Frances Billes

Amity Shlaes

not a simple story to tell in a dramatic or eloquent way.

After becoming president, Coolidge said, "I'm really going to cut the budget." Then he did that. When Coolidge left office, the budget was lower than it had been when he came in, which means the budget reduction was real. He cut the tax rate below 28%—which is the gold standard for political conservatives and Reagan's top tax rate—down to 25%. By doing so, and tightening the budget, Coolidge set the stage for prosperity. The country's economy grew throughout Coolidge's sixty-seven months in office.

His domestic economic success allowed him to guide the country toward being humane toward Europe. After World War I, European nations had massive debt. Mellon and Coolidge together entertained one European leader after another, and all of them wanted lower interest rates on their debt owed to the United States—they basically wanted to refinance. Because of how strong they had made the American economy, Mellon and Coolidge were able to lower the interest rate for the Europeans, which made it possible for them to get their houses in order quicker post-war. Not all nations managed that. But the Mellon refinancing helped.

With a tight budget, the expectation of inflation was reduced. Here's how tough

Coolidge was on doing what it took to cut the budget. Every half year he brought his Cabinet officials into a meeting with his budget director, and told them, "In your budget, you each received one pencil. I think by now you've used one-half a pencil, so I'd like you to return the pencil stub."

BOSTON So he was keeping track of the half pencils.

SHLAES He kept track of the pencils the same way he kept track of the number of letters being written by the people in his administration. He made it clear that he wanted fewer letters written because letters were expensive. He used his budget director, Herbert Mayhew Lord, as a bad cop, and it was a very effective way to manage all costs—even on items that otherwise appeared to have a low cost. Coolidge emphasized many nickel-and-dime budget targets for purely theatrical purposes. The tactic worked because he managed to intimidate the government into spending much less than it otherwise would have.

Another partner in this effort was that other silent guy, Andrew Mellon. The pair wrote all their fancy tax legislation after conversing in private about it. We all know executives like that—grunt, grunt, decision made.

BOSTON Something that comes through loud and clear in this book, and demonstrates Coolidge's incredible ferocity at managing the budget and looking at every single half pencil and the cost of every letter written, is that by doing this year after year, his pursuing constant extreme savings took its toll not only on Coolidge, but also on everybody in the federal government who just got worn out working in a mode of non-stop diligence about cutting expenses. "You want me to explain my half pencil? You mean I can't write this letter?" After having to operate in this relentless cost-cutting mode for a few years, many of them finally quit their jobs in the administration, essentially saying "I've had all this that I can stand." So ferocity in budgeting is a good thing, but one of the lessons of Coolidge's presidency is that it wore his people out.

SHLAES Correct. It's not always a good thing.

The Treasury Secretary rapped Coolidge for being penny wise and pound foolish. Mellon wrote a memo to Coolidge explaining that he had just lost a top lawyer in the Treasury Department. The attorney had left him to go to work in the private sector. In the memo, Mellon conveyed how much he needed the Treasury lawyer and how much time and money it would cost to replace him—such that staff turnover was costing the government more than Coolidge realized.

People knew Coolidge's fiscal discipline was genuine. They knew he wasn't cutting government spending just to be harsh, but because he wanted people to have "more money for themselves," as he put it. There's one video that shows Coolidge speaking, (it's on YouTube), and in it he says, "I want people to have more for themselves." To paraphrase him: "That's why I want to save money. Not because I'm a scrooge."

COOLIDGE'S FAMILY TRAGEDY

BOSTON During his presidency, Calvin Coolidge lost his teenaged son, Calvin, Jr., to a staph infection and also lost his beloved father. As time passed after those deaths, your book suggests that he became more distant from both his wife Grace and his surviving son John. In the midst of this grief and family estrangement, Coolidge did not have a close friend with whom he could talk things through or who could give him a tough love wakeup call.

Did Coolidge just stuff his personal feelings or did he have some outlet for his emotions, other than smoking cigars?

SHLAES One outlet was an electric horse. This horse was like a merry-go-round horse, and he rode it to relieve stress. It was his aerobics equipment and he was a good rider. The horse now can be seen at the Forbes Library in Northampton, Massachusetts. I liked what Evan Thomas said about Nixon two days ago here at King's College. But I don't think Nixon or Coolidge or many of their peers (who were not near as troubled as they were) would have agreed that they needed to see a therapist. Therapy is really a modern way of dealing with depression—that the person needs someone to talk to. Coolidge would have said, "I have consulted my conscience," as many other depressed people of his era would have said, too. So I'm not sure his talking to someone about his grief over the deaths in his family would have helped.

He was incredibly sad over the loss of his son. He said, "If I hadn't been president, my son wouldn't have died." My impression is that Coolidge turned to faith and his church at this point.

BOSTON His son got a staph infection playing tennis on the White House tennis court. So Coolidge thought that if he hadn't been president, his son wouldn't have played tennis on the White House tennis court, wouldn't have gotten the staph infection, and, therefore, wouldn't have died. So he blamed himself.

SHLAES Yes, he did. Calvin, Jr., had just gone through a growth spurt and his sneakers likely didn't fit during that fateful tennis match. He died because there was no penicillin to kill an infection in those days. It was an especially hard blow to lose his son Calvin. Calvin was a lively extroverted child, and was very bright and magnanimous. One summer during Coolidge's presidency, Calvin, Jr., worked in a tobacco field in Massachusetts. Someone said, "If my father were president, I wouldn't be working in any tobacco field." Calvin replied, "If your father were my father, you would." Calvin was a very lovable child, and actually a good representative for the family even at the age of sixteen.

I've been working on a book with Professor Jeffrey Engel at SMU's Center for Presidential Studies on the subject of presidential crisis, to be published by Harvard University Press. In it, I compare Coolidge to Lincoln, who also lost a son in the White House. They both prosecuted wars amidst that—Lincoln, with the Civil War, and Coolidge, with his tax and budget war. Despite their deep grief, they did not fail in waging their respective battles. There's a psychology book by professor Robert Gilbert from UMass Amherst. The hypothesis is that Coolidge simply gave up living after the death of his son Calvin. I don't think that's the case. Coolidge was suffering, and he was depressed, but he continued relentlessly with his work.

BOSTON Your book mentions how after Calvin Jr.'s death, the family went to Vermont, found a tree there, and then transplanted it to a spot beside the White House tennis court. President Coolidge could see the tree from a window in his office, and it reminded him of his late son. It had to be rough for him to look at that tree every day.

SHLAES We found out about the tree in a letter from Grace.

COOLIDGE'S FOREIGN POLICY

BOSTON Coolidge received great adulation for his work in negotiating the Kellogg-Briand Treaty in May 1928, the final year of his presidency. He did it along with his Secretary of State Frank Kellogg, thinking that it might be an international motivator to prevent future wars by laying out a "network for peace."

Was his motivation for Kellogg-Briand as much about saving money—since wars are always so expensive—as it was about aspiring to spare lives in future combat?

SHLAES No, I don't think so. Coolidge was not a fighter by temperament. He wasn't one who would want to build up a huge powerful navy so it could be used in future wars.

Yes, building up a navy would have cost a lot, but he believed that the United States should aspire to exist and thrive in a peaceful world, and hoped that other nations would follow our lead with Kellogg-Briand. He didn't believe the United States needed to intervene militarily everywhere, and knew that when we had intervened in the past, it was not always productive. Coolidge was no neocon.

The Kellogg-Briand Pact attempted to ban war. It was much mocked because the idea of an international prohibition on future wars was beyond illusory. The pact just happened to line up with Coolidge's philosophy, which was, "We will all agree that we will follow the law and not take up arms." He believed that through the rule of law, and through example, the United States would help to tame and civilize the world. Did it work? Maybe not, but the idea of there being a formal written commitment to a network of peace, nation by nation, with everyone complying with the rule of law resonates and appeals today. That was Coolidge's overriding goal in pushing hard to bring the Kellogg-Briand Pact to fruition.

BOSTON We're now out of time and I want to say thank you to the wonderful Amity Shlaes.

Although no one regards Herbert Hoover as a great president, he was a significant one because the Great Depression started during his time in the Oval Office. **DAVID DAVENPORT** is a research fellow and public policy scholar at the Hoover Institution at Stanford University and the co-author (with Gordon Lloyd) of *The New Deal & Modern American Conservatism: A Defining Rivalry* (Hoover Institution 2013). He and **AMITY SHLAES** (see chapter thirteen) have an ongoing debate about who deserves the most credit for originating the modern American conservative movement—Davenport says it was Hoover; Shlaes says it was Coolidge. I interviewed them together on October 6, 2015 as part of the presidential symposium held at The King's College in New York City on the issues raised by their Coolidge-Hoover debate.

"Was Hoover on sound economic footing in the steps he took after the Great Depression hit? According to the economic understanding of the time, the answer is: 'Yes.' In particular, what he did was on sound political footing. The American people suffering during the Depression simply didn't have the patience to say, 'Let's just do nothing.' Coolidge might have had a very serious problem if he had remained president during the Depression and chosen to do nothing about it. It would have been his instinct to do far less than Hoover did, and maybe he would have done nothing; but if he did nothing, the American people caught in the crisis would not have accepted quietly a president's refusal to take action." **– DAVID DAVENPORT**

CHAPTER 14

DAVID DAVENPORT AND AMITY SHLAES
ON
Hoover, Coolidge, & the Birth of Republican Conservatism

RESPONSE TO THE EMINENT DOWNTURN PRE-GREAT DEPRESSION

BOSTON Amity, in the last year of Coolidge's presidency, he could see a major stock market decline coming because the Dow Jones had spiked—mainly due to people buying stocks on margin.

What, if anything, did President Coolidge do to address the looming, eminent downturn?

SHLAES Coolidge believed that if the president tried to do something in response to a falling market, it would set a precedent of intervention that would be worse than any market crash. His doing nothing was an intentional show of strength. Coolidge tried

Gordon Lloyd & David Davenport

Courtesy of Hoover Institute Press

keeping the Treasury Department and the Federal Reserve from doing anything, because in his eyes, as he said, "Everything seems okay to me."

He's been much maligned for having allegedly said in 1929 after the stock market crash, "Everything is absolutely sound and stocks are now cheap." Actually we've now established that Coolidge made no such statement after the crash. If Coolidge was here tonight and asked about the events of late 1929 and the decade that followed, he would say the crash was inevitable, but the Depression wouldn't have been so "great" if there had been less government intervention.

BOSTON David, along those same lines, obviously Hoover ran for president in 1928 and won with a huge margin.

During his campaign, did he see that a crash was likely to occur during his presidency?

DAVENPORT Hoover was secretary of commerce under Presidents Harding and Coolidge, so he served in the Cabinet eight years before becoming president. There had been a recession in the early twenties, and both Coolidge and Hoover anticipated a recession coming again in the late twenties, though neither saw a Great Depression coming. In responding to the Depression, it's fair to say Hoover was a bit more active in addressing it than Coolidge would have been. Coolidge was known as "the Great Refrainer," while Hoover was more of an activist.

COOLIDGE, HOOVER, AND THE ELECTION OF 1928

BOSTON Prior to the 1928 election, Coolidge famously said "I will not run for another term" without providing any explanation of his decision to the press. When he made that announcement, Hoover was the fair-haired boy wonder secretary of commerce, a fabulously successful businessman,

and a full-fledged crowd pleaser to the media—meaning he may have been more beloved than President Coolidge at the time.

When the American voter went to the polls in 1928, did they understand that there was a meaningful difference in political philosophy as between Coolidge and Hoover—inactive vs. active? Or did they think Hoover was just going to pursue a mere continuation of Coolidge's political approach?

SHLAES The Republican Party at that time was as neurotic as it is today. They were very happy with Coolidge because he'd won an absolute majority in a three-way race in 1924 and was good at getting the ethnic vote. The party members had something of a nervous breakdown when Coolidge decided not to run, and when Hoover was vetted, he was perceived to be a candidate who would continue Coolidge's policies. Everyone soon realized that they were not the same type of person. To me, Hoover was like Mitt Romney—he was definitely from "outside" and not from the inside part of the party. Coolidge was an inside Republican Party man all the way up. So voters recognized that the two men had risen to the top from very different places, but they expected their policies would be more similar.

HOOVER'S INITIAL RESPONSE TO THE GREAT DEPRESSION

BOSTON Hoover was inaugurated in March 1929 and Black Tuesday came in October. With Hoover's being more of an activist, what were his first actions in response to the Great Depression?

DAVENPORT During and after World War I, well before he went into politics, Hoover had been involved in international relief projects, and had fed millions of people in Europe, and probably saved millions of lives there. Because of that experience while secretary of commerce, his style of addressing any fallout from an economic crisis was with a voluntary approach. After the Depression hit, President Hoover called business leaders and attempted to be the nation's cheerleader in rallying voluntary support for needed relief.

Like Coolidge, Hoover felt obligated to say that the country was capable of working its way through the crisis, and ultimately a sound economy would be restored. His message to business leaders was to encourage them to keep their wages up, avoid layoffs, and everybody should work through the crisis together. So he was active in that respect before he began engaging in any type of government intervention.

COOLIDGE AND HOOVER'S DIFFERENCES ON WHEN GOVERNMENT SHOULD BE ACTIVE AND WHEN IT SHOULD BE INACTIVE

BOSTON Amity's book *The Forgotten Man* contains the following statement: "Hoover believed action was necessary to make the country live up to its potential. Coolidge, the Great Refrainer, on the other hand, preferred inaction and frequently said it was more important to kill bad bills than to pass good ones."

I'd like both of you to weigh in on the difference between Coolidge and Hoover on when and in what areas the federal government should be inactive and where it should be active.

SHLAES One example where they had different perspectives was with labor prices. Coolidge believed that when employers were in trouble, they might have to pay lower wages. That's what had been done in prior recessions. Henry Ford had encouraged employers to keep wages up so their workers would have the money to buy cars. Coolidge thought Ford's idea sounded good. But sometimes when employers decided to maintain high wages, they would have to lay people

off because there would necessarily have to be that type of trade-off. Coolidge saw it was more inhumane to lay off people than to cut their wages. Hoover preferred higher wages, and if that meant layoffs, so be it.

Another area of difference between the two men was that Hoover scolded Wall Street—"You bad Wall Street speculators! You've caused this depression!" Coolidge never talked to business leaders in that fashion because he respected markets and recognized that sometimes, unpleasant things happened. When stocks go down, government should leave markets alone and respect the fact that prices will ultimately find their own level.

BOSTON David, do you want to add to what Amity has said about any material differences between Hoover and Coolidge on what the federal government should and shouldn't do in times of serious economic crisis?

DAVENPORT I can certainly affirm the differences Amity pointed out and can add some more. Hoover was much more of an activist. While secretary of commerce, he wanted President Coolidge to do something about the stock speculation and the stock prices that were getting out of hand. He also wanted Coolidge to do something about some of the things happening then in the agricultural sector.

When Hoover became president, besides cheerleading with business leaders after the Great Depression hit, the government became active in public safety, health, and national defense because of his belief in what he called, "constructive government." He had very clear ideas about where government should be active, which meant he was *not* the Great Refrainer like Coolidge.

BOSTON From a philosophical standpoint, did either Coolidge or Hoover believe that there were certain dire circumstances where the federal government should extend some sort of welfare benefits to those in need?

SHLAES There was a kind of tragic litmus test in 1927. A terrible flood of the Mississippi River occurred. The water rose to fifty feet high, people drowned, and hundreds of thousands were displaced. Coolidge sent Hoover, his commerce secretary, down to investigate the damage but Coolidge didn't go down to see it. Why? Because there was significant infrastructure legislation before Congress at the time and the president knew that if a photo was taken of him where the flooding damage had occurred, then his veto of that legislation would be overridden by the progressives in Congress. A senator commented acidly that if the flood had happened near Coolidge's home in Vermont instead of on the Mississippi River, he definitely would have run home to address the emergency.

Then, in a form of divine or political retribution, a few months after the Mississippi River flood, there came a terrible flood in Vermont. The Christmas tree crop in Vermont was completely wrecked. The waters washed out a hundred bridges. At the time, Vermont relied heavily on railroad transportation and the floods completely wrecked the railroad system. Vermont's lieutenant governor drowned trying to get out of his car.

So Coolidge was faced with a challenge: in the first half of the year, he had refused to visit the places damaged by the Mississippi River flood. Would he also refuse to visit his home state where the rivers there had flooded? He knew that the good-hearted thing to do would be to go home, but he refused to go home as a matter of principle. One commentator summed it up: "He can't do for his own what he didn't do for others." Coolidge took a very rigid principled stance. It was painful to him and damaged his reputation in his home state, but he believed that the president should not be seen as a domestic rescuer or favoritist.

I've spoken about how Coolidge dealt with the floods during his presidency with President Bush, 43, because of the crisis he faced in having to respond to Hurricane Katrina. The situations were clearly analogous. Federalism is a key issue here.

BOSTON David, where did Hoover draw the line on the circumstances by which, in an actual emergency, the federal government should appropriately extend some type of recovery or welfare benefits to those in need?

DAVENPORT Hoover's view was like Coolidge's—that basically the helping hand should come from churches and volunteer organizations, and maybe from cities and states, but it really wasn't the federal government's job to be providing direct aid.

As the Great Depression became worldwide and the fallout grew deeper and deeper, Hoover recognized that different phases of the crisis required different approaches by the federal government. In the first phase of the Depression, as I've mentioned, he pursued voluntary rallying of business leaders to maintain their wages. In the second phase, he and Congress passed legislation to support some of the banks, railways, and key industries that were in a position to help the economy and provide jobs.

Finally, in the last year of his presidency, against his principles but in the face of the Depression, he began delivering some direct aid to those in serious need of it from the federal government. It was a line he really did not want to cross, and a precedent he did want to set, but as the Depression grew deeper, his hand was forced.

A president dealing with a major depression has to combine economic theory with political leadership. Yes, maybe principles tell a lower level official not to go to a flood site, but for the president, the nation's top political leader, not to visit the flood site? It's very hard for a president to stay away from places where he knows some people have died and others are facing dire straits. A president has to balance his economic theories with fulfilling his leadership responsibilities, and both Hoover and Coolidge had to face that tough choice.

THE TWO MEN'S VIEWS ON THE ROLE OF THE FEDERAL GOVERNMENT IN REGULATING PUBLIC UTILITIES AND RESTRAINT OF TRADE

BOSTON Here's a quote from Herbert Hoover's book, *American Individualism*: "Our massive regulation of public utilities and our legislation against restraint of trade is the monument to our intent to preserve equality of opportunity."

My question for both of you is did Coolidge and Hoover agree that these two subjects were appropriate for federal regulation?

DAVENPORT Hoover certainly did. Hoover coined the term, "rugged individualism" and his essay in the book you just quoted from was all about that. He said that in America, rugged individualism had to be coupled with equality of opportunity. He recognized that markets didn't always deliver equality of opportunity and sometimes the federal government had to get involved to make sure it happened. Those were two examples of things Hoover thought government could and should do, and those two ideals—rugged individualism and equality of opportunity—were Hoover's core philosophy, and they needed to be in balance.

BOSTON Amity, was Coolidge in alignment with that?

SHLAES Coolidge certainly believed in education and conservatives fault him for being a little too active on the federal side in education. He always strove for equality of opportunity through enhancing education for everyone.

I'm teaching a course now on Lyndon Johnson's Great Society. During the Great Society, equality of opportunity morphed into equality of results. Neither Hoover nor Coolidge sought equality of result. As David said, there are different phases to a man's

political philosophy. Coolidge was a "state progressive." As governor of Massachusetts, he took progressive measures such as signing off on minimum wage or hours for women legislation. He just didn't think the federal government should address most social and business issues. At the state level, in a progressive way, he sought to establish equality of opportunity early on.

BOSTON Are you saying then, that as far as Coolidge was concerned, public utilities should not be regulated by the federal government and the federal government should not have legislation that it was against restraint of trade?

SHLAES Trade is a complex issue because Coolidge was from the Republican Party. At that time, the Republicans were *the party* of the tariff. They also pursued anti-trust regulation. When he was a young man, Coolidge sponsored a bill for the state of Massachusetts to break up a theater trust. So Republicans of the era took their position on government's role in addressing trade issues to extremes. That's the main thing to understand.

BOSTON What was Coolidge's position on the need for government to regulate public utilities?

SHLAES If he favored it, it would only be for regulation at the state level. I don't recall him being a big fan of the need for utility regulation though. Franklin Roosevelt was from New York. That state had significant water issues and FDR believed government needed to take action when it came to utilities. I doubt Coolidge would have favored much government intervention in the utilities sector. He vetoed federal dams at Muscle Shoals—which we call the Tennessee Valley. He killed a bill for government operations with a pocket veto.

THE CONFLICT BETWEEN COOLIDGE AND HOOVER

BOSTON As David mentioned, before his presidency, Hoover served eight years as secretary of commerce under Harding and Coolidge. Even though they were alongside each other at the top of the executive branch, Coolidge and Hoover didn't get along—such that, toward the end of his six-year presidency, Coolidge said, "Hoover has offered me unsolicited advice for six years—all of it bad."

Amity, what bad advice from Hoover was President Coolidge referring to?

SHLAES We don't know, but it probably related to Hoover's beliefs about the need for federal intervention. Hoover had a great desire to standardize. He wanted the Department of Commerce to be bigger and more powerful. In business, standardization is considered as a good thing—we want a mattress or a screwdriver to have a standard size. Hoover wanted the Commerce Department to be involved in maintaining standardization, and Coolidge saw that as the federal government's interrupting commerce. I'm not sure Coolidge liked having a Department of Commerce at all. He asked, "Why doesn't Hoover ever go home?" He

disliked Hoover's activism and didn't believe anything good came of it.

Differences between Coolidge and Hoover also arose from their different temperaments. Hoover was an active person—like Theodore Roosevelt—even though he came from a business background. His activity produced amazing achievements in his life. Coolidge, on the other hand, disfavored high activity in anything. If the two men took a career aptitude test, they'd come out as totally different kinds of guys. Coolidge definitely had the temperament of an attorney (which he was) or an accountant. Both types of temperaments feature merits and demerits.

BOSTON David, during Coolidge's presidency, can you identify some areas where Hoover in fact gave Coolidge advice that Coolidge rejected or bristled at or anything—where they had a clear face-to-face disagreement?

DAVENPORT First of all, I agree with Amity that some of their differences arose because of their temperaments and occupational experience, and that was the main cause of their friction as opposed to any particular unappreciated advice that Hoover attempted to give Coolidge. Hoover said that when Coolidge did nothing, nine out of ten times he would be right and the problem wouldn't grow large because government did not intervene in it. However, the tenth time Coolidge did nothing, the problem would worsen as Coolidge refrained from taking action.

So Hoover's unpopular advice to Coolidge surely involved a recommendation that the government be more active. He was the one sent to the flood by Coolidge. He was the one who, as secretary of commerce, helped develop ways to oversee new fields like radio communications and air flight, both of which were developing at the time.

As a businessman, Hoover had run huge worldwide engineering projects and was used to tackling challenging situations in a hands-on way. When he became president, he believed the country had sat on its hands too long and, therefore, he intended to be a more active president than Coolidge. Surprisingly, both parties actually wanted Hoover to run for president, since he was considered one of the best and brightest men of his time. Six months into his presidency though, when the Depression hit, his became an emergency presidency and it changed the whole character of what he did.

THE EFFECT OF HOOVER'S LONG-TERM RESPONSE TO THE GREAT DEPRESSION

BOSTON Now let's talk about the emergency that arose from the Great Depression. During his presidency, shortly after Black Tuesday in October 1929, Hoover responded by ratcheting up the federal government's role in trying to turn the Depression around by, among other things, getting Congress to pass legislation to build highways and bridges and imposing one of the highest tariffs in US history in hopes of protecting American's domestic producers.

David, did Hoover's efforts at using the federal government in hopes of turning around the Depression have any meaningful positive effects?

DAVENPORT That's impossible to answer. Ben Bernanke, the long-time chair of the Federal Reserve, has said that finding the causes of the Great Depression is the Holy Grail in the field of economics. Today, we still can't answer the question, "What actually caused the Great Depression?" Milton Friedman argued that it was caused by our monetary policy; another excellent economist at UCLA has said it was caused by holding wages too high for too long. There are about a half a dozen theories, and the proponent of each is absolutely sure his theory is right. But as Bernanke says, we don't really know what caused the Great Depression.

So, turning back the clock, can we say whether Hoover's efforts were effective? Well, they didn't stop the Depression—but neither did Franklin Roosevelt's New Deal efforts. We didn't return to pre-Depression employment levels until World War II. It's hard to know how effective Hoover's policies were or how much worse things would have been without his efforts.

Was Hoover on sound economic footing in the steps that he took? According to the economic understanding of the time, the answer is: "Yes." In particular, what he did was on sound political footing. The American people suffering during the Great Depression simply didn't have the patience to say, "Let's just do nothing." Coolidge might have had a very serious problem if he had remained president during the Depression and chosen to do nothing about it. It would have been his instinct to do far less than Hoover did, and maybe he would have done nothing; but if he did nothing, the American people caught in the crisis would not have accepted quietly a president's refusal to take action.

HOW COOLIDGE WOULD HAVE RESPONDED TO THE GREAT DEPRESSION

BOSTON Let's imagine Coolidge had chosen to run again in 1928. He surely would have been re-elected, and, therefore, would have been in office when Black Tuesday hit in October 1926.

Amity, what would Coolidge have done in response to the Great Depression as opposed to how Hoover responded to it?

SHLAES Hoover signed the Smoot-Hawley Tariff bill. Coolidge also would have signed it. Republicans were for tariffs.

A difference: The Hoover administration raised taxes dramatically, and Coolidge would have been reluctant to raise taxes. He also would have been very reluctant to exhort business to maintain pre-Depression wages. Lee Ohanian is a professor who's

made the argument that government-influenced high wages prolonged the Depression, and his books add to the understanding. Wages stayed relatively high during the downturn at Hoover's urging, and Coolidge would not have encouraged that. Many believe today that government pressure on wages raised unemployment.

The other issue on which Coolidge and Hoover disagreed was letting markets find their level. For prices to go back up, they first have to go down. The market has to collapse and then go up. That's what had happened in all the preceding crashes. At first, when the Depression hit, the market went down by 45 or 50%. During Coolidge's presidency, it had gone down over 40% a number of times and then come back. So Coolidge believed that the government should not interfere, and should let the market collapse and then it would get back on its feet again and find its level. There's a famous Andrew Mellon quote, which he may or may not have said, "Liquidate, liquidate, liquidate." That didn't mean to be like Dorothy and the witch in The Wizard of Oz and liquidate; but rather it meant people should sell their stocks and let the markets

find their prices. That type of conduct didn't happen much in this downturn. The result was that traders were unsure of prices.

If the question is whether the Great Depression would have been as bad had the government intervened more and used persuasion less, Coolidge would have answered, "Yes, it would have been bad regardless of any government intervention." A big reason why that was true was because the UK went off the gold standard, which caused money to stop flowing around the world and that caused a round of bank failures here.

THE IMPACT OF EUROPE'S POST-WAR PROBLEMS ON THE GREAT DEPRESSION

BOSTON David, when you were talking a minute ago about there being so many different theories on what caused the Great Depression, in your book you say that Hoover believed that the cause and continuation of America's Great Depression was the inability of Europe to have a healthy political and economic post-war recovery. Is that the same thing Amity just talked about or is that different?

DAVENPORT It's a bit different. Hoover's view was that the Depression was a worldwide event triggered by the debts European nations owed after World War I. Hoover believed that the United States should have been more proactive in helping European countries get relieved of their debt—either by our forgiving debt or by providing them with foreign aid.

SHLAES Or by reducing our interest rates on the debt they owed us.

DAVENPORT Hoover recognized that we had achieved a high production level during World War I, but then after the war, nobody in Europe had money to buy our goods. Hoover felt like if we would be more proactive in forgiving the debt Europe owed us, then that would allow countries to increase their trade with us and buy our goods, which would help us come back to a post-war equilibrium.

BOSTON Did he forgive any debt?

DAVENPORT Yes, he began to do so as president. He had wanted Coolidge to forgive the post-war debt, but Coolidge refused to do so. That was another disagreement between the two of them.

SHLAES Coolidge didn't believe we should forgive the debt Europe owed us; rather, he believed we should allow Europe to refinance the debt because of the importance of preserving the honor of the contract. If contracts are no longer honored, people would stop making loans. He wanted loan transactions to continue. So Coolidge's strategy was not inhumane; it was just different.

There's another point that needs to be made on this subject as we think about the future of today's Republican Party. It is the incredible hypocrisy of the Republican Party in that period, whether during Coolidge's or Hoover's presidency. On the one hand, they were talking about refinancing the debt owed by Europe, and working hard to do that. On the other hand, they were imposing tariffs on goods Americans bought from Europe. The tariffs made it impossible for Europe to make enough money off the sale of their goods to pay the debts it owed to the United States.

What about that, gentlemen? If we had really wanted to help Europe, why make the repayment of loans easier? Why not just open up trade? So Hoover, who believed more in trade and knew a lot more about how businesses operate than Coolidge, signed Smoot Hawley, a big tariff, and that sent a political signal to Europe, "Take care of yourself," at a time when European democracies were incredibly fragile.

DAVENPORT It's ironic that the big story on the front page of *The New York Times* today is about a free trade agreement and

lowering of tariffs with the nations on the Pacific Rim. So these economic policies are in the news today. Amity's right. Republicans today have "come around" largely to the view that having lower barriers and more active trade is a good thing. In Coolidge and Hoover's terms in office, it was thought to be important to build tariff walls that would protect American industries from other countries. We see more clearly *now* that that's a bad idea, but it's important to realize that trade with foreign countries was a small part of America's economy at that time, such that our signing Smoot Hawley, though a bad idea, was not one of the major factors that caused the Great Depression.

THE IMPACT OF HOOVER'S ECONOMIC POLICIES ON THE NEW DEAL

BOSTON Getting back to this idea of Hoover's responding to the Great Depression with a philosophy about the role of government needing to be more active in addressing the emergency situation, he did increase the budget in an effort to help the situation.

Did Hoover's efforts to increase the federal government because of the Great Depression in any way prime the pump for FDR's New Deal?

DAVENPORT That argument has been made by Murray Rothbard and Steven Horowitz. Their argument is that during the last year or two of Hoover's presidency, when he allowed the government to spend more money on relief and undertake more debt as the Depression deepened, his policies became more New Deal-like and in effect lit the fire for the New Deal; and when Roosevelt came in, he just put more gasoline and matches to the fire Hoover had already started.

If you look at the economic record, there is a large difference between what Hoover did even in his last year compared with what FDR did. In Hoover's first year, the federal debt actually declined, but the second year, it went back up to what he had inherited. There is much more discontinuity between Hoover and FDR than there is between Hoover's early and later phases.

So yes, he created some constructs for economic intervention that Coolidge would not have done and that Roosevelt more than doubled, and then increased some more.

CONSERVATIVE ECONOMIC POLICY'S BEING REJECTED BY PRESIDENT BUSH 43 IN THE 2008 MELTDOWN

BOSTON It's interesting. In the 2008 subprime mortgage collapse, the Bush 43 administration was run by some very conservative people and they faced a similar situation to what Hoover faced. President Bush ended up taking actions that surprised many people. The head of Bush's Council of Economic Advisors in 2008 was a Hoover fellow and a colleague of mine. He never believed in bailing out businesses and always believed in letting markets work. But when a president and his team are staring at the abyss and think their administration is about to be responsible for the *second* Great Depression, that situation makes people do things that don't necessarily fit into their longstanding economic philosophy.

BOSTON I had an opportunity three years ago to have a one-on-one conversation with President Bush in Dallas and he talked about how the bailout and other parts of his response to the crash of 2008 were obviously in conflict with his principles and philosophy but he said he was *not* going to allow the second Great Depression to occur on his watch. Amity may think that what he did was irresponsible and/or unprincipled.

SHLAES It was very difficult for President Bush to respond as he did but what happened was so unusual because the markets had gone crazy. Some might say that the

Republican rescue set the stage for the Great Recession or the "slow recovery" on the Democratic watch. The quality of the recovery, although it's pretty good now, we owe to one sector—energy. The rest of the recovery since 2008 has not been good. During the Obama administration, wages have not been high and new opportunities have not been created except in the regulatory sector. That's in part because of there being great uncertainty over where the government will intervene next. Laws like Dodd-Frank and Sarbanes Oxley come out of the new government impulse to control markets—in hopes of avoiding the repeat of situations like "too big to fail."

Perhaps President Bush and his treasury secretary, Hank Paulson, could have intervened less. They didn't know whether a great depression was definitely coming; they just knew something bad was happening. They did the best they could. If you go back and look at what journalists wrote in *The New York Times* about how Bush responded to the meltdown, they too were shocked and awed, including yours truly. No president wants to be responsible for an incredible economic disaster on his watch.

HOW COOLIDGE AND HOOVER WOULD HAVE REACTED TO THE 2008 COLLAPSE

BOSTON That may be a good way to distinguish between Coolidge and Hoover. Let's assume, hypothetically, that both Coolidge and Hoover were president in 2008 when the economy tanked.

What would Coolidge have done on the abyss, facing a major depression, as opposed to what Hoover would have done?

DAVENPORT I would love to see what Coolidge would have done in response to either the Great Depression or the Great Recession of 2008. Why? Because Amity and a lot of economists argue that the federal government's interventions in both those two historic situations actually made the economy worse—they delayed the recovery and weighed it down with a lot of regulation that was not helpful toward preventing a recurrence.

We've never really tried just letting the market correct itself in such an economic crisis. If Coolidge had been president during those two meltdowns, I believe he would have done nothing, let the market correct itself, and then we would finally have a test case. The fact that Coolidge would have done nothing in the face of a major economic crisis is evidenced by the fact that he was going to let his home state, Vermont, drown under a major flood without having the federal government do anything, so it wouldn't bother him to do nothing while the economy crashed.

SHLAES Let's look back at what happened in the other downturns, which we discussed. The market first went down 40% and then went down close to 50%. Coolidge's life parallels the Dow-Jones Industrial Average, so it's easy to track it. He entered adulthood after he graduated from Amherst in 1895 and that's around when the Dow got started. And in 1901, 1907, and 1921 the market dropped by just about half, but there wasn't any great depression after those recessions. After a while, it always went back up after the recession had run its course. So there is a precedent in the United States of allowing a major economic decline to happen and then, without there being any government interruption, allowing it to come back.

BOSTON Were people jumping out of windows?

SHLAES No, but there was incredible suffering. One thing that's important to remember is that right now, we have a little machine we wear on our wrist and it takes our pulse and measures our blood pressure. The data we get from it causes us to focus a whole lot more on what's going on with our body. In the first two decades of the

twentieth century, there was no national unemployment data available for Americans to look at to gauge the status of their economy. There was nothing to study on Friday mornings. They didn't know what the unemployment level was. There was terrible suffering in the crashes before 1929, and the '29 crash was probably the worst, but that '29 suffering was also much more publicized. Massive news coverage of an economic collapse or any type of tragedy can distort how bad it is.

Today, when you hear something on the radio or see something on television, such as a refugee from Syria crossing a border, then people cry out that the particular refugee must be rescued; though behind him are a thousand refugees who don't happen to get on film for the television. So you don't want to be too prejudiced in looking at the past because of the distortions increased news coverage would have caused Coolidge. He and his team were not inhumane. On the contrary, they felt incredible agony for those in trouble. It was just that they felt they would reduce the length of the agony by sticking to market principles.

THE HOOVER-FDR DEBATE ON THE ROLE OF THE FEDERAL GOVERNMENT

BOSTON David, on page 2 of your book, you say it was Hoover's and FDR's writings and speeches, beginning with the presidential campaign in 1932, and especially after the New Deal began getting implemented in 1933, that started the progressive-conservative debate that has dominated the American political policy landscape for the last eighty years.

Amity, before, during, or after his presidency, did Coolidge engage in a progressive-conservative debate with *any* Democrat on the order of Hoover's with FDR that helped frame the future political and policy landscape?

SHLAES Insofar as he ran for election, of course, his policies were debated against his opponents. It's important to remember that in the 1920s, the Republicans were the progressive party. Theodore Roosevelt was a Republican. Many of the policy debates transpired within the Republican Party, where Coolidge was the old wing and Hoover the new wing.

BOSTON David's book talks of there being a framed debate—where you've got FDR saying one thing and Hoover saying another, and they're saying it publicly year after year in speeches and editorials, and there's this big intellectual political clash that went on between them. I'm asking if Coolidge ever had a counterpart with whom he had an ongoing debate on the order of Hoover's with FDR?

SHLAES In 1924, Coolidge ran against John Davis and there's a wonderful book by my fellow Coolidge trustee Garland Tucker. Tucker makes clear that there was very little difference between the Democrats and the Republicans in 1924. Both were conservative. In Coolidge's time, there was a remarkable consensus that politicians should be fairly conservative. The Progressives enjoyed support, but lacked electoral punch. They were more an impulse than an abiding force.

BOSTON So it really took an FDR and his advocating a more extreme position about the role of government in order to really frame the debate?

DAVENPORT My view is that the New Deal was like our French Revolution. Edmund Burke, the father of modern conservatism, developed his political philosophy in response to the French Revolution. The major conservative to examine the New Deal, America's version of the French Revolution, in detail was Herbert Hoover. He was initially disturbed by the reality of its policies, and then became more and more offended by it, which motivated him

to become more aggressive about criticizing it and pointing out its excesses as time went on. Even though we say that the beginning of modern American conservatism came in the 1950s with Russell Kirk, William F. Buckley, and *The National Review*, the first voice in the wilderness making the case for modern conservatism was Herbert Hoover in his speeches and editorial debates with Franklin Roosevelt in the 1930s.

THE IMPACT OF HOOVER'S UNSUCCESSFUL PRESIDENCY ON HIS IMPACT AS AN IMPORTANT CONSERVATIVE THINKER

BOSTON That leads to my next question. After his presidency, Hoover was a prophetic voice crying in the American wilderness of the 1930s, pointing the way toward what has become modern conservatism. We'll all acknowledge that he was a great political thinker.

Is it Hoover's dismal record in having almost no success in dealing with the Great Depression that has caused him to be largely overlooked as modern conservatism's prophetic voice?

DAVENPORT I'll say a couple of things about that. First, Hoover himself acknowledged that he was the only public figure who ever had a depression named for him. So being president when the Great Depression started was not a happy circumstance for his ultimate political legacy.

Second observation: Hoover was much more of a political philosopher than most presidents. He wrote a 1922 essay on American individualism that's considered to be one of the finer pieces of political philosophy that was done in the twentieth century. During his post-presidency, he used his time writing, speaking, and really honing his political philosophy, and Roosevelt gave him plenty of material to work with in expressing his conservative views.

David Davenport

BOSTON What I'm saying is that people like me, in 2015, who are not fellows at the Hoover Institution at Stanford University, really have no awareness of Herbert Hoover's being this prophetic voice in the wilderness political philosopher until I read your book.

DAVENPORT That's why we wrote it.

BOSTON Most people's first reaction to Hoover is Hooverville and the Great Depression, so is that part of the fight you have in attempting to elevate this man and his brilliance?

DAVENPORT When I give tours of the Hoover Institution in Palo Alto, I take people first into a room that's devoted to what Herbert Hoover did before he became president of the United States, and also shows what he did after his presidency. Before he became president, he was the best and the brightest at everything he did. He was arguably the wealthiest businessman of his time. He was an orphan who was completely self-made and ran mining projects all over

the world. With his food relief projects in Europe after World War I, he saved more lives than anyone in the world.

After his presidency, he did important things that people haven't focused on like framing the conservative response to the New Deal. George Nash, recognized as Hoover's official biographer, went into the Institution's archives and found a book Hoover wrote that was never published, called *The Crusade Years*. In it, it made this same case against the New Deal in his post-presidency that he crusaded about in his editorials when Roosevelt was president.

BOSTON After Roosevelt beat Hoover in 1932, and then ranted at FDR and his government more than anybody, is there any evidence that Hoover regretted having increased the size of government during his presidency in response to the Great Depression?

DAVENPORT No, I don't think so. He saw the New Deal as being something entirely different in both kind and amount than what he had done as president. He saw FDR going off on what he called "economic regimentation"—which was a whole different approach than Hoover had taken. He had always attempted to hold the line about America's being a country of individuals and he recognized the need to defend the role of individuals in our society. He felt Roosevelt's New Deal was really being pursued for the purpose of changing America's political economy and political system.

THE TENSION BETWEEN RUGGED INDIVIDUALISM AND COMPASSION

BOSTON Speaking of rugged individualism, did Hoover's concept of the desired American trait of rugged individualism have any component of compassion in it?

DAVENPORT Absolutely. His great essay on "American Individualism" in 1922 pointed out that in the United States through our history, rugged individualism has always been combined with something else, and he thought that something else was equality of opportunity. They kept trying in Hoover's day to make rugged individualism sound like *laissez-faire* economics—with his thinking being along the lines of, "Let the robber barons and fat cats on Wall Street do whatever they want to do." Hoover said that was an incorrect assessment because rugged individualism was not just economic *laissez faire*; instead it was American individualism coupled with equality of opportunity as a philosophy.

HOW GOVERNMENT SHOULD DEAL WITH "THE FORGOTTEN MAN"

BOSTON Amity wrote a book that focused on FDR and how he rose to power by appealing to all the downtrodden people harmed by the Great Depression, who he called "The Forgotten Man"—that's the title of her book.

I want you both to answer the following question from Coolidge and Hoover's viewpoint: What concern, if any, should the federal government have for the forgotten man?

SHLAES There are several forgotten men. One forgotten man is the homeless man, at the bottom. Before Coolidge, there was a famous philosopher named William Graham Sumner, and he pointed out that another forgotten man is the taxpayer. What he said was, "Who is forgotten? The man who pays, the man who prays, and the man who is not thought of—the regular guy." There has always been a great tension among these different types of forgotten men. What do we do for the homeless? What do we do for the party who is already bearing a large part of the country's tax burden? The circumstances of all forgotten men raise important questions.

BOSTON Let's address the forgotten man who's homeless and unemployed—the guy who's in the ditch and his family is in the ditch.

From Coolidge's and Hoover's standpoint, what was the federal government's responsibility to that forgotten man?

SHLAES The federal government's responsibility was to respect the role of states, communities, and churches, and let them help all the forgotten men.

At that time, states, cities, and churches collectively were a bigger part of America's relief efforts to those in need than the federal government except in time of war. Coolidge felt that the states' experiments in dealing with the homeless were very useful and that they were leading the way in how to respond. His approach was not inhumane; it was just that he believed different authorities should deal with the problem of serious poverty.

DAVENPORT Hoover's view would have been the same. One of the great philosophical questions throughout time is: What are the essential things that a federal government needs to do? Coolidge and Hoover in the 1920s and '30s had pretty similar views, though they had different dispositions and temperaments. They had similar views on what subjects the federal government should address; and the issue of providing relief to individual people in high economic stress was not one of the essential things they thought a federal government should be doing.

BOSTON We have time for a question from the audience.

HOW HOOVER AND COOLIDGE WOULD FIT INTO THE REPUBLICAN PARTY IN 2015

AUDIENCE MEMBER In today's political and cultural landscape, there's a shift going on in our ideology toward expansive government. In the 2016 election, Bernie Sanders is a self-proclaimed Socialist and he's gaining ground; and on the conservative side, Donald Trump has supported policies like universal healthcare and progressive taxes.

Amity and David, would you say there's still room for a modern day Coolidge or Hoover type of conservative in today's political landscape?

DAVENPORT Amity and I have a friendly disagreement about this question. I like Amity's book on Coolidge very much, and I like Calvin Coolidge very much. Although he was president in the twentieth century, he was actually more like a nineteenth century president. His values were formed growing up where his dad was a local official and a farmer in Vermont. He viewed debt, for example, as a moral thing—you've got to repay your debts. In the modern economy, debt is a tool of economic policy; it's not just a moral question. So Coolidge's views were pre-modern.

The New Deal completely transformed the American political and economic systems, and therefore, I'm not sure we can go back to the 1920s and determine how a pre-modern thinker like Coolidge would fit into the modern era. Herbert Hoover could be a strong candidate for president today because he had a very strong philosophy about the Constitution and what the role of the federal government should be as he confronted the New Deal.

The question though is whether somebody like Hoover could win an election? There are still people like Hoover out there, but the generation of Americans now in their twenties and thirties—like my children—have lived their whole lives with big government, and they don't see it as a problem. It's hard for them to think about individual liberty as something that is really worth protecting because of what's been happening throughout the era in which they've grown up.

Every once in a while, we have a "liberty moment"—like when my son discovered that when he bought his healthcare, he was going to have to pay for pregnancy coverage and other things he didn't want that cost extra money. I told him it was a "liberty moment," because he could now realize how the government was getting into his affairs. Selling conservative principles to the electorate has become more difficult now because we're used to big government in our lives. Our country's moving back toward embracing conservative philosophy is very much needed, and I'd love to see a candidate in a campaign holding others accountable to that sort of conservatism.

AMITY But Coolidge was modern. His conservative philosophy is very modern. If you look at the economy during his presidency, it's what we hope a modern economy can be. Today we prize innovation. There was an incredible patent rate during his presidency in the mid-1920s, and that's the gold standard for productivity gains, which are the most important part of economic growth. Today we prize new technology. In the twenties, people got electricity, cars, household appliances, and toilets. He might have appeared a dour and unusual character in a morality play, but actually Coolidge presided over a state of affairs that we envy today.

Could a Coolidge be elected today? Shortly after the Coolidge book came out, Mrs. Thatcher passed away. I wrote a column in tribute to her. Writing it made me think about how in the 1970s, England embraced compassionate conservatism. The Tory Party was soft on the idea of markets being able to correct themselves, and also believed that those who made hard market arguments were obsolete. Then terrible economic troubles came to England. All of a sudden someone Victorian in her demeanor became incredibly popular and led the country out of trouble through sticking to her conservative economic principles which had previously been judged as being too harsh. Thatcher was the UK Coolidge—in modern times.

Our interest rate right now is too low for us to want to implement tough measures. One day though, when the interest rate goes up, our budget will fall apart, and then we'll go looking for a figure like Margaret Thatcher or Calvin Coolidge. The circumstances are what will cause a conservative such as Coolidge to appeal. Those circumstances are missing now. It's only when there's deep trouble that people start looking for a tougher type.

BOSTON You've been a great audience. Let's have a round of applause for David Davenport and Amity Shlaes.

IV.

Thirties Through Fifties

FRANKLIN D. ROOSEVELT

HARRY S. TRUMAN

DWIGHT EISENHOWER

JAMES TOBIN is a past winner of the National Book Critics Award in biography. His fourth book, *The Man He Became: How FDR Defied Polio to Win the Presidency* (Simon & Schuster 2013), makes the compelling argument that Franklin Roosevelt became president not in spite of polio, but because of it. The interview took place December 12, 2013 at the Rosewood Crescent Hotel ballroom at a luncheon sponsored by the World Affairs Council of Dallas/Fort Worth.

"What polio did was to allow FDR to prove—as much to himself as to anyone else—that he had a depth of courage that had never been tested before the virus hit him. There are some things in life you don't find out about yourself until you're put to the test. Confronting polio was his great test. Because of polio, Franklin Roosevelt learned what he had inside him." **– JAMES TOBIN**

CHAPTER 15

JAMES TOBIN
ON
Franklin
D. Roosevelt

THE IMPACT OF POLIO ON FDR

BOSTON Jim, we're here this afternoon to talk about your newest book, *The Man He Became: How FDR Defied Polio to Win the Presidency.*

Most people think of Franklin Roosevelt as the president who took us through the Great Depression and most of World War II. We also think of him as one of our great presidential communicators—we remember his famous statement, "We have nothing to fear but fear itself" in his famous first inaugural address, and also his Fireside Chats.

But I have to say that after reading your book, I now think of him more than anything else as the man who was able to defy polio, and had the strength

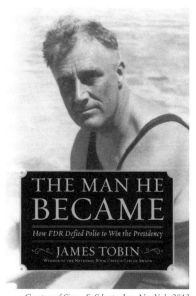

Courtesy of Simon & Schuster, Inc., New York, 2013

of character not to be set back when he lost the use of his legs at age thirty-nine.

Is it your perception that his response to polio tells us more about the essential Franklin Roosevelt than any other component of his life?

TOBIN I don't know if I'd go that far. You'd have to put the influence of his family first. The Roosevelts were an extraordinary family. Franklin was inspired as a young man by the example of his distant cousin, Theodore Roosevelt, whom he came to know quite well. Then there was the Delano family, which was, in its day, a more powerful family than the Roosevelts. FDR's formidable mother, Sarah Delano Roosevelt, always liked to say, "Oh, Franklin is really a Delano." When I got to know a little bit more about the Delano family, I realized what she was talking about. That heritage was a deep sense of noblesse oblige, in the best sense, and that, more than anything else, was the foundation of FDR's character.

What polio did for FDR was to allow him to prove—as much to himself as to everybody else—that he had not only an amazing family background, but also a depth of courage that had never been tested before the virus hit him. There are some things you don't find out about yourself until you're put to the test. Confronting polio was his great test. Because of polio, he learned what he had inside him.

BOSTON There was definitely a link, though, between the courage to overcome polio and his incredible ambition.

TOBIN No question about that. When I was working on the book, someone asked, "Wasn't it really Eleanor who drove his ambition?" Answer: Not in the slightest. I hope nobody thinks that. During his early life, FDR was the most ambitious man alive. He wanted the presidency from the time he was a kid. He could never give up that ambition. So you're right—it was absolutely a push and pull relationship between the polio and

his ambition. The quest for the presidency defined him. In some sense, it was the quest to fulfill the kind of belief his parents had in him, and at the same time to match the example of Theodore Roosevelt, who was a powerful force in his life.

HOW FDR CONTRACTED POLIO

BOSTON On page 70 of your book, you raise questions that presumably Franklin Roosevelt asked of himself, and so many other Americans did at the time (as to those who had any passing familiarity with polio as of 1921), once the diagnosis was made. The questions: Was it really possible for a thirty-nine-year-old Anglo-Saxon in excellent health, who lived in the best surroundings with the highest standards of cleanliness and safety, to contract infantile paralysis? Wasn't polio a disease that struck only children, especially poor, unfortunate children of the slums?

TOBIN Here's how I think it happened. What you said was the perception at the time, but not the truth of the matter. In fact, many children infected with the poliovirus actually lived in circumstances of good sanitation.

Polio, unlike many other terrible childhood illnesses, is—strangely—a disease of good sanitation. How did he get sick? In the first place, FDR had always been susceptible to germs. There was clearly some weakness in his immune system. He was brought up as an only child on a fairly isolated country estate on the Hudson River. His mother did not like to see him playing with the village boys. So he did not pick up the germs that most of us picked up when we played with our childhood playmates; we get sick and develop immunities to those germs. He didn't develop those immunities, and that made him sick all the time—before and after polio—with various minor and some serious illnesses. So there was that.

He had run for vice president in 1920 on the Democratic ticket headed by James Cox that opposed Warren Harding, and they had been defeated. On July 28, 1921, FDR was trying to remake his career as a New York state politician, and was getting ready to run for the Senate or governor, and so he was making the rounds. He was very active in many charitable organizations and political organizations around New York, and one of the jobs he took on was the chairmanship of the New York Area Boy Scout Council. His kids were Boy Scouts. So he went to a huge Boy Scout campout at a state park up the Hudson River from New York City, and it was there, almost certainly, that he encountered the poliovirus.

We know this based on how many days later he started to show symptoms. The day he spent at the Boy Scout camp must have been the day he picked up the virus, either from one of those kids, or as the book makes clear, from polluted water in the state park. There was an obscure New York state public health report (that I found only through the magic of Google) showing the presence of the E. coli bacteria in water sources at the park's camping areas. That means human waste was in the water. That's how the poliovirus got spread around. So we can't know for sure if he contracted the virus from a kid or from bad water, but it almost certainly happened that day.

BOSTON One of my favorite sentences in the book that speaks to what you were talking about is on page 28. You were trying to explain how this polio happened at a Boy Scout camp, and you put it in plain words: "Children playing outdoors in the summer time are apt to shit in the woods."

TOBIN I have a historian colleague at Miami University (Ohio), where I teach, who is not a prude, but she happened to read that passage when the book was still in manuscript and she told me: "You cannot say this." When she said that, I thought, "Well, yeah, now I am definitely going to say that."

THE DIFFICULTY IN UNDERSTANDING FDR'S MINDSET

BOSTON A major challenge in writing a biography of FDR is the fact that he never opened up about what he was really thinking. Your book talks about his "heavily forested interior;" how his mind had "subterranean streams;" and was a "complex tapestry." He realized that, maybe even delighted in it, to the extent he once told movie star Orson Welles that he considered himself an actor in the way he presented his persona.

So how did you get past FDR's opaqueness in drawing conclusions about what made him tick?

TOBIN I probably never did get past his opaqueness. That "forested interior" remark is a quotation from the great playwright, Robert Sherwood, who worked as a speechwriter for FDR. Sherwood was a brilliant guy who was very perceptive about the human character and the human condition. In a first rate biography of FDR, Sherwood wrote, he said, "I tried to look into that forested interior, but I never could figure out what was going on in there."

The fact is, I tried to determine Roosevelt's state of mind and motivation, but due to his closed personality, much of what I said is more in the nature of conjecture than conclusion; though it's the best conjecture I can give based on the best evidence I had, and much of the evidence was fragmentary.

David McCullough wrote a wonderful essay about the great nineteenth century biologist Louis Agassiz, who was known to tell his biology students, upon delivering a dead fish for them to examine, "Look at your fish." Then he would leave the room, and come back a few minutes later and say, "What have you observed?" All the students were thinking, "What the hell? It's a dead fish." So they'd come up short and he would say to them, "All right then, look at your fish." And he would leave again and then

come back. Finally, they started to realize that if they looked hard enough, they could come up with very astute observations. He would reward them finally by saying, "Yes, yes, you've got it. That's brilliant. Now for your next assignment, look at your fish."

David McCullough tells that story as a kind of object lesson for historians, that we should look at the documentary material all historians look at when we're analyzing a major character like Roosevelt. I was reviewing materials at the Franklin Roosevelt Library in New York that many biographers and historians have examined before. I was trying to look at my fish. I was trying to see things that others maybe had missed. I don't know for sure that I did that, but I sure tried to. I was looking for little fragments of evidence.

I'll give you an example. FDR, in the weeks and months after he became ill with polio, began to write letters to his many contacts around the country. He had a million friends, and because of his 1920 vice presidential campaign, he had made many new contacts in the Democratic Party. He was trying to nurture and stay connected with them. From the moment he began to write people, he said, "My doctors have assured me I'm getting along beautifully, and I'm far exceeding their expectations with this quick recovery I'm making." Now, I had access to his doctors' letters between each other, not to FDR, but the doctors writing each other, and they weren't saying anything like, "Oh, he's going to make a miraculous recovery." So I kept asking myself, "Why would he write such positive things about his health to people? Even though his doctors may not have been fully frank with him, he must have known that what he was telling his friends was vastly over-optimistic. Why would he do that?"

I started to realize that the pattern in his letter writing was powerful. He was telling *himself* that this is what was going to happen. He would never admit to anyone else, to his family, to any of his doctors, or to himself, that there was a possibility he might not recover the ability to walk. In fact, he did recover the ability to walk by himself, though only with the help of braces and crutches. But it was by that insistence, keeping at bay any possibility of despair, that he was able to make this work. I've described him before as a gigantic optimism machine, and it began right from the very beginning. That's what I tried to do: stare at those letters over and over again, and try and see patterns in them that perhaps other people had missed.

HOW POLIO LED FDR TO THE PRESIDENCY

BOSTON To your knowledge, has any FDR biographer besides you concluded that polio, and the inspiring story associated with FDR's defying it, and then his actually using that disability to his political advantage, was a main cause of FDR's rise to the presidency?

TOBIN No one's been as brilliant. Thanks for pointing that out. As a matter of fact, yes, earlier biographers have pointed out some of the benefits of polio in his later career. What I did was try to put that insight, which is not original to me, front and center, and develop the case for it. You see, my book only covers the period from 1921 (when he got polio) to when he was elected president in 1932. I had the liberty of trying to expand and develop that thesis at greater length. I do think it's a convincing one, and I'm not sure anyone else has shown how FDR make use of his physical comeback as part of his political comeback—how he used that when he ran for governor in 1928 as a prelude to running for the presidency, which he fully intended to do. With polio, he was able to present himself in a way he never had before.

FDR had enormous advantages in politics, starting with his golden family background, and the greatest name in American politics. He had been to Harvard. He had had early success in politics and government. What he didn't have was any kind of a common touch. What he could do in coming back from this terrible, devastating illness was to present himself as somebody who had had great difficulty and then surmounted it.

One of his top political aides was Jim Farley, who became his campaign manager in 1932, and later became his postmaster general, and was basically the political consigliere in the Roosevelt administration. Farley had once been the boxing commissioner for the state of New York. During FDR's presidential campaign in '32, Farley said the greatest accolade in sports writing was: here was a fellow who had been down on the deck and then got up and came back to win. That could now be said of FDR. His recovery from polio allowed him to present himself as a man of the people in a way he never could have done before.

ELEANOR'S RESPONSE TO FDR'S POLIO

BOSTON As of 1921, when he contracted polio, FDR and his wife, Eleanor, had been estranged for three years because it had

been that long since she discovered the love letters between FDR and her assistant, Lucy Mercer.

Given that they hadn't been close in their marriage and had been leading at least semi-separate lives for three years, how did Eleanor respond to the polio?

TOBIN She was amazing. After he betrayed her and the marriage became very tense, she came to his side. She literally nursed him for a number of months. As a young woman, she had received nurse's training and done nursing work before. Although she didn't believe he could possibly have another career in politics, she thought it was important for him to believe in that possibility, so she supported his ambition. She brought people into their home to have conversations with him and keep his interest and ambition alive. She acted above and beyond the call of marital duty, and was amazing in that role.

BOSTON Another incredibly powerful moment in the book is Eleanor's description of the look on her husband's face when he was told by a doctor for the first time, "You have polio."

TOBIN When she was asked the question many years after FDR's death, "How did your husband react when he was given the news that he had polio?", she said there was only one other time she saw an expression on his face like that: December 7, 1941, when he was dealing with the destruction of much of the American fleet in Hawaii, at Pearl Harbor. Same reaction.

FDR'S CIVIL WAR OF CONFLICTING EMOTIONS

BOSTON All right, getting back to his "complex tapestry" personality, in the book you talk about his multi-dimensional response (which you would expect from a "complex tapestry" personality) to the polio, going through the negative emotions of inner rage, deep grieving, denial, fear, and depression. At the same time, he always maintained a positive, cheery, defiant exterior attitude, intolerant of anyone who expressed any type of pity to him.

With these conflicting emotions going on simultaneously, was there something of a civil war going on inside FDR's head after he contracted polio in 1921?

TOBIN I suppose that's right. I hadn't thought of it that way. The reaction people have had to a severe trauma like this did not come out of my reading of FDR's materials, because he was never candid about those dark moments he surely had, and never wrote about them, and never spoke about them, as far as we know.

I drew my conclusions about these negative emotions that had to well up inside him from reading the memoirs of other people who had polio and were severely disabled. The pattern of reaction to getting hit by polio is so uniform that we can be pretty sure Roosevelt felt this way. He had to be fighting one emotion with another. He had this insistence that everything was going to be okay, and that is not an unusual reaction to trauma. There is a will to believe that everything's going to be all right. That's how you keep the shock and despair at bay. So I think you're right—there *was* a kind of interior civil war going on inside FDR.

HOW THE MEDIA COVERED FDR'S POLIO

BOSTON To present the story of Roosevelt's battle with polio to the American people with a positive spin involved three main characters besides FDR himself—his wife Eleanor, his assistant Louis Howe, and his doctor, George Draper.

For the most part, did the press take Eleanor, Howe, and Draper at their word, such that there was very little investigative reporting regarding the seriousness of his illness?

TOBIN There was not much press inquiry. This turned out to be an interesting part of the story. How did they announce the news and keep the press abreast of his progress? It got complicated.

In the first few weeks, Eleanor and Louis Howe were reluctant to release much information. That was largely because FDR's mother, Sarah Roosevelt, who was always very close to his affairs, was overseas on her annual European tour, and they couldn't get word of his illness to her before she got on her liner, crossed the ocean, and came back. So they tried to keep the news under wraps to protect her.

When she returned from her trip, they had already received a definitive diagnosis, and told Sarah the bad news. FDR then returned from their summer place in Maine, to their home in New York City, and then they allowed the news to be fully released. After that, for a long while, it was assumed FDR's political career was over. So once the story of his polio happened, there was no longer much to tell, as far as reporters were concerned.

I'm a former journalist, so I know how these things go. A famous and successful young man is crippled by a virus—that's a tragedy, and thus a good story. After that, not so much. He was out of the news. There wasn't much incentive to find out more about how he was doing. So you don't find much in the newspapers about him for three more years until FDR discovered the amazing mineral springs in Warm Springs, Georgia. Then, there was a new story to be told—a comeback story! Louis Howe, FDR's press agent, started to put that story out. That's when the reporters started paying attention again, and the story was: "Here's a guy who was finished—and now look how well he's doing!"

Photo credit: Myra Klarman Photography

James Tobin

WHAT AMERICAN VOTERS KNEW ABOUT FDR'S POLIO

BOSTON He came back into politics with his first big appearance at the 1924 Democratic Convention, and then for the next eight years, he rose to the point of getting elected governor of New York and then received the Democratic nomination and got elected president in 1932.

During his political rise, did most Americans know he had polio? How much was really understood about his condition?

TOBIN In 1924, at the Democratic Convention, Governor Al Smith of New York was nominated. FDR was Smith's long-time political ally, so Smith chose FDR to give his nominating address because he needed Roosevelt's backing and big name. It was absolutely clear to the thousands of people inside Madison Square Garden that this man was crippled and could not walk without assistance. The national newspaper coverage at that time made it perfectly clear what the story was and how disabled he

had been by this disease. The same was true when he ran for governor in 1928.

His difficulty in walking was central to most of the coverage. So people did know about it.

This gets to one of the points that the book makes, which is the view that many of us have today—the widespread belief that FDR concealed his condition. This myth has come in part because of the FDR Memorial in Washington, DC created during the 1990s.

THE PROBLEM WITH THE FDR MEMORIAL IN WASHINGTON, DC

BOSTON Speaking of the FDR Memorial, one of the images we have from it is of the statue of him sitting in a wheelchair. What's wrong with that image?

TOBIN FDR wasn't in a wheelchair very much. That's another thing we hear—that he spent the rest of his life in a wheelchair. No. FDR used a wheelchair a couple of times a day when he was wheeled around from one room to another, and that was behind closed doors. Once he entered a room, he sat in an easy chair or an office chair, not in a wheelchair. When he was out in public, he would walk and he was capable of walking. He had his braces on, and a cane in one hand and his assistant's arm to hold onto with the other. That was his public presentation.

In private, he used the wheelchair just to get from one place to another. So the wheelchair image in the statue is a little misleading. There's a wonderful statue of Roosevelt in London—the British thought very highly of FDR for obvious reasons. It shows him standing with a cane. That was his public presentation in the US and the rest of the world. That, to me, is a more fitting way of presenting him. On the other hand, I understand why people wanted him portrayed in a wheelchair, and it does present one facet of the reality about him.

FDR'S IMPACT ON AMERICA'S ATTITUDE TOWARD THOSE WITH DISABILITIES

BOSTON Here in Texas, one of our state's most successful politicians is Greg Abbott, currently our attorney general but who's now running for governor [and in 2014, was elected governor of Texas]. Shouldn't Greg Abbott thank Franklin Roosevelt for his being in a position where nobody talks about his being in a wheelchair anymore? Is that part of FDR's legacy—how he transformed the American mindset toward those with disabilities?

TOBIN There is still a stigma. Everybody knows someone with a significant disability and that friend or relative of yours will tell you, when speaking honestly, that it's still difficult for him to have normal interactions with people who are not disabled. But there's also no question that people with disabilities now can have a full participatory role in American life. FDR started that. FDR's example was an absolutely irrefutable argument that somebody who could not walk on his own could still play a whole role, could do what he wanted to, as other people did. Even though FDR did not set himself up as a disabilities crusader, that example, more than anything else, laid the foundation for where we are today.

TOBIN READS HIS FAVORITE PASSAGE FROM THE BOOK

BOSTON My last question is really not a question, but I want the audience to have the opportunity to hear the rhythm of your language in the writing. Whenever I go to buy a book in a bookstore, I always look at the first page and the last page because if those are really great, then I buy the book. If they're not, then I know the book's not going to be very good. Jim, you get an A+ for your ending. For the benefit of the crowd, please read the last four paragraphs, which tie a ribbon around *The Man He*

Became, and bring it all together in a perfect Christmas bow.

TOBIN When you first talked about me doing this, Talmage, I thought about a guy who writes about books on the Internet and has a great blog. His test for deciding whether he wants to buy a book is: when he picks up a book in the bookstore, he goes to the 99th page. He says he knows authors work hard on the first page of their books and on the last page, but on page 99, the author might be thinking, *Let's just keep it moving here.* I think that's a pretty good test. Luckily, you did not ask me to read my page 99, and my ending is something I did work a little harder on.

"If a person's sense of self—his belief about who he really is—is the story of his own life that he carries in his mind, then FDR as president must have drawn power from the turn his story took between 1921 and 1932. He knew he had done something terribly difficult. Through exercise, practice, and compromise with his own highest hopes, he had recovered some of the strength and mobility he had lost to the poliovirus. But more important and more difficult, he had defeated the stigma that prevented people with disabled limbs from participating fully in life's struggles. That victory required a fierce will, many wiles, and a lot of help. The wiles and the will lay somewhere inside the thirty-nine-year-old man at the moment he became ill. He might have retreated into a comfortable retirement. Instead, he chose to exert his will and exercise his wiles, and that act of choosing, more than anything else, revealed who he was. His close friend and aide of the later presidential years, Harry Hopkins, once said: 'The guy *never* knows when he is licked.' Hopkins said that was a defect. Maybe it was, but obviously it was also a strength. As the journalist John Gunther put it, 'Because he had beaten his illness, Roosevelt thought he could beat anything.'

"Nearly half a century after Roosevelt died in 1945, the anthropologist Robert

Murphy told the story of his own paralysis in an extraordinary memoir titled *The Body Silent*. Murphy observed that because all of us are wounded, visibly or invisibly, the struggle of the disabled represents the struggle of every man and woman. It stands for 'the battle of life's wounded against isolation, dependency, denigration and entropy, and all other things that pull them back out of life into their inner selves and ultimate negation. This struggle is the highest expression of the human rage for life, the ultimate purpose for our species.' Paralytics, and all the disabled, are characters in a Passion Play, mummers in search of Resurrection. One cannot help but see FDR's pursuit of the presidency as the embodiment of Murphy's idea.

"Roosevelt's best epitaph might be the offhand remark he made when an aide listening to him spin yet another grand plan said, 'Mr. President, you *can't* do that.'

"The President looked at him and said, 'I do a lot of things I can't do.'"

BOSTON Isn't that great?

TOBIN Thank you.

BOSTON That passage highlights what the book is really about. To me, it's so much more than a man and his battle with polio. It's about what it takes to have the strength and character to overcome any type of adversity, so I can't imagine a better story than what Jim has created.

GEOFFREY C. WARD has been Ken Burns' right-hand man for many of the highest rated documentaries, including *The Civil War, Baseball, Jazz,* and *The Roosevelts.* Through their collaboration, and his work for the PBS program The American Experience, Geoff has won seven Emmy Awards. His first book about Franklin Roosevelt won the National Book Critics Circle Award and was a finalist for the Pulitzer Prize. He's written a total of four books with a focus on FDR, the most recent being *The Roosevelts: An Intimate History* (Knopf 2014), and also served as the editor of American Heritage. The interview took place May 20, 2015, in the offices of the Jackie Robinson Foundation in New York City at a program organized by the Foundation's CEO Della Britton.

"FDR, like his cousin Theodore, commanded every conversation. Anyone who went to see either of them was lucky to get in a word edgewise. His Interior Secretary Harold Ickes always tried to schedule his meetings with FDR at lunchtime. That way, Ickes could talk whenever the president stopped to take a bite." – **GEOFFREY C. WARD**

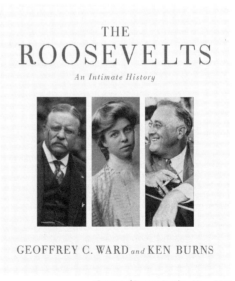

WARD Yes. I came from a good Democratic household and FDR was a hero to my parents, so I grew up hearing a lot about him. I was born in 1940 and at nine I got polio. My mom died recently at 101 and I regret now never having asked her whether she and my father had consciously encouraged me to be interested in Roosevelt because he, too, had developed the disease. But I know I began learning about him early on.

When I was eleven, something I read made me question FDR's 1940 decision to run for a third term when no president before him had dared to do so. Why it bothered me I can't now remember. But I somehow felt the only way to find out why he did it was to write Eleanor Roosevelt and ask her. So I sat down and wrote her a letter and addressed the envelope to "Eleanor Roosevelt, New York City." Somehow it got to her and I received an answer from her within a week and a half—a handwritten letter explaining that for a time, the president himself had not been sure whether he should break the precedent set by George Washington and run for a third term. It was the rise of Hitler that persuaded him he had to do it. That experience made me think that all famous people would write me back right away if I sent them a letter. To this day, she's the only one who ever did.

To go back to polio, my bout with it has been nowhere near as severe as Roosevelt's was. He was basically paralyzed from the waist down and for the most part couldn't move his legs. I'm nowhere near being that badly affected, but I know my having polio had something to do with my being interested in FDR.

I'll always be grateful to Ken Burns because he read my *A First-Class Temperament* about FDR many years ago, and understood how incredibly important polio was in the life of Franklin Roosevelt. If you're going to understand Roosevelt, you've got to understand that when he wanted a glass of water, he had to find somebody to get it for him; and if he wanted to pee in the Oval Office,

somebody had to bring him a bottle. Polio affected every hour of every day.

Earlier books about him said that he had "conquered" polio. Well, no one ever does that. Roosevelt learned to live with it. He never took a step by himself from the age of thirty-nine on, though he managed in all sorts of ways to make people think he was walking. He was a great actor as well as a great president. He really did once tell Orson Welles that there were two great actors in the United States and that, he, Welles, was the other one.

To my eternal gratitude, Ken gave us two hours in the documentary to develop FDR's struggle with polio. Episode Four is almost all about the disease and its impact—about a man who spent seven years of his life trying to get back on his feet without success, and then decided he was going to go on with his political career and pursue the presidency in spite of it.

HOW POLIO IMPACTED FDR'S STATE OF MIND

BOSTON On page one of her Pulitzer prize-winning biography about Franklin and Eleanor Roosevelt, *No Ordinary Time*, Doris Kearns Goodwin described how during his presidency, FDR, before he went to bed at night in the White House, would often visualize himself as a boy at Hyde Park sledding down a hill and then walking up the hill. She said his going through that ritual at night "liberated him from his paralysis through an act of imaginative will" and allowed his mind to settle down so he could go to sleep.

Is going through that type of ritual common among polio victims?

WARD It's a terrific book and Doris is a friend of mine but no dream could liberate him from polio paralysis for more than a few moments. He still had to wake up the next morning, unable to dress himself.

What he did have was a serene sense of himself that polio somehow couldn't undercut and therein lies the great mystery. I've spent most of my life trying to figure out how the hell he maintained such serene self-confidence through it all. We'll never know for sure but that's why I started writing about him.

One day years ago, when I was the editor of *American Heritage* magazine, a professor called. He was an expert on relations between the United States and Japan during a particular period before the war and he had devoted his life to that subject. "I just found some recordings of FDR at Hyde Park. They were made in the fall of 1940 and appear to be secret conversations. Would you be interested in that?" I pretended to be only mildly interested, but in fact I became instantly obsessed with the prospect of hearing them.

It became clear that FDR had had a microphone installed in a lamp on his desk, attached to a wire recorder in the White House basement. His object had been to record press conferences so that he couldn't be misquoted. But he often forgot to switch the system off. The professor who'd called me had been interested only in Roosevelt's discussion of Japan but I was fascinated by the other topics that came up—campaigning, political scandal, integrating the armed forces.

And by something else. The Franklin Roosevelt on those recordings — whether he was talking politics or complimenting his secretary on a brand-new dress —was precisely the same man he was when addressing the nation—good-humored, self-confident, seemingly ready for anything.

Here's a guy in a wheelchair who's been president for eight years. He was surely tired. It was 1940 and the world was going to hell. And he seems unchanged. I thought to myself, "How the hell does somebody do that?" I've spent the last forty years trying to figure out how he did it. I still don't know, but I've had a lot of fun trying to find out.

ELEANOR'S IMPACT ON FDR'S POLITICS

BOSTON In the book, you describe the great irony of Franklin Roosevelt, despite being a child of privilege, somehow becoming a champion of the working man. You also say that Eleanor Roosevelt was Franklin's "liberal conscience."

Would FDR have been the champion of the working man without Eleanor's vigilant presence as a spur in his life, asserting her forceful liberal conscience into his mindset?

WARD He would not have been as liberal, that's for sure. From the first, FDR was a progressive Democrat who shared his Republican cousin Theodore's belief that the federal government had a responsibility for the well-being of the people. But Eleanor was a constant goad throughout his life. She was always telling him he could do better, do more, win passages of bills he knew Congress would never vote to enact. "Goad" is the right word, I think. She sometimes irritated him but she also made him a far greater man than he would have ever been otherwise.

Eleanor Roosevelt was a miracle of the human spirit. It's almost impossible to understand how she became the woman the world came to revere. She never wanted for material comfort as a child but everything else seemed to conspire against her. She was an orphan raised as a poor relation by grim, dutiful relatives in an emotionally parched atmosphere that taught her that nobody could be expected ever to love her for long. The only way she thought she might win people's affection would be by doing things for them. She spent her whole life doing exactly that.

It's hard to understand how she developed, given her childhood, given what was expected of women in her era, given all the easy choices she could have made. Maybe she could have been merely the wife of a politician, but she insisted on being more than that—she was her own person. Though she came out of a girlhood where she never wanted for food or physical comfort, nevertheless, it was an emotionally parched, arid childhood in which nobody loved her.

BOSTON On the "goad" issue, as I read history, between the time Franklin Roosevelt became president until the start of World War II, that being the era when he was obviously focused on the New Deal and getting the United States out of the Great Depression, it seems he was a lot more receptive to Eleanor's liberal conscience during the first two terms of his presidency. Then once World War II came along, obviously he had to focus virtually all his attention on the war effort, although she stayed consumed with her liberal social issues, such that Franklin and Eleanor were much more compatible before World War II than during the war.

Is that accurate?

WARD I don't know that they were more or less compatible during the war years, but what you say is basically true. He could not do all the domestic things she wanted him to do during the war. But we shouldn't forget that in the midst of the war he called for an Economic Bill of Rights, promising every American a living wage, a decent home, a good education and medical care. He also signed the GI Bill of Rights that transformed the American Middle Class.

FDR'S DEVELOPING MENTAL TOUGHNESS THROUGH CHILDHOOD, PREP SCHOOL, AND COLLEGE

BOSTON You talk in your books about how when Franklin Roosevelt was growing up, he was something of an outcast during his teenage years at Groton School and later at Harvard; though he tried not to acknowledge the stress of not fitting in to those two student bodies.

Did the emotional strength he developed during those formative years of refusing

to show disappointment and sadness over social rejection become the foundation for his having the strength and self-discipline to defy and never show disappointment over the many stresses he had later in life— polio, loneliness, dealing with the Great Depression, World War II, dealing with his disappointing children? In other words, was he able to keep the smile on his face and the upbeat tone in his voice throughout his life, regardless of major obstacles and setbacks, because of his maintaining his smile through high school and college when things weren't good?

WARD I think it goes back farther than that. He was an only child of a very strong-willed mother and a much older father. When his parents married, Sara Delano was twenty-five years old and James Roosevelt was fifty-six. Women cried at the wedding because a young woman was marrying such an old man.

Their marriage was a happy one and Franklin, an only child, was the absolute object of his parents' adoration. If you've ever been to Springwood, their country home at Hyde Park, you get some sense of it, He was really treated like the Sun King up there. Not only did his parents dote on him, but the tenant farmers who worked their large country estate all called him "Master Franklin" and took their hats off to him whenever he rode by on his pony.

I received a letter after "The Roosevelts" ran on PBS last fall from the grandson of a tenant farmer at Hyde Park who remembered his grandfather telling him about a double-sided saddle the Roosevelts liked to use—two wicker baskets attached across a pony's hack, so that a child could sit on either side and take a ride. But if only one basket was occupied there was the danger that the whole business could be thrown off balance and the precious passenger might fall. This kid's grandfather had been the same age and size as FDR, and so, whenever they wanted young Franklin to go for a ride on his side of the basket saddle, he was imported to provide balance.

The sledding FDR dreamed about was not as strenuous as you might think because there were other kids on the family's estate who were allowed to ride down the hill with him, but then they (not Franklin) had to pull it back up the slope so they could do it again. He also had a velvet-lined horse-drawn sleigh which had once belonged to the emperor of France in which to ride around his father's estate.

FDR was raised to be the center of the world and I believe he saw the presidency as in some ways simply the natural order of things.

But when FDR was nine or so, James suffered a heart attack and young Franklin and his mother entered into what they called "a loving conspiracy" to make sure they never did anything to worry the old man because the doctor had told them that if James was ever again startled or surprised, it might bring on another fatal attack. Maintaining this "conspiracy" to make sure nothing ever surprised his father became, in his kid's mind, a huge responsibility.

Anything unpleasant was to be hidden, a teaching already common to members of FDR's social class, but driven home by the precarious health of his father.

Here's an example of the boy's remarkable stoicism. The Roosevelts had a private railroad car. One day when they were aboard, a steel curtain pipe fell on Franklin's head and cut him badly. Blood poured down his face. His mother was terrified. Franklin wiped away the blood, put on a cap to cover the wound and stepped out on the observation platform to keep his father from being alarmed.

When the time came for Franklin to go off to prep school, he had been taught two things: he was not to show distress and he was the center of the world.

Well, at Groton—and later, at Harvard—he was distinctly not the center of the world. He managed to hide his disappointments well but they ate at him inside.

His problems at school also had something to do with having been raised by a much older father and taught the importance of pleasing older people. His prep school and college professors all liked him. A good many of his contemporaries didn't. They found him too well-mannered, too eager to please. He couldn't ever quite understand why he had been rejected by Harvard's most exclusive club and had not been chosen to be president of his class. He had to learn that it was his responsibility to figure out how to achieve his goals, because they were not going to just be conferred on him.

People have asked me about whether we discovered anything new when we worked on *The Roosevelts.* Since I had previously written three books about him, there wasn't much "new" for me to find, but there were two photographs we came across which I had never seen before. One of them was taken at Groton. I had written some thirty pages about FDR's experience at Groton in my first book, and thought I had it pretty much covered, but this one photograph says it all. Our Florentine Films team found it in the Groton archives, and I don't think anyone had ever seen it before. It's a picture of two Groton seniors in school sweaters, just like out of a movie. They're kind of slouching against a wall, and laughing as they look down at a slender miserable-looking Franklin Roosevelt, who is doing his best to slink out of the picture. I know of no other picture in which he looks like that, but that's what it was like for him at Groton.

The other picture we found of which I'm even fonder, needs to be put in the context of recognizing that FDR very nearly worshiped his older cousin, Theodore. We knew from Mrs. Roosevelt's memoir that Franklin had gone to see TR sworn in as president in March 1905, but that was all we knew. I said to myself, "If he was there, there are lots of pictures of TR's inauguration. We might find him in one of those pictures." So we got a great glass plate negative of the inaugural crowd—one of those incredibly detailed photographs—and using a magnifying glass, we went over every inch of that huge crowd and sure enough, as TR raised his hand to take the oath of office, we found FDR's absolutely unmistakable profile. You can just imagine him saying to himself, "Boy, that looks like fun. I want to do that."

FDR'S STYLE OF LEADERSHIP

BOSTON After he'd been at Harvard awhile, Franklin finally found his niche at the *Harvard Crimson* newspaper, where he became its managing editor and president. There, he showed for the first time his gift for leadership through his "geniality and frictionless command," a gift he would obviously demonstrate for the rest of his life.

We know that as he grew up, FDR's greatest hero was his cousin, Theodore Roosevelt, who most definitely did not lead with geniality and frictionless command. So did FDR have a role model for his personal style of leadership or was his style entirely created by his own personality and imagination, which you call in your first book his "first class temperament"?

WARD That's a really good question. TR was very charming. If he wanted to charm you, you got charmed. People just fell in love with him. When they left his office, somebody said, they "had to wring his personality out of their clothes". But he was

not frictionless. He loved to fight and FDR did *not* love to fight.

FDR's capacity to avoid friction largely came from the determinedly quiet household he grew up in. He dreamed of being a hero and a leader and he admired TR extravagantly, but I don't think he ever felt he was going to lead like his older cousin did. He was not going to charge up San Juan Hill. Rather, he would find a way to maneuver into leadership positions. That went back to his childhood. In order to deal with a very strong-willed mother, he had to learn how to maneuver around her if he wanted to get what he was after.

FDR, like TR, saw the presidency as a bully pulpit from which a leader could make moral arguments. That pulpit allows a president to tell people what he believes they should do and explain how the government can help them do it. In that sense, he was very much in Theodore's mold and no one has ever been better at it. But behind closed doors in the Oval Office, things were different. He didn't harangue people, he wooed them.

Each Roosevelt commanded the conversation. Anyone who went to see either of them was lucky to get in a word edgewise. Harold Ickes, the Interior Secretary, who lasted through all twelve years of Roosevelt's administration, always tried to schedule his meetings with FDR at lunchtime. That way, Ickes could talk whenever the president stopped to take a bite.

THE TENSION BETWEEN FDR'S MOTHER SARA AND ELEANOR

BOSTON Getting back to Eleanor, she was most definitely an amazingly independent, strong-willed person, yet for almost forty years, she constantly yielded and acquiesced to her mother-in-law, Sara Delano Roosevelt.

Why couldn't Eleanor assert herself around Sara the way she did around every other person she came in contact with, particularly after Sara served as an active force in distancing Eleanor from her husband and her children?

WARD You're harder on Sara Delano Roosevelt than I am. In some ways she's my favorite Roosevelt. And the caricature of her in *Sunrise at Campobello* is just that—a caricature.

First of all, here's my definition of a good mother: if you inculcate into a child the belief that anything he sets his mind to he can achieve, then clearly Sara Delano Roosevelt was a great mother.

She was a more complicated mother-in-law—though even there she's been somewhat misunderstood You have to remember that Eleanor never really had a mother whom she could emulate, had no model for how to be a conventional wife or mother during that period. None. She was frightened of babies for fear she'd drop them, confused by the conflicting advice she found in parenting books. For a long time she was grateful to her mother-in-law for filling the breach: Sara hired and fired nannies and advised her on her duties as a conventional wife. There are letters from Eleanor thanking her mother-in-law for the help she'd given her—saying things like she didn't know what would happen to the children if we didn't have you—that kind of thing. So they had a complicated relationship. Their relationship did grow more difficult as Eleanor became more independent.

ELEANOR'S INABILITY TO PROVIDE UNCEASING DEVOTION TO FDR

BOSTON We know Franklin Roosevelt greatly favored certain women who gave him unceasing devotion and attention over the course of his life. First was his mother, and then his one-time lover and later close friend, Lucy Mercer. Also his personal secretary, Missy Lehand, then Princess Martha of Norway, and his cousin and closest

companion Daisy Suckley all hit the mark in their constant devotion and affection for him.

At least in the early years of her relationship with Franklin, (that is, during their courtship, engagement, and honeymoon pre-children phase), did Eleanor *ever* have an unceasing devotion attitude toward her husband but then later lost it due to having nonstop babies (six in the first eleven years of their marriage) and an overbearing mother-in-law OR did she never have the capacity to provide unceasing devotion to Franklin?

WARD I don't think she ever had it. She had a very strong moral sense that people should always do their absolute best—that they should always strive to do better. That personality trait is initially encouraging but becomes annoying over time. She and Franklin were certainly in love with each other. It was a real partnership, but I don't think she ever gave him the kind of unquestioning devotion that he wanted and found in other women.

I don't mean by that that he should be put on the list of womanizing presidents. He seems to have had some kind of sexual relationship with Lucy Mercer when they were young, long before he became president—though we cannot know that for sure -- but all the rest of the women you mentioned, including Lucy in his final years, but as far as I know, were only admiring friends.

BOSTON After he got the polio, do we know in fact whether he was physically capable of having sexual relations?

WARD That was not a problem. I was going to say, "Trust me."

Photo credit: Diane Raines Ward

Geoffrey C. Ward

THE IMPACT OF TRAUMA ON FDR AND ELEANOR

BOSTON Franklin and Eleanor Roosevelt each suffered a major life-changing trauma that, with 20-20 hindsight, can be viewed as blessings-in-disguise. For FDR, as we discussed previously, his big trauma was contracting polio, but everybody concluded that it caused him to become more empathetic toward the suffering of others less fortunate than he, such that the crippling of his body was instrumental to expanding his sensibilities.

For Eleanor, her big trauma was learning of Franklin's affair with Lucy Mercer. That betrayal disconnected her from him from an intimacy standpoint, as she immediately moved into her own bedroom, but the disconnect caused her to create and assert her own separate existence, which caused her to become a highly inspirational leader for dozens of worthy social causes—always pursuing new avenues of making herself useful to society.

Again, we're going to have to speculate, but that's the fun part of history. Is it likely that Franklin and Eleanor would have risen to their respective heights without having suffered these two major traumas?

WARD Well, that's also a good question. I think what you've suggested is true. Each trauma had its own peculiar good result. Besides empathy, I think Franklin also developed patience after he contracted polio. He'd been a terribly impatient person while he was physically active, but once he started asking people to help him get through his daily life activities, he learned to be patient. That's something that just happens. Anyone who loses the use of their legs has to figure out how to get things done.

I honestly don't know how much the Mercer affair betrayal affected Eleanor. Would she, all on her own, have gone out and done the things she did as Eleanor Roosevelt, but not Franklin Roosevelt's wife? I don't think there's any way to know the answer. She was conventionally deferential to her husband in public during his presidency and insisted throughout her widowhood that she be introduced as "Mrs. Franklin D. Roosevelt." At the same time, she was fiercely independent personally. So exactly how things would have worked for her independently, if she hadn't had that sort of disguise of being the governor's wife, and then the candidate's wife, and then the president's wife—I honestly don't know.

BOSTON But would she have emerged as a thoroughly independent, high-achieving woman without having the impetus to do so because of FDR's affair with Lucy Mercer?

WARD I don't think her learning of the Mercer affair changed Eleanor much. She was already showing signs of the kind of independence that alarmed her mother-in-law before the Lucy Mercer business happened. It undoubtedly sped things up.

BOSTON You don't think the Mercer affair accelerated Eleanor's assertion of her independence?

WARD It did make it much easier for her to be her own person publicly and privately. She no longer had to justify her independence to her husband. FDR knew why she was operating more independently and could do very little about it even if he'd been against it—which he wasn't.

FDR AND ELEANOR'S PARENTING DEFICIENCIES

BOSTON As virtuous and accomplished as Franklin and Eleanor were in their respective public arenas, they both would not get high marks in the way they went about parenting their children, who each had disappointing personal and professional lives. Here's an amazing statistic: Out of their five children who survived infancy, they had a total of nineteen marriages.

Eleanor would have been able to explain this family disconnect between her and her kids due to the disruption caused by her mother-in-law Sara and by her not having had good role models for parenting by her own parents, but how would Franklin have explained his disconnect from his children? Or would he simply refuse to explain it because he never wanted to acknowledge anything disappointing?

WARD I think the fact that the Roosevelt children had so many difficulties in life had comparatively little to do with their grandmother. I talked to two of his sons. Both remembered that, for the most part, their memory of their mother was of her being on the road. They found what maternal love and comfort hey got from their grandmother. She spoiled them. But she was what they had.

BOSTON But what about Franklin's disconnect from his children? After polio hit him, for a period of years, his children barely saw him as he was trying to figure himself out politically.

WARD I think the key to it is polio. For seven years, he spent almost all his time away from his family trying to figure out how to get back on his feet. He was either on a houseboat off the Florida coast or in Warm Springs in Georgia. Those kids, during their critical teenage years, were without a father.

But also the truth of the matter is that Franklin Roosevelt enjoyed playing with his kids when he happened to be home but he wanted all the disciplining and the hard parts of parenting to be done by his wife—who also often wasn't home.

HYPERACTIVITY AS AN ANTIDOTE FOR DEPRESSION

BOSTON Eleanor was Theodore Roosevelt's niece. Her father Elliott was Teddy Roosevelt's brother, and he was a drunk. Eleanor and Theodore both dealt with the grief and disappointment they suffered in their lives by attempting to live in the arena at high speed. Do their lives demonstrate that dealing with sadness and grief by engaging in a hyper-hectic lifestyle is a successful or an unsuccessful life strategy?

WARD It was certainly successful for both of them. TR and ER both suffered from terrible life-long depression. If they were ever alone and not furiously doing something, darkness descended.

I'm sure the reason Mrs. Roosevelt wrote me the letter I mentioned earlier, (and I'm sure it wasn't the only letter she wrote that day), was because she would sit up till 3 AM personally handling her correspondence. Her taking the time to do that was wonderful from my point of view, but it was also what someone did if she didn't dare lie down to deal with her own thoughts. Eleanor had to totally exhaust herself in order to go to sleep. She became so depressed in her last years that she even considered suicide, and that mostly had to do with what her children did, over which she had no control and for which blamed herself.

Theodore Roosevelt suffered the same thing. He could not stop. He read three or four books a day, every day, and he was obsessive that way.

At his home at Oyster Bay, there's a great big piazza in the front. He used to sit out there in a rocking chair during the summer and read. His wife used to sit next to him because as he sat in a rocking chair, he read with such ferocity that he would rock himself closer and closer to the edge and not notice. And she would have to say, "Theodore, move back. Move back!" He couldn't read the way the rest of us read. He had to fill his mind all the time. He had to be thinking about something, planning something, shooting something, riding something. That approach to living life at high speed worked for him and his beloved niece.

THEODORE ROOSEVELT'S IMPACT ON FDR

BOSTON Franklin Roosevelt's political career followed virtually exactly in his cousin Theodore's footsteps—New York state legislator, assistant secretary of the US Navy, governor of New York, and president of the United States.

Was that step-for-step career path by Franklin deliberate or coincidental?

WARD Before he started in politics, FDR was an indifferent law clerk at a Wall Street firm. One afternoon, nothing much was happening, so the young lawyers began talking about what they wanted to do in the future. Franklin said, "I think I'll be president of the United States." He laid out his climb to power, rung by rung Now, he was twenty-five years old then, but his cousin Theodore was president at that time. There are always people who sit around idly and say, "I think I'll be president of the United States one day." FDR not only said it—he did it, so that's different. The person who remembers FDR's prophecy at the law firm was Grenville Clark, who later became a distinguished figure in the law, so I believe the story. Franklin also told at least one girl he dated while at Harvard that he planned to become president one day and it caused

her parents to burst into laughter, and he did not marry that girl.

BOSTON Something that seems surprising to me was their both having the job Assistant Secretary of the Navy. I wonder if FDR would have even known whether that job existed if Theodore had not had it. Guess he thought, "It worked for him; it should also work for me."

WARD Yes, and when he first arrived in the New York legislature, Franklin tried to act like Theodore Roosevelt, which meant operating in a way that did not really fit his personality—confronting and denouncing the political bosses.

BOSTON Now one of the points behind the theme of putting the Roosevelts together in one book was how much overlap there was between Theodore Roosevelt's aspirational progressive political agenda during and after his presidency, as compared to Franklin Roosevelt's actual New Deal political agenda that he accomplished prior to World War II.

WARD There was a lot of overlap and FDR used a lot of the same people who had been enlisted in Theodore Roosevelt's 1912 Progressive crusade. Franklin saw himself fulfilling those progressive dreams. What Theodore wanted to do but didn't do, Franklin could do and did. FDR was deferential toward the memory of his cousin Theodore for quite a long time, but during the last parts of his presidency, when people compared him to TR, it began to annoy him. He understood that he was having a far greater impact on America than Theodore Roosevelt ever had.

THE ROOSEVELTS' MARRIAGE VS. THE CLINTONS' MARRIAGE

BOSTON My final question brings us into 2015. As I kept reading about this marriage/political partnership between Franklin and Eleanor Roosevelt, of course, I thought about the Clintons.

WARD They've thought about the Roosevelts, too.

BOSTON As a historian and a person who's still actively keeping up with politics, in 2015, what are the most important comparisons between the Roosevelt and the Clinton marriage/political partnership?

WARD They are very different people, but there are similarities. It is true that FDR had a romantic relationship and the Roosevelts decided to stay together. That's a rough parallel, I guess.

Mrs. Clinton is an enormous admirer of Mrs. Roosevelt. She used to joke she communed with Eleanor's ghost. She however, is a much more practically-oriented compromise-inclined politician than Eleanor Roosevelt was. I think that's the main difference between them.

Bill Clinton is a great admirer of FDR. I got to know him a little bit when he was running for president. I saw a picture of him on the front page of the *New York Daily News* coming out of a debate, and he was carrying *A First Class Temperament*. So I wrote to thank him for all the free publicity. He wrote me back a handwritten note and wanted to talk about FDR. That doesn't mean Bill Clinton necessarily desired to emulate Franklin Roosevelt; it meant he was interested in him, especially in his early political years when his reputation was that of an able, ambitious, charming but somewhat unreliable charmer.

BOSTON But let's talk about the dynamics of the marriage—onthe one hand, husband and wife, and on the other hand, a political partnership—in other words, this is a man, this is a woman, they've got twenty-four hours in a day together, how does it work? I don't think Hillary's politics are in conflict with her husband's, though Eleanor was ahead of Franklin on the liberal social agenda front. What I'm interested in is your perception of comparing the dynamics in the two marriages.

WARD I don't really know enough about the Clintons. I agree that there doesn't seem to be very much difference between the Clintons as far as their politics go. I think they both probably have a better sense of politics as "the art of the possible" than Eleanor Roosevelt did.

But Eleanor was a tough cookie. When Carmine DeSapio, the head of Tammany Hall in New York, torpedoed her son Franklin, Jr.'s bid to become governor she said, "I'm going to get him." It took her eight years. She campaigned against him relentlessly, and when he finally lost his district leadership post from Greenwich Village, she couldn't have been more pleased. "I said I was going to get him," she told a friend, and I got him."

People in politics learned it was best not to mess with her. In order to win over liberals and win the Democratic presidential nomination in 1960, Jack Kennedy, had to go and pay obeisance to Eleanor at her home at Val-Kill. Her grand-daughter had just been fatally injured in a riding accident. Kennedy offered to cancel. Mrs. Roosevelt said to come ahead; she understood how difficult it was to make last-minute changes in a campaign schedule. Then at age seventy-five, she proceeded to dazzle Kennedy who said as he left something to the effect that she was the most extraordinary woman he'd ever met.

Certainly, she was the most extraordinary woman I have ever tried to write about.

BOSTON Geoff, our time has run out. Thanks so much.

DAVID McCULLOUGH and my interview of him is described in my introduction to the chapter on John Adams. This chapter is devoted to the part of our interview where we discussed his Pulitzer Prize-winning biography of *Truman* (Simon & Schuster 1992).

"I grew up in a very Republican family and had become interested in politics. The night of the election, I tried to stay awake to see who won, but as some of you know, the final count didn't come through until about two in the morning. I probably fell asleep about eleven o'clock. The next morning, my father was in the bathroom shaving, and I asked him who won. He said, in a tone of full-blown gloom, "Truman!" Twenty or thirty years later I was back home in Pittsburgh and after dinner one night Dad started talking about how everything in the country was going to hell. Then, all at once, he stopped, paused, and said, "Too bad ol' Harry isn't still in the White House." **–DAVID McCULLOUGH**

CHAPTER 17

DAVID McCULLOUGH
ON
Harry S. Truman

COMPARISON OF JOHN ADAMS AND HARRY TRUMAN

BOSTON David, here's my transition question between our two subjects in tonight's interview. When John Adams was elected president, a Baltimore newspaper gave this description of him: "a tough, hardy, laborious little horse that works very hard and lives upon very little and is very useful to his master at small expense."

When I read that description of him in your biography *John Adams,* I thought to myself, "Couldn't those same words be used to describe Harry Truman?"

McCULLOUGH Absolutely. The two men had many similarities. Both grew up on farms, and lacked

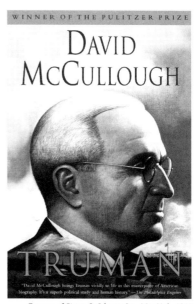

Courtesy of Simon & Schuster, Inc., New York, 1992

money or advantage. Neither was handsome or particularly charming in terms of first impressions, although that could change once people got to know them. Both enjoyed a good drink. Both liked to tell stories. Both were tough physically. Both did what they thought was right when they had major responsibility.

As president, both had to make unpopular decisions—and they made them. During his presidency, Adams kept us out of a war with France, which at the time would have been catastrophic. Most of the politicians, including Adams' fellow Federalists, were ready to go to war with France. But Adams knew better.

Like Adams, Truman, too, was a great reader. Truman, as few could have imagined, read Latin for pleasure, and we're talking about a man who never went to college! One of the things to remember is that high school education at the time of Truman's adolescence was in many ways comparable to a college education of today. I've seen the history test Truman passed in his senior year at high school. I doubt many history majors in our colleges and universities today could pass that test. I'm not sure I could. Truman had an excellent history teacher in high school, Miss Margaret Phelps, and he loved history all his life.

His knowledge went beyond history. During his presidency, Truman would go to the national symphony, not for a photo opportunity, but because he wanted to hear what was on the program that night. If it was one of his favorite composers like Mozart, he would take the score with him.

Harry Truman was no simple Missouri nobody who had failed as a haberdasher. He was in many ways a born leader. Look at what he did in World War I and you see exactly what kind of leader he was, even as a young man.

At the heart of the story of these two remarkable men are character and courage. Not just physical courage, but the courage of their convictions. And Truman knew who he was. "I tried never to forget who I was,

where I came from, and where I would go back to," he said.

One of my favorite Truman stories took place in the Oval Office when he was about to appoint General George Marshall Secretary of State. One of his political advisors cautioned him, saying, "Mr. President, you might want to think twice about making that appointment." Truman asked why. "Because," said the advisor, "if you appoint General Marshall Secretary of State, in two or three months people will start saying he'd make a better president than you are." "He *would* make a better president," Truman answered, "but *I'm* the president, and I need the best people possible around me."

Consider what he accomplished in his presidency. Imagine desegregating the armed services with one sweep of his pen. He just used his right as commander-in-chief and signed the military desegregation into law.

The Marshall Plan, one of our greatest steps ever as a nation, came to fruition during Truman's time in office. His accomplishments just go on and on. This supposed nobody became one of our best presidents ever.

It's important to keep in mind about Truman that he'd been through a great many setbacks in his life. He had learned how to handle failure, as Adams had, too. If you want to judge someone on how they're going to act in the office of the presidency, take a look at how many times they experienced failure, because every president is eventually going to have failures of some sort to contend with. How does one handle it? Do you get feisty, angry, touchy? Do you start blaming others? Or do you get back up on your feet and keep going? Do you learn from mistakes and failures? Do you let those around you see that you have the courage of your convictions?

I would like to tell one more story because I think it's important. After he was appointed as Secretary of State, General Marshall held a press conference. A reporter asked him if he thought he had received a good education at the Virginia Military

Institute where he went to college. "No," Marshall answered. The reporter followed up, "Why not, sir?" "Because they didn't teach us history," Marshall said.

Truman once said, "The only new thing in the world is the history you don't know."

Truman's passion for history was essential to his life in general and his presidency in particular. It is not coincidental, in my view, that some of the most effective presidential leaders we've had were those who had a major interest in history. A number of them actually wrote history themselves—Woodrow Wilson and Theodore Roosevelt, for example. It is a sad statistic that today 82% of American universities and colleges no longer require any history in order to graduate. What a mistake that is! We have to know who we are; and how we got to be where we are; and how very much we owe to those who preceded us and provided us with so many blessings and opportunities that we ought not ever take for granted.

TRUMAN AND FDR

BOSTON David, another extraordinary fact that is so impressive about Truman is how he became president. When he was named the Democratic Party's vice presidential candidate in July 1944, it was clear to everyone who saw him up close that Franklin Roosevelt's days were numbered. When Harry Truman had tea with Roosevelt in August 1944, the president's hands shook so badly that he poured more tea in his saucer than he put in his cup. He could no longer stand up to give a speech, and he started getting confused when he gave speeches.

Upon being chosen as FDR's running mate, and up until their inauguration, did Truman realize that he would probably become president in a very short period of time?

McCULLOUGH Of course he did, but he never said anything about it. He couldn't help but notice Roosevelt's condition. What was so distressing and unfair was how

Photo credit: Leo Hessler, Hessler Studio of Washington DC, Courtesy of Harry S. Truman Library.

Roosevelt treated Truman. FDR did not tell his vice president much of anything about anything—including the atomic bomb. For Truman to step into that job all of a sudden—Oh, my God! It took exceptional character and determination to handle things as he did.

It's interesting to note that Truman rarely complimented Roosevelt. I think he felt Roosevelt had a kind of class objection to him. Certainly Roosevelt indicated little or no interest in Truman. Truman thought George Marshall was the greatest American of the time.

TRUMAN AND THE ATOMIC BOMBS

BOSTON Let's talk about his decision to drop the atomic bomb, which occurred when Truman had been president less than four months. Yes, Truman knew that the bomb would kill Japanese civilians and therefore knew he would have "blood on his hands," and also knew that it would be a dangerous sign of the future world order; though he also knew the incredible amount of man hours and money that had already been spent toward developing the bomb; and knew that dropping the bomb would save hundreds of thousands of lives because it would probably mean that the Americans would no longer have to invade Japan.

With those facts in front of him, how much did Truman struggle with the decision before he pulled the trigger to drop the atomic bomb?

McCULLOUGH Among those directly involved in the decision, no one opposed it. It wasn't just that we would save the lives of so many Americans by not having to invade Japan. We knew that thousands of Japanese lives would be lost; but had we not dropped the two bombs there would have been many more deaths on both sides from the protracted fighting that almost certainly would have gone on for some time.

As the years since 1945, with no new revelations coming to light, the stronger has become the consensus that, regardless of how horrible it was, dropping the bombs was the correct decision. It was really the decision Truman *had* to make because the momentum was such that all the rationale behind creating and dropping the bomb was hard to challenge. Sure, there would be those against it.

Discussion and arguments have gone on, and will continue. Churchill called it the decision that was no decision.

Photo credit: William B. McCullough

David McCullough

ON WRITING HISTORY

BOSTON David, there are a lot of lawyers who aspire to be great writers like you. Last week, when I read your account of the events leading up to the dropping of the bomb on Hiroshima, it was so compelling, I almost began tingling. It's a story that had been covered hundreds of times by other journalists and historians before you decided to write about it in your *Truman* biography.

What was your approach in trying to come up with something new or fresh, that would also be powerful in the way you described the dropping of the atomic bombs?

McCULLOUGH My approach has been the same with every book I've written—and that is to try and get inside the history. Get inside what happened. Get inside the people involved, get to know them, and to be there, as it were. It requires telling a story—not listing a sequence of events.

History is human. That's the essential reality. In Jefferson's famous line, "When in the course of human events," the operative word is *human*. This means empathy and understanding are essential and digging below the surface in order to know those about whom you're writing. In the case of Truman, John Adams, the Wright Brothers—so many I've written about—it has been primarily through their personal correspondence that I've come to know them. They could pour themselves out on paper—in letters, diaries—in a way few of us do anymore. In fact, we're not going to leave much about ourselves, much about who we are, what we thought, what we worried about, what we loved.

Nobody keeps a diary anymore, because as you lawyers know, it could be used against you in court! Our children and grandchildren scarcely ever write anything down on paper, and, from what I've been told, the electronic communication that we so depend on is not likely to last very long.

If any of you happen to be interested in immortality, you might start keeping a diary.

Write about whatever you wish. And when you get to the point where you think maybe the curtain's going to come down, give the diary to the library here at SMU. It will be quoted for hundreds of years. It will be the only diary in existence.

Adams and Truman both kept diaries and wrote letters. Truman even wrote famous letters wherein he expressed his outrage, though then, on second thought, he customarily tucked them away in his desk drawer—with the exception of one to a music critic who didn't like Margaret Truman's concert performance.

BOSTON Truman's daughter was a professional singer who some music critics regarded as a mediocre performer, and she once received a bad review from a critic at *The Washington Post*.

McCULLOUGH Yes, the poor guy wrote the review, and Truman's letter seemed almost to threaten him with his life.

But Truman's letters to Bess and his family during World War I, for example, help us to understand him far better—as do his letters to Bess during much of his time in the Senate and the presidency. She did not like Washington, and she, Bess, had two brothers with drinking problems, so she felt she was needed to be back home. Truman wrote marvelous letters about how lonely he felt, how life was on the Hill and in the Oval Office. And we come to see and appreciate the kind of human being he really was.

TRUMAN'S ROLE IN AVOIDING WORLD WAR III

BOSTON Arguably, the greatest achievement of Harry Truman was that during his almost eight years in the Oval Office, when the world was in post-war chaos, he played the largest part in avoiding World War III—no small task with the threat of the atomic bomb fresh on everyone's minds, the Soviets taking over Eastern Europe, and the Chinese providing major military support

to the North Korean army during the war in Korea. It led Churchill to tell Truman in 1954, "You saved Western civilization."

In those instances, during Truman's presidency—with the a-bomb as the ever present elephant in the room, the Russians in Eastern Europe, and the Chinese in Korea—how close did we get to World War III?

McCULLOUGH Very, very close, just as Churchill said. Yet through all those tense and troubled years, Truman never lost his balance. Very important to his capacity to maintain his equilibrium came from knowing how to work with the other side, the Republicans. And they liked each other. They disagreed on some issues, of course, but they weren't enemies.

One of the more obvious lessons in history is that little of consequence is ever accomplished alone. Truman understood that. Oh, if we only had more politicians today who would heed that obvious historic fact! We've got to work together!

Truman's popularity declined sharply during his presidency, but as time passes we begin to see historic figures differently. Harry Truman said it takes at least fifty years for the dust to settle.

I was in high school in 1948 when Truman ran against Dewey, and everybody knew Truman was going to lose.

BOSTON Amazingly, shortly before that election, they asked the fifty top political pundits to predict who was going to win. All fifty of them predicted Dewey would be the winner.

McCULLOUGH I grew up in a very Republican family and had become interested in politics. The night of the election, I tried to stay awake to see who won, but as some of you know, the final count didn't come through until about two in the morning. I probably fell asleep about eleven o'clock. The next morning, my father was in the bathroom shaving, and I asked him who won. He said, in a tone of full-blown gloom,

"Truman!" Twenty or thirty years later I was back home in Pittsburgh and after dinner one night Dad started talking about how everything in the country was going to hell. Then, all at once, he stopped, paused, and said, "Too bad ol' Harry isn't still in the White House."

TRUMAN AND THE CONSTITUTION

BOSTON David, some of Truman's biggest crises during his presidency came from labor strikes. In dealing with them, he was fearless, though arguably reckless, such that when he nationalized the steel industry and then tried to draft the steel workers into the military to stop them from striking, the United States Supreme Court held that he had violated the Constitution.

We know that Harry Truman was not a lawyer. In fact, he said at that time, that as for the steel workers, "We'll draft them and think about the law later."

Was his attorney general or anyone else advising him on whether what he planned to do with the striking steel workers was constitutional or did he simply decide to act without constitutional authority in order to keep the country functioning?

McCULLOUGH The latter, and it was a mistake, no question. He made mistakes during his presidency, and that is one of the more obvious ones, though you have to remember he was a deeply patriotic man and also a war veteran. He'd been through hell in World War I and the idea of steel workers going on strike at a time of national crisis was to him disloyalty beyond acceptance. While the strike went on, he was being pretty badly beaten up politically and his popularity was going way down, so he tried to draft the steel workers based on those considerations.

TRUMAN'S STATURE AND LEGACY

BOSTON When he first took office, Truman was the most popular president we ever had. People often forget that. He had an 81% approval rating in 1945. I must have interviewed well over a hundred people who knew him and worked with him, because my book was written long enough ago [copyrighted in 1992] that there were still plenty of them alive. I would ask each of them, and particularly those who were in some position of consequence in Washington at the time, "How did you feel when you heard Franklin Roosevelt had died, and Harry Truman had become president of the United States?" Without exception, every single one of them said, "I felt good." I asked why. Their answer: "Because I knew the man."

When he left the presidency, Truman didn't have much money. He made some from writing his autobiography a few years after retirement. But there was no presidential pension then. Yet he refused to serve on any board for pay or to take fees for speeches. To do that, he said, would be disrespectful to the office of the presidency. He believed that no one should cash in on the presidency.

BOSTON How about that!!!

McCULLOUGH When he learned that the Kennedy campaign was going to have $1,000 a plate dinners, he said, "There goes democracy." Today we have $50,000 a plate dinners. It's out of control—and something has to be done about it. We have to assemble people with backbones who will stand up for what's right.

BOSTON Absolutely. David, thank you so much for your wisdom and insights tonight.

JEAN EDWARD SMITH is a past winner of the Francis Parkman Prize, awarded annually by the Society of American historians for the best book in American history during a calendar year. At the time I interviewed him on June 16, 2015, at Georgetown College, Jean was eighty-three years old and drove by himself from Huntington, West Virginia, to Georgetown, Kentucky, allowing me to interview him about Presidents Grant and Eisenhower for almost two hours. Suffice it to say, age has not slowed Jean down a bit, as this interview demonstrates.

"When you look at the historical record, Eisenhower ranks next to Franklin Roosevelt in terms of accomplishment during the twentieth century. When Ike became president, we were bogged down in a war in Korea. He immediately made peace there and after that, not one American was killed in combat for the remaining eight years of his terms. No president after Eisenhower can make that statement."

– JEAN EDWARD SMITH

was a member of the class of 1954. It was a lily white class of 750 people. There were also no blacks in the class of 1953, the class before me. There were only two in the class of 1952, and that was it. I think it is too easy for us to forget how entrenched segregation was in those days and how decisive Eisenhower's action was at the time. It was probably premature to make any more of a move toward potent civil rights legislation until Lyndon Johnson did it. John Kennedy didn't do it. Eisenhower's record on integration and desegregation goes beyond appointing judges and sending troops into Little Rock.

Back in January of 1942, when the United States was going to send two divisions of reinforcements to Australia, Eisenhower was working in the War Department in Washington as chief of operations. The Australian ambassador came to Ike and said that in those two divisions we were going to send over, he didn't want any black troops. Eisenhower said, "Fine. We won't send any troops then." Thus, Eisenhower forced the Australians to accept black troops.

Then, when he became president, he immediately ordered the desegregation of the armed forces. Harry Truman is given credit for desegregating our military because he signed the order stopping segregation of the armed forces, but during Truman's presidency there was no real enforcement of the order. General Bradley testified that the military couldn't do it, which meant that when Eisenhower took office, our military was still 90% segregated. He immediately put an end to that and also ordered the Navy yards to desegregate their work forces and also the schools on military bases. He made integration move forward.

EISENHOWER IN WAR AND IN PEACE

BOSTON The title of your book is *Eisenhower in War and Peace*. To me, one of the most fascinating aspects of the

Eisenhower presidency was that despite his having been European commander of the Allied forces during World War II, during his years in the White House, he was totally dedicated to keeping the US out of war. To accentuate his quest for peace, in his farewell address a few days before he left the presidency, he famously warned the American people of the dangers associated with the expanding military industrial complex.

Does your book's epigraph (Ike: "I hate war as only a soldier who has lived it can") explain why the consummate warrior was such a consummate advocate for peace?

SMITH That statement in the epigraph was true of both Eisenhower and Grant. They had both seen war at its worst and didn't want to be involved in it again. I'd like to say a word about the title. You see the title *Grant* for my Grant biography and *FDR* for my Roosevelt biography. I wanted to call this book "Ike" and let it go at that, but the year before it came out, someone published a book called *Ike* and I couldn't use it. So I had to come up with a multi-word title which I really didn't want to do.

BOSTON Talk about the circumstances that led to the Eisenhower quote in the epigraph.

SMITH Eisenhower made that statement at Ottawa in 1946 I believe. He had seen war and didn't want to go there again. One of the difficulties the United States has faced after the Eisenhower administration is that it became much easier for our military to intervene in foreign wars. Henry Kissinger is partially responsible for that by talking about the necessity for choice in pursuing our foreign policy as it pertains to the military. Each president after Eisenhower has tended to involve American troops in places where war was a possibility. Eisenhower, however, did not send troops to Vietnam when he faced that situation, and military intervention there during the 1950s would have been an easy thing for us to do.

THE TWO SIDES
OF EISENHOWER

BOSTON In David Brooks' current *New York Times* best seller, *The Road to Character*, he relies on your biography of Eisenhower at length, and references it several times in identifying his mother Ida's impact on Eisenhower. Besides instilling Ike and his brothers with the desire to be high achievers through her constant love and affection, she empowered them to construct a character, particularly for Ike, which gave him the strength and self-control to conquer his hot temper by inspiring him to practice small acts of self-control which developed into his lifetime habit of constant self-repression. This allowed him to create what David Brooks describes as his "second self".

Given the complexity of Eisenhower's personality, do you agree with David Brooks that Eisenhower, in fact, had two selfs?

SMITH Absolutely. Eisenhower was raised in a very fundamentalist household in Kansas—so fundamentalist that his parents later became members of Jehovah's Witnesses. None of the six brothers grew up to embrace a fundamentalist faith, but it was important to all of them in building their character and keeping them under control.

BOSTON As we recognize this "second self" in Eisenhower's complex personality, when you interviewed his son John Eisenhower for your book, he basically said, "Good luck in trying to figure out my father." And once Mamie Eisenhower was asked if anybody really understood her husband. She answered, "I don't think so."

So go a little deeper into the complexity of Ike's personality and his having two selfs.

SMITH Throughout his life, Eisenhower played lots of poker and bridge, and that became a good metaphor because, as far as his personality went, he always played his cards close to the chest. Don't forget that beginning in 1930, Eisenhower was working as

the executive assistant to people very high in the government. He became MacArthur's aide when the general was chief of staff in 1931, and stayed with him four years in Washington, and then was with him for another four years in Manila when MacArthur commanded the Philippine army. Then, after Pearl Harbor in December of 1941, he came back to the War Department in DC where he became Marshall's assistant in charge of war plans. Because of those experiences, Eisenhower knew how the military and the federal government worked at their highest level and recognized the necessity of keeping his cards close to his chest and not telegraphing his intentions beforehand.

EISENHOWER'S HIGH LEVEL OF SELF-CONTROL—IN ENDING THE SUMMERSBY AFFAIR AND STOPPING HIS SMOKING HABIT

BOSTON Getting back to his high level of self-repression and self-control that came from his mother's addressing it at a young age, the two best pieces of evidence of his maintaining that regimen was the way he

immediately ended his three year affair with Kay Summersby at the end of the war and also the way he ended his four pack a day smoking habit cold turkey in 1949 after (as he said) he "gave himself an order" to stop smoking.

SMITH That's right. Eisenhower was very much in command of himself. Let me talk about the smoking incident first. Before 1949, Eisenhower smoked between three and four packs a day. It was a habit he had learned at West Point illegally and he continued it, and didn't care what brand he smoked. When he became president of Columbia University after the war, his doctor told him that his smoking was creating a serious heart problem. So, as you said, Ike simply "gave himself an order," and then stopped a thirty year addiction overnight.

Now the other situation involving Kay Summersby, his mistress during World War II, where he demonstrated his high level of self-control is more difficult.

Eisenhower and his family have gone to great lengths to portray Kay as simply Ike's driver during the war, much to the dissatisfaction of Sergeant Dry, who in fact *was* Ike's driver during the war and remained his driver until he retired from the presidency. Eisenhower met Kay in London when he first went over, and then got to know her better when he was stationed in London before the North African invasion. At the outset of their relationship, she did drive the car for him. She then went with him to North Africa, and there became his executive assistant and retained that position through the rest of the war.

Before going to Tehran, President Roosevelt stopped in North Africa and wanted to take Ike's measure before he met with the Russians and before giving him responsibility to execute D-Day. After spending three days in North Africa, Roosevelt wrote his family a letter that said Ike was having an affair with Kay. The affair was well-known, but army officers having affairs at that time wasn't unique. Walter Bedell Smith, Eisenhower's aide, had an affair with the woman regarded by most as the most beautiful girl in the nursing corps there, so affairs were relatively commonplace. George Patton had an affair with a woman he referred to as "his niece" throughout the war.

Eisenhower's relationship with Kay was a loving affair and in 1945, after the war ended, Eisenhower wrote General Marshall and said he wanted to divorce Mamie and marry Kay. Marshall wrote back and said, "That's fine, but if you do, I'll relieve you as supreme commander." Eisenhower was a five star general at the time and if both he and Marshall had followed through, then he would have stayed at that rank, but would no longer have been supreme commander. So Eisenhower essentially gave himself an order (just like he later did with smoking), and decided not to marry Kay, though they continued to live together until Eisenhower returned to the United States in November of 1945. I should add, the British provided a castle for Ike and Kay to live in on the Scottish coast until he returned to America in late 1945.

Kay thought that when Eisenhower returned home in November of 1945, she would be going with him. The day before he was to leave, however, she received orders transferring her to General Clay's headquarters in Berlin. This is another example of Ike's turning on a dime. She received these orders without any prior knowledge, and Eisenhower and his party left Europe and returned to the United States. Once Ike got back to Washington, he wrote her a "Dear John" letter which probably stands at the pinnacle of "Dear John" letters for its being cold and devoid of passion.

THE EISENHOWER MARRIAGE

BOSTON Let's talk about Ike's relationship with his wife Mamie. The marriage lasted over forty years until he died. From reading your book, I'm not sure what tools Mamie had in her tool kit that earned her a place in Ike's heart or that she deserves much of a place in American history except for the fact that she was First Lady for eight years.

Was Mamie anything more than a Canasta playing, pulp fiction reading, soap opera watching, simpleton and social butterfly?

SMITH There was more to her than that. Mamie was very attractive as a young woman. Eisenhower met her in 1915 just after he graduated from West Point at Fort Sam Houston where he was stationed. She came from an extremely wealthy Denver family—the Douds—and they were married on July 1, 1916, shortly after he met her. Their early life together was quite affectionate. They had one son, Little Ikey, who died from scarlet fever as an infant in early 1920s, and that placed a severe strain on the marriage.

After Ikey's death, Ike went to Panama, and Mamie didn't like Panama, so she came back to live with the Douds in Denver where she delivered their second son, John. Ike was transferred from Panama to Paris shortly after John was born, and their marriage thrived there. After their time in Paris, they returned to Washington and lived just off Connecticut Avenue in a large apartment, and the marriage continued to thrive.

When Ike went with MacArthur to the Philippines in 1935, Mamie did not want to go, and so she didn't go for the first year Ike was there. That was a very difficult time in their marriage and I don't think it ever got back on firm ground for many years because after his service in the Philippines, the war came, Eisenhower went abroad, and Mamie was left in Washington.

After their affair ended, Kay Summersby wrote two books about Eisenhower. The last one was published in the early 1980s, and was entitled "My Love Affair with Ike." When it was released, Eisenhower's son John decided to publish Ike's wartime letters to Mamie to show that there really was nothing to the Summersby affair.

During the war, Eisenhower wrote Mamie at least once a week. They were handwritten letters because Mamie didn't want them typed, feeling sure that someone else would be typing them for him. When I was doing research for my book, I went out to the Eisenhower Presidential Library and asked to see the letters. The librarians said, "We don't have the originals. John sold them. We just have copies." So I read the copies of Ike's wartime letters to Mamie. In them, Ike was clearly responding to Mamie's letters, although her letters to him have disappeared. The official story regarding their disappearance is, "Ike didn't save them." The unofficial story is that those letters have disappeared and I believe someone has them somewhere. It's in the letters from Mamie to Ike during the war where she was clearly raking him over the coals for his having an affair with Kay, and the Eisenhower family has chosen to keep a lid on it.

MAMIE AS FIRST LADY

BOSTON She was First Lady of the United States for eight years. Of course, Eleanor Roosevelt set the standard for First Ladies becoming activists for special causes. Jaqueline Kennedy made her cause renovating the White House; Lady Bird Johnson had as her cause the preservation of wildflowers along our highways; and Laura Bush, a librarian, started the big book festival in Washington, DC.

Did Mamie do anything as First Lady in furtherance of any cause?

SMITH Don't forget she was succeeding Bess Truman, who really didn't do anything as First Lady. I can think of one thing Mamie did—she saved Camp David. Roosevelt had called the presidential retreat facility "Shangri La" when it was constructed. It was about to be deactivated when Eisenhower took office and Mamie decided they should keep it.

By the time of his presidency, their relationship had changed. Eisenhower was in his sixties. He had learned a lesson from the Kay Summersby affair, and was never involved again extramaritally. They were actually closer than many presidential couples. Eisenhower went to work in the White House very early in the morning, and when the work day was over, he and Mamie spent their evenings together. So in that way, she did play a positive role as First Lady.

EISENHOWER'S GOOD LUCK

BOSTON Going back to World War II, so many huge opportunities came Ike's way as an army officer that led to his becoming the Allied Supreme Commander from having amazing military mentors who led, protected and advanced him; to his being assigned to write the history of the Western Front after World War I; to his being assigned to work under General Pershing on the Battlefield Monument Commission, thereby gaining an encyclopedic knowledge of the European battlefields and terrain; and finally to FDR's choosing him over George Marshall to lead Europe even though Ike at that time had no prior command experience in war time.

Did Ike live under a lucky star or was it just a case of him making most of his luck—that is, was his luck the residue of his own design?

SMITH You can argue that both Ike and Grant were lucky, but at the same time, Ike worked very hard. From the time he left West Point, he worked a seven day week and that's very rare in the peacetime army. Eisenhower was a very hard worker and though he tended to knock off early in the afternoon, he was consumed by the task at hand.

He did benefit greatly from his relationship with people higher up who saw his ability, wanted to use it, and, therefore, promoted him.

In fairness, like Ike, going into World War II, General Marshall never had a military command either. Marshall was chief of staff, but he never commanded troops in the field. The British made it clear that they did not want Marshall to command the invasion and so Roosevelt looked for an alternative. Eisenhower became that alternative. Unlike Grant, Eisenhower was not a battlefield commander. With the exception of the Battle of the Bulge, Eisenhower took no direct part in any battle during the second World War.

EISENHOWER'S MEMOIRS

BOSTON On several occasions in the book, you point out where Ike's wartime memoir and his presidential memoir involved his reconstructing history inaccurately in a way that was obviously favorable to him and his legacy.

In doing your research, were you surprised that he would engage in essentially intellectual dishonesty?

SMITH I'm not sure it was intellectual dishonesty so much as him exaggerating his decisions—like after the invasion of France on the breakout.

BOSTON What about the Guatemala coup that occurred during his presidency where he said we had no role and obviously we did?

SMITH If you were to ask me what was the low point of the Eisenhower administration, I would say his approvals of the coups in Guatemala and Iran which toppled Mosaddegh and brought the Shah back. To some degree, his decision about Iran is the root of the problems we confront there today.

BOSTON Was it surprising to you, as you read what he said about what happened in his memoirs, while you were independently researching what happened, and you realized that his books were not accurate?

SMITH If you've been in history and writing biographies and looking at the record

Jean Edward Smith

as long as I have, you're not surprised by something like that.

BOSTON That's my next question. You've read dozens, perhaps hundreds, of wartime memoirs. Did Ike fudge the truth any more than his peers?

SMITH I don't think so. In fact, Eisenhower's memoir of the crusade in Europe is probably the best memoir to emerge from the second World War. From a literary standpoint, it doesn't quite reach the level of Grant's memoirs, but it's probably the best book written by a general of the second World War or at any time after that.

EISENHOWER AND THE ATOMIC BOMB

BOSTON Ike had a curious history with the atomic bomb. When he first learned of it in 1945, he was opposed to it and he remained steadfast about America's not using it; but then as president, his successful foreign policy was tied at least in part to the way he consistently bluffed about the possibility of using the A-bomb to quell an uprising.

In his presidential memoir, did Ike acknowledge how he put his extraordinary card playing skills to use in the way he bluffed using the atomic bomb to avoid World War III?

SMITH He didn't talk about it in those terms, but you're exactly correct. Twice Eisenhower rejected recommendations from the National Security Council that the United States use atomic weapons— once to defend the French garrison at Dien Bien Phu; the second time to protect the islands which the nationalist government on Formosa held against invasion by the Chinese government.

Eisenhower was not about to deploy atomic weapons, though he did use them as a bluff and the military policy of the Eisenhower administration was based on the threats regarding the United States' potential use of atomic weapons. That approach to foreign policy was what caused Henry Kissinger to write his book *The Necessity for Choice,* where he argued that the United States needed to have a choice in its various military options, and not rely entirely on the threat of using atomic weapons in its diplomatic efforts. That's when the United States developed its "limited war" capability which President Kennedy used to get us involved in Vietnam, which President Johnson also used, and has been used by presidents ever since. It's a little hard to say that Eisenhower was wrong in keeping us out of "limited wars".

PRESIDENT EISENHOWER'S DEFENSE BUDGET PRIORITIZING

BOSTON Getting back to our discussion a few minutes ago about Eisenhower's attitude during peacetime, talk about how he shifted the defense budget from the use of conventional troops toward focusing more on the Air Force.

SMITH I'm not sure he reduced the overall defense budget, but he certainly reduced the army's budget and reduced the United States' ground forces because he did not want to get us involved in a ground war anywhere. Eisenhower believed that the risk of an atomic war was so great that no country would dare confront or provoke the United States on that issue. Who's to say he was wrong?

EISENHOWER AND McCARTHYISM

BOSTON Let's talk about Eisenhower's handling of Joseph McCarthy and his witch hunts. Ike's strategy was to avoid making public comments about McCarthy and essentially giving him enough rope to hang himself, which McCarthy ultimately did. Many historians say Eisenhower should have been more proactive and confrontational in order to take McCarthy out of commission sooner.

Do you agree or disagree?

SMITH Oh, no. The establishment position now is that Ike played the McCarthy situation very well. Mr. Greenstein at Princeton deals with how Eisenhower handled it by using what he calls "the hidden hand presidency." Eisenhower thought that for him to take on McCarthy directly would enhance McCarthy's prestige; so to deal with the situation, he definitely called the shots, but from offstage. It was Eisenhower who determined the army's strategy during the Army/McCarthy hearings. It was Eisenhower who approved the appointment of Welch as the attorney to represent the Secretary of the Army in those hearings. It was a typical Eisenhower maneuver—he did McCarthy in, but without exposing himself, and it was a total victory in many respects.

I was a Princeton undergraduate when the McCarthy hearings took place. In those days, no one had a TV in his dorm room, so we all went to Cuyler Hall to watch the Army/McCarthy hearings on television. We didn't know at the time that it was Eisenhower who was behind the scenes calling the shots in the Army's strategy, but he was.

BOSTON At the time, was there mumbling among the Princeton crowd about, "Where's Eisenhower? Why doesn't he take on this so-and-so directly?"

SMITH Absolutely. Everyone was wondering that, but Eisenhower thought it was better to organize and execute his plan from behind the scenes. Looking back, most people now realize that he was right.

BOSTON You mention a speech during the height of McCarthy-ism where George Marshall's American credentials were being challenged, without merit obviously, and Eisenhower had a paragraph in his speech where he stood up for Marshall. Then, because of who was in the audience, he took it out of the speech. There's a lot of people still dismayed that he did not stand up for Marshall in that instance.

SMITH That took place in the 1952 election. Eisenhower instructed the people running his campaign, "Don't have me speak in Wisconsin." He didn't want to speak there because McCarthy was running for re-election and he didn't want to take issue with that. Ike's campaign schedule got screwed up though, and his train passed through Wisconsin on the way from Chicago to Minnesota so he had to give a speech there. He became highly annoyed about it. He had a paragraph in the draft of his speech praising General Marshall (who McCarthy had falsely attacked as being a communist), but at the recommendation of Wisconsin's Republican Party, he deleted it because the Wisconsin Republican leaders said, "If you leave that part in, McCarthy may lose the election." So Eisenhower reluctantly removed the paragraph. He knew at the time it was a mistake and he regretted it the rest of his life.

PRESIDENT EISENHOWER'S CONDUCT IN GUATEMALA, THE CONGO, AND THE SOVIET UNION

BOSTON You mentioned a few minutes ago that Ike made much use of the CIA covert activities throughout his presidency, particularly in Iran where he put the Shah into power after ousting the elected prime minister; and also in Guatemala, and finally in the Congo.

Were there no rules, restrictions, or democratic principles that mattered to Ike during his administration that took priority over protecting the US's oil supply and/or discretely waging war on communism in the third world?

SMITH You have mentioned probably the low point in the Eisenhower administration. Eisenhower was not worried about a war between the United States and the Soviet Union or the possibility that the relationship between the two world powers might lead to a major military confrontation. But he was concerned about communist penetration abroad. So he allowed himself to be led by the CIA and the Dulles brothers, and that became a low point in his presidency.

Let me add a sidebar to that: The Paris Summit was scheduled for the summer of 1960, Eisenhower's last year in office. There he was to meet with Khrushchev, de Gaulle, and the British Prime Minister, and the plan was for them to move decisively on German reunification. Before the summit, Eisenhower had authorized the last U-2 spy flight of Francis Gary Powers to fly over Russia, and Powers was shot down. Khrushchev gave Eisenhower numerous opportunities to blame Dulles for the U-2 spying, and say it took place without his approval; but Eisenhower had approved the flight, so he declined to make Dulles the scapegoat. His taking personal responsibility resulted in torpedoing the Paris Summit which really was unfortunate, but it says something about Ike—that having approved the final U-2 flight, he didn't want to say he hadn't approved it, so there was a certain integrity there. On the other hand, the cost of the U-2's getting shot down over Russia really set back US-Soviet relations for many years.

BOSTON I don't recall a single instance either during the war or his presidency when Eisenhower ever threw a subordinate under the bus.

SMITH I think that's absolutely true, and you could say the same for Grant. They were both prepared to take the blame.

EISENHOWER AND VIETNAM

BOSTON You talked a few minutes ago about Vietnam. My high school years took place during the height of the anti-war movement when Nixon made a very protracted withdrawal from Vietnam. Historians often say that what happened regarding America's involvement in the Vietnam War really started with Truman, then Eisenhower kept the ball rolling, then Kennedy stepped it up, and then Johnson escalated our involvement big-time; such that there was a continuum among American presidents in succession that ultimately led to the Johnson administration's escalation.

Do you think Ike had any role whatsoever in the circumstances that led to the escalation of the America effort in Vietnam?

SMITH Only in that he did not simply wash his hands of the situation altogether. Don't forget Eisenhower ended the war in Korea. He also declined to intervene to protect the French interests at their garrison at Dien Bien Phu. He told his Cabinet, "My goodness! We can't use atomic bombs on the Asian people twice in ten years."

He declined to say whether he was going to use atomic weapons to protect Formosa, and that was his position on Vietnam as well. He retained a purposeful murkiness in his public statements. Maybe he should have been more forceful and said that what was going on in Vietnam was none of our business, but he did *not* get us more involved there, and he did not send troops there. America started sending troops there during the Kennedy administration, and from an intellectual standpoint, it actually began with Henry Kissinger's book *Necessity for Choice.* Eisenhower placed all his chips on the threatened possibility of nuclear war, and he didn't want the United States to become involved in anything below the nuclear threshold. It was Kissinger's book that prompted our foreign policy to begin considering using our military forces below the nuclear threshold, and that's the step that led to our military involvement in Vietnam.

EISENHOWER AND TRUMAN

BOSTON I want to wrap this up by talking about Eisenhower's relationship with two presidents: the first, Harry Truman. Both Ike and Truman are today ranked in the historical polls as top ten presidents. They got along during Truman's presidency until the 1952 election, where Truman, a Democrat, was the outgoing president, and Eisenhower ran as a Republican to be Truman's successor. On inauguration day, Ike jerked Truman around in terms of not coming up to the White House, thereby making Truman come out to his car, and they didn't really reconcile for over ten years until after John F. Kennedy's funeral.

Ike had so many positive relationships with Democrats throughout his adult life. Why couldn't he get along with Truman from 1952 until 1963?

SMITH Let me begin my answer by remembering that in 1945, at the time of the Potsdam Conference, Truman had Eisenhower and Bradley in his car, and they were looking at the ruins in Berlin. Truman then offered Eisenhower the Democratic nomination for president in 1948 if he wanted to take it. Truman said he would step back from the presidency and

become Ike's vice president. In 1951, before Eisenhower went to Europe to command NATO (per Truman's appointment), and get it off the ground, Truman again offered Ike the Democratic nomination in 1952, and Eisenhower again said he didn't want it. Their relationship went way back, as Ike's older brother had actually roomed with Truman in Kansas City, Missouri, in the early 1920s in the same boarding house.

As the 1952 campaign approached, in the run-up to the Republican convention, Truman said that if Robert Taft got the Republican nomination, then he would run as the Democratic candidate; but he also said he would not run against Eisenhower if Ike got the nomination, so Truman was essentially encouraging Eisenhower to take the Republican nomination. Up until that point, they were still friends.

The disconnect between them occurred during the campaign. Joe McCarthy was going to give a speech attacking Governor Stevenson because of his alleged sexual orientation. The FBI had leaked (by Hoover's quietly releasing) documents to McCarthy which suggested that Stevenson was gay. McCarthy let it be known that he intended to mention it in a nationwide television address. Truman said that if McCarthy did that, then Truman would release the letter Ike had written to Marshall saying he wanted to divorce Mamie and marry Kay. This caused the Republican leadership to tell McCarthy to back off and not mention the claim about Stevenson.

Eisenhower got really ticked at Truman for having made that threat because Ike knew the letter was there, so that's what caused their falling out. That explains why Ike would not get out of the car on inauguration day to go and have coffee with President Truman and Bess inside the White House, as is customary. That's why they barely spoke on the ride up to Capitol Hill. They remained at arms-length for over a decade until after Kennedy's assassination and the funeral.

One more thing: after Eisenhower was inaugurated, I'm certain that the first thing he did when he got into the White House was attempt to locate the letters between him and Marshall about Kay Summersby. Someone told him Truman had burned them. Truman had indeed burned the letters after the election was over so that no one could ever use them again. He told that to his biographer Merle Miller many years later.

The letters had been seen (before they were destroyed) by Garrett Mattingly, a distinguished professor of history at Columbia who during the war was in military intelligence in Washington. His job was to read the outgoing correspondence in the Pentagon and so forth, and he saw the Summersby letters between Eisenhower and Marshall.

EISENHOWER AND NIXON

BOSTON For my last question, I want to talk about Ike's relationship with Richard Nixon, his vice president all eight years of the Eisenhower presidency. After Nixon had been named his vice president on the Republican ticket, there was a controversy that soon arose regarding his personal finances that led to the famous "Checkers" speech in 1952. Eisenhower expected Nixon to end that speech by announcing his resigning from the ticket, but Nixon didn't resign. His refusal did permanent damage to their relationship, such that Nixon became a largely removed, irrelevant vice president for eight years and a pariah in Ike's eyes.

Assuming all of that's true, how did Nixon win the Republic presidential nomination in 1960 since he obviously didn't have Ike's coattails to ride, since there was no positive relationship between them?

SMITH You're right all the way through. Eisenhower tried to get a replacement for Nixon as vice president in 1956, but didn't want to confront Nixon on it. He offered Nixon the position of Secretary of Defense or Secretary of this and that, hoping Nixon would step down, but Nixon wouldn't.

You asked how Nixon got the Republican presidential nomination in 1960. It was like the Democratic nomination in 2016. Nixon was the major figure in the Republican Party at that time who could succeed Eisenhower. There was no other candidate who was possible. It's like Mrs. Clinton today and the Democratic ticket. I think that's a useful analogy. There was no one to contest him for the nomination.

BOSTON Our time's up. Let's give one final round of applause for Jean Edward Smith.

V.

The Modern Era

JOHN F. KENNEDY

LYNDON B. JOHNSON
& THE CIVIL RIGHTS MOVEMENT

RICHARD NIXON

THE NIXON TAPES 1971-1972

RONALD REAGAN

GEORGE H.W. BUSH

BILL CLINTON

THE POST-WORLD WAR II "PRESIDENTS CLUB"

SHELDON M. STERN served as the historian at the John F. Kennedy Presidential Library from 1977-2000 and has written three books on the Cuban Missile Crisis, the most recent being *The Cuban Missile Crisis in American Memory: Myths vs. Reality* (Stanford Nuclear Age Series 2012). I interviewed Sheldon as my JFK historian on October 13, 2015 at the Kennedy Library and his candor revealed some surprising conclusions about the thirty-fifth president of the United States.

"There was something major that was missing in Kennedy's televised speech on October 22 when he told the country what was happening in Cuba. He made no reference, of course, to the fact that before the Russians started sending missiles to Cuba, his administration was actively pursuing a secret war that included American efforts to assassinate Fidel Castro. Prior to the Missile Crisis, the CIA had been behind terrorist activities in Cuba, such as burning sugar cane fields and factories, and everything the CIA did was completely secret to the American people—we knew nothing about it. Nikita Khrushchev, Castro, and the Cubans, however, knew exactly what the CIA was doing." – **SHELDON M. STERN**

CHAPTER 19

SHELDON M. STERN

ON

John F. Kennedy

JFK AND THE CATHOLIC ISSUE IN THE 1960 ELECTION

BOSTON Sheldon, the United States has obviously come a long way since 1960, particularly in our concerns about the religious beliefs of political candidates. National religious leaders Billy Graham and Norman Vincent Peale both came out strongly in 1960 expressing major concerns over the possibility of having a practicing Roman Catholic as president. In 2015, we're incredulous to think that such well-known religious leaders could think that way during our lifetime.

What's your explanation for why the majority of Americans in 1960 decided that the Catholic issue would not impact their vote for president?

STERN First of all, I'm not sure that's true. If you look carefully at the analyses that have been done of the vote in 1960, it's very clear that Kennedy was definitely hurt by the religious issue. I vividly remember doing oral history interviews here at the Kennedy Library on the 1960 campaign, and spending time in Ted Sorenson's and others' papers from that campaign. I was stunned by the virulence of the anti-Catholic material. There are folders after folders after folders of this stuff and they're absolutely loony. There were things in there from 1928 when Al Smith ran as the first Catholic presidential candidate. When you read that anti-Catholic material it becomes clear that things weren't very much different from 1928 to 1960. From 1960 to now, thank goodness, attitudes are extremely different.

Most people know the basic history— Kennedy had to enter and win the primaries to show the Democratic bosses, most of whom were Catholic, that a Catholic could win the presidency. John Bailey in Connecticut didn't want a Catholic to run for president because he thought a Catholic candidate would lose the election, which would cause the Democrats to lose control of Congress.

The first major test was in Wisconsin, right next door to Hubert Humphrey's home state of Minnesota. Humphrey was Kennedy's primary rival. Kennedy got 56% of the vote in Wisconsin, but lost the Protestant vote. That made him decide to enter the West Virginia primary, since the total Catholic population there was less than 5%. It was quite a gamble and he put a huge amount of resources into West Virginia and won—proving he could attract the Protestant vote.

Throughout the campaign and since, there have been claims that the Mafia was behind JFK because his father was allegedly involved with the Mafia. Some claimed that there were people sent down to West Virginia carrying satchels of money which they gave out in appropriate circumstances to make sure they won.

The Catholic issue would not go away though, even after JFK won West Virginia. He had to confront it again in September before the Greater Houston Ministerial Association. Even at the very end of the campaign, there were three bishops in Puerto Rico who issued a statement saying no Catholic should vote for a candidate who does not support the church's position on abortion and birth control. That hit the newspapers and television all over the country three days before the election, and it caused panic in the Kennedy campaign. I remember finding in Ted Sorenson's papers that Kennedy was going to make a statement about the Puerto Rican situation and Sorenson advised him to ignore it and hope it would blow over. Whether it did or not, who can say?

The fact is the 1960 election was essentially a tie in the popular vote. Therefore, in my judgment, there was clearly a serious Catholic issue in the campaign that definitely impacted Kennedy's numbers. If he had been a Protestant, and everything else had been the same, he would have won by at least 5% more. Today, I doubt if 5% of Americans know or even care that Vice President Biden is the first Catholic VP in our history.

JFK AND EISENHOWER

BOSTON When Kennedy was elected as Eisenhower's successor, Ike was viewed as being old (at that time he was the oldest president to date), and also being passive and inactive as a leader. The criticism was that he played too much golf and was naïve about foreign policy. In fact, in the Kennedy-Nixon debates, Kennedy said that if voters liked the way things were under Eisenhower, then they should vote for Nixon. Over the last fifty years, the historical evaluation of Eisenhower has substantially changed for the better—so that in the most recent polls, he's rated as a top ten president by most historians, given that for eight years, he maintained peace and prosperity.

How did JFK and obviously a majority of the voters fail to appreciate the success of the Eisenhower presidency?

STERN A lot of it has to do, interestingly enough, with historians. There was a view of Eisenhower—particularly by people like Arthur Schlesinger, Jr.—that he was basically an amiable bumbler who didn't understand the issues. Schlesinger and others claimed that Ike was a figurehead for John Foster Dulles in foreign policy, and that Sherman Adams, the Chief of Staff, ran the White House.

That was the dominant view of many historians until the 1980s when they opened up his private papers and diaries at the Eisenhower Library. What they found in those documents just blew away all past perceptions of Ike. Fred Greenstein called the Eisenhower years the "hidden hand presidency" and demonstrated how Eisenhower was involved, for example, in bringing down Joseph McCarthy. He got things done in ways where his fingerprints weren't on anything. He was very, very clever in the way he used his power and his "hidden hand" approach was very much *not* JFK's style. Of course, given Ike's remarkable leadership in World War II, it is remarkable—but not really surprising—that historians could ever have been so biased.

The biggest problem for Kennedy with Eisenhower was that by saying, "If you're satisfied with the way the country is now, then vote for Nixon," that meant JFK was implicitly being very critical of Eisenhower who was very popular at the time. It was widely assumed at the time that Ike could have won a third term if the Constitution and his health permitted. It was a very difficult dance for Democrats to be critical of Nixon without coming across as being hostile to Eisenhower.

Privately, Kennedy referred to Eisenhower as "that old asshole," while Eisenhower referred to Kennedy as "Little Boy Blue." They had actually met very briefly in 1945 at Potsdam; but they finally met seriously for over an hour on December 6, 1960, after the election, and it went quite well. Eisenhower was quite impressed by Kennedy's grasp of the issues. Kennedy wanted to keep Eisenhower on board during his administration—especially on foreign affairs. From Day One of his presidency, Kennedy had several Republicans in his administration—especially Doug Dillon, his Secretary of the Treasury, and John McCone, later head of CIA—who had both served under Ike and were responsible for keeping Eisenhower informed. They especially kept Ike in the loop during the Missile Crisis. The worst thing for Kennedy would have been for Ike to break with him publicly.

BOSTON Along those lines, Eisenhower was not informed beforehand of the decision to invade the Bay of Pigs. Obviously, it was a disaster and when it was over, Kennedy invited Eisenhower to Camp David, where Eisenhower famously took JFK to the woodshed. At the end of that tough conversation, though, Ike basically affirmed Kennedy as president.

Was that really the lesson of the Bay of Pigs—that you don't exclude Eisenhower in foreign affairs?

STERN That's an interesting way of looking at it; I've never thought of it quite that way. But Kennedy never did exclude Ike again and I've often wished that there were a tape of that post-Bay of Pigs conversation at Camp David. Those who talked to Ike afterwards about the conversation thought he just skinned JFK alive over how badly he had mishandled the Bay of Pigs.

Kennedy made a terrible mistake during that conversation with Ike at Camp David. He talked about the complexity of dealing with something like the Bay of Pigs invasion. Who was he talking to? The guy who ran D-Day! Comparing the Bay of Pigs to D-Day! So Eisenhower naturally took him to the woodshed.

BOSTON I read in Herbert Parmet's biography of Kennedy's presidency that in their December 1960 conversation a month prior to the inauguration, Eisenhower gave JFK his best advice on running the White House and it went in one ear and out the other, because Kennedy didn't think he needed Eisenhower's advice. He planned to run the White House his way and thought this old guy didn't really know what he was doing anyway. Then he became president and soon decided to invade the Bay of Pigs—which turned out to be a colossal failure. All of a sudden, Kennedy realized that maybe Eisenhower's advice was actually pretty good.

Is that consistent with your understanding?

STERN That's overstated in my judgment. They were never close; it was a limited political relationship. As a matter of fact—and this illustrates it—on November 22, 1963, Eisenhower was chairing a meeting of key Republican leaders about how to defeat Kennedy in the upcoming 1964 election. The meeting was broken up by news of the assassination. So there it is in a nutshell.

IMPACT OF THE KENNEDY-NIXON TELEVISED DEBATES

BOSTON The 1960 election obviously involved two of the biggest names of the twentieth century—Kennedy and Nixon—our thirty-fifth and thirty-seventh presidents.

Is the ultimate conclusion to be drawn from the 1960 election that television charisma triumphs over everything else in a presidential election?

STERN That appears to be the consensus view.

BOSTON When you read about the 1960 debates, and see the videos of them here at the library, there was Kennedy—handsome and wearing the dark blue suit that set him off against the white background; while there was Nixon with a five o'clock shadow and a light gray suit blending in to the white background.

STERN The people who organized the debate invited both candidates to come and look at the set and ask for any changes. Nixon didn't go. He had just been discharged after spending two weeks in the hospital battling a serious knee infection from an accident on the campaign trail. Everything was wrong about his appearance—the wrong color suit, his lazy shave, and his sweating for all to see. It gave viewers a bad, "Tricky Dick" impression. Clearly, Kennedy won from a visual television standpoint, though apparently Nixon won substantively, because the poll taken of the radio audience said that Nixon had won.

BOSTON Bottom line, wasn't it a situation where Kennedy truly understood the power of television—how to look and perform best on television as opposed to Nixon who hadn't yet realized the importance of television at that time?

STERN That's true, even though Nixon had a remarkable staff of people running his campaign. The only other major mistake he made was not using Eisenhower enough.

BOSTON Would you agree that the perception of the performances in the televised debate really was the tipping point in the election?

STERN Things changed dramatically in the polls after the first debate; Kennedy's crowds became much larger and more enthusiastic. But remember that all of a sudden at the very end, in the last five days of the election, things suddenly tightened up tremendously because of the combination of the Puerto Rican bishops re-opening the whole Catholic issue and due to Eisenhower finally campaigning for Nixon.

JFK, CIVIL RIGHTS, AND LYNDON JOHNSON

BOSTON For a Northern Democrat, Kennedy had a remarkably slow awakening about the historical importance of the Civil Rights movement in the early '60s. Martin Luther King, Jr. accurately told an aide in early 1962 that the Kennedy Administration had a "schizophrenic" tendency when it came to aggressively pressing for civil rights legislation.

What impact did JFK's inertia towards civil rights in '61 and '62 have on African-Americans who were obviously pushing hard for civil rights legislation during those years?

STERN When he became president, JFK, in my judgment, really didn't understand what the civil rights struggle was about. In his personal life until then, black people had been essentially absent. Even the servants to the Kennedy family were white—usually young women they brought over from Ireland.

He thought of civil rights as being primarily a strategic, political, legal issue. You see this very clearly in the transcripts or tapes from the James Meredith crisis at the University of Mississippi. Nowhere in the tapes when the Kennedy brothers were talking to Governor Barnett (and other people in Mississippi) did they ever say that segregation was wrong or against American principles or that it had been ruled unconstitutional in 1954. They just talked about strategy and law. Of course, the legal/constitutional argument was the only one Barnett might understand. He clearly did not think that segregation was wrong. JFK and RFK sounded politically sympathetic—saying essentially, "We understand what you're going through," but also stressing that Meredith needed to be enrolled safely; and Governor Barnett double-crossed them, which made them furious.

Then in June 1963, there was a sea change in the White House, especially after the televised violence in Birmingham, Alabama, and the confrontation with Governor George Wallace over integrating the University of Alabama. Kennedy understood, as he never had before, that he had no choice—he had to side with ending segregation and pursuing racial equality. And he made a historic speech about it.

BOSTON First, he gave a fabulous speech about civil rights in June 1963; and then, he submitted a civil rights bill that was stuck in committee until his death. After the assassination, along came Lyndon Baines Johnson who had the legislative genius and experience Kennedy lacked (since he'd never been particularly active in Congress even though he served there for fourteen years). And it was LBJ who got the ball over the goal line in getting the Civil Rights Act passed, and getting cloture to stop the filibuster.

Is the best thing that happened for the advancement of the Civil Rights movement in the first half of the 1960s the assassination of John F. Kennedy?

STERN If your yardstick is that the Civil Rights Act was passed, I can understand that statement. But there is compelling evidence it would have passed under Kennedy had he lived. There was a call made by a top Larry O'Brien aide to JFK in Fort Worth just before he left for Dallas, telling him that a great breakthrough had occurred and that they had gotten the House Ways and Means chairman to allow the bill to reach the floor. Also the GOP leaders of the House and Senate had come on board and it seemed sure to pass by 1964.

So it probably would have passed under Kennedy, but I think there's a very important and related issue that your question suggested which is the relationship Kennedy had with LBJ. He failed to use LBJ adequately during his vice presidency. It's a long and complicated story. Robert Caro has done a fabulous job of telling how Johnson was or wasn't treated. Johnson was an incredibly difficult man to deal with. I don't want to get into psychological terminology, but he was very neurotic about many things. The big problem with Johnson was he was not temperamentally suited to be number two—he was only temperamentally suited to be number one. The Kennedy administration failed miserably to use Johnson adequately and make him feel used. Yes, he was given the space committee and sent on foreign trips, but he knew what that was all about. His favorite term for it was "more of this Kennedy horseshit."

BOSTON Here LBJ was, "the master of the Senate," and yet the president who had Johnson and his legislative skills by his side as vice president, refused to use him.

Wasn't that in large part because the president's closest advisor, his brother Robert, so despised Lyndon Johnson that he wasn't about to give him a meaningful role?

STERN Yes, that's absolutely true. Robert Kennedy's influence in his brother's administration was extraordinary. Bobby Kennedy was very much at the center of JFK's administration, but his hatred of Johnson went back to a meeting they had years before. It really wasn't based on anything specific. Robert Kennedy just didn't like Johnson—didn't like his swagger or anything about him.

And we know the story about how Bobby tried to retract LBJ's vice presidential nomination at the 1960 Democratic convention; and whether or not he had his brother's approval for that is disputed to this day; though I find it hard to believe Bobby acted without his brother's at least covert agreement.

The place we really see Kennedy's failure to use Johnson was in civil rights. Here was Johnson who had gotten through the 1957 Civil Rights Act, with all its flaws and inadequacies. It was certainly better than nothing, and was the first civil rights act that had been passed since Reconstruction. When the Meredith controversy happened, Johnson was in Texas and the Kennedy brothers never asked him for any input. He was never consulted about civil rights.

BOSTON Getting back to my question, though, in terms of the greatest thing that happened in civil rights during the sixties was the assassination of Kennedy; in fact, in every Johnson speech, memo, etc., after November 22, 1963, LBJ capitalized on the tragedy of the assassination, and told Congress and everybody else, "Passing this bill is the best possible way to honor the memory of our fallen leader"—that's entirely where his focus was. In that respect, Johnson's strategy on civil rights used JFK's memory for getting the bill over the goal line.

STERN Sorenson was incredibly impressed by Johnson's passion on the issue. Johnson, for example, spoke publicly that his family cook, who had been with him for thirty years, had to drive four hundred miles through the South to visit friends and family and most of the time she could not use a restroom or find a place where they would let her get a bite to eat. "Goddamn it," he said, "she's an American. Her son is in the United States Army! He goes and risks his life for this country, and she can't even use a restroom..." That kind of passion was not in the Kennedy administration at least until after the George Wallace confrontation at the University of Alabama in 1963 and the June 1963 civil rights speech.

JFK AND RFK

BOSTON Getting back to the subject of the relationship between JFK and RFK, so much has been made through the years of Joseph Kennedy's political ambition for his sons. Because of Papa Joe's insistence, John F. Kennedy named his brother Robert as his attorney general even though Robert had virtually no prior legal experience.

Since JFK was not a lawyer himself, how could he feel that he would have a competent attorney general to handle the legal affairs of the United States with such a total novice at the helm?

STERN Well, it turned out that Robert Kennedy was a hell of a good attorney general, and all the histories of that period have demonstrated that.

BOSTON That's looking at it with hindsight. I'm saying on the front end, President Kennedy essentially put into place to run the Justice Department a baby lawyer with no legal experience.

STERN JFK wanted Robert as close as possible—and saying "no" to his father was not a good idea. There's never been a relationship in the White House between two people equivalent to the relationship between JFK and RFK. It was unique. I find it hard to imagine there ever will be one like it again.

When I first began listening to the tape recordings of their telephone conversations here at the Kennedy Library, I often wondered what they were talking about. You'd hear "ring, ring," and then "Yep, yeah, alright, good"—not "Hello. How are you? How are the kids?" It would be difficult to even know who was on the phone, but somehow they knew. Their conversations went like this: "On the 16th?" "Yes." "What about Tuesday?" "Yeah, alright." "Good, fine." "Thanks." "Bye." What in the world was that about? Somehow they always understood each other. Conversations like that happened over and over again.

The one time when it was very, very different was when the two brothers were alone. There was only one time when they were taped while alone together in the Oval Office. The door was closed and it was just the two of them. It was completely different. First of all, they used obscenities, which nobody ever used during formal meetings. Their tone was so different when it was just the two of them.

The Cabinet members all said that Robert Kennedy was JFK's fiercest protector, and he protected his brother in ways President Kennedy could not do himself. The ultimate proof was when push came to shove on Saturday, October 27th, on the last day of the Cuban Missile Crisis. Who did the president send to Ambassador Dobrynin with the compromise proposal about trading the missiles in Cuba and Turkey? He sent his brother who was dead set against the compromise—despite what he later wrote in *13 Days*! Although Bobby was against it, JFK knew Bobby would never break his word and would do what he was told to do. His loyalty to his older brother was instinctive.

JFK AND KHRUSHCHEV

BOSTON Throughout the Kennedy presidency, the Cold War was at its hottest; and Kennedy's communist counterpart was Soviet leader Nikita Khrushchev.

In the dialogue they had, and the tensions they had, was Berlin the focal point?

STERN It was, without any question. Fred Kaplan has written that people today would find it impossible to understand what the word "Berlin" meant in the early 1960s—Just saying the word, "Berlin." For Kennedy, it was his touchstone. "If Berlin is not kept safe…"

The city of Berlin was divided between the Soviet and the Allied side, and it was located two hundred miles inside East Germany. That meant trucks had to cross the border into East Germany and then drive two hundred miles just to get to Berlin. Of course, the Russians always made as much trouble as they could for the trucks, and they escalated that trouble during the Missile Crisis.

Khrushchev was determined to find a way to prevent the endless bleeding of the population of East Berlin and East Germany into West Berlin. Eventually, building the wall was the solution—and it wasn't much of a solution, but it worked from Khrushchev's point of view. When he met Kennedy in Vienna in June 1961, he was *brutal*—that's the word Dean Rusk used to describe Khrushchev's behavior. Khrushchev told his son Sergei, "How can

I talk seriously with someone who's about the age of my oldest son?"

The issue of Berlin was absolutely front and center for Khrushchev. He threatened in Vienna to sign a separate peace treaty with the East Germans. At the end of the Missile Crisis, on the day after Khrushchev agreed to remove the missiles from Cuba, Kennedy met in the Oval Office with several members of the joint chiefs. It was a very relaxed meeting after the crisis had passed. And at one point JFK said, "Maybe we can use the settlement in Cuba as an entry to finding a solution over Berlin, which is now an impossible situation." The JCS replied, "Maybe we can." Of course, nothing happened.

JFK AND VIETNAM

BOSTON One thing Kennedy and Eisenhower agreed on was the "Domino Theory" in Southeast Asia, which provided the basis for the decision to commit significant American resources to address the looming, potential communist takeovers in Laos and Vietnam. Obviously, after Kennedy's death, Vietnam became LBJ's responsibility, and he soon substantially escalated the American military effort there using many of JFK's foreign policy advisors, believing he was doing what was necessary in order to prevent the fall of South Vietnam.

What's your assessment on whether JFK, if he had lived, would have done what LBJ did in Vietnam in order to prevent the South from falling?

STERN I can speak on this with some degree of authority because I did half a dozen oral history interviews on it and spent a great deal of time reading the then-classified documents on Vietnam here at the Kennedy Library. It was a real eye-opener to listen to the tapes of the meetings on Vietnam. Having said all that, I'm sorry to say I can't give a definitive answer to your question.

BOSTON Give us your best shot.

STERN My best shot is—and I'm convinced of this—is that at the time of his death, Kennedy had not made up his mind about what to do about Vietnam. I think if you had been with him in Fort Worth on the last morning of his life and asked, "Mr. President, what are we going to do in Vietnam?" His reply would have been something like, "Damn! I don't know what the hell we're going to do in Vietnam." That's what he was thinking at the time.

BOSTON I suspect Lyndon Johnson had no idea what to do in Vietnam. I don't think anybody knew what to do in Vietnam.

STERN In my judgment, the documents prove that. When he published his memoir, Robert McNamara made a big thing out of a National Security Council meeting on October 2, 1963. I remember listening to the tape of that meeting. McNamara said in the meeting that a decision was made to withdraw 1,500 troops at Christmastime from Vietnam. A red flag immediately went up in my head, and I said to myself "No, no, no, no, Secretary McNamara; that wasn't the conclusion of the meeting." They discussed several possible options, one of which was to remove 1,500 troops, another of which was to *add* troops. And there was no decision made at the end of that meeting.

So that's where things were on October 2, 1963—a month and a half before the assassination. To me, what was said at that meeting reflects the fact that Kennedy was moving on parallel tracks in Vietnam. One of the tracks was to go in with more troops and the other track was to pull out the troops, and find a way to get out. He had not made up his mind.

BOSTON But if he had gone the second track, realized that America's involvement in Vietnam was a quagmire, and pulled the troops out, didn't he think that would mean the fall of every domino? Did he ever dispute the Domino Theory?

STERN Not to my knowledge. But there was a meeting of the National Security Council in 1962 at the end of which, George Ball, the number two person in the State Department under Dean Rusk, and the resident dove in the administration, came up to the president and said essentially this: "Mr. President, if you continue to send troops into Vietnam, then down the road in a few years, there will be a half a million American soldiers lost in the jungles of Vietnam and it's going to be the biggest political disaster in American history." That's not a bad description of what eventually happened. Kennedy replied, "George, you're just crazier than hell. That's never going to happen."

Johnson and Kennedy had different attitudes about the military. Kennedy didn't trust the military, and had never trusted the military. Johnson felt that he didn't know enough to know whether to trust the military. Johnson was an absolutely brilliant man, but he was not well educated and did not know much about foreign affairs, so he depended on what the military told him.

BOSTON And Johnson's military experience had been almost zero whereas Kennedy had been a World War II hero.

STERN Yes, exactly. It's ironic, isn't it? Kennedy was a war hero, yet he had a very low regard for the military.

BOSTON That's like Eisenhower, who often told the joint chiefs that their recommendations were wrong.

STERN Ike also told them that they were spending too much money and told them many other things that they did not like.

So, my judgment is that if Kennedy had lived, he would have had to face the first big problem in December 1963, only a month after his assassination, when the first North Vietnamese regular army units crossed

the DMZ (demilitarized zone) into South Vietnam—a huge escalation on the part of North Vietnam. There is little doubt that they did it precisely because the president had been assassinated and there was a new president and, therefore, they thought there was uncertainty in Washington. If Kennedy had been alive, would the North Vietnamese have sent troops into South Vietnam? Perhaps. If so, he would have had to make a decision whether to escalate America's military effort.

I agree here with McGeorge Bundy, who said that Kennedy would have been, on the whole, indistinguishable from Johnson during the '64 campaign. If he had run against Barry Goldwater, the worst thing he could have faced from Goldwater was the claim that he was soft on communism. So JFK would have taken a position during the campaign very similar to the one Johnson took. Then after the election, that's where we don't know. Would he have sent more troops? Perhaps lots more? Bombing? Perhaps.

BOSTON Would he have allowed South Vietnam to fall?

STERN If push came to shove, I think so—after the 1964 election—which is what happened anyway in 1975. But that is really a historian's informed hunch—but still a hunch.

BOSTON I know that's what happened anyway, but are you saying that he changed his mind about the Domino Theory and would have been willing to accept the consequences of having the first domino fall?

STERN In the speeches he made about Vietnam when he was still a senator, he said Vietnam was not central to American security. He never changed his mind about that but was very aware of the domestic political dangers. But I think he would have been willing to let it fall as the lesser of two evils.

JFK AND THE CUBAN MISSILE CRISIS

BOSTON Let's now talk about the Cuban Missile Crisis. Sheldon, your three books on the Missile Crisis revolve around the 42-1/2 hours of tape recordings of what was actually said by the Kennedy administration leaders around the table at the Executive Committee of the National Security Council, (shortened to "ExComm meetings") during late October 1962, where decisions were made over the course of thirteen days. As you point out in your books, the tape recordings of the ExComm meetings tell a very different story of what happened during the Missile Crisis meetings as compared to the book *Thirteen Days*, written by RFK and completed by Ted Sorenson, and also different from the film *Thirteen Days* released in 2000 that starred Kevin Costner, and was directed by Roger Donaldson.

Let's start with the book. What are the major areas about the Robert Kennedy-Ted Sorenson book, *Thirteen Days*, that you regard as a material distortion and/or an outright lie as compared to what the tapes reveal about what was actually said?

STERN In one word—everything. When I speak to audiences about the Missile Crisis, I sometimes start by saying, "Forget everything you think you know about the Missile Crisis because most of it is simply wrong." And that's true. Here is the standard version of what many believe happened during the Cuban Missile Crisis, based on what appears in the RFK-Sorenson book:

"On October 16, 1962, JFK and his advisors were shocked to learn that the Soviet Union, despite repeated denials and totally without provocation, was installing nuclear missiles in Cuba. Eight days later, Kennedy announced in a nationally televised speech that he had imposed a US naval blockade around Cuba and demanded removal of the missiles. Khrushchev blustered and threatened, but Kennedy and the best and brightest around him held fast and the two sides went eyeball-to-eyeball. Eventually, through a combination of flexibility, toughness, will, nerve, wisdom, and brilliant crisis management, Kennedy prevailed. Khrushchev agreed to remove the missiles, and nuclear war was averted."

That is a summary of the book *Thirteen Days*—and it's not true. It's hard to know where to start in explaining what really happened and all the ways the book's portrayal is inaccurate. Let's start with the notion that Khrushchev and the Russians had sent missiles to Cuba "totally without provocation." There was something major that was missing in Kennedy's televised speech on October 22nd when he told the country what was happening in Cuba. He made no reference, of course, to the fact that before the Russians started sending missiles to Cuba, his administration was actively pursuing a secret war that included American efforts to assassinate Fidel Castro.

Prior to the Missile Crisis, the CIA had been behind terrorist activities in Cuba, such as burning sugar cane fields and factories, and everything the CIA did was completely secret to the American people—we knew nothing about it. Nikita Khrushchev,

Castro, and the Cubans, however, knew exactly what the CIA was doing.

Why did Khrushchev put missiles in Cuba? During a vacation in the Crimea near the old Tsarist palace, he looked across the Black Sea to the border of Turkey. He knew that just a few miles inland from there, in Turkey, were American Jupiter missiles which could reach the Soviet Union in a matter of five minutes. Khrushchev likely said to himself, "Damn it. If the Americans can put missiles in Turkey five minutes from us, why can't we put missiles in Cuba? And we'll do it secretly and then when I speak to the UN in November I'll reveal to the world that there are Soviet missiles in Cuba." That would have been an enormous propaganda victory for the Soviets and Khrushchev. So he decided then and there to send missiles to Cuba.

There was a lot of opposition to it in Moscow. Most of his Kremlin colleagues who supposedly understood American politics, said, "Oh, God! Don't do it! You just don't understand. The Americans have something called the Monroe Doctrine that has defined their relationship with South America and Central America for over a century. They feel that they control South America and Central America. They will not allow a foreign country to have a base there. Don't do it." Khrushchev was certain, however, that the missiles would not be discovered until the sites were completed. His son Sergei, a nuclear engineer, said to his father, "These missiles are enormous, Papa. We'll never be able to hide them." Khrushchev replied to his son, "We can cover them with coconuts and palm leaves and the American U2 planes will go right over them and they won't see them." So that's what he did. So, first of all, there was *plenty* of provocation by Kennedy and the CIA to warrant Khrushchev's decision to send missiles to Cuba. From Khrushchev's point of view, he had everything to gain and nothing to lose by putting missiles there. At the time, there was serious domestic unrest within Russia. In the summer of 1962, there

had been bread riots, and several teenagers involved in the riots were shot. Missiles in Cuba would divert attention from the unrest. Also at the time, Khrushchev was constantly being criticized by the Red Chinese. Mao Tse-tung referred to him as the "running dog of American imperialism"—meaning Mao thought Khrushchev wasn't tough enough with the Americans.

Putting missiles in Cuba would show Mao and the Chinese that Khrushchev was very tough with the Americans. Finally, he favored the idea of helping Cuba because Khrushchev was really a romantic Marxist. He believed the whole Marxist philosophy and to him, Castro was a genuine Marxist leader of "a real people's revolution." He said Castro reminded him of himself at a young age. So he really wanted to help Castro after the Bay of Pigs, and supplying him with missiles seemed to be the solution. It was a cheap and quick way to protect Cuba against a second Kennedy administration invasion.

There was also another reason for the Russians to put missiles in Cuba—they knew their own ICBMs (intercontinental ballistic missiles) were inadequate. There had been a lot of talk during the 1960 American presidential campaign about there being a "missile gap," and how the US trailed the Soviet Union in missile strength. It was exactly the opposite of the truth. In fact, the Soviet Union was way behind the United States in missile strength and the idea of there being a "missile gap" arose because the Russians had fooled the CIA about the number of their missiles. The CIA thought the Soviets had 300 ICBMs, when actually they had only about twenty.

Khrushchev had also been told by his military advisors that there were lots of questions about the accuracy of their guidance systems and they were not even sure whether if they fired them, they could reach the US. So Khrushchev came up with a wonderful solution. Take their MRBMs— medium range missiles—and put them in Cuba, where they were only five minutes from Florida, and sixteen minutes from the northern part of the East Coast. It would change the balance of power—politically and perhaps even militarily. Putting all those factors together, moving missiles to Cuba was a no-lose situation for Khrushchev, and he didn't think they would be discovered.

Once they *were* discovered, of course, President Kennedy kept it secret from the American people for more than a week—from Sunday, October 14 to Monday the 22nd. It was eight days after the discovery that Kennedy went on television and told the American people what had been going on. The tapes establish that what actually happened in the ExComm meetings of President Kennedy and his team of advisors is as different from the account in the RFK-Sorenson book *Thirteen Days* as night from day.

REASONS FOR RFK'S AND SORENSON'S MISREPRESENTING THE FACTS IN *THIRTEEN DAYS*

BOSTON Having said what you just said, that the book *Thirteen Days* was in total conflict with the actual statements made and tape-recorded during the ExComm meetings, what's your best assessment of what led Robert Kennedy to totally fabricate what had occurred at the meetings?

STERN The principle reason for RFK's misrepresentation was understandable: the trade of America's Turkish missiles for Russia's Cuban missiles, which was the deal that ended the Missile Crisis, was a secret. Politically, the administration did not want to reveal that they had cut that deal. So Robert Kennedy (and later Ted Sorenson) needed some way to explain how they had gotten out of the Missile Crisis without mentioning the secret trade.

They came up with a brilliant idea to explain how the crisis ended without telling the American people about the secret missile trade's being consummated and here's how it played out. On Friday

night, Khrushchev's message arrived, which had been sent through regular diplomatic channels. In it, he said, "We disagree with you. The missiles in Cuba are *not* offensive weapons, but we'll take them out if you make a public pledge not to invade Cuba." On Saturday morning, the Kennedy team met to discuss Khrushchev's cable of the night before. Then suddenly, in came press secretary Pierre Salinger who told the group that there was a new message from Khrushchev that had just been broadcast over Moscow radio—so it was public; not a secret diplomatic communique like the night before. The whole world now knew that Khrushchev had just said he would take the missiles out of Cuba if we would take our missiles out of Turkey. Then, for the rest of that unbelievable day, without question the most dangerous day in human history when things could have gone in any number of different directions, they debated what to do.

By the end of the day, every adviser in the room, including Robert Kennedy, was against the public missile trade proposal. RFK and McNamara were the strongest opponents of the trade—but Rusk, Bundy, McCone, and JCS chair General Taylor were also against it. There was only one participant who was really in favor of the trade, and that happened to be the only person with the authority to actually make the decision—the president.

The debate went on, back and forth, all day long. Every time questions were raised about the possibility of making the missile trade, President Kennedy said, "We can't possibly reject this public offer precisely because it's a public offer." He said at one point that any rational person who looks at this situation is going to say that this trade makes a lot of sense and is completely reasonable. I'm paraphrasing him now, but JFK basically told his advisors, "How are we going to explain going to war over a bunch of useless missiles in Turkey? Who cares about those missiles particularly when we're soon going to replace them with Polaris missiles on submarines which are even more effective and far less vulnerable to attack? Are the Jupiter missiles in Turkey reason enough to risk a nuclear war?"

BOSTON So why did Robert Kennedy (and later Ted Sorenson) misrepresent what they and others said during the discussion?

STERN The first element, as I just said, was to cover up the secret missile trade deal which was actually made but was not disclosed to the public until 1989 at the conference in Moscow.

The second reason for their fabrication was Robert Kennedy's own political ambition at the time he wrote the book. Bobby started working on the book in December 1962 and there's very little known about what he had done on it over the next eleven months.

Then, after his brother was murdered, the book's whole focus changed. There is a memo here at the Kennedy Library which suggests that RFK initially wanted to finish the book in time to use it for JFK's reelection campaign in 1964, just the way they had used John Hershey's article on *PT109* in JFK's first campaign for Congress in Massachusetts in 1946, and later used *Profiles in Courage* in the 1960 presidential campaign. Then suddenly, his brother was gone, and the 1964 campaign would now be completely different.

The change in the book came between the assassination and the spring of 1964. Kenneth O'Donnell, a close JFK aide and friend, put his finger on the change when Bobby Kennedy first showed him the draft of the book and asked him to read it. O'Donnell said he would take it home and read it over the weekend, which he did. They met the following week and Bobby asked him, "What do you think?" There was another person present during this conversation, and I learned of O'Donnell's response from the other person—who happened to be Dan Fenn, later the first director of the Kennedy Library. O'Donnell looked at Bobby and

said, "I thought *your brother* was the president during the missile crisis?" So what had O'Donnell perceived? That the book was now obviously being written to promote Robert Kennedy's political future. Later in that same meeting, O'Donnell asked Robert Kennedy, "Do you think Jack would like this?" Robert replied, "Jack wouldn't mind. I'm now the one running; he's not." Bobby was then running (successfully) for the U.S. Senate from New York.

When Anatoly Dobrynin, the Soviet Ambassador, two days after Khrushchev had agreed to remove the missiles, brought a letter from Khrushchev to Bobby, and asked him to deliver it to his brother, Bobby read it and said, "No, no, no, no. This letter has a reference to the secret missile trade deal in it. You cannot make reference to what is absolutely secret. If you refer to it, we will repudiate it." Then Bobby said to Dobrynin, "If this were to come out, it could do incalculable damage to my own political future." RFK also later falsified an important memo to Rusk in order to cover his tracks on the missile deal.

BOSTON You've now written three books on the subject of the Cuban Missile Crisis as well as many articles. In one of your recent articles, you mention that as of 2012, the Belfer Center for Science and International Affairs at Harvard's JFK School of Government was still recommending the book *Thirteen Days* to teachers who taught courses on the missile crisis. Do you happen to know whether they are still recommending the book in 2015?

STERN It's a casualty of academic politics.

BOSTON Does the Belfer Center have any of your books on the list of recommended books for those who teach on the Cuban Missile Crisis?

STERN No.

Photo credit: Jennifer A. Stern

Sheldon M. Stern

BOSTON I know from your books and our conversations that through the years, there have been upgraded transcripts made of the tape recordings from the ExComm meetings.

Does the Belfer Center direct the teachers who teach the Missile Crisis toward the transcripts of the tapes?

STERN Yes, they do.

BOSTON That's encouraging.

WHY JFK RECORDED THE EXCOMM MEETINGS

BOSTON Only John F. Kennedy and Robert Kennedy knew that the ExComm meetings were being taped. Nobody else at the table knew they were being recorded. When Sorenson finished *Thirteen Days* after RFK's assassination, presumably he was not aware that there was a better record of what had been said at the meetings.

STERN The existence of the tapes was not made public until 1973. I'm not certain

whether Sorenson knew before that. Probably not.

BOSTON At the time of the recording of the ExComm meetings, is it your assessment that the Kennedy brothers agreed that there would be recordings for the same reason President Nixon wanted his conversations taped—that is, because they wanted to use the tapes to write accounts of their administrations and they believed that the tapes would never be released into the public record.

STERN That is absolutely true. Richard Nixon believed right up to the end he would never have to release the tapes, and that was especially true for the Kennedys. In 1962, when the tapes were made of the ExComm meetings, it was before the passage of the Presidential Records Act, before the passage of the Freedom of Information Act, and before Watergate. No one ever imagined in 1962 that these tapes would ever be made public. They were considered to be the president's private property. Now, of course, the Presidential Records Act has changed that.

BOSTON When was that enacted?

STERN It was enacted after Watergate. Everything changed after Watergate. Who could ever have imagined something like Watergate?

INACCURACIES IN THE MOVIE *THIRTEEN DAYS*

BOSTON The film *Thirteen Days* directed by Roger Donaldson might have made some reference to the tapes at its beginning, but then depicted a story that was totally in conflict with the tapes, and was totally consistent with the fabricated story in the book *Thirteen Days*.

When the movie came out in 2000, was there any adverse reaction to its being historically flawed like the controversy we saw over the recent movie *Selma*?

STERN I don't believe there was any reference to the tapes in the film. McNamara, Sorenson, and Schlesinger were the only three major ExComm people who were still alive when the film came out, and they were all very critical of the movie.

BOSTON Because it was inaccurate?

STERN Yes. They each cited examples of inaccuracies, especially the fictional central role for Kenneth O'Donnell in the crisis; although it's hard to imagine that they would ever take the position that I've taken based on the tapes. That's just not what they were all about.

BOSTON Schlesinger wrote a biography of RFK published in 1978 that essentially rubber stamped what had been in the book *Thirteen Days.*
STERN But in fairness to him, when he wrote that book, he did not have access to the tapes.

BOSTON But then after the first transcripts of the tapes come out in '97, Schlesinger made a public statement that the tapes *confirmed* what had been said in his RFK biography and in *Thirteen Days.*

STERN That's right. When I criticized the movie, I specifically cited Schlesinger, and said I was initially willing to give him a lot of leeway because the tapes were still closed when he wrote the biography. But, before the movie came out, he had had four years to read the transcripts and find out that Robert Kennedy's account of the Cuban Missile Crisis was completely false, and for him to say that the tapes confirmed the RFK-Sorenson book was outrageous.

BOSTON Do we know if he even listened to the tapes or read the transcripts?

STERN He must have read the transcripts because he published a review of the first volume of transcripts and said it was an historic achievement and that they were magnificent.

BOSTON Did anybody challenge him at the time?

STERN Not that I remember. The reviews of the 1997 transcripts were effusively positive and no one made an effort to check them for accuracy until my 2003 book. The errors in the 1997 transcripts are egregious and in many ways inexplicable.

JFK AS THE SOLE HERO OF THE CUBAN MISSILE CRISIS

BOSTON As you mentioned a minute ago, based on what the tapes reveal, John F. Kennedy was the "hero" of the ExComm meetings, particularly for accepting Khrushchev's missile trade offer that ended the crisis.

Give us a quick summary of exactly what the president did in connection with making the right decision on the missile crisis.

STERN It's easy in hindsight to conclude that he made the right decision because there wasn't a nuclear war—and that's a pretty good outcome. But from the third day of the crisis—the 18th—he first raised the idea of making a trade for the Turkish missiles. His statement is right there on the 18th. By the way, Adlai Stevenson had suggested a missile trade idea to JFK on the 17th, so it's quite possible Stevenson put the bee in his bonnet; but in any case, President Kennedy mentioned it at the ExComm meeting the next day.

Then throughout the subsequent eleven days, there were approximately a dozen times where Kennedy received—in my judgment—terrible, provocative, dangerous advice and in every case but one he rejected it.

For example:

When they realized the Soviets had transport planes big enough to carry missiles by air, McNamara told JFK he should consider preventing Soviet planes from flying into Cuba. Kennedy said the only way to stop a plane was to shoot it down and he didn't think that would be a good idea in such a dangerous situation.

The Soviet escalated harassment of the trucks entering East Germany to go to West Berlin, and demanded to search and open everything inside the trucks. Ambassador Thompson, our former ambassador to the Soviet Union, said we should not let them make those searches. JFK replied that the Russians had five times the number of troops on the ground in Berlin that the US had, so we were not in a position to make a big deal over their inspecting the trucks—if they want to inspect the trucks, let them inspect the trucks.

McNamara wanted to use flares to light up the Cuban landscape so our U2 spy planes could take pictures at night. Dean Rusk said that was a terrible idea because in World War II (only seventeen years earlier), flares were always shot off before the beginning of a night bombing attack and the Russians would think they were about to be attacked, which might provoke them to launch the ICBMs against the US. Kennedy agreed and wouldn't do it.

Russian ships began approaching the quarantine line where the American Navy ships were waiting. Some of the Soviet ships suddenly turned around—presumably the ones actually carrying the weapons—and Bobby Kennedy said we should stop them anyway in order to confiscate and analyze their weapons. Dean Rusk said, "No, no, no, no. The Russians are already as sensitive as a boil. Look at the quarantine proclamation. It says we are only to prevent weapons from entering Cuba, period. It doesn't say anything about seizing and analyzing Soviet weapons. If they are going to turn their ships around, let them go home." Kennedy sided with Rusk.

The ultimate example came when a U2 plane was shot down on Saturday afternoon on the 27th and the pilot killed. When it happened, the room went into a state of shock. Kennedy said, "This is a major escalation by them, isn't it?"—and it was, without question. All around the room people said, "They've fired the first shot. They've drawn the first blood. We must now respond. We should bomb all the ICBM missile sites. Short of that, we should bomb the surface-to-air missile site—that launched the missile that shot down the plane." Two days earlier, Kennedy had agreed with General Taylor that if they should launch a SAM missile and bring down an American plane, we should then destroy all their SAM missiles or at least the one that actually fired and Kennedy agreed. Two days later it happened and Taylor said, "Well?" And Kennedy replied, "I don't know yet. We don't know why that happened. Who issued the order to shoot down the plane? Did it come from Moscow? Let's get more information before we do anything so dangerous and provocative."

It turned out the order wasn't from Moscow and when Khrushchev found out about the U2 being shot down, he blew his cork. Sergei Khrushchev was with his father when they got the news, and said his dad was furious. "Who did that? What a stupid thing to do—to shoot down an American plane! We're hanging by a thread over nuclear war. Find out the name of the bastard who launched that missile and send him to Siberia for the rest of his life."

It turned out the order came from a captain in the Red Army, and Khrushchev was absolutely furious that the order to shoot down the plane had come from a Russian officer on the scene without authorization from the Kremlin. The situation persuaded him (as he said later that afternoon to Andrei Gromyko, the foreign minister), "We have to find a way to help Kennedy get out of this because he's facing his crazy military, and I'm facing my crazy military, and they all want a military conflict. If we let that happen, there's going to be a nuclear war."

The one exception referred to earlier was that JFK reluctantly agreed to use so-called "practice depth charges" against Soviet submarines near Cuba after McNamara and Taylor assured him that they would not damage the submarines. In fact, at least one submarine was damaged and the air control system was knocked out. The temperature rose to 120 degrees and crewmen began to faint. The captain assumed that war had already begun and ordered the arming of his two nuclear-tipped torpedoes. He was going to surface and launch them against American naval vessels. Fortunately, cooler heads prevailed.

JFK'S POLICY TOWARD CUBA AFTER THE MISSILE CRISIS

BOSTON After the crisis ended, did JFK change his Cuban covert war tactics?

STERN No, though he cancelled Operation Mongoose in the spring of 1963.

BOSTON Was that the code name for the effort to assassinate Castro?

STERN It included the assassination of Castro and it was reconstituted under a different name later in 1963. In November, at the time of Kennedy's death, there were thirteen separate CIA covert operations going on seeking to destabilize the Cuban economy and the government of Fidel Castro.

I first learned in this building (the JFK Library) three years ago at the conference in October of 2012, the fiftieth anniversary of the Missile Crisis, that at the moment Kennedy was killed in Dallas, an American agent was making a final agreement with a Cuban agent for another assassination attempt on Castro. The only problem was that the Cuban agent was a double agent working for Castro, which of course the American agent did not know.

HOW THE CUBAN MISSILE CRISIS IMPACTED LBJ

BOSTON One of the points you make in your book is to speculate on whether his experience at the ExComm meetings impacted Lyndon Johnson's foreign policy after he became president. What's your conclusion on that?

STERN That's an extremely important point. On October 27, 1962, meetings were held virtually non-stop from 10:00 am to almost midnight. Can you imagine how tired and terrified they must have been? At around 8:00 pm, JFK went back to the Oval Office and asked seven of the fifteen people who had been in the ExComm meeting room to join him. At that rump meeting, there were a total of eight people including the president. He said, "I'm sending Bobby to Dobrynin with the offer to remove the missiles in Turkey if he will remove their missiles in Cuba." They all finally acquiesced. They had no choice because the president had made his decision.

BOSTON Was Johnson in the Oval Office at the rump meeting?

STERN That's exactly the point, Talmage. No, Johnson was not in the room. Johnson became president a year later believing that Kennedy had prevailed in the Missile Crisis by being tough and inflexible—not because he had accepted the public missile trade deal that Khrushchev had proposed. Johnson had no idea that Kennedy had actually compromised and cut a deal in which he gave the Russians a lot—certainly enough to help Khrushchev save face.

BOSTON How did that impact LBJ's foreign policy?

STERN Historian Max Holland found two places in the tapes of LBJ's early years as president when Bundy and Rusk failed to tell President Johnson about the trade deal that ended the Missile Crisis. When the issue came up, they should have said, "Of course, you realize that President Kennedy did *not* force the Soviets to back down to end the Cuban Missile Crises. We ended the crisis by reaching a secret missile trade compromise"—but they said nothing about the deal to Johnson. They claim that the reason they didn't tell him what really happened was because President Kennedy had pledged them to absolute secrecy at that rump meeting on the night of October 27, 1962.

In my judgment, that pledge of secrecy should have been completely voided once Lyndon Johnson had become the president. If he were still the vice president, it would have been appropriate to maintain their pledge of secrecy—but by then, LBJ was the president. He should have been told about the terms of the missile trade deal (the way FDR's advisers told President Truman about the atomic bomb) and then *maybe* he would have handled Vietnam differently. Who knows? The model in Johnson's head for how to conduct foreign policy was a very different one because he didn't know why the Cuban Missile Crisis ended the way it actually did.

"WHAT IF" SCENARIOS POST-MISSILE CRISIS

BOSTON   Do you care to hazard a guess regarding how the world would have changed had President Kennedy not reached a diplomatic solution to end the Cuban Missile Crisis?

STERN   If you have seen the movie *Groundhog Day*, it's about reliving the same day over and over again. I'll use that as a metaphor to answer the question. Roll back time to the morning of October 16, 1962 when Bundy came to Kennedy's bedroom and said, "Mr. President, these pictures show that the Russians have missiles in Cuba." Kennedy was absolutely furious—"They're not going to do this to me. They can't get away with this."

If you could start all over again, and let the crisis happen from that morning right through to the end, and did that a hundred times, I don't think there's the slightest doubt that there would have been a nuclear conflagration in many of those hundred reruns. There was an enormous amount of luck involved in 1962. There were many things that happened which nobody could have predicted. For example, a US plane near Alaska flew accidentally into Russia, and the Soviets reacted rationally and escorted the plane out. It would have been very possible for Khrushchev to overreact, thinking that the plane was the beginning of a secret attack by the US. In addition, there was the practice depth charge incident mentioned earlier.

THE KENNEDY MARRIAGE

BOSTON   Finally, since we're running out of time, I've got two final areas of inquiry. First, let's talk about the Kennedy marriage. Jackie obviously knew of her husband's non-stop sexual shenanigans. In his book *JFK: The Presidency of John F. Kennedy*, Herbert Parmet says they spent most weekends apart during the thousand days of his presidency.

Having read extensively many sources about the lives of Jack and Jackie Kennedy, as well as talked to people who were part of his administration, what's your perception of the nature of that marriage?

STERN   Let me first say that it was a different time. There was a turning point in how the press covered the personal lives of presidential candidates which began in 1984 with Gary Hart. That was the first time that kind of thing really hit the fan. The fact is that in 1960, the public didn't know a lot of the things, but the journalists who covered Kennedy did. Several of the journalists I interviewed when I was doing oral histories for the Kennedy Library specifically said that. I think it was Bob Pierpoint, White House correspondent for one of the networks, who told me that JFK made no effort made to hide this behavior. Pierpoint once mentioned it to his wife and she said, "That's Jackie's problem, not yours"—in other words, that's not our business. So that's an important thing to understand about how different things were in the 1950s and 1960s.

I know for a fact, for example, that there was a woman in Northern Virginia who claimed to have pictures of Kennedy visiting a young woman's apartment when he was still a Senator. She sent them to many media outlets of one sort or another and no one would touch the story. That in itself speaks volumes about how things were different in the fifties and early sixties. The one media source that did publish the photos, by the way, was the newspaper of the American Nazi Party! I happened to come across copies of it once while researching an interview. Needless to say, keeping a president's extramarital activities private today would be impossible.

The other thing I want to say is that I have very little firsthand information about the Kennedy marriage. I've read some of the books—such as Sally Bedell Smith's book *Grace and Power: The Private World of the Kennedy White House*, which is a pretty sobering book, and there are several others—so most of what I know is second or even third hand. While working at the Kennedy Library or doing interviews or reading documents, I never came across very much. If you ask me if what's been written about the Kennedy marriage is true, I would say that on the whole, the answer is yes, though not everything that's been written is true.

BOSTON I understand the importance of recognizing the context of the times. I also recognize your not having firsthand knowledge. But I want to go a little deeper—regardless of the context of the times, regardless of how the media covered it—in terms of the oral histories that you did and what you've derived about the nature of the Kennedy marriage—particularly Jaqueline Kennedy's awareness that her husband, throughout their marriage and during his

presidency, was continuing to have extra-marital affairs.

Is there anything you've learned from people who seemed like reliable sources about how she was able to accept her fate being the First Lady in that type of marriage?

STERN My sense is that by becoming a Kennedy woman, there were certain things she knew were true before she married him. She just learned to live with it, the same way Rose Kennedy did and Joan Kennedy did. I know about the claims that Joseph Kennedy paid her off in order to stop her from divorcing JFK, though I have never seen any document that verified that claim. Does the claim sound credible to me? It does, but I would not go to the wall over it because I don't *know* that it's true.

I can cite a few examples which come closer to being first-hand. One of Kennedy's aides told me about Jackie tongue-lashing JFK in Ottawa because she had to shake hands with a woman she described as "a blonde bimbo" who was in the receiving line at the airport when they were returning to Washington. Jackie was furious at having to directly encounter this woman, and said, "It's bad enough that I have to deal with this stuff and now you want me to shake hands with her?" The aide who told me about the incident was right there and I have no reason to believe he would not have told the truth.

One other thing about this subject just occurred to me. When Judith Campbell Exner published her book about her relationship with President Kennedy, she mentioned that when she went to see Kennedy the first time in the White House, she went to the East Gate and told the security guard she had an appointment with Jackie. She didn't have a photo I.D. for identification, so she used a credit card, which was fairly unusual in those days. When the White House gate logs were declassified those details were verified—the east gate, the date, the alleged appointment with Jackie, and the credit card. So Exner appears to have told the truth about that.

Finally, in an oral history interview with a former State Department official, I was told that Dean Rusk was asked to be involved in recruiting female companions for President Kennedy when they went on foreign trips. Rusk refused and made it clear that if he were compelled to do it, he would resign as Secretary of State. So he was never asked again.

JFK AND HIS BOOKS

BOSTON   For my final questions, I'd like to discuss the two books that JFK allegedly authored. It's been often said that Kennedy's book *Profiles in Courage*, for which he won the Pulitzer Prize, and which was certainly instrumental in his rise to the presidency at such a young age, was not actually written by JFK, but rather was written by Ted Sorenson or perhaps others.

Based on everything you've read and heard and understood, what's your perception of who actually did the research and writing of *Profiles in Courage*?

STERN   I think Herbert Parmet's conclusion is spot on and I don't question it at all. Joseph Kennedy, a man with powerful connections, intervened with the Pulitzer Prize committee, and that helps explain why JFK won the Pulitzer.

Parmet is a very careful researcher. He concluded that Sorenson wrote the book, though there were scraps of paper with notes and such that JFK passed along to Sorenson—particularly when he was in the hospital having back surgery. There is no reliable evidence that Kennedy wrote the book and, as I said earlier, the circumstances that led to his winning the Pulitzer Prize were very dubious.

In the early 1980s, a senior staffer at the Kennedy Library attended several meetings that included Sorenson. According to that source, on the final evening after they'd completed all their work, the group went

out to dinner and had some drinks. After the dinner ended, he shared a cab with Sorenson, who, he claimed, said straight out that he had written *Profiles in Courage*.

BOSTON   Do we know if JFK wrote the book *While England Slept*?

STERN   Most of what I know comes from secondhand information—but it appears he wrote a draft that went to his professor at Harvard who was not terribly impressed with it. Then it was reworked by Arthur Krock, the journalist with *The New York Times*, who was a close buddy of Joseph Kennedy. It was also edited by a man who worked at Ambassador Kennedy's office in London. It was Krock who actually came up with the title, so we can say *While England Slept* was Kennedy's work, with an asterisk—like Barry Bonds' home run records.

BOSTON   We're out of time. Thanks so much, Sheldon.

On Christmas Day 2014, the movie *Selma* was released and generated major controversy because of its flawed depiction of President Lyndon Johnson's role in leading the federal government's effort to pass the Voting Rights Act of 1965. Who better to provide historical commentary on the symbiotic relationship between LBJ and Martin Luther King, Jr. than America's premier civil rights historian (and Pulitzer Prize winner) **TAYLOR BRANCH** and the Director of the Lyndon B. Johnson Presidential Library (and LBJ biographer) **MARK UPDEGROVE**? On April 22, 2015, I interviewed Messrs. Branch and Updegrove on the LBJ-MLK relationship and what actually occurred in Selma, Alabama, during March 1965 in front of Mike Cramer's class on Media and Culture at the University of Texas at Austin.

"President Johnson told Dr. King that he wished the *Brown v. Board of Education* decision had been about voting rights instead of schools, because he believed voting rights were the essence of the Constitution's founding principle, 'We the People.'" **– TAYLOR BRANCH**

"By using the words 'We Shall Overcome' at the end of his speech to Congress eight days after Bloody Sunday and the night before he submitted his voting rights bill to them, our president was announcing that he had heard the message of the Civil Rights movement loud and clear, and was willing to do something about it." **– MARK UPDEGROVE**

CHAPTER 20

TAYLOR BRANCH AND MARK UPDEGROVE

ON
Lyndon B. Johnson & the Civil Rights Movement

THE LBJ-MLK RELATIONSHIP IN REALITY—AS OPPOSED TO HOW IT WAS PORTRAYED IN THE MOVIE *SELMA*

BOSTON Mark, Doris Kearns Goodwin recently told a large crowd at SMU that the tragedy of the *Selma* movie was that it failed to tell the wonderful true story about the fantastic collaborative black/white, MLK/LBJ triumphant effort that led to the passage of the Voting Rights Act in 1965.

Do you regard how the *Selma* movie treated the LBJ/MLK relationship, as it existed in 1965, as a tragedy?

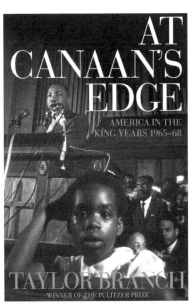

Courtesy of Simon & Schuster, Inc., New York, 2006

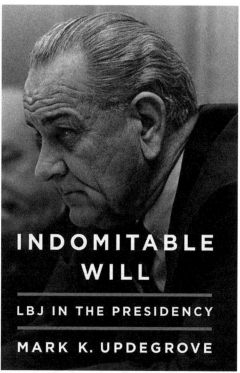

INDOMITABLE WILL

LBJ IN THE PRESIDENCY

MARK K. UPDEGROVE

Courtesy of Penguin Random House LLC

UPDEGROVE Tragedy might be over-stating it since all we're talking about is a Hollywood movie. So many young people in particular get their history from movies, and think that there is a standard in place to ensure historic accuracy. Maybe there should be some sort of regulatory body that screens movies based on history, and then weighs in, and says, "This part is accurate, but this isn't, so it needs to be tweaked," but obviously there is no such body.

The unfortunate thing is that many people who see movies regard them as in-trinsically accurate, and that's certainly not the case in *Selma*. It's a missed opportunity because it would have been a better story if the film had more faithfully captured the consequential and symbiotic relationship between Martin Luther King and Lyndon Baines Johnson regarding the advancement of the Civil Rights movement.

LBJ, J. EDGAR HOOVER, AND THE WIRETAPPING OF MLK

BOSTON Taylor, although LBJ was improperly villainized in the film, in fact there were some genuine villains in the Selma movement—people like George Wallace and J. Edgar Hoover. LBJ is often quoted on the subject of Hoover, saying "I'd rather have him inside my tent pissing out than outside my tent pissing in." Hoover's wiretapping of Martin Luther King came with the authorization of then Attorney General Robert Kennedy, not because LBJ authorized it. However, LBJ presumably knew about Hoover's taping activities, which were clearly aimed at destroying Martin Luther King's reputation.

Is there any evidence that LBJ ever did anything to stop Hoover's taping activities or was it a situation where the president knew that if he tried to shut it down, then the FBI director would leave the tent, go outside, and start pissing in on the White House?

BRANCH Wow. It is still an open ques-tion exactly why in October 1963 Robert Kennedy signed the authorization for Hoover to wiretap Dr. King. It's something historians should wrestle with because it's a very complicated question. Part of the rea-son why Kennedy did it was to protect his brother, and part of it was politics, but the history is unsettled.

On the subject of LBJ and Hoover, LBJ aggressively tried to restrict wiretaps. I've talked about that several times with the late US Attorney General Katzenbach, (who succeeded Robert Kennedy and was Attorney General in 1965). He said he'd get phone calls from LBJ, where the president asked, "Nick, have I ever ordered you to wiretap or bug anybody?" Researchers can find and listen to these calls today on the LBJ Library website.

We need to understand there's a dif-ference between a wiretap and a bug. A "wiretap" is a remote intercept that records a phone conversation. A "bug" requires someone to break into a physical space (such as an office, home, or hotel room), and plant a hidden microphone that will capture every sound in range, not just what's said on the phone. Bugging was much more controversial because it required trespass like a burglary and violated privacy rights extending even into the bedroom.

Bugging was not authorized by the attorney general, and was done solely on Hoover's authority. Johnson tried to get Katzenbach to shut down Hoover in his bugging activities, and said, "The FBI must obtain authority before it can bug. Hoover can't bug people at his own will."

In my first King book, [*Parting the Waters*, pp. 562-569], I discuss the authority Hoover presumably relied on for bugging inside people's property, and say that there's no honest way to summarize the basis for his presumption of authority that's not embarrassing to the dignity of the United States. There was a unanimous US Supreme Court decision in the 1950s that outlawed bugs. The court held that "bugs," (that is, hidden microphones, placed inside property by trespass, without a court order), were illegal. Hoover ignored this ruling after he received a memo from the US Attorney General saying: "Here's this seemingly plain and definitive unanimous Supreme Court decision that bugging is illegal; but in really serious cases, we may have to plant bugs anyway." Once Hoover got that memo, he assumed he had the legal authority to plant bugs whenever he wanted.

Most of the aggressive eavesdropping on Martin Luther King was of the two-stage variety. The FBI used a phone wiretap to learn in advance where King was going to go. Then, the FBI would go to the hotel where he planned to stay before King arrived, and Hoover's men would go to the hotel manager and say "We're the FBI. We want to reserve the room directly above Martin Luther King's room," and then they'd install their bugging equipment. It was not very pretty.

LBJ had nothing to do with Hoover's bugging except he tried to get rid of it. Most of it was done entirely by Hoover and he was the aggressive force behind it, though to some degree, Bobby Kennedy was involved. The historical record shows that Bobby Kennedy was compromised by the fact that Hoover had all sorts of damaging information about his brother, the president, so this was a nasty, tangled situation that can be very easily oversimplified.

UPDEGROVE Taylor, what was at the root of Hoover's concern about King? Was it because he thought King had a communist affiliation, or was it just because he was a black man who was gaining power?

BRANCH In my view, Hoover was America's foremost skilled bureaucrat. By the mid-1960s, he had been at the FBI almost fifty years. The consistent thing about his career was that he always identified and publicized things Americans were afraid of, and then he would say, "The FBI will protect you."

In World War I, Americans were afraid of Bolsheviks and immigrants, and young Hoover led government efforts to deport them. In the 1930s, he publicized the threat of gangsters and said, "We'll save you from them." Then, it was Nazi saboteurs during World War II, and communists all through the Cold War.

In 1960, when the Civil Rights movement came around, Hoover said, "What's going on with this movement is a scary thing." He made sure to keep a fear factor in place.

Hoover's formative years were in Washington, DC during the early years of the twentieth century, when the Ku Klux Klan would march proudly down Pennsylvania Avenue. It was universally assumed from the Ivy League on down, that there was a scientific hierarchy of races and the white race was superior. Hoover grew up with that belief and he embraced it. He had five FBI agents who were black, but three of them were his chauffeurs and two his butlers. The only reason they were called FBI agents was so he could fire them more easily. His world was profoundly threatened by King's demand for civil rights and voting rights, but even the FBI had to recognize the change that was coming in the way of rights for African-Americans.

WHAT THE TAPES AT THE LBJ PRESIDENTIAL LIBRARY REVEAL ABOUT THE LBJ-MLK RELATIONSHIP

BOSTON Mark, the disagreement between LBJ and Martin Luther King in the early part of the *Selma* film was over their having very different ideas about when a voting rights bill should be pushed through Congress. In fact, they *did* have different ideas on timing, as reflected in their December 18, 1964 conversation, although Andrew Young at last year's Civil Rights Summit at the LBJ Library called it a "gentleman's disagreement."

What could director Ava DuVernay, director of the *Selma* film, learn about the LBJ/MLK relationship and whether their disagreements were bitter or whether they were, in fact, gentlemen's disagreements, if she had listened to the tapes at the LBJ Library?

UPDEGROVE Without question, she would learn that they had a gentlemen's disagreement on timing. They both had the same objective: They wanted equal rights for all Americans, and without question, after the Civil Rights Act got passed in 1964, the next phase in seeking to ensure equal rights for all Americans was to pursue the issue of voting rights. LBJ wanted more than anything else to get a voting rights bill enacted, but he was a political pragmatist and knew what was happening in the halls of Congress in late 1964 and early 1965. Before becoming Kennedy's vice-president, he had been probably the most powerful Senate majority leader of the twentieth century, and maybe

in our country's entire history. Johnson was a master of the legislative process and knew instinctively that he couldn't get a voting rights bill passed so soon after passing the very controversial Civil Rights Act of 1964, which had broken the back of Jim Crow.

What LBJ wanted, and you can hear it in the tapes of his telephone conversations, was for King to identify and then highlight the very worst example of voting rights oppression in the South. There's a great conversation that happened on King's thirty-sixth birthday, January 15, 1965, in which LBJ said to Dr. King: "If you take your people, and find the very worst of what's happening down there—and then talk about that situation in the pulpits, in meetings, on TV, and on the radio—then there won't be a fellow who doesn't do anything but drive a tractor who won't say, "That isn't right. That isn't fair."

LBJ had faith in the American people and knew that if they were exposed to what was happening toward the oppression of voting rights in the South at that time, they wouldn't stand for it. That's exactly what happened when Bloody Sunday occurred in Selma. Americans saw on television all the African-American marchers get beaten and clubbed by the local Alabama policemen and state troopers, and they were outraged about it; and that gave LBJ the moral impetus to push the bill through Congress. LBJ never let a good crisis go unused or unexploited, and that was certainly the case with voting rights.

LBJ, MLK, BLOODY SUNDAY IN SELMA, AND THE VOTING RIGHTS ACT OF 1965

BOSTON Taylor, regarding that January 15, 1965 phone conversation that Mark just mentioned, I've read the transcript of it. To me, LBJ was telling Martin Luther King to choose the best story he could find about how unfair the voting practices were in the South at the time, and then keep getting it publicized over and over again until the guy on the tractor had heard it and recognized it as unfair; and then that guy would write his Congressman to get this thing changed. I *don't* read the transcript as LBJ telling Martin Luther King to organize several hundred people into a fifty-four-mile march from Selma to Montgomery into the face of a local and statewide bigoted power structure as existed at that time in Alabama.

When LBJ first learned of Martin Luther King's Selma-to-Montgomery march plan, prior to Bloody Sunday, did he support it?

BRANCH Bloody Sunday—boy, there's so much rich context here. Remember that when they had that conversation on January 15, 1965, King was already in Selma. He had gone there on January 2 and announced that his team was coming in, and in fact they had been working there to lay the groundwork even before then. So Selma was a movement that King and his team had worked on for a long time before January 15.

In the January 15 conversation, LBJ was essentially telling King to keep doing what he was doing, and find as many examples as possible that could make news, because we need to shift public opinion so people will understand how much voting rights were being violated.

There was a lot of interaction between LBJ and King after the January 15 phone conversation up until March 7 when Bloody Sunday occurred. King had become frustrated that his team had received no publicity over their daily demonstrations in which his people were getting arrested and getting hit

When King went to jail in Selma in February 1965, he and his team put an ad in the *New York Times*, saying "This is Selma, Alabama. There are more Negroes in jail with me here than there are on the voting roll." He had originally planned to write a letter from the Selma jail, echoing the letter he wrote in 1963 from the Birmingham jail, except this letter would be about voting rights. However, he got depressed in the Selma jail and decided to get bailed

out. When he did, his staff objected that a leader of his stature could not leave jail like that for personal relief. They said, "You can't do that. You have to say publicly that you came out for a reason. We'll say you bailed out to meet with President Johnson about voting rights." That announcement caused Johnson's aides to go nuts. They said to King, "You can't just announce on your own that you're going to talk to the president of the United States." Then the White House staff orchestrated a compromise for King to meet with the vice president.

When King arrived and began talking with Vice President Humphrey, Johnson "accidentally" wandered in, so he and King actually did talk. The net effect of what King's aides got from this forced meeting was that they angered Johnson's aides, but then everyone calmed down, worked together, and they had a private meeting in the White House, where Johnson told King, "Keep it up!"

When March 7 rolled around, nobody knew that the march from Selma over the Pettus Bridge was going to be on the news or that it would be a big breakthrough. They thought the marchers were just going to get arrested and go to jail, like they had been doing for two months. King wasn't even in Selma on March 7. So it was not like anyone planned that the march would turn into a focal point in civil rights history.

Having said all that, I'm not sure I know whether the march planned to take place on March 7 was controversial in the White House before it turned into Bloody Sunday. President Johnson was intent on not introducing a voting rights bill in Congress until he thought it could pass. A whole element here that the film didn't get into was that LBJ's Justice Department did not really want to prepare a oting rights bill because it was not going to be easy to write. The Constitution says that the *states* are in charge of qualifications for voting; so attempting to enact a federal voting rights bill would be entering into an incredibly sensitive area.

To this day, the Voting Rights Act and its justification is a matter of enormous controversy. Nick Katzenbach told me, and this is confirmed on the tapes, that by early 1965, the Department of Justice already had over a hundred lawsuits seeking to enforce the Civil Rights Act. After the Act had gone into effect, there were still lots of restaurants that refused to desegregate. He believed that the country's adjusting to the Civil Rights Act was going to take at least five years.

On top of that, drafting a voting rights bill that was constitutional and, therefore, could survive Supreme Court scrutiny was another problem. There was also the issue of the poll tax. Put it all together and there were all kinds of questions that baffled the Justice Department lawyers and so LBJ ordered Katzenbach, despite thinking it was premature, to get his best attorneys working on drafting a passable and constitutional voting rights bill. They were working on it, but it wasn't finished when LBJ was talking to King in January and February 1965. All of this context is about something that was laudable but very difficult to execute; and it was all caught up in a number of different political agendas, including the Justice Department's troubles with ending segregation.

On the very day the Civil Rights Act was signed on July 2, 1964, a local restauranteur in Atlanta welcomed his first black customer to his restaurant door with a gun and said to him, "I don't care what this law says. You're not coming in here and I'm doing you a favor because black people should support segregation, too." He then chased the black customer off his parking lot with his son right behind him holding an axe handle. The case brought against that Atlanta restaurant owner by the Department of Justice was one of many of the test cases going forward on desegregation all over the country as of early 1965.

The reason I mention it is not just to show what was going on in the aftermath of the Civil Rights Act when King and his team were talking about moving forward with the voting rights issue; but to give a sense of the political climate at that time. The restaurant owner I just mentioned got elected governor of Georgia—Lester Maddox—simply because he was a symbol of resistance to the Civil Rights Act.

LBJ knew better than anybody that he was in a hornet's nest of a political climate as of early 1965, and he wanted a voting rights bill that his Justice Department lawyers had confidence in. He would then introduce it when he knew he had the public support to get it passed through a reluctant Congress that he knew would likely choose to filibuster the bill. Remember it took four months to beat the filibuster in 1964 before the Civil Rights Act could be brought to the floor.

UPDEGROVE I would just add that originally there was a Voting Rights plank in the Civil Rights bill, but LBJ advocated taking it out because he knew it would make the bill top heavy. At least from a legislation standpoint, he looked at the Civil Rights movement on an incremental basis. First, he wanted to break the back of Jim Crow and *then* he'd be ready to move on to voting rights, though he recognized that getting a voting rights bill passed would be challenging because Congress would be very reluctant to pass another civil rights bill so soon after the first one. He thought getting voting rights for the African-Americans in the South could possibly be achieved through courts' enforcing the Civil Rights Act itself—that is through litigation, and not by having to pass a new bill.

I'd also like to go back to something Taylor mentioned. One of the things the *Selma* movie got right was its depiction of the very fractious nature of the Civil Rights movement. It was not monolithic. You didn't have *all* African-Americans lining up uniformly behind Martin Luther King. As Taylor said, there were many who told King that he needed to stay in jail in Selma. But King answered, "No, I need to get out for my own psychological well-being." The movement was very fractious. People in it differed on timing and tactics just as President Johnson and Dr. King differed on timing and tactics, though everyone had the same overall objective.

BRANCH I don't have total recall about all the things Johnson told King, but the president did say to King that he wished the *Brown v. Board of Education* decision had been about voting rights instead of schools, because he believed voting rights were the essence of the Constitution's founding principle: "We, The People." Voting rights were the essence of our whole democratic venture, our whole self-government experiment.

The school issue got people all tangled up with their emotions because it involved their children, whereas voting rights were and are so fundamental to the promise of democracy. President Johnson wished that the Supreme Court had said in the *Brown* case, "Wait a minute. We're doing something fundamentally wrong here about equal citizenship where black people are involved."

I mention this to underscore how much LBJ saw voting rights as being as fundamental as it was, and still is. I would hope that if anybody here is interested in equal rights going forward, and restoring the optimism and capacity of the government to fulfill that promise, then you need to recognize the importance of voting rights.

By "voting rights," I mean how voting gets done, how to make sure votes get counted, how to make sure they're counted equally, how voting districts are apportioned, and when is the most appropriate time to vote? There are a whole host of issues on voting rights connected to what "We, The People" in our Constitution means. Ultimately, the main question is, "How do we best determine the will of the people?" These voting rights issues will be vital throughout your lives. We haven't yet settled everything on voting rights, by any means.

UPDEGROVE Taylor, you're absolutely right about what Johnson said to King about the

Brown decision, but by the same token, one of the ways he tried to pacify King regarding the timing of the voting rights bill was by his pushing through the Elementary and Secondary Education Act, which started the first real infusion of federal money into our education system. LBJ essentially said to King, "Yes, I'm for voting rights and you're going to get your voting rights bill, but getting federal attention on education is really important, too. If we succeed in leveling the playing field in education, then ultimately there may not be a need for any more civil rights bills because the doors of opportunity will open for all." In addition to getting a voting rights bill passed, and an education bill passed, he was also trying to get a load of other things passed in 1965 that would also help level the playing field among the races, including Medicare, which desegregated many hospitals for the first time. There were many different battles being fought in the war for civil rights in 1965.

THE TENSION OVER LBJ'S SIMULTANEOUSLY SUPPORTING BOTH CIVIL RIGHTS AND LAW AND ORDER

BOSTON I'm going to ask a question of both of you. If I'm Lyndon Johnson and I'm president of the United States in 1965, I therefore have a strong interest in leading a country where there's less disorder, less conflict, less violence, and more rule of law. In spite of having that interest in law and order, I have this very hot issue in front of me where African-Americans are getting organized and leading marches in the Deep South where the Ku Klux Klan has thousands of members, and there are several racist governors and police chiefs. So Martin Luther King's advocating a movement that was highly likely to result in violence and disorder had to be quite a challenge for a president who aspired to maintain law and order.

After Bloody Sunday took place on March 7 and then King and his team

Photo credit: LBJ Library Photo by Yoichi Okamoto

President Lyndon B. Johnson meets
with Martin Luther King, Jr.

planned the second march over the Pettus Bridge on March 9, wouldn't Johnson expect there to be a second round of beating and violence in Selma on national television that would again embarrass us around the world? So I'd like both of you to speak on the president's challenge in dealing with those two competing areas of national interest: number one, wanting to maintain order; and at the same time, wanting to support civil rights and voting rights.

BRANCH Maintaining order during the Civil Rights movement was difficult. Dr. King recognized it as a difficult issue because he was always being criticized for his civil disobedience. His answer to the criticism was that maintaining order was not as important as working toward implementing justice. He believed that the only lasting order that could ever come about would be through achieving justice. Actions that were not violent in nature but which might precipitate violence by demonstrating the lack of justice in American society he believed were, in the long run, steps toward achieving a lasting order that rested on a higher form of justice. Those are real, real paradoxes.

If you look back on this period, every time there was major violence in the Civil Rights era, the history books written at the time negatively portrayed the violence. The Klan tried to support segregation with violence. In 1963, they bombed the little 16th Street church in Birmingham which was what inspired the marches there. Those marches in '63 helped get President Kennedy to introduce the civil rights bill. As the media coverage of those marches showed violence and attack dogs and fire hoses attacking children, the whole country rose up, and said, "We need to do something about this." So there was a very paradoxical relationship between maintaining order and pushing for civil rights.

When I speak at college campuses, I say there's no more salient topic to young people in order to understand our American culture than the role of violence, but it's not studied very much. How effective is violence? How do people react to it? The Civil Rights movement was a nonviolent movement built on the notion that its supporters made up the only army where they were tested by their willingness to die for something, but not to kill for it. They were the only army at the time in which women could be generals and leaders. It was dedicated to the proposition that the heart of America would react against violence when good innocent people become the victims of violence. King proclaimed it religiously, saying, "Unmerited suffering is redemptive."

King's message resonated with LBJ to some degree because King was leading a *nonviolent* movement about voting rights. I'm amazed that most people never think about it, but King preached about how people react strangely to nonviolence. They think it's esoteric or wrong or chicken, but King asked, "What is the heart of democracy but a whole system of votes and what is a vote? Every vote is an act of nonviolence. We agree to manage our conflicts through nonviolent means in the form of votes."

So it was not an unwise thing for Ghandians and Buddhist monks to believe that nonviolence was something they should be committed to. Yet Americans historically have had trouble understanding a nonviolent process because the president is the commander-in-chief and he goes out on aircraft carriers and advocates violence as a solution to problems. Pursuing a major societal change through nonviolence is an issue where Americans are still divided. In the long run, what King was trying to say was, "Unless there is justice to the extent that 'We the People' transcends race, nonviolence is the most useful weapon to expose injustice in a constructive way."

UPDEGROVE Violence complicated things for LBJ. Every summer from 1965 throughout the remainder of his presidency, many cities burned—Watts in Los Angeles, Detroit, Washington, DC, Newark—and the violence and unrest that ensued greatly complicated things for LBJ. Conventional wisdom is that the Vietnam War compromised President Johnson's Great Society agenda and to some degree that's true; but so did the riots. Congress began losing its appetite for passing bills that offered great domestic reform. Martin Luther King realized that, too. The riots compromised his ability to influence the country's political agenda.

BRANCH Remember—and this is a key difference: the Civil Rights movement was a black-led movement that involved nonviolently marching while violence was being inflicted on them by white people, and this advertised their cause in one way; the violence in the riots and burning from 1965-1988, was violence to some degree initiated by black folks. It was not initiated by or part of the nonviolent group; rather, it was a rebellion complicated by doctrines of "Black Power." When people were seeing and worrying about violence, it was hard for them to sift out any moral message. The violence was aimed at benefiting the cause of civil rights, but it complicated things terribly.

THE ROLE OF THE FEDERAL JUDICIARY IN THE SELMA STORY

BOSTON Taylor, getting back to the specific facts of what happened at Selma, one of the main game-changers after the Bloody Sunday first attempt to cross the Pettus Bridge on March 7 was when federal judge Frank Johnson signed a restraining order on March 9, 1965, that was intended to stop the second march at the bridge before it began.

Was Judge Johnson's restraining order issued at his own initiative, or is there any evidence that LBJ told Judge Johnson he needed to sign the order?

BRANCH I have interviewed most of those people involved in what happened at Selma, including John Doar, the US Attorney who told Dr. King that the restraining order had been signed and was on its way to being served on him before he got to the bridge. I do not have confirmation that LBJ directed Judge Johnson to sign the order.

Immediately after Bloody Sunday, lawsuits with crossed purposes were filed in Judge Johnson's court. The lawsuit filed by the leaders of the Civil Rights movement said that the Bloody Sunday violence had been done to them, and, therefore, they wanted the judge to order protection for them because they wanted to march over the Pettus Bridge and go from Selma to Montgomery. At the same time, George Wallace had his Alabama Attorney General file a lawsuit in the same court that said all attempted civil rights marches in Selma were illegal, and were intended to do terrible things, and the state wanted the judge to order the voting rights advocates not to march. So Judge Johnson had both sides in front of him with the two lawsuits: the extreme segregationists and the Civil Rights movement. Each side was saying that something terrible had happened at Selma and the other guy was at fault.

After he signed the restraining order in hopes of preventing a second Bloody

Sunday, Judge Johnson said, "Let's have a hearing in a few days. I can't decide all these complicated issues immediately regarding something that just happened twenty-four hours ago." The Department of Justice definitely wanted to first have an evidentiary hearing and then they wanted Judge Johnson to sign an order that would allow the march from Selma to Montgomery to take place; but they didn't want him to do it blindly and they understood that he couldn't.

Judge Johnson could see how complicated the situation was. From his point of view, the worst thing that could happen would be for him to issue a restraining order that prohibited the march from proceeding and then have it be disobeyed because that would necessarily mean that King and his team were undermining the federal court's authority. Knowing the risk of that happening, by his ruling, he essentially said to the parties, "Let's call time out. I'm signing a restraining order and then we're going to have a hearing in a few days and then I'll decide this after I've heard some evidence and considered the pertinent statutory law and the case law.

What Judge Johnson didn't realize when he signed the restraining order on March 9 was that two nights before, on the very night of Bloody Sunday, King sent out telegrams to religious leaders all over the country saying, "Come to Selma and march with us in the same place where you saw people getting beaten up on television. A terrible thing has happened here in Selma and we want you to not just protest where you live or write a letter. We want you to come to Selma and march with us." The first march (Bloody Sunday) was made up of all black people, but when religious leaders from all over the country started getting these telegrams on the evening of March 7, only a few hours after the beatings on the first march, they started flocking into Selma the next day, such that they were ready to march over the Pettus Bridge on Tuesday, March 9.

I think it's hard to communicate the remarkable degree of mobilization that took place throughout the country then, almost instantly, by people who didn't know much about what was going on in Selma; but once they got the telegram from Martin Luther King (decades before Travelocity, Expedia or anything else like that came along), they immediately traveled to a remote town in Alabama with no preplanning within twenty-four hours. Nobody knew this army of people from all over the country was going to arrive in Selma in short order ready to participate in the second march.

Judge Johnson certainly didn't realize that at the time he issued his restraining order on March 9, King had already gotten almost seven hundred people to come there and march with him. So what was King going to tell these people? That after traveling hundreds or thousands of miles, they now couldn't march because of a restraining order? So as King led them to the middle of the Pettus Bridge on March 9 after being served with the restraining order.

MLK'S MOMENT OF DECISION IN THE SECOND ATTEMPTED CROSSING OF THE PETTUS BRIDGE IN SELMA

BRANCH That's why I think the second attempted march across the Pettus Bridge is the most interesting one of the three because what happened then was wrapped up in issues of federalism, political leadership, law—all these things. King was trying to manage a huge movement that had just made a huge breakthrough in national publicity, and he had gotten lots of priests, nuns, and pastors down there to join him with his team and thereby risk their lives. Many of those on the bridge with King were justifiably terrified when they learned of the restraining order. They certainly didn't want to violate a federal court order. Then they heard that Governor Wallace actually wanted King and his supporters to disregard the restraining order and march toward

Montgomery because that would align Wallace with the federal government. They were also concerned that nuns from other parts of the country would be marching out into the middle of Alabama, an incredibly hostile environment, who were not really prepared to march, and they might be caught in a trap.

So as he stood there in the middle of the bridge on March 9, King had been negotiating with all three branches of the federal government. He was worried about what Wallace was doing, and also was trying to manage a divided movement. The movie screenplay got it almost right in having King say, "I have to march. All these people have come here at my request; I have to do something with them." He got halfway over the bridge and saw that the troopers who had been preparing to block the march, all of a sudden opened their blockade, like the parting of the Red Sea. When they opened up, King and the marchers had to decide, "Is this a trick? Is this a temptation to get us to violate the restraining order and then march out into the middle of nowhere? Is Governor Wallace trying to trap us into doing that? Or—Is this liberation? Is this like Moses, such that we can and should march right on through and head toward our destination of Montgomery?"

King stopped midway across the Pettus Bridge on that second march, said a prayer, and then told the crowd behind him, "We will go back to the church now." Then he turned around and went back to Selma. As he was walking back, some people who had planned to march with him said, "Martin Luther King is a chicken. He should have marched," and they started singing "Ain't Going to Let Nobody Turn Me Around," which was a movement song; although King had just turned them around.

This was King's greatest moment of leadership during Selma, and he only had a few seconds to make his decision. In essence, what he was saying was, "I have got to hold this movement together, but what we are really wanting here at Selma is to do

what it takes to get a law that will enable voting rights to become effective in the South. It will take the federal government and the president to change the law, and I have to have faith in them and their promises that the hearing that will take place in a few days in Judge Johnson's court, and it will not be a trick where the judge would ultimately order us not to march. If that happens, my whole movement would dissipate." It was an act of faith in the federal government and its courts for King to turn around mid-bridge on the second march and comply with the restraining order by returning to Selma.

BOSTON Obviously, Martin Luther King was assassinated before he ever had a chance to write his autobiography. Did he ever fully explain what went through his mind during those few seconds where he was halfway across the bridge, saw those policemen open their blockade, and didn't know if it was a trick, but knew he had been counseled by US Attorney John Doar and former Florida governor Leroy Collins, who had both told King, "Don't violate this restraining order. It's a federal court order, and you want the federal courts to be on your side."

Did he ever explain his thought process in making the decision to turn around and return to Selma?

BRANCH I didn't get to talk to him, I am sad to say, but I did talk to a number of his aides who were there with him on the bridge and afterwards. There are clues based on his testimony at the hearing a few days later. Judge Johnson did an unusual thing at that hearing. Although he had lawyers for the Civil Rights movement and for the State of Alabama in his court for that hearing, from the bench, Judge Johnson himself questioned King as a witness.

The restraining order had been served on King before he stepped on the bridge. It said he was enjoined from taking a step on the bridge, yet he and the other marchers took several steps and walked across the bridge before they stopped and turned around. Because of those facts, Judge Johnson asked King, "What did you do? What did you intend to do when you marched onto the bridge after being served with the restraining order?"

There were a lot of clues about what went through King's mind in making the decision based on his testimony. King testified, "I was in a terrible position. I had to make the most difficult decision of my life. I had to decide upon the most promising long range solution to accomplish our goal of marching to Montgomery to make a stand for voting rights." King's lawyer Clarence Jones supported King's making the decision to turn around on the bridge and go back to Selma. Some of the FBI wiretap evidence corroborated King's testimony (even if it was politically wrong to wiretap), and showed that he did what he had to do in order to hold the movement together on a long-term basis—and that required him to show Judge Johnson that he took the restraining order seriously, and that's why he turned around and led the marchers back to Selma.

LBJ, MLK, AND THE EVENTS OF SELMA

UPDEGROVE King was a controversial figure during the events of Selma. There are three things we've touched on that made him controversial. Number one was his bailing out of jail in Selma in February 1965. Number two was his not marching in the first march on March 7, 1965, now known as Bloody Sunday, because there had been death threats made against him, and he was afraid that his being there might compromise the other marchers, so that's why he wasn't there for the first march. Finally, there was this Turnaround Tuesday on March 9, when he decided not to march across Pettus Bridge to ensure that he wasn't violating a court order. As Taylor mentioned, being depicted as a chicken by people in his own movement was remarkable but he withstood

it. In Selma, he had the weight of the world on his shoulders.

BRANCH I want to correct one thing there. The reason King wasn't there for the first march on Bloody Sunday was because his father didn't want him there. His father at the time was losing membership at his Ebenezer Baptist Church (where he was the pastor) because he was gruff and difficult. King, Sr. told King, Jr., "You are the co-pastor here. You *have* to preach this Sunday on March 7."

The other civil rights marchers didn't really anticipate that the crossing of the Pettus Bridge on March 7 was going to be any big deal. They didn't know there were going to be six hundred people to join that march until they all showed up. Most of these six hundred people were from another county—the county where Jimmie Lee Jackson (the voting rights martyr) was from. Jackson was not from Selma, but from a town in Perry County forty miles away. A lot of people showed up unexpectedly on March 7, and they thought they might get arrested, and after that, the desire to complete the march would keep going, and King would then come over and march with them later. So the march scheduled to take place on March 7 wasn't expected to be that big of a deal.

Bloody Sunday was an unexpected wakeup call, and the whole thing built from there. Everyone wondered, "Are they going to march again? Will they make it? What is LBJ going to do? How is Judge Johnson going to rule after the hearing? Is Congress going to get involved?" It went on and on.

LBJ brought the Congressional leadership into the White House on Sunday night, March 14, exactly one week after Bloody Sunday. The publicity had been building all week and President Johnson described for them the urgency of the voting rights bill. He also told them how irresponsibly Governor George Wallace was behaving. He spoke that Sunday night in such passionate and persuasive terms that Speaker of the House John McCormick said, "My God,

Mr. President. Why don't you talk with this kind of moral force to the people?" LBJ replied, "At the right time, I will." Johnson was very well aware of how public opinion was moving as he waited for Judge Johnson to make a final ruling after having heard all the evidence at the hearing. The president knew that things were getting more favorable for the Civil Rights movement by the day. In fact, by the end of that March 14 meeting, the Congressional leaders had talked him into coming before Congress the very next night to address the situation and talk about the need for a voting rights bill.

That next night became the right time and his March 15th speech, known as the "We Shall Overcome" speech, is powerfully eloquent and arresting from its very first sentence: "I speak tonight for the dignity of man and the destiny of democracy." Instantly, he framed the Bloody Sunday marchers as being part of the vanguard of American historical patriotism—right up there with the American Revolution militia who fought at Lexington and Concord and the Civil War leaders at Appomattox, which was a stunning comparison when you think about it. There was an all-black nonviolent movement going on in Selma, Alabama, that the president believed was right up there in the pantheon with earlier Americans who had been instrumental in the fight for basic freedom.

It is a masterpiece of a speech full of passion and written by Doris Kearns Goodwin's husband, Richard Goodwin. He wrote at least the first draft of it, but I talked to the people who rode up to the Capitol that night in the limo with the president and they said he was editing it all the way until he got out of the car.

UPDEGROVE What Taylor referred to as the "We Shall Overcome" speech has an important title because the song "We Shall Overcome" was the anthem of the Civil Rights movement. When LBJ included those words in his speech for voting rights on March 15, 1965, to highlight the need to overcome bigotry and injustice in America,

it was very meaningful to those on the front lines of the movement who were waging that battle. By using those words, our president, the most important person in the free world, was announcing that he had heard the message of the movement loud and clear and was willing to do something about it. Civil rights leader John Lewis (now a US Congressman) was watching that speech on television with Dr. King at the home of the parents of Jimmie Lee Jackson (who Taylor just mentioned had been killed the week before, thereby becoming the Selma movement's first martyr). When LBJ said, "We Shall Overcome," John Lewis saw Dr. King cry for the first time, and King said, "We shall march from Selma to Montgomery. The Voting Rights Act will pass." That's exactly what happened.

THE DISRUPTION TO LBJ'S FOCUS ON CIVIL RIGHTS CAUSED BY THE VIETNAM WAR

BOSTON So many times in studying history, we forget that the president of the United States is a human being who can only do so much and process only so much information and stress. Taylor, in your book you mention that while Selma was going on in March of 1965, LBJ was dealing with another huge issue: figuring out America's proper role in the Vietnam War. *Time* magazine had an article recently by historian David Kaiser who said, "LBJ was making the best and the worst decisions of his presidency at the same time."

Give us your analysis, and Mark feel free to chime in, regarding whether the Vietnam situation disrupted LBJ's focus on executing his vision for voting rights and the rest of his Great Society agenda in the spring of 1965.

BRANCH Wow. It is absolutely correct that LBJ's having to decide what he needed to do about voting rights and Vietnam was going on at the same time in February and March 1965. The notion that they affected

Photo credit: Jean-Pierre Ishendjian

Taylor Branch

president, "We must retaliate with bombing raids." And he and the president were discussing whether the US should start bombing raids in Vietnam when Martin Luther King arrived at the White House uninvited.

These things were tumbling over each other right from the beginning because if we were going to start bombing raids, then we would need some combat troops to protect the air fields in Vietnam. So the first thing Johnson did in February 1965 was to say, "Okay. We are going to send in some Marines to guard the air fields." He would not send the first actual combat divisions to Vietnam until late that summer, but the American war effort was beginning to start up. The Marines he sent to protect the airbases landed on March 7—the day of Bloody Sunday. They landed in Da Nang and came ashore where Vietnamese people put flowers around our soldiers' necks, and welcome them, since they were the first people coming over there to protect the airbases.

So these decisions were going on at the same time, although nobody had any notion then that the Vietnam War was going to turn into a major war, let alone the first war America ever lost. In fact, as of the spring of 1965, very few Americans had even heard of Vietnam. It was an inside game going on in Washington, and most of the country didn't know much about it.

I think the most important thing I could say about whether the president's attention got stretched too far over deciding issues of Vietnam and the Civil Rights movement simultaneously is that because the Vietnam War became *the* biggest issue of the Sixties going forward, the fact that Johnson's early decisions about it occurred while he was also making decisions about how best to advance civil rights made the two of them together become part of the same historical conversation about that era.

Some people have ultimately concluded that Johnson was an ogre on how he handled Vietnam; some have concluded he didn't understand what was going on there; some have concluded he was duped by his

one another in President Johnson's mind was not a conscious thing, but it may have been subconscious. Here was a nonviolent movement seeking justice at home versus what America should do about a violent war going on across the globe; and they were both considered to be about freedom and America's standing up for freedom - in one case, by resisting communism overseas, and in another, by standing up for voting rights at home.

I mentioned earlier how offended White House advisors were when after Dr. King bailed himself out of jail in Selma in February 1965, he announced that he got out of jail in order to come see President Johnson in Washington, DC. Immediately after that announcement, King did fly to Washington, and arrived just as National Security Advisor McGeorge Bundy had come back from Vietnam where he had traveled because the Vietcong had just over-run a US Marine establishment there at Pleiku. During his trip, Bundy saw Marines blown to smithereens. He had never before seen anything like that, and he told the advisors; some have concluded it was an imperialist war that was fought for money; and some have concluded LBJ was a militarist and blood thirsty.

The thing I want to say is that I am so grateful we have these tapes here at the LBJ Library where you can actually listen to President Johnson as he made those decisions in real time. To me, it was a revelation because I lived through this. This was a very big deal in my life. For many years I wondered, "What were we really trying to do in Vietnam?" It was a great revelation for me to listen to those tapes in the Nineties when they were first released. I listened to hundreds of them, and I had to transcribe them myself.

What you get out of hearing them is Johnson's anguish. He sensed that we might lose the war at a time when nobody thought it was possible for the mighty United States to lose a war in the jungles against a fifteenth rate power that nobody had ever heard of. But *he* knew it, and he kept saying things as he kept increasing our war effort over there like, "My answer is yes, but my judgment is no." Hearing him say that made chills run up my back, but he believed that the American people would forgive him for anything except being weak. To me, that is the crux of it. Johnson felt he was going to lose the war and that would cause him to lose the political support to do any of the good things on the domestic front that he wanted to do. He, therefore, had to stand and fight. He told Dr. King, "I have killed a few people, we had 265 casualties out there last week, but it could easily have been 265,000 if I didn't manage it correctly. They are on me to have a big war and to bomb and I am trying to resist it. I am just trying to do what is right." To me, the tapes show that in the beginning of a historical appraisal that we haven't really completed yet, LBJ was showing true anguish as he tried to manage the situation in Vietnam.

UPDEGROVE Anguish is absolutely right—anguish and profound ambivalence. As early as 1964, he was talking to his national

Photo credit: LBJ Library Photo by Jay Godwin

Mark Updegrove

security advisor McGeorge Bundy and said, "I don't think Vietnam is worth fighting for and yet I can't get out. It's the biggest damn mess."

To your point, Taylor, he further asked Bundy, "What in the world is Vietnam worth to me? What is it worth to this country?"

Ultimately, his actions spoke louder than those words because Vietnam did mean something to him. He escalated troop involvement, because he didn't see a way out, and he didn't want to look weak. Paradoxically, he was afraid of the Kennedys to some degree. John Kennedy had been elected president as a staunch cold warrior, and Johnson was afraid of looking weak and bearing the scrutiny.

There was this crushing weight he felt about making those decisions and he just didn't believe America could let communists and insurgents win in that part of the world. At the time, the prevalent theory in American foreign policy was that if we let communists win anywhere in the world, then that would embolden China and the Soviet Union to take other more important countries, and then the dominos would start to fall.

BRANCH The most striking part of the tapes for me involved hearing Richard Russell, the senator from Georgia, who for decades was like a father figure to LBJ. Russell was the leader of the Southern segregationists, and what happened between the two men involving civil rights and Vietnam proved the miraculous power of Lyndon Johnson. They continued to have a father-son type relationship even after LBJ said, "Dick, I love you, but I am going to run over you on civil rights. I am telling you that because you are like my daddy, but you are wrong on segregation." Somehow Russell continued on as Johnson's closest advisor and in one of the conversations on tape where LBJ was anguishing about what to do in Vietnam, (and this was very early on before he sent any troops over there), he asked Russell for advice. Russell said, "We are just like a cow stuck over a fence in Vietnam. We can't get back and we can't go forward. We can't win the war and we can't get out." This came from a guy who was regarded as a stereotypical hawk who supported our every military thrust and was the Congressional face who most advocated our doing what we were doing during the Vietnam War.

So it was a real shock for me to hear Senator Richard Russell telling Johnson regarding the situation in Vietnam that we were like a cow stuck halfway over a fence, and Vietnam didn't mean a damn thing to us strategically. After he said that to Johnson, Russell said, "I don't know what to do."

In fact, Russell told Johnson a couple of times, and he said it halfway as a joke, "I would like to install a government in Vietnam that would tell us to leave. Then we would be covered because we could say politically that we left because we were told to leave." In retrospect, I am not sure, but maybe Russell meant that comment to be taken more seriously than it was taken, but Johnson didn't take it seriously, or I don't think he did. Russell also said about Vietnam, "I'm afraid it's another Korea."

APPORTIONING CREDIT FOR THE VOTING RIGHTS ACT OF 1965

BOSTON In wrapping up this issue of the Voting Rights Act and the controversy over whether Martin Luther King was its grand champion, or was LBJ the grand champion, or was it a 50/50 partnership. A year ago at the Civil Rights Summit here at the LBJ Library, Andrew Young was on a panel with Taylor and said, "We could have not have gotten the Voting Rights Act passed without President Johnson and his legislative skills and we could not have gotten it passed without Martin Luther King and his execution of the nonviolent Selma masterpiece."

Richard Goodwin who we mentioned before as LBJ's speechwriter who wrote the first draft of the "We Shall Overcome" speech, in a recent *Washington Post* editorial said, "The moral imperative of a social movement became the legal imperative of the government. It was not a black moment or a white moment, but an incandescent American moment."

Hearing those statements from Young and Goodwin, and knowing what you know about history, do you give 50/50 credit for the passage of the Voting Rights Act to LBJ and MLK?

BRANCH First of all, I don't think it matters. Getting the Voting Rights Act passed was a collaboration between an active citizen's movement and a responsive government acting in a way reflecting how our system was designed to work. Regardless of whether it was 50/50 or 60/40, either way it was that kind of collaboration. I would say one other thing though. Selma was not all Martin Luther King. Selma was not even King's idea. It was a big surprise to me to find out Selma was the idea of some twenty year olds who were responding to the Birmingham Church bombing, who determined that they had to do something to redeem these four little girls who got killed. They brought the plan for what became

Selma to King, and they hectored him all through 1964 until he finally agreed to it.

So the idea for what happened at Selma came essentially from college students who couldn't vote themselves, but who nevertheless designed a plan to take action. It became historic and King agreed to it. So young people had a stake in this, too. They were part of the active citizen's movement and were the initiating part, with King becoming the symbol of it.

LBJ, THURGOOD MARSHALL, AND PRESIDENT OBAMA

BOSTON If you ask anybody to name the three most important African-Americans in history, one of them would be Martin Luther King who we've been talking about today at length; another would be Thurgood Marshall, our first African-American US Supreme Court Justice; and the third would be President Obama, our first African-American president.

For the final comment for this program, and relying on certain passages in his splendid new book *Destiny for Democracy*, I would like Mark to tell us where LBJ stood in the eyes of Supreme Court Justice Thurgood Marshall and President Barack Obama.

UPDEGROVE Thurgood Marshall revered Johnson. He was named Solicitor General by President Johnson in 1965. He became the first African-American to hold that position and then became the first African-American Supreme Court Justice in 1967, nominated for that position by Johnson as well.

There was a wonderful conversation that we have on tape at the LBJ Library where Johnson was speaking with Marshall at the time when Johnson offered him the Solicitor General job. If Marshall accepted, it would be a major pay cut and he would have to move from New York where he was then living and working for the NAACP, and would have to move to Washington. It would be historic for him to become the first African-American Solicitor General in

history, but it would also be a major family decision for him. Marshall told President Johnson, "I'm going to have to talk to my wife, so it's going to take some time." Johnson said, "Well I understand. Get back to me tomorrow."

Then, in 1967, President Johnson offered Marshall the position of Associate Justice on the Supreme Court. These nominations of Marshall by Johnson were historic decisions. Johnson was not just passing the Civil Rights Act and the Voting Rights Act; he was trying to integrate government as well. Thurgood Marshall stated in no uncertain terms that he regarded Lyndon Johnson as the greatest civil rights president in American history.

President Obama said to me when we had a few moments alone at the Civil Rights Center last year, as he looked at the original draft of the "We Shall Overcome" speech (an exhibit in the LBJ Library's Great Hall), "I view Johnson as one of our six greatest presidents." That is high praise and puts LBJ in the presidential pantheon with folks like Abraham Lincoln, George Washington, Thomas Jefferson, and FDR.

BOSTON Thanks so much, Taylor Branch and Mark Updegrove.

EVAN THOMAS spent much of his career as a journalist at *Time* and *Newsweek* magazines. He served as *Newsweek*'s Washington bureau chief and editor at large. He's written nine books about history, and the most recent is *Being Nixon: A Man Divided* (Random House 2015). I interviewed Evan twice about his Nixon biography—using two sets of questions—first in front of a large group of students and faculty at The King's College in New York City on October 5, 2015, and then in front of a private gathering of lawyers, accountants, and clients sponsored by Winstead PC law firm and the Dallas office of Ernst & Young at Arlington Hall in Dallas, Texas, on October 15, 2015. I then intergrated the two transcripts into one.

"Another reason why he didn't have deep conversations was because he was a loner. He didn't like to talk to people. The joke on Nixon's staff was that his best friend was a yellow legal pad where he was always making notes to himself. His notes would describe the person he wanted to be—Joyful. Serene. Inspiring. Confident. Optimistic—and Nixon knew he was none of those things. I think he knew that at some level, he was locked in a terrible internal struggle trying to be the optimistic, upbeat person he could never quite be."

– EVAN THOMAS

CHAPTER 21

EVAN THOMAS
ON
Richard Nixon

NIXON THE CHILDHOOD DREAMER

BOSTON Let's start with Nixon's childhood. Your book states that throughout his youth, Nixon received very little nurturance from either his mother or father. In fact, Henry Kissinger once said of him, "Can you imagine what this man would have been if somebody had loved him?" You make reference at least twice to the image of Nixon as a boy lying on his back on the grass, looking up at the sky.

In that moment, Evan, I'd like for you to be Nixon. Be his heart. Be his mind. There he is, lying on the grass, looking at the sky, feeling unnurtured and lonely. What do you think his inner voice was telling him?

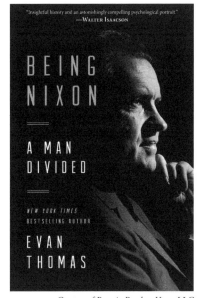

Courtesy of Penguin Random House LLC

THOMAS Get me out of here! His father was a bully. He said his mom was saintly, but she was a passive-aggressive saint. All his life, Richard Nixon hated personal confrontation after watching his mom and dad fight. He was unloved as a kid in many ways. He was unpopular—other kids didn't like him very much, but he was smart. He received a scholarship to attend Harvard, but he couldn't go because there wasn't any money to send him.

He was a lonely little boy, but when he was staring up at the clouds, he dreamed. One thing that ran through his writings and conversation all his life was a sense of destiny. This homely little boy who didn't have many friends, somehow believed he was destined to do great things. Maybe he had big dreams to defy his humble background. Who knows? But he had big dreams of being destined to do great things—no doubt about it.

NIXON'S LACK OF SELF-AWARENESS

BOSTON Throughout the book, you frequently mention Nixon's lack of self-awareness, and say, "Nixon, at times, seemed to deny he had an inner self." But then you ask, "How many great men of history were truly self-aware?" Again, Evan, "be Nixon," and explain your lack of self-awareness and your refusal to attempt accessing your inner self.

THOMAS Nixon, like a lot of great people, felt he couldn't get up in the morning and worry about who he really was. He felt that in order for a person to do great things, he had to just be a great person. To do that required keeping his eye on the ball and not look left or right, and not stopping to look inside.

There's a lot to be said for somebody with a single focus on forging straight ahead. Nixon had unbelievable drive and he was always prepared. His nickname in law school was "Iron Butt" because he studied so much it seemed like he never left his

chair. But there's always a cost that comes with obsessive ambition. This is the story of human nature because the tradeoffs that take place are complicated, and strengths can sometimes become weaknesses.

His particular weakness was that he had trouble seeing his own weaknesses. I found a few places in his records where he said, "A person needs to know his own weaknesses," but then he would move on quickly and not dwell on that thought or his weaknesses.

He had one particular weakness. He could not forgive his enemies. He collected grudges, and nursed them, and finally would lash out at his enemies. As president, he had the power to act on his grudges, and this doomed him because he picked fights with people who could get back at him. For example—*The Washington Post*. Never pick a fight with a newspaper. They always have the last laugh. They've got the printing press.

He enabled his enemies to feel righteous about attacking him because he so often was underhanded in his attacks on them. He had lists of his enemies. Of course, the lists leaked out and his enemies found out about them, and it emboldened them to go after him. And they did.

Many of his wounds came because he brought them on himself by being so vengeful and sometimes even committing criminal acts. He deserved to be driven from the presidency, but his story is like a Shakespearean drama because so much of the damage he suffered came from self-inflicted wounds.

I searched the record to find evidence of his having any awareness about his weakness of not forgiving his enemies. The only place I found anything was at the very end of his presidency, just as he was leaving the White House when he was about to get on the helicopter and fly away. His last words to his staff were, "If you hate your enemies, they win, and you destroy yourself." Hello! Too late! Did that just occur to him on the day he resigned as he was getting on the helicopter to fly into disgrace and exile? You won't find that statement in his records—I

4444444444

looked and looked without success for any evidence that he had ever made the statement before leaving the White House.

I wondered whether Nixon ever read Greek tragedies or Shakespeare, so I looked in his school papers, which have survived. He went to Whittier College, a good Quaker school, and there he read Shakespeare's *Julius Caesar*, and wrote a paper about it in 1930. I read it and it's a terrible paper. He totally missed the point! He failed to see the play's basic message about hubris—that over-weaning pride cometh before the fall. Whittier is actually a pretty good college, but, as a student, (and he was a good student), Nixon did not absorb the central lesson that over-weaning arrogance leads to the fall. If only he had read more Shakespeare, Sophocles, and Euripides, and grasped them, things might have turned out different.

He read a lot of political philosophy in college, which is implicit in *Julius Caesar*, but he didn't really focus on the true tragedy. He was an intellectual, but he missed the essential lesson that could have saved his presidency.

BOSTON Besides it being a good idea not to make enemies with *The Washington Post*, a president also shouldn't make an enemy of a federal judge. In your book, you tell the story of John Sirica, the federal district judge in DC who ordered the production of the Watergate tapes. Long before Watergate, Judge Sirica came to Nixon informally and mentioned that he'd like to be named a justice on the US Court of Appeals. Nixon ignored him, which Sirica didn't appreciate, and he ended up being the judge who brought the president down.

THOMAS Right. Don't burn bridges with people you may meet down the road.

NIXON'S INABILITY TO HAVE INTIMATE CONVERSATIONS

BOSTON Along the same lines, you say that Nixon was not capable of participating in any soul-baring, frank, personal conversations—not even with family or friends.

Was he incapable of having a soul-baring conversation with anyone since he never found a way to access his own soul?

THOMAS There are 3,700 hours of tape recordings of Nixon talking to his aides—the largest record of any president in history. Nixon put a taping system in his Oval Office, in his hideaway office at the Executive Office Building, and all over the White House. We have a record of what he said all day long and at night, too.

In all his taped conversations, there are no intimate, soul-baring conversations. He had deep conversations about policy, and about his enemies and how to get them, but no deep personal talks except for an occasional tiny flicker. For example, he mentioned that strange things were happening that could only happen in his White House—referring to the fact that the Pentagon was spying on the president of the United States. They had people going through the garbage looking for the so-called "burn bags" where Nixon's people put top secret documents to be destroyed. People on the Pentagon staff fished out of the trash top secret documents so they could tell the joint chiefs of staff and the Pentagon generals what Nixon was doing. The military was spying on the president and stealing secret documents. Nixon caught them doing it, and knew that the admirals were behind it. When he recognized this, Nixon said on the tape, "Did I do this? Did I create such a toxic environment that the generals in the Pentagon are spying on their commander-in-chief?" It was just a little flicker of self-awareness by Nixon. And then he quickly moved on and said, "I want to get those bastards!"

I looked and looked to find any further traces of his having any deep conversations with anyone. Part of his problem was that he had a sense of propriety. He felt it was undignified for a man to bare his soul. He equated self-knowledge with weakness—thought it was whiney and too confessional—thought people who went to psychiatrists were weak. He never understood that seeking psychological help is a sign of strength, and that people go to psychiatrists when they're in trouble in hopes that the treatment will make them stronger.

As president, although he wouldn't see a psychiatrist, Nixon had no problem with the idea of seeing a quack doctor who prescribed drugs which, not surprisingly, made him much worse. This guy gave Nixon various narcotics to medicate his pain, but he never talked to Nixon about his pain.

A historian has to look for hints of what's really going on inside the person he's studying. I read an oral history from his daughter Julie. She described her father coming home at night, and when he came through the door of the White House or at their home in New York, he'd whistle, and turn on all the lights, and put a Broadway show tune on the record player. At dinner, he wanted nothing but happy talk. He wanted to be upbeat and optimistic.

At the time, he was fighting his demons and struggling with all kinds of turmoil, but his routine of whistling, lighting up rooms, playing show tunes, and engaging in only happy talk at dinner strongly suggests that he was mirror imaging—trying hard to be upbeat because he felt so low. It's like the dog that didn't bark in the old story. He did the opposite of what he was feeling. All those happy activities suggest that Nixon was hurting, and stuck in his darkness. Late at night, when he was alone, he would brood and drink too much and talk about how much he wanted to get his enemies.

Another reason why he didn't have deep conversations was because he was a loner. He didn't like to talk to people. The joke on Nixon's staff was that his best friend was a

yellow legal pad where he was always making notes to himself. His notes would describe the person he wanted to be—Joyful. Serene. Inspiring. Confident. Optimistic—and Nixon knew he was none of those things. He made notes about the person he wanted to be. I think he knew that at some level, he was locked in a terrible internal struggle trying to be the optimistic, upbeat person he could never quite be.

BOSTON For the better part of Nixon's career in national politics, his "best friend" was a guy named Bebe Rebozo. You would assume that he would have intimate conversations with his best friend, but from everything I've ever read, when they got together, Nixon did all the talking and Bebe Rebozo just sat there and listened.

THOMAS Or both of them would say nothing at all. A president always has to have Secret Service protection. Bebe would take Nixon out on his boat and they would sit up on the top deck while the Secret Service guy sat down below within earshot. There would be hours of silence where neither man spoke. They'd just sit in the sun. Nixon valued that Bebe didn't ever press him about anything that was going on, and occasionally would entertain him with a dirty joke. Nixon found it very relaxing to say nothing, swim, laugh, and drink with Rebozo.

NIXON'S DUAL APPROACH TO CONFRONTATION

BOSTON Nixon had a lifelong problem of being averse to personal confrontation, which was a factor in why he mishandled Watergate so egregiously. You say that as a boy, he witnessed ugly confrontations between his father and brother that were so ugly, it made Nixon want to avoid confrontations for the rest of his life.

Did Nixon not know that there are emotionally intelligent methods of confrontation that can be managed in a way that don't have to be angry or ugly?

THOMAS He knew it in some ways. He was actually a statesman who was good at negotiating with the Soviet Union. He was the first president to go to Moscow to negotiate a major arms control treaty. That's confrontation at a very high level—"Your nuclear missiles against our nuclear missiles." Nixon was great at that. He never preached at his adversaries or lectured them. He didn't say, "American ideology is better than communism." He showed respect to those who tried to upset him. He would stay cool, lower his voice, and talk about areas of interests—not competing ideologies. He was always well prepared. In that context, he could handle confrontation.

Where he was bad at confrontations was with his friends and staff. He didn't really want to know what they were up to. So in summary, as a statesman acting for the interests of the United States, he could handle confrontation; but when it was personal and intimate, he could not.

NIXON'S REACTION TO REJECTION

BOSTON A recurring theme throughout Nixon's life was rejection followed by triumph. It was true of the girls he wanted to date, who originally rejected him but then he finally got to date the girl he wanted in high school; and later he got the greatest object of his desire—Pat Ryan, who became his wife. In college at Whittier, where no fraternity wanted him, he became student body president. Later, in national politics, he dealt with rejection by Eisenhower when he was Ike's vice president; then rejection by the voters in the 1960 presidential election and the '62 California gubernatorial election; but then he ultimately triumphed in the '68 and '72 elections.

So, although he ultimately found ways to succeed, what role did all these rejections play in causing Nixon's emotional instability that bottomed out during his presidency?

THOMAS Rejection was a powerful motivator for him to do better and get what he wanted, but he nurtured and wouldn't let go of grievances and grudges. He was socially awkward and extremely shy and uncomfortable, but learned how to compensate by being able to remember names. He also had a keen sense of being on the side of the outsiders against the insiders.

At Whittier College, a Quaker school, when he ran for student body president, his platform was to allow dances on campus—a radical thing to do for an uptight Quaker school. Why did he do it? Because he understood that rich kids could dance anytime they wanted at the local country club or nice restaurants. It was the poor kids who couldn't find a place to dance, so he won overwhelmingly.

NIXON'S CHOICE OF POLITICS, DESPITE HIS BEING AN INTROVERT

BOSTON You've already said tonight that Nixon was a loner and an introvert. Yet he pursued a career in politics—the ultimate business for an extrovert.

What drove him into politics—a bad fit with his personality?

THOMAS This is one reason why I wrote the book. I couldn't understand why somebody so shy would go into national politics. Nixon took shyness to extremes—to where the buses don't run. When his Deputy White House Chief of Staff Alexander Butterfield was first introduced to him, Nixon literally could not get a word out. Butterfield's account of that first meeting is backed by H.R. Haldeman's account in his diary. Haldeman, Nixon's chief of staff, didn't want to introduce his deputy to Nixon because he was afraid of what would happen—that this socially shy speechless president of the United States would be unable to say anything. Nixon had a way of working around his shyness problem and was prepared to overcome it at times. He wasn't speechless shy in every circumstance. For example, he was comfortable when he met Elvis Presley of all people; but at times, he just couldn't get any words out.

BOSTON Why would anybody that shy go into politics? Did he think political achievement was the only way he could validate his own life? Obviously, he grew up in poverty. He was a man who truly pulled himself up by his own boot straps—rags to riches. Was politics his only method of validation?

THOMAS Yes, in several respects. First, many actors are shy and deal with it by performing onstage. They're only comfortable there, and in no other settings. Nixon had a bit of the actor in him. One of his favorite places to be onstage was to go face-to-face with angry crowds in front of cameras. In film clips of Nixon, you can see that he often held up the "V" for victory sign that Eisenhower and Churchill had used in World War II; but by 1970, the "V" sign was the peace symbol for the anti-war activists. Nixon liked to wave to the crowd of peaceniks with the "V" sign and it really drove them crazy. He liked that kind of confrontation.

THE NIXON MARRIAGE

BOSTON Let's talk about the Nixon marriage. Your book details how, like her husband, Pat Ryan Nixon came from very humble beginnings. She was either ferociously loyal to her husband or else ferociously ambitious as evidenced by the way she campaigned for him during their marriage. She said she believed her husband was a man of destiny—and, therefore, she presumably saw herself as a woman of destiny; though with each year of the marriage, she hated politics more.

Staying with her husband through all the media attacks, and all the protests against him during his presidency, and through the humiliating ordeal of Watergate, have we ever had a mentally tougher First Lady than Pat Nixon?

THOMAS She was a very affecting woman. The picture we have of her in our minds is of someone who looks drawn, tired, and sad. That's an unfair picture. In my book, there's a photograph of her in 1953 and she was a knockout then—a real beauty. In that picture, she's standing there and Nixon's next to her and he has this look on his face of a guy who can't believe his good luck in having married somebody so beautiful.

While they dated, on occasion Nixon would drive Pat on her dates with other men. He'd read a book in a hotel lobby while she went out on her date; and then he'd drive her home. He did this for a couple of years and finally just wore her down.

She had grown up poor and saw in Nixon a sense of destiny that made her stick with him, no matter what. She hated politics, though at least five times, when he got depressed and wanted to get out of politics, she told him, "You can't," because she understood that if he did, it would destroy him.

By Watergate, things got pretty tough. Their daughter Julie wrote that her mom and dad were drinking a little bit too much then—translation—they were drinking a *lot* too much. Typical Nixon, after he was driven from office, he rebuilt his marriage. If you google "Pat Nixon funeral," you'll see a video of Richard Nixon who wasn't just crying, he was bawling. He was undone by the death of his wife.

NIXON, ALGER HISS, AND THE MEDIA

BOSTON His political star rose nationally as a young congressman in the late 1940s with his investigation of Alger Hiss, an East Coast Ivy League darling who Nixon proved was a communist spy working in the State Department. You say that Nixon's rough treatment of Hiss adversely impacted his relationship with the national media and Washington social in-crowd of that era.

Why weren't the media and the in-crowd pleased that someone had caused a prominent communist spy to be identified and imprisoned?

THOMAS We're all members of different tribes, and beginning in high school, Nixon consistently embarrassed the cool kid tribe. For Nixon, who had been the nerd at the high school table and spent the rest of his life playing that role, bringing down Hiss was his great chance to embarrass the cool table—exposing one of theirs as a communist spy. The cool people didn't appreciate what the nerd had done, so rather than focus on the fact that Hiss was a communist spy who had been caught, they focused on the fact that the nerd had embarrassed them. Not all of them did this, but many of them did.

Nixon lived under the shadow of this for a long time. Of course, it embittered him because he felt he wasn't being given his due for exposing a dangerous spy, and instead was being mocked and vilified by the cool crowd.

This brings me back to your question about why Nixon went into politics. Although Nixon was shy, he was an effective politician because he understood how to appeal to outsiders. After all, there would always be more of them than insiders. When Nixon got to Whittier College, he discovered that, as in most colleges, there was a cool kids' fraternity and they were called the Franklins. So Nixon started a fraternity for the uncool guys, and they called themselves the Orthogonians, and there were more of them. Nixon wanted to be a student politician, so he rallied the outsiders against the insiders—and he won a majority of the vote by doing that.

He did this throughout his political career. In 1969, he gave a famous speech about the "silent majority." The United States in 1969-1970 was almost on the verge of revolution. Cities were burning. Campuses were in uproar and the liberal establishment seemed to be encouraging the disruption. Many people in the United States became upset about it, though they didn't raise their voices. They weren't out

there demonstrating and protesting, but they didn't like what was going on. Nixon understood this, so he appealed to them.

In 1972, Nixon won the presidential election by one of the largest landslides in history. As a Republican, he won 35% of the Democratic vote by appealing to people who were outsiders and felt that the establishment wasn't looking after their interests. Nixon appeared as the candidate who could be their voice.

NIXON'S RELATIONSHIP WITH DWIGHT EISENHOWER

BOSTON Let's talk about the relationship between Dwight Eisenhower, our two-term thirty-fourth president, and Nixon, his vice president for all eight years. Ike learned almost immediately after choosing Nixon at the 1952 Republican Convention that the two of them were out of sync, and Ike definitely wanted Nixon off the ticket in both 1952 and in 1956.

Why didn't Dwight Eisenhower just pull the trigger and remove Richard Nixon as his running mate?

THOMAS Because Nixon could hang on by his fingernails. Ike barely knew Nixon when he chose him as vice president. It was a political choice. Nixon was from California and appealed to the far right. Then, right after Ike picked him, Nixon blew it. The first time he came in and met Eisenhower, he greeted Ike with, "Hi, Chief." No one called Dwight Eisenhower, the top general of the army, "Chief." So they got off on the wrong foot. Then right after the convention, Nixon got caught up in a phony little scandal over his maintaining a private account for funding his personal expenses.

BOSTON Which led to the famous Checkers speech.

THOMAS Yes, Nixon had to go on national television to explain the account, and he gave what some people thought was an overly sentimental speech, but it worked, and Eisenhower kept him on the ticket. Then again in '56, as you mentioned, Eisenhower tried to dump him. Again, Nixon basically hung on for dear life. Then, in 1960, when Nixon was running for president, Eisenhower was asked at a press conference if he could identify something Vice President Nixon had done to further his foreign policy, and Eisenhower answered, "Well, if you give me a week, I'll think of something"—pretty cruel.

BOSTON A question about that remark by Eisenhower was actually asked of Nixon during the Nixon-Kennedy televised debate.

THOMAS It was the first question: "Why did Eisenhower say that about you?"

BOSTON In 1952, after Nixon had been named Eisenhower's vice president on the Republican presidential ticket, the press went after Nixon for having the same type of political fund to pay his personal expenses that the Democratic presidential candidate Adlai Stevenson had, though the press didn't go after Stevenson at all.

Did the media's obvious double standard toward Nixon justify his paranoia?

THOMAS Even paranoids have enemies and Nixon had enemies, but this was a classic "turn the other cheek" moment. Although the press clearly set out to get Nixon, it was unfair how they vilified him. By lashing back and fighting the press, however, Nixon picked a fight he could not win. If you make the national press your enemy—particularly in the pre-internet days when the press was so centralized and controlled by *The New York Times*, *The Washington Post*, and the three television networks, then you've made an enemy with folks who cannot be beat. He tried to go over their heads by connecting with the silent majority voters, but the media was a powerful enemy and Nixon lived to regret going to war against them.

BOSTON Was his paranoia justified?

THOMAS It was justified, but not entirely justified. It was still stupid and wrong. These issues are always complicated. Although the New York and Washington press were pretty liberal, there were many conservative newspapers all over the United States. Nixon actually received a majority of the newspaper endorsements in 1960 because a lot of them were Republican-owned. So the press wasn't quite as one-sided as it seemed, but it was the concentrated East Coast liberal media elite whom Nixon was obsessed about. They made him uncomfortable, and he showed his discomfort.

When he ran against JFK in 1960, Kennedy was cool, smooth, and handsome. The reporters loved him and liked to hang out with him. Kennedy knew how to play them, and it drove Nixon crazy because he was so different from Kennedy—so bumptious and ill at ease. The liberal press delighted in making fun of Nixon and again, his life was like it had been in high school. The cool clique mocked Nixon and instead of taking it with equanimity—instead of turning the other cheek, if you will—instead of rising above it—instead of finding a way to handle it—he let it get to him.

NIXON'S PERFORMANCE AS VICE PRESIDENT

BOSTON It's amazing to me that despite his being personally disconnected from Eisenhower, as vice president, Nixon did a fabulous job as an international superpower diplomat in Russia, Peru, Venezuela, and elsewhere.

Because of what he accomplished in that capacity, should Nixon be rated as one of the most influential vice presidents in history?

THOMAS Yes. Little known fact—on top of what he did in international affairs, Nixon was Eisenhower's point man on civil rights. He became close to Martin Luther King, Jr.

Republicans in those days did better with African-Americans than they have in recent years.

In foreign affairs, he was smart, well-informed, and a very successful roving ambassador. On the tapes, whenever you hear Nixon, his comments while he was in his office were pretty bad. But when he met with foreign leaders—like Chou En-Lai, Mao Tse-Tung, Adenauer, or De Gaulle—he was great! They liked him. He didn't make small talk with them because he didn't know how, but world leaders usually don't want to make small talk. He did not preach or lecture to them. He was not ideological with them. He kept his conversations with world leaders focused on national interests—Soviet interests, Chinese interests, American interests. He was always well-prepared and well-read before meetings, and cool and commanding on the world stage—a very different person than we hear on the tapes when he was in his office.

BOSTON He faced down hostile crowds in Latin America and came back a hero. With all of his international success, why did Eisenhower say, "I'm not sure what he ever did in foreign affairs. Give me a week …"

How could Ike forget what Nixon had done?

THOMAS Eisenhower could be a cold fish. In that particular case, Eisenhower was at the end of his presidency and was getting questions from reporters about why are you playing so much golf, Mr. President? So Eisenhower was on his heels. The question about Nixon came at the end of a press conference and Ike was in a testy mood so he just said something stupid that was obviously cruel and harmful to Nixon. I think when Eisenhower gave the answer, he betrayed his true feelings towards Nixon, but he also said it because he was tired of being badgered by reporters that day. Dwight Eisenhower's son, John, told me, "My father gave himself an order to like Dick Nixon."

BOSTON That's like Ike famously gave himself an order to stop smoking and he went from smoking four packs of cigarettes a day to cold turkey instantly.

THOMAS Actually, like a lot of Eisenhower stories, it's not true.

BOSTON I'm quoting Jean Edward Smith in his recent Eisenhower biography on that, so if I'm wrong, then Jean Edward Smith is wrong.

THOMAS Eisenhower told that story, but here's the true story. He was unable to quit. When he took away all the cigarettes, for a while, he cheated. Then he had a psychological insight that caused him to fill his office with cigarette boxes, and carry cigarettes with him. Every time somebody came in, Ike would offer him a cigarette and it made him feel morally superior not to take a cigarette while the other guy smoked. That was the motivation that got him to quit.

THE 1960 NIXON-KENNEDY PRESIDENTIAL ELECTION

BOSTON Let's talk about the Nixon-Kennedy election in 1960. You make the point in the book that that's where the Kennedy machine taught Nixon the art of the political dirty trick.

Was being on the receiving end of Kennedy's many dirty tricks during that campaign a tipping point in Nixon's career as a politician?

THOMAS I think so. In 1960, Nixon ran against Kennedy and it was a pretty even race all the way through. It went right down to the wire and scholars now believe that in two states—Illinois and Texas—the election was probably stolen. In Chicago, the ward bosses basically stole the vote for the Democrats. In one precinct there were more votes for Kennedy than there were people living there. The same kind of thing happened in Texas.

Nixon could have challenged the outcome and gone to court and raised hell. He didn't protest though because the country was in the middle of the Cold War—facing off against the Soviet Union. Nixon thought it would be bad for the country if he staged a political fight in the middle of the Cold War, so in that situation, he did turn the other cheek. He gracefully accepted the outcome, though it embittered him especially because he knew the Kennedys had played plenty of dirty tricks on him—and not just in Chicago where the bosses controlled politics and in Texas where LBJ (Kennedy's vice presidential candidate) controlled the machinery.

In Watergate, Nixon got in trouble for using the Internal Revenue Service to audit his enemies. Nixon himself had been audited three times by the IRS—in 1961, 1962, and 1963—at the order of Attorney General Robert Kennedy, President Kennedy's brother, who fully understood personal politics. So as president, Nixon abused his enemies with the IRS, and he got the idea to do that from the Kennedys.

BOSTON On a smaller scale, the Kennedys had a master political dirty trickster on their side named Richard Tuck. Nixon's campaign would organize a political parade and Tuck would get the street signs turned around—this was in the day before Mapquest or iPhones—such that people trying to get to the parades couldn't find them because all the street signs had been changed. Tuck was a master at totally disrupting Nixon's events.

THOMAS Tuck would get a pregnant woman and put a sign around her neck saying, "Nixon's the one." It was all done in a joking way. When Nixon got in the White House, he wanted his own Dick Tuck—"Don't get mad, get even"—but he didn't get even. He got brought down by his dirty tricks.

NIXON'S ABSENCE FROM POLITICS FROM 1962-1968

BOSTON After the 1960 presidential loss, he ran for governor of California in 1962 and lost to Pat Brown. After losing that race, he said at a press conference, "You will never have Nixon to kick around anymore. This is my last press conference."

What happened between 1962 and 1968 (when he decided to run for president) that caused him to reverse his prior statement about getting out of politics?

THOMAS Nixon believed in public service, and he devoted himself to it almost all his life. When he was defeated in '60 and '62, he was driven out of it for a while. They wrote his political obituary. He then went to New York to make some money, but he still wanted back into public service.

One of the tragedies and ironies of Nixon is that Watergate gave such a bad name to government service and made people so cynical that they didn't want to serve in government. It was a tragedy because Nixon himself was a public servant who wanted to serve and who did serve. He was not in it to make money. He was not a greedy guy. He really believed in serving his country. He was actually very patriotic. It's just heart-breaking that his disrespect for his own office turned a whole generation and really a whole country away from government service.

BOSTON Well, to the extent any of you decide to pursue a political career, if you have any sort of success—and Nixon had a lot of success until 1960—being involved in politics becomes oxygen. With the applause, the crowds, the adulation among your supporters, it all becomes something many politicians just can't live without.

THOMAS That's certainly part of why Nixon reentered politics after 1962, but it was also because Nixon had a sense of his own destiny. This was a shy little kid who was unpopular, but he believed he was destined to do great things. He stayed up all night talking to a friend after his loss in 1962 in California, and said to him, "If I don't get back into public life, I am going to be mentally dead in two years and physically dead in four." He believed public service in politics was his destiny.

NIXON AND LBJ'S MATCHING WITS OVER VIETNAM IN 1968

BOSTON Evan, in the fall of 1968, a presidential election year, an intriguing battle of political wits took place which the American public didn't know about until many years later between President Lyndon Johnson and the Republican presidential nominee Richard Nixon clashed over America's effort to bring a diplomatic conclusion to the Vietnam War. In that situation, Johnson was trying to expedite a peace settlement in order to help Democratic presidential nominee Hubert Humphrey and Nixon was trying to delay peaceful

resolution of the Vietnam War in hopes of preserving his lead over Humphrey.

Were Johnson and Nixon equally culpable of putting presidential politics above our national interests?

THOMAS This is a messy, complicated story. On the face of it, it appeared that they were putting politics first. Johnson had arranged a bombing pause during the negotiations in Paris to make Hubert Humphrey (the Democratic candidate) look like more of a peace candidate in hopes of beating Nixon. Meanwhile, Nixon had his own backchannel communication going on with President Thieu in South Vietnam, through the wonderfully named Dragon Lady, Madame Chenault, who signaled the South Vietnamese that they should not agree to the deal being advocated by Johnson. The message from Nixon was: "Don't make the deal; things will go better if I'm president." Johnson, of course, was eavesdropping—the CIA was wiretapping the offices of the South Vietnamese ambassador and President Chou's office; so Johnson knew what Nixon was doing and declared it to be treason.

BOSTON Although he only declared it privately.

THOMAS That's an important point—privately. Publicly, he never said anything about Nixon's secret communications to the South Vietnamese. Both sides collected dirt on the other routinely. I love it that for Johnson, his chief dirt collector was the saintly Bill Moyers, who collected dirt on Barry Goldwater. In those days, each side had dirt on the other, but they would not fire their missiles. They used the information only as a means of trying to keep each other honest. In this case, even though each side had dirt on the other, they never used it.

Johnson and Nixon had a weird respect for each other. Even though Johnson said Nixon had committed treason, he never publicly aired it. Nixon, by the same token, never publicly complained that Johnson was trying to make a peace deal just to get Humphrey elected. The truth here is murky. Actually, it wasn't Johnson's idea to do a peace deal—it was done at the behest of his generals and diplomats. He was actually a little bit against it and he didn't actually like Humphrey much. There are always wheels within wheels in politics.

BOSTON Humphrey had started criticizing Johnson's handling of the Vietnam War as the campaign wore on, so that certainly didn't endear him to LBJ.

THOMAS That's right. I think Johnson knew that Nixon would conduct the war more like Johnson had, so we have to follow the bouncing ball. On Nixon's side of the story, he was a funny guy. He would threaten to do things, but he then didn't always do them. On the whole question of whether he really perverted the peace process, most scholars now realize that no matter what Nixon was signaling, President Chou was not going to go to Paris and make a deal. So it's not that Nixon actually changed events because Chou was never going to take the deal anyway, regardless of what Nixon did. Historically, it didn't make much difference, but it sure sounds bad when they're eavesdropping on each other, and one side accuses the other of being treasonous, and then they decide to keep it all secret.

NIXON'S HANDLING OF THE VIETNAM WAR

BOSTON Given how long it took Nixon to get us out of the Vietnam War, what kind of a grade do you give him for the way that he handled that quagmire?

THOMAS C+, but it's easy for me to hand out grades. Vietnam was a tough road. He inherited the war. There were 550,000 American troops in Vietnam when Nixon was sworn in. The war had been dragging on for years, we were losing it, and the North Vietnamese didn't show any signs of

giving up. They had defeated the Japanese and the French before we arrived, so they'd been fighting that war a long time and were quite willing to fight it forever.

Nixon didn't want to just quit, go home, and let the government of South Vietnam topple because that would make the United States look weak to the rest of the world. The United States was regarded by everyone as the great superpower standing against communism. If we had gotten in airplanes and boats and gone home, it would badly tarnish our international image. He had to find a way to extricate us from Vietnam without losing face, and it was a difficult proposition.

He wanted to withdraw American forces gradually and he started doing that, but he also wanted to negotiate with the North Vietnamese to get some kind of face-saving settlement. It's hard to negotiate from a position of weakness as you're drawing down your forces. Where was our big stick? If we were slowly taking our stick away, how could we force the enemy to do anything?

He got us out of Vietnam in fits and starts. He had us engage in bombing campaigns that felt like spasms. Eventually, he made a deal. It took him over four years and it wasn't a very good deal. After everyone signed off on it, South Vietnam toppled twenty-two months later and it was a sad ending to a sad war—the only war America has ever lost, and we definitely lost it.

BOSTON Recognizing what Nixon was trying to do—achieve peace with honor—by bombing one day and then backing off the next, as I read your book, it sounded to me like both Nixon and Kissinger, his top advisor, were bona fide hawks about Vietnam. Is that correct?

THOMAS Yes—but with an asterisk. They were bona fide hawks. Together they used what they called the "mad man strategy," whereby Kissinger and the president wanted the North Vietnamese to believe that Nixon was going crazy, and might just start dropping atomic bombs, and they thought that threat would scare the enemy into giving up.

Nixon soon realized that he had to pull back our troops because of all the dissent at home. There was so much unrest on the campuses, and so many people demonstrating in the streets, that Nixon became afraid that if he went all out against the North Vietnamese, then American cities would blow up, our campuses would blow up, and the country would just revolt against him—so he backed off.

He may have been a hawk, but he was a politically pragmatic hawk. He backed off and he and Kissinger regretted it. They both wished that they had hit the gas at the start of Nixon's presidency.

BOSTON Right now, at the Newseum in Washington, DC, there's a special exhibit about how the media covered the Vietnam War. It goes into detail with plenty of great footage about what Evan was just talking about in terms of American soldiers' experience in Vietnam as well as all the uproar here in opposition to the war.

THOMAS It shocks you. You students here at The King's College are young. Long before you were born, this country was real messy. The night Martin Luther King, Jr. was murdered in Memphis in 1968, there were race riots in sixty-eight American cities. There were machine gun emplacements on Key Bridge in front of the US Capitol. Fourteenth Street—right in the middle of Washington, DC—was in flames. I went to college at Harvard and in the spring of my freshman year, they had to close the campus for a while because when Nixon invaded Cambodia, it caused students to raise hell. Things were that far gone.

IMPACT OF THE ANTI-WAR MOVEMENT ON NIXON

BOSTON Throughout his presidency, there was a huge anti-war movement in America that Nixon, for the most part, tried to ignore.

Did he ever make a decision about Vietnam based on his concern about the anti-war movement?

THOMAS He did. He actually wanted to ignore them, but he didn't. Nixon had this idea that when he first came in, if we gave a sharp military jolt to the North Vietnamese by bombing them heavily, then they would quickly come to the peace table. He and Henry Kissinger in 1969 cooked up a strategy to bomb the hell out of North Vietnam and it was called "Duck Hook." I don't know where that name came from—it's a golf shot.

Here's the answer to your question. They were getting ready to go forward with Duck Hook and then came the moratorium in October 1969. The moratorium made it clear to Nixon and everyone else that the peace movement in the United States was no longer made up of college hippies. It now included civilians who met in town squares. Nixon saw that and called off the Duck Hook bombing strategy because of the moratorium.

When I interviewed Kissinger for the book, he told me his biggest single regret as national security advisor was that they did not carry out Duck Hook in the fall of 1969, which caused the war to drag on for another four years. They basically later carried it out in May 1972 when they mined the harbors and then bombed Hanoi. That's pretty much what they planned to do in the fall of 1969 before the moratorium changed their minds. They finally followed through with it three and a half years later, and thousands of American boys had died in the intervening years.

BOSTON President Nixon said in the context of Vietnam, "If when the chips are down, the world's most powerful nation, the United States of America, acts like a pitiful helpless giant, the forces of totalitarianism and anarchy will threaten free nations and free institutions throughout the world".

Do you believe that's timeless advice that should be heeded by all presidents, including President Obama?

THOMAS I do, but as you know, speeches are all about context. I believe that statement by Nixon is true. If we're a helpless giant, then the world becomes chaotic. We are, for better or worse, the world's superpower—the greatest force the world has ever seen for peace, order, stability, freedom, and democracy. The world has never seen anything like it before, and if we go away, there will be a return to darkness.

When Nixon said those words you just quoted (which were actually written by his most hawkish speechwriter, Pat Buchanan), it was the wrong time to say them. He said it shortly after the Kent State shooting, and it inflamed the country. In that moment, saying those true words was politically unwise.

NIXON AND KISSINGER

BOSTON Regarding the relationship between Nixon and his foreign policy advisor Henry Kissinger, you talk often about their conducting our international affairs in a backchannel mode.

Why did Nixon want to disconnect himself from his own State Department?

THOMAS Nixon set up his presidency to keep foreign policy in the White House. He really wanted to be his own secretary of state and he put a pal, Rogers, in as secretary of state knowing that Rogers was not particularly interested in foreign policy. Rogers had been attorney general during Eisenhower's second term, and was a good lawyer, but he was not knowledgeable about international affairs, so he was basically just a placeholder as secretary of state. Real foreign policy happened out of the White

House run by Nixon and his national security advisor Henry Kissinger and it worked pretty well.

Kissinger was a brilliant advisor who also executed Nixon's policies. Problems arose because he often bragged about his own achievements and liked to take credit for anything good that happened. For example, he hinted that the opening to China had been his idea when it was actually Nixon's idea. When H.R. Haldeman, Nixon's chief of staff, told Kissinger that the boss was going to China, Kissinger's first reaction was, "Fat chance."—he didn't think it was possible. He did carry out the policy on China for Nixon and deserves credit for that, but it drove Nixon crazy for Kissinger to brag about and distort the actual record.

So what did Nixon do to make sure that the record would be clear about whose ideas were whose? He put in the tapes. That's why the taping system got installed in the White House. In February 1971, two years after Nixon was sworn in, per Haldeman's diary, he put in the famous White House taping system to be able to rebut Henry Kissinger's version of events. Kissinger later said Nixon certainly paid a big price for putting in the system. They were a great team in a lot of ways, but there was plenty of jealousy between them. It was a wonderful and awful relationship at the same time.

NIXON AND HIS DÉTENTE FOREIGN POLICY

BOSTON The Nixon-Kissinger foreign policy objective was to achieve détente, the balance of power, by using a triangular strategy aimed at causing one's enemy to become one's friend, thereby pushing the world's superpowers away from the brink of nuclear warfare.

Do you regard détente during the Nixon presidency as among the most brilliant examples of foreign policy ever executed in American geopolitical history?

THOMAS I'm not sure I'd go that far, but it was a hell of a smart thing to do. Nixon was the first US president to go to Moscow. He personally negotiated the first ever arms control treaty, and that was an important step in easing tension between the United States and the Soviet Union. We had this enormous arsenal that could destroy the world in fifteen minutes and Nixon, although a big anti-communist, was the one who took the initiative to check and retard that process.

For years, Nixon was attacked by the Far Right as being too soft on communism—a sell-out to the communists—because he made the arms control deal. My own view, as Churchill said, "Jaw-jaw's better than war-war,"—better to talk than to fight. Nixon understood that. He had a grand geostrategic vision. That sounds pompous, but it's true. Because Nixon didn't like to talk to other people, he would stay up all night reading, thinking, and writing. Long before he was elected president, he could see the opening into China, and his pursuing it was a radical thing for a Republican president to do. Nobody had been to China for twenty-five years. It was closed off to the world and through the secret diplomacy of Henry Kissinger, Nixon opened the door and brought China into the world—a major achievement.

BOSTON When we think about American foreign policy since World War II, is there anybody else who is on the level of Nixon and Eisenhower in terms of having a vision and then executing on it?

THOMAS I don't think so. Most presidents get their feet tangled up on foreign policy because it's easy to do. It's a messy world out there and Vietnam obviously was tough for Nixon. He did end it but it took him four years and another 30,000 dead Americans. Every American president gets faced with intractable foreign policy. Most of the world depends on us and also hates us. How would you like to be the head of a corporation where your customers loathe you but need you? That's the way it is. That's the burden of being a superpower.

NIXON'S OVERALL PERFORMANCE AS PRESIDENT

BOSTON In 1968, Nixon was elected our thirty-seventh president and in most ways, he more than measured up to the job. Your book details his many achievements as president, both on the international front and also in the area of the important domestic legislation he put through.

But for the Watergate train wreck that caused his resignation, do you rate Richard Nixon as a top ten president?

THOMAS Not top ten, but certainly top twenty. He accomplished a lot on the international front—most notably, arms control with the Soviet Union, and opening up relations with China. In 1970, China had been closed for twenty-five years. Nobody went there. It was under communist rule, but was very insular. Nixon had been aggressively anti-communist throughout his political career until then, but he was always brilliant about confounding and outflanking his enemies—doing the unexpected and then pulling things off in victorious fashion. "Nixon goes to China" is now a phrase used in politics to describe a situation where somebody does something totally unexpected and it leads to major success. People can do it only because they have enough credibility with their supporters and enemies to get away with it.

BOSTON His anti-communism started with Alger Hiss, which set the table for the rise of Joe McCarthy.

THOMAS Because of his past history, he knew the anti-communist crowd was not going to criticize him. He was one of them. They were not going to criticize him for reaching out to the Chinese Communists.

So he was perfectly suited to be the one to open up China. It was a brilliant strategy—way over the horizon and politically a very brave thing to do—and it worked.

Domestically, he outflanked his enemies and created the Environmental Protection Agency. At that time, Democrats were trying to get control of the environment as their issue in the early days of that movement. Nixon cleverly advanced past them on the issue by creating the EPA instead of letting the Democrats do it. He was a very hard guy to predict. As his attorney general John Mitchell said, "The key thing was to watch what we do—not what we say."

Nixon talked the conservative rhetoric talk, but he did some moderate and even liberal things. One example was civil rights. Nixon tried to appeal to Southerners by intimating that if the Southern Democrats became Republicans, they'd probably get a better shake. It was known as the "Southern Strategy." Some of it was pandering and some of it was a little raw and arguably racist; yet Nixon became the guy who integrated the public schools in the South. It's surprising that in 1969, only 10% of black kids in the deep South went to integrated schools; the rest went to all-black schools. After Nixon had been president two years, 70% went to integrated schools.

That wasn't easy to do—even as late as 1970—but Nixon found a way to do it quietly under the radar screen. He didn't make a big show of it, but he did it because he understood that black kids needed to go to schools that were just as good as white schools. He knew that "separate but equal" wasn't equal, so he made integrated schools happen.

NIXON'S RESPONSE TO THE PUBLICATION OF THE PENTAGON PAPERS

BOSTON As I read your book in terms of his becoming unhinged as his presidency went on, it seemed to me the tipping point was the publication of the Pentagon Papers in *The New York Times* in 1971, which disclosed many of the lies that had been made to the American people by Nixon's predecessor, Lyndon Johnson, about our involvement in the Vietnam War.

THOMAS The name Richard Nixon is not even in the Pentagon Papers.

BOSTON Why did the release of the Pentagon Papers, which obviously were very harmful to Lyndon Johnson's legacy, become the basis for Nixon's tipping point into his downward mental health spiral?

THOMAS Nixon was terrible when he talked on the tapes about the Pentagon Papers. He ordered his aides to break into the Brookings Institution to find some documents and his ordering that break-in proved he was totally nuts. Why did the Pentagon Papers cause Nixon to twist off? He was obsessed with secrets, and he hated leakers, and he hated *The New York Times*, and he was conducting secret diplomacy with China that he didn't want anyone to know about. Kissinger was secretly going to China at the time, and Nixon was afraid there would be leaks about that.

There was something else going on at the time, and this is why historical context is so important. For years, presidents of the United States used the FBI to spy on their enemies. I know that sounds wrong, but they did. J. Edgar Hoover was FBI director for forty years and he stayed in power because he blackmailed presidents partly by digging up dirt on them and partly by doing their dirty work by spying on their opponents. The FBI had spied on LBJ and on dissident Democrats at the 1964 Democratic Convention. By 1970-1971, Hoover saw that things were changing. The FBI had been sued for illegal wiretapping and he blamed the Supreme Court, which had become more liberal and was starting to uphold the Bill of Rights. Hoover saw that the wind was changing and it was no longer good for the FBI to spy on behalf of the president anymore. So without having the FBI around to do his spying, what did Nixon do? He went in-house and created the "plumbers," his own in-house spies, who were incompetent and screwed up their attempts to spy on Nixon's enemies.

BOSTON They called them "plumbers" because they were supposed to stop the leaks to the media.

THOMAS They weren't dastardly criminals. They were just misfits from the FBI and CIA who'd been dumped, in classic bureaucratic fashion, on the White House to get rid of them. They were run by a guy named Bud Krogh, whose nickname at the White House was Evil Krogh. It was a joke. Evil Krogh was wonderful, nice, and warm, and been an Eagle Scout. His buddies called him Evil as a joke. He was totally the wrong guy to run some super-secret sleuth operation that broke into buildings and then screwed up and got caught. That's how the Watergate scandal happened.

WATERGATE

BOSTON You and I lived through Watergate. The five most central figures in it were Nixon; his attorney general John Mitchell; and Bob Haldeman, John Ehrlichman and Charles Colson on his White House staff. Out of those five people, I'll give you 100 points. Allocate the blame for the Watergate debacle among those five people.

THOMAS You could spread it around evenly. The greatest puzzlement and the greatest lesson to me about Watergate involved H.R. Haldeman, Nixon's chief of staff. He was a very good chief of staff—ran a tight ship. There was a lot of accountability, responsibility, and clear lines of authority during his watch. Although it was a well-run White House, somehow, Haldeman could not save Nixon from himself in Watergate. He let the scandal get out of control. Frankly, I don't

know what the hell happened, but my theory is that Haldeman just got exhausted.

Haldeman was smart enough to not carry out the crazy orders that Nixon often issued. He knew not to do that. But after having been at Nixon's beck and call twenty-four hours a day, seven days a week, over four years, Haldeman became exhausted.

He should have realized that he had run out of the energy needed to do the job, and resigned from the job. They should have changed chiefs of staff. He couldn't see what was coming because he was worn out. He wasn't a criminal lawyer capable of recognizing the illegality of all that was being done. Haldeman just let it get out of control and he was later saved by his faith—a Christian Scientist. The president's White House chief of staff went to prison for eighteen months and was revived by his faith afterwards, but his faith didn't help him while the wrongdoing was going on, and it's a tragedy and a puzzlement.

BOSTON There's a great scene in the book, and it gets back to Nixon's inability to confront difficult interpersonal situations, where Nixon wouldn't go to John Mitchell and say, "John, what did you know and when did you know it? What have you done?" And he wouldn't do that with Haldeman, or with Ehrlichman, or with Colson. So, he finally arranged a meeting where they were all in the same room at the same time.

THOMAS And when it happened, they all talked past each other because nobody wanted to confront the elephant in the room—the cover-up that was going on. They didn't want to talk to each other—and by then, it was too late. The breakin at the Watergate happened in June 1972. Nixon did not call a meeting to get everybody in one room until March 1973. Nine months of cover-up had already gone on, felonies had already been committed, and it was too late.

The message is obvious. When you get in trouble, you've got to step up to it sooner, not later. You can't allow these things to fester. If you've got a problem, deal with it. In time, because no one was willing to deal with it, things got worse, people covered up, and then they duplicated their mistakes.

If only Nixon had stood up when the problem hit, and dealt with it immediately, he would have finished his second term, and been the successful president that he could have been—but he didn't. He couldn't confront Haldeman or any of his guys and they did not help him. Unwinding and addressing a situation like Watergate has to be a reciprocal thing. It was the job of the chief of staff to force the president to deal with the problem—and Haldeman didn't do it.

BOSTON Explain President Nixon's relationship with John Mitchell.

Photo credit: Ode Thomas

Evan Thomas

THOMAS Nixon, like all politicians, needed somebody in his administration he could talk to and tell him the truth and he thought Mitchell, his former law partner, was the right guy to be that person. Mitchell had been a bond lawyer in New York, which meant he was involved in bond issuances, which resulted in his knowing mayors and governors—so he knew politics from that vantage point. He was a smart, tough guy and was willing to tell Nixon the truth.

Mitchell became Nixon's attorney general, and he wasn't good at the job—as proven by his mistakes. He suggested that Nixon nominate Clement Haynesworth and Harold Carswell to the US Supreme Court, and both those nominations were rejected by the Senate.

So with the fallout over his mistakes, Mitchell became sick of being attorney general and wanted to go back and be a lawyer again in New York. By 1972, as he was wanting to leave, he started drinking too much in large part because of his crazy, lethal wife Martha, who would also get drunk and then call reporters in the middle of the night and tell them all kinds of crazy things. Mitchell stood by her, but he was consumed by her. He just wanted to go home to New York.

Unfortunately, after stepping down as attorney general, Mitchell became the head of the Committee to Re-Elect the President. In that position, he took his eye off the ball and Watergate happened. It's still unclear how much Mitchell really knew about the Watergate break-in and whether he gave the break-in order or not. The testimony is conflicting on this, and the facts are so murky because when people started testifying, they kept changing their stories.

Mitchell never went to Nixon and said, "We've got to cut this thing off here. We've got to deal with this now. We can't let it fester." If only John Mitchell had been more alert, and been the grownup in the room, and gone to Nixon and said in June 1972, "Whoa, boss. There's a problem here. Let's cut our losses. Let's take our lumps now because they won't be as bad as they will be later." Instead, Mitchell and Nixon let it drift. Soon, they crossed the line and paid hush money—which meant obstruction of justice. Buying the silence of people meant they were committing felonies.

BOSTON Now throughout the seemingly endless days of the Watergate crisis, his daughters, Tricia and Julie, continued to beg their father to stay in office, and not resign. No father wants to disappoint his daughter.

As I read your book, it sounded like the Nixon girls were highly influential in his decision to remain in office as long as he did.

Should we blame Tricia and Julie for the last several months that our country suffered through Watergate?

THOMAS That's a good question. His family was super loyal and they stood by him. The last people to throw in the towel on the Nixon presidency were Pat, Tricia, and Julie. Nixon, ever the politician, threw in the towel when he counted the impeachment votes in the US Senate and House. When the votes weren't there anymore, he resigned.

The family, more sentimental, was saying, "Dad, never ever, ever quit." It was painful for them. There were plenty of tears shed in the family quarters. It was a poignant time because they would always try to keep things upbeat. Even in the darkest days of Watergate, they wouldn't talk about it at dinner, but they would write little notes to each other and leave them on their pillows at night. Frank Gannon, Nixon's ghost writer for his memoirs, told me that the Nixon family came right out of a Tolstoy novel—they would leave sweet little notes at night to reassure each other as things got darker and darker and darker.

BOSTON Didn't his wife Pat suggest that he burn the tapes?

THOMAS Yes. This is an interesting thing. Pat Nixon was a good political advisor to Nixon in many cases. But by 1971 or 1972, she had been cut out of the political dialogue by H.R. Haldeman, Nixon's chief of staff. In the White House, there was a big staff around the president. Haldeman and Ehrlichman led the staff and they created a wall around Nixon. Pat was outside the wall. She was not asked about what to do with the tapes so she did not get to share her own view, which was to "burn 'em."

Hers was the correct view. He had about two days before the subpoenas arrived when

he could have burned the tapes. There would have been a storm and all hell would have broken loose if he had burned the tapes, but I think his presidency would have survived. It was the tapes that killed him, because they're so ugly when you listen to them. Billy Graham, Nixon's great friend and spiritual advisor, actually threw up when he first heard the tapes. His was the correct response. The parts of them where they're talking about Watergate are pretty bad, but then on some of the other tapes, he sounds like a very thoughtful, considered, deeply read president. Not many presidents, other than Theodore Roosevelt, read a lot in the White House. Nixon, who didn't like talking to people, read all night.

BOSTON He didn't have any friends.

THOMAS That's right—he didn't have any friends, so it left a lot of time to read. His private library is now at his presidential library in Yorba Linda. I asked to see it, and it's like a graduate student's library. As president, he was reading political philosophy and underlining parts and putting stars in the margin. This is how he came up with his carefully considered geostrategic theories. Most presidents don't think that way. Nixon did, and at times, he talked that way on the tapes. You can hear him ruminating and thinking deeply, and it's pretty impressive—that's the "good Nixon."

But then there's the "bad Nixon"—like when he's counting the number of Jews in the Bureau of Labor Statistics. He was just off the charts crazy paranoid and profane—it's sad. One thing about it though. My wife Oscie and I listened to lots of these tapes, and we got the strong impression that whenever Nixon was being profane, he did it to show off—it was an act. He was trying to posture himself to whoever he was speaking to as a tough guy, and he wasn't very good at swearing. If you want to hear good swearing, listen to LBJ's tapes. Nixon's swearing rang phony to me—like he was trying to prove something—trying to be somebody he really wasn't.

BOSTON Your book has a memorable scene of very dark humor. It was on the Nixon family's last night in the White House, after they had taken one last family photograph in the room. Tell that story so the audience can gain an appreciation that there are some laughs in your book.

THOMAS On their last night in the White House, the family was in Nixon's bedroom and they heard loud voices outside. Pat thought the crowd was chanting, "Hail to the chief. Hail to the chief," so to hear them, they walked over to the window. When they got there, they realized that the crowd was actually chanting, "Jail to the chief. Jail to the chief." It was a tough moment.

NIXON'S MENTAL INSTABILITY IN THE END

BOSTON You create a very vivid picture of Nixon's becoming increasingly unhinged in the White House during his last two years in office—first over Vietnam and the anti-war movement, and then over Watergate. Do you regard Anthony Hopkins' portrayal of Nixon as a bona fide psycho in the Oliver Stone movie as an accurate depiction of him?

THOMAS It's too harsh—it's Hollywood. I love Anthony Hopkins as an actor, but he portrayed Nixon as a grotesque version of the man. It was too crazy to see him talking to portraits and being a sick drunk. Having said that about the movie, in fact, things did get pretty bad for Nixon at the end of his presidency. Even his daughter Julie has said that he and his wife, Pat, were drinking too much during their final months in the White House.

Nixon was clearly brooding a lot because of paper trail he left. There's a lot of paper generated in every presidency, and it shows what each president did every day in office.

Nixon's paper trail is extensive until about October 1973, and then it just stopped. He didn't leave office until August 1974, so for about his last ten months in office, the lack of paperwork shows that nothing was happening at the White House. Nixon was basically just sitting in his office brooding, worrying, and hoping something good was going to happen, and probably drinking too much.

At the end, there was a brutal scene. Nixon was a Quaker and although he seemed very cynical and expedient and certainly didn't advertise his faith, he actually got down on his knees and prayed at night. There was a terrible scene, two days before his resignation, where Henry Kissinger was with him. Kissinger, Nixon's national security advisor, is a Jew; not a Christian. In his faith, you don't pray on your knees. Kissinger has never admitted that he got down on his knees with Nixon, but this I do know. Kissinger went back to his office and said, "You won't believe what just happened. Nixon wanted me to get on my knees with him and pray with him." As he was telling his aides what happened, the phone rang. It was Nixon, asking Kissinger not to tell anybody what he had done because it would be hurtful. Kissinger put one of his aides on the extension and it was written up in *The Washington Post* two days later. That's what life is like in power. You've got to be prepared for the worst, there is no privacy, and there are no secrets.

NIXON AND TODAY'S REPUBLICAN PARTY

BOSTON One of the most important conclusions in your book is your claim that it was Nixon, not Reagan, who created the modern Republican Party—although obviously the Republican Party in 2015 is a total mess.

Do Nixon's political beliefs have any connection to those being spouted these days by Donald Trump, Ben Carson, Carly Fiorina, or Ted Cruz?

THOMAS Yes and no. Nixon was a great master at peeling away disaffected Democrats. In 1972 when he beat McGovern in a landslide, he won 35% of the registered Democrats. Reagan typically gets credit for attracting the so-called "Reagan Democrat" to the Republican Party, but Nixon did it before him. His Democratic supporters were typically blue-collar people who didn't like the establishment. Nixon had a great sense of appealing to outsiders against insiders, because he knew there were always more of them. He was brilliant in appealing to people who didn't like *The Washington Post, The New York Times,* Wall Street, and Harvard, and felt like the elites were out to get them.

This populist thread runs all the way through American politics back into the late nineteenth century. You can see it today, too. The fact that the three top frontrunners in the Republican Party today (for the 2016 presidential nomination) are non-politicians means that they're populists—their support comes from there being resentment by the outside against the inside. They're sending a message to the elites in the establishment: "We don't like any of your people." Being part of the existing scene in Washington alone disqualifies a candidate from serious consideration. And that's why today there's a strange order of people who are now leading the pack in the Republican Party. Nixon would have understood Trump's playing against the elites as the outsider. Nixon wasn't Trump because Nixon himself (as a former congressman, senator, and vice president) was an insider, but he certainly would have understood what Trump is trying to do.

BOSTON We've run out of time. Thanks so much, Evan.

DOUGLAS BRINKLEY refined his talents as a historian at the feet of his mentor Stephen Ambrose, with whom he co-authored three books and taught under at the University of New Orleans. Prior to his death, Ambrose called Doug "the best of the new generation of American historians." Among his achievements: He's written biographies of several twentieth century presidents, served as the editor of *The Reagan Diaries* (Harper Collins 2007), and with Texas A&M history professor Luke Nichter, he collaborated on *The Nixon Tapes: 1971-1972* (Houghton Mifflin 2014). On November 11, 2014, I interviewed Doug in Dallas at Arlington Hall in Lee Park to talk about *The Nixon Tapes* at an event for the clients and professionals of my law firm and the Dallas office of the Ernst & Young accounting firm.

"I have never encountered a president who loathed not just the Soviet Union but the Russian people, like Nixon did. The whole China gambit came about as a way to punish the Soviets and give us some negotiating room. He thought the twenty-first century was going to be the China/US century, and Russia was the Mafia he had to work around."

– DOUGLAS BRINKLEY

CHAPTER 22

DOUGLAS BRINKLEY
ON
The Nixon Tapes 1971-1972

BRINKLEY'S CONNECTION TO NIXON

BOSTON Doug, before now, you've written books about several presidents—Theodore Roosevelt, FDR, JFK, Gerald Ford, Jimmy Carter, Reagan—but we're here today to talk about Nixon. Obviously, you can choose to write about anyone.

What was it about Nixon that made you decide your newest book would be about him and his famous tapes?

BRINKLEY I became a teenager during the Nixon presidency, and it was during those years that I began homing in on American politics. My parents had been for Kennedy in '60 and Johnson in '64, but something

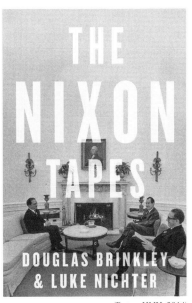

(Boston: HMH, 2014)

about the '68 election turned them to Nixon, and they were strong for him again in '72. I remember watching his presidency unfold on television, and during the whole Watergate situation when everybody was riveted on "What did he know and when did he know it?" We all soon learned the cast of characters and wondered whether our country could sustain the hit—with so many people going after Nixon, and then we began anticipating the impeachment process. That was an unforgettable time in American history.

On top of my fascination with Watergate, another reason for my doing this book is because for years, I've taught a course at Rice University called "History of the Cold War." You can't teach the Cold War without getting into the Nixon years in a big way—the SALT (Strategic Arms Limitations Talks) process, the ABM (Antiballistic Missile) Treaty, the Vietnam War, the Cambodia Incursion, the recognition of China, and the Middle East shuttle diplomacy with Henry Kissinger. When you start getting into the foreign affairs of the Cold War era, Nixon stands out on a large scale.

The Nixon Tapes book really got its start when I did a book on John Kerry, our current secretary of state, called *Tour of Duty*. In doing my research, he let me see his Vietnam War letters and diaries. When I asked him if Nixon had ever commented on his [Kerry's] running the Vietnam Veterans Against the War in Vietnam, he said, "I don't know. Some people say Nixon was talking about me in the tapes, but I never looked into it." So *I* looked into it. It turns out there's a guy down here at Texas A&M named Luke Nichter who has spent ten years listening to the Nixon Tapes every day, deciphering.

BOSTON Sounds like hell on earth.

BRINKLEY Luke just had a kid, and he's worried the boy's going to think Nixon is his grandfather because his voice is floating in their house all the time.

It's difficult work to do exact transcriptions from the tapes because Nixon bugged the entire White House. FDR did a little taping, as did Kennedy and Johnson, but they taped selectively or just had the Oval Office telephone taped. Nixon voice-activated everything. So when you listen to the Nixon Tapes, you're hearing plates sliding on tables, forks clanging, and people coughing. You hear all those noises and have to listen around them to hear the key conversation moments.

When Nixon was in the Oval Office with Henry Kissinger, you know they were talking about serious things. But at unexpected times, the tapes confirmed that Nixon *had* talked about Kerry and was worried about the veterans' protesting America's involvement in the Vietnam War, though he couldn't have cared less about the rest of the anti-war movement.

Once we retrieved Nixon's conversations about Kerry, Luke and I decided to collaborate and find out what happened on the rest of the tapes. We're voyeur historians when you get down to it. We read other people's mail for a living. There are archival collections and letters of all our presidents, but the Nixon Tapes are the most accurate records of what happened during any American presidency. They covered Nixon, day by day, hour by hour, through the life and times of an American president. Nixon studies are going to grow as more of these tapes become available. This book is sort of our opening salvo. The last big batch of tapes got released by the National Archives in August 2013 and hence our book came out in 2014.

THE NIXON TAPES' STILL HAVING CLASSIFIED INFORMATION IN THEM

BOSTON You say in the book's introduction that there are 700 hours of tape which are still classified either because of national security concerns or to protect the privacy of individuals, including Nixon, his heirs, or people still alive who were secretly recorded.

How can there still be national security concerns about information that's over forty years old?

BRINKLEY That's what I want to know! I promise you, I tried to get all of them. Nixon never thought that guys like Luke and me could ever bring out a book like this. He thought the tapes belonged to him, and that this was going to be the grist of his great legacy. He was very legacy-oriented, and loved reading Winston Churchill's books, trying to learn how Churchill did things. Nixon envisioned himself as a major historical figure on the order of Churchill— the president who would either win the Vietnam War or get us out of Southeast Asia, the president who won two historic elections; the president when Neil Armstrong walked on the moon, the president who created the Environmental Protection Agency and worked to get clean air and water on the domestic front, the president who developed the détente strategy with the Soviets while going behind their back with Mao Tse-tung, and on and on. He was truly a global strategist.

He planned to take the tapes back to San Clemente after his presidency ended, hire a staff, get them transcribed, and then use them for his own memoirs and books on a variety of topics that were going to add to his greatness. He never thought to his dying day that anybody should own the tapes except him. But the Supreme Court ruled eight to zero that for the most part, they belonged to the American people. The Court also held what didn't belong to the American people, and those were the conversations about national security and also those between Nixon and his wife, and his children.

There were some national security conversations that took place in the White House during the Nixon years, and haven't yet been released. As best I can tell from the redactions, they mainly deal with Saudi Arabia, Israel, and the situation in the Middle East. Our government always redacts Middle East stuff. Always. If there were a bunch of documents requested of an archivist today, and somebody sought information about the Grenada invasion of '83, if a requested document has a link to the Middle East, then that part would get deleted out. That's where I think those 700 hours are.

The Nixons have kept the tapes of their family conversations, and I don't know what they'll ever do with them, but they aren't going to be released. We're now arguing that all the Middle East taped conversations need to be released. We'll see. I think we'll get some more—probably another 300 hours out of that 750.

THE BOOK'S LENGTH COMPARED TO THE TOTAL LENGTH OF THE TRANSCRIPTS

BOSTON Your book is thick (over 700 pages); yet compare the size of it to the size of the total transcripts.

BRINKLEY If I took what has been transcribed, and stacked it up, it would go from the floor to the ceiling. As a presidential historian and Cold War scholar, I had to go through the stack and select what was important, and that's what's in the book.

One of the main things you notice when you listen to the tapes is how much Nixon loved to curse and swear and make ugly remarks about people. You could do a book on "Ugly Nixon." I couldn't get over how often he was doing that. I put only a few of those conversations in the book to give the reader an example of that but I didn't want it to be an "I gotcha" book with so much swearing that it overshadowed all the important things he was talking about and dealing with.

Nixon was born in Yorba Linda, Orange County, California. You probably think of that as a great place to live today, but it actually was a very hard, warm desert, Great Depression community. He grew up

Photo credit: Courtesy: The Richard Nixon Presidential Library and Museum (National Archives and Records Administration)

exceedingly poor, unbelievably bright, but a total geek, in a very male cowboy culture. When he got older, he began compensating for being a geek by talking tough. He'd curse a lot in the Oval Office to get control over his conversations with men, but not with women. With men, he'd come in and say, "You bastard, where were you last night?" or "We'll bomb the bejesus out of them!" His language jars you when you hear it on the tapes, but you realize he was in charge and that's the way he was. He would go on a very dark tantrum about people from certain countries because he did not like other countries and their people very much, except China.

He felt Mao Tse-tung and Zhou Inlay were honorable people and he knew the breakthrough to China was his big play. At all costs, he wanted to see the Soviet Union destroyed. I have never encountered a president who loathed not just the Soviet Union but the Russian people like Nixon did. The whole China gambit came about as a way to punish the Soviets and give us some negotiation room. He felt the

twenty-first century was going to be the China/US century, and Russia was the Mafia that he had to work around.

NIXON'S UNCONVENTIONAL APPROACH TO FOREIGN POLICY

BOSTON In your capacity as a Cold War scholar and teacher, one of the principles that comes out in this book is how Nixon's approach to foreign policy was so unconventional. You have a quote where Kissinger tells Nixon, "You're changing the whole approach to foreign policy. Because all the wise guys who told you 'ABM will kill SALT'—that's been proved wrong. And they told you, 'Go to Beijing, it will drive the Russians crazy'—that's been proved wrong. And they told you, 'If you play it tough in Jordan, there will be a war'—the opposite was true. It ended the war." You quote Senator John McCain's father, Admiral John McCain, who disagreed with Nixon's war strategies and said the entire senior command of the armed forces disagreed with them, too.

Give us your perspective on Nixon's unconventional approach to foreign policy. Was it a necessary component to his success in that arena?

BRINKLEY There are always some senators, Lindsey Graham being one today, who are known for their expertise in foreign affairs. They're always beating that drum. That was Nixon. He loved and collected books on foreign policy. He came to see himself as smarter than any other people in the room on foreign affairs. Even when Kissinger was with him, it was Nixon who knew more than Kissinger. He disdained his own State Department led by Secretary of State William Rogers. He thought Rogers was a lightweight and that the State Department was a sieve filled with leaks. He wanted to run everything about foreign affairs out of the White House by himself with his little group.

There's one telling bit on the tape when he was talking to Bob Haldeman. Nixon said, "You know those damn Kennedys. How do they sell this Camelot stuff? And people are buying it. I knew Jack. He was not a great man or a literary man or a philosopher. And he didn't have all the courage. The Kennedys sold America a bunch of baloney, but they sold it. Why aren't we able to sell something?" Then Kissinger responded saying, "Sir, we're selling your competence. You're great at being competent." Then Nixon said, "Competence? I want guts. I want to be known as the president with guts, not competence! The American people demand competence from a president. To be seen as a great president, you've got to be seen as having guts. Go sell guts. Nixon equals guts."

He really does deserve a good grade for having guts. Nixon made big moves and took big risks; and to answer your question, much of what he did in foreign policy was highly unconventional. He believed that to be a historic figure, you have to roll the dice and gamble. He gambled all the time on where to take the country and what to do.

He was also a loner except for his marriage to Pat and relationships with his children. He didn't have many friends. But he was deeply patriotic about all things America. Everything he ever did was ultimately about justifying to himself that what he was doing as president was in America's best interest. The Watergate debate came about because of Nixon's believing our country would go down the drain if we had a George McGovern presidency. Nixon believed that if McGovern got in, our position in the world would become dangerously weak. He justified his Watergate activities by saying, "I've got to do what I've got to do or else the Democrats will blow our entire military strategy."

The downside with Nixon was the paranoia he carried. I've never written about two people more opposite in style than Ronald Reagan and Richard Nixon, two Californians. Reagan had no paranoia about

people. He'd come in here and say, "I'll tell you this..." But Nixon would come in and be wondering, "What's your inside game?" And he'd be thinking about that every minute. Being paranoid all the time wears on you. It shows a cunning, an intelligence, and an insightfulness in Nixon; but before long, it wore him down. Reagan never would have had an enemies list and part of Nixon's legacy is his enemies list.

NIXON AND KISSINGER

BOSTON Besides Nixon, the other main character in your book is Henry Kissinger. Obviously, together they crafted an incredible foreign policy. Based on the transcripts, though, it seems that whenever Henry left the room, Nixon would seize on the opportunity to criticize him behind his back. At different points, Nixon said, "Henry's just so jealous of letting Haig come in." "He's not a good negotiator." He feared Henry was "going to be a dictator." He said to others on his staff, "Henry divides us" and "He's a very difficult individual to have around."

The tapes make clear that on the one hand, Nixon and Kissinger were dependent on each other in explaining and executing America's foreign policy, yet at least from Nixon's perspective, there was real hostility between them when they weren't around each other.

BRINKLEY When those two got together it was dark on dark. When Kissinger was with Gerald Ford, it was a perfect relationship, because Ford had such a light view of things. Throughout his time in government, Kissinger was always trying to get credit for everything and Nixon did not want history to think Kissinger deserved all the credit. Henry mastered the East Coast media, which made Nixon respond, "What about me? The press isn't giving me credit for anything. They're giving it all to Henry." In many ways, they had a very dysfunctional relationship, but Kissinger was pretty much the errand man—running errands around the world for Nixon and Nixon treated him like an errand man.

When Henry was in the Oval Office, though, you had a sycophantic Kissinger. When he left the room, Nixon would begin firing darts at him in front of whoever else was there. It's not pretty to read.

What they shared, what they're famous for regarding all their diplomatic achievements came about because they needed each other. Kissinger went to China first and laid the groundwork for Nixon's visit, and set the table for Nixon's ultimate arrival. So they definitely had a symbiotic working relationship, but it was pretty dark.

The funniest story regarding the tapes and how Nixon would backstab others when someone left the room involved George Herbert Walker Bush. When Bush learned what we were doing and knew our book was coming out, he asked us, "What's on the tapes about *me*." "What did Nixon say about *me*?" So we told him what Nixon said about him, and it was mixed. But then Bush asked the follow-up question: "What did Nixon say about me when I left the room?"

That's the golden question. Nixon did this a lot of ways. He would respectfully ask someone, "Did you have a good meeting with so-and-so? Tell me all about it." Then when that person walked out, Nixon would start babbling, "Can you believe what a jackass he is? He belongs back in Idaho." All this is on tape. Everybody from that era is terrified about what was said about them, because nobody knew the taping was going on. Kissinger never knew he was being taped. Nobody knew. It was just voice-activated all over. At Camp David, the lodge room was bugged. People thought they were relaxing at Camp David on a retreat and little did they know that everything they were saying or muttering was being recorded. It was a nasty thing to do to people.

BOSTON There are a lot of statements in the book from Kissinger that I'm sure he's not happy to read. Have you gotten any feedback from him on the contents of his remarks that are in your book?

BRINKLEY This is Henry: "Don't believe the tapes." What he means by that is, "There was more going on than just what we were saying. Yes, we said all that stupid stuff, but we were getting this and that policy done."

The tapes have been nothing but a source of embarrassment for Kissinger because they shrink who he was and build Nixon up more. Once Nixon became a pariah figure after Watergate brought him down, Kissinger wrapped his legacy around Jerry Ford. Now he lives in New York City and Connecticut and has wrapped his legacy around the establishment and Wall Street people.

Henry does not need to be reminded of his awkward moments with Nixon. Nixon's like a curse, an albatross around his neck, because Kissinger has spent his adult lifetime being so brilliant at explaining what the two of them were trying to do. For example, with the Indo-Pakistani War, Kissinger's written about it very eloquently, saying, "Here's what we were doing with India and Pakistan. This was our strategy." His books and memoirs go into detail about it. Then suddenly the tapes came out and showed everything Henry said in his book was the opposite of what was actually said in the tapes. Kissinger often spun it in such a way in his books to make himself look big when in fact it was other people who deserved the credit. So, yes, Kissinger does not like the tapes.

BOSTON There are parts of the book where it seems Kissinger was aspiring to have an upper hand in what was going on. You detail an April 20, 1972 conversation where Haig told Nixon that Kissinger's prime concession in Moscow was going to be that the US would allow 100,000 North Vietnamese troops to remain in South Vietnam—which would make it the most significant reduction in American expectations since the start of the Peace Talks, and Nixon knew nothing about it. In October

1972, when Kissinger got to Paris for a new round of talks with the North Vietnamese, he received a proposal from them that he didn't even share with Nixon.

Reading these stories made me wonder, "Who was the president here? Who was the commander in chief?"

BRINKLEY The Paris Peace Talks in Vietnam were all Henry. Nixon loathed the very idea of sitting in Paris and negotiating all day long on minutiae. That was all Henry's gambit. What Nixon always wanted Henry to make clear with the world leaders was to create the impression that he (Nixon) was a little crazy. Nixon very pragmatically said, "That's what you want. They need to think you're going to bomb them. That you're not bluffing. To be a great leader—you have to be feared." So when the US was engaged in the Peace Talks, Nixon was saying on the tapes in the Oval Office, "Great, talk about peace—but let them know that we're going to bomb the hell out of them while the Peace Talks are going on. And if the Peace Talks collapse, I'm gonna bomb them more. You let them know that. I have to be believed in. We have to increase the bombing while you're negotiating, Henry, so that they know I mean business."

This is the reality of Richard Nixon, which at times can be inspiring and other times very tragic, because he did not have a human rights moral compass. He was very much *realpolitik* in foreign affairs. He was all about the big power chess game type of reality. What I mean by that is Nixon was not at his best, for example, in a Bangladesh humanitarian crisis. His response was, "Where is America's interest in Bangladesh? Can't we get the Red Cross to give them some money? Why does the federal government have to give them funding?" He apparently never thought, "Oh those poor people, the flood was bad. We need to help them…" You don't get that with Nixon.

The big debate in foreign affairs is the tradeoff between human rights and realism. It's okay to be the realism person that

Douglas Brinkley

Nixon was, but a leader needs to have at least a strand of the humanitarian side in him. For example, look at what George W. Bush did with AIDS in Africa. A good president must have a human rights component in him, and Nixon didn't have it.

He liked statistics. He'd say, "We'll bomb there and we'll kill 200 thou," and he'd move on without thinking about the consequences of that. Then you stop and think, "Wow, 200,000 people killed!" Nixon said it so casually.

Kissinger has said, "Look, we knew Nixon was exaggerating and he was just trying to be macho. We knew we weren't going to go bomb 200,000 people. That was Nixon's way of letting us know 'I want business, you guys are soft.'"

NIXON'S STRATEGY FOR ENDING THE VIETNAM WAR

BOSTON When Nixon and Humphrey ran for president in 1968, the biggest issue in their campaigns was that they both committed to getting the United States out of Vietnam. It took Nixon his entire presidency, and in the last two years of it, as you just mentioned, he engaged in heavy bombing—Operation Linebacker I and II.

How do think history is going to evaluate Nixon's approach to ending the Vietnam War?

BRINKLEY The main point about Vietnam on the tapes was Nixon saying, "Look, this is Kennedy's war and it's Johnson's war and I inherited the mess. Right now, right this minute, if I want to be popular, I could pull our troops out of Vietnam."

Remember Nixon was Eisenhower's V.P. He knew Ike got elected in '52, was sworn in in '53, and six months later, got us out of the Korean War. Nixon said, "I can pull an Eisenhower and get us out of Vietnam. The media will love me. I'll be a darling. I'll be the one that got us out while those two Democratic presidents got us in and botched it."

But he didn't think that a fast Vietnam pullout was right for the United States. He thought the war was not about democracy flourishing in South Vietnam; it was about our relationship with China. His fear was that if we just pulled out and didn't get our POWs back, didn't build some infrastructure, didn't find ways to get more intelligence in the region, then that would damage our standing in the world—particularly with China. Nixon did find a way to make China realize that just because we lost in Vietnam did not mean we wouldn't go into a full world war mode if they dared touch Taiwan or intervened in the Philippines.

It was sort of a World War II generation perspective in response to what the Japanese did at Pearl Harbor. He was always very cognizant of how Vietnam could impact his ultimate plan for China. He thought, "We've got to get out of Vietnam with honor—peace with honor, but we've got to let China know that just because we're bailing here does not mean we're not coming in wolverine fierce if you dare move Chinese expansionism into our American zone of interest."

That was the reason behind his strategy of increased hitting, hitting, and more hitting. In the end, he didn't achieve the desired result in Vietnam because some things exploded on him, like the release of the Pentagon Papers in 1970. The incursion into Cambodia made a lot of people question the constitutionality of his actions, and that led to a new wave of protests here at home, including the Kent State killings. Also, there was a very liberal, anti-war media reporting on Vietnam all the time, and Nixon was always butting heads with them.

In truth, he *was* constantly getting us out of Vietnam. He *was* definitely pulling out our troops, but his strategy was, "While we're withdrawing, that's the time to bomb heavy. Withdraw and bomb." We're seeing that in Iraq right now. No boots on the ground, but we're using precision bombing.

The net result of Nixon's tactics was that none of our Vietnam peace strategy worked because South Vietnam's government collapsed with the fall of Saigon once we left there. Then the Khmer Rouge came in. So I don't give him high marks on Vietnam for dragging it out as long as he did, and I think he underestimated the domestic cost of a slow withdrawal. He never had a good strategy for dealing with America's civilian mindset about what he needed to do over there. So although it was not Nixon's war, he didn't end it. It was Jerry Ford who ended the war.

NIXON AND CHINA

BOSTON The only way the United States could succeed in building a relationship with China was to diminish our relationship with Taiwan. And that was obviously a delicate balance and required Nixon to pivot away from Taiwan toward China. Was that a hard decision?

BRINKLEY Yes. That's a good question. When Ronald Reagan was Governor of California, he called Nixon on the phone and told him to either get the US out of the

UN, or at least withdraw our ambassador to the UN (who was George Herbert Walker Bush at the time) over the Taiwan issue. That was when they were seating China on the Security Council, and Taiwan was starting to be the forlorn country—no longer the real China. Reagan was a Taiwan diehard, and Nixon knew China was going to get a Security Council seat.

It's an interesting difference between two Republican views: Nixon the internationalist saying, "NATO is what matters, I don't like the UN much, but I'm not going to pull out my ambassador and make a big stink of this"; and Reagan the conservative ideologue saying, "You can't do this. You're punishing the Taiwanese, and they're our great ally." There's the split in the Republican Party and it still exists today in different ways. Nixon was more moderate. He trained under and was not that different in his views from Dean Acheson or John Foster Dulles. He believed we had to have global intervention and always needed to stay mindful of the big powers. China was a big power; Taiwan wasn't, so Nixon had less interest in Taiwan.

BOSTON Doug, thanks so much. We're out of time.

H.W. ("BILL") BRANDS makes sparks fly when he starts talking presidential history with high speed precision. Shortly after the two-time Pulitzer Prize finalist came out with his thorough biography, *Reagan: A Life* (Doubleday 2015), I did two onstage interviews with him (using two sets of questions) on May 15 and 25, 2015—one in Houston, one in Dallas—for my law firm's clients and professionals in those two cities. I then integrated the two transcripts into one, which explains why this chapter is longer than the others.

"What we learn from studying his life is that there was the rhetorical Regan and then there was the practical Reagan—but it was the practical Reagan who actually governed the country. Republicans need to remember not just what he said, but also what he did, which was often different from what he said." –H.W. BRANDS.

CHAPTER 23

H.W. BRANDS
ON
Ronald Reagan

COMPARISON BETWEEN REAGAN AND LINCOLN

BOSTON Bill, throughout the book you make comparisons between Reagan and Lincoln. Both of them were the great communicators of their era. Lincoln led the country to win the Civil War while Reagan led the country toward ending the Cold War. All politicians today have to get right with Lincoln, while at least all Republican politicians have to get right with Reagan. They have many historical parallels and yet Lincoln is rated number one in the presidential polls, while Reagan is ranked anywhere from eight to eleven, depending on the poll.

How close to Lincoln does Reagan belong in the presidential rankings?

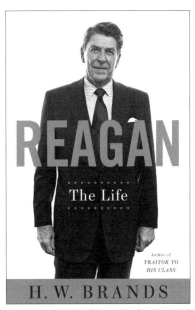

Courtesy of Penguin Random House LLC

BRANDS The first thing to remember is that Lincoln would not have been rated near the top if you had done the poll within thirty years of his presidency, if he had not been assassinated. His being killed in office turned him into a martyr, which skewed at least some people's evaluation of him. It takes a long time before historians, political scientists, and the general public can come to any kind of consensus about the meaning of any particular presidency. If you had asked anybody in Texas what they thought of Abraham Lincoln in 1875, they would not have rated him near the top.

Almost thirty years removed from his presidency, Reagan seems to me to be one of the two most important presidents of the twentieth century. The first one is Franklin Roosevelt. The second one is Ronald Reagan. This is because, more than any others of the twentieth century, those two presidents changed the direction of America's political conversation and the trend line of American politics.

COMPARISON BETWEEN REAGAN AND FDR

BOSTON Okay, then, let's talk about Reagan and Franklin Roosevelt, about whom you've also written a biography. Again, we know that both of them were obviously great communicators—FDR on the radio; Reagan on television. Both also had the important gift of being able to make Americans feel better about themselves in depressing times. Both also tipped the national scales in favor of his party's brand of politics during his era. Both were also resilient: FDR defied polio; Reagan defied an assassin's bullet.

Despite all those similarities between them, in most presidential polls, FDR is rated number three behind Lincoln and Washington; and that's five to eight places above Reagan (depending on the polls).

Is the main reason FDR ranks higher than Reagan in the polls because he led America through a victorious war effort whereas Reagan only led us to the end of the Cold War?

BRANDS I think that's the basic reason, yes. If you lead the country to victory in an existential crisis, you get chops for that. Abraham Lincoln. Franklin Roosevelt. You list the top three—great triumvirate of American presidencies—Washington, Lincoln, and Roosevelt.

Washington gets a nod and is essentially grandfathered in as being among the top three ranked presidents partly because he was the first. He did, of course, lead the country to victory in the Revolutionary War, but that had nothing to do with his presidency since the office didn't even exist until after the war. As president, Washington set a number of precedents, including the fact that the presidents these days are limited to two terms largely because of Washington's decision to leave the office after two terms.

Besides Washington, our greatest presidents (according to the polls), Lincoln and FDR, are the ones who led America to victory through our country's two greatest wars. It actually speaks well for Reagan that he ranks as high as he does because he accomplished what he did without the benefit of winning a war. There's sort of a rule of thumb in presidential polls: if you want to be a really great president, you have to preside during a moment of great crisis.

For the most part, as much as we grumble about it, the American political system works well. If you think about the long course of American history, you realize that what our political system has accomplished for over 200 years is really the great success story of modern world history. So we're doing something basically right. Voters recognize this every four years by choosing, at least most of the time, middle of the road status quo candidates who usually don't have a chance to push the envelope very far from the norm. It's only when the system breaks down most spectacularly, as it did during the Civil War, the Great Depression, and World War II, that a president has the maximum opportunity to show his greatness. So for Reagan to accomplish what he did when the United States was not at war, and when the economy was floundering but not in serious crisis, makes his being ranked in the eight to eleven spots in the various polls truly remarkable.

REAGAN'S HIDDEN PERSONALITY

BOSTON Let's talk about the inner Reagan. You say that Reagan's growing up with an alcoholic and often-unemployed father was a major reason for his inability to get close to people throughout his life. You note how he "protected himself by holding back" and also say that "his heart had limited capacity." This feature of his personality disconnected him from his children, and the only close friend he ever really had was his wife Nancy, who acknowledged that her husband often "had a wall around him." His shutdown interior, as you point out, was also the source of his acting career's demise.

How could Reagan have had such a massive passionate political following with such a locked up personality?

BRANDS There are some politicians and public figures who exude charisma and people will follow them almost anywhere. For example, people who knew or served under Andrew Jackson said they would have marched into hell under Jackson. There are people in recent times who have also had that touch—like Bill Clinton. There are lots of people who dislike everything about Bill Clinton's policies but once they meet him, they're charmed. Reagan was not that way.

One of the basic puzzles I had to try and solve (and I'm not sure I did, but I put my best answer in the book) is the basic puzzle of: "How did Reagan accomplish what he accomplished?" It's such a puzzle because he did not have the type of personality that made people think, "This is a guy I would do anything for." Reagan seemed friendly

from a distance. He was amiable. He was really good at delivering speeches. He told jokes as well as any president since Abraham Lincoln. He would always start a speech or any important conversation with a joke and people would chuckle. As they chuckled, their resistance and skepticism toward him would diminish and they would open up to what he wanted them to do.

Lots of people thought Reagan was a friendly guy and somebody they would really like to know or go out and have a drink with. The closer people got to him though, the more they realized he was aloof. He got cooler the closer a person got to him. Nancy Reagan was really her husband's only friend. I would say, with a little hyperbole, that if Reagan hadn't been famous and attracted the attention he did, no one would have come to his funeral except Nancy. There were people, of course, who flocked to Reagan because he was powerful but Reagan never gave of himself the way you have to do in order to form true friendships. One of the things Reagan understood though, as governor of California and later as president, was that to be a political leader, he didn't have to have friends; he only needed to have supporters. He exuded enough warmth for people to want to support him.

One of the striking things about Reagan, and the reason he remains an icon for Republicans and conservatives, is he was that very rare, almost unique example of a cheerful conservative. Conservatives generally grumble about how the world is going to hell in a handbasket. The essence of conservatism is: hold what we have because change is usually for the worse. Reagan firmly believed that America's brightest days were ahead of it. I happen to think Americans generally tend to be conservative in their politics because of their preference to do things themselves rather than have government do it for them; but when most conservative politicians speak with a stern lecturing tone, it often doesn't resonate with voters.

I don't know how many of you remember Barry Goldwater, but his political philosophy was the same as Reagan's. In fact, you could hardly find any philosophical differences between the two of them; but in terms of their persona, they were worlds apart. That's why when Reagan broke onto the national political scene in 1964 speaking on behalf of Goldwater (that year's Republican presidential nominee), and Republican voters saw this new guy and then read his speech, they said, "Okay. He's saying exactly what Goldwater believes." But what they really saw was a man with an engaging presence who drew people in. This was the first time Reagan had ever been seen on national television in a political context, and Republicans all over the country immediately said to themselves, "Oh my gosh, we nominated the wrong guy. We should have nominated Ronald Reagan instead of Goldwater." The very next day, Reagan for president committees began getting formed, and this happened before he had ever run for anything in politics. These committees were formed in states all over the country and shortly thereafter, he ran for governor of California and won. So Reagan's speech for Goldwater in 1964 was what started his political career; not because of his having a warm fuzzy personality because personal warmth was not really in his toolkit.

WHY REAGAN WENT INTO POLITICS

BOSTON Let's talk about his transition from acting to politics. You say in your book that whereas some people enter politics seeking power, Reagan entered the arena "because he wanted attention, a stage, an audience, and applause" at a time when his star turn in Hollywood had essentially ended. That sounds like a pretty shallow reason for getting into politics.

Wasn't a big part of Reagan's going into politics in the mid-sixties tied to his genuine burning desire to reduce the size and influence of government, turn free enterprise loose, and also get tough on communism?

BRANDS What you've just described was Reagan's political agenda and he was sincerely attached to that agenda.

As I look at the course of Reagan's life, you can see the adult coming out of the child. One of the things biographers do is look for a personality story line. To find that line, after completing our research, we ask ourselves, "What is it that we can see from the young life that carried into the adult life?" The title of my book is *Reagan: The Life*, but my name at the bottom of the dust jacket cover is almost as big as Reagan's. The reason I mention this is not to boast, but just to warn the reader that this book is *my* interpretation of Reagan's life, and other people can have interpretations about him of their own.

Reagan himself actually wrote two memoirs—one when he was running for governor of California in 1965, the other after he left the presidency. In both of them, he told the story about the joy he had when he first went on stage as a young child. This happened when he was growing up in a household with his alcoholic father.

I was doing a book tour for my Ulysses Grant biography a couple of years ago. During the tour, I did a radio interview and toward the end of the hour, the host asked me what my next project was. I told him I was writing on Ronald Reagan. At that point, he put his hand over the microphone and said, "When we get off the air, there's something I want to tell you." Believe me, I was all ears! I wondered if this guy was a closet expert on Ronald Reagan.

When we got off the air, he said, "If you want to understand Ronald Reagan, there's one thing you must always keep in mind. And I said, "Oh, yeah. What's that?" I'd already been working on Reagan for a couple of years as of the time of that radio show, so I wondered if there was something I'd missed. He said, "You have to remember that Reagan was the son of an alcoholic father." I didn't know exactly how to respond to that comment at first, because his dad's being an alcoholic was a matter of public record in that Reagan had written about it in his memoirs. Then the radio host said, "I speak as the son of an alcoholic father. There is a characteristic emotional style for people who grew up in that situation. It comes from the fact that while growing up, every young boy always looks to his father as a role model and someone who's always there to provide emotional support. When that person who's supposed to serve as a rock of stability is, in fact, utterly unreliable, then it permanently impacts the boy's personality. One day, that boy comes home from school and his dad's playing ball with him, taking him out for ice cream, and is his best friend. The next day, the boy comes home, and his dad beats the daylights out of him. So the boy never knows when he wakes up which dad he's going to have to deal with that day."

I listened to the radio host, and thought to myself, "Okay, that's interesting," and just sort of filed it away to see what I could make of it. Reagan tells the same story in both his memoirs about the day he came home from school himself in his hometown of Dixon, Illinois. It was during the winter, so it was cold with snow on the ground and the temperature below freezing. It was late in the afternoon and he saw his father passed out in the snow. As Reagan told the story, he stood there for a moment trying to decide what he should do. Should he wake his dad and get him into the house or should he just walk on by and let him freeze to death? For an eleven-year-old kid to be making what amounts to a life-and-death decision about his father is a major event in a young life. And for that kid to entertain the thought, "My life might actually be better if my father was dead"—well, that's quite a remarkable thing for a kid to have to deal with. In both memoirs, Reagan described how when he was growing up, the worst times were the holidays. That's when everything was supposed to be warm and

nice, but that's when his father Jack (Ronald Reagan and his brother always called their parents by their first names) would fall off the wagon.

The moment when Reagan felt most comfortable as a child was when he performed on stage. His mother hosted skits, musicals, and plays at their church. She would get little Ronnie into her shows because he was a cute kid and he could perform. While he was writing at age eighty, Reagan could remember the first time he heard applause. For him, it was like music. He said, "The applause music calmed my anxieties and made all my troubles go away." For the eighty-year-old Reagan to remember that about the ten-year-old kid I think was very significant.

If you track Reagan's career, when he was ten, twenty, thirty, forty, even fifty years old, he had no idea he would ever want to go into politics. What was he looking for throughout his life? He was looking for an audience. So he participated in school plays, and college plays, and then he went into radio. His audience kept getting bigger. When he went to Hollywood, the audience got even bigger.

So when people say, "Reagan became president because he wanted to get political stuff done," I'll acknowledge that, but that leaves out the question of, "What made him want to go into politics in the first place?" Before 1964, Reagan was not a political kind of guy. The way I see it, he was looking for a stage and the stage that opened up for him was politics. So he stepped onto it, and he turned out to be pretty good at it.

THE IMPACT OF REAGAN'S ACTING CAREER ON HIS POLITICAL CAREER

BOSTON Let's go a little deeper into Reagan the actor and the connection to Reagan the politician. Anybody who's ever seen a Ronald Reagan movie knows that he was not a passionate actor like Marlon Brando or Robert DeNiro.

Was there a connection between his being a dispassionate actor and his being an effective communicator as president?

BRANDS In the first place, if Reagan had been a better actor and bigger star in Hollywood, he never would have gone into politics. Acting would have been his whole career and he would have been quite happy at that. The reason he went into politics was that he had failed as an actor. By the 1950s, he couldn't get any good roles in movies, so he was demoted to television. He worked eight years as the spokesman for General Electric because he was the host of the General Electric Theater, until he got fired from that job.

In 1964, when he in effect auditioned for a role in politics by giving a speech on behalf of Barry Goldwater, he was basically looking for a new line of work, and politics presented itself to him. Politics suited him quite well because one of the things that's conducive to success in politics is the ability to perform before the public. Reagan had this ability to perform so well in politics because his acting career had primarily been performing in front of a camera. With a camera, you have to imagine an audience because you don't actually have the audience in front of you. His movie and television experience turned out to be very helpful because by the time Reagan became president, political audiences were rarely in-person audiences. They were audiences beyond the television camera. So, as an actor, Reagan learned how to imagine the audience out there beyond the camera and it served him very well.

Reagan was often criticized as being merely an actor. The implication was that actors can only read lines written by others and are, therefore, likely to be empty heads. Yet, as a matter of fact, Reagan wrote more of his own lines than any president since Woodrow Wilson. Reagan took great pains in writing his important speeches.

The signature line of perhaps his most important speech as president was the one where he was standing in front of the Brandenburg gate in Berlin and said, "Mr. Gorbachev, tear down this wall." He wrote that line himself. The draft of the speech was sent off to the State Department to vet it and make sure it wouldn't raise too many problems. The State Department said, "You've got to take that out. It's going to alienate the Russians; it's going to upset the Germans." Reagan said, "Put it back in." And they tried to take it out again, and Reagan said, "Put it back in." Reagan actually wrote more of his own lines than he was given credit for.

The other thing Reagan gained from acting that helped his presidency was that he understood that being president was a role in which success requires you to meet certain popular expectations, one of the most important being that the president, uniquely among American elected officials, is somebody who speaks for the nation as a whole. Senators speak for their states. Members of Congress speak for their districts. It's the president who has to embody and articulate the vision he has for the country as a whole, and Reagan understood how to do that.

In many ways, Jimmy Carter was better prepared to become president than Ronald Reagan. Carter knew more about policies and had a greater understanding of the way all the pieces of government fit together. But Jimmy Carter did not know how to perform the presidency and speak for the country as a whole, whereas Reagan did. That's one of the many reasons Reagan is considered a much more important president than Jimmy Carter.

THE REAGAN MARRIAGE

BOSTON Let's talk about the Reagan marriage. Your book confirms that because President Reagan would not address any type of personal conflict or any of the discord among the people in his administration, he left all the unpleasant confrontation dirty work up to Nancy.

Have we ever had that type of marital dynamic before or since in the White House?

BRANDS There probably has not been a First Lady so involved in the administration of her husband as Nancy Reagan, with the possible exception of Woodrow Wilson's second wife, Edith Wilson, and Edith's becoming a major player in her husband's presidency sort of fell into her lap. Woodrow Wilson had a stroke in 1919 when he still had a year and a half left to go in his presidency. At that time, we didn't have a Twenty-Fifth Amendment, so we didn't know what to do if a president became incapacitated. Wilson wasn't dead after his stroke, but someone had to take charge of his administration, and Edith stepped into that role. I have occasionally suggested to my students, "Should Hillary Clinton be elected in 2016, she will be the second woman president of the United States; with the first being Edith Wilson, who served as sort of a de facto president."

The relationship between Reagan and Nancy is really interesting. I'm going to put a question to this audience and want to see what the reaction is. Nancy Reagan always called her husband "Ronnie" to his face. In her memoir, (which, by the way, is one of the most revealing memoirs by anybody in public life that I've read in the last fifty years), she described how her husband would sometimes put up an emotional wall between them (though most of the time they were each other's soul-mate and each other's entire emotional universe). Even the Reagan children got sort of pushed to the outside in terms of what their family life was like.

So, Nancy called him "Ronnie." Do you know what he called her? "Mommy." Now I just heard "Ooooh…." When I tell this to my students, I get, "What?"

The reason I put it to you (and to almost every audience I've spoken to about Reagan), is to see what you make of this, or whether you make anything of it at all.

How people respond to the Reagan's pet name for Nancy tends to be generational. People who are fairly close to Reagan's age often say that his calling Nancy "Mommy" is not particularly remarkable because when a couple has children, the husband often calls the wife "Mommy," and the wife calls the husband "Daddy." For my students, who these days are about twenty years old, they think what he called Nancy is really bizarre.

I don't quite know what to make of it, and so in the book I don't really make anything of it—I just put it out there. I say, "This is what he called her." The simplest explanation is that she was the mother of two of his children and so, when you have little kids, you say, "Okay, go see Mommy," and then he just sort of extrapolated from that to address her as "Mommy" the rest of his life; but I think there's more to it than that.

In the book, I suggest that when Reagan's father proved to be so unreliable, his mother became his rock of strength. She was the one who held their family together. This idea actually ties into his first marriage to Jane Wyman. After Reagan had been in Hollywood a couple of years, he married Jane Wyman. To Hollywood, it seemed to be a marriage made in heaven because they were both rising stars. The marriage then broke up after a few years because Jane Wyman decided he was boring, and he wasn't what she was looking for. She had had a difficult childhood just like he did. Reagan was devastated by the divorce. He thought he had found Jane Wyman as sort of a substitute for his mother—a new figure in his life in whom he could invest all his emotions because he couldn't really do that to anybody else except his mother. Then Jane dumped him, and it devastated him.

He was floundering and didn't know what he was going to do. Then Nancy Davis came along and found him and they decided to get married. When I said Nancy Reagan's memoirs are candid, one thing she pointed out in her book was she gave the date of the marriage, then the date of the birth of their first child, Patty, and then she

Photo credit: Courtesy Ronald Reagan Library

said (sort of in parentheses), "You do the math," because Patty was born seven months after they were married. I'm not going to impute anything to Nancy for this, and it all did turn out for the best. There is this sense that Nancy was her husband's sole emotional support, and that was great for Reagan on a personal level, though one can ask whether it was the best thing for the country. I'll stop here.

BOSTON Where do you come out on how much Nancy set the White House agenda during Reagan's presidency based on the advice of her astrologer, Joan Quigley?

BRANDS You mentioned earlier that Reagan survived an assassination attempt. There were six bullets fired, and one of them hit him and lodged within half an inch of his heart. Whether he would survive that was literally touch-and-go for a while. He survived and recovered pretty well, physically and emotionally.

The largest effect of this brush with death for Reagan was it deepened his religious conviction. He believed that all of us are put on earth for a purpose and the assassination attempt reminded him that his

life could end in an instant, so he darn well better focus on the important stuff. Reagan was never a detail man. He never really sweated the small stuff, but more than ever after surviving the bullet, he said, "I'm going to focus on the big stuff—the kind of things that will really make this country make the world better."

Famously, when he went into surgery to have the bullet removed, he said a line that instantly became famous. They were about to put him under the anesthetic, and he looked around at the doctors and nurses, and said, "I sure hope you're all Republicans." So he was able to handle the surgery and, again, this is somebody who was always on stage. He knew he had an audience there in the emergency room. In fact, he used that line twice. The first time was when he had just entered the emergency room, and everybody was bustling around, and he said, "Hey, I hope you're all Republicans," but nobody was listening because they were trying to stabilize him and make sure he didn't die. He realized that the joke wasn't heard or didn't go over, so he waited until they were just about to put him under. By then, everybody was looking at him, again he used the line, and then he got his laugh.

With Nancy, the effect of Reagan's near-death experience was transformative because he was her entire emotional universe. She didn't think she could live if her husband died. She knew that presidents are often subject to assassination attempts. She also knew about the twenty-year curse on the White House—that is, how as of 1980, every president elected in a year divisible by twenty, ever since 1840, had died in office. Not all of them died by assassinations; some died by natural causes.

When her husband was nearly killed, (and of course he had been elected in 1980) she thought, "Oh my God, fate is coming to get him." After he nearly died, there was a period of about six weeks when she couldn't eat and couldn't sleep. If you remember the mental image you have a

Nancy Reagan, she was a slight woman to begin with. She lost fifteen pounds shortly after Reagan was shot. People thought she was dying of something. She had a slightly greater capacity for making friends than Reagan himself did. Her friends began worrying that there was something seriously wrong with her. Merv Griffin was one of her buddies from Hollywood. Merv Griffin told her, "There's somebody out here in California who can help you." He referred Nancy to a woman named Joan Quigley who was an astrologer.

Now Nancy was a smart cookie. The fact that she fell for the line I'm about to tell you indicates how desperate she was after the shooting. She got on the phone with Joan Quigley, and the astrologer said, "I could have told you that the day of the assassination attempt was going to be a bad one for your husband." Nancy replied, "Oh, really." Predicting things that have already happened is pretty easy. Under other circumstances, Nancy would have taken Joan's after-the-fact prediction with several grains of salt, but she was desperate for something or someone who could make her feel less fearful. From then on, Joan Quigley essentially became Nancy's counselor and they conducted weekly and sometimes more frequent meetings by telephone. What Nancy always wanted to know from Joan was, "What days are going to be especially dangerous for my husband?" Joan Quigley would then identify the good days and the bad days.

During Reagan's first term, the go-between Nancy had with the White House staff was Michael Deaver. He was deputy chief of staff and a long-time family friend. Deaver knew about Nancy and the astrologer. He knew enough to be a buffer between the California astrologer and the White House scheduling book, and he was very discrete about it. There were other people on the White House staff who had this sense that there was an odd kind of force shaping the president's schedule because nobody could just make an appointment for the president.

Before an event could be scheduled, it always had to be checked out with various people and the process seemed to take longer than it should have.

The secret about Nancy and her astrologer was kept very closely through the first term and into the second term when James Baker was replaced as White House chief of staff by Don Regan, who had been a Wall Street CEO before becoming Reagan's secretary of treasury during his first term. Regan had exactly the wrong personality for being a chief of staff. People who are White House chief of staff are not supposed to make the front page of the newspaper. If they do, the administration has problems. Nancy Reagan got repeatedly upset with Don Regan for getting himself on the front page. So she had it in for him, and finally had him fired after the Iran-Contra scandal blew up. She blamed him for not keeping an eye on what was going on in the West Wing.

After Regan left the White House, he felt he had been deeply wronged in the way he had been treated because he knew Nancy Reagan had gotten him fired and nobody had elected her to anything. He believed an astrologer should not have any role at all in how President Reagan's schedule got planned. Regan knew that when Reagan was going to meet with Mikhail Gorbachev in Reykjavik to discuss the fate of the world and potentially negotiate the end of nuclear weapons, it had been Joan Quigley who said, "You have to fly over on this day rather than that," and this made Don Regan beside himself. The most powerful man on earth, the leader of the free world, was beholden to a crackpot astrologer in California. So when Regan got fired at Nancy's behest, he broke the story about the astrologer on page one of his memoir, and it became a huge embarrassment to the Reagan administration.

Now, I'm sort of mildly interested in Joan Quigley, and slightly more interested in Don Regan, but I'm really interested in Ronald Reagan. Why did Ronald Reagan go along with Nancy and her astrologer's advice?

There's no indication that Ronald Reagan himself believed in astrology, but he knew his wife was desperate after the assassination attempt. He knew that Nancy's having Joan Quigley to talk to and to get this kind of advice from comforted his wife. So Ronald Reagan decided he would risk the embarrassment over having his schedule set by an astrologer if it made Nancy feel better.

This is one of those cases where you have to credit the guy's love and affection for his wife. It's very touching, but at the same time, he was president of the United States, and didn't he have another responsibility as well to the American people?

THE IMPACT OF LUCK ON REAGAN'S POLITICAL RISE FROM 1966 TO 1980

BOSTON It wasn't until reading your book that I connected the dots on the amazing timing on Reagan's ascension to the presidency. In 1966, he was elected governor of California at age fifty-five, and fourteen years later, at age sixty-nine, he was elected president. You can't run for president the first time when you're in your seventies, so he was elected president in the last possible year.

During those fourteen years between 1966 and 1980, LBJ decided not to run for a second term after the Vietnam disaster; Nixon got his second term cut short because of Watergate; uncharismatic Jerry Ford pardoned Nixon, which was a big reason for why he lost in 1976, after being president less than three years; and Jimmy Carter, as we all know, was the father of the "Misery Index" and was an easy foil for whoever the Republican candidate was in 1980.

So recognizing the circumstances of the four presidents who preceded Reagan, was it the twentieth century version of Manifest Destiny that all this luck would fall into Reagan's lap by the time he reached sixty-nine, which allowed him to become president?

BRANDS There was absolutely nothing inevitable about the ascendancy of Ronald Reagan in 1980. The longer I study, the more I realize that success in politics, especially at the presidential level, requires all sorts of things to happen that no one has any control over. If Reagan had come along a couple of years earlier or a few years later, he probably wouldn't have been elected president at all.

It took Reagan three times (in 1968, 1976, and 1980) to even secure the Republican nomination. In certain respects, Reagan was really pressing the envelope. He challenged Gerald Ford for the Republican nomination in 1976 and this alienated a large part of the Republican Party. There's an unwritten rule: You don't challenge a sitting president of your own party. That's the first rule you're supposed to learn. Although Reagan was and is an icon of the Republican Party, he was never a good Republican team player. He didn't play by the rules of the party, but instead went for the opportunity he saw.

He broke the unwritten rule and challenged Ford in 1976 for two reasons: the one that he admitted was he thought Ford was too moderate. I won't call Reagan a hardline conservative, but he was a staunch conservative and he looked at Jerry Ford and said, "This guy is not conservative enough." This is the story that Reagan told himself to rationalize why he was challenging President Ford.

The other reason he ran against Ford was that Reagan himself (along with everybody else) figured it was 1976 or never. If he didn't get the nomination in 1976, he thought he would be too old to run in 1980. He lost the nomination to Gerald Ford and that embittered Ford as a result. Ford and his people blamed Reagan for Ford's loss to Carter in 1976 because of the energy Ford had to expend in trying to beat back the Reagan challenge.

Reagan was also not a good loyal Republican in terms of pulling the wagons together and going out to campaign on behalf of the person who defeated him. Reagan essentially sat on the sidelines in the fall of 1976, which antagonized Ford even more. After Ford lost to Carter in 1976, Reagan decided, probably with the help and encouragement of Nancy, that he was too young to retire and he couldn't figure out what else to do, so he began campaigning in 1977 for the 1980 nomination. Of course, he ultimately got it and was elected.

THE IMPACT OF LUCK ON REAGAN'S PRESIDENCY

BOSTON Another bit of good fortune for Reagan during his presidency was the fact that two men who he did not appoint played huge roles in his success. The first was Paul Volcker, the head of the Fed who was instrumental in getting inflation under control during his first term. The second was Mikhail Gorbachev who, during Reagan's second term, became the first Russian leader who an American president could actually talk to and negotiate with. So, again, was Reagan incredibly lucky that two of his biggest achievements, for which he is best remembered, were aided greatly by people who essentially fell in his lap?

BRANDS He was very lucky. Long before he became president, Reagan articulated two goals for the American government; number one: to shrink government at home; number two: to defeat communism abroad. So when Reagan became president, he started out trying to shrink government at home and he made some progress there. He brought taxes down, he didn't get spending down as much as he wanted, and he wanted to defeat communism abroad. At the end of the book, I gave Reagan sort of a grade on a scorecard. So for my grades, out of the two things he wanted to accomplish, he accomplished one and a half.

The one he accomplished completely, of course with the help of Mikhail Gorbachev and George H.W. Bush, was that he defeated communism. Within two years after

Reagan left office, communism was a dead letter in world politics and it hasn't come back to life since. So give him a full mark on that one. On shrinking government at home, he did half of what he set out to do. He brought taxes down, but spending stayed up. In both cases, Reagan wouldn't have accomplished what he did without Paul Volcker and Mikhail Gorbachev.

The American economy revived in the 1980s after a bad patch in the 1970s. It revived partly because of the Reagan tax cuts and partly because of deregulation during the Reagan years, but probably more than anything, it revived because Paul Volcker engineered a recession that changed people's expectations about rising prices. He basically ran the inflation out of the economy.

Volcker could get away with engineering a recession in order to control inflation because he was an unelected official, and, therefore, he could be absolutely as unpopular as he needed to be. If Volcker had been appointed two years earlier and had undertaken his anti-inflation, tight money policy, then it's quite likely that the economy would have improved sufficiently for Carter to have been re-elected in 1980—and beaten Reagan. If Volcker had come along a couple of years after Reagan's election in 1980, then Reagan would have had trouble getting re-elected in 1984. The recession that hit during Reagan's first term was timed so that the worst of it came around the time of the 1982 mid-term elections. Reagan's party, which had won the White House in 1980, got hammered in the mid-terms. If the recession had come along in 1984, it probably would have swept Reagan away and he would have been a one-term president.

REAGANOMICS

BOSTON Reagan was the first president to advocate supply-side economics, which is based on the idea that reduced taxes stimulate the economy, and the increased revenues coming from the economic stimulation should prevent any adverse effect on the federal deficit.

George H. W. Bush, before he was chosen to be Reagan's vice president, labeled the plan "voodoo economics." In fact, Reagan's economic policy, which became known as "Reaganomics," did cut taxes, and it did stimulate the economy, but it substantially increased our federal deficit to record levels.

Would you describe Reagan's supply-side economic policy as a success, a failure, or something in between?

BRANDS I would say it was both a success and a failure. I don't think you have to call it one or the other, and I'm not even sure you have to say it was something in between. Reagan's supply-side economic policy was a success in that it definitely revived the economy, which had been very strong ever since the 1940s and through the 1950s, but by the end of the 1960s, inflation started to creep up and the deficit started to grow. During the 1970s, the deficit got out of control along with inflation.

The federal deficit wasn't so high (and this is a critical part of the Reagan story) until Reagan came along. The litmus test for Republican conservatives on fiscal issues has always been the balanced budget. Since World War II, conservatives have always said, "You've got to balance the budget. Households have to balance the budget. The government needs to balance the budget." Until Reagan became president, it was only the Democratic Party that was willing to tolerate deficits. Then Reagan came along preaching tax cuts and spending cuts, and how they were going to balance each other. This was what he preached, but what Reagan practiced was something different.

I still haven't quite decided when Reagan made the fateful decision to decouple tax cuts from spending cuts—whether he overestimated his persuasive ability or whether he simply understood that he was not going to get spending cuts but he could get tax cuts, and maybe later he would starve the beast and then he could slow the

rate of government growth. What Reagan did in his first year in office was to propose tax cuts and spending cuts to Congress, controlled at that time by Democrats led by Tip O'Neill. By and large, they resisted the spending cuts, but they were willing to tolerate tax cuts if it was part of a deal. Reagan realized he could get the tax cuts quickly in exchange for promises of spending cuts later. So with his big victory mandate from the 1980 election, in the summer of 1981, he got Congress to pass a tax cut over three years, and the top personal tax rate went from 70% down to less than 30%—a huge cut. It was a major victory for the Reagan administration.

On the spending side, his administration got promises from Congress to cut spending in future years and Reagan accepted the deal. This proved to be a fateful choice because, as Reagan discovered, tax cuts are actually easy to get. Oftentimes, Democrats will resist making tax cuts but every incumbent running for re-election likes to go to his constituents and say, "I cut your taxes." Getting Congress to cut taxes is almost like getting a baby to accept candy. Getting spending cuts is a whole lot harder. When Reagan made the decision not to hold the tax cuts hostage to the spending cuts, he got the tax cuts but he never did get the spending cuts. Reagan blamed the Democrats because they refused to make the cuts but of course, shifting blame is what every politician does.

Reagan might have done better on the deficit side if he had not simultaneously insisted on increasing America's military arsenal. For Reagan, growing our defense was the big deal. When asked, "If you had to choose between building up the military arsenal or eliminating deficits?" he'd say, "I can accept the deficits because the arsenal is absolutely necessary." Ever since Reagan, as you pointed out, we have lived with these massive deficits, and now, it's pretty much built in.

By the way, Reagan refused to touch the big entitlement programs, meaning Social

Security and Medicare were off the table. You take those off the table, you cut taxes, you ramp up defense, and there's no way you're going to recoup that and be able to balance the budget.

PRESIDENT REAGAN'S SUCCESS AT WORKING WITH CONGRESS

BOSTON One of the things most people don't realize was that as president, Reagan was very successful at working with Congress and, in fact, caused a lot of important legislation to be passed at his direction and under his influence. Currently, we have a president who has a great deal of trouble working with Congress and getting anything done.

Did Reagan know something about governing that President Obama does not know OR are we living in a new era where it is virtually impossible for a president to move with fluidity in dealing with Congress?

BRANDS Some of Reagan's success at passing bi-partisan legislation was due to his innate characteristics of leadership. He was an appealing individual and people responded to his kind of appeal. The answer to your question, though, is it's the latter.

If you look at the history of American political parties from the Federalists and the Jeffersonian Republicans in the 1790s, through the Whigs and the Democrats of the mid-nineteenth century, through the modern Republicans and Democrats through the first half of the twentieth century—in all those cases, both political parties were ideological coalitions. There were always conservative Republicans and liberal Republicans. There were always liberal Democrats and conservative Democrats. That situation persisted into the 1960s.

It began to change when President Lyndon Johnson made civil rights reform the essential cause of the national Democratic Party. By doing so, he gave

permission to all Southern Democrats who were conservative (and other things being equal, they should have been Republicans all along), and who had been legacy Democrats because the South remembered the Republican Party as the party of Lincoln, and the party who had waged war on the South. So a hundred years after the Civil War, Johnson's actions gave those Southern conservatives permission to leave the Democratic Party and join the Republican Party, with which they had a more natural philosophical affinity. In some cases, congressmen and senators actually switched parties. In other cases, those who were older just remained Democrats, but when they retired or died, their places were taken by younger people in the South (conservatives) who were members of the Republican Party. The great migration of Southern conservatives out of the Democratic Party into the Republican Party began in the 1960s.

I should add that Lyndon Johnson realized exactly what he was doing. On the night he signed the Civil Rights Act in 1964, he turned to Bill Moyers, his secretary, and said, "Bill, I have just delivered the South to the Republican Party for a long time to come." And he was right.

By the time Reagan became president, this great migration of Southern Democrats into being Southern Republicans was about half completed, so there were still lots of conservative—mostly Southern—Democrats, and those "Reagan Democrats" as they were called during the 1980s, were a crucial part of the Reagan constituency. They allowed him to accomplish things that a president of either party today would have a much harder time accomplishing, because today, the two parties have sifted out ideologically almost 100%. You would have to look really hard today to find a liberal Republican anywhere in the country and you would have to look really hard to find a conservative Democrat. Essentially, if you are a Democrat you are a liberal, if you're a Republican you are a conservative, and the between meets no more. Add to this the fact that with computers and polling it is possible, and it has been accomplished almost purposefully, to write congressional districts so that they are safe for a particular party.

So we're now in a situation with respect to Congress where the South always was during the days of Jim Crow, in which the important election was always the primary election—in those days, the Democratic primary. These days, in most races for Congress, the most important election is the primary—which means that Republican incumbents only have to look over their right shoulder because that's where the challenge is going to come from in the primaries and Democrats only have to look over their left shoulder.

Under these circumstances, there is almost no political incentive for a member of one party to become a part of any kind of common cause with a president of the other party. This was true to a large degree for George W. Bush, it has been even more true for Barack Obama, and I don't see any sign that it's going to get any easier for the next president.

REAGAN'S ATTITUDE TOWARD AND CAPACITY FOR COMPROMISE

BOSTON During the last few years in the Republican Party, the Tea Party phenomenon has emerged. Right now, with the recent elections of Ted Cruz, Dan Patrick, and Ken Paxton, it's clear that the Tea Party controls Texas. On the one hand, Tea Partiers lionize Reagan as their greatest political hero, but on the other hand, they speak loud and often about how the word "compromise" is a dirty word used only by politicians who lack the courage to stand on their principles.

Was "compromise" a dirty word to Ronald Reagan?

BRANDS Not at all. Ronald Reagan understood that progress comes through compromise. Reagan was re-elected in

1984 with 60% of the popular vote. That's a landslide. There were only one or two elections in American history before that one which had a greater margin of victory, but Reagan won one of the biggest landslides in American history. But what did it mean? It meant that 40% of the country didn't vote for him because they voted for the other person. Reagan understood that. He understood that a president is a president and not a tsar. He also understood that progress toward a political goal almost always comes in steps.

Philosophically, Reagan was and remains the model for everybody in the Republican Party, including the Tea Party activists. Reagan gave essentially one speech his entire career. Details changed, the opening joke changed, but the message was always the same: shrink government at home and defeat communism abroad. Everything he said was a variation on that theme. Communism is not a big issue for Tea Party activists today but shrinking government certainly is. You can quote Reagan chapter and verse and it's exactly what the Tea Party is looking for.

In that respect, Reagan has been a man for all Republican seasons. What we learn from studying history is there was the rhetorical Reagan and then there was the practical Reagan, but it was the practical Reagan who actually governed. Reagan is the last towering conservative to occupy the White House. He knew, though, that if he was actually going to make progress toward his goals, given that 40% of the country disagreed with him, and that the Democrats had a majority in one house of Congress, he would have to make compromises.

Reagan understood that the point of getting elected was not to make speeches, but rather was to score points and make progress. When I interviewed James Baker for the book, he told me that if Reagan told him once, he told him 15,000 times, "I would rather get 80% of what I want than go over the cliff with my flag flying." That was Reagan. He understood that he didn't have to get to his goal all at once. He knew if he could get 80% today, then he could come back the next day and shoot for the last 20%. This is why Reagan should remain an icon for everybody in the Republican Party.

The Republicans need to remember not just what he said, but also what he did, which was often different from what he said. The various people who have criticized Reagan for compromising are people who have never been president, and most of them have never held an executive position where they were actually responsible for getting things done.

REAGAN'S SUCCESS AT SAYING ONE THING AND DOING ANOTHER

BOSTON Given that Reagan was very good at saying one thing to get elected, but then doing something different in order to govern or to make things happen on the world stage, that may have had something to do with Reagan's not having to operate in the 24/7/365 news cycle.

With today's angry, vigilant watchdogs on television, would it be possible today for a president to lead the country in 2015 who was so good at saying one thing and doing another?

BRANDS It would be harder, but not impossible. That's because there is this fundamental understanding on the part of voters that what people say in campaigns is one thing, but what they actually do in office can be something else. It doesn't mean candidates were insincere when they were campaigning. When politicians campaign, they promise the moon. That's what you do when you campaign. You lay out your full agenda and say, "This is what I will do if elected and if everything falls into place." Once a candidate gets elected into office, however, they realize that there are other people around them who are pushing against them.

Since the book came out, I've been asked "Could Ronald Reagan get the nomination of the Republican Party today?" The question is usually posed by Democrats, who, over the years, have decided that Ronald Reagan was not that bad a president because they recognize Reagan as having been much more moderate than most Republicans today. So they expect me to say, "No, he couldn't get the nomination today," and therefore they think that the Republican Party has now run itself into this ditch on the right-hand side of the road. That's the implication they're looking for.

The answer I give them is, "Yes, he could get the Republican nomination today"—in fact, he could get it in a minute—if—and this is a really big "if"—if he hadn't actually already been president of the United States for eight years, because Reagan was a brilliant conservative candidate in a way that no other conservative has been able to duplicate. Reagan's message throughout his political career was 100% conservative. From studying American history, I happen to think that the way we Americans like to think of ourselves is slightly right of center, in the sense that we Americans like to think of ourselves as individualists and we would rather do things for ourselves than have government do things for us. That's the essence of conservatism.

The problem Reagan would have if he ran as a Republican for president today is that he would have to run on his record as president in the 1980s. He would have to deal with the fact that although he cut taxes in a big swipe in his first year, he then agreed to tax increases four or five times over the rest of his presidency (depending on how you define "tax increases.") Reagan was skeptical of Social Security from its earliest days, but he engineered Social Security reform that gave it a sound footing for another thirty years.

Thus, Reagan, as president, was quite the pragmatist and that's one of the main reasons he was able to accomplish as much as he did because he understood that to govern requires pragmatism. When you're a candidate you make speeches. When you're a president, you continue to make speeches, but in Reagan's speeches, he never acknowledged the fact that he was making these compromises. His speeches still said the same thing, but with Reagan, you had to watch what he was doing as opposed to just listen to what he was saying.

THE PERFORMANCE OF REAGAN'S WHITE HOUSE CHIEFS OF STAFF

BOSTON Reagan famously governed as president at a 35,000-foot level and never liked to be bothered by details. That worked just fine as long as James Baker was his chief of staff. Then once Baker left, that changed. Details started bubbling up that Reagan either didn't address or refused to address and his second term was less successful than his first.

What do we learn about best practices and worst practices for a White House chief of staff based on the performance of James Baker, Don Regan, and Howard Baker during the Reagan presidency?

BRANDS When James Baker left his position as chief of staff—and this is in his papers at Princeton—he wrote down something he had learned from one of his predecessors, Donald Rumsfeld, who was chief of staff for Jerry Ford, who created what he called "Rumsfeld's Rules," on how to be a good chief of staff. The first Rumsfeld's Rule was, "Remember, you are not the president." Then there were several other Rumsfeld Rules, and number eight was, "Remember, you are not the president." Then there were several more and the last one was, "Remember, you are not the president."

The success of Baker as chief of staff started with his remembering that he wasn't the president. The failure of Don Regan's term as chief of staff was that he either never read or else forgot Rumsfeld's Rules because the biggest complaint that people had, starting with Nancy Reagan, was that Donald Regan acted as though he was the president. He would give interviews that featured him and all the things that he had done. Jim Baker never did that kind of thing. A successful White House chief of staff has to understand the style of the person he is working for.

You characterized Reagan's first term as more successful than his second term. That was generally the perception, but in a certain important respect, the perception was misleading because Reagan's second term, which of course was known for the Iran-Contra scandal, had to do with Reagan's governing style and Donald Regan's mismanagement of his position. Reagan's second term, however, was also the term in which he made a breakthrough with Mikhail Gorbachev on arms control. Both of those reflect on his style of management. Reagan focused on a couple of really important issues at the expense of nearly everything else. For example, Reagan was on top of policy toward the Soviet Union and if you read (and I was able to read because they have been declassified, minutes of National Security Council meetings) the minutes of the policy group in the White House, whenever the discussion turned to "what's our policy toward the Soviet Union?" (even including arms policy which can get pretty esoteric), Reagan was on top of his game. When you read the transcripts of the weekend Reagan spent at Reykjavik with Gorbachev, it's surprising because Reagan was the guy about whom Richard Nixon said, "Do not let Reagan in the same room alone with Gorbachev. Gorbachev will eat his lunch." Well, in fact, Reagan went toe-to-toe with Gorbachev and was as fully the master of his brief on the technology of arms control as Gorbachev was. It was a very impressive performance and that's one of the reasons I devote substantial pages in my book to this negotiation because it shows Reagan at the top of his game.

The Reykjavik summit was going on at precisely the moment that the Iran-Contra

Photo credit: Marsha Miller

H. W. Brands

scandal was going on because Reagan understood that there are only so many hours in a president's day, and if he wants to make progress on the big things, he's going to have to give up control of some of the small things. So while Reagan was focusing on the Soviet Union and arms control and making landmark progress there, Iran-Contra was bubbling up on the side and he wasn't on top of that. That almost proved his undoing, but not quite because people liked Ronald Reagan. The reason he survived Iran-Contra was the reason why Richard Nixon did not survive Watergate. It was not because Iran-Contra was less serious than Watergate. In fact, in the eyes of the rest of the world, Iran-Contra was a much bigger deal than Watergate, because most people in the world outside the US thought nothing more than Watergate was a spat between the political parties, while Iran-Contra was a violation of several American laws and flew in the face of announced and imposed American policy. George Schultz was flying all over the world trying to get other nations to join America's armed boycott of Iran and then the world discovered that the White House was sending arms to

Iran. It was a horrible thing. But Reagan survived because people liked Reagan and they didn't like Richard Nixon. There's this very simple thing. Political elections, when it comes right down to it, are a popularity contest. If people like you, you've got a big advantage over an opponent that people don't like however smart and experienced that person might be.

BRANDS' APPROACH TO GRASPING THE ESSENTIAL REAGAN

BOSTON Last question. One of America's leading historians, Edmund Morris, the Pulitzer Prize-winning biographer of Theodore Roosevelt, was given the opportunity by the Reagans to shadow the president from 1985 to 1988 as he made his rounds, in hopes Morris would one day turn out a great presidential biography. It didn't happen. After fourteen years of research, Morris finally wrote the book titled "Dutch" (Reagan's nickname through the first twenty odd years of his life), but it was subpar and strange in that Morris inserted himself as a fictional Reagan observer character into his non-fiction biography. Morris explained his weird approach to the book by saying he had to do something because he was simply unable to get a handle on Reagan's personality.

You wrote your Reagan biography about a dead man you never met. Edmund Morris wrote his book about a live man whom he spent countless hours with. Was it easier to grasp the essential Reagan from afar after his death as opposed to trying to grasp him up close and personal?

BRANDS I have nothing but respect for Edmund Morris. I think he's a brilliant writer and I think his three volumes on Theodore Roosevelt are a terrific read. I think he really missed the point of Ronald Reagan and I'm not going to cast aspersions on his honesty in explaining it the way he did. There are various ways of explaining things.

I think the thing Morris didn't get about Reagan is that the importance of Reagan was not internal to Reagan; rather, it was in Reagan's connection to American public life during his era. I've encountered Edmund Morris on a number of occasions and I have heard him say that he finds politics boring. Actually, that's not so bad if you're writing about the young Theodore Roosevelt because young Theodore was not in politics. By the way, if you've read Morris' trilogy on Theodore Roosevelt, the best one is the first one about the young Theodore Roosevelt. The second volume was about TR's presidency, and the third volume was about the post-presidential years. Of the three, the volume on Roosevelt's presidency is the least interesting because it's the most political.

With Reagan, let me put it this way: if Theodore Roosevelt had never become president of the United States, he would have made a fascinating subject for biographers because he was a very big personality. If Ronald Reagan had never become president of the United States, we would not be having this conversation, because no one would be interested in Ronald Reagan. The secret of Ronald Reagan was his relationship to politics, not his personality.

In writing my book, the puzzle I had to solve was not so much, "What made Reagan tick?" but, "How did this person of rather unremarkable talent become such a political superstar?" If somebody looked at Ronald Reagan at age fifty (recognizing that his big speech for Goldwater in 1964 happened when he was fifty-three), and the questions got posed to the masses, "What do you make of this guy? What do you think? Does he have a future?", almost everyone would have said, "No, he has no big future." That would have been the answer because he was never the smartest person in the room, and he wasn't particularly charismatic. At age fifty, he had been a modestly successful actor but his entertainment career was essentially over. Then, beginning at age fifty-three, he became the most important president of the second half of the twentieth century.

When you're looking at history and trying to explain the Reagan phenomenon, and when you look at it from a biography side, there's a temptation to look for the sources of the greatness in the individual, so as to be able to conclude that this person must have had remarkable talents in order to produce remarkable results. Reagan's talents were not exactly remarkable. There were plenty of people in his era who had more talent than Reagan, but Reagan had the gift of understanding his times which gave him the power to motivate the American people.

This is the gift Reagan shared with Franklin Roosevelt, who was Reagan's first idol in politics. Even though their political views diverged as time passed, FDR remained Reagan's model for how to be president. What Roosevelt demonstrated, and what Reagan discovered and also demonstrated, was that a president who has the capacity to channel the power of the American people into his voice can accomplish a great deal.

Having said that, I'm going to add that Reagan's success as president benefitted tremendously from good timing. If Paul Volcker had not been named chairman of the Federal Reserve just before Reagan became president, then the economy would not have turned around the way it did during Reagan's first term. The recovery wasn't caused by Reagonomics. It came about largely because Volcker squeezed the inflation out of the economy; and as chairman of the Fed, he could afford to be unpopular by refusing to lower interest rates, whereas a president couldn't. The timing was perfect. The recession of Reagan's first two years in office caused by Volcker's tight fiscal policy devastated the Republicans in the 1982 election. If inflation had slowed down two years earlier during Carter's presidency, then Reagan wouldn't have been elected in the first place; and if the recession caused by the fiscal policy (that brought inflation under control) had come during the last two years of Reagan's first term, he would have been swept out of office running for re-election in 1984. So Volcker should get a lot of the credit for the recovery of the economy, though the Reagan economic program of tax cuts didn't hurt.

Then on the foreign policy side, if Leonid Brezhnev, the general secretary of the Soviet Union, had lived a few years longer until 1988, then Reagan's role in ending communism in the Soviet Union wouldn't have happened. Reagan needed an interlocutor on the other side in order to move the needle toward ending the Cold War. In March 1985, at the very beginning of Reagan's second term, along came Mikhail Gorbachev, someone who was willing to talk to the United States, and that gave Reagan his opportunity.

When you're in the history business, you don't really deal so much with the "what ifs;" rather, you deal with what actually happened. Thus, for a variety of reasons, Reagan was responsible for shifting the direction of American politics during his era. From FDR until Reagan came along, the trend line in American politics was in a bigger government moving in a more liberal direction. Since Reagan, the conversation has changed. It turns out that government is hard to shrink, such that ever since Reagan became president, government hasn't shrunk, but the conversation has changed. Certainly, people on the street have taken the position that government generally messes things up, so our society would work much better if government got out of the way.

On the foreign policy side, there's another parallel between Franklin Roosevelt and Ronald Reagan. On the domestic policy front, Roosevelt pushed the pendulum in a liberal direction to the left, whereas Reagan pushed it back to the right. Neither one was particularly radical, and therefore, neither one pushed it very far from center. They both just gave it a nudge. In foreign policy though, it was Franklin Roosevelt who was primarily responsible for defeating fascism, the first version of twentieth century totalitarianism; and then Reagan became the one who vanquished communism, the second version.

BOSTON How great is Bill Brands! I don't think I've ever absorbed this much information in this short of period of time in my life.

JON MEACHAM'S three presidential biographies on Andrew Jackson, Thomas Jefferson, and George H.W. Bush have all been *New York Times* bestsellers and received major critical acclaim—and his Jackson book won the Pulitzer Prize. I interviewed Jon twice (with two different sets of questions)—once in Dallas and once in Houston—when his book *Destiny and Power: The American Odyssey of George Herbert Walker Bush* (Random House 2015) was released in late 2015. I then integrated the two interviews into one, which hopefully flow together as a smooth read.

 "President Bush packed eight years of action into four years. You mentioned several of them—Tiananmen Square, the fall of the Berlin Wall, the end of the Soviet Union, the unification of Germany, the first Gulf War, the negotiation of NAFTA, the passing of the Americans with Disabilities Act, the passing of the Clean Air Act, the 1990 budget deal— which Bill Clinton will tell you at length (which is redundant I realize!) set the terms of prosperity for the 1990s. The list of the major events of his presidency just goes on and on. As you quoted Henry Kissinger a minute ago, "It was the most tumultuous period in our history since Truman."
– JON MEACHAM

CHAPTER 24

JON MEACHAM
ON
George H.W. Bush

WHY BUSH 41 APPROVED OF THE BOOK'S COMING OUT DURING HIS LIFETIME

BOSTON Jon, when you were in town almost three years ago, you told us that Bush 41 didn't want this biography (that you were then working on then) to come out until after he died. You said his words were that he wanted to be "paws up" when it came out. What caused him to change his mind and allow your book to come out now while he's still alive?

MEACHAM He really believes in getting history straight. In particular in the last three years, he has become incredibly comfortable with what he did—and believes that a fair minded assessment of his life and

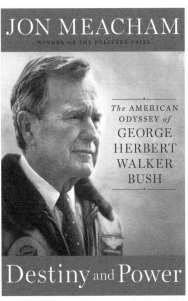

JON MEACHAM
WINNER OF THE PULITZER PRIZE

The AMERICAN ODYSSEY of GEORGE HERBERT WALKER BUSH

Destiny and Power

Courtesy of Penguin Random House LLC

career will show him to have always tried to put the country first.

I'd love to say he changed his mind because he wanted to read the book, but I suspect that's not the case. When I took it down to him three weeks ago, it was the first time he'd seen it. This is a no conditions book. There was no review of it by the Bush family before it was published. Nobody could edit anything out of it. When I took it to him, he looked at it and loved the pictures. I asked his staff a few days later, "Did he look at any of it?" They said, "Well, he really doesn't read books about himself because, as he puts it, "I know how the story turns out." Mrs. Bush, as ever, is a different matter. So I'm having lunch with them later today, and I have a feeling that if I'm served two courses, then she will have liked it; but if it's only one, we'll know what happened.

BUSH 41'S TAPE RECORDED DIARY

BOSTON Regarding his tape recorded diary (that Bush 41 kept intermittently before and while he was vice president, and much more regularly when he was president), that you cite throughout the book, given that he never wrote his authentic full-blown presidential memoir, (but only wrote a book with Brent Scowcroft limited to his foreign policy), why do you think he kept the diary?

MEACHAM He just needed some place to talk and he had an idea that someday what he was dictating would be valuable for history, and thank God he did. Very few people—even his closest aides—knew he was doing it.

He kept it for a couple of reasons. First, it was honestly therapeutic. Remember, we're talking about the consummate WASP and, as a repressed WASP myself, I was particularly well tuned at his being so inclined to complain about whatever happened to be going on. He didn't believe in whining or complaining to others about being

president. As he put it to me, "Nobody wants to hear a president say, "Oh woe is me," because everyone knows that whoever serves in the Oval Office is just damn lucky to be there.

So part of why he kept the tape-recorded diary was that he could not complain to anyone except to himself. Again and again and again, he would have had a bad day, he would have read the newspaper, and maybe what he read made it a bad day, and he would be fairly harsh about whatever it was that distressed him; but then he'd always talk himself back into the game—back into knowing he was so fortunate to be where he was and he had worked so hard to get there.

The other thing he said about why he kept the diary was that when he was hospitalized in May of '91—when his thyroid condition had been manifesting itself into a small heart episode—he said that if something were to happen to him, then Barbara could use his thoughts on the tapes and do a book, and support the family. So I think he kept it for history preservation, and also for providing his wife with a way to enhance her financial security if he died suddenly.

As a historian, I thank the Lord he did the diary, because it's a truly remarkable record of what it actually felt like to be president. He usually dictated very early in the morning, as part of his morning routine. He would wake up at 5:00, and drink a lot of coffee, and then read five or six newspapers and the White House news summaries. To dictate, he might go into the Treaty Room which he used as an office up in the residence. He would take a shower with his dog Millie. (That's a little disturbing, but again I'm an historian; and I have an obligation to say the truth). He would also dictate at Camp David almost every weekend where he might catch up on his week; and on Marine I and Air Force One. You can hear on the tapes the blades of the helicopter and the engines of the jet. He'd fill up these sixty minute tapes and then send them down to Houston, where they'd be transcribed and kept, and then the transcripts would be sent back to him. They were kept in some safe in the residence.

GEORGE AND BARBARA BUSH'S COOPERATION WITH MEACHAM IN THE BOOK

BOSTON He authorized you to become his biographer in 2006, and, to me what he did with you was somewhat similar to what Ronald Reagan did with Edmund Morris in terms of a president's authorizing a biographer to write up his life, although Morris worked on his book during Reagan's presidency, while you wrote your book long after Bush's presidency.

Since George H.W. Bush wasn't going to write a presidential memoir, was he planning for your authorized biography to essentially become his memoir?

MEACHAM I'm actually not his authorized biographer, because in the classic sense, an authorized biographer is simply someone with whom the subject of the memoir cooperates, and, as the term is used, it means the person who's the subject of the book had final approval over the content. It was very important to me and to President Bush that that not be the impression any reader could get from the book.

My pursuing this biography started when I went to the Bushes. I knew about the diary. My initial request of him was, "Let me have the diary, and I'll edit it the way Michael Beschloss did with the Johnson Tapes." Then, the more I read the diary's transcripts, the more I realized that this was a man who deserved full treatment in a complete biography.

In that sense, George and Barbara Bush did choose to cooperate on the book due to my initiative. What I hope comes out of the final product is that it truly reflects the spirit of what the president wanted from me, which was to call it as I saw it, with no punches pulled.

The only condition on anything I read from the Bush family's papers had to do

with Mrs. Bush's diary, which she kept from 1948 forward. For anything that I wanted to use from her diary, I had to clear any quotation with her—not the context, not the conclusion—just the words themselves as they appear in her diary. I delivered to her ninety pages from the draft of the book that had her diary quotes in them, and she took nothing out. We were sitting in their home in Houston, and she was reading along, and said, "My, I was an opinionated thirty-eight-year old woman". And it was all I could do not to say, "Well, you know ma'am, the apple didn't fall too far from the tree." At eighty-nine, she hasn't exactly retired from having strong opinions.

BUSH 41, PRESIDENTIAL POWER, AND MASTERING THE ART OF RELATIONSHIPS

BOSTON Jon, you use the word "power" in this book's title and you also used it in the subtitle to your Thomas Jefferson biography.

Is the essential ingredient in presidential "power," as you use the word, having the capacity to master the art of relationships?

MEACHAM It certainly was for George H.W. Bush. He could not have been President of the United States without a quiet, persistent charisma. I suspect most people in this room have spent time around him, and more than a few of you may have received notes from him. We know the things in him that are missing from a charisma standpoint. We don't think of him as a glamorous figure, like we do John F. Kennedy, or Ronald Reagan; but he would not have been the President of the United States if he had not mastered the art of personal relationships, person by person by person by person. Jefferson did the same thing.

My definition of "power" ultimately is when a person can bend history in the direction he wants—when he can take a set of clinical, historical, and political factors headed in one direction and move them in another direction, if that's what he wants to do. Presidents tend to do that by amassing power through accumulating political capital, though the only way one accumulates political capital is to accumulate trust. What's the most fundamental political transaction? "I need your vote. I need you to believe that your fate and your children's fate, at whatever level—whether at the school board or the nuclear authority, or in the White House—will be safest in my hands." To me, George Herbert Walker Bush became President of the United States because he convinced enough people that their fates would be safe in his hands.

BARBARA BUSH AS FIRST LADY, AND THE COUPLE'S ROADS TAKEN AND NOT TAKEN

BOSTON Let's talk about Barbara. Every woman who becomes First Lady has her own vision of exactly what a First Lady's role should be. What did Barbara aspire to do as First Lady?

MEACHAM Chiefly, she believed her role was to support the man whom she essentially fell in love with over the holidays in December 1941 at the Greenwich Country Club Christmas Dance. He was seventeen, and she was sixteen. He was the first boy she kissed, and she was the first girl he kissed. It's one of the great love stories in American public life. I don't think he would have ever become president without her. Together, they traveled lots of roads and also decided on lots of roads not taken.

For a biographer, it's fascinating to think of those moments where if things had gone this way or that way, things would have turned out differently. There were three critical moments for George H.W. Bush. First, was his making the decision to marry Barbara Pierce.

Second, was moving to Odessa, Texas, after he graduated from Yale in 1948. Barbara's mother, Mrs. Pierce, was so convinced that Texas was the frontier that

she sent boxes of soap and laundry detergent down here from Rye, New York, so her daughter would be clean.

His last fork-in-the-road decision came when he first got seriously interested in politics in Texas, and was offered the chance to join the John Connally faction of the Democratic Party—which means he could have chosen to become a conservative Democrat in what was then largely a one party state. There are those who have argued that George Bush has always been essentially a creature of ambition. If that was the case, he would have taken Connally's offer and run for office as a Democrat; but he was a Republican. It was in his DNA. His father was a Republican Senator from Connecticut; so he stuck with his convictions.

IMPACT OF BUSH 41'S MILITARY SERVICE ON HIS PRESIDENCY

BOSTON George H.W. Bush was a bona fide war hero as a young aviator during World War II, and was shot down in the Pacific in a situation that claimed the lives of his two crewmen. As president, he made the most difficult decision a president can make—and that is to send American troops into harm's way into both Panama and Kuwait, and we lost lives in both interventions.

Did Bush's World War II experience in combat impact his willingness to use military force in order to achieve his foreign policy objectives?

MEACHAM I think so. He understood what war was really like. He was not trigger happy, but he was also keen to project American power when he believed that American interests were at stake and he could meet the tests laid out by Colin Powell, in particular, of a clearly defined mission and appropriate level of overwhelming force.

The diaries of youth show his concern over the lives of his fellow troops because he had lost John Delaney and Ted White to die on September 2, 1944 when he was shot down over Chichi-Jima. He told me he has thought about them every day since September 2, 1944, always wondering, "Did I do enough? Why was I spared?"

You listen to him now and read his diaries during the Panama intervention, and during the Gulf War, and he was always worrying about our soldier's worried parents, and their worried spouses, and worried kids. If you ask him what the toughest thing about being president was, the first thing he always said was, "The president has other people's lives and other people's children in his hands." I think his World War II service affected him deeply and I think it's one of the very interesting things we have in recent times as the military has moved to a volunteer force. President Bush is our last president with a combat record, and there's no plausible potential next president who has one.

VICE PRESIDENT BUSH DURING THE IRAN-CONTRA SCANDAL

BOSTON Let's talk about the Israel-Iran arms-for-hostages transaction which was integral to the Iran-Contra affair and became the glaring scar on President Reagan's second term while Bush was Vice President. You said last night at the Bush Library that you pulled no punches in the book, and in the description of this incident, you are quite critical of Bush's failure to be forthcoming at the time about "what he knew" and "when he knew it," and also because he failed to recognize that arms-for-hostages was a badly misguided policy.

Does Bush now acknowledge his lack of candor to the American people about the arms-for-hostages trade?

MEACHAM No. What he says is that he disagreed with the execution of the policy but he didn't think an operation of this sensitivity should go through a third party; so he didn't think they should have gone through Israel to try to get the hostages out of Iran. If you're going to run an operation like that, you should have full control.

Basically, I think this is the one place in President Bush's career where he did not tell the truth. The phrase I used in the book is, "It was unworthy of his essential character;" but as the former head of the CIA, he was an old spymaster, and he was totally loyal to Reagan. They were motivated for all of the right reasons. They wanted to get these hostages away from Hezbollah, and they wanted to negotiate with Iran. To do that, they wanted to open a channel. So you can pull out the factors and justify what they did.

It's a fascinating story. It all started in the same week basically—November 4, 1986—when Bush started his presidential campaign diary. They had lost the Senate, and a publication in Lebanon revealed the arms-for-hostages deal, and it happened in the same week. That's a big week! When Vice President Bush was first asked about our having made an arms-for-hostages deal, he denied it altogether. He said, "That's crazy." He also asked his press secretary to deny it altogether.

Then George Schultz, Reagan's Secretary of State, went to Bush at the vice presidential residence at the end of that week to have a drink. Schultz said, "You can't deny this. You were there. You approved it." And Bush got very snippy and said, "Don't you understand that there were strategic reasons for this?"—meaning there were strategic reasons for improving the relationship with Iran as opposed to getting the hostages out. Schultz said, "That doesn't matter. You were there." It was not the most pleasant cocktail hour George Schultz and George Bush ever had.

After Schulz left, Bush began to realize that Schultz was right, and that he had to stop denying that the US had agreed to an arms-for-hostages deal. Bush then became an advocate for trying to get as much of the truth out about the situation as possible. So there was a brief moment where his instinct was to cover up. He then offered to do two things. First, he volunteered to go to Langley and take a lie detector test particularly on the subject of the Contra diversion. He knew he would pass that and then he could run an investigative panel to try to figure out what went wrong. Neither thing happened. Of course, it was John Tower who ultimately came in and ran a very fine investigation of the Iran-Contra scandal. I don't think we know much more thirty years later than what Senator Tower, General Scowcroft, and Senator Muskie found out in the short term that they conducted their investigation.

The whole situation was a dark moment for Bush and for the Reagan presidency. What's amusing about it, too, is that the way Bush held fast to support President Reagan went straight to Bush's vision of the vice presidency, which was that he, as vice president, was a senior confidential advisor without portfolio to the president and that he did not want anyone, including the secretary of state, the chief of staff, or the secretary of defense, to know the advice he was giving the president, which is a very different view of the vice president's responsibility to maintain a high level of confidentiality with the president he serves as opposed to the view of the job that people like Gore, Biden, or Dick Cheney have had.

ASSESSMENT OF VICE PRESIDENT QUAYLE'S PERFORMANCE

BOSTON In 1988 at the Republican Convention, Bush 41 surprised lots of people by naming Dan Quayle as his vice president.

Give your assessment of whether President Bush was well served by Dan Quayle as his Vice President.

MEACHAM I have a complicated answer to that, and I come at it having interviewed both President Bush and vice president Quayle at some length on this subject, and

also having thoroughly reviewed President Bush's White House diary, which contains a great deal about it.

Quayle was chosen above all because Bush wanted to surprise everyone and he certainly did that. If he had totally had his druthers, I think he would have put Senator Alan Simpson on the ticket, but Simpson was a little too close to being pro-choice for the Republican base, so that eliminated him from consideration. Bob Kimmitt, who was handling the vetting, brought large boxes of files to New Orleans with Jack Kemp's, Bob Dole's, and Dan Quayle's information in them. They were the finalists for vice president. Bush had even flirted very briefly with putting Elizabeth Dole on the ticket, and may have also considered Sandra Day O'Connor. Quayle got chosen without Bush's ever having an "open kimono," "final gut check," (pick your cliché), meeting about Quayle with his closest campaign advisors—James Baker, Lee Atwater, Roger Ailes, Nick Brady, and Bob Mosbacher.

One of the very few slightly tense moments President Bush and I had in doing the interviews for this book over nine years, came when I asked him about his process for selecting Quayle, because there clearly wasn't a process. The choice was made by reason of George Bush, the old director of Central Intelligence, compartmentalizing the decision. He didn't want Bob Kimmitt, who was doing the vetting, to tell anyone else who he was vetting.

People wonder, "Why did he go it alone? Why, on such a big decision, did he not have his gold level team of advisors weigh in?" I think the answer is psychological more than anything else. Bush had not been able to make his own independent political decisions since the Republican National Convention in Detroit in 1980. Finally, after eight years, the 1988 Republican Convention would provide the moment when he was going to be in a position to make his own decision. He wanted to surprise people—even his own people. He didn't tell Jim Baker he had chosen Quayle until they were on Air Force 2 going to the convention.

So in the interviews for the book, I kept asking President Bush, "Why? Why would you not discuss this important decision with your closest advisors? You were putting a man a heartbeat away from the Oval Office, and you didn't want anyone else's opinion?" I'm not going to say he snapped, but he finally said with urgency in his voice, "Sometimes you just don't want people telling you what to do all the time," which is a classic Bush formulation.

There is a streak in the president of pridefulness and a kind of stubbornness, and his pridefulness and stubbornness were engaged in choosing Dan Quayle. Once he made the decision, his significant loyalty gene kicked in, and he would not be shaken from it.

That gets me to your question, "How did Quayle do as Vice President?" He had one of the leakiest offices in Washington. Bill Kristol was his chief of staff and basically had an open line to most political reporters. What often happened was that the Office of the Vice President, through Kristol, would position Quayle to the media as the "true conservative" in the White House, with the idea that presenting that spin would cause everyone on the far right to feel comfortable because Quayle was around to ride to the rescue and save everybody from the moderate leaders.

I'm going to use a technical historical term—what Kristol and Quayle did absolutely drove President Bush "bananas." According to his diary, though, the president rarely said anything to Quayle about it. He would talk to his diary about how pissed off he was, but he wouldn't discuss it directly to Quayle.

I talked to Quayle about it, (who's a lovely man by the way), and he was a pretty good student of George Bush, except when it came to this, (which is like saying, "besides that, Mrs. Lincoln, how was the play?"). Quayle told me that whenever George Bush

got mad, he didn't yell; he just got quiet. It made me think that there must have been some really quiet times between them during their four years together.

Bush would sometimes say in his diary, "I've got to talk to Dan about getting off these television talk shows," or "Bill Kristol's got to stop doing this," but, when I took some of these diary entries and showed them to Vice President Quayle and Bill Kristol, they were shocked at how angry the president was with them, which tells you something about George Bush.

As I mentioned before, the diary for him was almost a therapeutic tool. He would unleash into it, but then try to run the White House calmly in a day-to-day way that allowed things to function. That's a long-winded answer, but it's puzzling to me that Quayle would not have learned more about how to better conduct himself in his office based on how Vice President Bush had performed under President Reagan.

BOSTON With a *New York Times* best-selling criticism of the way he performed as vice president, have you heard from him since the book came out?

MEACHAM He knew before the book came out what was in it about Bush's thoughts on this subject. One thing I tried to do before I sent the final manuscript to the publisher was to give those who were possibly going to be unhappy about what was being said about them in the book a chance to respond to the criticism. Regardless of how they responded, I didn't change any of the criticisms in the book, but I wanted them to have a headsup and not have to learn about it for the first time after it came out.

Photo credit: Courtesy of the George Bush Presidential Library and Museum

BUSH'S LIFELONG COMPETITIVE FIRE AND ITS IMPACT ON HIS ASSESSMENT OF HIS ONE-TERM PRESIDENCY

BOSTON Part of George Bush's lifelong code has been maintaining his competitive drive—his all-consuming ambition to win and always be Number One. That went from being captain of the Yale baseball team, to tennis champion of his country club, to being the oldest guy to ever jump out of an airplane—while maintaining outward humility to camouflage his competitiveness. That code obviously took Bush all the way to the presidency, yet in your book you say that when you interviewed him, he "felt like an asterisk," and believed he had a failed presidency.

Is there a moral to this story about having a lifelong obsession to be Number One, and then constantly succeeding in achieving that goal, and yet in the end, where does all that Number One recognition get you, if you think you're a failure?

MEACHAM I think his assessment of his presidency has now changed a little bit since he said what he said in those interviews several years ago, which are quoted in the book. When I was with him last year in College Station, at the twenty-fifth anniversary of his inauguration, there was a lot of reminiscing going on about his presidency. We were standing in the corner and I asked him, "How does it feel?" He replied, "It's hard to believe, but it seems to me that it's kinder and gentler all over the place."

I will say, to rephrase your very erudite question, writing this book seemed a little bit like writing a biography of Dana Carvey. "Not gonna do it". Only George Herbert Walker Bush could produce an afternoon like I had this past summer where, in the course of one hour, I had three phone calls fact checking things. One was from Dick Cheney, one from Henry Kissinger, and one from Dana Carvey, who spoke to me in Bush's voice—so it *may* have been the president on the line.

I think that the moral of George Bush's story is that he was always driven to win, driven to compete, driven to serve. To serve, you had to succeed, and to succeed, that meant someone else had to lose. That was just fine with him. The loss of a second term was devastating and catastrophic emotionally. He said it was "ghastly." There are those who believe that he didn't really snap out of it until George W. Bush became Governor Bush down here, two years later in 1994. His brother, Jonathan, told me that he thought President Bush was depressed when he saw him in Houston after 41 had just left the White House.

The moral is—if you want a smooth ride, politics is not the business to go into. Ultimately, George H.W. Bush knows that. Any man who was at 89% in his approval ratings after the first Gulf War in January 1991, and ended up having only 37% of the country wanting him to keep his job in November 1992, understands that things can change rapidly in politics.

BUSH 41 AND HIS "KINDER GENTLER" APPROACH TO WORKING WITH BOTH SIDES OF CONGRESS' AISLE

BOSTON A big part of President Bush's success in working both sides of Congress came about because throughout his presidency, he created a "kinder and gentler" culture in Washington—doing things like hosting Democrats inside and outside the White House, playing paddleball at the House gym, etc.

Is it possible for a president in the twenty-first century to create a kinder and gentler culture given how much polarization and discord there is now?

MEACHAM It's possible, though obviously it's more difficult. In fact, it became more difficult during President Bush's term for three reasons. First, the rise of freelance partisanship made it hard to maintain any sort of equilibrium for governance. If you're looking for the "rosebud" moment that produced what we're now seeing in the 2016 presidential campaign, watch the footage of George H.W. Bush, Bob Dole, George Mitchell, and Tom Foley, going out into the Rose Garden to announce the 1990 budget agreement, while Newt Gingrich went out the other door of the White House on his way up to Capitol Hill where he was greeted by his supporters, (I reiterate: *his* supporters, not George Bush's supporters), who held a rally supporting Gingrich for his having rebelled against the president for having broken the "read my lips; no new taxes" pledge.

That kind of freelance reflexive partisanship was anathema to Bush. It wasn't part of his ambient reality. Newt Gingrich built his movement by giving speeches covered by C-SPAN to an empty House chamber. He would go to the chamber late at night and just talk. The cameras never panned the room, so television viewers didn't realize he was only talking to the camera, though it

allowed him to talk to the country. This rise in freelance partisanship led by Gingrich caused the press to talk less about a politician's supporters and more about his donors. The rise of the phrase "donor class" is particularly important, and it began to happen during the 1990-1992 time frame.

The second reason for the decline of the "kinder, gentler" political culture was the rise of the twenty-four-hour news cycle. President Bush did not have to deal with the internet, but he did have to deal with CNN and the explosion of talk shows—Rush Limbaugh and other talk radio figures—who for two hours a day, (or however long their programs were), needed controversy. The never-ending news cycle was a machine that needed the gasoline of controversy. A program can't attract viewers by supporting an administration whose essential compass was a moderate conservative "Eisenhower Republican" compass.

That's a key thing to understand about George H.W. Bush. He was not a "moderate," in the sense we use that term today. He was a moderate conservative—like Dwight Eisenhower, Gerald Ford, and Ronald Reagan.

Being a moderate conservative means George Bush did not define his identity with the belief that conservative principles should be used to advance a more active agenda. He was very much a traditional conservative in that he accepted the world as he found it, and attempted to reform it modestly as best he could. In many ways, George H.W. Bush was a more classically conservative figure than Ronald Reagan, though it's impossible to imagine talking in terms of a "Bush revolution." A Reagan revolution makes all the sense in the world, but not a Bush revolution.

The third thing that changed the state of our political culture during Bush's presidency was the rise of what I call "confessional politics"—the idea that every emotion a politician can manufacture inside his body should be put on display for public consumption. Bill Clinton was the master of this.

A scene on this subject moved me so much I put it in the book's prologue. George H.W. Bush and Barbara lost their daughter, Robin, to leukemia in 1953. In about 1987, while he was vice president, he was being shown into a children's leukemia ward in Krakow during an overseas visit. He realized where he was, and the press pool was standing behind him. He immediately began to tear up as he saw the children with leukemia, but he didn't turn around. He knew that if he did, with tears in his eyes, the story of his visit to the hospital would have become about him and not about the children. Now I know a lot of politicians, and I like most of them. I admire them for going into the arena and attempting (by and large) to make the life of the nation better; but I don't know many of them who would not have turned around to show their tears to the cameras. The essence of George Bush is that he was not going to detract the attention away from those children.

BUSH'S PROBLEMS WITH REPUBLICANS ON THE FAR RIGHT

BOSTON With respect to the freelance partisanship led by Gingrich during Bush's presidency, would it be accurate to say that Bush 41 had more problems with the Republicans on the far right than he did with the Democrats?

MEACHAM He certainly had more intractable ones. Chase Untermeyer (who's here in the audience today) is the Samuel Pepys of Reagan and Bush's Washington, and has published three volumes of George Bush's diaries, which I highly recommend. Chase worked for Vice President Bush early on, and the first volume is called "When Things Went Right," and it was incredibly valuable to me.

In the diary is a description of a scene in 1981 when an invitation to the Conservative Political Action Committee

National Convention had just come in. Bush looked at it, said, "Well, I guess we should go, but we realize that I've been doing this for thirty years, and the nuts are never going to be for me." Going back to 1963, in Mrs. Bush's diary, she said, "the nuts will never love him," about her husband. That caused her husband at one point to say, "Labels are for cans"—his attempt to try to avoid the kinds of unfair blanket assessments that those in the far right love to make.

The right wing of the Republican Party never fully trusted George Bush. They believed they were proven right in their maintaining distrust on the 26th of June, 1990, the Pearl Harbor Day abyss for the president, because it was the day when he broke the "Read my lips; no new taxes" pledge. On that day, everybody in the far right said, "See there! He wasn't an heir to Reagan."

The irony of this is that Ronald Reagan trusted and genuinely liked George Bush. 41 did what he did on increasing taxes partly because he had insurmountable obstacles in the Democratic-controlled Congress along with the Republican rebellion against him. Saddam invaded Kuwait in the middle of the budget negotiations, on the 2nd of August, 1990. Newt Gingrich went to President Bush that day and said, "I have a plan. Now that we're at war, you can renege on the "no new taxes" pledge again. If you do that, then all the Republican candidates can go into the mid-term elections in November, and tell the voters, "If you want a tax increase, vote for the Democrats; if you want to support the president and troops, support our budget."

That idea from Gingrich was beyond George Bush's realm of comprehension. The idea of playing partisan politics in a midterm election with troops in the field just didn't compute for him. So the Republican revolt led by Gingrich gave the Democrats an even stronger hand.

The final budget deal in 1990 actually included something that the original deal didn't. The original tax increase agreed to by Bush was only about a gas tax and a tobacco tax, but it left marginal income tax rates unchanged. The final deal raising marginal rates, and it came about only because the far right Republicans had bolted away from the president's original plan.

"READ MY LIPS: NO NEW TAXES"

BOSTON Regarding his famous "Read my lips: no new taxes" line in his speech at the 1988 Republican Convention, the violation of which played a part in his not being reelected in 1992, before that speech was given, Richard Darman, who would soon become Bush's budget director, said, "Take those lines out," because he didn't think freezing taxes for four years was going to be possible. Peggy Noonan had written the speech and she kept them in.

Did Bush 41 have an awareness that he was making a promise at the 1988 convention that he might well not be able to keep?

MEACHAM I talked to Michael Dukakis about the "no new taxes" pledge. He told me that during their post-election visit in December of 1988, something about the deficit had been in the headlines, and Bush said to Dukakis, within a month of beating him in the election, "Well, I certainly can't raise taxes in the first year". And Dukakis thought, "In the first year??? This guy just killed me with this promise not to increase taxes, and he was obviously just thinking of it as a smaller provisional promise."

It's probably the thing I hold President Bush most accountable for. In a fundamental act of presidential leadership, he did not believe words mattered as much as they do. He did not embrace the bully pulpit and the spirit of Theodore Roosevelt. When he broke the "no new taxes" pledge in June 1990, he didn't speak out in public about it for three days. He just thought he was doing the right thing by raising taxes in order to get a budget deal done, and believed that it would lead to the right result, so he wasn't going to explain it. It was a colossal political mistake.

Dan Quayle made a marvelous observation to me about this. Vice President Quayle said that President Bush always saw things through the lens of results orientation. Bush believed that if he achieved the right result, then people would ultimately be with him, and he didn't understand that he had to explain and convince them that he had done the right thing to get to the right result.

It's very hard to believe that a man who was in public life for half a century didn't recognize the importance of words and maintaining a strong line of communication with the voters. He first got involved in politics when he was one of the three Republicans in Midland, Texas in 1952, and acted as the Eisenhower publicity chairman that year in West Texas at a time when his father was the Republican US Senator from Connecticut. I asked him what the Eisenhower publicity chairman did in Midland in 1952, and he said, "I kept my head down." For a man who was in politics that long, for some reason, large acts of communication, such as when he spoke at the 1988 Republic Convention, were not George Bush's strong suit.

BUSH'S POLITICAL INDEPENDENCE

BOSTON To me, that's amazing, because he was obviously a brilliant guy, a very well-read guy, and history teaches everyone that to be a great leader, you've got to be a great communicator—Lincoln, FDR, Churchill and Reagan as the prime examples. How could he miss that essential point if he had any hopes of transforming things—or maybe the answer is that he didn't really want to transform things. He just kind of wanted to keep things going.

MEACHAM I'm with you until the very last point. He was a conservative centrist. He wanted to make things as conservative as possible but he did believe in the public sector.

I hope you'll appreciate this, I believe it explains the presidency. When George H.W.

Bush got elected to Congress in '66, who was the president of the United States? A Democrat from Texas. He got to Washington in '67 and in '68, and he voted with Lyndon Johnson 53% of the time. Let me say that again. A Republican from Houston voted with a Democratic president 53% of the time. Then, Richard Nixon became president in January of 1969, and Bush served under Nixon as president the same amount of time he served under Johnson. The percentage of the time he voted with Nixon, a president from his own party, skyrocketed to 55%.

What does that tell you? It tells you that George Bush came of age in a political universe where people actually thought about what they were voting on and actually thought it was a good idea to work with the president on issues where you agreed with him. So he voted with Johnson on the Vietnam War, on foreign policy, on a few domestic issues, and he voted against him on most domestic policy issues.

He went to Washington at a time when presidents were not demonized reflexively. I'm not saying it was Valhalla then. I'm not saying that this was some sort of magical kingdom forty years ago; but the reality was that George Herbert Walker Bush came of political age at a time when you cooperated with the other side if you thought the other side had a point. He expected that to happen when he became president, and what happened? His own party walked out the front door on him. When he announced the budget deal, what happened? Newt Gingrich, the House Minority Whip, said, "I can't back it," and he left the White House. The next time you see 41, ask him about that. He's still mad because it was just beyond him. He wouldn't have done that to a Democrat, and the idea that a Republican leader would walk out on a Republican president was just anathema to him. So the rise of reflexive partisanship in his presidency was one of the things that surprised him the most about being president.

BUSH'S FOREIGN POLICY AND HIS ADVISORY TEAM

BOSTON Bush 41 executed a highly successful foreign policy during his four years, which Henry Kissinger has said were the most tumultuous four years in our history since World War II—the high points being Tiananmen Square; the end of the Cold War; the unification of Germany; and, of course, the Gulf War's removal of Iraqi troops from Kuwait.

How much of President Bush's success in foreign policy do you attribute to his Secretary of State James Baker?

MEACHAM A huge amount, as President Bush 41 would be the first to acknowledge if he were sitting here. He would say he had an amazing team—Secretary Baker, Brent Scowcroft, Dick Cheney, Colin Powell, and Bob Gates who was Deputy National Security Advisor at the time. He was very well served by an unusually harmonious team.

One of the quickest ways to learn to hate someone is not marriage, but by becoming the National Security Advisor and then have to deal with the Secretary of State. These are epic rivalries. Whether it's Cyrus Vance and Zbigniew Brzezinski or William Rogers and Henry Kissinger, that's the way it has almost always gone; but Brent Scowcroft and James Baker made a pact that worked for them and Scowcroft was brilliant about it.

Baker had been Bush's first appointment announced here in Houston the day after the 1988 election. Scowcroft, who had been President Ford's National Security Advisor, had first gotten to know Bush as the Director of the Central Intelligence Agency. They had come to like and appreciate each other, but Scowcroft knew who the senior foreign policy partner in the administration was going to be—James A. Baker III. In what I consider to be a brilliant diplomatic move—Scowcroft went to Baker and said, "You're the senior guy. I'm not going to go on television or talk publicly about foreign policy unless you give the okay." It was such an un-Washington thing to do that it took Baker aback. After a month or two, Baker said, "Brent, do whatever you want to do." So there was extreme harmony and stability on that team.

From 1970 until he got elected president in 1988, George Bush focused mainly on foreign policy in his career. He spent four years in the House (from the Seventh District here), but then he was at the UN; then chairman of the Republican Party during Watergate (which was a great lesson in diplomacy, or at least diplomatic survival); then envoy to China; then director of the CIA; and then vice president of the United States.

President Reagan depended on him for two things chiefly. One was to perform the political chores often associated with the vice presidency, but the other was foreign policy. I have a whole chapter in the book on Vice President Bush's going to Western Europe and selling them on the need to deploy the Pershing II weapon system at a critical moment in the Cold War. Though skeptical at first, the Europeans finally agreed to it. This prompted *The Washington Post*, (not exactly a pro-Reagan, pro-Bush publication), to publish an editorial when Vice President Bush returned, the headline of which was, "George Did It." And *he* had done it.

So during his presidency, George Bush was very much in charge of George Bush's foreign policy. In fact, on matters related to China, the people around him used to joke that Bush might as well have been the State Department's Desk Officer on China. He just loved dealing with every aspect of the job—large or small.

I don't say this in any way to minimize Secretary Baker's or General Scowcroft's role. I've seen both of them recently, and blessedly, they are both in amazing health. Apparently one key to long life is to have a stressful professional life, so y'all are doing pretty well. Good luck. Richard Nixon

couldn't have done what he did without Kissinger. Baker was essential to President Bush, but 41 was very much in charge of his own foreign policy.

BOSTON History shows that there are always plenty of brilliant people involved in America's foreign policy, but what was unusual in the Bush 41 administration was how well they worked together.

MEACHAM Absolutely. Dean Atchison once said that the subtitle of every Washington memoir should be, "If Only They'd Listened to Me." No one ever comes out second best in their own anecdote. It just doesn't happen. So it was highly unusual for the Bush foreign policy leaders to function as smoothly as they did. Reagan went through something like six National Security Advisors, and two Secretaries of State, the first being Al Haig, who had a hard time working well with anyone.

The way his team worked together is a tribute to President Bush. That type of collaborative spirit comes from the top. Bush 41 wanted a harmonious team, and he got it.

BUSH AND THE GULF WAR

BOSTON President Bush has always acknowledged that his passion while acting as the nation's chief executive was foreign policy, not domestic policy, which had a lot to do with the fact that in foreign policy, he had much less involvement with Congress; and throughout his four year presidency, both houses were controlled by the Democrats.

His aversion to confrontation with Congress was so extreme that during the days leading up to the Gulf War, he seriously considered bypassing Congress in committing our country to war, which he acknowledged more than once would have exposed him to impeachment, and yet he was still going to do it.

Had he lost his mind?

MEACHAM No. He did what he believed was necessary. By the 5th of August 1990, when he said, "This will not stand," after Iraq invaded Kuwait, he had decided that it would require military action to get Saddam out of Kuwait. His heart was into diplomacy. I think Jim Baker did a masterful job in those months until the war began on the 13th of January, 1991. What Bush said about impeachment was that if Congress did not vote to approve the use of military force and pass a resolution to support the UN resolutions, then he was going to send our troops into battle anyway; and if it had gone badly, he expected to be impeached. Daniel Inouye, Senator from Hawaii, went to President Bush and said, "If you don't get Congressional authorization and we start to lose a lot of boys in the desert, then you're going to be impeached." Regardless of that, President Bush was determined to do it anyway.

The issue of dealing with Iraq while it was led by Saddam Hussein during the presidencies of Bush 41 and 43 is very important historically and also it's relevant to the Shakespearian nature of the way we sometimes think about the Bush family. There was a George Bush who was very unilateral about Iraq, who talked about Saddam Hussein as "the epitome of evil," and that George Bush was George Herbert Walker Bush. So, father and son George Bush were not as far apart in their reactions to Iraq as the popular narrative sometimes has it.

ROSS PEROT AND THE 1992 ELECTION

BOSTON Regarding Bush 41's defeat in the 1992 election. I suspect he believes that the main reason he lost was because of Ross Perot. That's what James Baker told me when I interviewed him last week.

Does Bush 41 acknowledge that it works both ways—and that the main reason his son won the election was because of Ralph Nader?

MEACHAM No, he doesn't realize that a third-party candidate caused his son to become president. I'm sure that idea has never crossed his mind.

Let me go back to the '92 election. With immense respect to President Bush and Secretary Baker, with whom I've talked through this on several occasions, I don't believe Perot cost him the election. Perot was definitely an exacerbating factor.

But if a person was so angry in 1992 that he was going to vote for Ross Perot, knowing that Perot was certainly not going to get elected, I don't think the Perot voter's second choice was going to be George Herbert Walker Bush. I know Secretary Baker and President Bush both disagree with me about this, but the political science, such as it is, supports what I'm saying.

SIGNIFICANCE OF THE 1992 ELECTION AND HOW BUSH FITS INTO TODAY'S REPUBLICAN PARTY

BOSTON Let's talk about that '92 presidential election where Bush, the war hero, lost to Clinton, the draft dodger. You said last night at the George W. Bush Presidential Library that the twentieth century, as we know it, ended when that election result happened.

Did the 1992 election establish that then and for the foreseeable future in America in the twenty-first century, "Duty, Honor, Country" no longer matters to the majority of voters; while showmanship in the media age is more important than character and integrity?

MEACHAM That's a risk. I'm not willing to say that it's happening, but I think that given the political climate of the moment, we have to be incredibly vigilant, as people engaged in the political process, to make sure that disregarding "Duty, Honor, Country" does *not* become the ultimate reality.

George Bush was the last president of the World War II generation, and Bill

Clinton was obviously the first Baby Boomer. They were shaped by different values and different experiences, and brought different things to the job.

If I may wander into current politics for a second, I think the Republican field for 2016 (at least if you look at the polls), does not necessarily reflect our traditional understanding of the kinds of candidates who seek office. We associate President Bush's generation with a sense of putting the country before its own political interest, and nobody did that more than he did. Three examples of that come to mind.

He ran for the US Senate in 1964, three years after John Tower had broken the barrier and become the first Republican senator to win in Texas since Reconstruction. During the '64 campaign, Bush said that he opposed the Civil Rights Act of 1964, which ultimately has become a piece of the American canon. He opposed it because at the time, he was a Goldwater Republican running in Texas. Then, after losing the '64 election to Ralph Yarborough, he ran for and won the US House seat for the Seventh District of Houston in 1966. While he was a Congressman in 1968 what did he do? He voted for the Open Housing Act. He voted to remove racial discrimination from the sale of all residences. After that vote, he went down to Memorial High School in Houston and faced a furious crowd. His constituents did not want open housing for all races. They said, "We didn't send you up to Washington to do this kind of liberal thing." So he said one thing to try to get elected, but once he had power, he did the right thing.

He put the national interest over his own political interest again in connection with what he did about his pledge to the Republican Convention in 1988 when he said, "Read my lips. No new taxes." He made that statement at the convention to hold the Republican Party's conservative base together in 1988. Two years later, he recognized what the country needed in order to get a budget passed that would

address the Reagan deficits, and that required him to give in on a couple of the tax increases. He knew that increasing taxes after promising *not* to increase taxes might cost him reelection. In fact, he recognized that in his diary and letters; but he put the national interest ahead of his own political interest in a very, very direct way.

Finally, he put his country over politics in the way he attempted to govern in the midst of dealing with an increasingly divided Congress. Let's be honest. The way the media goes after people in politics is not exactly a game of cricket or lawn darts. It's more like war. But what did he do when he became president? He actually created a kinder and gentler political culture, where he hosted Democrats inside and outside of the White House, and still used the House gym to play paddle ball, and got in the sauna with House Ways and Means Chairman Dan Rostenkowski.

BOSTON A picture of that is *not* in the book.

MEACHAM Vin Weber, the former Congressman from Minnesota, told me a great story about how President Bush tried to maintain civility and respect for those Republicans having a different political perspective. Newt Gingrich had just gotten elected House Minority Whip, and everybody was saying, "Gingrichism is on the rise. Reflexive partisanship is on the rise." So what did President Bush do? He invited Gingrich and Vin Weber, (who had run Gingrich's campaign in the Southern caucuses and, as Vin told me, "No one had ever invited the House Whip's campaign manager to the White House—only Bush would think to do that") to the White House. So they were sitting upstairs, having a beer in the Residence, and Gingrich and Weber could tell that there was something Bush was not quite saying. So Weber asked, "Mr. President, just tell us. What is your biggest worry about us?" This was in the spring of 1989. Bush replied without hesitating, "I worry that your idealism may get in the way of what I think of as sound governance." Weber said he knew that only George H.W. Bush would have used the word "idealism". He didn't say your "nuttiness," or "purity," or "ideology." He gave them credit for their idealism—essentially saying, "These are your ideas. You believe we shouldn't cooperate. I believe we should."

Then in 1990, after Gingrich refused to agree to the budget deal President Bush had negotiated, Weber said that this split among the Republicans was the very thing Bush was concerned about when they had that earlier White House conversation.

My sense of George H.W. Bush is that he was a one-term president for many reasons. One is that he was living on borrowed historical time. We hadn't had twelve consecutive years of one party rule, with the exception of Roosevelt and Truman, since the founders. So the American people historically like switching out the party of their president every eight years. The other main reason for his being president only one term was because of his insistence on putting the national interest over politics. I call President Bush "the Last Gentleman." It was a different kind of politics then. It was a politics where personal relationships mattered.

BUSH'S PERCEPTION OF HIS LEGACY

BOSTON Although Bush 41 lost the '92 election and thereby became a one-term president, since leaving office, his political legacy has done nothing but go up—such that he and James K. Polk are regarded as the two greatest one-term presidents in American history.

With this type of recognition, is he satisfied with his place in history?

MEACHAM I don't think he thinks about it very much. He doesn't like talking about the "L" word—legacy—or the "D" word—dynasty. There are a lot of character words he just doesn't like to talk about very much. He believes he attempted to

serve his country from his eighteenth birthday forward as best he could. On June 12, 1942, he turned eighteen and joined the United States Navy right after graduating from high school. From that point forward, with the possible exception of the time he spent building an oil business over twelve to fourteen years before he became Harris County Republican Chairman in the spring of 1962, he always attempted to put the country first.

The fact that he was a one-term president reflects his being part of a historical aberration. We had not had more than eight years of one party White House rule since Roosevelt and Truman, so Bush was living on borrowed historical time by being a Republican president from '88 to '92 after Reagan's presidency from '80-'88. It's fascinating that Bush's stature fell as low as it did with both the media and the public in 1992 until he lost the election to Bill Clinton. After the election on November 3, 1992, his numbers immediately started going up. It was as though we had a fever about him and then it broke. Only after it broke did we realize how good he had been as president. He left Washington with an approval rating of about 51%—twice what Harry Truman had when he left Washington.

My own view is that he packed eight years of action into four years. You mentioned several of them—Tiananmen Square, the fall of the Berlin Wall, the end of the Soviet Union, the unification of Germany, the first Gulf War, the negotiation of NAFTA, the passing of the Americans with Disabilities Act, the passing of the Clean Air Act, the 1990 budget deal—which Bill Clinton will tell you at length (which is redundant I realize!) set the terms of prosperity for the 1990s. The list of the major events of his presidency just goes on and on. As you quoted Henry Kissinger a minute ago, "It was the most tumultuous period in our history since Truman.

BUSH 41'S CRITICISM OF BUSH 43'S ADMINISTRATION

BOSTON Which brings us to the point that's been the subject of virtually every article written about your book. That point is that during Bush 43's presidency, Bush 41 never criticized any aspect of his son's performance, yet in 2008-2010, as you interviewed him for the book, Bush Sr. was critical of Vice President Cheney's being too "iron ass" hawkish during his son's presidency and he even said that Cheney caused his son 43 to become too hawkish.

I tried to imagine you sitting there, Jon, and there was Father Bush criticizing his son, and you knew you were going to have to put that in the book. Were you shocked that Bush 41 would essentially violate his family loyalty code to support his son?

MEACHAM I'm not sure I accept the premise of that. I don't think he was violating a code. I think what he was doing, in response to questions I put to him, was reflecting as a former president on what he believed to be an overly hawkish tone—not actions, but tone—that he (41) believed had not served the president (43) well and that improper tone included his son's use of the phrase "axis of evil".

I think the two men were much closer in substance than we think. They were different in style and I think the context for him saying what you just described in the book was important. At the time of the interviews, it was during the last year of his son's administration and the first two years of the Obama administration. The context of what he said was more about the real conservative talk at that time about expanding the war on terror beyond Afghanistan and Iraq to possibly include Iran. What's important to remember is that I think he made these comments about Cheney because he wanted to make the point about what had occurred during the 2006-2008 time period—that force and diplomacy did not have to be competitive with one another, but

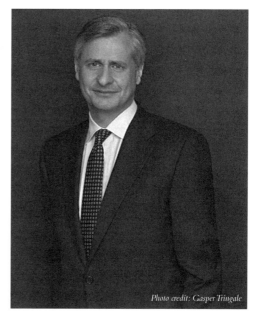

Photo credit: Gasper Tringale

Jon Meacham

should be complementary. Vice President Cheney was actually very pleased to be called an "iron ass" when I told him about 41's comment.

BOSTON It was a compliment.

MEACHAM Damn right. Liz Cheney said she was going to have "iron ass" t-shirts made up for the grandkids. I told her I wanted one.

The senior Bush did not think Cheney was in charge of his son's administration. He absolutely understood that George W. Bush was fully in charge. I would tell anybody in this room that I would defy anybody to spend three minutes with George W. Bush and not come away knowing that he is fully in charge of anything he wants to be in charge of. So it's a myth that Cheney was ever in charge and Bush 43 wasn't, and Bush 41 wasn't really saying that. What he was saying is that there were a lot of people around Cheney who were talking tough in kind of a swaggering culture that was centered around the office of the vice president, and George H.W. Bush did not think it served the president well.

BOSTON On the subject of *tone*, when the Berlin Wall fell down and the Cold War ended, as a matter of tone, George H.W. Bush did not gloat in any way. That produced all kinds of good results in maintaining a harmonious relationship with Gorbachev.

What do you think would have been the tone of Bush 43 and Cheney if they had been president and vice president during the fall of the Berlin Wall?

MEACHAM That's a great question. I don't know.

BOSTON Speculate.

MEACHAM Cheney was there in Bush 41's administration as the Secretary of Defense, and was more forward-leaning even then. Cheney had said on television that he thought Gorbachev was going to fall in 1989. In fact, during that year, after Cheney had said on a Sunday morning television talk show that he thought Gorbachev would be ousted soon. This caused Baker to call Scowcroft immediately and say, "Dump on Dick with all alacrity."

Here's the thing about the nuance that gets lost. There's the first term George W. Bush and the second term George W. Bush. During his second term, he had a lot more in common with his dad diplomatically than he did during his first term. So I think we need to give George W. Bush hypothetical credit to a hypothetical question, and say that, like his father, he himself would have put the interest of the country first and would not have, as President Bush 41 put it, "stuck it in Gorbachev's ear."

BOSTON Is it your perception that what's been revealed in your book about 41's thoughts on 43's presidency has damaged any relationships as among father, son, Cheney and Rumsfeld?

MEACHAM No, because everyone already knew there was not a good relationship

between Rumsfeld and 41. Rumsfeld has been the one person who put out a statement after the book came out, and he said, "President Bush is getting up in years." The phrase that President Bush uses in the book to describe both Rumsfeld and Cheney, "iron ass," has now become my contribution to the vernacular of American politics. I wrote 800 pages in this book and that's my sole contribution.

In fact, at the unveiling of Vice President Cheney's bust at the Capitol earlier this week, President Bush 43 said in his remarks to the crowd, "I told Dad I was coming for this ceremony, and he said to give his best to old iron ass!"

To be quite serious, I admire very much the way both President Bush 43 and Vice President Cheney responded to what was said about them in the book. They were both gentlemen about it. I also admire so much that President Bush 41 wanted his assessments to be on the historical record, because they make the record very clear about how he feels. He'd felt his son's administration was too swaggering and that Cheney and Rumsfeld had exacerbated an unfortunate tendency to talk and attempt to be too tough. If someone who he's criticized doesn't like his assessments, George H.W. Bush knows that truth is an absolute defense.

BOSTON We have time for one question from the audience.

THE BEST TIME IN BUSH 41'S LIFE

AUDIENCE MEMBER What do you think George H.W. Bush's favorite time was in his life—whether in his public career or his private career?

MEACHAM I think it was probably Friday, January 20, 1989 until the end of the one hundred hours when our ground forces finished the job in Kuwait with Operation Desert Storm. I think he loved the presidency in 1989 and 1990 and during the first couple of months in 1991.

After the Gulf War ended, he reached a discernable point at which he became despondent. He was as unsatisfied with the conclusion of the Gulf War as a lot of Americans were. What kind of a victory is it when the other guy is still in power? He never celebrated that even privately. He knew long before the pundits that the economy and domestic policy would decide the 1992 election. It's in his diary in March of 1991. I speculate in a sentence or two that part of the reason for why he felt such deep satisfaction over the way the Gulf War was carried out was that by his putting together a coalition of thirty-five nations on a limited mission to realize FDR's vision of a new world order after World War II but before the Cold War really got going. I think to some extent he knew at some psychological level (almost certainly unconsciously) that the work he was put on earth to do was done and I think he just never really got back in the game fully after the Gulf War.

I think his health mattered. He was diagnosed with Graves' disease in 1991, and his acuity went up and down. His energy levels were not what they once were. Bush was mentally and physically about fifty years old for a period of about fifteen years, and then he was sixty-five for about twenty years, and then when he turned eighty-five he became an old man. I first met him in 1998, so he would have been seventy-four, and he was like a thirty-five-year-old totally. So he's been kind of ageless in stages, but I think that the joy of the White House and the presidency was fully realized when he put together that amazingly successful coalition in the Gulf War. He was probably the happiest then, out of all his years in the White House as he remembered that for me during our interviews.

BOSTON I was hoping your answer was going to be that his happiest time was when he played baseball for Yale. He was the

captain of the team, went to the College World Series twice, and got to shake hands with Babe Ruth.

MEACHAM Can I get in one baseball story? I have three children—a thirteen-year-old, an eleven-year-old, and a seven-year-old. The seven-year-old thinks it's very odd that I've written a book about someone called George Jefferson. Sherman Helmsley didn't keep a diary, so—But my son and I were once with George H.W. Bush about five years ago. My son was probably eight at the time and we are big Yankee fans, and the president asked my son, "Who's your favorite player?" And my son said, "Derek Jeter." Then I said, "You know President Bush once met Babe Ruth." Then there was a 4-5 sentence exchange between 41 and my son about who was better—Babe Ruth or Lou Gehrig.

Who do you think George H.W. Bush was for? Answer: Gehrig because he showed up for work every day, was steadfast in his duty, wasn't flashy, never hot dogged it, and just did his job. Ruth was the big home run hitter, the glamor guy who was great. I've always thought that to some extent, Ronald Reagan is the Babe Ruth of modern American politics and George Bush is Lou Gehrig.

BOSTON There is no better way to end the program than with that comment. Thanks so much, Jon.

DAVID MARANISS won the Pulitzer Prize for national reporting for his work at *The Washington Post* covering presidential candidate Bill Clinton during the 1992 campaign. On top of that, he's a three-time Pulitzer finalist and the author of seven critically acclaimed, best-selling books—including *First In His Class: A Biography of Bill Clinton* (Simon & Schuster 1995). On September 8, 2015, I interviewed David on the subject of Bill Clinton in front of a group of friends at the Anne Wexler Briefing Room at the office of Wexler/Walker in Washington, DC.

"Bill Clinton is a remarkably astute person about everything in the world except himself. He could see the issue of the downside of combining political success, power, and sex very clearly as early as 1969 when Teddy Kennedy had his incident at Chappaquiddick, but when it came to his own behavior, he always had a blind spot." – **DAVID MARANISS**

CHAPTER 25

DAVID MARANISS

ON

Bill Clinton

ON THE CLINTONS' REFUSAL TO COOPERATE IN MARANISS' BIOGRAPHY OF BILL

BOSTON David, you won the Pulitzer in 1993, and *First In His Class* came out in 1995 during Bill Clinton's first term. In your preface, you mention that the Clintons refused to be interviewed for the book and also their aides were not helpful to you.

What's your best guess regarding why the Clintons refused to cooperate with you in the writing of this book?

MARANISS I did interview Bill Clinton eight times at length when he was a candidate during the 1992 campaign; but once I signed the contract to write the

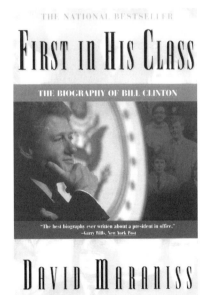

THE NATIONAL BESTSELLER

FIRST IN HIS CLASS

THE BIOGRAPHY OF BILL CLINTON

"The best biography ever written about a president in office."
–Garry Wills, New York Post

DAVID MARANISS

Courtesy of Simon & Schuster, Inc., New York, 1995

book, there was a two year period where he was first president-elect and then president for the first two years in office, where I had interviews with him set up several times, and at the last minute, his press secretary would call and say, "He's just not quite ready to talk with you."

Right before the book came out, but after I had finished writing it, I did an interview with Hillary Clinton in the White House for a piece I was writing in *The Washington Post*. She said, "David, I regret that we didn't talk to you, but our attorney, Robert Barnett, instructed us not to because he thought our being part of your book would potentially cause problems with what we'll put in our memoirs after we leave the White House."

I don't think that's really what happened, but I'm sure Barnett did tell them not to talk to me, though the notion that anything they would have told me would have competed with their own post-presidency memoirs is preposterous. Presidential memoirs sell regardless of what's in them and my biography covered completely different ground compared to what they were likely to put in their books. Maybe Barnett said what Hillary told me, but I think there were other reasons involved in their refusing to be interviewed for my book.

The most interesting thing that happened regarding a direct connection between my book and the Clintons came when Mike McCurry had just been appointed as Bill's press secretary right before the book came out. He called me then and said, "David, the president wants to know why he didn't talk to you first." I said, "Well, that's an interesting question, Mike. That's a good introduction for you in understanding the president. He didn't talk to me because he didn't want to talk to me. He didn't want a serious investigative journalist rooting around in his life right at the time he was in his early presidency." I'm sure Bill Clinton was just uncomfortable with the situation and what it might lead to. So, to answer your question, I think his refusal to

be interviewed for my book was because of timing and politics.

I didn't take it personally. The truth is I wanted to interview him for the book and I had many questions for him, but if he had spoken with me, it would have created other difficulties for me. It's always tough to write a biography of somebody who's alive. It's even more difficult to write a biography of someone who is alive and president of the United States.

My policy from the beginning of doing the research for my book was to treat him as though he was not available because he was president. Every day, every week, every month there's a different angle on him. He's up or he's down. There's a pressure in writing a political biography to address what's going on at that moment though you can't write that way for history. So the fact is I had to treat him as if he wasn't around and available.

The fact that I didn't interview him for *First in His Class* made writing it easier in some ways. I interviewed over 400 people for the book and got access to many primary documents he had written (letters, diaries, and so on), and this collection of information was probably a more accurate reflection of his life than what he might have tried to remember in an interview.

THE CLINTONS' FEEDBACK AFTER THE BOOK'S RELEASE

Once the book came out, and contained some unflattering parts about Bill Clinton in it—particularly about his draft avoidance as well as the sexual escapades—did you get any feedback from either him or Hillary about it?

MARANISS This actually has an interesting connection to Anne Wexler, whose conference room we're now sitting in. My book was the first serious biography ever written about Bill Clinton, but as I say in the introduction, it was not a book that was intended to be about his sex life. If the reader wants to dine on that part of his life, he should go elsewhere.

There are moments where the subject of our public figures' private lives presents a really difficult question to deal with in modern America's political culture. My decision in how much attention to give his private life was that I chose to write about it only when I saw an intersection between his political life and what he was doing outside his marriage.

One of the points where I did talk about it was in 1987, when he was considering running for president in the 1988 election, and he called all of his closest friends down to Little Rock for the announcement. The night before he planned to announce he was going to run, he met with his political advisor Betsy Wright, who eventually worked here at Wexler/Walker for a while and was a friend of Anne Wexler's. That night, Betsy went over a list of the women in his life who would be problematic for Bill Clinton if he ran, and they talked about how to deal with them. When I interviewed her, she told me about that conversation in detail.

A frustration I have to deal with is that when I write, my goal is to explain someone in the context of the fullness of their life. The book came out and, of course, everybody focused on those three pages of the book that covered what was said in Betsy's conversation with him. That's the way our culture works, and there was nothing I could do about it.

The day that story broke, I refused to talk to the press. My publisher didn't like my doing that, and I don't know whether I made the right choice or not, but for my own sense of integrity, I wanted the book to be perceived as something more than what he had done in his private life, but in any case, the story of that conversation came out.

The story about Betsy Wright's meeting Bill Clinton was something that infuriated Hillary for one reason and infuriated her husband for another reason, so the Clintons immediately called Betsy over to the White House. The next thing that happened was

Betsy issued a non-denial denial saying that I might have misinterpreted what she told me. So that became the story of the day and Betsy denied what I had said about her conversation with Bill in 1987 and the White House also denied the conversation's ever taking place.

Those were the days when you still had answering machines with tape recorders on them. At 2:00 a.m. that night, Betsy Wright called my phone at *The Washington Post* and said, "David, they pressured me into doing this. I'm sorry. What I told you was the truth." She then went on to describe some more things. So the next day, Mike McCurry was about to start his daily press briefing and he called me. I told him, "Mike, believe me, you don't want to deny Betsy's 1987 conversation with Bill Clinton again." So he backed off on that.

I later found out that President Clinton would actually read aloud parts of the book to his staff. He enjoyed certain parts of it and he didn't enjoy other parts of it. I can't worry about that. I just have to write what I consider to be the truth and put it in context. Because of the temporal nature of the media and politics and how everything is judged superficially, the storm of that moment passed and people soon saw the book for what it really was.

THE MIRACLE OF BILL CLINTON IN LIGHT OF HIS GENETICS

BOSTON Bill Clinton was the product of two very racy and unaccomplished people. His mother Virginia loved to smoke, drink, gamble, make herself up garishly, flirt, and she outlived three husbands. His probable father, William Blythe, was a traveling salesman who had been married five times when he died in a car wreck at age 28 before Bill Clinton was born.

So from a genetic standpoint, it's easy to understand where Bill got his charismatic sex appeal; but can you speculate as to where in Bill Clinton's genetics he got his off-the-charts high IQ brilliance and his spectacular political networking skills?

MARANISS When you study high achievers, it's not uncommon to find that they sometimes come out of nowhere from a genetic standpoint. In terms of his IQ, it was highest in the area of emotional intelligence. He does have a near photographic memory. He can meet someone who he hasn't seen in twenty years and say, "Let's call your parents," and he would remember their phone number. He has that kind of memory.

You alluded to his probable father, William Jefferson's Blythe, who was married to Bill's mother, whose name was Virginia Cassidy at that point. They had only been together for a month before he was sent off to war and they spent very little time together. Bill was then born a month early, which explains away the fact that nine months before his birth, Bill Blythe was in the military outside the country. There are people in Hope, Arkansas, who are still curious about whether Bill was Blythe's progeny. I don't want to speculate too much about that aspect of it, but even assuming William Jefferson Blythe was Bill Clinton's father, it's not uncommon for genius to come out of unlikely parents.

BOSTON Regarding genetics in another area, you say that Bill Clinton and his half-brother, Roger (who's a rock musician, a college dropout, and been in prison for selling cocaine), are two sides of the same coin. How so?

MARANISS Well, it's clearly their mother—largely. And Roger and Bill Clinton were both performers. They both have certain tendencies toward addiction. When his brother Roger was arrested and convicted on drug charges, Bill actually went and talked to some social workers about addiction and his own difficulties there. So they had certain commonalities, but Bill was the one who had all the other positive attributes. I've always described Clinton as

an exaggeration of all of us—for better or worse—with a huge appetite for life in every possible respect.

IMPACT OF BILL CLINTON'S UNUSUAL FAMILY LIFE

BOSTON I love that image—the big appetite for life. Your book mentions how he would get an apple and devour it in four bites, including the core. Now that's an appetite!

You say on page 21 that central to understanding Bill Clinton is recognizing that in his formative youth, he had essentially two actively involved mother figures—his mother and his grandmother—for whom he was the psychological center of their lives; and also that he had no real father figure.

Explain that. How did having two mother figures and no father figure impact Bill's character and personality?

MARANISS He was born in Hope, Arkansas—a small town in southwest Arkansas—in August 1946. When he was brought home, his mother was living with her parents, and his supposed father had already been killed. Virginia was the mother and Edith was the grandmother, and they both competed for little Billy's attention. It was not a particularly healthy relationship between the two of them. In many ways, Edith wanted to be Bill's mother even though she was the grandmother, and they both worshipped him.

There were periods during his first five years of life when Virginia, his mother, went away for many months to study in nursing school, ultimately becoming a nurse anesthetist. During that period, Edith was Bill's primary caregiver. There was always this sort of tension or jealously between the two of them over Billy. At the same time, he had no father in the house until Virginia married Roger Clinton, which came a little later. Bill's grandfather Eldridge was a nice older man who ran a grocery store in Hope, but he was not a particularly strong force in the house. So from the very beginning—and you find this fairly commonly with success-ful politicians—early success came from the women in their lives, because that's where all the positive energy came from.

BOSTON You mentioned Virginia's second husband, a car salesman and bootlegger named Roger Clinton. He was an alcoholic who abused Virginia physically and verbally in the house where Bill Clinton grew up. H.W. Brands in his new biography of Ronald Reagan says that a huge key to understanding Reagan's personality comes from knowing he grew up with an alcoholic father.

To understand Bill Clinton's personality, is it important to know that he grew up in a house with an alcoholic stepfather?

MARANISS Absolutely. I think that a lot of the characteristics you see in Bill Clinton throughout the rest of his life in some ways were shaped by those childhood years when he had to deal with an alcoholic stepfather. There's a theory about children of alcohol-ics to the effect that someone in that family often becomes sort of the "family hero." Bill Clinton saw himself in that respect, trying to go out and achieve in order to redeem the family, and bridge the difficult tensions within the home.

You see in Bill Clinton the capacity to try to please everyone. I think it's shaped in part by those experiences growing up in a house with his stepfather. I think also in Bill Clinton there was a tendency later to just push past all the unpleasantness in his family life by becoming "compartmental-ized," which is almost a cliché. Many of his childhood friends didn't even know he had troubles at home—or that his stepfather was an alcoholic. You can see three major characteristics that came from responding to growing up with this stepfather: trying to please people; being able to bridge gaps by compartmentalizing, and having the desire to achieve. All three came in part because of his circumstances at home while he was growing up.

Photo credit: William J. Clinton Presidential Library

BOSTON On a possibly related note, both Reagan and Clinton had the political gift of being able to communicate optimism to the masses regardless of how bad things were.

Does this capacity for projecting extreme optimism in dire circumstances have any connection to growing up in a house with an abusive alcoholic stepfather?

MARANISS To some degree I think it does. Like I said, part of that has to do with the desire to go out and achieve and to com-partmentalize and not show the difficulties within. So Bill Clinton had to present to the outside world his positive face, even though he had all this tension and difficulty inside his home. In his memoir, he talked about the inner turmoil he had growing up which he didn't show to the public. I assumed that to be the case, but didn't know it was as strong as he described it in his book. I have always spoken of Bill Clinton as someone who could wake up every day, forgive him-self, forgive everybody else, and go from there; and I think he developed that capacity because of his childhood.

BILL CLINTON'S UNRIVALED POLITICAL SKILLS

BOSTON A few years ago, you wrote a biography of Roberto Clemente, a man born with the skills to become a consummate baseball player which he obviously developed to the fullest. As I read *First In His Class*, it seemed to me that Bill Clinton was born with the skills to become the consummate politician, which he developed to the fullest beginning as early as the second grade. His second grade teacher said, "This kid's going to be president." From early on, he has bowled people over with his people skills, his oratorical skills, his sheer brilliance at synthesizing vast amounts of information, his boundless energy, his unbridled ambition—and he had all these talents operating at a high octane, non-stop level before he was ten years old.

Has America ever had a better natural born pure politician than Bill Clinton?

MARANISS Well, I'm not going to say "ever," but I would say that in the course of the 40 years I've covered politics, I've never seen anybody like him in those regards, and he had it from the beginning. His mother was telling everybody in first grade that he was going to be president someday. In second grade, his second grade teacher actually talked about it, and so did his other teachers going up through high school, where he won so many elections for offices that the principal finally had to stop him from running for senior class president.

When he went to Boy's Nation in the summer of 1963, all the other young men from around the country who I interviewed described to me how it was Billy Clinton who raced off the buses when they got to the White House and made sure he was first in line to shake John F. Kennedy's hand and get his picture taken with the president. So everyone could see his political ability and desire to win people over beginning at an incredibly early age.

Besides having a combination of emotional intelligence and the desire to win people over, he also had great organizational skills. Before he ever ran for public office in Arkansas, he had an index card file containing thousands of names of people who might help him along the way. His being a great campaign organizer along with being a great campaigner is a rare combination.

BOSTON In fact, regarding his having a political network early on, one of the points you made in the book came during the 1972 presidential election when George McGovern was the Democratic nominee. Bill Clinton and Taylor Branch (who later became a Pulitzer Prize-winning civil rights historian) were in charge of the McGovern campaign for the State of Texas and they lived in Austin. Of course, the campaign for the Democrats that year was hopeless and McGovern got blown out. You point out that from his McGovern experience, Clinton realized that a successful politician must have a network and one of the many reasons McGovern lost was because he really had no network. By golly, that was not going to happen to Bill Clinton with his system of 10,000 index cards!

MARANISS Absolutely. Clinton learned a lot from working in losing campaigns. In the McGovern campaign, the lessons were two-fold: one was the organizational aspect of it; and the other was recognizing what it would take for someone with essentially progressive leanings and instincts to prevail in the modern political culture. He saw the mistakes McGovern was making and some of the places where the McGovern ideology wasn't going to work for Democrats as of 1972.

BILL CLINTON THE SEX ADDICT

BOSTON You discuss throughout your book (as we mentioned a few minutes ago), how Bill Clinton has always had a voracious appetite for all aspects of life, which has its disadvantages when it includes a voracious appetite for sex with mass quantities of women.

On page 218, you mention a comment he made in the aftermath of Ted Kennedy's incident at Chappaquiddick, when Clinton said to a friend, "Politics gives guys so much power and such big egos that they tend to behave badly toward women. I hope I never get into that."

Obviously, as a politician, Bill Clinton did get into that. While he was the governor of Arkansas during the 1983-85 time period, a state trooper on Clinton's security staff acknowledged that he was asked to solicit one hundred different women for the governor—essentially a new woman every week for two years.

Is it accurate to describe Bill Clinton as a prototypical sex addict who, as far as anyone knows, has never sought treatment for it?

MARANISS He did consider treatment at one point, after seeing his half-brother go through his drug problems, when he spoke with people about addictions and it was clear that he was talking about his own sex addiction.

At that time, he was trying to deal with his whole family's situation and it's as close as I could get to seeing that he was at least starting to address his own addiction, though obviously he didn't succeed at it.

Regarding what he said about Teddy Kennedy, in my opinion, Bill Clinton is a remarkably astute person about everything in the world except himself. He could see that larger issue of the downside of combining political success, power, and sex very clearly as early as 1969, but when it came to his own behavior, he always had a blind spot.

It's not in the book, but the first time I ever interviewed him for a story about his 1992 presidential campaign was right before the Gennifer Flowers story broke, which was the first of the campaign stories alleging his sexual misbehavior. We were in the backseat of a limousine somewhere in rural Maryland driving to an event. I brought

up Gary Hart and how he had been a very talented person who disappointed a lot of people because of his behavior. Clinton completely dismissed Hart in a discouraging way and I was a little confused by his answer. Then two days later, the Gennifer Flowers broke.

BILL CLINTON'S AVOIDANCE OF MILITARY SERVICE AND THE MEDIA'S COVERAGE OF IT

BOSTON One of the major focuses of your book is describing what Bill Clinton had to do to avoid military service during the Vietnam War which was obviously true of many young, well-educated men his age during the late 1960s. As you point out, Bill knew that being perceived as a draft dodger would surely hurt his chances for later political success, so he moved very carefully in playing the draft avoidance game "like a chess player"—to use your term.

Once his political career began in Arkansas, you recognize that he clearly misrepresented the specifics of his draft avoidance journey in order to create a more positive but inaccurate spin on why he never served in the military or the reserves.

Did Dan Rather and CBS News ever pursue the story of how Bill Clinton avoided the draft like they did in pursuing the story of President Bush 43 and his time in the Texas National Guard?

MARANISS During the campaign in 1992, the first story broke in *The Wall Street Journal* about the letter Bill Clinton wrote to the ROTC at the University of Arkansas. From that moment on, there were plenty of stories about Bill Clinton and the draft, so there certainly was a great pursuit of that story by many in the media.

In attempting to understand Bill Clinton's efforts to stay out of the military, I had the luxury of having two years when I got to interview everybody, and get all the documents, and I tried to lay it out in a careful fashion about what Bill Clinton really did and the way he maneuvered in order to avoid military service. First of all, as you say, in the larger context, hundreds of thousands of young men didn't want to serve in Vietnam and figured out ways to avoid that. Either they didn't believe in the war or else they were acting out of fear or self-interest, and usually it was some kind of combination of the above. That's the way human nature is, and Bill Clinton was in that category.

He didn't believe in the war; he didn't want to fight in it; he had other things he wanted to do; but unlike almost every other one of the millions of similarly situated young men of his generation, he also had his eye on a larger prize in the future. So he was very careful and tried to calculate every step of the way to make it appear that he wasn't specifically avoiding the draft though he would find a way to end up not being drafted. Two-thirds of the way through that story, he lucked out in terms of his getting a high draft lottery number and that resolved a lot of the issues. Before that point, he definitely played it very carefully and effectively so that it would probably look as though he wasn't trying to avoid the draft, but he was, and it wasn't until the 1992 campaign that the story actually broke which explained how he did it.

BOSTON My question is really about the media and bias, or lack of bias. Obviously, the way Dan Rather and CBS handled the Bush 43/Texas National Guard story led to Rather's being fired for shoddy reporting. I remember having an awareness before I read your book (which lays it out in great detail), that Bill Clinton had done something to avoid going to Vietnam.

So since you've been a journalist for quite some time, I'm curious if it was your perspective that there was the same attempt to "get Clinton" over what he did to avoid military service like there was when Rather and CBS tried to "get Bush 43" with the Texas National Guard story?

MARANISS "Attempt to get" Clinton or Bush is not a phrase I would use, but I would say that from the Whitewater scandal on, the press has not given Clinton an easy ride. To go to the larger question, first of all, it's hard to talk about the press as a monolithic thing. Secondly, every human being has political bias and every reporter has his own preferences; but almost every journalist who I know and respect in the large serious newspaper press—*The Washington Post, The New York Times, The Wall Street Journal, The Los Angeles Times*—finds ways to transcend his bias, such that his interest is in the story and the truth, and not in making his own political point. Regardless of whether they were right or wrong about the way they covered Clinton regarding what he did to avoid military service, I don't think the reporters who covered that story were politically motivated.

BILL CLINTON, ANNE WEXLER, AND THE DUFFY CAMPAIGN

BOSTON One of Bill Clinton's first huge breaks in politics came during his time at Yale Law School when he became highly involved in the Joe Duffy for US Senate campaign in Connecticut. There he learned lifetime lessons from one of his great political mentors, Anne Wexler (whose conference room we're now sitting in for today's interview). What were the lessons he learned from Anne Wexler as a young man that have stayed with him throughout his political career?

MARANISS The Duffy campaign was in 1970, and the Vietnam War was still the main issue then. Joe Duffy and Anne Wexler both had been strongly supportive of the McCarthy presidential campaign in 1968 and active in the anti-war movement. What Bill Clinton learned from Anne was mainly about how to deal with people in a straightforward but tactful manner and how to understand the dynamics of politics at a level he had not known before.

The title of my book is *First In His Class*. He was never first in his class at any school he attended and at Yale Law School, he was almost never in class at all. All three years at Yale were spent doing something else, including that first year when he was the organizer in the Third Congressional District in Connecticut for the Duffy campaign, which included essentially all the area around New Haven. It's a very ethnically diverse place with lots of working class people and utterly unlike anything he had encountered in Arkansas. What he learned during the Duffy campaign from Anne Wexler, along with the organizational skills, was how to relate to a wide variety of people. He already had the innate ability to work with whoever he had been around before, but it wasn't until he got into that race that he had to practice it with such a huge breadth of people.

Joe Duffy was perhaps, in Clinton's mind, too intellectual for the Connecticut Democratic working class vote and Clinton saw the tension that arose from that circumstance—the sort of separation that existed between the suburban liberal anti-war voters and the urban ethnic Democratic voters. He saw those rifts in that campaign for the first time and he had to deal with them the rest of his career. So the Duffy campaign was a very illuminating and political career-shaping campaign, and Anne Wexler was the glue in it.

BILL CLINTON'S BEING SEEN AS PRESIDENTIAL MATERIAL PRIOR TO ENDING HIS FORMAL EDUCATION

BOSTON I remember Dave Wexler telling me years ago how his mother Anne, like so many people in his past, identified Bill Clinton as a guy who was going to be president one day. I don't know if she mentioned that to you when you interviewed her or not.

MARANISS As I worked on the book, after a while, I began hearing it *from everybody*. In fact, it was more nota*ble when someone didn't say it.* There were a couple of people who said they originally didn't think this guy was goi*ng anywhere, but not very many.* Before he got to Connecticut and Yale Law School, he was a Rhodes Scholar. That was my favorite little subset of "friends of Bill" because with that group, you had forty young men—there were no women Rhodes Scholars then—and they were all on this ship heading to England where they would study. When the boat left America, all forty of them thought they would be president someday, but by the time the boat landed in England, they all knew there was only one guy among them who really had what it took to become president.

BOSTON On the boat was *a fellow Rhodes Scholar:* Robert Reich, who later became Clinton's *Secretary of Labor.* Another person on the boat—and he was not a Rhodes Scholar—was Bobby Baker who had already been brought down over some corruption issues, though for quite a while, had been LBJ's fair-haired boy and the ultimate Washington, DC political insider. On the ride across the Atlantic, Bill Clinton just couldn't get enough Bobby Baker stories.

MARANISS Most of the other Rhodes Scholars on that ship were sort of revolted by the presence of Bobby Baker. He was in the ship's lounge regaling women with stories and braggadocio and this trip happened during the counterculture period. This was the fall of 1968 and Baker seemed passé and old school and everything about him was anathema to most of those brilliant young men who were largely anti-war—not all, but most of them—and they were from an utterly different culture from Baker. Bill Clinton though was totally fascinated by him and sat at his side, learning as much as he could about the interworkings of politics from Bobby Baker.

THE CLINTON MARRIAGE

BOSTON You do a good job in the book explaining why Bill wanted to marry Hillary and vice versa. The way I read it, their attraction was tied to their mutual high-flying political ambitions. You said they've always had a reversal of gender stereotypes with Bill being the person with charm and sex appeal while Hillary is the straightforward and self-possessed one; and Bill being the one who massages others' toes, while Hillary is the one who often steps on other's toes. Their marital union has always been fully consumed by their political ambitions, such that when it came time for them to get married, Hillary had no interest in planning any aspect of the wedding; the conversation at the wedding reception was consumed with talk of Bill's next campaign; and they didn't go on a honeymoon following their wedding.

MARANISS They finally went on a honeymoon a few months after their wedding, and Hillary's parents and brothers went with them, and Bill took a book along with him by Earnest Decker, *Denial of Death*. So it was an odd honeymoon.

BOSTON With that predicate, at least from a political partnership standpoint, their marriage has been a great success. So even though they've had constant storminess in the personal aspects of their relationship, given that they've both always been totally obsessed with politics, if they were in this room right now, and we asked them if they'd had a successful marriage, would they both answer, "When we look at everything, we have had a very successful marriage"?

MARANISS It would be a longer answer, but yes, that would be at the end of their answer. When Bill Clinton was the president of the United States, Hillary was the First Lady, and Al Gore and Tipper were the vice president and wife, who would have predicted which marriage would last after

the Monica Lewinsky story broke? Human nature is unpredictable, but I always maintained that the Clintons would stay together through everything and I saw the bond between them from the very beginning.

They've certainly had a shared political ambition throughout their marriage, but it's more than that. They share a lot of intellectual curiosity together. As the years went on, in every politician there's a battle between idealism and ambition, and the Clintons' battle over those two drives is more exaggerated.

As his personal problems have created difficulties for them politically, they have also clearly affected their personal relationship, yet in some ways, they've strengthened it. They always knew that they could get places together that they couldn't get to apart. From the beginning, she was someone who was incredibly valuable to him. I think she was head-over-heels in love with him in the beginning and blinded to some degree or at least willing to accept certain things, while he was impressed by her intellectual capacities and organizational skills. Their political skills complement each other as a team.

She's had her difficulties as a candidate because of being compared to him, who is unlike anyone else in terms of his emotional intelligence and political skills. She doesn't have the same skills, but the skills she has have always been valuable to him. For these reasons, I've never been surprised that they lasted as a couple through thick and thin. I'm sure it's a love-hate relationship, although one never knows the internal dynamics of any marriage outside of one's own.

BOSTON You mention in the book that Hillary says her political partnership/marriage role model has been Eleanor Roosevelt, who led a separate life apart from FDR, at least most of the time. Have Bill and Hillary aspired to have that same type of marriage, leading separate lives, like Franklin and Eleanor did, particularly after they became empty nesters when Chelsea left for college and then when Bill left the White House in January 2001?

MARANISS I don't think they aspired to have separate lives, though that's largely been the case at times. The parallels with Eleanor Roosevelt that Hillary would like to draw have more to do with her own political interests and commitments than with her distant personal relationship with her husband. She hasn't tried to necessarily model her personal relationship with her husband after Eleanor and Franklin's relationship. Even if she did, I don't think it was intentional; it just happened. I think she has tried to model herself after Eleanor Roosevelt as a strong woman with political commitments who didn't always have to be in sync with her husband.

Photo credit: Lucian Perkings

David Maraniss

BILL CLINTON'S TWO SIDES—TIED TO LOSS AND RECOVERY

BOSTON Throughout the book you recognize that there's always two sides to Bill Clinton—there's the big hearted and the small; the sincere and the devious; the humble and the ambitious; the mediator and the predator; the chameleon who says different things to different groups; and when he's down, he's about to rise, and when he's up, he's about to fall.

About his many conflicting sides you say, "These internal contradictions coexist. There's no point in trying to separate them because they're so integrated into each other."

You mentioned a few minutes ago the term "compartmentalize." Is that the only way we can understand Bill Clinton—by recognizing these compartments within him that produce these conflicting parts to him?

MARANISS The way I understand Bill Clinton and have always tried to explain him is that his life is a perpetual cycle of loss and recovery. As you pointed out, when he's down, he's always finding his way back. When he's on top, he'll find a way to get in trouble, and he's maintained that cycle of loss and recovery throughout his life. It started at a very early age and has continued. That's why when my book came out, which was before Monica Lewinsky, and the major troubles of his presidency, I predicted his fall. If you read the book, you see what's going to happen in his presidency, even though the book is not about his fall.

There's something larger to explain about the cycle-of-loss-and-recovery part of him. When he was president, a lot of people who had faith in him and wanted him to succeed, would always say, "If only..." "If only he didn't have this other part to him, he could be great." I would respond to that by saying, "You can't say that. There is no 'if only' to Bill Clinton. He would not have been president if he didn't have the other parts to him." The loss-recovery cycle is all part of his personality that drives him for better and for worse. I think that's true of almost everybody. You can't separate those aspects of people because usually someone's strengths are their weaknesses and their weaknesses are their strengths in different ways. As with everything else with Bill Clinton, it's just an exaggeration of that fact with him.

BILL CLINTON'S FUTURE AFTER 2015

BOSTON I realize your book ends with him announcing that he would be running for president in 1992, but obviously you've continued to observe him since then. You've mentioned the possibility that when Hillary's moment in the sun ends, which could be a long time from now, you plan to do another biography of him; but on page 451, close to the end of your book, you say, "No single world can keep Bill Clinton for long."

My question is, when you think about him today in 2015 at age sixty-nine, a man who is now rich—and he's gotten rich by giving the same speeches over and over again; who is largely out of the power stream and barely tethered to his wife who is obviously a top contender to be elected president in 2016—can you think of any potential avenue in 2015 and the coming years for Bill Clinton where he will find a new avenue for contentment?

MARANISS I don't know about contentment. I don't think he'll ever be content. When he was leaving the presidency, people would say "What is he going to do?" I would answer, "He's going to run for president the rest of his life." That's essentially Bill Clinton. He's always had that need. In some sense, Hillary's campaign for president in 2012 and now going on is an extension of that, although it is driven by her own desires as well as his. He's still largely beloved around the world and the polls show he is pretty popular in the United States as well. So I don't think he necessarily has anything to prove to himself any more.

I don't think he's content, but I think the life he has now is pretty much going to play out unless he becomes the "First Man." I don't have a hard time thinking that Hillary could be president of the United States, although I've got some questions about whether she'll get elected. But I do have large doubts about what the heck do you do with this big dog if she's in the White House? What does he do? How does he handle that? It's extraordinary to think about because he's such a huge character.

BOSTON I read one time that before he left the presidency, he had some constitutional lawyer examine whether the Twenty-second Amendment (which says you can't have more than two terms in a row), would be violated if he sat out a term or two, and then ran again.

MARANISS That's not true.

BOSTON Okay. That was a vicious rumor.

MARANISS He's too smart. He knew he couldn't do that. But he would have happily served a third, fourth, fifth term if it had been allowed. He'd like to be the pope even though he's not Catholic. When he went to college at Georgetown, one of the seminarians took him out for a hamburger and said, "Bill, you ought to think about going into the seminary." Bill said, "Don't you have to be a Catholic first?" The guy didn't even know Bill wasn't a Catholic because he's always been so good at absorbing whatever culture he's in. So what about his becoming UN secretary general? That's not going to happen, but all those types of things on a world scale he'd be happy to do. Contentment though is a different animal and I don't think I could consider Bill Clinton ever content.

BOSTON I think that point is well taken, but since he's left the Presidency he's done some very positive things in the international scene and the American scene—post-Katrina around New Orleans and places around the world—but I guess he can only do so much of that.

MARANISS I think Jimmy Carter has set the standard for post-presidency that Clinton has modeled in some ways and not in others. I think that with the Clinton

Foundation, as with everything with Bill Clinton, there's a very strong positive aspect and there's a questionable aspect to it. I'm not saying he shouldn't make money. His speeches—he's made $50,000,000 off these speeches since he left the presidency—are just a function of supply and demand. But what the Foundation is doing for good and what it's doing for other purposes is at least debatable, but there's something good going on there. So I think he would certainly like to be as involved in humanitarian causes as much as people will allow him to be.

BOSTON Those are all my questions. Thanks so much David.

MICHAEL DUFFY is the Deputy Managing Editor of *Time* magazine, where he has worked since 1985. He and *Time's* current managing editor Nancy Gibbs have written two wonderful *New York Times* best-selling books on our post-Coolidge presidents, the second one being *The Presidents Club: Inside the World's Most Exclusive Fraternity* (Simon & Schuster 2012). Michael is a fabulous storyteller as shown in the following transcript of an event on February 7, 2014, that we did together for the clients and professionals at my law firm and the Dallas office of Ernst & Young.

"The main reason behind the presidency's attracting so many loners is that in order to become president these days, you have to be extremely guarded and careful. We're kind of breeding this type of isolated individual to become president and that's probably not good for politics." **– MICHAEL DUFFY**

CHAPTER 26

MICHAEL DUFFY
ON
The Post-World War II "Presidents Club"

THE IDEA BEHIND THE BOOK
THE PRESIDENTS CLUB

BOSTON Michael, what was the seed that blossomed into The Presidents Club?

DUFFY Nancy Gibbs (now *Time's* managing editor) and I were writing a book on Billy Graham and his relationships with all the presidents since Truman; and we kept stumbling on moments where presidents—former presidents, sitting presidents, and future presidents—were secretly doing deals, making agreements, getting into arguments, and trying to kill each other. Just when we were finishing the Graham book, we realized that a book about all these inter-presidential dealings and relationships would make for a great

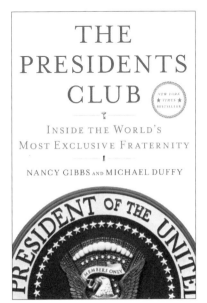

Courtesy of Simon & Schuster, Inc., New York, 2012

next project. Nancy is a faster writer than I am, so she finished her chapters on Billy Graham first. One day she called me and said, "We're doing the wrong book," which is the worst thing you can say to a co-author before he's finished with the first book.

When we had both finished the Graham book, our initial thought was to recognize that as of 1965, we still had three presidents—Ike, Johnson, and Nixon—who were all on stage at the same time; but by 1992, there were five living presidents. With more people connecting with each other at a time, you obviously have more potential for great stories. The back-channel maneuvering between them is just fascinating, so we thought, "Why don't we just write about that?" The book took off from there.

IN THE PRESIDENTS CLUB, OPPOSITES ATTRACT

BOSTON To my surprise, The Presidents Club shows that true friendships among the Club are more likely to arise between people of the opposite party. Herbert Hoover and Harry Truman became great friends, as did Jimmy Carter and Gerald Ford. Bill Clinton became very good friends with the Nixons, as well as with both Bushes. On the other hand, true hostility has arisen between some members of the Club from the same party. Reagan didn't get along with Nixon or Ford. Carter and Clinton have never gotten along. How do you explain this opposite attraction?

DUFFY It is one of my favorite parts about the Club because it's the last thing you'd expect. When Truman and Herbert Hoover first connected, Hoover had not been invited back to the White House by FDR in thirteen years. When Hoover left DC after his Presidency, he essentially left town with people throwing tomatoes at his car. Truman brought him back into the fold by putting him to work as a form of redemption nearly two decades after he had left town. Truman asked Hoover to find and deliver food to

the starving world in Europe after WWII ended, because he knew Hoover had done that same job after WWI and was the only man Truman knew who could get that big job done. He gave Hoover a plane and a staff and he sent him all over the world. In 1947, Hoover and Truman started doing deals together, and then they started doing radio addresses together. They became such good friends that in 1953, when Ike was being sworn in, Hoover walked up to Truman on the dais of the Capitol during the swearing in and said: "Let's start a Presidents Club." Truman replied "Great. You be the president, and I'll be the secretary." They were kidding, except that's how they functioned.

It would also be how Carter and Ford functioned. Here were two men who had opposed each other in the '76 election, yet they ended up doing twenty-five projects together over the next quarter of a century. They realized that both of them had been tossed out of office early, both still had long lives left to live, both did not like Ronald Reagan, and they were not that far apart politically. So they became great friends, and each man vowed to the other to give the eulogy of the funeral of whomever died first—an astonishing tribute that each man paid to the other. There are stories like this throughout history. It's an amazing feature of this special brotherhood.

THE CLUB'S TWO BLACK SHEEP: NIXON AND CARTER

BOSTON In reading the book, it's clear that the Club has had two black sheep: Nixon and Carter, who simply could not stay on the sidelines after they left the White House. Whenever they received international assignments from sitting presidents, they both had this bad tendency to go rogue. How do you think history is going to evaluate the post-presidency years of Nixon and Carter?

DUFFY Both Nancy and I came out of writing this book liking all the presidents more than when we started the book, with the possible exceptions of Nixon and Carter, who were just difficult. Both men left office earlier than they had planned, and Nixon spent twenty-five years trying to redeem himself in public. That led him to overcompensate at times. Carter is right now the longest living former president in American history—he's still active thirty-three years and a little over a month since he left the presidency. That's the longest any former president has ever lived after leaving the Oval Office.

BOSTON And he's likely to live a lot longer.

DUFFY Carter is the black sheep of the Club. He gives all the other members something to complain about. He's amazing. He's done a zillion things, and he's won the Nobel Peace Prize, and he's really set a very high bar for all the others. But he's just a difficult man, and that has not changed since he left office.

Carter has this wonderful phrase: "I think I am a better former president than I was a president." It's because he's been a former president seven times as long as he was the president! But he gets in trouble when he says, "I became a better former president than the others." He keeps on saying things like that that are clearly best left unsaid. I don't think history will be kind to either Nixon or Carter for obvious reasons, but they do make the Club an interesting place. Even now, Carter is an interesting piece of work. President Bush Sr. is the oldest of the four who are alive, not counting Obama. Carter is just about six months behind him.

BOSTON For those who were at the Bush 43 Presidential Library dedication, Jimmy Carter tried to be gracious to Bush in his remarks, but still had to remind the crowd that Bush 43 became president only after the election got thrown into the Supreme Court. That's Jimmy Carter's best effort at being gracious.

EISENHOWER'S IMPACT ON JFK AND LBJ'S FOREIGN POLICY

BOSTON Michael, an example of a former president who actually helped a sitting president came when Eisenhower was called back into service, first by JFK after the Bay of Pigs, and then by LBJ as Vietnam went into a downward spiral. Is it accurate to say that Eisenhower, a former president, actually helped shape the foreign policy of his successors?

DUFFY There is no question about that. He saved Kennedy. When Kennedy went into office in 1961, he sort of pretended to ask Ike for advice, and Ike gave it, and told him: "Here's how you ought to set up the White House. I've been doing it for eight years and it works well." Kennedy then completely ignored Ike's advice.

Eight weeks later, we had the Bay of Pigs fiasco, and Kennedy suddenly looked like someone who didn't know what he was doing. He was the youngest president since Theodore Roosevelt. So Kennedy invited Ike to Camp David two days after the Bay of Pigs, and Eisenhower, the oldest president in a century, took JFK for a literal trip to the woodshed. Eisenhower just let him have it: "What did you ask? Who did you ask? What questions did you put to the generals?" It immediately became clear that if Kennedy had followed Ike's earlier advice, some of the bad outcome from the Bay of Pigs wouldn't have happened. So Eisenhower gave Kennedy a tour of Camp David (where Kennedy had never been before), took him to the woodshed, and then, after he had taken this beating, Kennedy and Ike came out in front of the cameras, and Ike said "I support him," despite everything that's happened; which would be really hard to imagine today, but it was standard then. That's the endorsement Kennedy wanted, and he got the picture.

Ike was also incredibly helpful to Johnson. Johnson would have Ike down to the White

House from Gettysburg (where Ike lived in retirement) to run National Security Council events. Imagine that today—Barack Obama inviting George W. Bush into the White House to run National Security Council events. Hard to imagine. It's a tradition that could go on for the next thirty or forty years in smaller ways, but there was an amazing partnership between Ike and Johnson.

THE FREQUENCY OF FRIENDLESS LONERS AMONG POST-WAR PRESIDENTS

BOSTON The book reveals that the Presidents Club, over the last seventy years, has been made up largely of men who were friendless loners: LBJ, Nixon, Reagan, Carter, Obama. The only close friends these guys have had are their wives, and it's touch and go with them sometimes.

Why does the presidency attract this type of isolated personality?

DUFFY This is the exam portion of the show. I think we can all draw conclusions from our wives.

It's a curiosity of American politics that we would elect men, and so far only men, who, as you said, in many cases are lone individuals, and I don't quite understand it. For every one of those, though, there are also those who are gregarious. But I think the main reason behind the presidency's attracting so many loners is that in order to become president these days, you have to be extremely guarded and careful. We're kind of breeding this type of isolated individual to become president, and in a way, that's probably not good for our politics. I don't have a better explanation than that.

I do know why the Club matters to all of them—that is, they alone have sat in that chair and have made those impossible decisions, which none of us can imagine. They alone have gotten the scars and the would-of, could-of, should-ofs, and the bruises you get from being at the top of anything—whether it's the president of

the United States, the president of a law firm, or the president of your garden club. No one else can understand what it's like except the people who have done it. They share that and it's the one thing they have in common. Even their wives can't understand what that's like. That's something that Jimmy Carter and Gerald Ford both could understand about the other.

President Bush, Sr. said to me, "When we get together, there is one thing we don't have to talk about, and that's what we did as president." As they live longer, everywhere they go, there's someone asking questions about "Why'd you do that?" and "What were you thinking when you did this?" When they're among themselves, they don't have to deal with those questions. It's a safe place.

LBJ, NIXON, AND THE PARIS PEACE TALKS

BOSTON Two of the most complex people to ever serve as president were LBJ and Nixon. They battled each other behind the scenes in the international arena as the Paris Peace Talks (aimed at ending the Vietnam War) were going on prior to Election Day 1968. After Nixon beat Humphrey in the '68 election, LBJ never revealed to the American people what he knew about the back door shenanigans Nixon had engaged in that sabotaged the Paris Peace Talks. Why did LBJ keep that information about Nixon secret?

DUFFY It's one of my favorite stories in the book, and it takes about three minutes to explain, so bear with me. As 1968 was ending, Johnson wasn't running again, Humphrey was running for the Democrats, Nixon was running for the Republicans, and it was a tight race. In about October of that year, Johnson found out (through some sophisticated electronic surveillance) that Nixon was quietly telling the South Vietnamese, "Don't do a deal with Johnson. Wait till I'm president. I'll give you better terms down the road." Nixon told them that at a time when Johnson was conducting the Paris Peace Talks. Johnson hit the roof. He said to his inner circle, "This is treason. He can't do this."

It put LBJ in a moral quandary: "Do I tell the American people what Nixon's been doing, and, perhaps tip the election to Humphrey (who Johnson wasn't that keen on)?" If Johnson didn't reveal it, then the election might go to Nixon. Johnson agonized about what to do, and two weeks before the election, he decided to simply let Nixon know that he knew what Nixon had done to sabotage the peace talks. LBJ essentially said to Nixon, "Cool it," but didn't threaten him; just said, "Cool it." The peace talks then fell apart, and Nixon was elected by the narrowest margin in one hundred years or so.

Then LBJ retired to the Pedernales, and Nixon spent the next few years taking very good care of Johnson—got him a plane when he needed it, got him a car, bought him this clubhouse on Lafayette Square. Johnson basically created a clubhouse for former presidents. So Nixon took very good care of Lyndon Johnson—celebrated his birthday, and named a national forest after his wife.

Everything was fine between the two of them until early January 1973, when the Senate began investigating Nixon for Watergate while Johnson was still alive. Nixon called Johnson and said, "I want you to call your friends at the Senate and tell them to back off this investigation or I'm going to tell them that you hacked me in 1968." Johnson came back at him and said, "If you do that, I'll tell them what you did in sabotaging the Paris Peace Talks." So there's a case of double blackmail by two club members. The Club has definitely had its moments of intrigue and backlash. The reason we know that is because Johnson dropped dead from a heart attack a couple of weeks later, and Nixon was reinaugurated in 1973, so that's the story. It's amazing, and it didn't come out until about a decade later.

NIXON AND FORD

BOSTON In your book, you suggest that by reason of the fact that Nixon got away with sabotaging the Paris Peace Talks, it emboldened him to think, "I can do anything! I can do Watergate!"

DUFFY One of the things we try to make clear is that in his conflict with Johnson, Nixon knew he had been taped by Johnson, and Nixon probably thought, "Aha! This is what presidents do! They tape!" In some respects, he wasn't wrong given Johnson's behavior. So, this story gives a slightly different slant that most people hadn't heard before on Watergate, and it reflects the complicated relationships between these very powerful men. I really like the story and think it's a good insight.

BOSTON Another story of Presidents Club members being conflicted came in Nixon's final days in the White House. The Supreme Court had ordered that the final tapes be produced. Once people listened to them, everyone knew the writing was on the wall, and Nixon would have to resign. So he sent his Chief of Staff Alexander Haig to Vice President Ford (soon-to-be President Ford), and Haig said, "Look, Nixon will resign quicker if you'll promise to give him a full pardon." When you first learned of that alarming proposal, what was your reaction?

DUFFY That came out some years before we did our research. My favorite part of the story is that Ford first said, "Okay," but then, a few hours later, he said, "I can't accept that." It's a tale of a man under pressure coming to the right decision just as he was about to become president of the United States, at what would have been an incredibly complicated and tempting moment for any of us.

I think what's missed about that conversation is that the political left thinks it was a deal, and maybe the political right thinks it was a conspiracy. What's interesting to me

Photo credit: Alex Ho

Michael Duffy

is that Ford and Nixon had been friends since 1949. Nixon got to the House in '47, and Ford got there in '49. The first person to come up to Gerald Ford on the floor of the House in 1949, after he got sworn in by Sam Rayburn, was Dick Nixon who introduced himself. Within a few months, they were carpooling together. These men were friends. They weren't strangers to each other. They weren't just president and vice president; they were friends of twenty-five years standing. Their wives were friends. How do you factor friendship into a moment like the one I just described?

We all know the complications of these friendship relationships as we get older. So you have to look at them as much from a political, and a legal end, as from a personal one. What we tried to do throughout this book was say, "How do you slice that prosciutto when you get handed that situation?" Ford stayed close to Nixon right to the end, but I don't think he ever misjudged him.

One of the facts to remember about Ford: Nixon dangled the vice presidency to Gerald Ford in 1960, then again when he was running in 1968, and then again in

1973, when he had to find another vice president after Agnew resigned. Nixon finally chose him, but it was only on the third try that Ford got it. By then, Ford knew everything he needed to know about Dick.

CARTER, BUSH 41, AND IRAQ'S INVASION OF KUWAIT

BOSTON An example of a former president trying to torpedo a sitting president involved Jimmy Carter and Bush 41 in the days leading up to the Gulf War, over how the UN should respond to Saddam Hussein's invasion of Kuwait.

Tell our audience exactly what Jimmy Carter did, and then tell us why you think President Bush 41 never told the public about Carter's conduct, which Bush and his insiders regarded as treasonous.

DUFFY Again, it's very similar to the Nixon and Johnson situation I described a few minutes ago. Before the Gulf War, as you remember, George Herbert Walker Bush had organized an astonishing coalition of sixty or seventy countries to liberate Kuwait. He and his diplomatic team got all these nations aligned together—Arab and Christian, Asian, and Western—it was just an amazing piece of diplomatic ballet. I haven't seen anything like it since. With that alignment in place, just as we were getting close to starting the war, Carter decided to write a letter. Only Jimmy Carter could have had this idea come into his brain. He wrote the other members of the UN Security Council, and said, "Don't go to war." Unlike Nixon, who did his post-presidency international politicking secretly, Carter did his first round of advocating a position contrary to President Bush's position in public, so everyone would know. This upset everyone because Bush was seeking the UN to support going to war.

Then Carter did a second round of letters, which were private. He started writing members of the individual Arab countries. Bush got even more furious about those letters. Like Johnson had done before with Nixon, Bush let Carter know that he knew about his letters, and asked him to cease and desist. Like Johnson with Nixon, what Carter did eventually came out.

I talked to Carter about this, and asked him, "If you had to do that one all over again, would you?" I was thinking, "This is a gimme. He's got to say, 'No. It's been twenty-five years. Everyone can see that what he did was a big mistake.'" And, of course, Carter said, "I did exactly what I wanted to do and if the opportunity ever arose, I would do it again the same way." So there are moments like this where they are backstabbing each other and some of it's public, but most of it's private.

BUSH 41 AND BUSH 43

BOSTON On page 476 of your book, you say that Bush 41's presidency did not define Bush 43's presidency; rather, it was the son's presidency which defined the father's presidency. Explain that.

DUFFY It's a funny relationship. People like to think about Bush 1 and 2 as a pair. I think that's really dumb because times change, threats change, and situations change. It was very convenient for people who didn't understand why George W. Bush was elected, particularly on the left, to think that there was some kind of large, dark, deep conspiracy about how 43 was an extension of Bush 41. If you knew the two men or their staffs, that clearly was not true. To me, they were always completely separate entities. They were the same family, and had the same personal traits. For example, the Bushes would always say, "Bring a gift, leave early, send a thank you note," and we all know now that that's how the Bushes do things.

But I think they were really different kinds of men, with different philosophies, different kinds of Cabinets, and different kinds of staffs. Most importantly, they were president in different eras. George H.W. Bush came out of an era where stability

mattered and a president could still manage it. He had sort of an Ike-esq "America rules the world" philosophy. He believed that philosophy had to be maintained, and that it could be maintained because during his presidency threats were known and diplomatic strategies were achievable. By the time Bush 2 came into office, the game was different. Threats weren't seen, risks weren't seen, and dangers weren't symmetric. He had to completely change the way he and all his team thought about foreign policy. When his father watched what was happening during his son's presidency, I don't think he was expecting that the world as he had known it was likely to continue. Bush 2 said, "It's a different era."

My favorite thing about the father and son is that during the second Bush presidency, most of the concern ran from Washington (Bush 2) back to Kennebunkport (Bush 1). How? The father was watching television all day, every day during his son's presidency. That was agonizing because of the criticisms and second-guessing of his son; yet, it was the son who called the father, and said, "Dad, I'm fine, I've got this. Turn off the television." The mother (Barbara) would call George 43, and say, "Would you call your father and tell him to stop watching television." This is the human part of the dynamic that everyone misses. You know that if you have sons, you naturally worry about them more than you worry about yourself. I don't think that's a big mystery or rocket science. But for some reason, the parent with all the moral human qualities of a family is still on stage while his child has also come on stage. People in politics never think about the family aspects that are most common to us. To me, that was an easy story.

OBAMA AS A FUTURE MEMBER OF THE PRESIDENTS CLUB

BOSTON Given the facts that by all accounts President Obama is a loner, and "guarded," and has had ongoing friction with Bill Clinton, and has continuously blamed Bush 43 for every failure to achieve the "change" that he thought he could get when he ran for president in 2008, what's your prediction on how Obama is going to fit into the Presidents Club after he leaves the White House?

DUFFY I have a photograph of all five of them standing together in the Oval Office. You've probably seen that picture. It was taken in the last week of George W. Bush's presidency. Obama had called Bush and said, "Would you get the Club together? I would like to have lunch with them." George W. Bush replied, "Even Carter?" They all got together. You might have thought that when the Club gets together, they would all talk about the Middle East or China, or whatever great crisis they could complain about. Instead, they talked about the one thing they all had in common: their daughters in the White House. They all had them—Bush 1, Carter, Clinton, Bush 2. They talked about how difficult it was generally to raise daughters, and how it was even harder on stage.

Of course, that luncheon was off the record, and no one was able to record anything that happened, but consequently Jimmy Carter told me all about it. He mentioned he didn't think there was enough food served; perhaps he thought the reception was a little meager. Bush 2 though said something fabulous at the lunch. He said to Obama, (in effect) "We're rooting for you, because we know more than anyone else in this entire world how impossible it is for you to do this job." All of them knew that in a country where almost no one knows how the federal government works, it's really impossible for us to have an executive who functions, and is powerful, and can get stuff done, and can move a ham sandwich from here to there. They love that. That's one thing they share. They know the presidency has to remain strong, even when they disagree about what to do with it, or who to appoint or where to go. They know the presidency has to function and work, particularly in a crisis.

How will Obama fit into the Club? Who knows? The Club is such a funky motley place. There are so many people who have been in it for so many years and it can transcend anyone. I'm not really worried about Obama fitting in, or whoever is the next president, but it's important for each of the members to stay active. I think having Clinton and Bush 1 go out and work on Katrina and the tsunami, and Clinton and Bush 2 go out and work on Haiti is a powerful signal to the country that those people from opposing parties who battled each other during their political careers can find a way to work together. There are a lot of powerful signals about that and it's important. It's not necessarily what they intended when they created the Club. It's just one of the things that goes along with it, and it's an important thing for us as a people to know about, until we figure out how to do things together better. I hope that more of this collaboration will happen soon, but we aren't doing it real well now.

CLINTON AND THE BUSH FAMILY

BOSTON To close, why don't you tell the story of the Bush family reunion where Bill Clinton was there, and the time came for the family photo.

DUFFY Okay. Clinton now is like the black sheep of the family. In the Bush family, they call Clinton "the brother from another mother." Barbara has said several times that 41 is the father 42 never had. Clinton's gotten so comfortable with the Bush clan that he invites himself to Kennebunkport and doesn't wait for the invitation. Among just us, I wouldn't try that.

About three years ago, they had a birthday party for Bush, Sr. at the Kennedy Center in Washington. All the former presidents and Obama attended. A series of tributes were made by the former presidents to the oldest member of the Club, and they were all very nice. Clinton's was the most extravagant of all. He stood at one point, looked at Bush 41, and said, "I love you." Now that is not the language of politicians. The "L" word was a strong card for Clinton to play in front of the rest of his family.

My favorite story about the event took place afterward. There were eighty-five Bushes there—the whole family—and Laura said "I want a picture." So everyone was organized and the entire clan was backstage at the back of the Kennedy Center in that dramatic black box stage. Off to the side were Rosalyn and Jimmy Carter, and Bill Clinton. Either George W. or Jeb said, "Hey, Bill, come on over." Sure enough, the family picture has eighty-five Bushes and Bill Clinton as the eighty-sixth person in it. That picture sits on the older Bush's credenza in his office at Kennebunkport. Like they say, "He's a brother from another mother." This may be the apotheosis of the Presidents Club when the families mix.

There was some of that with Carter and Ford. There was some of that between Truman and Hoover, who both felt overshadowed by FDR. There are elements of redemption in this for all ages and generations of presidents, as well as all the other things that we didn't expect and found out about in ways that just continue to surprise us.

BOSTON Thanks so much, Michael.

VI.

Presidential Insiders

LYNDA JOHNSON ROBB & LARRY TEMPLE
ON LYNDON B. JOHNSON

HENRY KISSINGER ON HIS LIFE, RICHARD NIXON,
& THE CURRENT INTERNATIONAL SITUATION

JAMES A. BAKER, III ON RONALD REAGAN
& GEORGE H.W. BUSH

JOHN SUNUNU ON GEORGE H.W. BUSH

ANDY CARD ON RONALD REAGAN,
GEORGE H. W. BUSH, & GEORGE W. BUSH

In 2014, America celebrated the golden anniversary of the Civil Rights Act of 1964, thought by many to be "the Bill of the Century." To commemorate this milestone, on June 27, 2014 at the State Bar of Texas' Annual Meeting in Austin, I moderated a lively panel discussion at the annual Friday morning Bench Bar Breakfast with President Lyndon Johnson's older daughter, **LYNDA JOHNSON ROBB**, and LBJ's final White House counsel, **LARRY TEMPLE**, to discuss their remembrances and insights about our thirty-sixth president and what he did during that historic time for our country. Lynda has a dazzling personality and a great sense of humor, and Larry is a wise, seasoned lion who has spent much of his adult life in service to LBJ and then the LBJ Foundation.

"Part of Lyndon Johnson's legislative genius—and it was genius, plainly and simply—was that he knew and understood the people with whom he was dealing, and he dealt with them with civility and understanding. He knew Congress and how to work with them, but he also knew when, where, and how to move, act, and react." **– LYNDA JOHNSON ROBB**

"Lyndon Johnson could be very soft and caring. Around the White House, he was always looking to do something nice for somebody. If I had been working fifteen to sixteen hours a day for several weeks, he would tell me to bring my wife over for lunch, and he'd bring her into the Oval Office and give her something—a chain or a pen or some token. He was very thoughtful and considerate to everybody. I think that was a part of his genius. He did that over a long period of time, and then he was able to encourage people to be reciprocal in doing something for him at a time when he needed help on a piece of legislation."
– LARRY TEMPLE

CHAPTER 27

LYNDA JOHNSON ROBB AND LARRY TEMPLE
ON
Lyndon B. Johnson

LBJ AND MLK'S CONVERSATION SHORTLY AFTER THE KENNEDY ASSASSINATION

BOSTON It's now time to celebrate the golden anniversary of what historians have called the Bill of the Century, the Civil Rights Act of 1964. Before my questions of Lynda Johnson Robb and Larry Temple begin, let's listen to the voices of the American Civil Rights movement's two most important leaders, President Lyndon Johnson and Martin Luther King, Jr., in a phone conversation they had shortly after the Kennedy assassination.

RECORDING **Johnson:** *I'm interested in your cooperation and communication, and a good many people told me that they heard about your statement, I guess on TV, wasn't it?*

King: *Yeah, that's right.*

Johnson: *I've been locked up in this office and haven't seen it, but I wanted to tell you how grateful I am, and how worthy I'm going to try to be of all your hopes.*

King: *Well, thank you very much. I'm so happy to hear that and I knew that you were of such great spirit. You know you have our support and backing. We know what a difficult period this is.*

Johnson: *It's just an impossible period. We've got a budget coming up. We've got nothing to do with it. It's practically already made. We've got the civil rights bill and it hadn't even passed the House. It's November and Hubert Humphrey told me yesterday that everybody wanted to go home. We've got a tax bill that they haven't touched and we just got to not let up on any of them and keep going. I guess they'll say I'm repudiating, but I'm going to ask Congress one of these days to just stay there and pass them all. They won't do it, but we'll just keep them here next year and they'll do it. We just won't give up an inch.*

King: *Uh-huh. Well this is mighty fine. It's so imperative. I think one of the great tributes we can pay in memory of President Kennedy is to try to enact some of the great progressive policies that he sought to initiate.*

Johnson: *Well, I understood them all and you can count on that; and I'm going to do my best*

to get other men to do likewise and I'll have to have y'all's help. And I never need it more than I do now.

King: *Well you know you have it, and just feel free to call on us for anything.*

Johnson: *Thank you so much, Martin.*

King: *All right. Call me when you have time.*

Johnson: *I sure will. Call me when you're down here next time.*

King: *I certainly will.*

Johnson: *Let's get together, and any suggestions you've got, let's bring them in.*

King: *Fine, I certainly will do that.*

Johnson: *Thank you so much.*

Photo credit: LBJ Library Photo by Cecil Stoughton

President Lyndon B. Johnson signs the 1964 Civil Rights Act as Martin Luther King, Jr., and others look on.

BOSTON Much has been said about the difference in the approaches to addressing the battle for civil rights between Presidents Kennedy and Johnson during their time in the Oval Office.

Robert Caro began his newest biography of LBJ, *The Passage of Power,* with the observation that, "At the time of Kennedy's death, every major administration bill before Congress, including the Civil Rights Act, was stalled."

Roy Wilkins, head of the NAACP in the 1960s, said, "John Kennedy didn't really know what was possible in Congress. Lyndon Johnson knew exactly what was possible."

Richard Rovere, in a 1964 article in *The New Yorker,* said, "President Kennedy's eloquence made people think. President Johnson's hammer blows made people act."

Today, to discuss the Bill of the Century, we're honored to have with us two people who knew the Civil Rights Act's wheel horse, Lyndon Johnson, better than anyone else who is still with us and active in preserving the legacy of Lyndon Johnson. Now they're going to share their thoughts about the president who stands at the top of the American history's mountain in the field of civil rights in 2014.

LBJ AND THE TRANSITION FROM VICE PRESIDENT TO PRESIDENT

BOSTON Lynda, let's start by going back to November 22, 1963. Your dad began that day as vice president, his least favorite position during his political career, a job he once described as being like a Texas steer in that he's lost his social standing in the society in which he resides. But on that November afternoon, he became president, the world's most powerful man, and he responded by assuming his responsibilities flawlessly.

You were twenty years old at the time, a student at the University of Texas at Austin. Give us a daughter's perspective on the transformation you think took place inside your father on November 22 and the days following as he left behind his vice president bum steer job and rose to lead the country after the Kennedy assassination.

ROBB Talmage has asked me to do something I'm obviously not capable of doing. Nobody could understand Lyndon Johnson's mind. I would be the very last person to try to speak for him. Nor might I add would Larry Temple try to do that.

But upon his becoming president, I think he recognized that here was the opportunity to get a lot of legislation through in memory of President Kennedy. It's important to know what to work for, but it's also important to look and say, "When can it be possible?" The civil rights bill had been stalled. Daddy had spoken at Gettysburg that August, and talked about the need to make the Emancipation Proclamation a reality and not just a phrase; and it was a very strong speech.

You understand the politics of this in Texas. There was a lot of concern with some people, not Daddy, but some people, who were thinking, "Wait a minute. Maybe we ought to start working on moving the civil rights bill forward in the beginning of '65, after we get reelected." But Daddy knew this was the time when we had a window of opportunity. He saw that on the very night of November 22. As you heard a minute ago in the telephone conversation, he really wanted to seize the moment and the hearts of the people in this country and he could see this was something he and Congress needed to do right then. In memory of President Kennedy, he wanted to work on making this a more just country. That's why he called Dr. Martin Luther King.

But he didn't just call Dr. King; he called everybody. He recognized this was not something he alone was going to be able to do. He needed the Republicans, he needed the religious leaders, he needed every constituency to work together to push this through; and then was the time, not after the election, but right after Kennedy's death, when it could have the most impact.

He started then in November, and with the help of many people, he got it through. We need to recognize, as wonderful as Daddy was, and as remarkable as Dr. King was, there were a lot of people—maybe not as rich as you all—but there were a lot of people out there in the hinterlands who were putting their lives on the line. Not only the African-Americans, but also white people, all across this country. It wasn't just a political line. Some of those people who came to meet us at the train station—when my mother and I traveled through the South after the Act was passed—were people who had marched in support of civil rights. They knew some people at their own church weren't going to like them anymore. They knew there were going to be some people saying, "I'm not going to buy anything from your store anymore." So it was not just Daddy, it was a groundswell of people all over the United States who recognized that we needed to make a change, and we wanted to do it with as little bloodshed as possible. It was a revolution not with spears but with votes.

LBJ'S CIVIL RIGHTS JOURNEY FROM 1937-1964

BOSTON Larry, Lyndon Johnson traveled a civil rights odyssey from 1937, when he came to DC as a congressman, through 1964 when the Act was passed. His voting record in Congress before 1957 matched up with his mentor, Senator Richard Russell, a Southern segregationist—meaning that in his first twenty-one years in Washington, LBJ voted against all civil rights bills. However, upon his gaining power as the senate majority leader in 1957, he pushed through the first civil rights bill in America since 1875, over Richard Russell's objection—though it was a weak law and had little effect on Jim Crow. Then, when Lyndon Johnson became president in late 1963, as Lynda just mentioned, he had maximum power. He broke the legislative log jam that was holding up the civil rights bill,

got it out of committee, onto the floor of Congress, and voted into law.

Give us your perspective on Lyndon Johnson's civil rights journey from 1937 through 1964 that culminated in his Oval Office accomplishments.

TEMPLE I'm like Lynda. Nobody knows what was in Lyndon Johnson's mind, and why he did what he did or why he didn't do what he didn't do. Lyndon Johnson was the ultimate pragmatist. He looked at the facts and dealt with them as they occurred. I think he didn't do anything about civil rights any earlier because he didn't have the clout and the time wasn't right.

When he started in Congress, he was a junior member of the House. When he started in the Senate, obviously he was a junior member of the Senate. He simply did not have the political clout to do what he otherwise might have wanted to do. He obviously had that clout when he became Senate majority leader in 1957.

If you listen to what he said when he spoke of civil rights in the 1960s, the genesis of his views on civil rights originated in Cotulla, Texas, where he taught in a one-room school to a group of Mexican-American children during his college years. He said he "saw in their eyes" the hunger they came to school with, the deprivation they had, and he always wanted to do something about that. I'm satisfied he wanted to do it in 1937 and 1945 and 1951, but he simply didn't have the political muscle to do it and the timing wasn't right. But when the time *was* right, and he had that political strength, he took advantage of it—in '57, '64, '65, '68. Once he had the power, he could do what he had always wanted to do.

ROBB And remember, he was one of three Southerners who refused to sign the Southern Manifesto [the 1956 document signed by 101 congressmen from Southern states that stated their opposition to racial integration in public places].

BOSTON He had a famous saying: "You don't try to kill the snake until you've got the hoe in your hands." It wasn't until he became president that he had the hoe in his hands.

LBJ AND HIS MENTOR SENATOR RICHARD RUSSELL

BOSTON Lynda, you grew up in Virginia when your dad was in Congress. And during those years, Senator Richard Russell, a confirmed bachelor, was your family's frequent houseguest. I read that you affectionately called him "Uncle Dick" and once said that "he helped raise you."

What was it like in 1964 knowing your dad was going head-to-head with his long-time friend and mentor, your Uncle Dick, who was his biggest obstacle to getting the civil rights bill passed?

ROBB First you have to understand those were different times. Daddy knew every member of the Senate and was friends with most of them. He might not have voted the way they did, he might not have agreed with all their policies, but there was a time when people actually talked to each other in Congress across the party lines, and they ate together.

There were a few things that ruined Congress. One was air conditioning—you got a lot more work for your money in those days. Congressmen would come to Washington in January and then everybody would go home in about July. They'd do all their constituent services at home during the rest of the summer, and then they'd come back again. They didn't just spend two days a week in Washington like they do today.

So everyone really knew each other, and our family loved Dick Russell. He was Daddy's sponsor in the Senate. He was his mentor, and it's very hard to go against somebody you love. But Daddy recognized that times had changed, and this was the time. He talked to Dick Russell about it, and basically said, "I'm gonna pass this civil rights bill, and if I have to run over you, I'm gonna do it."

Now I want you all to know that Dick Russell was not a mean, nasty racist. He was a man who was born in a different time. When this bill came along, it was just too late to try to change the way he had been, as they say in that song, "carefully taught." When he lost the civil rights vote, the man who walked him back to his office was Clarence Mitchell, the lobbyist for the NAACP. Dick Russell told Clarence that the Act's getting passed wasn't the outcome he wanted, but it was now the law of the land, and he thought everyone should follow it.

BOSTON To follow that up, I read that when Clarence Mitchell passed away, you gave the eulogy at his funeral.

ROBB I did! I did give the eulogy. He was a wonderful man.

In those days, as I grew up, my experience in the summers and after school involved my going up to the Senate office building and helping. I folded mail. I was asked to show constituents around. I thought I was very important. So I knew the senators then better than I did when my husband Chuck was a senator. I knew where their offices were, and went around and visited with them. Luci and I didn't think anything about it. We loved it.

TEMPLE Talmage, let me elaborate on something Lynda said, because I think it's really insightful about Lyndon Johnson. Those who may have seen the Broadway play, *All The Way*, which is about LBJ and the '64 Civil Rights Act, may have left that play wondering, "Was Lyndon Johnson for civil rights because he deeply believed in it or was he for civil rights because he thought he needed that for reelection in '64?" That question has been posed on many occasions. There was the meeting [with Richard Russell] that Lynda talked about that was recorded by Jack Valenti, who was there.

In his book, Jack said present at the meeting were he, Lyndon Johnson, and Richard Russell sitting together in the Oval Office. President Johnson said, "Dick, I love you and I owe you, but I'm going to pass this civil rights bill. If I have to run over you to do it, I'm gonna run over you to do it; but I'm going to pass it, and we're going to pass all of it. We're not going to pull pieces out and pass part of it. I just want you to know I'm going to do that if I've got to run over you."

Then there was a pause, and Richard Russell said, "Mr. President, you may very well do that. But I'm here to tell you that if you do, you will lose the South, and that might cause you to lose the election this year." To which Lyndon Johnson said, "Dick, if that's the price I have to pay to pass this legislation, I will gladly pay it." That one conversation tells you how much Lyndon Johnson was committed to getting the Civil Rights Act passed.

ROBB Daddy knew that the Civil Rights Act wasn't going to help him a bit in the South. Those people had been his biggest supporters, yet he did it. He knew what he was going in for, and he knew the time was right.

IMPACT OF THE CIVIL RIGHTS ACT OF 1964

ROBB There's an interesting piece I read recently, and I'm not sure if this was in Georgia or somewhere else in the South. The person telling the story said there was a young African-American military officer who had just moved into this Southern town. He went to a hamburger joint to get something to eat, and came up to the counter, and gave his order. The person serving him said, "Officer, I don't understand this. I'm from New Jersey, but in this town, I can't serve you here, but if you'll come around back, I'll give you the hamburgers." The young officer said, "I'm not that hungry" and walked away. Then right after the Civil Rights Act passed, the next

day, the soldier went back to the same hamburger joint, and he was served. That young serviceman was Colin Powell.

So there were a lot of places in the South where, once the Act was passed, as Dick Russell said, people knew, "It's the law now, and I'm going to follow it."

LBJ'S LEGISLATIVE GENIUS

BOSTON In 2014, we don't seem to have anybody in Washington capable of getting legislation passed. History proves that nobody could do it like Lyndon Johnson. No one could horsetrade like Lyndon Johnson, no one could go for his adversary's jugular like he could, and no one knew how to seize the moment with perfect timing like he did. He proved this first as Senate majority leader and then as president.

Larry, give us your perspective on Lyndon Johnson's unique ability to get legislation passed.

TEMPLE Remember that he grew up in the Congress. He was in the House, and then the Senate, and he understood both houses of Congress. Historians will tell you that of our forty-four presidents, no one understood and worked with Congress better than Lyndon Johnson. That's where he got his start, and he understood what would motivate a particular congressman. It may be a member of the House that wanted help in getting appropriation for a dam in their district—LBJ would help get the appropriation for the dam. It might be a senator that had somebody he or she wanted appointed to a judicial position—LBJ would see if that could be done or expedited. Sometimes, it was a threat—"If you don't do that, you're not going to get my help on X," and sometimes it was the softer approach—"You really need to do this for your country."

There's a very famous story, I don't know if it's true, but I love it. In 1964, Everett Dirksen was the Republican leader in the Senate. In order to get Dirksen to be very active in support of the civil rights bill,

President Johnson was telling him about his place in history, and said, "You know, Ev, you get out front on this, and one hundred years from now, school kids will only know two names when it comes to civil rights: Abraham Lincoln and Everett Dirksen." Dirksen wasn't totally dumb, but I was around several times when the president and Dirksen were together, and there was enough ego and vanity there. Ev thought, "This might be true." So he became quite the advocate for the bill.

One thing about Lyndon Johnson—if you watched him through the years—that man knew and took advantage of circumstances, knowing when the time was right for the country to take action or for Congress to take action. Think about it just a moment. He had three civil rights bills that he got passed as president. The '64 Civil Rights Act that we're talking about today came immediately after the assassination of President Kennedy. He said that we need to do this to honor our fallen president. Go back and look at that civil rights bill. It started out being the civil rights bill that President Kennedy wanted, but it was expanded to be all the things LBJ wanted—yet he always called it "Kennedy's bill." "This is President Kennedy's bill that we gotta pass." He took advantage of the grief in this country to pass that legislation.

Then, the next step was to try to get the voting rights legislation passed. For a while, he couldn't get it done. It was stalled. In March 1965, in what became known as Bloody Sunday, there was a group of African-Americans who attempted to make a peaceful march from Selma to Montgomery. They crossed the Pettus Bridge and Congressman John Lewis, who was one of the march's great war horses and is still in Congress today, was there as a young man. As they crossed the Pettus Bridge, they were met by the local police who had guns and fire hoses, dogs and batons, and the marchers literally got beat up. What the law enforcement people doing the beating didn't realize was that it was all

Photo credit: LBJ Library photo by Arnold Newman

on television. It was being beamed to this country on television, and people got upset. That's when Lyndon Johnson said all they wanted to do was register people and give them the right to vote. *Now* we've got to pass the Voting Rights Act. And they got it passed in part, not solely but in large part, because of the circumstances in the country involving the public's outcry over what happened in Selma.

Then in 1968, the president wanted to pass the Fair Housing Act. I remember being there, and it was stalled in Congress. The Fair Housing Act said that there would be no discrimination in the buying and selling of housing, in the financing of housing, and in the rental of housing. When it stalled, he waited until the right time—which turned out to be when Dr. Martin Luther King was killed. The next day after Dr. King's assassination, the president said, "We can move now and we're gonna move now," and he got the Fair Housing Act passed.

So a part of his legislative genius—and it was genius, plainly and simply—was that he knew and understood the people with whom he was dealing, and he dealt with them with civility and understanding. He knew Congress and how to work with them, but he also knew when, where, and how to move, act, and react.

ROBB He was also a friend to so many of those people, even the ones he differed with on voting. I have now lived in Virginia for fifty years. My husband, Chuck, who's here this morning, was the governor of Virginia and the senator from Virginia, and he's also a lawyer. I must say I have paid for the education of two lawyers and I haven't gotten a bit out of either one of them, in terms of providing legal advice. A lot of good things about them, but they haven't helped me as lawyers. Senator Byrd of Virginia was very important in Daddy's time. When Daddy was president, he got Senator Byrd to vote on a bill that was supported by labor. Someone asked, "Why, did you vote for that bill? Why did you let Lyndon Johnson get that bill out of committee?" Byrd said, "When my niece died, there was a terrible snow storm. Lyndon Johnson was the only member of the Senate who came to her funeral."

So we all have to recognize that having friendships across party lines, knowing people, caring about them, that makes a big difference. That was something Daddy knew and used it to his best advantage. He was there for them, and they were there for him when he needed them.

For the civil rights bill, he purposely crossed the line and urged everybody, including Republicans, to vote for it because he recognized that if he passed a law with both Democrats and Republicans voting for it, then he'd be much more likely to get it not just passed, but have it effective and enforced all over this country. Everybody bought into that approach, and there ended up being only six Republicans who didn't vote for the Civil Rights Act. One of them was Senator Tower; another was Barry Goldwater. But the majority of the Republicans voted for it and it wouldn't have passed without them.

There were a lot of Republican heroes. Imagine a Democratic president giving the first pen he used to sign the bill into law to the Republican leader, Everett Dirksen, but Daddy knew Dirksen and all those people had put their political lives on the line. There were people in Peoria who were not going to be happy about Ev Dirksen's vote and support for the Act. So a big part of Daddy's success came from knowing the people in Congress well, a great advantage.

LBJ AS A READER OF MEN

BOSTON Lynda, it's been said that your father's expertise in the science of politics came because he was a reader of men, not of books. Hubert Humphrey said he was "like a psychiatrist in the way he could size people up and look into a man's heart and know his innermost worries and desires." Give us your perspective on those descriptions of your father.

ROBB I think that's true. I've become more interested and more educated about the passage of the Civil Rights Act in recent years. Believe it or not, they did not pass the law with me behind the scenes pulling all the strings. I was twenty years old in 1964, and I had other things on my mind then. But Daddy was behind the scene pulling strings. He tried to get everybody to live up to the best in them. His first choice was to appeal to their hearts. If you listen to his conversations with George Wallace [that you can hear at the LBJ Library], for instance, he said: "Governor Wallace, you started off as a Populist. Remember you came into government to help the little man. Do you want what's on your tombstone to say 'I was a builder, or do you want it to say, um –'"

TEMPLE "Or do you want what's on your tombstone to say 'I hated'?" I think that resonated with George Wallace, but he was still pretty entrenched in his racism.

ROBB Yes, but he did ask him. Daddy knew viscerally how much the South hated what happened to them in Reconstruction with the Union troops coming down. So he wasn't going to send federal troops into the South when the Selma conflict arose without being asked. He appealed to George Wallace, and that's why Wallace asked him to bring in troops to keep order in Alabama. When Martin Luther King finally marched across the Pettus Bridge, nobody was hit with any batons, and it was a very successful, nonviolent march. But my father got George Wallace to ask him so it was not the president acting on his own in sending troops down. They went to Alabama because Wallace asked for them.

LBJ'S SOFT SIDE AND POWER OF PERSUASION

BOSTON Larry, let's go a little deeper. Are there any characteristics about Lyndon Johnson that you think most people don't know or don't appreciate that came into play in getting the Civil Rights Act passed?

TEMPLE Although I wasn't there in '64, I think Lynda probably has put her finger on it. I think people have a perception of Lyndon Johnson as this big, tough, demanding, overpowering person who would threaten somebody or grab them by the lapels and talk to them, and he did do that, and it was effective. When he got onto somebody, he would get right in his face—even have his nose within three or four inches of the other person's nose. At six feet four [inches tall], he'd be looking down and the other guy would be looking up. I was in that situation on occasion. I know what that does to a person.

But there was also a softness to LBJ that I think has never been fully understood. This mention of attending Senator Byrd's niece's funeral—that was quintessential LBJ. He remembered when somebody had problems, when there was a death in the family, when there was an illness in the family. And he got

people to vote with him like Senator Byrd, not because of what he did in connection with that vote, but because of what he had done over a period of a lifetime with the relationship between the two.

He could be very soft and caring. Around the White House, he was always looking to do something nice for somebody. If I had been working fifteen to sixteen hours a day for several weeks, he would tell me to bring my wife over for lunch, and he'd bring her into the Oval Office and give her something—a chain or a pen or some token. He was very thoughtful and considerate to everybody. I think that was a part of his genius. He did that over a long period of time, and then he was able to encourage people to be reciprocal in doing something for him at a time when he needed help on a piece of legislation.

This will be a little advertisement for the LBJ Library—but you can listen to all the tapes in the exhibits throughout the library. There are about ninety separate telephone conversation tapes. When you do that, you don't have to hear Lynda Robb or Larry Temple tell you about Lyndon Johnson. Lyndon Johnson will tell you about Lyndon Johnson, and you'll hear him say multiple times, "This isn't the president asking you to do this. This is not Lyndon Johnson asking you to do this. This is your country asking you to do this." He would put his request for something on that kind of basis, and people responded.

THE "LADY BIRD SPECIAL" TRAIN RIDE AFTER THE PASSAGE OF THE CIVIL RIGHTS ACT OF 1964

BOSTON Lynda, in your opening remarks you mentioned that immediately after the Civil Rights Act was signed into law, you and your sister Luci joined your mother on a nineteen-car train that the press called "the Lady Bird Special," and traveled from Washington, DC to New Orleans, making forty-seven stops in eight states.

Photo credit: Clay Blackmore

Lynda Johnson Robb

How did Southerners react to the Lady Bird Special's journey in the aftermath of the Civil Rights Act's passage in July 1964?

ROBB Mother particularly wanted the Southern people to know we loved them. Mother said to the crowds during the train tour, "You may not like what I'm saying, but you'll understand my voice when I'm saying it." There was a lot to that. She grew up in deep East Texas and had lots of relatives in Alabama and throughout the South. We tapped into all those relatives when the train came to their area. You can be sure they all came to the train station. We also took along with us on the train a lot of very nice respectable women.

Not long ago, I was speaking to a lady who was with us on the train, and was a little older than I. I asked her, "Your father was a senator from the Deep South. What did he think about you riding on that train going through the South after the Civil Rights Act passed?" She said, "Oh, Lynda, he loved your daddy so much. He understood."

I think there were a lot of people in the South who recognized that even though they didn't like what was in the Civil Rights Act,

and didn't want it, what it called for was going to happen. They could be ugly and mean about it, or they could just accept it and understand that times were changing. Before we went on that trip, Mother called the senators and governors of the states we were going to be going through, and said, "I just want you to know I'm coming down. I didn't want to come into your state without telling you I'm coming. We'd love to have you come and ride through the state with us on the train." "We'd love to have you meet us when we come to Richmond," or whatever.

When Chuck was governor of Virginia, I had all the governors and their spouses come to the Governor's Mansion. The ladies gathered around and told stories about what our 1964 train trip was like for them. One of the stories was about Governor Godwin. In Virginia we do everything differently, and we have off-year elections because we're not going to be influenced by the federal government. Senator Byrd made our election cycle go that way. So the story was that we were going to Virginia on the train. Mother called the sitting governor, and he didn't really want to come to the train station, so he sent his lieutenant governor (who was part of the Byrd machine) to meet us in Richmond, who was Mills Godwin. Mills later told me, "I never would have been elected governor if I hadn't come to meet you and your mother at the train station." He was a Democrat, and he had been a good governor, particularly good on education. He said, "I knew if I hadn't come, the moderates—let's not use that bad word—the liberals in the Democratic Party in Virginia, would have opposed me in the primary, and I wouldn't have been elected governor." He recognized the importance of that gesture and what a difference it made.

We went through a lot of states. At first, there were bomb threats. The biggest scare for me, though, was not the bomb threats. We would always send a cart through ahead of us, and hope that if there was a bomb on the train bridge tracks, it would wipe out that little push cart. The main worry was the fact that the people in these towns were so polarized that you would get the African-Americans and the supporters of the Civil Rights movement on one side, and then you would have the very anti-civil rights people on the other side, and then maybe they would get into a fight and that would be the story.

In some places we went, people said, "Down with the Black Bird," and many other things that were not near as nice about us traveling through their part of the country. We really worried about what might happen if those two groups clashed. In some places it was very violent. In her speeches, Mother would have all her dignity, and say, "All right. You've had your opportunity to speak; now let me have mine." Her demeanor carried the day. So the people who opposed us quieted down a bit, and would let her speak.

There were places where they would deny us the use of the facilities in the area. You had to stay really close to the train. It was an interesting, scary time. There were a lot of brave men, members of the Democratic Party, who came out to meet us. We were lucky all around. We had good people, and good religious leaders who supported us and came out to meet us. We had a lot of people who came and were willing to put their names on the line too, and risk everything, including their livelihoods. It was an exciting time. We felt we could really make a difference in this country, and I think we did make a difference.

One of the many good things about having anniversaries, like the fiftieth anniversary of just about everything in the next two or three years, is that you get to hear so many wonderful stories about people you never knew about. Recently, there was a story in the paper about the Job Corps. You all know about George Foreman being in the Job Corps as a young man. When he won his belt for being the heavyweight champion, he sent it to Daddy because he recognized it was the Job Corps that gave him the opportunity to be a great fighter. Somebody

Larry Temple

wrote in and said, "I'm the man you're talking about in the story about the Job Corps." He said his parents didn't support him financially like he needed, and so at sixteen, he went into the Job Corps. He said, "I got my GED in the Job Corps, then I went on to college, then I got my law degree, and now I'm the chief judge of Idaho." And when my daughter Catherine was doing a triathlon in Idaho, she talked to that judge. Some of you out there in the audience may have been affected by some of those laws passed in the '60s. We all benefited. Being on Medicare now, I'm very pleased.

LBJ'S LEGACY AS THE GRAND CHAMPION OF CIVIL RIGHTS

BOSTON Larry, let's close with your observation, as the chairman of the Lyndon Baines Johnson Foundation, of where President Johnson's legacy is today as our champion of civil rights.

Do you believe all the activities during the fifty-year anniversary of the Act have confirmed in the public mindset that it was President Lyndon Johnson, more than anyone else, who succeeded in getting the American civil rights heroic effort codified into the books of law?

TEMPLE I don't think there's any question about it, and that's not just my opinion. My opinion is biased and I acknowledge that. But we had at the LBJ Library in April what we called the Civil Rights Summit to recognize the fiftieth anniversary of the '64 Civil Rights Act's passage. Broader than that, we focused on all three planks of the civil rights legislation—the '64 Act, the '65 Voting Rights Act, and the '68 Fair Housing Act. We had all the great leaders of the Civil Rights movement of the '60s here. John Lewis, whom I mentioned earlier, was here. Some of you may not know about John Lewis. What a remarkable human being he is. When he was twenty-two or twenty-three, he literally got beat up and almost killed on Bloody Sunday in Selma at the Pettus Bridge in March 1965. Now he's one of the great, distinguished members of the Congress. Andrew Young and a myriad of other people came here. Every one of them said, "Lyndon Johnson is the civil rights president," and "We would not have had the advancements in civil rights if it had not been for Lyndon Johnson."

Then we had four people that came with a bit of credibility on the subject of who was *the* civil rights president. On Tuesday night of the summit, President Jimmy Carter came. On Wednesday night, President Bill Clinton came. At noon on Thursday, President Obama came, and on Thursday night, we had President George W. Bush. The only missing one in that group was President George H. W. Bush, who was invited, and wanted to come, but he didn't feel like he was up to it physically; but he asked to have his name attached to the summit, and be an honorary co-chairman of it.

We had five presidents involved, and all four who came here said, and President Obama said repeatedly—a dozen or more times—"Lyndon Johnson is civil rights." He is the one, and history will say that one

hundred years from now, two hundred years from now, and I think there's absolutely no doubt about it. As I said, my opinion is biased, but we've got some pretty good objective opinions that have reached the same conclusion.

BOSTON Lynda has something she wants to read to us to close the program.

ROBB In our family, we have a motto: "Take a breath, lose your turn," because we all often talk over each other. As President Reagan said: "It's my mike." So I'd just like to finish up.

One of the things Daddy recognized was the importance of getting the Civil Rights Act passed. The first papers that were opened here at the LBJ Library were the Civil Rights papers. We had a big meeting there on that occasion, and it was in December, and it was cold, and Daddy was having heart trouble. His doctor told him he could not come to the opening of the summit, and warned him, "If you go to that, you might die." Daddy replied: "What better way to go!" That day, when he opened the civil rights papers, he reminded us that justice and the fight for equal status were never ending. He concluded his remarks that day by saying, "If our hearts are right, and if courage remains our constant companion, then my fellow Americans, I am confident we shall overcome."

We're now fighting some of these battles fifty years later. It's not up to members of Congress alone or the president. It's up to every one of us to make sure that those things done in the 1960s, that belief that all have an obligation to help every person live up to the best that God gave us, then those must be *our* goals today, and not just the goals of the politicians.

Thank you for letting us come and talk to you about it. I hope you will go out strengthened to work to make this a better country. Thank you.

DR. HENRY KISSINGER served as our national security advisor and secretary of state for Presidents Richard Nixon and Gerald Ford. He is the recipient of the Nobel Peace Prize and the Presidential Medal of Freedom. I interviewed him on March 15, 2013 at the Hilton Anatole Hotel Ballroom at an event sponsored by the World Affairs Council of Dallas/Fort Worth.

"Because of the way it all ended, I look back at Vietnam with great sadness because our country should never have been that divided. If the vast majority of Americans had understood what we were up against, I think they would have come to very similar conclusions like we did. Our basic view was that we would be very flexible in our military activities, but we would not turn our backs on people who chose our side in reliance on the Americans' word. We would not turn them over to the Communists." – **DR. HENRY KISSINGER**

CHAPTER 28

HENRY KISSINGER
ON
His Life, Richard Nixon, & the Current International Situation

KISSINGER'S JOURNEY INTO PUBLIC SERVICE

BOSTON Dr. Kissinger, knowing you to be a great baseball fan, let me begin by saying what a thrill it is to be here with the Babe Ruth of international statesmen.

Let's begin at the beginning. You started your international affairs career as an academic at Harvard. After receiving your PhD, what happened that made you set your sights on being a player on the field and not just a commentator on the sidelines?

KISSINGER Actually, I didn't start out my career anticipating that my field would one day be international affairs. When I came to this country in 1938 as a teenager, my first job was working in a shaving brush factory. When it was time for college, I went to school at night and studied accounting at City College in New York. Then, when the United States began participating in World War II, it was in the army where I got the idea to try to do public service at some point. After the war ended, under the GI Bill of Rights, I went to Harvard.

At the outset of my time in academia, I didn't have a fixed plan of how to get into public service. I usually tell my students who want to participate in public service: "Do what interests you most while you're studying in college. If you write something significant, sooner or later they will find you."

If you try to plot my life, you see how things seem to have fallen into place. I was appointed national security advisor by Richard Nixon, whom I had never met before. Before that, I had been a foreign policy advisor to Nelson Rockefeller, who was Nixon's principal opponent in the 1968 election. Seeing how things have gone in my life, I don't think you can plan public service. What you can do is think about where the country should go and what contribution you might make, and then let life take care it.

KISSINGER ON NIXON

BOSTON You've certainly done a good job of that. Regarding your service with President Nixon, in your book, *Years of Upheaval*, you said, "There was no true Nixon. There were several warring personalities which struggled for preeminence in the same individual."

Obviously, there was a very good Nixon and there was a bad Nixon. Fortunately, you connected with the good Nixon in your many foreign achievements. Did you ever figure out who or what was motivating the bad Nixon?

KISSINGER No. I never the saw the bad Nixon, and I don't accept the general media notion about there being a bad Nixon. From my perspective, Nixon was a distinguished president who performed great service for the country. He suffered from some personal insecurities and that made his human relationships more complex than they should have been. In order to balance his insecurities, he sometimes did things in order to avoid direct personal confrontations.

If you look at the actual decisions he made, in both domestic and foreign policy, his overriding principle was, "You pay the same price for doing something halfway as for doing it completely, so you might as well do it completely."

I have always urged people to look at what Nixon did and not at what happened with the Watergate situation, which was a series of people doing some pretty stupid things, some of which he wasn't even directly involved. I think over time Nixon will be seen as an important president.

KISSINGER ON THE LEADERS WHO MOST IMPACTED THE WORLD IN THE TWENTIETH CENTURY

BOSTON On the subject of great international leadership, in your book *Diplomacy*, you say that "top political leadership involves bridging the gap between experience and vision," which "requires an instinctive grasp of historical currents," and also requires "being bold enough to operate at the limit of what a situation permits."

Using that definition, not including yourself, whom do you regard as the two or three top political leaders in the world over the last one hundred years?

KISSINGER De Gaulle, Mandela, Sadat, Franklin Roosevelt, Theodore Roosevelt, and Mao. I'm applying the criteria you gave. I'm not saying necessarily that I'd vote for them.

BOSTON Mao?

KISSINGER Although he was responsible for many deaths, he qualifies as a top leader based on his impact on the world and his own Chinese society.

KISSINGER ON THE FALL OF SOUTH VIETNAM

BOSTON Going back to the time you spent as President Nixon's national security advisor, one of the greatest challenges you assumed was being the lead negotiator to bring us out of the Vietnam War. On behalf of people my age, I want to thank you for doing that.

From your perspective, after you succeeded in getting us extricated from the war, what was it that caused South Vietnam to fall as fast as it did?

KISSINGER The tragedy of the whole Vietnam experience was that America entered that war with the absolute best motives. We wanted to achieve in Asia what we had achieved in Europe—namely to keep countries out of the control of Communist pressures.

The Kennedy and Johnson administrations got us involved and they did not estimate correctly that the challenge in Vietnam was different than it had been in Europe—because Vietnam had no history of being a state. So our efforts there were in the context of coming to the aid of a state that was just getting built while it was in the middle of a civil war.

Then, sometime after we became involved in the war, America turned on itself. The issue of the Vietnam War became a huge debate on the theory that our government was somehow guilty of something, which caused people to begin pressuring the government.

I worked with Presidents Kennedy, Johnson, and Nixon. Nobody had a greater incentive to get our country out the war than the president of the United States. On the one hand, we were dealing with an adversary, yet we Americans approached dealing with that adversary at the outset of our involvement with a strategy of seeking to achieve compromise. To our Vietnamese enemies, compromise was defeat, so they had no desire to compromise. Their goal was to bring down the entire South Vietnamese political system.

By 1972, in the negotiations I conducted, the whole situation had turned into a nightmare, such that our adversaries would read to me statements condemning what we were doing in Vietnam that came from members of the US Senate and from *The New York Times*. Then I would say, "Here is our position. We don't pay attention to that."

Photo credit: *Courtesy of The Richard Nixon Presidential Library and Museum (National Archives and Records Administration)*

Finally, by the end of 1972, we got an agreement. Could that agreement have lasted? Who knows? We thought it could. But then came Watergate, and at the same time, Congress cut the budget for Vietnam from $2.5 billion to $700 million at a time when oil prices were quadrupling, which caused the South Vietnamese Army to ration artillery shells and limit flights. Then Congress prohibited any American military action in support of making sure the settlement agreement was enforced. If you make an agreement that you're not willing to enforce, it's a kind of surrender.

Because of the way it all ended, I look back at Vietnam with great sadness because our country should never have been that divided. If the vast majority of Americans had understood what we were up against, I think they would have come to very similar conclusions like we did. Our basic view was that we would be very flexible in our military activities, but we would not turn our backs on people who chose our side in reliance on the Americans' word. We would not turn them over to the Communists. If they want to vote themselves into becoming a Communist regime somewhere down the line, that's their problem.

Right now, I believe that America's involvement in the Vietnam War is not being taught at universities in any objective way. Someday, we will really have to ask ourselves, "How did we come to split our country so much over this war?" The community who protested our government's activities during the war caused the split. In my view, they are the reason why South Vietnam collapsed so quickly. Could it have maintained itself indefinitely? I don't know. Maybe—maybe not—but maybe it could have gone the way South Korea did. It certainly had the resources.

KISSINGER'S EXPLANATION FOR AMERICA'S RECENT LACK OF SUCCESS IN FOREIGN WARS

BOSTON You were one of our first foreign policy experts to recognize that America has limits on what it can do in international affairs. Obviously, our nation's ambitions exceeded our military commitment and probably our political will in Vietnam, Iraq, and Afghanistan.

Why does America keep entering wars that it doesn't know how to end?

KISSINGER It happens because we have a tendency to deal with foreign policy as a missionary enterprise, such that we define our purpose in entering wars around the world as an effort to transform the world to our principles. As a general objective, that is of course what we prefer to happen when we make the decision to participate in a war, but when you apply that rationale to concrete cases, you always must ask yourself, "What are the limits of what America can do?"

For example, take Iraq. There, a third of the country is Shia, a third of the country is Sunni, and a third of the country is Kurd. They were put together into a single country in 1920 by the British, who wanted to block Iran and also wanted to block the Arab national resurgence. The British had

no idea how to make such a divided country work when they formed it.

Our objectives in entering into the Iraq War were absolutely noble, but we didn't take into account that the Shias and Sunnis have been fighting each other in a religious conflict since the ninth century. The Kurds are yet another group that have been striving for independence. On the whole, we've actually been fairly successful in what we did in Iraq in a ten-year period, but then the American public support ran out.

We have fought four wars that we entered with great enthusiasm, and all were fought with 80% public support initially, but then we didn't know how to end them. The reason we didn't know how to end them was because we did not translate our general objectives into political objectives that could lead to a successful negotiation, or we did not understand properly the extent of the other side's thinking.

One of the big tasks in front of our country now is in analyzing the issues in the world in which we may want or need to exercise our influence. We have to divide these issues intellectually among three groups: those which are so important to us that we would be willing to pursue them alone, if necessary; those that are important to us but which we can't succeed in carrying out unless we have widespread support; and finally, those that are significant, but we cannot act on them. We have to start thinking this way in how we go about analyzing situations and what we are going to do about them.

The second thing we have to recognize is that we have fought in these troublesome wars where the front lines were in the interior of Asia, and, therefore, the enemy would win if it only survived. Time was totally on their side. We have to have a more peripheral strategy in those types of wars and determine how to maximize our geographic position. If you look at how Wellington defeated Napoleon, it wasn't by fighting a war at the center of the continent at first; it started at the very edge of the country.

So these are general observations about our lack of success in some recent wars; but when you talk of American failures, you also have to talk about American successes. We won the Cold War. We restored Europe. The international system is more or less following market principle maxims. But when we became too enthusiastic about the social and political engineering we thought we could do in countries like Vietnam, Iraq, and Afghanistan, we were not successful.

KISSINGER ON THE SYRIAN SITUATION (AS OF MARCH 2013)

BOSTON Which brings us to Syria. Obviously that's now a hot situation. Last week, you said America should do what we can there, short of using ground forces. But with over seventy thousand killed and over a million people having fled the country in the last year, and now with Iran stepping up with substantial military assistance to the Syrian government, there appears to be little prospect of things settling down there. If you were president of the United States today, what steps would you take regarding the Syrian crisis?

KISSINGER The first step I'd take is to get the smartest people I can find to analyze the problem and tell me what is the issue there, and then let them reach a conclusion.

When instability in Syria started, a lot of American attention was focused on how to get rid of Assad, as if it was a question of dealing with a single individual. Now the thing we need to remember about Assad is he started life as an ophthalmologist. I'm sure he's sitting in Damascus now, mourning the day when his father pulled him out of his ophthalmology practice in London because his older brother had been killed in an automobile accident.

So, Assad represents not just himself as an individual; he represents the Alawite minority and the Shia minority that has been governing Syria since the 1970s. They also supply all the army officers. So what's happening in Syria is really an ethnic struggle between Alawites on the one hand, Sunnis on the other, where most of the other minorities, including the Christians, are supporting the Alawites because they are afraid of Sunni domination.

When you look at an ethnic conflict, of course you could say that if you utilize overpowering force, you might be able to get it under control. Then, however, if you do that, you might also find yourself in a situation like Iraq, where we found ourselves in the middle of the civil war of all against all.

So we have to ask: What is our national interest? We certainly have an American national interest in preventing Iran from emerging out of this upheaval as a dominant country in Syria. So I would support any approach by which we support forces that fight the Iranians.

Regarding the most desirable outcome, what is most conducive to our principles would be an outcome in which every ethnic group can lead a certain autonomous existence and they can all come together in a benign central government. When you say that, however, that's like the person who allegedly said that the way to solve the submarine problem is to heat the ocean and boil them to the surface. Somebody else then replied, "How do you do that?" Then the first fellow said, "I've given you the idea. The technical implementation is up to you."

So, as a general rule, if we can identify ethnic groups that support an outcome like I have described, I would favor supporting them. What I don't think we should do though is to get into another open-ended commitment where we put military forces into a country in the midst of a civil war that has been going on for a long time. If we do that, then it will end like Afghanistan.

In Syria, Russia could be helpful. Russia's fear is that they have thirty million Muslims in their country, and if radicalism spreads too much in Syria, it will reach Russia very quickly. So we should attempt to get together with the Europeans and Russians to come up with some guiding principles and then find groups that, after we achieve success, will govern according to these principles. If we can't do these things, then Syria will remain a tragedy, but we can't solve every tragedy by using American military presence on the ground.

KISSINGER ON CHINA (AS OF MARCH 2013)

BOSTON When most people hear the name "Kissinger," the first word that comes to mind is "China," and the diplomatic revolution that you and President Nixon engineered there. Earlier this week, new Chinese President Xi said his number one priority is for China to surpass the US as the world's top military power, and he predicted a marathon contest for global dominion. What's your reaction to that statement at a time when our congressmen in Washington, DC are aggressively pursuing ways to cut America's defense?

KISSINGER Xi is the newly-installed president of a country where he almost certainly has less power than the American president in the sense that he cannot just walk into his office and order something to happen. China is a country run by a constellation of various constituencies in which Xi is clearly the dominant figure. So whenever I see his speeches, I like to see what audience he's addressing.

In the history of the world, when you have a country rising like China is, and a country that's well-established like the United States, that situation very often leads to conflict. Many people say World War I started because Germany was on the rise and Britain was established, and the established country and the new country went to war. That's true. But then you have to ask yourself, "If the people who went to war in 1914 had known what the world would look like in 1918, would they have ever gone to war?" I doubt it.

So here we have China, a country with a different culture, undergoing considerable development. You ask, "Can they outdo us in a military way?" I can't conceive that they could reach that conclusion; but if they try, then we will have a conflict.

I realize pursuing peaceful relations with China would work only if they would join us. I'd like for us to see whether, in a world in which there are so many problems to be solved, can we and China evolve into a cooperative model? From a purely military point of view, it's very hard to see how either country could really defeat the other, but when you have energy, non-proliferation, and cyber issues—which really is sure to happen, given all the new technology that they are developing—I think a cooperative effort is needed to see whether our discordant relations with China can be harmonized.

If China really did what their president has said, and they'd have a long way to go before they can do it, then of course we will resist, and our resistance would emanate from a very strong position. Look, China is a country that right now has to move four hundred million people from the countryside into the cities. They have, by their own terms, a significant problem of corruption. They have to move the center of gravity of their country from the coast into the interior, and to do all of this in the midst of a military-type conflict with the United States would be very short-sighted from their point of view.

I think we should know what our national interest is—that we will not permit the hegemony of any country in the world—but we should also recognize that we are living in a new world. Look how the energy pattern has changed, in which the significance of the Middle East is diminishing because of our own development of energy sources in our own country. I think we should trust our own evolution, and if military conflicts are necessary, we'll of course have to engage in them, but first we should try to construct a more peaceful international system.

KISSINGER ON THE ISRAELI-PALESTINIAN RELATIONSHIP (AS OF MARCH 2013)

BOSTON During lunch, before we started our program, we had many photographs of you with a number of Israeli and Arab leaders over the last several decades. Of course, we're mindful of your success in ending the Yom Kippur War by playing a lead role in initiating the meetings that brought to fruition a resolution through shuttle diplomacy.

Let's again assume that today, you are President Kissinger. Would you be taking the lead in getting discussions going between the Israeli and Palestinian leaders in hopes of brokering a settlement?

KISSINGER In 1973, when I was active and started a number of these resolution efforts, the situation was that the people armed by the United States had won the war. So those people who wanted a change realized that we were the key to the solution, and that gave us a very strong bargaining position to lead the parties toward resolution.

In the present world, we have the Arab Spring, which started as an expression of local resentment but has now brought every country into key positions, including the Muslim Brotherhood, which for decades has dedicated itself to being an anti-Western pro-Sharia-type movement. Because of this, the objective conditions and the calculations people make have become more uncertain.

Still, I think an effort should be made by the United States to promote a Palestinian-Israeli negotiation. The question is whether we should aim at a negotiation that settles everything all at once or whether we should go step-by-step. I prefer step-by-step because when you want to do the whole thing, and you want to get guarantees and verification of every aspect, it gets so complicated and so dependent on domestic changes that it often blows up in your face. But I would be open-minded, and I think it's a worthwhile effort for the administration to support that process.

KISSINGER ON THE US-IRAN RELATIONSHIP (AS OF MARCH 2013)

BOSTON For my last question before we get to questions from the audience, we have to talk about Iran, a country that has bedeviled the United States now for several decades. You've said recently several times that the next twelve months are crucial and that President Obama has important decisions, policies, and strategies that he needs to implement involving this very volatile situation.

Again, let's assume we have President Kissinger instead of President Obama. What do you do during the next twelve months about that situation?

KISSINGER You would have to change the Constitution.

BOSTON Let's assume we've gotten past that.

KISSINGER I'm often described as a realist. I think that's got to be a good way of looking at this issue. The right way to look at these problems is to ask: What are we trying to do? What are we trying to prevent? And what are the facts in the case, (which you would do as a lawyer)?

Now, the facts in the case are these—for at least fifteen years, the United States and its allies have said that an Iranian nuclear military capability is unacceptable, but they've never exactly defined what they mean by "unacceptable" and what they mean by "military capability."

There are three elements to military strategic capability: delivery systems, physical material, and warheads. The Iranians have already finished building the delivery systems. They are out of our control and they are very hard to stop. Now they are in the phase of acquiring physical material. That is the most difficult part, but once they get it, making a warhead is relatively easy.

So when I say something has to be decided in the next twelve months, I mean

Photo credit: Jurgen Frank

Dr. Henry Kissinger

this: If this process by the Iranians goes on much longer, Iran could accumulate so much physical material—and scientists would have to tell you the exact amount—that they could go at any moment to the warhead phase, just like the Koreans have been doing. If that happens, it would change the situation in the region completely because then the other countries would do their utmost to buy or build nuclear weapons. Those are the stakes.

Now the issue is that we are engaged in a negotiation. We have to look at this negotiation to determine whether we are making a progress that enables us to say we have stopped the enrichment process at the point where they could not make nuclear weapons, except by a huge violation extended over a long period of time. I think we're getting very close to the point where this point could be reached. But to get the Iranians to agree to that, the president has to decide whether to step up sanctions and use other pressures, or whether he wants to make some settlement along whatever lines he wants without stepping up the sanctions.

I'm bothered by the fact that if you compare the original position the United States took fifteen years ago with where

we are now, an Iranian could come to the conclusion that rejecting American proposals doesn't cost much because Iran gets a better offer every time there's a new negotiation. It's a very tough decision that has to be made, and we have to remember in making it not to get ourselves into another open-ended conflict. But that's where I think we stand and that's why I say we can't carry this process as a negotiation much further without either getting an agreement or else making a significant increase in applying economic sanction pressure to them.

KISSINGER ON AMERICA'S PLACE IN THE WORLD AND DEALING WITH NORTH KOREA (AS OF MARCH 2013)

JIM FALK (CEO, World Affairs Council of Dallas/Fort Worth) Talmage, thank you so much and you can imagine the number of questions we've received from the audience. We have time for only one or two more. Many have asked Dr. Kissinger, "What really worries you the most today that affects our national interest and world security?" There were also many questions about the changes in North Korea and the recent aggressive posture of its new leader.

KISSINGER Let me say first that it's in the essence of a discussion like we're having now that you talk about problems. You're bound to ask questions of things that bother you. But if you think about the future of the world in the next thirty years, you might ask yourself why should the United States not be able to be at the beginning of a great period? The change in energy production, which we look at as a daily story, should mean great things for our country. If we become self-sufficient or substantially self-sufficient in energy, the significance of some of the regions of the world who have been able to blackmail us will be significantly different. We also know that the manufacturing sector in the United States should pick up significantly when our energy costs go down—as they will. So if you look around the world, ask yourself: Whose hand would you rather play than the American hand? So I am actually optimistic about the long-term for our country despite all the threatening situations that exist around the world.

You mentioned North Korea, which is an absolutely weird regime. Communist regimes normally have a party and some kind of structure, but the North Korean regime is a family enterprise run by one family in an unbelievably brutal manner. For example, North Korea's a country where every house has a radio in it that the inhabitants cannot turn off so that the government can talk to them twenty-four hours a day. North Korea used to be the industrial base for Korea. If you compare North Korea and South Korea, North Korea is now a basket case from an economic standpoint in almost every respect. At the cost of horrible famines, they have managed to build a few nuclear weapons and their conduct in international affairs is based on irrationality, so they threaten they will go to war; but I don't think they have enough reserves to go to war for more than two weeks. This is not a strong country. It's a ruthless country that, if it fires artillery into Seoul, could do huge damage, but I'm not worried about its nuclear weapons—certainly not *vis-a-vis* us.

One of the dangers is, however, that North Korea is a country that matters a great deal to China, Japan, and now to us. I could imagine that if the North Korean regime collapses one day, then the responses to that by China, US, Russia—everybody—to try to calibrate this could lead to a very dangerous situation. So this is something that we ought to address.

The capacity of North Korea to threaten anyone for more than a suicide attack is in my opinion extremely limited, but it's an extremely ruthless regime, though not a very strong regime. There's huge suffering there which they exact by terror, but it's a subject on which the surrounding countries really ought to come to some understanding and not let themselves be sucked into a conflict by these really irresponsible bunch of leaders.

KISSINGER ON THE CHANGES IN THE MEDIA'S COVERAGE OF WORLD AFFAIRS

FALK One last question, Dr. Kissinger. "So much has changed in the role of the media since you were secretary of state. How have those changes affected the conduct of our foreign policy now?"

KISSINGER Well, I hate to be nostalgic about the role of media. We had a tough time with the media that existed when I was secretary of state. The way the media has changed is that during the period when I first came into government, we had the evening news on three networks and it was the main daily television event about news.

Now we have a twenty-four-hours-a-day news cycle on many networks. The presenters have to get your attention, so they recycle crises, and then they have to have controversy whose central nature is rarely explained, such that the level of the public's concern is heightened, but it's not focused on anything sufficiently concrete.

In the print world, and God knows I did not enjoy that part of the media either, when I led the State Department, there were a few columnists doing serious work over extended periods of time whose opinions were influential at the time. I don't know any columnist today who has that degree of influence sufficient to compete with twenty-four-hour television news cycle.

Another thing about the media that has changed is the way knowledge is acquired. When you read something, you have to put it into some context in order to retain it in your mind because otherwise, it won't stick. But when you can acquire knowledge by pressing a button, and meet your immediate need by looking it up on Google, and then you can forget it because you know you can always go back and find it instantly, then the total impact of this method of processing information requires less conceptual understanding.

Real knowledge, in my opinion at least, consists of getting a view of how you go from where you are to where you haven't been. You can't look that up. You can only acquire that, and in studies of statesmen that I have concerned myself with, the people who have been best have been the ones who had a sense of history, and our society now is getting deprived of that to some extent.

Again, on the positive side, there are so many technical means of addressing what I have just described that once it's recognized, then it will hopefully be addressed. I don't want to leave you with the pessimistic impression. I have described problems because I was asked about problems. If you ask me for the overall situation, if we straighten out our own thinking, this could be the beginning of a great period for America, not a period of retreat. That would be my basic message to you.

FALK And that is a wonderful message for us to thank you and to end on. Dr. Kissinger, thank you for the contributions you've made to our nation's history.

JAMES A. BAKER, III has been recognized by many as "the man who made Washington work" while serving as President Ronald Reagan's White House chief of staff and secretary of the treasury, and then President George H.W. Bush's secretary of state. I had the privilege of interviewing Secretary Baker at Rice University's Baker Institute of Public Policy before a large group of students, professors, and admirers on December 2, 2015.

Photo credit: Michael Stravato/Polaris

"My view of pragmatism has always been to get stuff done without sacrificing principle, and Ronald Reagan was also very much a principled pragmatist. I can't tell you how many times I was with him in the Oval Office, just the two of us, talking about some effort we were working on right then on Capitol Hill, and he would look at me and say, 'Jim, I'd rather get 80% of what I want than go over the cliff with my flag flying.'" – JAMES A. BAKER, III

CHAPTER 29

JAMES A. BAKER, III
ON
Ronald Reagan & George H.W. Bush

BOSTON Let's begin with the presidency of Ronald Reagan.

REAGAN, BAKER, AND THE FAR RIGHT

BOSTON Secretary Baker, even though you opposed him in the Republican presidential race in 1976 when you were leading Gerald Ford's campaign, and also on the opposite side of him for the first five months of 1980 when you were leading George H.W. Bush's presidential campaign, Reagan obviously saw something in you he liked, even though you were a "moderate" Republican while Reagan's followers were the "true believers"

of the Far Right. Then, after George Bush dropped out of the race in 1980, Ronald Reagan asked you first to be the head of preparing him for the presidential debate, and then later named you as his White House chief of staff, arguably the most important position in his administration.

As Ronald Reagan kept calling your number during the last half of 1980, how did you read the tea leaves about Reagan's commitment to the true believers on the Far Right?

BAKER I really wasn't too concerned about his views of the true believers on the Far Right after he asked me to be his

White House chief of staff and I accepted the position. I knew we would have an administration that would be oriented toward getting things done, and everyone—including President Reagan—knew that the Far Right believed the word "pragmatist" was a dirty word.

My view of pragmatism has always been to get stuff done without sacrificing principle, and Ronald Reagan was also very much a principled pragmatist. I can't tell you how many times I was with him in the Oval Office, just the two of us, talking about some effort we were working on right then on Capitol Hill, and he would look at me and say, "Jim, I'd rather get 80% of what I want than go over the cliff with my flag flying."

People think he was an ideologue, but he wasn't. Yes, he was very conservative and held very firm beliefs that were strongly conservative. He understood though that we judge our presidents not just on their beliefs, but more importantly on the basis of what they get accomplished—meaning how much of their programs and policies they can get through the Congress.

He used to tell a joke—and nobody was a better joke teller than Ronald Reagan—and said that somebody in the press was interviewing him, and told him how conservative, and how far over on the right he and his people were. Reagan said he heard the guy out, and then replied, "Yeah, you know sometimes in our administration, our right hand doesn't know what our far right hand is doing."

REAGAN'S AGE AND MENTAL ACUITY DURING HIS PRESIDENCY

BOSTON Shortly into his presidency in May 1981, President Reagan was shot by an assassin but then obviously survived to lead the country until January 1989. In the last couple of months, there's been an uproar over Fox television pundit Bill O'Reilly's best-selling non-fiction book, which purports to be history, that's entitled *Killing Reagan* and it's premised on the idea that after President Reagan was shot, he went into a mental decline that lasted the remainder of his presidency. The book has been discredited by many, but it does raise the age issue.

Was there any time after President Reagan regained his health following the shooting that you ever sensed any mental decline at all until he left office in January of 1989?

BAKER The answer is: No. Never.

I don't buy the argument that somehow in the latter years of his presidency, he began suffering from Alzheimer's. That's just not accurate. I never noticed anything about his being in any sort of decline, and I was his treasury secretary during his second term up until July of '88 when I left to run George H.W. Bush's campaign for presidency. While at Treasury, I was with him often—though not as much as when I was his White House chief of staff and was at his right hand every single day—and I never noticed any slowdown at all.

The first time I noticed anything about his decline came in 1993, when I went to a Republican National Committee event after President Bush and I had just been involuntarily retired from public service. President Reagan was there, and as I went up to shake hands, I heard Nancy tell him, "It's Jim Baker, Ronny." That was the first time I became aware he was going downhill, and that was in 1993, after he had left office in 1989. He wrote his letter to the American people acknowledging his Alzheimer's in 1994.

THE JOB OF WHITE HOUSE CHIEF OF STAFF

BOSTON In describing your job as White House chief of staff, you've said that a major responsibility was to catch the javelins aimed at the president. During your four years, did you miss any?

BAKER Probably missed a bunch of them, but that's part of the chief of staff's job. The person holding the position is a semi-gate-keeper. But I'll tell you that President Reagan didn't want to be isolated or in-sulated. We had a post office box where anybody could write him—and they did—during the four years I was chief of staff. A lot of people would write him, and he would answer their letters in his own per-sonal hand. Martin and Annelise Anderson have written a book that documents this correspondence. He was by no means pro-tected, and there was no praetorian guard around Ronald Reagan. He didn't want it and we didn't have it.

What the chief of staff mainly tries to protect the president from is people com-ing at him with requests that begin with, "Oh, by the way…" By this, I'm referring to when there would be a Cabinet meeting, and we were talking about something do-mestic, and one of the Cabinet members on his way out of the meeting, would say, "Oh, by the way, Mr. President, I think we need such and such." My job was to kill these "Oh, by the way…" requests—and I did.

BAKER AS REAGAN'S POLITICAL PRISM

BOSTON As White House chief of staff, you also said in your book that a big part of your job was to advise the president on policy questions through your "political prism."

In H.W. Brands' new biography of Reagan, he said you definitely did that for President Reagan when there was an ef-fort to pursue social security reform in '81 (shortly after he came back from the shoot-ing), which was being advocated by then Secretary of Health and Human Services Richard Schweiker. You decided that Schweiker's initiative was not something the president should initially have his name on; but rather that it should be Health and Human Services who was the lead promot-er of it, because you could see it was going to sink.

Do you think it was your handling of that social security reform effort early in his administration that caused Ronald Reagan to view you as his lodestar to guide him through Congress' political waters?

BAKER No, I don't think so. The job of the White House chief of staff is to navigate the intersection between politics and policy. By virtue of the position, the chief of staff is to serve as the president's political advisor when it comes to decisions involving policy. This social security deal in 1981 was some-thing cooked up by Dick Schweiker and David Stockman. When it was presented to us, it had not been vetted, and there had never been any discussion about it in the Cabinet Council or anywhere else. In the Oval Office, we had never talked about it.

We knew we were going to take on social security at some point. But in those very early days in the administration, we regarded social security as the third rail of politics—anyone who touched it would get electrocuted. President Reagan very much wanted to do something about social securi-ty. We all did. But I thought it was a mistake for the president's name to be on it right out of the box. I thought the proposal from HHS and Schweiker should come from them with their name on it. Then later, if it looked like it might get somewhere, the president could support it. And that's what we did.

After Schweiker's bill got voted down unanimously by Congress in 1991, we proposed our own plan for reforming so-cial security, and the president was quite happy with it. We formed a Social Security Reform Commission and made some changes in social security aimed at protect-ing the sovereignty of the system for the next thirty years. We bumped the retirement age up a little bit and increased the contri-butions people had to make. Therefore, the bill we ultimately submitted to Congress had something in it for Democrats and something for Republicans, and we got it passed in 1983. It was the last time anybody has been successful with any type of social security reform.

The way we achieved social security reform demonstrates what I said about Reagan. He was not hung up on idealism at all costs. He understood the importance of getting things done and what he ultimately did with social security is a good example.

Tax reform is another example. We passed the Tax Reform Act in 1986. That's the last time there's been any tax reform and it was the first time it had been done in a hundred years. We did it because of the Gipper's leadership and with Democratic votes. To get to the goal line though, we had to deal with a rebellion at one point from some of the more hardline Republican members in the House. President Reagan finally went up to Capitol Hill and said, "Fellows, this is what we need to do and what I want done."

The reason for the rebellion was because we had to first get the bill through the House Ways and Means Committee, which has always had jurisdiction for all tax measures. Dan Rostenkowski was chairman of Ways and Means then, so for it to get through the committee meant it would necessarily have to be a Democratic bill. Some Far Right Republicans didn't support it for that reason. President Reagan wanted all Republicans to vote for it, and his message to the hardliners was: "Hey, fellows, vote for this. Get it out of the House. We'll fix it in the Senate where we have a majority; and if the Senate doesn't fix it, then I'll veto it."

That approach wasn't good enough for some of the Republicans and they started rebelling against President Reagan. Finally, he went up to the Hill and Dick Cheney tells a great story about this. Dick says that right before President Reagan went up to talk to the House caucus, there had been a terrible accident out at Fort Meyers, Virginia, where some of our servicemen had been killed. Reagan stood up to the assembled House caucus meeting and spent his first thirty minutes talking about the tragic accident and the heroism of these

fine young Americans who had served their country and lost their lives. After that, he said, "Now, fellows, let's talk about the tax bill." Dick Cheney had been one of the leaders of the rebellion and said at that point, it was all over.

The president then had the hardline Republicans in tow, and they voted for it, and we sent what had passed in the House over to the Senate, and they fixed it in the Senate, and lowered the top marginal tax rate from 70% to 28%. It was a really fundamental change in our tax code, and it kicked off sustained noninflationary economic growth for about eighteen years with only one or two small dips down during that time.

Today, we have a president who talks about tax reform but isn't willing to do anything about it. Tax reform is a good issue to bring Democrats and Republicans together because you lower marginal rates—and Republicans love that; and you also get rid of loopholes and deductions—and Democrats love that. You compensate for having lower margin rates by getting rid of loopholes and deductions.

Some Republicans rebelled against it because they thought we were eviscerating some of our best voting blocs by taking out double declining balance, which would hurt the real estate industry. I remember Donald Trump coming into my office in Treasury and raising hell, and saying to me, "You're going to kill the real estate industry if you do this!"

Anyway, the Tax Reform Act of 1986 was quite an achievement and had not been done for a hundred years and hasn't been done since. We needed a leader like Reagan to get it done.

BOSTON We also need a leader like James Baker, secretary of treasury, in order to get it done.

BAKER We needed a leader who was willing to go to his own troops and say, "Hey, I want to get this accomplished. No, this isn't a good bill here in the House, but we're going to fix after it leaves here, so please vote it out of the House. Give us a shot at it." And that's how we got it done.

REAGANOMICS AND DEFICITS

BOSTON That leads us to Reaganomics, which was obviously a big part of President Reagan's domestic program. He made the tax cuts shortly after he became president, and they continued throughout his presidency. They definitely succeeded in stimulating the economy. However, in large part because of his commitment to defense, we were not successful in reducing the amount of spending, which, according to Jon Meacham, caused the amount of our federal deficit to quadruple during Reagan's eight years.

From your standpoint, was President Reagan's inability to deal with the deficit problem the biggest domestic failure of his presidency?

BAKER No. The deficit may have tripled or quadrupled, but as a percentage of GDP, it was nothing—I repeat, nothing—compared to what it is today. I got a request from the current president in 2009, to answer his question: "What's the number one priority I'm now facing?" He asked it of me, Brent Scowcroft, and Henry Kissinger. I suspect he thought I would answer his question by identifying a foreign policy issue. But I told him, "The biggest problem you're facing, Mr. President, is the huge debt bomb that's overhanging our economy."

We have a debt to GDP ratio today of 100%. The debt to GDP during President Reagan's and George H.W. Bush's administrations was nowhere near that. Yes, the deficit did increase some when I was in Washington, DC because we couldn't get the Democratic-controlled House to cut spending. As a matter of fact, we agreed to some tax increases if they would agree to cut spending. But we never got our spending cuts.

People don't seem to realize that for both of President Reagan's terms, he had to live with a Democratic controlled House of Representatives. Actually, the government was shut down seven times during the Reagan's two terms, primarily by Tip O'Neill, who as speaker of the house was the titular head of the Democratic Party at the time.

It was too bad we couldn't get those spending cuts, but the tax cuts sure generated one hell of a lot of economic growth, which generates revenues and creates jobs. That's the whole idea behind supply-side economics, which some people condemned way back at that time as "voodoo economics." I don't know who in the hell would have done that.

I tell people, "Yes, I ran a presidential campaign for George H.W. Bush in which we claimed that Reagan's economic program was voodoo economics." And then I became Reagan's treasury secretary and learned from experience that we were wrong in our criticism of the plan. So I'm a reformed drunk when it comes to supply-side economics. It really worked, and it's too bad we can't capitalize on that kind of policy today.

THE IRAN-CONTRA SCANDAL

BOSTON The biggest scar on the Reagan presidency was the Iran-Contra scandal, which happened during his second term while you were his secretary of treasury. To me, Iran-Contra shows what James Baker meant to the success of the Reagan presidency because in Ronald Reagan's memoirs, he said that if you had been his national security advisor, then Iran-Contra would not have happened—and, as Reagan knew, you had actually tried to become national security advisor after your departure as chief of staff, but it didn't work out. Then Nancy Reagan, in her memoir, said that if you had stayed on as White House chief of staff, then Iran-Contra wouldn't have happened.

As you watched Iran-Contra unfold from your position at Treasury—and you said you weren't seeing him every day, but obviously you were aware of what was going on—were you ever tempted to come to his rescue because he clearly wasn't getting good advice?

BAKER He got bad advice and that's what happens any time the National Security Council goes operational. The National Security Council (NSC), is designed to advise the president. It's located there in the White House and it has grown exponentially in recent years. It's way too big now, and when it gets the idea it's going to implement the country's foreign policy, then that's when there's going to be trouble. The job of executing our foreign policy is given to the State Department by statute. They're the ones who are legally accountable and have to testify before the Congress. The NSC staff is considered only as presidential staff.

What happened in Iran-Contra was that our NSC advisors got operational and went rogue, and did a lot of unauthorized stuff. I'm convinced Ronald Reagan didn't know what they were doing. The testimony from the Iran-Contra Commission shows that. People argue, "Reagan should have known about what his NSC people were doing. Surely, he had some signs of what they were doing." I don't know.

I will tell you one anecdote about it. Admiral John Poindexter was the National Security Advisor who had taken over that job from Bud McFarlane during President Reagan's second term. At the time, I was still on the National Security Council because when I switched jobs with Don Regan—from White House chief of staff to secretary of the Treasury, and vice versa—I made sure I protected my position on the National Security Council; yet Poindexter didn't invite me to the NSC meetings when they discussed Iran-Contra. He came to me after the scandal broke out and said, "I'm really sorry I didn't invite you to those meetings, Jim." I said, "Sorry? Boy, you did

me the biggest favor you ever could have done." It really was too bad. It was a stain on Reagan's presidency, and it didn't have to happen.

REAGAN AND THE COLD WAR

BOSTON President Reagan justifiably gets lots of credit for the way he moved the ball forward toward ending the Cold War. Give us your perspective on why Ronald Reagan was the right person—maybe the only person at that time—who could change history and restore America's place in the world by the way he stepped up to the Soviet Union and reasserted our authority in the world.

BAKER He was the right person at the right time. On the other hand, I think we should recognize that every American president—Democrat or Republican, from Harry Truman through George H. W. Bush—did their part in winning the Cold War. They were all steadfast in resisting Soviet totalitarianism and Soviet expansionism.

All of them deserve some credit, but Ronald Reagan gets a huge part of it because he came in after Jimmy Carter, when the country's self-confidence was at a real low. He restored our pride and confidence. He rebuilt our military to the point where the Soviets couldn't compete with it. He had "Star Wars," and the Soviets were deftly afraid because they couldn't finance a system of their own to compete with it.

Then, as he so often did with everything, he communicated to the American people, as only he could, about the importance of steadfastness in our opposing the Soviets. When he went to Berlin and said, "Mister Gorbachev, tear down this wall," that was extraordinarily important.

All our post-war presidents deserve credit for being steadfast in the face of Soviet aggression, and George Bush gets a lot of credit too, as well he should, for the adroit way in which he managed the end game. People criticized George Bush 41 when the

Berlin Wall came down because he didn't dance on its ruins. People asked him, "Heck, why aren't you showing some emotion? This is something we've been working to happen for forty years and you're responding to it lackadaisically." Well, he knew we still had business to do with Gorbachev and Shevardnadze and he wasn't going to stick it in their eye.

BOSTON Let's move on to the presidency of George Herbert Walker Bush.

GEORGE H.W. BUSH AND THE COLD WAR

BOSTON You were President Bush's secretary of state during the most tumultuous four-year period in world history since World War II, according to Henry Kissinger.

Following up on what it took to ultimately bring an end to the Cold War, in his new biography of Bush 41, Jon Meacham says that in May of 1989, you told President Bush it was "time to be bold" and "get ahead of the power curve against Gorbachev." What brought on that advice? What was happening that needed to be stepped up?

BAKER You need to understand the context. We had a friendly transition from Reagan to Bush 41 because we had one Republican president succeeding another. We had not had that type of transfer from a president to his vice president via an election since we went from Andrew Jackson to Martin Van Buren in the 1830s. You always want the president's imprimatur to be on the policies of the administration and it was important for George H.W. Bush to have his own imprimatur on the foreign policy of the United States. Our most important foreign policy issue for the previous forty years, of course, had been our relationship with the Soviet Union. So President Bush and I and our team undertook a review of the US-Soviet relationship. Some people thought we were

worried that President Reagan and my pal, the former Secretary of State George Schultz, had been going too far with the Soviets. That's not what it was at all.

This review during the Bush administration was purely political. I hate to bust anyone's bubble, but occasionally things are done with our foreign policy for political reasons and this was purely political, designed to put George Bush's imprimatur upon the nation's foreign policy and it was successful.

After Bush was sworn in, he soon started getting some heat for dragging our feet too long. "Why aren't you engaging with the Soviets? What's the matter?" And so forth. What you're quoting from Meacham's book took place in about April or May 1989. That's right about the time we scheduled the first summit—the Malta Summit. President Bush told the Soviet leaders at Malta, in no uncertain terms, that he wanted some bold arms control proposals. He didn't want them to tell him why they couldn't do it. He wanted them to tell him how they could do it, and it turned out to be the right approach.

NATIONAL VS. INTERNATIONAL POWER GAMES

BOSTON While you served President Reagan as White House chief of staff and then secretary of treasury, you obviously were very successful in turning the president's policies into federal laws—and, therefore, became known as "the man who made Washington work." Then, upon becoming President Bush's secretary of state, you moved into the arena of international diplomacy on a full-time basis, and basically became "the man who made the world work."

What was the biggest difference in playing the power game at the national level as opposed to the international level?

BAKER Not a lot really. Negotiating skills are something you learn practicing law, and they're extraordinarily important in conducting business at both the national and international level. As secretary of state, it's not unlike representing a client in a business transaction negotiation except you're representing your country, but the same principles apply. You need to make every effort to understand what the political constraints are upon the guy across the table; and to the extent you can, you need to establish a relationship of trust with him. You've got to keep your word so he trusts you, and make sure he keeps his word so you can trust him. Only with mutual trust can you move forward and get things done. That doesn't mean you give up on your principles. You never sacrifice your country's principles to establish a relationship with trust.

BOSTON I was watching the PBS show "James Baker, the Man Who Made Washington Work" yesterday to prepare for today's interview, and David Gergen said, "National politics is like two-dimensional chess, whereas international politics is like three-dimensional chess." Is there anything to that?

BAKER Maybe two-and-a-half dimensional chess. That's very precise, and I'm not sure I can be as precise as David Gergen. By the way, David Gergen worked in the first Reagan administration. He was our communications director and his nickname at the time was "Tall" because he is really tall. He's made a great career for himself as a CNN commentator and by teaching an extraordinarily good class in political leadership at the Kennedy School at Harvard.

TIANANMEN SQUARE AND US-CHINA RELATIONS

BOSTON On June 3, 1989, the Chinese Army attacked the demonstrators at Tiananmen Square while the world watched in outrage. How difficult was it for you and President Bush to contain your anger and temper your response to the Chinese leaders in order to maintain the otherwise positive

relationship that you'd been developing between the US and China?

BAKER It wasn't too hard. As I wrote in my book, the desk officer for the US-China relationship in the presidency of George H.W. Bush was George H.W. Bush because he'd been our first ambassador to China and knew China better than anybody in the administration, and certainly better than his secretary of state did. He had a really good feel for how to deal with the Chinese, and that was an extraordinarily difficult time because what happened at Tiananmen Square was a very brutal thing when they put down those demonstrators.

After the massacre, we had a lot of pressure on us to sanction China big-time and break off our relationship with them. People were all over us, asking, "How can you sit back and do nothing when these brutes are doing this to their own people?" We did sanction them, but we kept the relationship alive and that was because of George Bush more than anybody else in the administration.

Brent Scowcroft was the absolute best national security advisor for President Bush 41. He knew how to do the job well since he had been Ford's national security advisor. When I first became secretary of state, he came to me and told me that Bush wanted to pick him as his national security advisor, and I told him, "You'd be great." Then a little later, he came to me and said, "I want to tell you something. You're secretary of state. I'm not ever going to go on television unless you tell me it's okay." Oftentimes, in most administrations, you'll see some conflict between the secretary of state and the national security advisor— and also between the secretary of state and the secretary of defense. We didn't have that in the Bush administration. George Bush understood foreign policy extremely well and made sure his foreign policy and national security apparatus functioned the way it should. That's why he had a very successful foreign policy presidency.

BAKER AND HARDBALL CONVERSATIONS

BOSTON Four days after the Tiananmen Square incident, you had a very tough conversation with Chinese Ambassador Han Xu. It was so in-your-face forceful that it reminded me of your conversation with David Stockman after his criticism of Reaganomics appeared in the *Atlantic Monthly* article fairly early in President Reagan's first term. Your words absolutely nailed Stockman right between the eyes.

BAKER I really shouldn't say this in public and especially since we're webcasting, but David Stockman had been Ronald Reagan's first budget director. He was an extraordinarily talented young man from Michigan who had been a congressman before he became budget director. He knew the budget better than anybody in the world. But a few months into Reagan's presidency, he gave a series of private interviews—or at least he thought they were private—to a guy named Bill Griner of *The Washington Post* in which he said, "Reaganomics is a Trojan horse for reducing spending." It was a very damaging interview, hurtful to the president personally and to the entire administration and our policies. In effect, here was one of our insiders saying, "Our economic policy is all a bunch of baloney." It wasn't baloney, but he was saying it was.

Many people in the White House wanted Stockman fired. Ed Meese and Mike Deaver wanted him fired, and Nancy probably did too. I didn't want him fired though because we didn't have anybody who came anywhere close to knowing the nuances of the federal budget—which is not uncomplicated—the way David Stockman did. President Reagan didn't like to fire anybody anyway, and I talked to him and said, "We really need to keep Stockman." The president went along with me, against the advice of the others, and said, "Okay, well bring him in here." I suggested, "Why don't

Photo credit: Provided courtesy of Rice University's Baker Institute for Public Policy.

you just read him the riot act, but don't fire him?" and he said, "Okay."

So I called Stockman into my office and said, "Stockman, you are in real trouble. The rest of the people up here want you fired, but the president has agreed to give some consideration to letting you stay, provided he talks to you. So you're going to have lunch with the president today."

I'm going to apologize in advance to this wonderful audience here today for telling you all this, but these are the exact words that I then told him: "You're going to have lunch with the president today. The menu is humble pie. And you're going to eat every mother-f'ing spoonful of it. And when you go into that Oval Office, I want to see that sorry ass of yours dragging the carpet."

David Stockman must have been wearing a wire on him that day, because he wrote every word of that conversation in his book. My mother, bless her heart, eighty-five years old down in Houston, Texas at the time, called me on the phone. She had just read the book and said, "Jimmy, darling, you didn't say those words, did you?" I said, "Of course not, Mother."

Anyway, we kept Stockman on as the budget director but he left a couple of years later.

BOSTON I don't think you used all of those words with the Chinese ambassador after Tiananmen Square.

BAKER Not all those words.

BOSTON But you were pretty strong with him.

BAKER I also got pretty strong with the Syrian foreign minister.

THE GULF WAR

BOSTON Let's talk about the Gulf War. You acknowledge in your books that the war powers as between the president and Congress have been a gray issue ever since the Vietnam War. President Bush told Jon Meacham in his new best-selling biography that if he had not received congressional support for sending our troops into war, he would have gone ahead and started the war anyway, knowing that he would have risked impeachment by doing that. Did you and he discuss the risk of impeachment if he disregarded Congress?

BAKER We didn't talk much about the risk of impeachment, but we did talk about his ordering the action whether we got Congress' approval or not. Bear in mind that we'd already gone to the United Nations Security Council and gotten its approval. By the way, the Obama administration tried to follow our model in getting UN approval first before pursuing getting the Syrian deal done.

Anyway, our getting approval for pursuing military action against the Iraqis in Kuwait was the first time that had ever happened since the UN had been organized— where the UN Security Council authorized the use of force against a member state. With the support of the UN behind us, we had some powerful arguments to use with the senators and the congressmen, though even we barely won in the Senate on a fifty-two to forty-seven vote authorizing the action to eject Iraq from Kuwait.

When we were working the issue, we would say to a senator, "You mean you're not going to vote for the president of the United States on this, Senator, while the president of Ethiopia—or the president of whatever the other country was—is going to support him?" It was very powerful. We barely won the vote in the Senate to get its approval for starting the war, but President Bush was going to do it anyway because it was the right thing to do, even if doing it would have risked impeachment.

BOSTON And you were okay with that?

BAKER Absolutely. Having gone to the UN Security Council and gotten international legal approval for the need for our doing it, yes, I was very much okay with it.

BOSTON Now when the Gulf War ended, Meacham's biography says that President Bush suffered a post-combat letdown while he was also battling a thyroid condition called Graves' disease, which caused him to have an energy loss. White House Press Secretary Marlin Fitzwater said President Bush basically seemed to "lose his zip" through the presidential campaign in 1982. Did you see any letdown and energy loss in President Bush after the Gulf War ended?

BAKER None whatsoever. I know that he had Graves' disease, but I want to tell you something about George Bush. He's about as competitive as anybody you will ever know. I remember during the 1992 election when people said, "Oh he really doesn't want it. He's not real exciting." In fact, he worked his tail off in that campaign. I know because I was sending him out there to all those events and he would call me from the road and say, "I'm ready to do another one if you want me to." So I absolutely do not believe he had any lack of energy and enthusiasm during that campaign.

THE 1992 ELECTION

BOSTON From your perspective, was the 1992 election primarily lost because of Ross Perot?

BAKER You got it. That's it. Look at it this way. We know from the polling that Ross was taking two-thirds of his votes from us. In the final election, he got 19%, Clinton got 43%, and we got 38%. You take two-thirds of 19%, and we would have gotten about 51% of the vote. So we know why we lost the election in 1992.

There was one big mistake we made in the aftermath of the Gulf War, at a time when President Bush's approval numbers were in the 1990s. When the Gulf War ended, we should have proposed something major for our economy. Dick Armand—who had worked for me at Treasury and at Commerce, and in the White House for President Reagan—suggested that in January of 1992, we should pursue a program called "Domestic Storm." We had been successful in Desert Storm and by pursuing "Domestic Storm," it would have given the country the idea we were going to focus on domestic problems and create something around which we could build a campaign. We didn't do that, and it was a mistake.

Primarily, we lost the election because of Ross Perot. It's also a fact though that George W. Bush won his first election in 2000 because of Ralph Nader. If Ralph Nader hadn't been in that race, as close as it was in Florida (537 votes), Gore would have been elected president.

This guy right now who's firing people up all the time—if he decides to go out and run as an independent in 2016, then that would bust next year's election for the Republicans for sure.

BAKER'S ROLE IN BUSH V. GORE

BOSTON My final question is about your role in the *Bush v. Gore* lawsuit as the quarterback of the legal team. Out of your top ten achievements in both national and international politics, where do you rate the successful outcome achieved in *Bush v. Gore*?

BAKER Let me give you an anecdote that will answer that question for you. I was walking down the street somewhere, and this guy walked up to me and said, "I know you. You're Jim Baker." I said, "That's right." He said, "Boy, thank you for what you've done for this country." I said, "Thank you very much. After all, I was the last Cold War secretary of state of the United States." He said, "No! I want to thank you for what you did in Florida." It was a very unique period in American politics.

BOSTON You say in your book that the final outcome in *Bush v. Gore* proved that our system works.

BAKER At one point, people said that by pursuing the litigation, we were trying to legally steal an election. My answer to them was that we were trying to legally *protect* an election. We were never behind in the vote counts. It was Gore who filed the challenges down there in Florida, and he and his team made a fundamental mistake. They asked for recounts in the four counties that were heavily Democratic counties. Their doing that gave us the moral high ground. They said, "Count the votes." We said, "Hell, the votes have been counted—once, twice, they've been counted a lot."

I don't know if we'll ever have a situation again where we have the Supreme Court of the United States resolving a presidential election. As I said in the book, the final outcome proves that the system works. I would get calls during that period from heads of states or from prime ministers or foreign ministers from other countries that I dealt with as secretary of state saying, "What's the matter with you? Can't you all run an election? I mean, you're supposed to be the cradle of the democracy. What's going on over there?" I replied, "I'll tell you what's going on. The system is working.

We're working this out. It's very emotional, but the system's working. The rule of law is going to prevail, and I bet if this was happening in your country, you might have tanks in the streets." Some of them admitted, "You're right. We might."

BOSTON Tell the audience what President Clinton told you on the day that you were up there when President Bush 43 was getting inaugurated.

BAKER He said, "You were good in Florida, real good." He was stealing a line from an Al Pacino movie, I think, where Pacino said, "You were good, real good." Clinton was about half pissed off because the Gore people didn't use him in Florida after the election.

He then said that he had told Gore and his team while the Florida re-count and litigation were going on, that "if they continued to play by the Marquis of Queensbury rules, they were going to get their brains beat in." We did beat their brains in.

BOSTON We have time for some questions from the audience. Does anybody have a question you'd like to ask Secretary Baker about his time in either presidency?

REAGAN'S ENDURING STATURE AMONG REPUBLICANS

AUDIENCE MEMBER Ronald Reagan is still the leading icon of the Republican Party, yet there are so many things he did and stood for that would prevent him from being nominated by the party today. Why is he still such an icon?

BAKER Because he had an extraordinary two-term presidency. He's the last two-term Republican president who had a completely successful presidency. George W. had two terms, but he had the problem of Iraq. Reagan is still seen to be the icon for that reason.

Someone said to me last year, "I don't understand why you Republicans stay focused only on Reagan. You had a hell of a president in Dwight Eisenhower. He was very successful and that ought to be a model for Republicans who want to become president." I tend to agree with that, too. I thought Ike was a terrific president, but Reagan is really the gold standard.

If you listen to the candidates today, I don't care where they're coming from—whether they're entertainers or politicians or whether they're outsiders or insiders—they'll all say they want to be a president like Ronald Reagan. Why? Because he was successful and he was good and he told people what he was going to do and then he did it. He held his beliefs viscerally, deeply, and fundamentally. Would he shave at the edges to get stuff done? You bet and that's where I think he's oftentimes misunderstood. People think he was a hard-core, right wing ideologue. He wasn't.

BAKER AND MEESE'S DYNAMICS DURING REAGAN'S PRESIDENCY

AUDIENCE MEMBER Secretary Baker, when you were chief of staff to Ronald Reagan, you shared a lot of responsibilities with Ed Meese. How did that relationship complicate your ability to execute the office of the chief of staff?

BAKER There were a lot of stories when we were in the White House about tension between the two sides of the White House, but those stories for the most part were overblown. Ed Meese has been and continues to be a really good friend of mind. I put him on the Iraq Study Group I chaired a few years ago. I also asked him to become a member of the National War Powers Commission, of which I was chairman. He and I are very close friends today.

Did we have differences in our views on some issues? You bet we did. But it wasn't the way the press would have you believe.

When Ronald Reagan asked me to be his chief of staff, the one thing he said to me was, "Make it right with Ed," because everybody had anticipated that Ed was going to be the White House chief of staff, since he'd been Reagan's chief of staff in California.

We were out at the Century Plaza Hotel after winning that overwhelming victory against Carter in the 1980 election, and I said, "Ed, we need to sit down," and we did over lunch. We prepared a one-page memo that we both signed. It delineated what each of our responsibilities and duties would be, and for the most part it held up quite well during the four years.

In fact, Ed Meese and I worked together for eight years because Ed became attorney general and I became treasury secretary during President Reagan's second term after we both left our positions in the White House. In those two Cabinet positions, we continued to work together quite closely, and we've worked together really closely since we've been out.

BOSTON I think that besides those rumors about the conflict between you and Meese, there were also tons of stories about the troika of you and Meese and Michael Deaver, and how well you worked as a team.

BAKER The three of us gave President Reagan the benefit of different views and that was very good for him. We used to tell a story about Ronald Reagan. We'd say, "Ronald Reagan doesn't like yes men. When he says 'No,' we all say 'no.'"

But you don't do any favors to a president unless you tell him what you really think. That's what Ronald Reagan wanted and that's what George Bush 41 wanted. He and I of course had been friends forever here in Houston. He was my daughter's godfather, and so forth. I could tell him anything I wanted and I did. The most important thing I ever told him was to get out of the race in 1980 before going to California or else he would piss Reagan off even more. And it would have, too.

BOSTON You were already seeing the likelihood that he would be in the race for being selected as Reagan's vice presidential running mate.

BAKER Let me tell you something. More people become president of the United States by having become vice president first than any other way. That's the best route to become president of the United States—get to be vice president. George said to me in May of 1980, "Oh, I don't want to be vice president. I've got people who are committed to me in New Jersey and these other states. I've been working hard and I can't let them down." I said, "Are you kidding?" He'll finally acknowledge now how bad things were going for him toward the end of the 1980 primaries.

REAGAN AND HIS DEFENSE INITIATIVES

AUDIENCE MEMBER Secretary Baker, on the subject of our winning the Cold War, it's very much still an open historical question in terms of what degree Gorbachev also played a role. You also mentioned "Star Wars" and the Strategic Defense Initiative (SDI), and how they impacted the Cold War. What was the environment within the administration at the time regarding SDI? The Russian sources I've read show that yes, they feared "Star Wars" and SDI, but there was a lot of doubt in terms of the system's potential effectiveness. *The New York Times* had a report about how what was first reported to be a successful missile test ended up being a complete farce because when they shot the missile up, the missile defense system was supposed to be able to hit it, and the scientific consensus at that time was that hitting it would be impossible. Was SDI simply a fear tactic that was Reagan's brainchild?

BAKER SDI was the brainchild of some of the people who advised President Reagan in the defense community, and it turned out to be a good brainchild. I'm not sure whether it would have actually worked or not, but it sure worked as far as the Soviets were concerned, and that extended through the time when I was secretary of state. During our arms control negotiations with the Soviets, they always wanted to find a way to get to our Strategic Defense Initiative and put restraints on it. The Soviets were always very concerned about SDI and that was pretty much enough for it to have served its purpose, regardless of whether it would actually work. The state of the Soviet economy was deteriorating at that time and it was collapsing pretty much on its own. We contributed mightily to that collapse by remaining resolute and strong in rebuilding our defenses and resisting Soviet aggression at every turn.

One of the big arguments we had with Gorbachev came whenever we talked about "winning the Cold War." He said, "Don't use the word 'winning!' That's demeaning to us. It's very tough on us in our own country for you to say you won the Cold War. Let's say that together we solved the problem of the Cold War, or something like that."

Gorbachev deserves lots of credit for the end of the Cold War because it was Gorbachev and his foreign minister Edward Shevardnadze, with whom I worked so closely and who made the decision not to use force to keep the Soviet empire together. Before they came on the scene, force had always been used to maintain the Soviet empire. Had they not made that decision, the Cold War certainly would not have ended peacefully as it did.

BOSTON In your book, you said the Cold War finally ended when the Russians supported the coalition against the Iraqi invasion into Kuwait.

BAKER That's when I think it ended. You can argue about a lot of events that occurred and say, "Here's where the Cold War ended." To me, the Cold War ended when Saddam invaded Kuwait. Iraq was a client state of the Soviet Union and the day

James A. Baker

after the invasion, we got the Soviet foreign minister to stand shoulder to shoulder with me, the secretary of state, in an airport in Moscow and condemn the Iraqi invasion. To me, that was the day the Cold War ended. Nobody would ever have dreamed our aligning with them as we did would be possible, and that they would stay with the coalition. Although they didn't supply troops to help us during the Gulf War, at least they didn't oppose what we did. They supported a number of UN Security Council resolutions, and that was really a change.

BOSTON Our time is up. You've obviously been a wonderful audience. Thank you so much, Secretary Baker, for your insight.

A former governor of New Hampshire, **JOHN SUNUNU** served as White House chief of staff for most of George H.W. Bush's administration after being actively involved in Bush 41's presidential campaigns in 1980 and 1988. I interviewed Governor Sununu on October 8, 2015 about his book *The Quiet Man: The Indispensable Presidency of George H.W. Bush* (Broadside 2015) on the campus of Colby-Sawyer College in New London, New Hampshire.

"Gorbachev said in his memoirs that the most important thing George Bush did on the day the Berlin Wall fell was to show discipline and say, 'This is a wonderful step, but it's only a step, and we will wait to see what happens after this.' President Bush didn't want to brag or gloat, and he had the self-discipline to avoid gloating, even as he was being attacked aggressively by the Democrats. Senator George Mitchell, in particular, made a big deal out of the fact that Bush wasn't going to the Wall to make a speech; but the president handled it in a way that maximized the overall result he wanted, which was a complete change in the Soviet Union and a Europe that was 'whole and free.'" **– JOHN SUNUNU**

CHAPTER 30

JOHN SUNUNU
ON
George H.W. Bush

THE JOB OF BEING WHITE HOUSE CHIEF OF STAFF

BOSTON Governor Sununu, your book details your being in the room with President Bush seemingly everywhere he was, for every major event during the first three years of his presidency, whether it was in Washington, DC, abroad, or anywhere else. I always think of the White House chief of staff as the president's gatekeeper, but as I read your book, I said, "No, you were more than that. You were the president's shadow."

For those of us who have not served in the White House, what exactly does the White House chief of staff do?

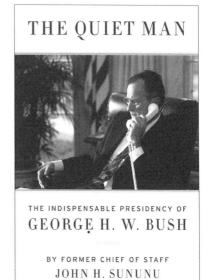

THE QUIET MAN

THE INDISPENSABLE PRESIDENCY OF
GEORGE H. W. BUSH

BY FORMER CHIEF OF STAFF
JOHN H. SUNUNU

Courtesy of Broadside Books

SUNUNU A chief of staff does whatever his president wants him to do. The job is really defined by the president, and it's different for different presidents. I had the good fortune to work for a president who had been in the White House as vice president and understood how complicated and, to some extent, how difficult the environment of the White House is. He recognized that there were certain advantages in selecting me to be his chief of staff because I had been through the political cauldron, served as a state governor, and dealt with legislatures.

President Bush defined a role for me, which was rather broad. Since we had gotten to know each other pretty well through the campaign, we continued to develop the relationship when I was chief of staff. What the position ended up being was one of highly trustful responsibility because he knew that if something had to be done, and he asked for it to be done, it got done.

SUNUNU'S POLICY-MAKING AND POLICY-EXECUTION ROLE IN THE BUSH ADMINISTRATION

BOSTON As I read your book, it appears that President Bush gave you a policy-making and policy-execution role on both domestic and foreign policy. Among other things, your book details how you worked with House Ways and Means Chairman Dan Rostenkowski and Budget Director Dick Darman on budget negotiations, and also participated in planning the Gulf War.

Explain with more detail the hands-on policy-making, policy-execution role you had during the Bush administration.

SUNUNU To answer that, let me give context to George Herbert Walker Bush's approach to the presidency on policy. While he was vice president during Reagan's second term, he recognized in '85 or '86 that he was going to run for president in 1988. The idea had been in his mind for a while, but he made a firm decision to do it then.

He always felt comfortable on the foreign policy side. He had been envoy to China and a delegate to the UN, and was serving as vice president to Ronald Reagan. He understood the nuances to foreign policy quite well; but he also understood, at that point, that he didn't understand domestic policy issues as well as he wanted.

Because of our state's early primary, governors of New Hampshire generally get to know presidential candidates quite well. It's one of the great things about being up here. So in the mid-eighties, George Bush would visit me in New Hampshire, and we talked domestic policy. Finally, he hired Lee Atwater to run his presidential campaign, and together they began to get serious about it. One of the first things they did was to come up to New Hampshire and spend some time with me. My recommendation to them was that the vice president should talk to Republican governors all around the country to find out about how to deal with issues like the environment, welfare, energy, or job creation. Those are the domestic issues Washington, DC has to think about, though the people who deal with them on a daily basis are governors.

He took that advice to heart and spent a year and a half visiting with Republican governors. He would ask me to gather a group of them together, and bring them to Kennebunkport to spend a day with him there. He would also visit National Governor Association and Republican Governor Association meetings so he could talk to clusters of governors there. Through that process, he really made a commitment to refresh his mind about the current nuances associated with those domestic issues.

When I got to the White House as chief of staff, he laid out for me the agenda of what he wanted to accomplish on domestic policy. He set guidelines on what he wanted to get done on the main issues, and basically said, "Go get me some legislation from the Congress that will produce these policies." The budget was certainly part of that responsibility.

So part of my job as chief of staff was to serve as the president's alter ego in legislative negotiations. When they put me on the cover, *Time* magazine said that I was the bad cop and President Bush was the good cop. My warmth and charm in doing my job was somehow not appreciated. Basically, I tried to put all the details together for a president who really had a much broader and more successful domestic policy agenda and he got more results than he ever received credit for. A main reason for writing my book was to let people understand how tremendous his accomplishments were on the home front.

WHY BUSH 41 NEVER WROTE HIS PRESIDENTIAL MEMOIRS

BOSTON In that regard, as you say in the introduction, your book essentially aspires to be the presidential memoir that President Bush never wrote. He did co-author a book with Brent Scowcroft about his foreign policy, but he never did a true presidential memoir that covered basically every aspect of his presidency.

Why didn't President Bush write his presidential memoirs?

SUNUNU It's part of the theme of my book. George Bush is a very unusual individual. He really hates to talk about himself. His mother used to admonish him, "George, don't brag about yourself; and bend your knees when you volley." There are two messages in that advice. One is, "Do well, but don't talk about yourself when you do well." The second is, "There's a right way to do things and whatever you do, do it the right way. The right way to volley is to bend your knees."

Those two components of his mother's advice really define the president I worked for. First, he really didn't like to talk about himself; and, second, he worked hard to get the right information from the right people so he could make the right decisions. I suspect that the only reason he even did

the book with Brent Scowcroft was that he really felt that the world needed to understand better how the monumental change in superpower relationships had occurred, thereby essentially providing a handbook for future presidents on how to deal with the same kind of situations.

BUSH AND "THE VISION THING"

BOSTON Getting back to your prior answer, in terms of his laying out what he hoped to accomplish on the domestic front, President Bush was famously criticized for lacking the "vision thing"—there was a cover of *Newsweek* about that—and yet, your book talks about how in both foreign policy and domestic policy, he had a very clear vision.

Is a political leader's likelihood of seeing and executing on a vision something that just can't be identified in advance, particularly by a media that in a modern era has such a partisan filter?

SUNUNU Whenever the media asks for something that corresponds to "the vision thing," they're really looking for a bumper sticker label. Lyndon Johnson had "the Great Society"—whatever that meant— that was his vision. George Bush had such a broad concept of what had to be done that a label for all of it just wouldn't fit on a bumper sticker.

On the foreign policy side, what he really wanted to do was take advantage of the unique opportunity that had come about because Ronald Reagan's "peace through strength" approach to handling world affairs had scared the hell out of the Soviets to the point where they were willing to come and talk about change. George Bush understood that there was an opportunity there to make a big difference, so part of his foreign policy agenda was to deal with that.

Part of the international agenda, however, gets thrust on you by events no one can anticipate—example: Saddam Hussein invaded Kuwait. Recognizing that reality, part of President Bush's broad agenda was to do what it took to stabilize the world. That specific action by Saddam destabilized things. So, because his "vision" agenda included creating stability, President Bush did what he had to do in the Gulf War.

On the domestic side, in the days between the election and taking the oath of office, he prepared a list of things he wanted to do. He knew he had to deal with the federal deficit because that was already a crisis he had to deal with. He also wanted to deal with the environment, and energy, and having a civil rights bill that didn't gut the rights of business. He had also been talking to a number of his friends about Americans with disability, so he wanted to deal with legislation on that issue in a constructive way while it was before Congress. He also believed that we put our farmers too much into a dependency role, so he wanted to take away some of the subsidies and instead create incentives for exports, which we ended up doing.

Then, within a few days after he got into office, we discovered there was a savings and loan crisis that would have to be addressed. Also, as a member of the Reagan administration, he certainly understood the difficulties President Reagan had run into with Congress in his last years over the Iran-Contra situation, so he knew he had to work out a process where he could start working and gaining credibility with Congress. Last on his list, he had heard from many governors and mayors that crime was a serious problem because local law enforcement officials were having difficulties dealing with the federal government, so he had a vision of what had to be done about that in terms of a crime bill.

How do you put a bumper sticker label on that collective set of visions associated with those important issues? We felt there was no way to summarize all that into a few words, and we got punished for it by the press because they were always looking for a short magic label.

SHARING THE FOREIGN POLICY LOAD DURING THE BUSH ADMINISTRATION

BOSTON Moving from domestic to foreign policy, a great mystery to me and probably to most people who have not served in the White House is exactly who has responsibility for doing what in the foreign policy arena?

During the Bush administration, explain how the foreign policy load was shared among President Bush, Secretary of State James Baker, and National Security Advisor Brent Scowcroft.

SUNUNU One of President Bush's greatest talents has always been cultivating true friends. He understood that there is a tremendous advantage in dealing with complicated issues with very smart people who also happen to be your friends. You ask how responsibilities were allocated or shared in our foreign policy, and it was almost as if the three men melded into one. They all had known each other a long time, and they also understood the president's vision: that here was an opportunity for the world if America would only lead well.

Frankly, with the exception of some arguments about nuances and details, there was virtually never a difference that we had in terms of what should be our approach and strategy. There were differences about tactics, and one of George Bush's other talents was that he was certainly willing to let those who worked for him argue with him when they felt that he wasn't going the right way; and he was smart enough to change his mind when somebody pointed out that things had to be changed. The chemistry there among the three of them—actually among the four of us—was really the key to the president's being able to get as much done as he did.

BOSTON Having said that, surely there were lines of authority, such as: the secretary of state is responsible for "X", the national security council advisor is responsible for "Y". You, as the chief of staff, obviously understood those lines, and so please explain those lines with more specificity.

SUNUNU There is no handbook that defines who has which responsibilities. The distribution of foreign policy responsibilities on day one immediately after the president took the oath of office was different than the distribution of responsibilities after the team had worked through some issues and circumstances had changed. There was never any specific allocation of responsibilities. Sitting down with the president in his office as issues were discussed, you just knew what was expected of you in order to get things done. Every individual in that room absorbed their assignment from the president almost by osmosis.

Since it was so easy to interact with this president, you could make the fine tune adjustments on who was doing what on an hourly or a daily basis as things went along. For example, in preparing for the Malta summit, the president had a whole series of meetings with outsiders. After he finished those, the four of us sat down to talk about what the president ought to do when he met with Gorbachev at Malta. It evolved that Jimmy Baker would put together a rough draft of the president's first presentation; Scowcroft would then go over it, I would then go over it, and the president would make the final cut. It wasn't that the president said, "You go do it." James Baker just knew he should start the process, and then it worked through the various hands that had to contribute to it.

BUSH 41 – THE MASTER OF BUILDING RELATIONSHIPS

BOSTON Throughout the book, you justifiably praise the president for his amazing capacity to build close genuine relationships with world leaders, with congressional leaders, and everybody else whom he needed to influence.

What did you learn from President Bush about the art of building relationships whenever someone is trying to achieve political objectives?

SUNUNU One of the things I saw in President Bush, and he did it better than anybody I've ever seen—and I've never really been able to do it myself—is at the start of a meeting, he had an uncanny knack for bringing in new acquaintances from the awkward moment of "hello" into the warmest level of interpersonal comfort in a very short period of time. He could deal with people he had just met and make them feel relaxed.

The best example I can give of that particular talent was the way he got things started with French President Francois Mitterrand. When George Bush took office, France and the US were not getting along. Mitterrand and Reagan had had a personality conflict and that made things rough between the two countries. Bush understood that in order to take advantage of the emerging opportunity with the Soviet Union while Gorbachev was at the helm, the best vehicle to move things forward would be with NATO. To do that, he knew that he would have to work with the three key European leaders of NATO: Margaret Thatcher of Great Britain, Helmut Kohl of Germany, and Francois Mitterrand of France.

President Bush was very much aware of Mitterrand's distrust of the US because of his discomfort with the personal relationship he had with President Reagan. So Bush told Scowcroft and me that he wanted to invite Mitterrand to Walker's Point at Kennebunkport. Scowcroft and I panicked because we knew Mitterrand was the classic European gentleman for whom the informality of Walker's Point just didn't seem to fit. But the president insisted, and he was the president.

So he invited Mitterrand, who arrived at Walker's Point in a helicopter, got off wearing a well-tailored suit, with his shoes shined to the ultimate, French cuffs on his shirt, perfectly dressed for an evening out for dinner in Paris. George and Barbara Bush are a little less formal. When Mitterrand got off the helicopter, you could see in his eyes that he fully expected not to enjoy his time there, and not to change his mood.

By the time George Bush finished spending time with Mitterrand in a day and a half, the French president had come to agree with the grand strategy Bush laid out for NATO, and they were calling each other "George" and "Francois." Mitterand actually took his tie off, and it was the beginning of an unbelievably close relationship. George Bush made building positive relationships an art form.

I can further define for you the warmth of that relationship by pointing out that a few years after President Bush left office, there was an event in Colorado Springs in which he, Margaret Thatcher, Gorbachev, Mitterrand, and Mulroney all sat down to discuss how they had collaborated to bring about the change in the Soviet Union. Mitterrand showed up and made a fantastic presentation, even though he was dying of cancer. In fact, he died less than two months later. That's how close George Bush was able to convert what was a difficult relationship into a great one in that day and a half at Walker's Point.

I also saw him do it with Margaret Thatcher, who was a little bit nervous about dealing with him because she had had such a great relationship with Reagan. He also did it with Gorbachev. He developed a relationship where people trusted him, and so they were willing to go the extra mile on agreements, strategy, and commitments.

BUSH'S HUMILITY

BOSTON Part of his art form in building relationships comes from President Bush's humility. You mention that his humility became strategically crucial to the way we responded to the fall of the Berlin Wall and the end of the Cold War. Explain how his humility produced the best possible result in those situations where it would have been easy to gloat.

SUNUNU It was a combination of humility and great self-discipline. Let's remember the time frame and the situation. We had started to work with NATO in the spring of 1989 to respond to the opportunity of perhaps inducing Gorbachev to pull some of the Russian military out of Eastern Europe's occupied countries—Hungary, Poland, Czechoslovakia, Romania, and so on—and that had begun. Bush put down a bold proposal in the spring of 1989 that we would reduce our troops to a certain level in Europe if the Soviet Union responded in kind. That process was taking place, and it allowed Gorbachev to start allowing a movement toward self-governments in the Eastern European countries. It was not happening as easily in Germany, because Germany was divided. The three allied post-World War II districts that had been occupied by the British, the French, and the Americans had all been merged into West Germany, but the Russians still held East Germany and had built the Wall separating Berlin.

As the changes began taking place in Eastern Europe, George Bush sensed that Gorbachev was getting pressure from the hardliners in the Soviet Union who didn't want this to happen. We understood the internal difficulties Gorbachev was having. One afternoon in November—maybe November 9—we were in the Oval Office and someone from the White House Press Office came running in and said, "You've got to go watch television in the next room. They're chipping away at the Berlin Wall and people are passing through the checkpoint." So we took a look, and it was true! The gateway at the Wall's checkpoints had been opened and people were being allowed to go from East Berlin to West Berlin and vice versa, and the Russian guards weren't shooting anybody. It looked like a party. Everybody was joyous.

So because this major event was taking place, we had to talk to the press. President Bush sensed that it was going to be a difficult, awkward situation because he understood that the last thing in the world Gorbachev needed would be for the United States to gloat over the collapse of the Soviet Union. His doing that would give the Russian hardliners an excuse to tell Gorbachev, "You're embarrassing us. This can't take place." Perhaps they would then attempt to remove him.

So they brought into the Oval Office a sampling of the press from the print media, radio, and TV—though it was not a full press conference—and they started peppering President Bush with, "Isn't this wonderful?" "Why aren't you cheering about it?" The next day, the newspapers condemned him for not making a speech on the fall of the Wall and gloating about it.

Gorbachev said in his memoirs that the most important thing George Bush did on the day the Berlin Wall fell was to show discipline and say, "This is a wonderful step, but it's only a step, and we will wait to see what happens after this." He didn't want to brag or gloat, and he had the self-discipline to avoid gloating, even as he was being attacked aggressively by the Democrats. George Mitchell, in particular, made a big deal out of the fact that Bush wasn't going to the Wall to make a speech; but the president handled it in a way that maximized the overall result he wanted, which was a complete change in the Soviet Union and a Europe that was "whole and free."

SUNUNU'S TRIP TO ADVISE THE SOVIETS ON BEST PRACTICES IN GOVERNMENT ADMINISTRATION

BOSTON As President Bush and Gorbachev developed this increasingly positive relationship, in 1990, Gorbachev came to the United States to discuss arms control and German reunification. While he was here, he asked the president if he would let you go to Russia to teach his team how to run an efficient administration, which you did.

When you got to Russia, what were the biggest flaws in their administration of government and what were your main

Photo credit: Courtesy of George Bush Presidential Library and Museum

President Bush looks on as Governor Sunu is sworn in as chief of staff by Vice President Quayle, January 21, 1989

suggestions on how the Russians could operate more efficiently?

SUNUNU Gorbachev came and saw that we had prepared schedules for the president, and that when papers were brought in to the president, there were guidelines on how he ought to deal with this. The White House is run extremely efficiently. Gorbachev realized that things in the Soviet Union going forward were going to have to be different. He had just been elected president by the representative body there. As he put it to Bush in not quite these words, Gorbachev was going to have to run the office of the presidency in the Soviet Union differently as a democratically-elected presidency as compared to how it had been run when it was essentially a dictatorship. When he asked if I would go over there, Bush replied, "Sununu can run an office either way—as a democracy or a dictatorship."

When we went there, and after we left, they unfortunately never could quite understand what I tried to teach them. There is a mentality there that's extremely difficult to deal with. We tried hard to communicate to them the things that they were going to have to deal with, not only in terms of operational and administrative issues, but also in terms of creating a new government process in their country.

One of the things I did before we went was to have the CIA translate *The Federalist Papers* into Russian and bind five hundred copies. We took them with us, and whenever we spoke to a group, we gave everybody a copy. They would come back the next day, and ask so many good questions, that we were positive they had read *The Federalist Papers* cover-to-cover. They wanted to talk about what they were struggling through and were astounded that we had dealt with those same issues two hundred years earlier in almost the same way—"What's the role of the legislative body? What's the role of the president? What's the role of the judiciary? Who appoints whom? Who has the last say? What kind of oversight is there in the process? What is the relationship of the central government to the governments of their equivalents of states or counties?"—All these things we had struggled through more than two hundred years earlier, they were going through live at that time. So we talked to them about that, but we also tried to talk to them about being efficient, and creating a schedule for Gorbachev, and creating a process where they could deal with the mundane.

When we got there, there was a huge table—like a huge dining room table—outside of Gorbachev's office. On the table were twenty or thirty yellow-green telephones. Each telephone went to a different department. Instead of having one phone with buttons on it, they had twenty or thirty individual phones. There were two people there who were responsible for answering them. My question was, "How do you know which one it is when it rings?" Their answer was basically that the art of knowing which phone rang was part of their job security. Just getting them to want to bring technology in to deal with an improved phone system and to recognize that Gorbachev should have a schedule with some forward vision to it—those were the kinds of suggestions we made, and I thought we were helpful.

I made my greatest contribution to making sure that the Soviet Union would never be a great power again when I suggested to their legislative body that they make sure that their committees should have oversight over the executive branch. That would be a sure way to create chaos.

BUSH, THE 1990 BUDGET, AND NEWT GINGRICH'S DISRUPTIVE TACTICS

BOSTON Moving from the international arena back to the home front, in the book you profile the heavy lifting done by the Bush administration that went into having a 1990 budget that the Democratic-controlled Congress was about to approve. Then after the deal was made, it came apart when House Minority Whip Newt Gingrich reneged on it.

How did President Bush, one of history's most consummate gentlemen, respond behind closed doors over the Gingrich betrayal on the 1990 budget—particularly at a time of high stress when he was trying to assemble a coalition to prepare for what would become the Gulf War?

SUNUNU That day when the budget deal fell through was probably as angry as I have ever seen President Bush—and it was only for a short period of time. When his brief spell of anger ended, he then said, "Well, we've got to go figure out how to fix it."

Let's remember what was going on then. George Bush had said, "Read my lips: no new taxes" in his acceptance speech at the Republican Convention in 1988 in New Orleans. The Democrats really felt his having made that promise was a big part of why he got elected. We succeeded in putting together a one-year budget our first year in 1989, which was the budget for calendar year 1990, that did not require a tax increase. We made some significant spending cuts in it and got it through Congress, even though the Democrats controlled the House 260 to 175, the Senate 55 to 45.

Then we got to 1990 and needed a budget for calendar year 1991. We recognized that the American economy actually needed a multi-year budget—a five-year budget at least—in order to lay out an agenda the world could see to show that we had gotten our deficits under control. The world had continued to buy US treasury bills during the Reagan deficit crisis, but they didn't buy them as much when they started wondering whether the US economy was falling apart. So that was the very big pressure weighing on the president in connection with getting a 1991 budget done during 1990.

At that point, the Democrats were absolutely determined to make President Bush pay the ransom of accepting new taxes as part of the new budget agreement. They had the votes in Congress to control the budget. They could pass what they wanted. The president might stop it with a veto, but that wouldn't produce a budget, and we had to get a budget in place.

So it was 1990, and we were going through the budget negotiations, and all of a sudden, Saddam invaded Kuwait on August 1 and 2. As we negotiated, we had known that if we didn't get an indication of there being an agreement on the budget soon, then we would have to begin planning for sequester, which would dramatically cut the defense budget. All of a sudden, George Bush was faced with a big cut in the defense budget at a time when he was trying to convince the Soviets that the US superpower was much stronger than the Soviets. At the same time, he was beginning to think about kicking Saddam Hussein out of Kuwait by sending our young men and women into harm's way. In that situation, the last thing in the world the president of the United States can tolerate is not having sufficient funds to support the needs of those young people who he's asking to put their lives on the line.

The pressure was on the president. He had to have a budget. For those of you who are looking with frustration at what's happening in Washington today, let me tell you that nothing happens in our federal government without presidential leadership. There is no way Congress can herd itself into taking prompt action because they are truly a herd of cats. The president has to manage the process, and both the incumbent party for the president and the opposition party in control of Congress at that time needed presidential leadership if a budget deal was going to get done.

So we went through this process in the summer of 1990 and we managed to get a budget in which the only significant tax increase was an increase in the gasoline tax, and we did that because it had not been adjusted for inflation in almost a decade. We were quite proud of what we had accomplished through hard negotiations, with new rules that required "pay as you go" for any new programs and caps on all discretionary spending. It was a budget that everyone should have been proud of. Newt Gingrich was very much a part of the negotiating team and said he would accept the budget if we met nine certain requirements. He gave Darman a typewritten copy of his criteria, and we met all nine of them.

We thought we had a wonderful agreement, so we invited everybody down to the White House to celebrate it. All the Democratic and Republican leadership came, including Gingrich. As we crammed into the Cabinet room, everybody said nice things about the budget, and the president took the key leaders out to the Rose Garden to sign the agreement, and then Gingrich slinked off and at the last minute, decided to oppose the presidential budget. As a result of his doing that, we lost the vote in the House, which really put the Democrats into control. They went back, eliminated some of the spending cuts they had previously agreed to, and converted most of the increased gasoline tax into an increase in the personal income tax. This concluded on October 30, and the president had to have a budget because we were getting ready to really begin the push to get Saddam out, and expected to take military action in January 1991. So the president had to sign a much less favorable budget than what we had had before Gingrich reneged.

In fact, Gingrich had claimed he didn't want an increase in personal income taxes, and by not supporting the increase in gasoline tax, he thereby caused an increase in personal income taxes, which obviously became a huge political problem for the president.

BOSTON You're saying that the Gingrich betrayal caused President Bush to get as mad as he ever got, at least in your presence?

SUNUNU Yes, and he stayed angry for about forty-five seconds; and then we decided we had to go and figure out how we were going to make things work.

"READ MY LIPS: NO NEW TAXES"

BOSTON Getting back to his pledge at the 1988 convention, "Read my lips: no new taxes," you suggest that because of the massive deficits that arose during the Reagan presidency (in large part because of Reagan's doubling the defense budget) that at the time Bush made that speech at the convention, he knew or should have known that keeping taxes where they were during a four-year term was essentially north of impossible if he planned to address the deficit crisis.

Why did a man of Bush's integrity make a promise that he knew he probably couldn't keep?

SUNUNU Let me explain what I really had hoped people would get out of it that part of my book. In 1990, we could have had a multi-year budget without any tax increases at all. We negotiated a five hundred plus billion dollar reduction in the deficit. We could have had a budget with only a four hundred billion dollar reduction in the deficit without increasing any taxes. The tax increase that finally passed was a little over a hundred

billion dollars. So it was possible, numerically, to have a budget without any tax increases, but the Democrats were determined to make Bush pay the ransom of having to accept taxes, and he wanted to reduce the deficit by a more significant amount.

I got nervous when I heard the president say, "No new taxes" at the convention because as a governor, I knew that there are always taxes and fees that you have to adjust for inflation. There are also always things that come in on legislation that you may not think are taxes, but people politically can call taxes. So I was nervous from a political point of view that he put himself in a position where he might not be able to prevent tax increases—not because numerically we couldn't deal with the deficit—but because I knew that in the course of normal business, there were creeping fees and taxes that you almost have to raise in order to adjust for inflation, so that you don't create a huge buildup of debt that somebody has to handle many years downstream.

BOSTON Are you saying that President Bush either overlooked or simply was not aware of this inevitable tax rise associated with inflation?

SUNUNU Look, that speech was written primarily by Peggy Noonan and vetted by Roger Ailes and the president, and in a way it was the right thing for him to say. It was right for him to define himself as an anti-tax Republican, and while such an absolute statement might have been rhetorically persuasive, we now see the problem it created. Darman (who became Bush's Budget Director) was part of the speech-writing team, and he wrote in his book that he tried three or four times to cross the "no new taxes" pledge out of the speech, but it kept creeping back into drafts of the speech, and he suspected it was because Peggy loved the phrase.

THE GULF WAR

BOSTON Let's move now to the Gulf War. You've mentioned Saddam Hussein's leading Iraq to invade Kuwait, which led to the Gulf War and Desert Storm in 1991. Play amateur psychologist. Why did Saddam refuse to leave Kuwait after being told in clear terms by President Bush and Secretary of State Baker that if he didn't leave, his troops would be bombed into submission. What kept him so adamant about staying there in the midst of those warnings?

SUNUNU There's a very good lesson in that. You have to remember that at that time, the US was still possessed by a post-Vietnam syndrome. We had not projected serious military power since Vietnam. I suspect that Saddam had advisers telling him that because of Vietnam, the US would not attack them in Kuwait, and that all our threats were just talk. Saddam just made a horribly bad calculation.

The easiest thing for a president to do in that situation is to not take action. It's easy not to send young men and women into harm's way. It is easy not to flex the muscles of the US to try and influence diplomacy. The hard thing is to make a positive decision to do that. Saddam simply believed that the president wasn't quite ready to fully engage our military, and obviously he made a mistake.

BOSTON He learned the hard way.

SUNUNU He most certainly did.

SUNUNU AND THE MEDIA

BOSTON You say that one of your biggest mistakes as White House chief of staff was how, unlike James Baker when he held the job during the Reagan administration, you made the decision to restrict your access to the media, and particularly to *The Washington Post*, and as a result of that, it motivated the press to criticize you on a very consistent basis as "the bad cop."

If you had to do it over again, during your years as White House chief of staff, would you have made yourself more accessible to the media?

SUNUNU There were actually two reasons why I distanced myself from the media. One, I didn't like them and didn't trust them. Number two, the president asked me to stay away from them. George Bush had the same feeling about the press that I did, and he had seen a Reagan White House in which leaks happened all over the place. He really had a strong aversion to his people talking to the press in the background. He essentially told us, "If you're going to talk to them, you ought to talk to them and be quoted."

Baker had created a weekly meeting with *The Washington Post* and maybe *The New York Times* where he would tell them all kinds of things that were happening from a background perspective. Baker recommended to me that I continue doing that. I asked the president about it and he said, "No." So, when you ask me what I would do differently, I wouldn't automatically go and have discussions with the press, but I would have fought harder with the president to allow me to do it. If the president still didn't want me to do it even after I fought harder, I would have abided by his direction and wouldn't have done it.

I absolutely believed that I had a constituency of one. My responsibility was to serve the president in the way he wanted me to serve him. If we ran into a situation where I felt morally or ethically uncomfortable, I'd leave, but as long as I stayed, my responsibility was to serve the president. If he didn't want me to talk to the press, I wouldn't talk to the press.

THE 1992 ELECTION

BOSTON Obviously, after three plus years in office, it became time for President Bush to run for reelection. In the book, you talk about the 1992 election in which Bill Clinton defeated President Bush, and how you believe there would have been a different result if Lee Atwater had not died of brain cancer in 1991. You also mention the "tepid team" that ran the president's reelection campaign in 1992.

Are you saying that Lee Atwater and a better team of campaign advisers could have overcome Ross Perot and also been able to overcome what you call "The Churchill Effect," (as described in your Introduction, about how people historically seek new leaders and refocus on domestic needs after a great foreign policy burden has been lifted from the electorate shoulders, as it had clearly been done with the Gulf War)?

SUNUNU Ross Perot, obviously, had a big impact on the 1992 election. He got 19% of the vote, two-third of which, I believe, were Republican votes that the president would have gotten, and that would have been enough to reelect President Bush. Atwater was as tough a political manager as I've ever seen—tough in the sense of running an effective campaign. If you remember, Ross Perot got in the race and then he got out, and then he came back in in October. I'm absolutely convinced that Lee Atwater would have made sure that upon returning to the campaign, Ross Perot would have been made to feel much more uncomfortable than he was. Not once did Ross Perot get attacked in 1992.

I left in March of '92, Roger Ailes had stopped working for the president about three or four months before that, and Atwater had died. Frankly, the three of us had been the rude and obnoxious people in the '88 campaign, so when we weren't around, there was nobody left who could bring toughness to the campaign and respond to all the charges the Clinton people

were making to Bush and all the horrible attacks he was getting from Ross Perot. The Bush campaign never aggressively went after Ross Perot for anything, including the fact that Ross Perot was attacking George Bush on taxes and proposed an economic plan that provided for about four times the amount of taxes that were included in the 1990 budget plan.

I use the phrase in the book, that Atwater "would have taken a two-by-four to the head" of Ross Perot—not really, but in terms of a strategy—because Ross Perot had a thin skin. He couldn't stand being criticized and the Bush campaign never made him uncomfortable for doing what he did.

BOSTON Your book is all about what a great president George Bush 41 was, and yet how could he be so great in organizing and executing during his presidency, but so bad at organizing and executing his re-election campaign?

SUNUNU It's because his style depended on a set of relationships with good friends who he trusted, and he ended up in '92 with a White House staff (I had left in March) and a campaign staff who he thought were going to be as close to him and would do as good a job as the people who had been with him since 1988. He discovered all of a sudden in the summer of 1992, that his new team wasn't as close or as effective. He then desperately tried to persuade Jimmy Baker to come back from the State Department and fix the broken campaign. Baker finally came back in August or September, but by then, the president and his staff were just completely out of sync.

One last point. In my opinion, Bush could have still won the election despite all the ineffectiveness of his campaign staff, Ross Perot, and the Churchill Effect, except for one thing that happened right before Election Day. Since Dwight Eisenhower, no party has held the White House for more than eight years except once, and that was the Bush continuation of the Regan administration. I feel in my heart that Bush could still have won the '92 election if on the last day of October, or the first day of November, the Special Prosecutor Walsh had not gotten former Secretary of Defense Weinberger indicted and tried and make a big deal again out of claiming that there had been criminal complicity in the Iran-Contra Affair. The Democrats used that indictment in the last week before Election Day to smear the president. There's actually polling data that shows that President Bush had virtually pulled even with Clinton seven days before the election and had the momentum going forward. Then, the day after the Weinberger indictment came out, the polling numbers dropped off.

Politics is complicated and tough and electorates are difficult to predict. There are lots of reasons he ended up losing in '92. We can only speculate which collection of them are the real reasons and which really didn't have much of an effect.

REFLECTIONS ON BUSH 41'S NOT HAVING A SECOND TERM

BOSTON Despite serving only one four-year term, President Bush's legacy has been growing every year since he left the White House in January 1993. We all know the historical record about our presidents usually having underwhelming and sometimes disastrous second terms.

From a historical legacy standpoint, is it a mixed blessing that President Bush lost the '92 election?

SUNUNU Let me answer that in a slightly different way. I'm often asked, "Did he regret losing the election?" Of course, he regretted losing an election, but for the Bush family, it turned out well. Not only has his legacy been growing, but if he had been re-elected, I don't think George W. would have run and therefore he would have not had a son as president and he would not have a second son running for president

now. So life is funny. Sometimes things that you think are not happy events turn out to be the predicate or precursor for things that are even better.

I don't think a Bush second term would have been as disastrous as some historical second terms because he really had a vision for what he wanted to do. He thought he had built up enough credibility in the Middle East with the Arab nations to begin to have a serious impact on the Israeli-Palestinian issue. He recognized that the relationship with the old Soviet Union could have been developed even further than it had. The new Russia, which was the successor to the Soviet Union, could have been a great energy supply trading partner for the United States and he could have built on the relationships he had. He also had a great vision that the unification of Germany set the stage for the European Union. He didn't quite have the vision of the European Union as it is now, but all these things were agenda items that he had in his head. He wanted to go with welfare reform which Clinton himself picked up and acted on, and so President Bush had a pretty clear vision of what his agenda would be and I expect that the relationships he had used so well in the first term would have continued in the second term.

BOSTON One thing presidential history teaches us is that the reason second terms are typically so bad is because the president is operating with a second string Cabinet and advisors since everybody from the first string basically gets burned out and quits before the second term.

SUNUNU It's true. That's a very true phenomenon and is actually parallel to what I was trying to say about the campaign team running in '92 versus the campaign team in '88. A president is able to bring his very best people in at the beginning. You use the phrase "second string" or "second team", but the people who he brings in to replace them are seldom as capable as the people who started.

BOSTON Those are all my questions. Does anyone in the audience have a question?

BARBARA BUSH AS FIRST LADY

AUDIENCE MEMBER What role did Barbara Bush play in the Bush administration? We always hear about the women behind the men and I'd be interested in your assessment of her role.

SUNUNU The best way to respond to that is to say that the Bushes really are a team. They talk a lot privately and she was smart enough not to stick her nose into policy publicly, but she was always there as a confidant. He trusts her judgment. She is not shy about giving her opinion to him, but, as I say, she's also smart enough not to stick her nose in policy publicly, and I think that's a big mistake that many First Ladies have made and she did not make that mistake.

PRESIDENT BUSH'S RELATIONSHIP WITH HIS PREDECESSOR RONALD REAGAN

AUDIENCE MEMBER You mention that during his presidency, George Bush was a continuation of the Reagan presidency more or less. What was his relationship with former President Regan during his four years in the Oval Office?

SUNUNU They really had a fantastic relationship. They were two people who were smart enough to know that so much more can be done by making sure their relationship stayed solid. I was with President Bush on probably half a dozen occasions where we met with President Reagan while we were in the White House, and were visiting California, and even after his presidency on one or two occasions, and it was always warm and friendly between the two men.

I think President Reagan really felt that George Bush tried to bring completion to some of the things Reagan started. Reagan put the Soviet Union in a position where they had to negotiate because of his "Peace Through Strength" policy and his building up our defense structure. George Bush took advantage of that and I think Reagan felt that he was the right man to do it.

BUSH 41'S CONDITION IN 2015

AUDIENCE MEMBER How is President Bush today and how often do you see him?

SUNUNU My wife and I went up to see him during first week in June and brought him a copy of the book, and had lunch with him and Barbara. He looked great—better than he did the year before when he had just come out of the bout with bronchitis. He fell this summer and was wearing a neck brace, and was a little cranky dealing with the brace, but other than that he's doing very well. When I was in the hospital five and a half weeks ago, he called me and we had a long conversation. He sounded very energetic and strong. He still swears he's going to jump out of an airplane again when he turns ninety-five.

BOSTON You all have been a wonderful audience. Thanks so much Governor Sununu.

ANDY CARD served in three different positions under President Reagan; as deputy White House chief of staff and secretary of transportation under President George H.W. Bush; and as White House chief of staff for most of George W. Bush's administration. I interviewed Mr. Card on October 8, 2015 on the campus of Franklin Pierce University, in Rindge, New Hampshire, where he now serves as the college's president.

"In the days after 9/11, the president actually addressed the world a couple of times in different forums. Basically, he told foreign countries, 'You're either with us or against us.' That was literally what he said. One of the first phone calls that came into the White House came from Muammar Gaddafi who said, 'I am with you. I am with you. I am with you. Yes, I am with you. Don't worry about me.'

Then we received a phone call from General (and President) Musharraf of Pakistan, who said, 'Please don't make me pick a team. Please, please, please. I want to be on both teams.' President Bush responded, 'No, you're either with us or against us.' His diplomatic challenge was quite significant and it caused many world leaders to discover a conscience. That doesn't mean they all chose the right answer, but they did have to confront their consciences."
– ANDY CARD

CHAPTER 31

ANDY CARD
ON
Ronald Reagan, George H. W. Bush, & George W. Bush

CARD ON REAGAN'S NATURE

BOSTON Andy, during the Reagan administration, you were special assistant to the president for intergovernmental affairs, then deputy assistant to the president, and finally director of intergovernmental affairs. In H. W. Brands' new biography of Reagan, he says that Reagan was clearly great at addressing the multitudes, whether in front of crowds or on television; but in person, he kept his distance from virtually everyone except his wife, Nancy.

Would you agree with that assessment?

CARD He had an infectious personality with a great stage presence, regardless of what stage he was on. He did not, however, invite people into his private life. His life was for us to witness rather than enjoy, but that doesn't mean he ever opened up his soul. He was tremendously engaging and a phenomenal communicator.

President Reagan was completely passionate about the people he included in his life and that had nothing to do with whether they agreed with him philosophically or in a partisan sense. Because he had been a governor himself, he had a unique empathetic relationship with every state governor. Frequently, my job was to convey messages to and from governors, and he often asked about a governor's personal life— "How are he and his wife doing? I understand his kids are having a tough time. Is there anything I can do to help?" His concern was sincere, even though he did not open himself up about his own life.

DIFFERENCE BETWEEN WHITE HOUSE DEPUTY CHIEF OF STAFF AND WHITE HOUSE CHIEF OF STAFF

BOSTON After Reagan left the White House, his successor was President George Bush 41. You served as his deputy White House chief of staff for three years while John Sununu was his White House chief of staff. Then, after the Clinton presidency, when President Bush 43 was elected, you served as his White House chief of staff for a period of over five years.

What's the biggest difference between being the deputy White House chief of staff and the chief of staff?

CARD As the deputy chief of staff, you're always the one who got it wrong. The chief of staff got it right. The deputy chief of staff is responsible for implementing whatever the chief of staff or the president wants to do.

The chief of staff has the greater responsibility because he's accountable for meeting the president's expectations—no small task. He also has the burden of making sure the president never has to make an easy decision. The deputy chief of staff is held accountable for the implementation of a decision, but the chief of staff is held accountable for which decisions the president is asked to make.

The average tenure for a White House chief of staff is twenty-three months. It's so short, you don't get a chance to vest in any pension program. I served as White House chief of staff for five and a half years and I overstayed my welcome several times, which involved situations when I didn't tell the president something he wanted to know or told him something he didn't need to know and then he worried about it. My test for speaking to the president was "taste your words before you spit them out."

Another test for a White House staffer is to avoid overplaying one's hand. The temptation to do that is always there because the arrogance of power at the White House is very inviting. Most people who work there have more power than they should, and don't want to do anything to lessen the impression that they're that powerful. To avoid overplaying one's hand takes tremendous restraint. The deputy chief of staff has to discipline those people who overuse their power to the detriment of the White House's ability to function.

Most people who work at the White House are very intelligent, but overconfident. The deputy chief of staff must respect the capacity of all staff members but more importantly must stimulate their intellects so the president gets their best counsel, and he usually needs more than one person's advice on an issue. High-powered staff members are usually capable and diligent, but sometimes they try to bully the president into making an ill-considered decision. Monitoring the situation when and how the president receives advice from many hard-charging people is quite a management challenge. The challenge of maintaining a well-functioning White House organization is to make sure everybody understands that his role is to serve the president. He personifies Article 2 in the Constitution.

The White House is kind of a caste system. The job of deputy chief of staff is to make sure the caste system works like a well-oiled machine. In the system are the president; the chief of staff and deputy chief of staff; the vice president; no more than twenty assistants to the president; about thirty deputy assistants to the president; and about seventy special assistants to the president. All of these people, except the vice president, are appointed by the president, and are called "commissioned officers."

Beneath them are directors appointed by the chief of staff; and beneath them are associate directors; and beneath them are administrative assistants.

Maintaining a disciplined line of authority within that caste system is the job of the chief of staff, and sometimes the deputy chief assists him with that job. He must make sure that no person beneath the president oversteps his authority, and every person respects the chain of command. Having said that, the chain of command must never prevent the appropriate people from getting needed information to the president which he should have in order to make a tough decision.

CARD'S MOST MEMORABLE EXPERIENCE WITH PRESIDENT GEORGE H.W. BUSH

BOSTON During the three years you served as deputy White House chief of staff, you spent considerable time with President Bush 41, and became very close to him.

What is the single most compelling memory you have of his presidency?

CARD When President Bush ran for office in 1988, the Dukakis campaign criticized him for his performance as director of the CIA regarding the drug trade business and government operation in Panama. Once Bush 41 became president, the situation in Panama worsened and had to be addressed. Manuel Noriega had been their military dictator for six years when in 1989, he arrested and then killed some Americans. President Bush and his staff then immediately began spending substantial time analyzing what should be done about Noriega.

There was a final meeting in the Oval Office to discuss the situation that included Secretary of State Jim Baker, Chief of Staff John Sununu, National Security Advisor Brent Scowcroft, Deputy National Security Advisor Bob Gates, the chairman of the joint chiefs of staff, and Vice President

Quayle. At that meeting, I mainly facilitated in displaying information to the group, while many options were presented and consequences considered.

At the end of the meeting, Secretary Baker stood up and said, "Mr. President, you've heard the information. This is *your* decision to make—it's not my decision or our decision. I'm going to leave you now so you can make that decision." He then walked out of the Oval Office, and everybody else followed him—except me.

As the low man on the totem pole, I stayed behind to gather the documents and easel that had been used during the meeting. President Bush went from the chair in front of the fireplace to the chair behind his desk. He sat, bent his head down, and shut his eyes. I think he was praying. Then he stood up. Although I was standing twenty feet in front of him, he did not look at me. He looked through me and said, "I am making a decision that will cost young men their lives." Then he opened the door that leads to the Rose Garden, went outside, and walked around the south side of the White House.

I remember leaving the Oval Office and saying to myself, "I just watched a president make a presidential decision." It was emotional. I felt gratified because I knew the president had made his decision—not based on theory, or emotions, or because of someone else's mission—but with full recognition of the pertinent facts and likely consequences. Young men and women would be asked to do things that would cause them to meet a fate no president ever wants to impose on anyone.

Although I was struck by what happened that day, my most unforgettable memory of President Bush is actually tied to a later day when the issue of Panama came up again in connection with his going to Cincinnati, Ohio, to make a speech. My job as deputy chief of staff included determining his travel logistics. To get ready, I found out what we intended to do there; who had invited us; what the message was he planned to deliver; who would be in attendance; and what the community was thinking about the president at the time. It turned out he was going there to deliver a major address on education to a group of students, parents, and teachers at a high school, and a policy team and speechwriters were already working on the message.

I then got into the details of what time he needed to arrive and leave, what else he would be doing while he was in Cincinnati, and I reviewed the letters that had come to the president recently from the zip codes where we were going. I received a computer printout that summarized the letters, and one jumped out at me. The headline describing the letter said, "A woman wrote the president after her son died in Panama and she wants to call the president a murderer to his face." Next to the detail of that letter was the appropriate action officer for the letter, who happened to be National Security Advisor Brent Scowcroft. I walked to General Scowcroft's office and asked, "Do you remember this letter?" He said, "Yes, and I sent it over to the Defense Department for them to handle. I also checked to make sure the president wrote a letter to the parents after their son died." He did.

At that moment, my pager went off letting me know the president wanted to see me. I went to the Oval Office, and although he had an issue he wanted to discuss with me, he started the conversation by saying, "You look troubled. What's going on?" I told him I was getting ready for the trip and had come across a letter that somebody in Cincinnati had written to him, and it was from an angry mother who wanted to meet him so she could call him a murderer to his face because her son had died in Panama. He said, "Of course, I should meet with her."

So I went back and finished organizing the trip. We went to Cincinnati and after the president spoke at the high school, I made arrangements for him to meet with the mother (and her family) who wrote the letter. When I walked into the room where

the family was, the mother was angry and reiterated what she wanted to do.

When he walked into the room, the president went over to the mother, and said, "I'm so glad to see you." She proceeded to do everything she said she would do, and he let her say everything she had to say, including calling him a murderer. Then he said, "Your son was a hero, and I couldn't do my job if it weren't for people like him. I want to know all about him. Tell me about your son." And she did. She talked with love about him and some good things that had happened when he was growing up, going to school, and playing baseball.

Then President Bush said to the brother, "Tell me about your brother." Then he said to the sister, "Tell me about your brother." Then he said to the stepdad, "He was a good son, wasn't he?" "Yes, he was."

There were tears in everyone's eyes. The president hugged the family, and then the mother reached in her purse, took out an envelope, and gave it to the president. "I want you to have this." He put it in his suit pocket and said goodbye. We walked out together, and got into a limousine. As we were driving toward Air Force One, the president opened the envelope and inside was a document written on white lined paper in pencil by a seventh grader. It said, "When I grow up, I want to be a soldier, and I'm not afraid to die for my country." It was written by the young man who had grown up and died for his country in Panama. The president was crying.

That was the most memorable moment I spent with President George H. W. Bush because it taught me the job of a president—that it requires making very tough decisions. Some decisions require sacrifices that no one would invite on anybody else. It also requires the president to appreciate the sacrifices made by others that are necessary for him to fulfill his oath. I witnessed the reality of a very tough presidential decision being made and the consequences that he had to live with. That's my story.

BOSTON That's an amazing story, Andy. It choked us all up.

CARD'S MEMORY OF SEPTEMBER 11, 2001

BOSTON Let's move to Bush 43's presidency. You were White House chief of staff and had been on the job less than eight months when the fateful day, September 11, 2001, arrived. You, the president, and others on the White House staff found yourself at the Emma Booker Elementary School in Sarasota, Florida. We could spend the rest of our interview time talking only about 9/11, so to allow some time for other topics, let's focus on a few areas of what happened on that day "when the world stopped turnin,'" to use Alan Jackson's words.

First, you were the one who had the job of telling President Bush what had just happened as he sat there in front of the school children.

What were the exact words you spoke in his ear and what was most important to you in how you said those words?

CARD I knew what the president had been told before he walked into the room. As we traveled to the school, two staff members, Dan Bartlett and Karl Rove, both asked, "Did anybody hear about the plane crash in New York City?" When we got to the school, the president went straight to a secure phone and called White House National Security Advisor Condoleezza Rice, though I didn't hear their conversation.

After I checked out where the president would speak, the classroom filled with second graders. The press corps was there to cover the event along with some White House staffers including the Secretary of Education. Standing at the door to the classroom was the president, the principal, and a Navy captain. The Director of the White House Situation Room Deb Loewer, then came up to the president and said, "Sir, it appears a small twin engine crop plane

crashed into one of the towers at the World Trade Center in New York City." That was all she said.

The reaction from the president, the principal, and me was the same: "Oh, what a horrible accident. The pilot must have had a heart attack or something." The principal opened the door to the classroom, she and the president went in, and the door shut. Captain Loewer then came up to me a minute later and said, "Sir, we just learned that it was *not* a small twin engine crop plane; it was a commercial jet liner."

My mind flashed to the fear that the passengers on the plane must have had. They had to know it wasn't gaining altitude. Then, a nanosecond later, Deb Loewer came back to me and said, "Oh, my God! Another plane hit the other tower at the World Trade Center!" My mind flashed to the initials: *UBL*. That's what we called Osama Bin Laden. I knew about him and the al-Qaeda network, and about their attacks on the World Trade Center in 1992 during the Clinton administration.

I then performed a task chiefs of staff have to perform all the time, and it's usually a tough task: Answering the question, "Does the president need to know this right now?" This time the answer was easy. Yes, he needed to know. I thought carefully about what to tell him. He was sitting in front of second graders with the press corps there, and I would need to walk into the room from backstage, right behind the president. I decided to tell him two facts, which I would do efficiently, and would also make one editorial comment. I wanted to say nothing that would invite a question or generate any dialogue with him because I knew everything said would be picked up by a boom microphone.

So I opened the door and walked into the classroom. The teacher was directing a conversation between the president and the children. I didn't want to interrupt that dialogue and the president didn't know I had walked into the room. Anne Compton from ABC News saw me and knew it was unusual for me to enter the room after the president had gone in, such that my being there, in and of itself, meant something major had happened. Then the teacher said to the students. "Take out your books. We're going to read to the president." That's when I walked up to him, leaned over, and whispered into his right ear, "A second plane hit the second tower. America is under attack." Two facts, one editorial comment.

I stood back so he couldn't ask any questions and he didn't turn to me. I went back to the classroom door, and watched his head bobbing up and down. He never turned back to me, and I left the room.

We knew we had to leave the school immediately. I was focusing on keeping the president out of danger. I know the Constitution places phenomenal responsibility on him. The job of the president is stated in his oath of office—to "preserve, protect, and defend." It's a phenomenal burden. I wanted him to meet his Constitutional responsibilities, which meant getting him in a safe place with good communications so he could fully operate as commander-in-chief. My job was to make sure he was in position to do his job.

So I told him, "We're getting out of here, Mr. President. We're going to fly in Air Force One to a safe place where we have good communications and then we're going to go to another safe place where we will have even better communication. Then, we're going to make sure things are done right to mitigate any unanticipated challenges—like getting all planes in the air down on the ground in case there are other terrorists on other planes planning on using them as weapons of mass destruction." Remember, the first plane that crashed into the World Trade Center had taken off from Boston, and the plane that crashed into Shanksville, Pennsylvania, had taken off from Washington. Another plane crashed into the Pentagon. I recognized the strong possibility that there were other planes in the air getting ready to crash into something.

BOSTON In a short period of time, after you whispered in his ear in the classroom, and the president came out to leave the school and get on Air Force One, and because America was under attack and it was a national emergency, immediate action was required. With the country in high danger, and everyone wondering what would be hit next, the decision was made for Air Force One to fly first to Louisiana, and then to Nebraska, because of the danger associated with the president's returning immediately to Washington, DC.

I know that when you advised the president of those travel plans, it was not pleasing to him. He wanted to go straight back to DC, but you stood your ground and insisted.

How hard was it for a White House chief of staff to tell a highly stressed president, "No, Mr. President. I know what you want to do, but we're not going to do that?"

CARD First of all, I tried to be really cool, calm, collected, and objective. On Air Force One, the president of the United States was pushing to go back to Washington, DC. I never said "No" to him. Instead, I said, "I don't think you really want to make that decision." Then, he said, "I'm making the decision. We're going back to Washington, DC." I again said, "I don't think you really want to make that decision right now." I kept repeating that and he kept yelling at me, "I am the commander-in-chief. I am making the decision. We're going back to Washington, DC." And I said, "Yes, but I don't think you really want to make that decision right now." I knew the Secret Service agent and the pilot on Air Force One didn't want him to make that decision yet.

Our mindset was that most people who had kidnapped planes in the past were seeking to go to Cuba, or get somebody released from prison, or make lots of money. We had never experienced somebody's choosing to kidnap a plane to use it as a weapon of mass destruction, so we knew we were dealing with people who had a completely different mindset. That's what we were concerned about as we left the Florida school, knowing that the president had plenty of work to do on Air Force One.

It impressed me that as he sat on Air Force One and we climbed to forty-eight thousand feet, facing a challenge nobody ever expected, without being prompted by anyone, he said, "Call President Putin. I want to talk to him." When Putin came on the line, President Bush said, "Guess what. We've been attacked. Don't think this is an excuse to go to war. We're not using it as an excuse to go to war. Don't mobilize. Don't go to Dep 63 Southern or whatever it is, but we are under attack. We are not looking for an excuse to attack you, and please don't use this to find an excuse to attack us." I thought his making that call was phenomenally insightful. It helped maintain a good relationship with the Soviets at a very stressful time.

In terms of the president and I having an argument about where we would go when we left the Florida school—yes we had an argument. It took him about a month to apologize to me. In his autobiography, *Decision Points*, he acknowledged that in those circumstances, he was really mad at me and I was really frustrated with him. And by the way, that wasn't the only time he was mad at me or the only time he frustrated me.

Working for President Reagan was very different from working for President George W. Bush, and working for President George H. W. Bush was very different from working for President George W. Bush. Why? Because of me. When I worked for President Reagan, he was like my grandfather. I was very deferential to him, like you would to your grandfather. If your grandfather tells you something you don't agree with, you still respond in a really nice way.

President George H. W. Bush was like my dad. When your dad tells you something you don't like, you tell him and then you feel guilty. George W. Bush was like my brother. When my brother told me something stupid, I called him stupid, and he called me stupid. And sometimes he'd say, "You're stupid," and I'd say, "No, you're stupid."

So my relationship with those presidents was generational more than it was political or even personal. It was always close. I had the courage to speak truth to every president I worked for, but I had different levels of courage in the battles I had with them. It's easy to say I should compare them as apples, apples, apples. No, it was my grandfather, my dad, and my brother, and I still feel guilty about thinking bad things about my grandfather. I will defend my father no matter how confused he may get, but I will still tweak my brother in no uncertain terms any time he gets confused about something. Those were the relationships.

BOSTON Once the president, you, and the team left Florida, and then went to Louisiana, and then went to Nebraska, the time came when it became safe to return to Washington, DC. Immediately, the president and his inner circle, (which included you), began planning the war on terrorism.

Given the lack of precedent in going to war with hidden enemies like al-Qaeda and the Taliban, how did the president, you, and the team go about setting priorities and coming up with a game plan for how America would go after those responsible for the attacks of 9/11?

CARD The president was very deliberate and not emotional in his planning which began almost immediately after he entered the holding room after I spoke to him in front of the second graders. He had full recognition of the challenge. Every discussion I had with the president from then on regarding what was happening in any aspect of what we might do in responding to terrorism always included a discussion about the consequences of our potential actions. When you plan for kinetic action in a war, you also have to determine such things as how many body bags need to be ordered. It's very sobering for a president to have to answer that question.

It so happened that the week of 9/11 was a very emotional week for me because on October 7, 2001, the war in Afghanistan had started. I don't forget that day and the fact that there were people who made sacrifices because of that day. Do I feel a party to the invitation to those sacrifices to be made? Yes, it is a burden to carry.

Congress authorized the president to do everything including going to war on September 14, 2001 —the Friday before the meeting at Camp David on September 15. It was a unanimous vote from the Senate (though there were two abstentions), and there was only one dissenting vote in the House of Representatives (with ten abstentions).

In the days after 9/11, the president actually addressed the world a couple of times in different forums. Basically, he told the world, "You're either with us or against us." That was literally what he said. It was not very diplomatic—kind of like Ronald Reagan's statement to Gorbachev, "Tear this wall down." The State Department didn't like it when Ronald Reagan spoke so directly, and didn't like it when George W. Bush did as well. It was a message he sent out to leaders around the world. One of the first phone calls that came into the White House came from Muammar Gaddafi who said, "I am with you. I am with you. I am with you. Yes, I am with you. Don't worry about me."

Then we received a phone call from General (and President) Musharraf of Pakistan, who said, "Please don't make me pick a team. Please, please, please. I want to be on both teams." President Bush responded, "No, you're either with us or against us." His diplomatic challenge was quite significant and it caused many leaders to discover a conscience. That doesn't mean they all chose the right answer, but they did have to confront their consciences. The coalition we built was surprisingly large.

BOSTON   Because of the way President Bush acted so courageously, eloquently,

and compassionately in every respect on and after 9/11, his popularity reached an all-time high. But then he had another seven years in office during which time his popularity came down during a time when President Bush had to operate in the highly toxic atmosphere in American politics exacerbated by 24/7 cable news and highly partisan blogs.

What was your and President Bush's game plan for staying above the fray in the toxic political and media atmosphere that was there virtually every day after the anguish over 9/11 had subsided until you stepped down as chief of staff?

CARD   The toxic media was there from the time the Supreme Court made the decision that George W. Bush would be president in December 2000 until September 11, 2001. Then there was a brief respite in America where partisanship in the media and in politics was largely abandoned, though not forgotten.

Then it reemerged once the election cycle opened up in 2002. The election cycle caused the partisanship to again rear its ugly head. Cable news, radio talk show hosts, and the news media all contributed to a climate where more passion is generated by anger than love. Passion often gets ignited by what comes into our brains through our eyes and ears, and what we input from the media causes us to gravitate toward and then get locked into our biases. Most people choose to watch either Fox News or MSNBC. Regardless of which station a person watches, he wakes up in the morning thinking he's really smart because he totally agrees with the guy he watched on television the night before.

BOSTON   We're now living in a world that operates in the aftermath of 9/11—a world of terrorism, suicide bombers, and all kinds of frightening possibilities. Regarding the Bush 43 presidency, a focal point of much of the criticism aimed at him comes from his decision to start the war in Iraq.

In your opinion, what would have happened if we had not commenced the war in Iraq, and there had been additional acts of terrorism committed at Saddam Hussein's behest? Would that have put George W. Bush in a class with Andrew Johnson at the bottom of the barrel of presidents for being so unresponsive to a world emergency?

CARD I think the nature of the president's reelection campaign would have been very different. We probably would have been challenged in the Republican primaries. And the Democrats probably would have challenged him for being too soft on terrorism. And John Kerry would have been the one to say (as President George H.W. Bush had once said about Iraq's activities after they invaded Kuwait), "We will not let this stand."

BOSTON We used to have a president who would follow through on a commitment about drawing red lines and then enforcing them.

CARD I'm going to quote Prime Minister Blair from his autobiography *My Journey in Politics.* It begins with him saying, "America wants to be loved, but America cannot be loved. It must be respected, admired, and feared. It must be respected by its allies, admired by neutrals, and feared by its enemies. America must always lead because if America doesn't lead, no other country will." That's an amazing thing for a prime minister of Great Britain to say and he credits President Bush with commanding respect; not necessarily winning a lot of admiration, but having enemies who feared him.

BUSH 43'S GOAL OF NATION-BUILDING AS PART OF THE WAR ON TERRORISM

BOSTON Neither of the wars in Afghanistan and Iraq had a successful end during Bush 43's presidency.

Was his stated desire to be a "nation-builder" for those countries an unrealistic and unachievable goal in the twenty-first century?

CARD When George W. Bush ran for president, he did not see himself as a "nation-builder," so he did not campaign for the office based on that. The reality of 9/11 and the failure of the regimes in Afghanistan and Iraq to accept the president's invitation to be part of the solution rather than part of the problem meant that the president had to make a tough decision to send troops in to make sure there were no safe havens for terrorists.

Along with that, once we went in, we had to deal with the mess made after we went in. Questions that have to be addressed: Can more stability be brought back into that country? Do we build a nation or just leave a tribe?

I'm not sure it was the president's desire to be a nation-builder. I think he legitimately believed that people have certain fundamental rights and one of them is self-governance. He hoped to encourage democracies in nations that would generate respect for human rights.

BOSTON In his speeches and writings, he made it quite clear that the "nation-building" ambition of his presidency did not occur until after 9/11. What I'm asking is, given the reality of the world post-9/11, is being a nation-builder for those third-world countries who aspire to be free, an unrealistic and unachievable goal in the twenty-first century, looking at it now with 20/20 hindsight?

CARD It's an aspirational goal. It's like excellence. Excellence doesn't mean you're done. If you become excellent at something, you still work for greater excellence. I think President Bush 43 would still say he'd love to see every nation on earth be one that's self-governed by the people. He'd still want to be a nation-builder rather than a nation destroyer.

Photo credit: Courtesy of the White House

BOSTON We all have that aspiration.

CARD Did things work out the way the president wanted? No. Were there plenty of strategic and tactical decisions made that did not live up to his expectation? Yes. Strategic decisions in Iraq, for example, had to be made where having realistic expectations was impossible. Do you want a top-down government or a bottom-up government? America started as a bottom-up experiment and most nations after participating in wars have ended up as being top-down. Much of the strategy in Baghdad was Baghdad-down, not Anbar-up.

Some decisions were strategic and some were tactical. Did we want a general from our own army to go in and be the proposed interim ruler or did we want a civilian leader who came in from the State Department? He brought in Paul Bremer, for example, to help try to put the bricks and mortar together to hold the government up and identify future permanent leaders and pass the baton. In Afghanistan, the loya jirga chose their leaders. Did it work out the way the president wanted it to? No. Are those nations better off today than they were when they went in? I don't know if we're confident to say if they are or they're not.

BOSTON I guess what my question is: knowing what you just said and recognizing that many things didn't work out the way we wanted, are those countries better off

than they were before? Answer: We don't know yet. With 20/20 hindsight, was it a good decision?

CARD As a win?

BOSTON Yes.

CARD I still believe we did the right thing. I wish the world wasn't like it was, but it was what it was; and the president was presented with only bad options. There wasn't one good option. "Mr. President, here are the eight bad options. Which is the least bad? You get to make the decision."

One of the most courageous things the president did was the surge in Iraq. Most people told him not to do it. But it was the least bad option in the president's view, and it became the best solution, even if it didn't produce a thriving democracy.

I don't think it was a mistake to go into Afghanistan or Iraq. Are there consequences to war that are unintended? Absolutely. I think the negative consequence of Iraq came about in part because of the decisions made by the president who followed President Bush 43.

BOSTON The line I'm trying to draw is, on the one hand, given what happened on 9/11, and in furtherance of the war on terrorism, of course you have to go into Iraq. Of course you have to go into Afghanistan for purposes of trying to destroy the terrorists. That's a given.

What, to me, is not a given is the answer to the question: If we've done all we can do in the way of removing the terrorists, while we still have troops in Iraq or Afghanistan, should we go ahead and try to help this nation reform toward democracy and freedom and all those good things?

CARD My answer is that I don't think America could just walk away. I don't think we could just go into a nation, go to war there, and then walk away. I don't think the world would let that happen. Maybe other nations can do that, but I don't think the US can.

BOSTON At least before the current president, that was true.

CARD I don't think a president can make the decision to go in; blow up their palace, their power stations, their electricity grid, their water treatment facilities; and then say, "Okay. We've gotten rid of the terrorists. It's all yours." That's not realistic. It might be good in theory, but I don't think it's good in reality.

CARD AND HURRICANES ANDREW AND KATRINA

BOSTON Let's now move onto some of the domestic issues you faced during your years in the White House. After you left the position of deputy chief of staff, President Bush 41 named you to the Cabinet post of secretary of transportation. While holding that position, you were sent to Florida after Hurricane Andrew to oversee the recovery. It then turned into a political football in the '92 presidential campaign when Bill Clinton and the Democrats claimed that the Bush 41 administration had underperformed in responding to the hurricane just as Democrats later complained that the Bush 43 administration underperformed in response to Hurricane Katrina in 2005.

What's your response to the criticism directed at the Bushes over their handling of Hurricanes Andrew in '92 and Katrina in '05?

CARD They were both inappropriate and politically motivated. My duties as secretary of transportation did not include disaster relief. I received a call from Jim Baker, chief of staff to President Bush in the last months of the administration, wondering whether if the president asked me to take over the disaster response to Hurricane Andrew from Federal Emergency Management Agency (FEMA), would I accept? I said yes; the president made the assignment the next

day; I immediately got on a plane and flew down to Florida; and took over the disaster response from FEMA. President Bush apparently had determined there was a problem with the traditional FEMA approach to hurricanes, which was the genesis of my going down there. Needless to say, FEMA was not happy when I showed up; and I ended up staying in Florida seven weeks.

BOSTON Were the Democrats' political attacks with respect to the administration's response to Hurricane Andrew aimed at FEMA's performance?

CARD They were aimed at President Bush because it was re-election time, and he was in the middle of his campaign. Hurricane Andrew hit the last week in August of '92— prime time election season. The conventions had already been held, so everyone was in full blown presidential campaign mode.

It was a life-changing experience for me to get down there and take over the disaster assistance effort. I remember being on the ground in Dade County and the head of their local disaster assistance effort was literally out on the front lawn of her building holding a press conference trashing the president, saying, "Where is he? Where's the cavalry? He hasn't sent anybody down here." There I was, sitting in her office, and she famously said, "Where's the cavalry?" I was waiting to meet with her *before* she went out for the press conference.

BOSTON Switching gears to Hurricane Katrina in '05, there has been much criticism of President Bush 43's handling of that. I've read his book, *Decision Points*, and have also heard him speak about it, but give me your perspective on the response to Hurricane Katrina.

CARD The president did more for pre-preparations as the South awaited Hurricane Katrina than had ever been done in history. He actually violated an existing law in order to do all the prepositioning he did. Under the law at the time, he did not have the authority to do anything until after there had been a declaration of a disaster, and a state governor's issuing a written request for assistance from the federal government. So even prior to the declaration and request being made by the Governor of Louisiana, President Bush had FEMA pre-position certain response mechanisms in anticipation of Hurricane Katrina's coming in, using the lessons learned from earlier hurricanes in Florida.

Because the year 2005 had already had a busy hurricane season, we had already done a lot in getting Florida ready. Then the storm hit. When it did, it wasn't as bad at first as everybody had expected, but then a surge came down from Lake Pontchartrain which broke the levees. After that, the disaster took on new meaning, and even then, the governor of Louisiana (in contrast to the governor of Mississippi) did not make the declaration and request required by law.

BOSTON Were people in the Bush administration coaching Louisiana Governor Kathleen Blanco regarding exactly what was required of her to allow the federal assistance ball to get rolling?

CARD Absolutely. I stayed on the phone with her from midnight until 2:30 in the morning and she kept making demands that were not credible. For example, she wanted the US military to be under her command as the head of the Louisiana Guard. She refused to request federal or military relief assistance unless it would be under her command.

BOSTON So she would only make the statutorily required request for federal assistance if it was on her terms—not the statute's terms?

CARD Correct—unlike Haley Barbour, who quickly got the forms in which allowed us to get relief promptly to Mississippi.

That's literally what had happened in Florida with Hurricane Andrew in 1992 where the governor of Florida, Lawton Chiles, only requested from the federal government six water buffalos (a water tank to put fresh water in) for the National Guard to use. I remember talking to the governor and telling him that when he made the request, he needed to put in his declaration form, "I need all the help I can get, Mr. President." Because we can't go in and provide full federal assistance without a written request from the governor, except in the event of an insurrection.

BOSTON In terms of all the media criticism of President Bush that followed, were people in the media simply ignoring the fact as to what the federal statute required and the substantial delay caused by the Louisiana governor?

CARD In all honesty, I don't know if they were ignoring the facts or not. I don't know what they were ignoring. They weren't reporting it accurately, and we already know that Brian Williams was exaggerating. Part of the challenge came from the fact that Louisiana is unique. They have a different form of government there than in any other state. Every levee has a separate political entity that controls it.

Another problem there was due to the fact that the Mayor of New Orleans was not cooperating with the Governor of Louisiana—which made their requests different. The jurisdiction over the Superdome was not with the local police; it was with the state police. So the mayor sent people to the Superdome while the state was saying the Superdome couldn't be used because they didn't have police there to control it. There was a huge jurisdictional battle going on between the governor and the mayor—and between the state police and the local police—and the governor was not requesting assistance from the federal government in a way that we could respond to it.

The president was ready to just push forward and deliver all the needed federal assistance despite the objections of the lawyers at the Defense Department and the White House Council, who said it was illegal to supply federal manpower without a written request from the governor. There was a huge debate going on. Harriet Miers, the White House Council, was very involved as were lawyers from the Defense Department, and the session went on all night long. I went home at 4:30 in the morning and came back an hour later.

I spent all night dealing with Governor Blanco on the phone. I could hear her husband—nicknamed "Coach"—telling her what to do. She was saying things like, "We know Karl Rove is making the decision. It's not the president." It was a very awkward time. We ended up cutting a deal where the Adjutant General, who's the head of the Louisiana military, and our US Army General Honore sat in the same office as they worked on the problems with essentially joint command over the relief effort. That way, we weren't putting the US military under the authority of the governor. So General Honore, with his strong personality and the fact that he was from Louisiana, helped mitigate some of the problems the governor had created, and that's how things finally started working.

BOSTON Looking back at the outpouring of criticism aimed at the Bush administration, unjustified by reason of all the jurisdictional issues and the governor's failure to comply with the law, should President Bush have done more to publicize the quandary he was in and better explain the reasons why his actions were taken when they were?

CARD I don't think anybody would have paid attention to any such efforts to explain the situation. We did talk about it whenever anyone from the press was around, but no one paid any attention. Our real focus was on saving lives, rescuing people, and addressing the reality that the levees had

been breached. Lots of lessons were learned. Many of the local levy board authorities' responsibilities could not be transferred to the mayor or governor's jurisdiction, and sign-offs were required from these political entities at a time when their leaders had scattered to the winds and some of them never came back. They moved out of the state, despite being elected officials in charge of these levees.

DEALING WITH THE STEM CELL RESEARCH ISSUE

BOSTON Let's move to another subject—one of the most intellectually and morally challenging decisions President Bush 43 had to make. It began on his ninth day in office. It's the issue of stem cell research—which had particular urgency after he received Nancy Reagan's plea that he allow the research to take place in hopes of providing answers to Alzheimer's victims like her husband.

How was the process orchestrated to allow President Bush to make the most informed decision on this issue that involved what he calls "a philosophical clash between science and morality" and overlapped with the abortion debate?

CARD How we handled the stem cell research issue is one of the best examples of how presidential decision-making should take place because the president had plenty of time to make the decision and wasn't operating in a crisis mode when he made it. The stem cell issue was presented to the president because of a budget issue. Stem cell research was not prohibited, but there was a need for government money to be spent on it. The National Institute of Health asked for money in their budget to fund the research. Our Budget Director Mitch Daniels, said to the president, "This is a budget issue you have to decide. It represents not just a policy question but also involves moral and philosophical questions. Mr. President, how do you want me to proceed?"

I asked Mitch when the decision was needed, and he answered, "before we actually file the budget document in late August/ early September"—which meant we had seven to eight months to make the decision.

The president was very methodical about the process. He wanted to talk to ethicists, scientists, medical researchers, victims of childhood diabetes, parents of children with diabetes, and people involved in Alzheimer's research. So we organized a comprehensive process getting information from all those constituencies to provide input to the president.

After he received the input, President Bush called a meeting in the Oval Office in July or August 2001. About fifteen of us gathered, and the president asked each of us what we thought he should do. Everyone offered an opinion and there were many different views.—"I'd fund it," "I wouldn't fund it," "I'd fund it but restrict it to the stem cell lines that were already in existence."

He then turned to me, and asked my advice. I said, "Mr. President, you know I always like to give you my counsel after everybody else is done and we're all alone." He said, "I know, but in this case, I want you to give your advice in front of everybody. I want the group to hear it." So I gave my view, but caveated it, because my view was parochial, influenced by my mother having Alzheimer's and my father's having Parkinson's. Then he said, "Thank you very much," and the meeting ended.

The next morning, he came in and I greeted him with my customary, "Top of the morning, Mr. President." And he said, "You're not going to be happy with me today. I made my decision and it's not what you recommended. I've decided to fund the research but only for work on those stem cell lines that have already been harvested." I told him I respected his decision and how it was made, and would proudly support it.

Then we moved into implementation mode. "Okay, Mitch Daniels, you can put the money in the budget." Then, working

with Karen Hughes, we determined a plan on how best to communicate his decision. Then he gave his speech on what he planned to do about the research from Crawford in the summer of 2001. It was one of his first significant addresses and it was on a complex issue where ethics, morality, theology, and science all came together.

BOSTON Thank goodness there was closure on it before 9/11.

CARD Right. But it was one of those rare opportunities where a tough presidential decision got made when there was plenty of time to prepare for it.

NOMINATING JUSTICES FOR THE SUPREME COURT

BOSTON Next subject. One of the president's most important jobs is to nominate justices to serve on the United States Supreme Court. During his terms, President Bush 43 filled two positions that ultimately went to John Roberts and Samuel Alito. We know that Chief Justice Roberts has not exactly towed the conservative line during his time on the court, among other things, twice voting in favor of challenges made to Obamacare.

What was the process for checking out John Roberts' judicial and political philosophies before he was nominated?

CARD Even before President Bush took office, a group was convened to start thinking about future Supreme Court justices. It included future White House Counsel Alberto Gonzalez, Attorney General John Ashcroft, Vice President Dick Cheney, and me. We started gathering the names of potential justices in case a Supreme Court justice dropped dead on Inauguration Day. We wanted to know who should be in the pipeline right from the start.

We met regularly, (though not every week or couple of weeks), and that way when an opening arose on the court, we'd have a list of proposed candidates ready. We reviewed resumes—trying to build a pool the president should consider. Our process included discerning their philosophical positions by reading their prior decisions, their writings, and speeches. We were sensitive to the president's desire to have diversity on the court—so we made sure the candidates weren't all white males or only people who had served on circuit courts of appeals; so we included some academics and others with prominent expertise.

When the first opening arose after Sandra Day O'Connor announced her retirement, we began interviewing candidates—some offsite, some at the White House. After the first group had been reviewed, the president told us to look for other names and he gave us some people who he thought should be considered. I called upon senators on the Judiciary Committee to see if they had any suggestions—and called both Republicans and Democrats. I remember having a particularly good conversation with Senator Kennedy about names he thought should be considered. Every name was then submitted to this group, we assessed them, and then the president sat down with us at regular meetings.

The president interviewed the leading candidates. John Roberts interviewed very well and was clearly the front runner. The president then nominated him. Because Justice O'Connor was leaving the Court, there was tremendous expectation that the president would nominate a woman, so when he chose John Roberts, there was some angst in the political world. Even Laura Bush wanted him to appoint a woman.

Then, shortly after the Roberts nomination announcement, Chief Justice Rehnquist died and the president had to consider another nominee. This time he was particularly interested in choosing a woman. I was tasked to see what qualified women should be considered. I again made a number of calls, including to Capitol Hill. I also spoke to some sitting Supreme Court justices to see if they had any suggestions.

We considered several names seriously and one that bubbled up in the process was Harriet Miers. I talked to the president, and he liked the Miers idea, and suggested we approach Harriet to see if she would be interested. She was and the rest is history. She was nominated. When her nomination did not gain the response we hoped it would, then Harriet withdrew and that was a very painful process—for her and for the president.

He then moved very quickly and, building on the interviews that had already taken place when he had appointed John Roberts, he proceeded to nominate Sam Alito, who interviewed very well, rose to the top, and became the nominee to replace John Roberts' associate justice slot since Roberts had been nominated to replace Chief Justice Rehnquist.

BOSTON I appreciate that accounting of the process for the two people who were actually named.

What was the process, though, for trying to discern a candidate's likely attitude on important social questions or moral questions? Was there any kind of checklist or identified points that the president wanted to have comfort on before he actually nominated someone?

CARD We tried to discern that, but no one was asked: "What is your position on abortion?" or, "What would you do if a particular case came before the Supreme Court?" To my knowledge, those types of questions weren't asked, and we would have considered it out of bounds to ask them. We knew justices go on the Supreme Court to deal with issues as they are presented in a particular case. Their process in making decisions on cases is not supposed to be philosophical; it's supposed to be based on the pertinent facts of the case, the applicable law, and their interpretation of the Constitution. Questions that were permissible and, therefore, were asked of the candidates were, "Do you believe in *stare decisis*? Do you think previous rulings of the court have been given disproportionate weight?"

BOSTON What I'm getting at is for people like me, who've never been part of this process, when you say asking those point blank questions was perceived to be "out of bounds," I'm curious how lines get drawn as to what's in bounds and what's not.

CARD The president drew the lines and he did that based on advice from the White House counsel's and attorney general's suggestions to be followed in the process. Everybody attempts to discern a person's philosophy and sense of morality, but I'm not sure it's appropriate to ask those direct questions.

BOSTON Given that I'm assuming the president wants a reasonable measure of certainty in his own mind about the person getting a lifetime appointment to the Supreme Court. I would have thought he would have asked point-blank questions.

CARD David Souter's nomination by President George H.W. Bush came on the recommendation, among others, of John Sununu and Warren Rudman. Justice Souter went on the Supreme Court with expectation that he would be a conservative justice. He ended up *not* being a conservative justice, and that was a major disappointment for many of us.

BOSTON President Bush 43 says the same thing in his book. He was very outspoken about his disappointment over Souter. That's what raises my question. Recognizing that Souter essentially went rogue, I would think that would cause people to be doubly careful to make sure tough questions got asked.

CARD Yes, but doing that would open up a can of worms in the nomination process. A member of the Senate Judiciary Committee always asks, "Have you already stated your position on any of the issues that have to come before the court?" If a judicial candidate said "Yes," it would be a death knell if the judge wanted be confirmed.

A candidate must say to the Judiciary Committee, "I will make my decision about that issue based on the information at the time in the case presented." I was involved in the judicial selection process for George H.W. Bush and George W. Bush, and both times, those were the expectations we had based on the advice we got from the White House counsel and attorney general.

PRESIDENT BUSH'S ATTEMPT AT SOCIAL SECURITY REFORM

BOSTON Next question: Another issue unsuccessfully undertaken by President Bush came at the start of his second term when he tried to reform our Social Security system. You and Secretary of the Treasury John Snow had primary responsibilities for this effort. It's clear from *Decision Points* that the Democrats were out to stymie any and everything President Bush did on every issue—that was a given.

Why did the Republicans in Congress refuse to step up and make Social Security reform happen?

CARD There were two issues where the same challenge existed. One was immigration reform; the other was Social Security reform. The reason the president had a hard time gaining support on those two issues from the Republican caucus was because he was a lame duck when he pushed both initiatives. Neither of his elections were perceived by anyone to provide him with a mandate because they were both very close. He's the only president I've worked for who got elected president but never went to a victory celebration. Without a mandate, as soon as he got reelected, auditions started for the next presidential nominee. So the people who supported the president (including me), didn't do the work necessary to provide the president with the platform for his initiatives that would have attracted a significant majority of support from his own party.

BOSTON Even without a mandate, as the president began his second term, obviously he wanted to focus on new initiatives that he thought had a high likelihood of achieving success—didn't he?

CARD He outlined Social Security as one of his priorities—he campaigned on it, as he did with immigration reform. Since the first days in his first term, the president had created a Social Security task force. In fact, we had study groups on every major issue.

BOSTON As part of the effort to pursue Social Security reform, had you met with the leaders of the Republican caucus and gotten assurances that the reforms the president wanted to pursue were going to meet with their approval?

CARD I don't know that we got assurances. We got acquiescence. It wasn't like there was enthusiasm.

BOSTON That's my question. Obviously, everyone knows Social Security will go bankrupt sooner or later. Here you had a president who was actually trying to confront an issue that most presidents wouldn't think about addressing.

Why were the Republicans in Congress not supporting their president on an issue everyone knew needed reform?

CARD Because they were still buying into the idea of politics' "third rail." Social Security is considered the third rail of politics. You can't touch it or else you'll get killed. That frustrated the president and he basically said to Congress, "Blame me, but grab onto the third rail. I'm not afraid to grab the third rail because if we don't do it now, we won't have a Social Security system that's sustainable."

I think that because his election victory came with such a close margin, the

troops in Congress were reluctant to grab the third rail. When you go into a subway, there are signs all over the place that say, "Stay away from the third rail. Don't touch the third rail," which is where the electricity is that powers the subway. Because the Republicans in Congress refused to touch the third rail, he couldn't move the train down the track.

ANDY CARD'S VIEW OF PRESIDENT GEORGE W. BUSH'S BEST DAY IN OFFICE

BOSTON Here's my final question. Describe what happened on your very best day while you were White House chief of staff during the Bush 43 administration.

CARD The day was September 14, 2001—the Friday after the attacks of 9/11. The dust had settled, the fog had lifted, and the reality and magnitude of the problems were evident. The consequences were beginning to be understood and the challenge was becoming recognizable. I woke up at 4:00 in the morning, and got to work at 5:45. I remember sitting at my desk and there was a big thick document called the President's Daily Brief (PDB), a CIA report. It contained very little analysis, but had a lot about "this threat" and "that threat" and "another threat." Then the little box on my desk started to flash, which meant the president was getting ready to come to work. It was about fifteen minutes before I expected him and I hadn't finished reading everything on my desk.

I ran down to the Oval Office. He walked in, and I greeted him: "Top of the morning, Mr. President. Let me tell you what your day is going to be like." He interrupted me and said, "I'll tell you what my day is going to be like." That troubled me because I was supposed to be in charge of his day. He told me he wanted me to get the FBI Director over there for a scheduling briefing. I said, "Terrific, we'll do that. Why don't we do it right at 8:30 in the morning after the CIA briefing?" He said, "Fine."

Photo credit: Kathleen Dooher

Andy Card

I called the FBI Director Bob Muller, and the Attorney General John Ashcroft, and said, "Come to the White House. We'll brief the president at 8:30." I went back and told the president everything was all set, and went back to my office.

After he met with the CIA, he then met with the FBI, and after hearing what their plans were for responding to the events of 9/11, he challenged them with these words: "I am more interested in what you're doing to prevent the next attack." That changed the mission of the FBI.

The president then turned to me, and said, "I want to meet with the War Council tomorrow at Camp David." Although there's no such thing as the War Council, I knew what he meant—and who he wanted to come to Camp David.

After the meeting with the FBI ended, his Cabinet Affairs Secretary Albert Hawkins and I got him ready for the Cabinet meeting. Albert gave the president 3x5 note cards, and we went over the protocol for the meeting, and then we walked to the Capitol where the meeting was.

Everybody stood at the Cabinet meeting until the president sat down. We began with a prayer offered by Secretary Rumsfeld. When the prayer ended, the president looked up and said, "We are at war. But while we are at war, we have a job of governing to do."

He then listened to a report from the secretary of state and the secretary of defense. He then looked at each Cabinet member, and with amazing specificity told them exactly what their job was. What he said showed his breadth of knowledge about the agenda he had for governing the country. He told the Cabinet that each of them had jobs to do while we are at war. Members of the press came in, took pictures, and everyone left.

Then we piled into a limousine and went to the National Cathedral. Every pew was filled with Senators, Congressmen, clergymen and women from virtually every faith in America, governors, ambassadors, and former presidents were there. It was unbelievable. Reverend Billy Graham gave a sermon. We said prayers and sang hymns. The president spoke and reminded us of a higher power. He prayed for us, we sang another hymn, and we left.

Then we went to Andrews Air Force Base, got on Air Force One, and flew to Trenton, New Jersey. When we got off the plane there, we were met by the Governor of New York and the Mayor of New York City. We got on a helicopter that became Marine One. We flew out to the coast of New Jersey, and then up the coast. We saw the Statute of Liberty, and she looked beautiful. There were no planes in the sky because nothing was permitted to take off from any of the airports. We saw smoke billowing from Ground Zero. Nobody said a word on the helicopter. We saw the rescue workers gathered around the base of the smoke pillar. We circled them twice, and then landed at Wall Street.

When we landed, we piled into limousine Suburbans and drove through the streets of New York. It was very eerie, unlike any other time I've been to New York with the president. As we approached Ground Zero, the president decided he wanted to get out of the limousine; but the Secret Service agents were uncomfortable with that because the people in the immediate area hadn't gone through any type of security screening. He got out of the limousine, and started working his way down to the disaster area. The people in the area began chanting "USA, USA, USA." Some were in tears, and some were cheering. It was just bizarre.

We got down to ground zero where there was a crushed vehicle. The crowd was still chanting "USA, USA, USA." I went to the president and asked, "Would you be willing to say something?" He answered, "Do you think it's appropriate?" I said, "Yes," and through Karl Rowe, we got Nina Bishop (the woman who worked as an advance person in the State Department) if she could get us a microphone. Somehow she found a bullhorn. The president got up on top of a crushed vehicle. We got a firefighter named Bob Beckwith and asked him to stand beside him.

As the president began to speak, somebody yelled out, "I can't hear you. I can't hear you." President Bush said, "I hear you and the whole world will hear us."

After he spoke, we piled into the limousine and went up to the Jacob Javits Center where several booths were set up. The president went to every single booth. In them were the rescue workers who came from every state in the union and thirty-eight countries. They had all volunteered to work at the rescue site and would become the next round of rescue workers. He had his picture taken with them, and thanked them for being there.

Again we piled into the limousine. He thought we were leaving the Javits Center, but instead we went to another part of it. He got out of the limousine when it stopped and there was a large room lined with blue drapes. He was told there was a podium, and could go in there and make some remarks. When the president learned the crowd was made up of the families of the policemen and firemen who were

missing at the World Trade Center, he didn't go to the microphone, but just walked into the room before any of the Secret Service agents did. He went directly to everybody in the room. There were tears, and hope, and fear, and anger, and resolve, and prayers, and hugs. The president didn't leave anybody out. We stayed there quite a while, much longer than scheduled.

As he was walking out, a woman came up to him. She had been one of the first people the president saw as he walked into the room. She stood in front of the president, looked him right in the eyes, held out her hand and said, "Mr. President, I want you to have this. This is my son's badge. His name is George Howard. Don't ever forget him." And she dropped the badge into the president's hand. Everybody was crying. I had tears streaming down my cheeks. The president was crying, but he said to her as tears streamed down his cheeks, "Mrs. Howard, America will move on, but I will never forget."

He finally walked away from Mrs. Howard and we followed him and got in the back of the limousine. I was sitting beside him, and he wasn't saying a word. We started to drive out of the Javits Center, and he reached into his pocket, pulled out the badge, and opened his hand. It was badge no. 1012. He then squeezed his hand, put the badge back in his pocket, and didn't say a word. We got to the landing zone, got out of the limousine, and he went over to have his picture taken with the firefighters and policemen protecting Marine One.

We all then got on Marine One. We lifted off and it was a long flight back to Trenton, New Jersey. Nobody said anything the whole ride. We landed and the staff got on a 747 and flew to Washington DC; and we got on a smaller plane that became Air Force One for that flight, and flew to Camp David.

We flew back to Hagerstown, Maryland, so we could go to Camp David to meet with those insiders in his administration who President Bush had just named his "War Council." The president slouched in his chair on the plane and shut his eyes. I'm convinced he was completely exhausted —physically, mentally, emotionally, and spiritually.

I said to him, "Mr. President, thank you." He opened his eyes, looked at me and said, "What?" I said, "Thank you. You are a great president. You did everything a president has to do and you did it in one day." He looked at me, leaned forward, and said, "What?" And I said, "Mr. President, today you changed the bureaucratic mission of the FBI and made it their mission to prevent the next attack. You called for an immediate meeting of the War Council. You charged the Cabinet that now that we are at war, we all have the job of governing to do. You prayed for the nation and the world, reminding us of a higher power and a greater calling. You told the world that they would hear us. You rallied the rescue workers and comforted the victims." All he said was: "Thank you."

BOSTON That's what you call a tour de force day.

CARD That was my most memorable day— September 14, 2001. It was also the day Congress passed the resolution authorizing the president to go to war. So from a constitutional point of view, it was a very memorable day, and, most importantly, it was a day when we witnessed the world coming together. That was my most memorable day.

BOSTON Thanks so much, Andy. Looks like we're out of time.

Closing Thoughts

NINE CONCLUSIONS & TEN COMMANDMENTS

Those who have completed the thirty-one interview transcripts in this book may now seek big picture conclusions at the thirty-five thousand feet level about what can be drawn from the lives of our most significant presidents. Here are the nine areas that struck me about a prudent approach to drawing conclusions about their legacies; followed by what I've derived from the interviews as the Ten Commandments of Presidential Leadership.

1. **A PERSPECTIVE ON PRESIDENTIAL STRENGTHS AND WEAKNESSES**

   As we size up performance, it's important to recognize on the front end that we have never had a flawless president—though Abraham Lincoln comes the closest and serves as the gold standard against whom all others are measured. Having said that, there is plenty to praise and condemn in all of them. To zero in on a president's particular strength or weakness makes comprehensive assessment impossible. There's more to James Madison's presidency than the day the British burned down the White House; to Ulysses S. Grant's than the corruption in his administration; to Woodrow Wilson's than his racial bias; and to Richard Nixon's than Watergate.

2. **EVALUATE A PRESIDENT IN HIS TIME AND PLACE**

   As a matter of fairness, a president is best evaluated in the context of his lifetime's setting since that was the arena in which he operated. Yes, Washington, Jefferson, Madison, and Jackson owned large farms in the South and followed the prevailing custom of their region and era in having slaves do the labor-intensive work on their plantations. As pointed out in the Heidlers', Peter Onuf's, and H.W. Brands' interviews (Chapters One, Three and Six), for the most part, during the eighteenth and early nineteenth centuries in the South—other than slaves—there were virtually no other available sources of agricultural workers in the area, and since mechanized farm equipment had not yet been invented, these plantation farm-owning presidents accepted the brutal economic calculus of their times, which, in retrospect, tarnishes their otherwise pristine legacies. Their having owned slaves has been used in recent years to demonize them and inspired efforts by some to strip away their historical significance.

Making such moral assessments about people who lived two centuries ago based on contemporary moral sensibilities in order to now pass judgment on men who lived by the norm and within the law of their times in their part of the country, should have the same logical appeal as a person's judging that apples are superior to oranges.

Caveat: A slave owner who repeatedly impregnated his slaves should be deemed immoral per se—in all circumstances and eras. Sorry, Thomas Jefferson. You reap what you sow—even if you're the fellow who blessed us with some truly marvelous rhetorical magic.

3. TIME NEEDS TO PASS BEFORE PAPERS GET GRADED

Grading a president's performance should occur only after several decades have passed since his departure from the White House, since it takes time for some decisions to play out; and delaying final assessment of performance allows us to put it into clearer perspective. Harry Truman wisely observed, "It takes fifty years for the dust to settle." As proof of this, witness the rise over the decades in the historical rankings of Grant, Truman, and Eisenhower; and the decline of James Monroe, Rutherford B. Hayes, and Grover Cleveland, after the six of them had passed over the horizon.

4. THE CRITICAL IMPORTANCE OF COMMUNICATION AND FOLLOW THROUGH

The American people have a constant burning desire to be inspired. In that regard, words, credibility, and tone are the coins of the realm in lifting up the masses. Jefferson and Lincoln were masters of the written word; Lincoln, Roosevelt, and Reagan of the spoken word. Surprisingly, George H.W. Bush never grasped the importance of ratcheting up his speeches, and he paid dearly for that omission.

To become recognized for true greatness though, a president's words must be credible and his walk must match his talk. He who makes powerful speeches with assertions based on fast-and-loose Pinocchio inaccuracies, and then fails to do what he said he'd do, becomes the proverbial emperor so consumed by his sense of elegance that he neglects to don his clothes.

5. PART OF THE JOB IS CROSSING THE AISLE

For a president to be deemed successful, he must have the wherewithal to push his favored pieces of legislation through Congress by gathering at least some bipartisan support. This requires heavy lifting; arm twisting; and, on occasion, pork. Lincoln did what it took to get Congress on board with the Thirteenth Amendment. Lyndon B. Johnson and Ronald Reagan consistently hit their domestic marks because they could cross the aisle and persevere toward getting their favored laws passed. When parties fracture and subdivide, as the Republican Party has been doing in the last quarter century, the degree of difficulty in building a Congressional majority on legislation doubles, as both George Bushes learned during their presidencies.

No one has ever said the job of president of the United States is a sinecure. A major part of the job description is confronting the reality of the push-pull process with Congress, and then rolling up one's sleeves, working hard to build relationships, and ferociously finding a way to end up with an acceptable (not perfect, but acceptable) law after remaining steadfast through the often grisly task of gaining legislative approval.

6. THE NECESSARY SUPPORT OF A PRESIDENT'S TEAM OF ADVISORS

A key to every president's performance is the strength of his supporting cast. No president is an island or has ever succeeded by himself. Who a president chooses to have in his inner circle speaks volumes about his wisdom and character, and has a major impact on his performance. One of George Washington's greatest strengths was recognizing that he was not the smartest guy in the room, and then having the wherewithal to choose the best and brightest to guide him as his team of advisors. Lincoln's "team of rivals" Cabinet caused his decisions to be battle-tested before he finalized them. Johnson's inept foreign policy team led him down the path of destruction on Vietnam. Nixon's inner amoral circle played a major role in the downward spiral that led to his resignation. Washington and Reagan performed much better in their first terms than their second because of the caliber of those who surrounded them during each term.

7. **LOYALTY TO THE COUNTRY IS A GIVEN**

We have had no disloyal presidents. Every president has aspired to achieve what he believes to be in America's best interest. Their hearts have all been in the right place. Sometimes, their minds and libidos twist off and go awry, but their desire to do what they believe is best for America cannot be questioned by an intellectually honest person—even during the darkest days of our impeachment/near impeachment Presidents Andrew Johnson, Richard Nixon, and Bill Clinton.

8. **CREDIBLE SOURCES ONLY**

In drawing conclusions about presidential performance, a person must lean on the most reliable sources of information. The Cuban Missile Crisis must be evaluated based on the taped conversations of what was actually said at the ExComm meetings; not by Robert Kennedy's politically motivated fabrication aimed at elevating his and his brother's greatness in the book *Thirteen Days*, completed after RFK's death by Kennedy family sycophant Ted Sorenson—the man who wrote *Profiles in Courage* and then let John F. Kennedy accept the Pulitzer for it. Presidential memoirs and presidential insiders' books typically obsess on the achievements of their administrations and invariably leave out mass quantities of unflattering pertinent information. As with a courtroom trial, historical evaluations must be based on the best available, most credible evidence that contains a minimum amount of self-serving bias.

9. **THE PRESIDENT AND FOREIGN POLICY**

Ever since George Washington, a president's performance in the vision and execution of his foreign policy in the constantly changing world is a big part of his legacy; nobody bats 1.000 at it; and voters seem to care less about it than historians. Wilson triumphed in World War I, but then self-induced his way into a massive stroke in his zealous, unsuccessful effort to persuade the American people that they should make their Congressional representatives vote to join the League of Nations. Truman hit a home run in authorizing the atomic bombs as a means of rapidly ending World War II, but then struck out with his war effort in Korea. Kennedy had his Bay of Pigs fiasco and his Cuban Missile Crisis success. Fairly or unfairly, given the unintelligible morass of information about the situation, Lyndon Johnson will forever be tarnished by his escalation of the Vietnam War and inability to conclude our involvement in it. Richard Nixon achieved historic diplomatic success by opening the door to China, but his excessive delay in removing American troops from Vietnam can't be ignored when the time comes to put grades on his foreign policy report card. Reagan successfully initiated the movement to end the Cold War, but then committed a major sin (of either omission or commission—we'll never know) in his handling of the Iran-Contra nightmare. George H.W. Bush came closest to having an unblemished international record during his presidency with the fall of the Berlin Wall, the unification of Germany, and the Gulf War; and despite his successes around the world, American voters would not give him a second term.

Attempting to find America's proper place in the world always involves shooting at a target that moves quicker than any commander-in-chief can accurately aim his foreign policy gun. David Gergen served under four presidents and has described a leader's attempt to orchestrate foreign affairs as being the equivalent of attempting to play chess in three dimensions—a game even geniuses know to avoid.

The Ten Commandments of Great Presidential Leadership

1. **A great leader serves as conscience-in-chief—acting always with high moral integrity, commitment, and direction.**
   Thank you, David and Jeanne Heidler, for accentuating this point about George Washington, and Ronald C. White, Jr., for doing the same with Abraham Lincoln.

2. **A great leader stays above the fray amidst partisan skirmishing; fully grasps all sides' position; and does what it takes to achieve a consensus position acceptable to the majority.**
   Thank you, Peter Onuf, for accentuating this point about Thomas Jefferson; and James A. Baker, III, for doing the same with Ronald Reagan.

3. **A great leader has self-awareness of his limitations; and prevails in spite of them, largely through prudent selection of and dependence upon top advisors, and the exercise of sound judgment.**
   Thank you, David O. Stewart, for accentuating this point about James Madison; and David McCullough for doing the same with Harry S. Truman.

4. **A great leader stays calm in a crisis, somehow finding a way to maintain a steady temperament.**
   Thank you, Jean Edward Smith, for accentuating this point about Ulysses S. Grant; Amity Shlaes, for doing the same with Calvin Coolidge; Sheldon Stern for emphasizing this virtue in John F. Kennedy; and John Sununu for focusing on it in connection with George H. W. Bush.

5. **A great leader has the steadfast resolve to withstand major setbacks.**
   Thank you, James Tobin and Geoffrey Ward, for accentuating this point about Franklin Roosevelt; and David Maraniss, for doing the same with Bill Clinton.

6. **A great leader has the courage to play hardball not only to defeat enemies, but also to keep allies in line.**
   Thank you, David McCullough, for accentuating this point about John Adams; H. W. Brands, for doing the same with Andrew Jackson; and Jean Edward Smith, for focusing on it in connection with Dwight Eisenhower.

7. **A great leader has a keen sense of optimum timing; and when the right moment arrives, he seizes it.**

   Thank you, Douglas Brinkley, for accentuating this point about Theodore Roosevelt; Evan Thomas, for doing the same with Richard Nixon; and Larry Temple, for focusing on it in connection with Lyndon Johnson.

8. **A great leader has communication skills that allow him to articulate the fears and hopes of his era's people.**

   Thank you, Ken Burns, for accentuating this point about the Roosevelts; Scott Berg, for doing the same with Woodrow Wilson; Sheldon Stern, for focusing on it in connection with John F. Kennedy, and H.W. Brands, for emphasizing it about Ronald Reagan.

9. **A great leader puts the national interest over his own political interest.**

   Thank you, Mark Updegrove, for accentuating this point about Lyndon Johnson; and Jon Meacham, for doing the same with George H.W. Bush.

10. **A great leader not only stays abreast of public opinion, but also devises and implements a strategy to shape it.**

    Thank you, Harold Holzer, for accentuating this point about Abraham Lincoln.

In discerning these conclusions and commandments, and then attempting to synthesize them, here's where I come out: the president of the United States is the most powerful person in the world, and has the most difficult and often the loneliest job in the world. To make hard decisions about sending American soldiers into war, knowing many will not come back physically and/or emotionally healthy, and some will not come back alive, requires a superhuman capacity to absorb stress, sorrow, and guilt.

For the most part, those who serve as our nation's chief executive have remarkable talents or else they never would have been elected. Despite these talents, they are flawed leaders surrounded by flawed advisors, who attempt to govern a country comprised of flawed people who operate in a world filled with flawed leaders, advisors, and people—making totally successful governance an impossibility.

Those who get elected president believe their skills make them the person most capable of doing the job better than anyone else in the country. Upon reaching the Oval Office, they soon realize that, contrary to their expectations, their talents somehow don't empower them to accomplish what they expected; and then they have no choice but to push through to the end of their term(s), giving it their best shot—with some good days and plenty of bad ones—and driving themselves beyond human limits, causing their bodies to age at an accelerated pace.

Presidents leave the White House with the satisfaction of knowing that on most of their days in the saddle, they did their best to achieve what they believed was in the best interest of our country; though they also depart from the job with the disappointment of knowing that what they pledged to accomplish when they ran for office turned out to be something that, for the most part, they could not accomplish. For all these reasons, those who have served as presidents of the United States deserve our highest appreciation for their public service, regardless of whether we agree with the decisions they made or admire the way they conducted themselves.

Acknowledgements

This book began in January 2015 when Lucy Chambers, the president of my publisher Bright Sky Press, read some unedited transcripts of my early interviews and pronounced them "book worthy." God bless Lucy Chambers, and her wonderful team at BSP: Lauren Adams Gow, Marla Garcia, Leslie Little, Eva Freeburn, and Fiona Bills.

Many key people helped it along toward its final execution. David O. Stewart had his biography of James Madison (see Chapter Four) released in February 2015 and his coming to Dallas for several events on his book's first day of publication kick-started the year. Later in 2015, David provided me with key introductions to David and Jeanne Heidler (see Chapter One), Peter Onuf (see Chapter Three), and Jean Edward Smith (see Chapters Nine and Seventeen). He also gave me important feedback on my Introduction. Most importantly, David showed me that in the twenty-first century, it's possible for a practicing lawyer to transform himself into a practicing historian. God bless David O. Stewart.

The years 2013-2015 turned out to be great years for presidential biographies. In addition to David Stewart's book, in 2015, David and Jeanne Heidler released their biography of George Washington (see Chapter One); Charles Slack came out with his book on John Adams, Thomas Jefferson, and the Alien and Sedition Acts (see Chapter Five); H.W. ("Bill") Brands brought out his Ronald Reagan biography (see Chapter Twenty Three); Evan Thomas had his Richard Nixon book (see Chapter Twenty One); and John Sununu and Jon Meacham both had biographies on George H.W. Bush (see Chapters Twenty Four and Twenty Nine).

These came on the heels of 2014's fine presidential biographies by Harold Holzer on Abraham Lincoln (see Chapter Seven), and Geoffrey Ward and Ken Burns on the Roosevelts (see Chapters Ten and Sixteen), which followed 2013's having strong books from Scott Berg, with his best-seller on Woodrow Wilson (see Chapter Twelve); Doug Brinkley, in collaboration with Luke Nichter with their first volume about the Nixon Tapes (see Chapter Twenty Two); and Jim Tobin with his book on Franklin Roosevelt (see Chapter Fifteen). I rode the wave of these highly readable and scholarly books, interviewing the authors at events as they were on the road promoting their good work. God bless these marvelous historians and the publishers who decided to publish their books since 2013.

Having become friends with several leading presidential biographers in years past, they were nice enough to make themselves available at onstage events I organized at various venues. These friends who made a special effort to make this book come to fruition included H.W. Brands (see Chapters Six and Twenty Three), Ronald C. White, Jr. (see Chapter Eight), Doug Brinkley (see Chapters Eleven and Twenty Two), Amity Shlaes (see Chapters Thirteen and Fourteen), Mark Updegrove (see Chapter Twenty), Evan Thomas (see Chapter Twenty One), David Maraniss (see Chapter Twenty Five), and Michael Duffy (see Chapter Twenty Six). God bless these friends who went the extra mile to make this book happen.

The Henry Kissinger (see Chapter Twenty Seven), Scott Berg (see Chapter Twelve), and Jim Tobin (see Chapter Fifteen) interviews were conducted at public events sponsored by the World Affairs Council of Dallas/Fort Worth, and were organized and executed by Jim Falk and Rachel Vogel of the WAC. The Ken Burns (see Chapter Ten) and David McCullough (see Chapters Two and Seventeen) interviews were conducted at events sponsored by the Dallas Bar Foundation, and were organized and executed by Elizabeth Phillip, Executive Director of the DBF. The Lynda Johnson Robb/Larry Temple interview (see Chapter Twenty Seven) took place at the State Bar of Texas' 2014 Annual Meeting. The Geoffrey Ward interview (see Chapter Sixteen) occurred at a gathering of the staff and friends of the Jackie Robinson Foundation in New York City made possible by my dear friend Della Britton. The James A. Baker, III interview (see Chapter Twenty Nine) took place at a program sponsored by the James A. Baker Institute for Public Policy at Rice University, and was organized and executed by Ryan Kirksey and Melissa Griffin. God bless these fine organizations and institutions that enrich their communities with high quality programs.

I'm pleased that many interviews took place in front of university students, faculty, staff, and alumni supporters, ranging from the Heidlers at an Air Force Academy history class (see Chapter One); Peter Onuf and Andy Card at Franklin Pierce University programs (see Chapters Three and Thirty One); Harold Holzer, Evan Thomas, Charles Stack, Amity Shlaes, and David Davenport at a presidential symposium organized by Kimberly Thornton and Amity Shlaes at The Kings College in New York City (see Chapters Five, Seven, Thirteen, Fourteen and Twenty One); Jean Edward Smith at a program organized by Todd Rasberry at Georgetown College in Georgetown, Kentucky (see Chapters Nine and Eighteen); John Sununu at an event on the campus of Colby-Sawyer College in New London, New Hampshire, organized and promoted by Kate Seamans at the instigation of my friends David and Marianne Harrison (see Chapter Thirty); Taylor Branch and Mark Updegrove in front of Mike Cramer's class in the School of Communications at the University of Texas at Austin (see Chapter Twenty); H.W. Brands' history class at the University of Texas at Austin (see Chapter Six); and Doug Brinkley's history class at Rice University (see Chapter Eleven). God bless these fine colleges and universities and the people who helped make these onstage interview programs possible.

My law firm, Winstead PC, determined a few years ago that our esteemed clients would be entertained and engaged by best-selling historians at breakfast events that we have co-sponsored with either the Dallas office of Ernst & Young or Comerica Bank. The David O. Stewart (see Chapter Four), Evan Thomas (see Chapter Twenty-One), Doug Brinkley (see Chapter Twenty-Two), H.W. Brands (see Chapter Twenty-Three), Jon Meacham (see Chapter Twenty-Four), and Michael Duffy (see Chapter Twenty-Six) interviews all took place in front of these client events. God bless Howard Mudrick, Kevin Sullivan, David Dawson, Tom Helfand, Greg Erwin, Teresa Schneider, Allen Fuqua, Jenny Winkelmann, Shannon Tipton, Rachel Guy, and Christina O'Neal at the Winstead PC law firm for their key roles in providing the funding and organization of these events; God bless Clint McDonough, Michelle Vopni, and Debra VonStorch of Ernst & Young for their roles in sponsoring and promoting these events; and God bless Scooter Smith, Pat Faubion, and Curt Farmer of Comerica Bank for their roles in sponsoring and promoting these events.

Two interview events came about thanks to two wonderful friends who provided the venues and their network of colleagues to attend them—Dave Wexler organized the David Maraniss program in the Anne Wexler Conference Room at the office of Wexler | Walker in Washington, DC (see Chapter Twenty-Five); and Harlan Crow provided the Old Parkland Board Room in Dallas on a Sunday afternoon for a gathering of friends and family at the Ronald C. White, Jr., interview (see Chapter Eight). God bless Dave Wexler and Harlan Crow.

Finally, thanks to an introduction provided by Herbert Parmet (who I met through Doug Brinkley), I became acquainted with my John F. Kennedy historian interviewee, Sheldon M. Stern (see Chapter Nineteen). Sheldon succeeded in getting use of a large conference room at the John F. Kennedy Presidential Library and also got many Library staff members to attend our interview program. God Bless Sheldon M. Stern.

Besides those previously mentioned, others have been crucial to my being in a position to conduct these interviews. Jeremi Suri and Jim Falk helped prepare me for the Henry Kissinger interview. John Williams facilitated all aspects of the James A. Baker III interview. My friend Bill Spears introduced me to Harold Holzer. Jeffrey Engle of SMU's Center for Presidential History and Alan Lowe of the George W. Bush Presidential Library gave me the opportunity to moderate a panel at one of their presidential symposiums—which led to my becoming acquainted with Amity Shlaes who, in turn, led me to Kimberly Thornbury and all the great people at The King's

College who made the presidential symposium there such a huge success. Ann Gagnon made the Peter Onuf and Andy Card interviews run smoothly at Franklin Pierce University. Cathy Sununu greatly helped facilitate my interview with her father John Sununu. Drs. Bill Lawrence, Todd Rasberry, and John Martin of SMU's Perkins School of Theology were instrumental in the school's sponsoring the annual Bolin Family Luncheon which provided the means by which I deepened my connections with Ronald C. White, Jr., Jon Meacham, Michael Duffy, Andy Card, and Taylor Branch. God bless these key facilitators and introducers.

In the last few years, Ken Burns has become a great friend. I have been honored to serve as both a Founding Director and a Board Director of the Better Angels Society, the non-profit that works to provide funding for the magnificent films created by Ken and his team at Florentine Films. Ken's Foreword for this book, by itself, gives it national credibility in presidential history circles. God bless Ken Burns.

In November 2015, I spent the better part of two days with David and Rosalee McCullough when they came to Dallas for three major events sponsored by SMU's John Tower Center for Political Studies, the Dallas Bar Foundation, and the World Affairs Council of Dallas/Fort Worth. David and I clicked at the interviews we did covering John Adams, Harry Truman, and the Wright Brothers. His endorsement of my interviewing work provides affirmation of the highest order. God bless David and Rosalee McCullough.

The endorsements on the back of my dust jacket from James A. Baker, III, Jon Meacham, Harold Holzer, Doug Brinkley, H.W. Brands, and Evan Thomas make all the blood, sweat, toil, tears, and heartburn that went into the book seem worthwhile. God bless my dust jacket endorsers.

My wife Claire stepped up to support this project and was with me every step of the way. Our children Scott and Lindsey have provided a constant stream of emotional support. My best friend of the last forty years, Marvin Blum, read parts of the book and gave me strong encouragement to see it through. God bless Claire, Scott, Lindsey, and Marvin.

This book simply would not have happened without the constant daily support of my assistant Jeanette Adams. Her calm spirit, high intelligence, and superhuman patience kept this ship afloat and moving in the right direction from start to finish. God bless Jeanette Adams.

This book is dedicated to my parents, Paul and Mary Jean Boston. Dad passed away in August 2011, though his spirit and life-long mentorship are still a big part of who I am. More than anyone else, Mom is responsible for my developing a love of presidential history beginning at age seven. She gave me a set of presidential trading cards in the first grade, and challenged me to memorize the presidents' names in chronological order—which I did—and it fooled everyone at Bunker Hill Elementary School in Houston, Texas into thinking I was smart. She also caused our family to take its summer vacation in 1963 on a tour of Washington, DC and the presidents' homes in Tennessee and Virginia. That experience brought to life the fact that our commanders-in-chief were real live people worthy of attention and study. She has remained steadfast in support of my efforts over the course of my life. God bless Paul and Mary Jean Boston.

Finally, I want to thank those members of the student body of the University of Texas at Austin who voted against me in the student body presidential election in the spring of 1975. By not giving me the victory, after several months of my participation in fierce campaigning on and off campus, the experience made me realize that the life of a political candidate was not for me. This proved to be a very good thing for all Americans because it brought to an end my dream of one day becoming president of the United States. Since that defeat in college, I've been freed up to pursue and fulfill other dreams that fit me far better than presidential politics ever could have—particularly, as we look at the sordid nature of it in the 2016 campaign. God bless Divine Providence which removed me from the presidential rat race once and for all in the spring of 1975—before I reached my twenty-second birthday.

Index of Topics Covered